Third-Party Effects of Arbitral Awards

International Arbitration Law Library

VOLUME 49

Editors

Professor Julian D.M. Lew QC has been involved with international arbitration for more than forty years as counsel, as arbitrator and as an academic. He is the founder and has been the Head of the School of International Arbitration, Centre for Commercial Law Studies, Queen Mary University of London since its creation in 1985. He is now an independent international arbitrator at 20 Essex Street, London.

Stavros Brekoulakis is Professor at Queen Mary University of London and an associate member of 3 Verulam Buildings (Gray's Inn). He is a leading academic in international arbitration and has led, or been involved in, several projects with ICCA, ICC Commission and ILA. He also acts as an independent arbitrator and has been appointed as chairman, sole arbitrator, co-arbitrator and emergency arbitrator under the rules of all the major arbitration rules.

Introduction

Since its first volume published in 1993, this authoritative practitioner-oriented series has published in-depth and analytical works on niche aspects of international arbitration, authored by specialists in the field.

Objective

This authoritative and established series covering in-depth analyses of niche areas appeals to both practitioners and academics. The series includes specific monographs and PhD dissertations of high quality, which are practical and cover issues not fully explored in general texts.

Frequency

A volume is published whenever an interesting topic presents itself.

The titles published in this series are listed at the end of this volume.

Third-Party Effects of Arbitral Awards

Res Judicata Against Privies, Non-mutual Preclusion and Factual Effects

Maximilian Pika

Wolters Kluwer

Published by:
Kluwer Law International B.V.
PO Box 316
2400 AH Alphen aan den Rijn
The Netherlands
E-mail: international-sales@wolterskluwer.com
Website: lrus.wolterskluwer.com

Sold and distributed in North, Central and South America by:
Wolters Kluwer Legal & Regulatory U.S.
7201 McKinney Circle
Frederick, MD 21704
United States of America
Email: customer.service@wolterskluwer.com

Sold and distributed in all other countries by:
Air Business Subscriptions
Rockwood House
Haywards Heath
West Sussex
RH16 3DH
United Kingdom
Email: international-customerservice@wolterskluwer.com

ISBN 978-94-035-1273-0

e-Book: ISBN 978-94-035-1265-5
web-PDF: ISBN 978-94-035-1271-6

Table of Contents

Foreword

International arbitration has developed in our time to become the dominant means of resolving cross-border commercial disputes. In light of its extraordinary growth, it is remarkable how many legal issues of fundamental importance remain to be resolved. The res judicata or preclusive effect of an arbitral award over third parties not named in the award exemplifies the point. All arbitration is premised upon the consent of the parties. The arbitration agreement is classically conceived as a bilateral relationship. Yet the purity of this legal model may be contrasted with economic realities. Corporate contracting parties frequently form part of a larger group of companies and a commercial transaction of any complexity will normally engage the rights and interests of numerous other persons beyond a simple bilateral model. It is left to general principles of the law to resolve the problems that arise when these principles collide. Yet such principles were developed to deal with legal problems in settings very different to the contemporary contexts of international arbitration.

For these reasons, I am delighted to welcome the publication of Dr Maximilian Pika's monograph: *Third-Party Effects of Arbitral Awards.* I had the pleasure of meeting Dr Pika in New Zealand during the course of his doctoral research. It was immediately apparent that here was a scholar with an incisive analytical mind, who had mastered the intricacies and obscurities of the different national law solutions and the larger international law framework and developed his own path of legal reasoning through the problem. The fruits of that research are now available to us all through the publication of this book. Dr Pika skilfully dissects the many different issues arising from the effect of arbitral awards on third parties and then synthesizes his conclusions in a clear analytical framework. The result is a work of real scholarly originality and practical utility, which can be real with profit as a monograph, but which will also form an essential reference tool in the international arbitration library.

Campbell McLachlan
Professor Campbell McLachlan QC
Victoria University of Wellington
Associé Institut de Droit International
Berlin, Germany
May 2019

List of Abbreviations

ALI	American Law Institute
ATF (BGE)	Official Collection of Decisions of the Swiss Federal Court
BGH	Bundesgerichtshof (German Federal Court of Justice - Supreme Court in Civil, Commercial and Criminal Matters)
BGHZ	Collection of Decision of the German Federal Court of Justice in Civil and Commercial Matters
BVerfGE	Official Collection of Decisions of the German Constitutional Court
CA	Court of Appeal(s); Cour d'appel (French Court of Appeal)
CAS	Court of Arbitration for Sport
Cass	Cour de cassation (French Supreme Court in Civil, Commercial and Criminal Matters)
Ch	High Court of Justice of England and Wales - Chancery Division
CIETAC	China International Economic and Trade Arbitration Commission
CISG	UN Convention on Contracts for the International Sale of Goods
Com	Commercial Chamber of the French Supreme Court
Comm	Commercial Court, High Court of Justice of England and Wales - Queen's Bench Division
Corresp	Correspondingly
CPC	Code de procédure civile (French Code of Civil Procedure)
CPR	Civil Procedure Rules (England and Wales)
CUP	Cambridge University Press
DST	Deutsche Schachtbau- und Tiefbohrgesellschaft
DIS	German Institution for Arbitration
ECHR	Convention for the Protection of Human Rights and Fundamental Freedoms

ECJ	Court of Justice of the European Union
EU	European Union
EWCA	Court of Appeal of England and Wales
FAA	Federal Arbitration Act (US)
Fasc	Fascicule
FRCP	Federal Rules of Civil Procedure (US)
HCA	High Court of Australia
HGB	Handelsgesetzbuch (German Commercial Code)
HKHC	High Court of Hong Kong
HKIAC	Hong Kong International Arbitration Centre
HL	House of Lords
ICC	International Chamber of Commerce
ICC Collection	ICC Collection of Arbitral Awards – Recueil des sentences arbitrales CCI
ICCA	International Council for Commercial Arbitration
ICDR	International Centre for Dispute Resolution of the American Arbitration Association
ILA	International Law Association
ILC	International Law Commission
JCl	Juris-Classeur
KG	Kantonsgericht (Swiss District Court)
LCIA	London Court of International Arbitration
LG	Landgericht (German District Court)
Model Law	UNCITRAL Model on International Commercial Arbitration
NYC	(New York) Convention on the Recognition and Enforcement of Foreign Arbitral Awards
NZCA	Court of Appeal of New Zealand
OGH	Oberster Gerichtshof (Austrian Supreme Court)
OLG	Oberlandesgericht (German Higher Regional Court)
OUP	Oxford University Press
PC	Privy Council
PCIJ	Permanent Court of International Justice
PILA	Private International Law Act (Switzerland)
QB	High Court of Justice of England and Wales – Queen's Bench Division
RGZ	Collection of Decision of the German Imperial Court of Justice in Civil and Commercial Matters
SC	Supreme Court

SCC	Stockholm Chamber of Commerce
SCIN	Supreme Court of India
SCNSW	Supreme Court of New South Wales
SGCA	Court of Appeals of Singapore
SGHC	High Court of Singapore
SIAC	Singapore International Arbitration Centre
SMA	Society of Maritime Arbitrators
SSRN	Social Science Research Network
sté	société (company)
TF (BG)	Bundesgericht/Tribunal Federal (Swiss Federal Tribunal - Supreme Court in Civil, Commercial and Criminal Matters)
TGI	Tribunal de grande instance (French District Court)
UK	United Kingdom
UNCITRAL	United Nations Commission on International Trade Law
UNIDROIT	International Institute for the Unification of Private Law
USf	United States (of America)
WIPO	World Intellectual Property Organization
Y.C.A	Yearbook of Commercial Arbitration
ZPO	Zivilprozessordnung (German Code of Civil Procedure)

Acknowledgements

This monograph is an updated version of my doctoral dissertation submitted at Heidelberg University, Germany in July 2018. In many countries, it is a good custom to commence the publication of a thesis with acknowledgements, and rightly so. Young researchers depend inherently on support, on guidance and, none the least, on conferred liberty of action. I am in the lucky position of having received such in manifold ways.

The 'father of my doctorate' (*Doktorvater*), as we aptly put it in German, has been an academic role model. A dedicated teacher, a mentor to his research and teaching assistants, and an author of the highest ethical standards, I am very lucky that Professor Marc-Philippe Weller has supervised my thesis and employed me at Heidelberg University's Institute for Comparative Law, Conflict of Laws and International Business Law throughout the three years of my research.

Professor Herbert Kronke of the Iran-US Claims Tribunal has not only provided very constructive comments in his swiftly issued examiner's report but also offered constant academic and practical advice to me. Professor Christoph Kern has served as the chairman of the examination committee at my *viva* and always kept an open door for me. Professor Chester Brown of the University of Sydney has provided very helpful suggestions in his swiftly issued expert opinion on my thesis' linguistic qualities, a necessity for English dissertations in Heidelberg. Professor Campbell McLachlan QC has not only honoured me with his Foreword, the conversations on my research in Wellington have been invaluable.

The Heidelberg Institute with its vast library on comparative and international law has been an extraordinary environment for my research. The German National Academic Foundation (*Studienstiftung*) has provided me with significant financial and ideational support both during my doctorate and my undergraduate studies. The International Max Planck Research School for Successful Dispute Resolution in International Law has funded my research during its early stages and hosted biannual seminars. The University of Montpellier, France has provided me with a research grant for my visit. Victoria University of Wellington has been particularly welcoming when

I arrived as Academic Visitor, which is above all owed to my host Professor Petra Butler.

During my presentations at these institutions, I was very lucky to receive feedback and suggestions from – in addition to those already mentioned – Professor Jürgen Basedow, Professor Giles Cuniberti, Professor Werner Ebke, Professor Burkhard Hess, Professor Mary Keyes, Dr Bevan Marten, Professor Pierre Mousseron and Professor Thomas Pfeiffer. Moreover, I profited significantly from the vivid discussions with and the proposals of my former peers Dr Björn Centner, Mirjam Escher, Dr Charlotte Harms, Mascha Hesse, Dr Leonhard Hübner, Professor Robert Magnus, Jan Mysegades, Professor Jens Prütting, Dr Bettina Rentsch, Professor Chris Thomale, Pierre Trippel, Dr Hannes Wais and Anton Zimmermann as well as the advice of the Heidelberg Institute's Director *emeritus* and nonetheless ubiquitous Professor Erik Jayme.

Kiran Gore, Eleanor Taylor and the entire team at Kluwer as well as at Newgen Knowledge Works have provided everything an author can ask for.

The final professional acknowledgement is owed to Professor Karsten Thorn of Bucerius Law School. I remain indebted for his mentorship during my undergraduate studies.

The actual end of acknowledgements is regularly reserved for family. And for me, again, rightly so. My parents and my grandmother did everything in their capacity to foster my education; my wife Carina's contribution to many of my ideas was the most significant, and the time spent with our two daughters born during the doctorate is the core reason why it will remain unforgettable.

Introduction

I THE PRIVITY OF ARBITRATION AS AN ANTONYM TO MULTILATERAL TRANSACTIONS

1. Founded upon the pillars of privity, arbitration has initially been conceived as a two-party mechanism. Yet, very few international transactions can be reduced on two parties only. Instead, the growing technical and commercial specialization as well as the increasing financial demand of global business necessitate: many transactions inherently affect more than two parties, e.g., construction, industrial and transport projects; commodity chains; distribution networks; or M&A transactions. Thus, further parties such as parent companies, subsidiaries, suppliers, wholesalers, sub-contractors, licensees, guarantors, sureties or insurers are frequently included in or affected by transactions. In these *multilateral transactions* (as they will be summarized in this book), arbitral proceedings involving all parties are often barred for jurisdictional reasons.[1] This lack of power of arbitral tribunals over third parties was identified as one of the arbitration's 'worst features' in the 2018 Queen Mary International Arbitration Survey. For such reason, parallel proceedings might occur and result in the '*nightmare*'[2] of inconsistent decisions. That could be prevented if it were permitted to invoke the result of a prior adjudication in subsequent proceedings, regardless of whether the parties to these proceedings are identical to the prior proceedings. Whether this is permissible is the ambit of this examination.

2. To exemplify two classic factual scenarios for this issue: *first*, indemnity claims scattered across different fora. For instance, when an arbitral tribunal awards damages for a deficient construction project to a principal against a contractor, the contractor might seek indemnity in court against the sub-contractor or an insurer. Then, the contactor might invoke the arbitral award in order to preclude the (for him) re-litigation of the construction project's insufficient objective quality. *Second*, arbitral awards are

1. *See infra* Chapter 1.
2. Hwang, (2015) 31 Arb. Int'l 195.

likely to be invoked in case scenarios of connected liability. Continuing upon the aforementioned example, in case the contractor defaults on his damages obligations, the principal might sue a guarantor or the contractor's parent company and invoke the arbitral award on the contractor's liability. In addition, the research project cannot only focus on effects to a third party's detriment. Instead, it might be the very third party itself that relies on an arbitral award in its *favour*; for instance, if the arbitral award held in favour of the contractor and the principal nonetheless sues the guarantor.

II EXAMINATION SCOPE: PRECLUSIVE, CONCLUSIVE AND FACTUAL THIRD-PARTY EFFECTS

3. Every adjudicatory decision might give rise to a certain non-binding inclination for other tribunals to decide accordingly in follow-up disputes. However, it is by no means impossible that a follow-up tribunal might interpret the related fact or debated aspect of the law differently. From a philosophic point of view, the mere possibility that a subsequent decision can deviate from an earlier decision on the very same issue might be considered a proof of the incomplete human judgment capacity. Legally, such risks have to be taken as a matter of fact. Effectively, the risks are pertinent, since it is estimated that 10% of non-prevailing parties do not deliberately honour an arbitral award.[3] Yet, both public and private rationales of justice, consistency, certainty and efficiency demand that there be an end to litigation. Hence, lawyers seek recourse to a doctrine establishing that an adjudicated matter cannot be raised anew: res judicata.[4] In this regard, '*the first lesson one must learn on the subject of res judicata is that judicial findings must not be consued [sic] with absolute truth*'.[5] Instead, res judicata establishes fictitious truth in that the prior adjudication's authority operates independently from its adequacy.

4. The very meaning of the term 'res judicata' raises a range of different understandings. Authors facilitate the term either in order to describe a decision's finality (particularly the exhaustion of appeals) or its relevance in follow-up disputes; in the latter case, it might be understood as a rule of jurisdiction, admissibility or a means of evidence; in either case because it facilitates the authority of the decision or a

3. Queen Mary University, *Report on International Arbitration*. *See* for critics *Redfern and Hunter* [11.02] ('first, because arbitration is a private process; and secondly, in any event, there is no particular reason why an arbitral tribunal should know whether or not an award has been carried out').
4. Latin for 'thing adjudged'. Despite the term's Latin origin, this treatise is not setting it in italics, because of the frequent use and visual rationales. The same applies to the term *lis pendens*.
5. Currie, (1957) 9 Stan. L. Rev. 315. *See*, *The Ampthill Peerage*, (1977) AC 547, 575-576 per Lord Simon of Glaisdale (HL) ('Important though the issues may be, how extensive so ever the evidence, whatever the eagerness for further fray; society says: "We have provided courts in which your rival contentions have been heard. [...] Since judges are fallible human beings, we have provided appellate courts which do their own fallible best to correct error. But in the end you must accept what has been decided. Enough is enough." And the law echoes: "*res judicata*", the matter is adjudged.').

modification of the claim.[6] Preferably, in an international examination, the term should be deployed as non-technically as possible. Accordingly, this examination adopts the broad, impact-based approach of international-arbitration scholarship. Res judicata describes that *a tribunal rejects any party's claim, request or argument under sole referral to a decision rendered in prior proceedings*. There are two sides of this coin, often associated with bipolar terms: on the one hand, the preclusive (negative) effect of a prior decision stating that duplicative claims are prevented (*ne bis in idem*); on the other hand, the conclusive (positive) effect of a prior decision stating that claims or matters decided cannot be re-raised as incidental arguments.[7] The examination summarizes both effects as 'res judicata', and occasionally, even more briefly, as 'preclusion'. Most importantly, the examination does not restrict 'res judicata' to the prior decision's cause of action as it can be observed sometimes – although not always – in common-law doctrine (claim preclusion). Instead, 'res judicata' also describes preclusion by virtue of a prior decision's incidental reasonings (issue preclusion), as it might arise in the first example mentioned above.

5. Whereas the above-mentioned construction scenario dealt with an arbitral award on the substance invoked in subsequent litigation, there are several other case scenarios which require due consideration in this examination. Particularly, the situation vice versa is that a court judgment is invoked *before* arbitral tribunals. Moreover, an arbitral award might be invoked in another arbitration or, in the case of a partial award, in the same arbitration. Finally, a court judgment in an arbitral matter, e.g., on the validity of an arbitration agreement or the *set aside (annulment)*[8] of an award, might be invoked in enforcement proceedings or arbitration. The instant examination will distinguish between these scenarios.[9]

6. This examination is particularly dedicated to res judicata in multilateral case scenarios. Accordingly, it will *not* provide any comprehensive discussion of all of res judicata's aspects; such ambition would exceed this thesis' constraints. The thesis can also build upon a considerable amount of examinations on res judicata's general operation both *of* arbitral awards and *before* arbitral tribunals.[10] Therefore, the thesis

---

6. *See infra* [96].
7. Cf. *ILA Final Report on Res Judicata* [15]; Brekoulakis, (2005) 16 Am. Rev. Int'l Arb. 184; Hanotiau, *Complex Arbitrations* 240; Hobér, (2011) 366 Rec. des cours 121; Kremslehner, in *Austrian Yearbook on International Arbitration 2007* 132; Radicati di Brozolo, in *ASA Special Series* 2; Schaffstein, *Res Judicata* [1-5]; Zeuner and Koch, in *International Encyclopedia of Comparative Law* [1]. *Crit.* on the bipolar distinction Wehland, *Multiple Proceedings in Investment Treaty Arbitration* [4.59].
8. This examination predominantly refers to the term 'set aside' found in Art. V(1)(e) NYC, Art. 34 UNCITRAL Model Law. For linguistic purposes, it will occasionally use the term 'to annul'. Synonyms under national arbitration acts are 'challenge' (s. 68 1996 Arbitration Act) and 'vacate' (s. 10 FAA).
9. *See infra* Chapters 4-9.
10. *See* on res judicata *of* arbitral awards *ILA Interim Report on Res Judicata*; *Born* 3747-67; Erk-Kubat, *Parallel Proceedings in International Arbitration* 162-177; Hobér, (2015) 366 Rec. des cours; Klement, *Rechtskraft des Schiedsspruchs*; Lühmann, *Die Rechtskraft des Schiedsspruchs* 28-112; Schaffstein, *Res Judicata* [4.14-4.121]. *See* on res judicata *before* arbitral tribunals *ILA Final Report on Res Judicata*; *Born* 3776; Debourg, *Les contrariétés de décisions* [501-570; 688-696]; Erk-Kubat, *Parallel Proceedings in International Arbitration* 231-246; Hanotiau,

will merely provide an overview on res judicata's general aspects in order to lay the foundation for a problem privy to multilateral transactions and largely undeveloped in arbitration doctrine: the application of res judicata towards parties that have been third parties to the prior decision, i.e., everyone not individually named as claimant, defendant or 'additional party'[11] within the prior decision. Such application will be summarized as 'third-party effect'[12] of a prior decision.

7. At a first glance on the topic, there might be a continuous understanding amongst jurisdictions and international scholars that arbitral awards and judgments comprised *no* third-party effect and could exclusively constitute res judicata between *the same parties*. However, the specific operation of this requirement in international arbitration is in fact highly uncertain. *First*, this applies to the summary of several parties as 'one' fictitious party. E.g., there might be a general consensus that a legatee and an heir can be considered as one party within the same-parties requirement. By contrast, other categories have not received any attention internationally, such as debtors and guarantors; assignors and assignees; insured and insurers; company and director as well as producer and wholesaler. Here, it is uncertain whether the same-parties requirement upholds the distinct legal personalities or whether the prior third parties can be exposed to res judicata as 'privies' to facilitate the common-law term. *Second*, it is disputed whether to entirely abandon the same-parties requirement where res judicata is invoked in favour of third parties. In the second case example, the parent company might invoke that, even if it were no privy, the principal's duplicative claim should be precluded.

8. The *third* case scenario in which an arbitral award might establish effects beyond the same parties significantly differs from the above-mentioned. Instead of justifying a preclusion of claims, requests or arguments in follow-up disputes, an arbitral award's sheer existence might trigger certain consequences under the law applicable to a follow-up dispute. For instance, in the construction scenario, the sub-contractor might reject any liability against the contractor and invoke that the sub-contractor's claim for a unique building material towards his distributor was rejected by a prior arbitral tribunal. Potentially, this might suspend the sub-contractor's obligations against the contractor under grounds such as objective impossibility, hardship or force majeure. The examination describes such *consequences stipulated for the claims conferred to and obligations imposed on a party, or their rejection by prior decisions*, as 'factual effects'. Sometimes, a case scenario might necessitate examining both res judicata and factual effects. In the second case example, for instance, the guarantor might invoke that the

Complex Arbitrations 239-256; Hascher, in *Travaux comité français DIP 2000-2003* 25-26; Mayer, in *Liber Amicorum Reymond* 187 et seqq.; Mayer, (2016) Rev. Arb. 92 et seqq.; Radicati di Brozolo in *ASA Special Series*; Schaffstein, *Res Judicata* [6.214]; Seraglini, (2016) Rev. Arb. 66-75; Zajdela, *L'autorité de la chose jugée devant l'arbitre*.

11. The rules of major arbitration institutions explicitly provide for such a possibility, e.g., Art. 2 (iii) ICC Rules; Art. 18 CIETAC Rules; Art. 27 HKIAC Rules; Art. 7 ICDR Rules.
12. This facilitation of the term is *distinct* to Brekoulakis, *Third Parties in Arbitration* [10.32-10.33] ('Res judicata mainly covers the claims or cause of action [...]. By contrast, the suggested third-party effect is limited only to a limited number of relevant issues [...].').

applicable law allows a guarantor to refuse payment if a prior tribunal has held the main debtor not liable.[13] Moreover, in France, the doctrine of *opposabilité* originated as describing factual effects and has recently – and controversially – been developed as a means for effectively applying issue preclusion.[14] In any case, factual effects inherently risk establishing adjudicatory effects erga omnes. They will thus be included by the term 'third-party effect' and this examination.

9. In assessing arbitral awards' third-party effects, the examination restricts its scope to international *commercial* arbitration. Accordingly, the problem of party identities in international *investment* arbitration will be largely excluded. Such problem has arisen where legally distinct, yet related investors exploited their capacity under BITs (bilateral investment treaties), multilateral treaties (such as the Energy Charter Treaty) or investment contracts and brought repetitive claims against host States.[15] Particularly, the instant examination takes the position that the two worlds need to be addressed separately because they regularly comprise distinct sources of adjudicatory powers, distinct subject matters and distinct causes for multiple proceedings.[16]

10. Finally, the examination focuses on *international* commercial arbitration. Hence, it concentrates on the cross-border dimension of res judicata. Particularly, such dimension increases the importance of res judicata. As domestic or regional (Brussels/Lugano) regimes can adequately handle parallel proceedings, they prevent the need for subsequent preclusion arguments. International settings, by contrast, fall short of such pre-emptive coordination. Here, res judicata is a pivotal means of '*fostering stability and unity in an inchoate international order*'.[17] The resulting assessment of res judicata in international arbitration adheres to the tasks of contemporary '*international private law*':[18] comparisons of national laws, determinations of the applicable law and statements as to possible uniform solutions.

III STATUS QUO: CLOSE TO A TERRA INCOGNITA OF INTERNATIONAL ARBITRATION SCHOLARSHIP

11. In comparative scholarship, there is a well-cited quote pursuant to which res judicata were a '*general principle of law recognized by civilized nations*'.[19] Yet, res

13. *See*, e.g., Art. 19 UN Guarantee Convention.
14. *See infra* [237-239].
15. *See CME Czech Republic BV v. Czech Republic*, UNCITRAL, Partial Award, 13 September 2001 (Kühn P, Schwebel and Hándl), [624]; *Grynberg v. Grenada*, ICSID Case ARB/10/6, Award, 2010, (Rowley P, Nottingham and Tercier); *Apotex Holdings Inc. v. United States of America*, ICSID Case ARB/(AF)/12/1, Award, 2014, (Veeder P, Crook and Rowley).
16. *See* more extensively *infra* [540-548].
17. von Mehren, (1980) 176 Rec. des cours 34.
18. *See* Boele-Woelki, (2009) 340 Rec. des cours [13] ('*[I]nternational private law* has a broader meaning [than private international law].').
19. *Charzów Factory* (*Germany v. Poland*), Judgment, (1927) 9 PCIJ Rep. Ser. A, 27 per Judge Anzilotti. *See also South West Africa* (*Ethiopia v. South Africa* and *Liberia v. South Africa*), Second Phase, Judgment, [1966] ICJ Rep 6; B Cheng, *General Principles of Law as Applied by International Courts and Tribunals* Ch. 17.

judicata's specific implementations might constitute one of the most delicate issues of international dispute resolution:

> Indeed, while the principle of res judicata can be considered a settled concept in the context of international arbitration, the less firmly settled questions lie in its application.[20]

12. As a starting point, the terms 'final and binding' often associated with arbitral awards in arbitral rules[21] are either perceived irrelevant[22] or at least little fruitful.[23] Hence, the issue of res judicata comes down to arbitration laws. Such are very diverse. Res judicata *'disguise[s] under ancient clothes very different concepts'*.[24] The significant differences amongst national concepts have, e.g., led the conference on the United Nations Commission on International Trade Law (UNCITRAL) Model Law to exclude the issue.[25] To name but a few divides: the point in time upon which res judicata operates, the relevance of adjudicatory reasonings and the doctrine of abuse of process.[26]

13. If the differences on such aspects might be called delicate, third-party effects will be characterized as precarious. Above all, detailed comparative scholarship on res judicata's third-party scope in arbitration is virtually non-existent.[27] Even intra-jurisdictional discussions are largely unsettled. Whilst French scholarship mainly focuses on the Supreme Court's *Prodim* jurisprudence concerning arbitral awards' factual effects, other jurisdictions comprise a little debated, yet open struggle between two solutions: the transfer of procedural rules for judgments and the relevance of the arbitration *agreement*'s third-party scope.[28] Given the assumption that more than

20. Poncet and Mockler, *Liber Amicorum Craig* 318.
21. For Example Art. 34 (2) UNCITRAL Rules; Art. R46 CAS Code; Art. 49 (9) CIETAC Rules; Art. 26 (8) LCIA Rules; Art. 32 (11) SIAC Rules; Art. 64 (b) WIPO Rules. By way of contrast, Art. 35 (6) 2017 ICC Rules, as well as Art. 35 (1) Model Law, only addresses the binding effect in order not to cause confusions about partial awards. The current HKIAC Rules and Swiss Rules contain no such clause.
22. Rubino-Samartano, *International Arbitration* at [1194-1200]. *See, e.g., Iran Aircraft Industries and Iran Helicopter Support and Renewal Company v. Avco Corporation*, [1993] Y.C.A. 596 (2d Cir. 1992) ('The terms "final" and "binding" merely reflect a contractual intention that the issues joined and resolved in the arbitration may not be tried do novo in any Court.').
23. *ILA Interim Report on Res Judicata* 23; Radicati di Brozolo, in *ASA Special Series* 5; Schaffstein, *Res Judicata Before Arbitral Tribunals* [4.103]. Whilst Art. 26 (8) LCIA Rules indicates a certain preference for issue preclusion, the indication does not result out of 'final and binding' but an extension: 'every award *including reasons for such award* shall be final and binding on the parties'.
24. Veeder, in *ICC Bulletin* 29.
25. UNDoc A/40/17 [259] ('A proposal was made to in article 31 a provision clarifying that the award made in the form provided in article 31 had the effect of res judicata. While not disagreeing with the general principle that awards were binding on the parties, the Commission did not adopt the proposal because it was considered that the term res judicata was a complex one which could have different applications in various legal systems.').
26. *See infra* [107-138].
27. *See* for existing overviews Brekoulakis, *Third Parties in Arbitration* [10.13-10.30]; Lühmann, *Die Rechtskraft des Schiedsspruchs* 113-183; Schaffstein, *Res Judicata* [4.29-4.31, 4.47].
28. *See infra* Chapter 4.

one-third of all international arbitration cases involve issues of third parties,[29] that there is a welter of jurisprudence concerning arbitral jurisdiction over third parties[30] and that those issues are likely to re-appear on a post-award stage, the situation will certainly evolve.

14. Turning to the cross-border circulation of arbitral awards, there is a strong distinction between res judicata *of* foreign arbitral awards in subsequent litigation and res judicata *in* subsequent international arbitration. As to the first aspect, the majority opinion follows a solution by means of *private international law*.[31] The discussion concerns whether res judicata is to be determined under the law of the arbitral seat, the law of the recognition forum or the law of the substance. In this regard, most arguments stem from the handling of foreign judgments.[32] By contrast, recent scholarly proposals seek to facilitate the New York Convention (NYC) in order to establish uniform rules for res judicata.[33] Moreover, the American Law Institute's (ALI's) recent Tentative Draft of the Third Restatement on Arbitration applies the NYC and the parties' expectations as requirements *in addition* to the applicable law.[34] In any case, arguments specific to the third-party dimension of res judicata are, yet again, virtually non-existent. Instead, the contributions usually focus on how to handle the entire res judicata of foreign arbitral awards.

15. Continuing to res judicata *before* arbitral tribunals, the solution method is shifting. Instead of a conflictualist approach, arbitration doctrine increasingly favours transnational solutions (substantive approach).[35] However, specific proposals on third-party effects are – for a third time in this Introduction – virtually non-existent. Foremost, the International Law Association's (ILA's) Report on res judicata before arbitral tribunals:

> refrain from formulating new rules in relation to the requirement of the identity of the parties [...]. There are too many different situations in relation to the question

29. Cf. Hanotiau, (2015) 32 J. Int'l Arb. 571.
30. *See*, e.g., Train, (2017) Rev. Arb. 391 (twenty-one judgments in France between 2012 and 2017).
31. The examination is going to facilitate the term established by Story, *Commentaries* § 9 instead of its counterpart (conflict of laws) favoured particularly in the US and first established by Ulricus Huber in 1689. *See* on the potential preferability Symeonides, (2016) 384 Rec. des cours 85-89.
32. *See ILA Interim Report on Res Judicata* 64; *Born* 3766-70; Debourg, *Les contrariétés de décisions* [494-495]; Hobér, (2011) 366 Rec. des cours 258-259; Kremslehner, in *Austrian Yearbook on International Arbitration 2007* 140; Radicati di Brozolo, in *ASA Special Series* 131; Scherer in Wolff (ed.), *New York Convention* Art. III [9]; Seraglini, (2016) Rev. Arb. at 52 et seqq.
33. *Born* 3741-42; Lühmann, *Die Rechtskraft des Schiedsspruchs* 309-312; Radicati di Brozolo, in *ASA Special Series* 8-9.
34. Restatement (Third) International Commercial Arbitration (Tentative Draft No. 2), § 4-9 and § 4-10.
35. *Born* 3776; Debourg, *Les contrariétés de décisions* [501-570; 688-696]; Erk-Kubat, *Parallel Proceedings in International Arbitration* 231-246; Hanotiau, *Complex Arbitrations* 239-256; Hascher, in *Travaux comité français DIP 2000-2003* 25-26; Mayer, in *Liber Amicorum Reymond* 187; Mayer, (2016) Rev. Arb. 101; Radicati di Brozolo in *ASA Special Series* 7; Schaffstein, *Res Judicata* [6.214]; Seraglini, (2016) Rev. Arb. 66-75; Yaffe, (2017) 34 J. Int'l Arb. 824. *See* Zajdela, *L'autorité de la chose jugée*.

whether a party, by virtue of assignment, succession, close relationship or otherwise, is bound [...] that these issues are left to the applicable law.[36]

16. Further, Article 28(2) ALI/UNIDROIT (International Institute for the Unification of Private Law) Principles,[37] and scholarly publications[38] leave third-party effects largely unaddressed. One exception favours a broad third-party effect of arbitral awards towards all commercially related third parties in order to avoid any inconsistencies between arbitral awards.[39] However, the author also argues that arbitral tribunals should no longer have to assess a third party's consent to arbitration when extending their jurisdiction but apply standards equivalent to those of courts.[40] Since such standards are inadmissible *de lege lata*,[41] the proposal on res judicata might maintain a certain connotation *de lege ferenda*. In summary, whilst res judicata has gained increasing attention in arbitration scholarship, its third-party dimension is yet to stand in the spotlight. Neither the comparative background, the impact of the NYC, the determination of the applicable law nor transnational principles have been specified. It is this ambition that the present work encompasses.

IV ARGUMENT AND AGENDA

17. The core thesis of this work is to take a restrictive position: an arbitral award's third-party effect requires the third-party scope of the underlying arbitration *agreement*. Only if the previous arbitral tribunal could have exercised personal jurisdiction over the third party, the thesis proposes to advance and apply procedural doctrines on third-party effects as they are either designated by means of private international law (before courts) or might apply by means of transnational principles (before arbitral tribunals). This restrictive position should not be confused with a restrictive position

36. *ILA Final Report on Res Judicata* [41, 46-49] ('The Recommendations maintain the traditional triple identity test, i.e. identity of the claims, of the causes of action and of the parties. [...] [They] refrain from formulating new rules in relation to the requirement of the identity of the parties. First, they do not formulate a requirement as to mutuality [...]. Second, [they] also refrain from formulating definitions as to the notion of parties. [...] There are too many different situations in relation to the question whether a party, by virtue of assignment, succession, close relationship or otherwise, is bound [...] that these issues are left to the applicable law. [...] The Committee notes that, in practise, important and delicate problems arise in relation to the identity of the parties, particularly in relation to groups of companies and BIT arbitrations. These issues are, however, too complex to deal with in [this Report]. [...] Moreover, different countries have different methods and theories for identification of third parties [...] (e.g. alter ago, agency, protection of legitimate expectations). Furthermore, the most important application of identification questions is in the field of piercing the veil of corporations and raises fundamental issues of international corporate law [...] which [...] deserved better and more elaborate treatment elsewhere.').

37. *See* Stürner, (2005) 69 RabelsZ 213 ('equally applicable to international arbitration').

38. Amongst the references in Note 10, brief proposals can be found in Mayer, in *Liber Amicorum Reymond* 199-200; Schaffstein, *Res Judicata* [6.119-120, 6.210-214].

39. Brekoulakis, *Third Parties in Arbitration* Ch. 9-10; Brekoulakis, (2005) 16 Am. Rev. Int'l Arb. 199.

40. Brekoulakis, *Third Parties in Arbitration* [7.43-7.45].

41. *See infra* [40].

towards arbitration in general. Instead, it is a manifestation of the perspective that res judicata can only operate in a fair and practically feasible manner when it is adjusted to other tools of *Forum Coordination*.

18. In particular, pre-emptive tools of Forum Coordination such as multi-party arbitration, consolidations or lis pendens can only operate within the jurisdictional boundaries established under the arbitration agreement (*see* Chapter 1, *infra*). Although res judicata is generally subjected to judgment principles under national arbitration laws (*see* Chapter 2, *infra*), the comprehensive application of judgment principles to multilateral case scenarios risks a severe disruption: in civil procedure, third-party effects of decisions inherently interact with intervention possibilities and are nothing but a *shift of the participatory burden* (*see* Chapter 3, *infra*).

19. By contrast, for arbitral awards, this very interaction can only be effective if the prior arbitral tribunal could have exercised jurisdiction over the third party. Therefore, albeit for individual scenarios only, national arbitration laws contain ample ground to submit that any third-party effect of an arbitral award requires a third-party effect of the underlying arbitration agreement (*see* Chapter 4, *infra*).

20. Whilst the inferences on this tension between arbitral jurisdiction and res judicata in multilateral case scenarios under national laws will mainly be developed in a *descriptive* nature that does not seek to submit on the evolution of national laws, the subsequent Chapters do seek to contribute to such very evolution for cross-border scenarios. They will describe the undeveloped degree of primary and secondary sources on arbitral third-party effects and propose what this examination perceives as doctrinally consistent, practically feasible and individually fair. Accordingly, the proposals remain positivist (*de lege lata*) in nature, albeit the borders to an assessment *de lege ferenda* blur, since the undeveloped degree of primary and secondary sources permits policy considerations.

21. In reaching its proposals, the examination will distinguish between res judicata before courts, on the one hand, and before arbitral tribunals, on the other. As to the former scenario, uniform law precedes any considerations of private international law. In this regard, the NYC has long been considered irrelevant. By contrast, it is the examination's core and genuine contention that Article V(1)(a) NYC can and should require that foreign arbitral awards' third-party effects must not exceed the underlying arbitration agreement. As to the remaining aspects of arbitral res judicata's operation before courts, a referral to national laws remains necessary (*see* Chapter 5, *infra*).

22. In this regard, the classic debate on the law applicable to res judicata is revisited. Whilst the examination will mainly favour the application of the *lex fori*, it submits that certain aspects of multilateral case scenarios which are governed by other laws should be applied as facts (*see* Chapter 6, *infra*).

23. The final mosaic to the third-party effects of international arbitral awards before courts is the unshaped factual effect which can be conferred upon arbitral awards, e.g., as a trigger for objective impossibility or hardship. In this regard, the examination submits that Article V(1)(a) NYC applies nonetheless (*see* Chapter 7, *infra*).

24. Advancing from third-party effects of awards before courts to the effects before arbitral tribunals, the examination considers the application of transnational principles feasible. In this capacity, it seeks to close the existing gap for third-party case scenarios. It proposes a multi-tiered approach adhering to preclusion agreements, the arbitration agreement's scope, comparative principles on due process and considerations of irreconcilability (*see* Chapter 8, *infra*).

25. Whereas the examination will largely focus on res judicata on the substance, the final Chapter addresses the conclusive effects of prior adjudications about *arbitral jurisdiction*. Although foreign judgment principles might be deemed applicable, the examination submits that third parties should only be bound under exceptional circumstances (*see* Chapter 9, *infra*).

26. Summarizing these proposals, the examination submits that its strict solutions are, from a practical point of view, preventing procedural tactics. Moreover, they are setting an incentive for multi-party arbitration and preclusion agreements. From a doctrinal point of view, they are contributing to the perception that international arbitration is a dispute resolution of judicial nature, yet build upon a consensual foundation (*see* Chapter 10, *infra*).

V COMPARATIVE METHODOLOGY

27. International commercial arbitration has taken an intermediate position between transnational and domestic law. On the one hand, it has become an increasingly transnational[42] topic based upon uniform rules and methodologies. On the other hand, many specific issues come down to national laws, either by virtue of the parties' choice or by court supervision. The thesis' methodology reflects this intermediate position in that it builds upon a comparative overview of national laws (*Chapters 1-5*) in order to propose solutions for cross-border issues under uniform, private international and transnational law (*Chapters 6-9*). In this regard, even though the classic method of comparative law might be increasingly exposed to criticism and evolutionary proposals,[43] the thesis' comparative methodology will focus on *functionality*.[44] In this regard, the study is *not* going to follow any strict country-report style. Instead and in

42. *See* Kronke, in *Liber Amicorum von Hoffmann* 1003 ('Inter-national […] implies that the rules […] are primarily designed to cater for transactions taking place between different jurisdictions and across borders. The shift to 'trans-national' paradigm reflects, first, that the global impacts the local […] and, secondly, that private actors are becoming more and more involved in the rule-making process […] reducing thereby the importance of sovereignty.').

43. *See* most recently the harsh criticisms from Legrand, (2017) (Special Issue) Am. J. Comp. L. 1 et seqq. and the responses such as Gordley, *ibid.*, 178-179 ('cultural and functional approaches […] are variants of a more general teleological approach'); Whitman, *ibid.*, 181-190. Cf. Kischel, *Rechtsvergleichung* 95-216.

44. Established by Zweigert and Kötz, *An Introduction to Comparative Law* 34. *See* Basedow, (2016) 71 JZ 269; Michaels, in *The Oxford Handbook of Comparative Law* 340 ('theory hardly exists').

conformity with contemporary arbitration treatises,[45] the thesis compares national solutions within pre-structured issues. This appears both more efficient (avoiding repetitions after country reports) and more effective (increasing the text dedicated to functional inferences). At the same time, the thesis will avoid any 'fusion fallacy':[46] although comparative arguments before national courts might be on the rise,[47] the examination will *not* infer that the law in country A results from a source of country B, but it will maintain the distinctions between national laws.

28. As to the jurisdictions examined: for civil law, the main focus will be on France, Switzerland (as predominant arbitral seats) and Germany (as UNCITRAL Model Law example[48]). Amongst common-law countries, the concentration is going to be on England and Wales as well as the law of the United States (US). References to legal sources of other Commonwealth states, particularly to the emerging arbitration capitals Hong Kong and Singapore, are going to be made when the latter are more specific than or particularly distinct to English law. With regard to common law, the thesis notes the diversity of the legal sources (common and statutory law; State and federal law; classic and mandatory, e.g., labour arbitration) insofar as possible. Yet, at many occasions, joint citations are necessary in order to simplify the illustration. Moreover, it is not only a civilist lawyer's temptation to refer to rule equivalents that leads this examination to focus on the ALI's Restatements within references on US law, but equally the constraints of this thesis.

29. An additional word requires the secondary references offered. Precedence constitutes one of the major divides between common and civil law. Yet, it is pivotal to note:

> [G]eneralizations are hazardous. Common law jurisdictions are by no means as wedded to strict notions of stare decisis as is commonly said to be the case, nor are civil law jurisdictions as averse to them.[49]

30. In this spirit, the examination adheres to the practical relevance of jurisprudence and predominantly cites case references. By way of contrast, academic authorities will be increasingly cited where jurisprudence is unavailable. Moreover, case examples will be continuously facilitated in order to serve illustrative purposes. Yet, it has to be proclaimed that the constraints of this thesis might sometimes prevent an adequately thorough display of some cases' facts.[50]

---

45. *See*, e.g., Bermann, (2015) 381 Rec. des cours; *Born*; *Lew Mistelis and Kröll*; *Poudret and Besson*; *Redfern and Hunter*; Rubino-Samartano, *Comparative International Arbitration*.
46. The term originates from the relation between common law and equity after the Judicature Act 1873.
47. *See*, e.g., *Roper v. Simmons*, 543 U.S. 551, 554 (2005) ('while not controlling our outcome, [EU law] does provide respected and significant confirmation for our own conclusions'); Häberle, (1989) JZ 913.
48. Legislation based on the Model Law has been adopted in 78 States in a total of 109 jurisdictions.
49. Bermann, (2015) 381 Rec. des cours [558].
50. *See* Hobér, (2013) 366 Rec. des cours 123 ('proper analysis [...] requires that each award be put in the proper perspective.').

31. Finally, even for civil-law sources, this examination cites English versions of statutes, decisions and publications as far as possible. Where official translations are unavailable, it offers its own translations of pivotal sources. In domestic debates, civil lawyers might less frequently refer to English contributions and facilitate their official language instead. Yet, for the instant topic, the widest possible facilitation of English publications appears feasible in order to enhance the readership's access to the sources and reflects the transnational *Zeitgeist*.[51]

51. *See* Jayme, (2015) 381 Rec. des cours 35 ('*Nous savons bien que l'anglais est en train de devenir la langue globale et mondiale [...]*').

PART I
The Dichotomy of Forum Coordination for Multilateral Transactions

32. One of the key arguments established in this examination is that the doctrine of res judicata should not be the ambit of an isolated discussion. Instead, res judicata is only one *out of several means of Forum Coordination*. Part I is dedicated to this perception in that it outlines the foundations of the doctrine of res judicata as well as its intrinsic connection to other tools of Forum Coordination. 'Forum Coordination' is a synonym offered for preventing multi-fora disputes and conflicting decisions. This might either occur on a pre-emptive basis (before any decision is rendered), or on a sequential basis (after a decision is rendered). *Chapter 1* is dedicated to the former case scenario and outlines the operation of pre-emptive Forum Coordination in international arbitration, i.e., multi-party arbitration, consolidation and lis pendens. It will reveal that all of these measures regularly require jurisdiction over all parties affected. Therefore, they inherently expose multilateral transactions to the risks of multi-fora disputes. This increases the relevance of sequential Forum Coordination - res judicata. *Chapter 2* summarizes the foundations of this very doctrine under national arbitration laws. In general, arbitration acts largely refer to proceduralist[52] doctrines of res judicata. This induces *Chapter 3* to examine res judicata towards third parties in civil procedure. It will reveal that judgments' third-party effects regularly interact with intervention possibilities. Therefore, a judgment's third-party effect is merely perceived as a *shift of the participatory burden*. Such inference highlights the inherent dichotomy against which the assessment of arbitral awards' third-party effects in Part II has to be undertaken: whilst the proceduralist connotation of res judicata inclines to transfer judgment principles, the latter are developed on the basis of courts' comprehensive jurisdictional power. For arbitral tribunals, such jurisdictional power does not exist. Instead, consent determines arbitral jurisdiction. This induces Part II to examine whether consent comprises additional relevance for the limits of arbitral res judicata.

52. The term comprises a dual connotation, i.e., *strict* and *procedural doctrine*.

CHAPTER 1

The Contractual Perception of Arbitral Jurisdiction as Trigger of Multi-Fora Disputes

33. Multilateral cross-border transactions give rise to the immanent need for coordinated dispute resolution. Respective measures known from litigation are plentiful. E.g., for a seller who seeks to hold both a purchaser and a guarantor liable, there are several applications in order to ensure that a potential issue as to the sold goods' conformity is decided consistently towards both opponents: from the outset, the seller could sue the purchaser and the guarantor in joint proceedings or apply for a measure of third-party notice. Eventually, in parallel proceedings against each opponent, the seller might seek consolidation. Alternatively, a measure of lis pendens could be considered. It is not until a decision against one of the opponents has been issued that the present issue of res judicata arises.

34. Against this outline, one might quickly reach the conclusion that the complex topic of res judicata was practically irrelevant in coordinating multilateral transactions. However, reality reveals the very opposite. In international arbitration, res judicata comprises nothing but a pivotal position. Particularly, multi-party arbitration can only operate under strict consensual boundaries (*see* §1.01, *infra*). Therefore, international multi-*party* case scenarios will frequently turn into multi-fora disputes, i.e., separate parallel proceedings on related aspects. Such multi-fora disputes comprise various detriments such as the potential for contradicting decisions (*see* §1.02, *infra*).

35. This leads to a focus on pre-emptive Forum Coordination such as third-party notice, consolidation and lis pendens. They correspond to each other in that they originate in procedural law where they operate on genuine criteria of connection between two disputes as to the facts, claims and parties. Yet, in international arbitration, these criteria have only limited efficacy. Above all, the consensual barriers of multi-party arbitration have a prolonged effect. Hence, pre-emptive measures generally adhere to the limits set by the arbitration agreement and require the tribunal's personal jurisdiction over third parties (*see* §1.03, *infra*). Certainly, in many scenarios the very arbitral jurisdiction itself is disputed and brought before various fora. Here, there are hardly any means for restricting each forum's prerogative in assessing the arbitral jurisdiction (*see* §1.04, *infra*). Accordingly, multi-fora disputes are an inherent risk to any multilateral transaction without a comprehensive multi-party arbitration clause. The structural conclusion for the potential application of res judicata is: *in multilateral transactions, res judicata comprises a crossroads position, first, of particular practical relevance and, second, with the potential to undermine consensual barriers to multi-party arbitration* (*see* §1.05, *infra*).

§1.01 MULTI-PARTY ARBITRATION'S OBSTACLES

36. In international litigation, various grounds for international jurisdiction such as the defendant's localization, the place of performance, a sufficient connection of joint defendants or exorbitant grounds can create *'Procedural Disorder'*.[53] Legally, this multiplicity has been held to be in conformity with public international law by the Permanent Court of International Justice (PCIJ).[54] Effectively, it is one of the major reasons why commercial parties opt for forum-selection and arbitration clauses.[55] The parties' immanent interest to avoid any procedural disorder and thereby reduce litigation risks is also the main rationale behind the law's inherent mandate to support such clauses.[56]

37. Such necessity is particularly given in the large number of transactions comprising more than two parties: construction, industrial and maritime projects; M&A transactions; commodity purchases or distribution chains.[57] In those situations, multiple parties frequently agree on multi-party arbitration. For example, roughly one-third of all International Chamber of Commerce (ICC) arbitrations now involve at least three parties.[58] Therefore, updates to the leading arbitration rules inserted provisions for arbitration with more than one claimant, more than one defendant or 'additional parties'.[59] The role of 'additional parties' illustrates the necessity to allow some parties

53. Ben Hamida, in *Procédures parallèles et décisions contradictoires* 19. Cf. Debourg, in *Procédures parallèles et décisions contradictoires* 74; Mayer, (2013) 4 J. Int Disp Resolution 407-410; Nicklisch, (1994) 4 J. Int Arb. 57; Mauro-Samartano, *International Arbitration* 902; Schneider, (1990) 6 Arb. Int'l 101.
54. *Lotus* (*France v. Turkey*), Judgment, (1927) 10 PCIJ Rep. Ser. A, 19 ('wide measure of discretion').
55. *M/S Bremen v. Zapata Off-Shore Co*, 407 U.S. 1, 13 (1972); *Reisman Craig Park and Paulsson* 9-86.
56. *See* Kronke, *in Liber amicorum Geimer* 397.
57. Cf. Revised Uniform Arbitration Act, § 10 comment 1 ('multi-party disputes are common in construction, insurance, maritime and sales contexts'); Böckstiegel, in *Die Beteiligung Dritter am Schiedsverfahren* 1; *Born* 2564; Hobér, (2013) 366 Rec. des cours 246; Schneider, (1990) 6 Arb. Int'l 102.
58. Cf. ICC, *2012 Statistical Report*, (2013) 24 ICC Ct. Bull. 10. *See* further Bond, *Multiparty Arbitration* 40; Whitesell and Silva-Romero, *ICC Bulletin – Special Supplement* 7.
59. For example Art. 8(1) ICC Rules; Art. 27 HKIAC Rules; Art. 24(1)(b) SIAC Rules; Art. 4(2) Swiss Rules; Art. 17(5) UNCITRAL Rules. Amongst statutes *see* s. 35 1996 Arbitration Act; Australian 2011 Arbitration Act, § 24; New Zealand Arbitration Act, § 6(2), Schedule 2, Art. 2.

to pursue their genuine interests detached from the claimant's or the respondent's side. For example, such an additional party might be exposed to a claim of the claimant and have an interest to immediately claim indemnity from the respondent.[60] Yet, despite its practical preferability for some situations, multi-party arbitration is facing significant limitations that can be summarized into three categories: general personal jurisdiction (*see* [A], *infra*), particular jurisdiction for connected contracts (*see* [B], *infra*) and post-jurisdictional aspects such as the selection of the arbitrators (*see* [C], *infra*).[61] These limitations render many multilateral transactions insusceptible to multi-party arbitration.

[A] Necessary Consent to Arbitration: The Salient Discussion on Non-signatories

38. Any multi-party arbitration rests upon *all* parties' consent. This necessitates that all parties have agreed to arbitration in general (personal jurisdiction) and that the relevant claims fall under the signed clause's scope (subject matter jurisdiction).[62] If any requirement is not met, the arbitral institution might reject to initiate the proceedings,[63] the tribunal might decline jurisdiction, the competent court at the arbitral seat might annul the award[64] or courts abroad will deny recognition and enforcement under Article V(1)(a) NYC.[65] Certainly, parties are able to facilitate model clauses such as the ICC's recommended clause providing for the guarantee of multi-party arbitration.[66] However, if they do not, significant problems arise. Therefore, in its

60. Cf. Schwab, in *Festschrift Habscheid* 287.
61. *See* Fouchard, in *Multiparty Business Disputes* 59; Hanotiau, *Complex Arbitrations* [3]; Meier in Arroyo (ed.), *Arbitration in Switzerland* Ch. 13 [27-47].
62. Also known as: 'jurisdiction to adjudicate' and 'jurisdiction to prescribe' in US law. *See*, e.g., Art. 7 UNCITRAL Model Law ('"Arbitration agreement" is an *agreement by the parties* to submit to arbitration *all or certain disputes* which have arisen or which may arise between them in respect of *a defined legal relationship*, whether contractual or not') (emphasis added); *Teamsters Local Union No. 764 v. JH Merrit and Co*, 770 F.2d 40, 42 (3d Cir. 1985).
63. *See*, e.g., Art. 6(4) ICC Rules ('The arbitration shall proceed if and to the extent that the Court is prima facie satisfied that [...] (i) where there are more than two parties to the arbitration [...] that an arbitration agreement under the Rules that binds them all may exist; and (ii) where claims [...] are made under more than one arbitration agreement [...] that all parties to the arbitration may have agreed that those claims can be determined together in a single arbitration.').
64. *See* Art. 34(2)(a)(i) Model Law ('An arbitral award may be set aside by the court [...] only if [...] the [arbitration] agreement is not valid under the law to which the parties have subjected it or, failing any indication thereon, under the law of this State [...].'). *See* correspondingly s. 67(1)(a) English Arbitration Act; Art. 1520 No. 1 French CPC; Art. 190(2)(b) Swiss PILA; s. 10(4) FAA.
65. 'Recognition and enforcement of the award may be refused [...] only if [...] the [arbitration] agreement is not valid under the law to which the parties have subjected it or, failing any indication thereon, under the law of the country where the award was made [...]'.
66. 'The parties to the present clause agree that: (a) If any such dispute raises issues which are the same as or are connected with issues raised in a related dispute arising in connection with a contract between a party to this contract and a third party, and provided that such related dispute is to be or has been submitted to arbitration under the ICC Rules, (b) and if the parties to such related dispute have themselves agreed., in their original arbitration agreement or any subsequent agreement, that such related dispute shall be finally settled in an ICC multi-party arbitration together with any dispute which might arise under a connected contract, (c) and provided that one or other of the parties to this contract also requires or accepts the same after

1994 *Delvolvé Report* proposing this very model clause, the ICC's Commission on International Arbitration concluded:

> The difficulties of multi-party arbitrations all result from a single cause. Arbitration has a contractual basis; only the common will of the contracting parties can entitle a person to bring proceedings before an arbitral tribunal against another person and oblige that other person to appear before it. [67]

39. Frequently, the very will of a third party that has not signed an arbitration agreement will be heavily disputed. In fact, arbitral jurisdiction over non-signatories that are parties to multilateral transactions might be regarded as one of the most heavily debated topics of international arbitration. It has caused a welter of appellate decisions, e.g., twenty-one in France alone during the past five years.[68] As jurisdiction is constantly going to lie at the heart of this examination's argument on res judicata, an outline of the jurisdictional debate appears feasible as to the substantive standard under arbitration laws (*see* [1], *infra*) and in private international law (*see* [2], *infra*). Yet, it has to be proclaimed that these issues would in themselves justify a treatise and the following paragraphs can constitute nothing but a very brief summary of the discussion.

[1] Standards under National Arbitration Laws

40. Nowadays, the general legal standard for the effects of arbitration agreements on such non-signatories that are affected by the underlying *substantive* transaction (e.g., guarantors, suppliers, parent companies, subsidiaries) is close to being undisputed: neither strict proposals that seek to focus only on an arbitration clause's signatures[69] nor lenient proposals foregoing consensual standards[70] prevail. Instead, it is a common ground of scholarship[71] and annulment/enforcement courts[72] that arbitral

learning of the said connected dispute, then such dispute hereunder and such related dispute shall be finally settled by the same arbitrator or arbitrators, who shall be appointed by common agreement amongst all the parties to the arbitration combined in this way, or by the Court of Arbitration of the ICC in accordance with the Guidelines for ICC Multi-Party Arbitration.'

67. Cf. *Final Report on Multiparty Arbitrations* published in (1995) 6 ICC Bulletin 26, [5].
68. *See* Train, (2017) Rev. Arb. 391.
69. *See* Poudret, (1995) Clunet 893-904; Mansel, in *Festschrift Maier-Reimer* 426 et seqq. *See* for invalidation of such concerns ATF 129 III 727, 735 with further references.
70. *See* Brekoulakis, *Third Parties in Arbitration* [7.25-8.42], discussed *infra* [517]. For choice-of-court agreements *see* Black and Pitel, (2016) 12 J. Priv Int'l L. 26 ('recent American decisions [...] have used both a closely related test and a global-transaction test to hold non-parties bound'); ECJ, 7 February 2013, *Refcomp*, C-543/10, ECLI:EU:C:2013:62; ECJ, 20 April 2016, *Profit Investment*, C-366/13, ECLI:EU:C:2016:13, [36].
71. *Born* 1417; *Poudret and Besson* [251] ('In the majority of cases, the status as party of a non-signatory does not result from the text of the agreement containing the arbitration clause, but from tacit acceptance.'); Park, in *Multiple Party Actions* [1.88] (providing an appendix of twenty-three arbitral awards and concluding that 'arbitrators usually look to theories related to implied consent and lack of corporate responsibility.'); Rubino-Samartano, *International Arbitration* 244; Sandrock, in *Liber Amicorum Lalive* 632 (providing eight brief conclusions); Steingruber, *Consent in International Arbitration* [9.30].
72. *See*, e.g., *Dallah Real Estate and Tourism Holding Company Co. v. Ministry of Religious Affairs of the Government of Pakistan*, [2011] 1 AC 763, [39] per Moore-Bick LJ (UKSC); *Stellar Shipping*

jurisdiction over non-signatories requires at least implied consent to the arbitration agreement (also by agency) or an extraordinarily frivolous action suspending the consent requirement (e.g., alter ego, piercing the corporate veil, estoppel). Whilst such lack of power of arbitral tribunals over third parties was identified as one of the arbitration's 'worst features' in the 2018 Queen Mary International Arbitration Survey, it remains the law.

41. In contrast to its establishment, the *application* of this standard is exposed to significant differences. The primary reason is the nature of the implied-consent standard, being '*fact specific*'[73] and assessed on a '*case-by-case basis, requiring a close analysis of the circumstances in which the agreement was made, the corporate and practical relationship […] and the intention of the parties.*'[74] Moreover, any factual assessment will heavily depend on a jurisdiction's leading cases, influential publications and its practitioners' notions. Whilst further examples will follow with regard to the specific transactions exposed to res judicata,[75] 'groups of companies' might be a preeminent example: although formally applying a universal consent threshold,[76] French[77] and arbitral[78] jurisprudence provide more lenient results than others in that they put an increased emphasis on the negotiation and performance of the contract. An

---

Co. LLC v. Hudson Shipping Lines, (2010) EWHC 2985 (Comm); *Peterson Farms Inc. v. C&M Farming Ltd*, [2004] EWHC 121 at [43] (Comm) (name borrowing). BGH, [2011] NJW-RR 1350, [23]; BGH, [2014] SchiedsVZ 151, [17 and 30]; ATF 117 II 94, 98; TF, 1 July 2014, 4A_450/2013, [3.2]; *John Wiley & Sons Inc. v. Livingston*, 376 U.S. 543, 547 (1964); *First Options of Chicago Inc. v. Kaplan*, 514 U.S. 938 (1995); *Thomson-CSF SA v. American Arbitration Association*, 64 F.3d 411 (2d Cir. 1995); *Smoothline Ltd v. NAFT*, 249 F.3d 147 (2d Cir. 2001); *Bridas S.I.P.A.C. v. Government of Turkmenistan*, 447 F.3d 411 (5th Cir. 2006).

73. Hanotiau, *Complex Arbitrations* [203, 206].
74. *ICC Case 9517*, Arbitral Award, 2000, (1996-2000) IV ICC Collection 876, [5].
75. *See infra* [254-274].
76. *ICC Case 4131, The Dow Chemical Company and others v. ISOVER Saint Gobain, Interim Award*, (1984) IX Y.C.A. 131 ('[T]he circumstances and the documents analyzed […] show that such application conforms to the *mutual intent* of the parties.'); *Fouchard Gaillard and Goldman* [500] ('Clearly, it is not so much the existence of a group that results in the carious companies of the group being bound by the agreement signed by only one of them, but the *true intention* of the parties.'); Train, (2017) Rev. Arb. 392 ('*recherhe de la volonté implicite des parties*').
77. Cass. (1e civ.), *sté Alcatel Business Systems (ABS) et al. v. Amkor Technology et al*, 27 March 2007, [2007] JCP I 168 No. 11 ('the effect of international arbitration clauses extends to the parties directly involved in the performance of the contract and any disputes that may arise in connection therewith.' – Translation by Mayer, *infra* [5.15]); Cass. (1e civ.), *Cotunav*, 25 June 1991, [1991] Rev. Arb. 453; CA Paris, *sté Korsnas Marma v. Sté Durand-Auzias*, 30 November 1988, [1989] Rev. Arb. 691; CA Paris, *sté Ofer Brothers v. The Tokyo Marine and Fire Insurance Co. Ltd et al*, Judgment 14 February 1989, also [1989] Rev. Arb. 691; CA Paris, *sté 2000 v. sté Project XJ 220 ITD et al*, 7 December 1994, [1996] Rev. Arb. 245; CA Paris, *SMABTP et al. v. sté Statinor et al*, 22 March 1995, [1997] Rev. Arb. 550. *See* therefore Mayer, in PCA (ed.), *Multi-Party Actions* [5.15] ('The Cour de cassation has [effectively] eliminated any reference to a supposed intent which, in certain decisions of the Paris Court of Appeal, rested on a double presumption: of knowledge of the arbitration clause and, as a consequence, of consent thereto.').
78. *See ICC Case 2375*, Arbitral Award, 1975, (1976) Clunet 973 (third-party signed protocol and performed part of the contract); *ICC Case 3879*, Westland Helicopters, Interim Award, 5 March 1984, (1986) XI Y.C.A. 127 (annulled on grounds of misapplication of international law on state defendants by TF, 19 July 1988, (1991) XVI Y.C.A. 174); *ICC Case 5894*, Arbitral Award, 1989, (1991) 2 ICC Bull. 25 (subsidiaries of parties to framework agreement); *ICC Case 8910*, Arbitral

infamous example of the resulting divergences is the *Dallah* case where the set-aside court in Paris considered the facts sufficient for the Pakistan Ministry of Defence to be bound to an arbitration clause as a non-signatory and the enforcement court in London – explicitly applying French law – reached the very opposite result.[79]

42. A distinct jurisdictional discussion concerns the case scenario in which third parties are not involved from the *outset*, but by virtue of *subsequent* actions, a topic aptly titled in a scholarly observation as the *'circulation of arbitration agreements'*.[80] In this regard, it appears highly feasible to distinguish between four scenarios. Primarily, in universal successions such as inheritances or corporate transformations, successors comprehensively acquire the predecessors' rights and obligations. The situation is equally unproblematic when an entire contract, including an arbitration clause, is transferred. Acquiring all rights and obligations under the contract's stipulations, the successors also acquires the position under the arbitration clause.[81]

43. The third, more complex scenario concerns the assignment of receivables. As a proclamation, the frequently used term 'transfer' of arbitration clauses might be misleading as the assignor can remain bound to arbitrate.[82] In any case, arbitration clauses are generally separate from the underlying contract's substantive rights and obligations. An assignment of individual receivables merely covers the latter. It stands against this background that courts in Russia[83] and Italy[84] held an assignee *not* bound to arbitrate. Yet, in this regard, the doctrine of severability is often over-displayed

---

Award, 1998, (1996-2000) IV ICC Collection 569 (tripartite arrangement with guarantee); *ICC Case 9762*, Arbitral Award, 2001, (2004) XXIX Y.C.A. 26 (state whose ministry was a signatory to the arbitration clause).

79. *Dallah Real Estate and Tourism Holding Company v. The Ministry of Religious Affairs, Government of Pakistan* [2010] UKSC 46; CA Paris, *Gouvernement du Pakistan – Ministère des Affaires Religieuses v. sté Dallah Real Estate and Tourism Holding Company*, 17 February 2011, 09/28533 09/28535 and 09/28541. *See* the comment on these two judgments by Schlosser, (2010) 15 ZZP Int 405.

80. Mayer, (2005) Clunet 251 (Title: *'La circulation des conventions d'arbitrage'*).

81. Germany: BGHZ 68, 356, 359; BayObLGZ 1999, 255, 266 f.; OLG Koblenz, [1990] NJW-RR, 1374 (obiter). France: CA Paris, *Al-Kawthar Investment Co. Ltd v. BNP*, 11 March 1993, [1994] Rev. Arb. 735; *ICC Case 2626*, Arbitral Award, 1977, (1978) 105 Clunet 980; *ICC Case 6754*, Arbitral Award, 1993, (1995) 122 Clunet 1009 (1995). England: s. 8(1) 1996 Arbitration Act ('Unless otherwise agreed by the parties, an arbitration agreement is not discharged by the death of a party and may be enforced by or against the personal representatives of that party.'); *Astra Insurance v. Sphere Drake Insurance and others*, [2000] 2 Lloyd's Rep. 550 at [20] per Steel J. (QB). *See Baytur v. Finagro*, [1991] 4 All ER 129 (CA) (after a company split into two companies, the Court of Appeal referred to an 'assignee' and required information and an intervention of the assignee). USA: *Fyrnetics (HK) Ltd v. Quantum Group Inc*, 293 F.3d 1023, 1029 (7th Cir. 2002) (successor company bound by arbitration agreement signed by entity that was merged into successor company); *AT&S Transp LLC v. Odyssey Logistics & Tech Corp*, 803 NYS2d 118 (NY App Div 2005). *See Born* 1463-1465.

82. Mayer, (2005) Clunet 251 [9 and 14-15] with references to two unpublished ICC Awards. *See* for transfer of debts ATF 134 III 565, [5.3.2]; TF, 8 March 2012, 4A_627/2011, [3.2].

83. CA Moscow, (2000) Riv dell'arb 499.

84. Corte di Cassazione, 12616, [1999] Foro Italia 2979. *Crit* Festi, *La clausula compromissoria* 272-284; *Poudret and Besson* [287].

whilst it essentially safeguards that tribunals can adjudicate invalid contracts.[85] Correspondingly, the default solution under the vast majority of jurisdictions is that assignees are bound to arbitrate.[86] Notably, English law requires notice to the debtor.[87] French law even assumes jurisdiction regardless of the assignment's validity.[88] In general, all of those jurisdictions require a justification as to the successors' consent to arbitrate. If addressed at all, the justifications vary from assuming an implied consent[89] to openly regarding the arbitration clause as ancillary or accessory to the legal relationship.[90] This discussion might be indecisive in that both concepts concur that an assignee is *not* bound to arbitrate if he explicitly expresses this intention (*intuitus personae*).[91]

44. The final case scenario concerns the transfer of property, e.g., in distribution chains. Generally, such transfer does *not* result in any obligation to arbitrate. Regardless of whether a jurisdiction assesses the property distinctively from the sales contract, chains of sales are generally not inter-related. An exception contains French law. Notably, already in substantive law, it allows direct claims (*action directe*). In arbitration, where former jurisprudence rejected the arbitration clause's extension in chains of sales contract,[92] there was a prudent change in 2001,[93] following the now

85. Mayer, (2005) Clunet 251 [8]; *Poudret and Besson* [284].
86. Switzerland: TF, 16 October 2003, ATF 129 III 727, 735. *See also* ATF 93 I 323 (forum-selection clause). Germany: BGHZ 68, 356, 359 (obiter); BGHZ 71, 162; BGHZ 77, 32; BGH, [1979] MDR 382; BGH, [1979] NJW 2567; BGH, [1998] NJW 371; BGH, [2000] NJW 2346. France: Cass. (2e civ), 20 December 2001, [2002] Rev. Arb. 379. Domestic arbitration: Cass. (1e civ.), *Taurus Films*, 8 February 2000, [2000] Rev. Arb. 280 (*'la clause d'arbitrage international s'impose à toute partie venant aux droits de l'un des contractants'*). Sweden: Supreme Court of Sweden, *MS Emja Braack Shiffahrts KG v. Wärtsilä Diesel Aktiebolag*, 15 October 1997, [1998] Rev. Arb. 431. USA: *Asset Allocation & Mgt Co. v. W Employers Ins. Co*, 892 F.2d 566, 574 (7th Cir. 1989); *Star-Kist Foods Inc. v. Diakan Hope SA*, 423 FSupp 1220, 1222-1224 (C.D. Cal. 1976); *SE* Pa. *Transp Auth v. AWS Remediation Inc*, 2003 WL 21994811 (E.D. Pa); *Cedrela Transp Ltd v. Banque Cantonale Vaudoise*, 67 FSupp2d 353, 354-356 (S.D.N.Y. 1999); *Donel Corp. v. Kosher Overseers Ass'n of Am*, 2001 WL 228364, 3 (S.D.N.Y.); *HT of Highlands Ranch Inc. v. Hollywood Tanning Sys Inc*, 590 FSupp2d 677, 684 (DNJ 2008). England: *Shayler v. Woolf*, [1946] LR Chancery 320 (CA); *The League*, [1984] 2 Lloyd's Rep. 259 (QB); *The Jordan Nicolov*, [1990] 2 Lloyd's Rep. 11 (QB); *Bawejem v. MC Fabrications*, [1999] BCIC 174 (CA); *West Tankers Inc. v. Ras Riunione Adriatica Di Sicurta SpA*, [2005] EWHC 454 (Comm); *Mustill and Boyd* 137-138. A Draft of the Arbitration Bill of 1995 pursuant to which separability did not affect the transfer of the arbitration agreement has not been adopted. *See* DAC Report §§ 44-46.
87. *Republic of Kazakhstan v. Istil Group Inc*, [2006] EWHC 448; *Baytur SA v. Finagro Holding SA*, [1991] All ER 129; *Eurosteel Ltd v. Stinnes AG*, [200] CLC 470; *Russell on Arbitration* [3-017].
88. Cass. (1e civ.), *Cimat*, Judgment of 28 May 2002, [2003] Rev. Arb. 397; CA Paris, [2004] Rev. Arb. 623.
89. Berger and Kellerhals, *Arbitration in Switzerland* [547-549] (with reference to separability and primary nature as court waiver). *See Fouchard Gaillard and Goldman* [707].
90. Mayer, (2005) Clunet 251 [10]; Seraglini and Ortscheidt, *Droit de l'arbitrage* [202], [205]; Loquin, in *JCl procédure civile* Fasc 1020 [144]. Switzerland: Kaufmann-Kohler and Rigozzi, *International Arbitration in Switzerland* [3.155].
91. TF, 13 October 1992, [1993] ASA Bull. 68, 70-71; ATF 128 III 50, 62; Cass. (2e civ), 28 May 2002, [2003] Rev. Arb. 397; *Fouchard Gaillard and Goldman* [720].
92. Cass. (1e civ.), *Fraser v. Compagnie européenne des Pétroles*, 6 November 1990, [1991] Rev. Arb. 73; CA Paris, *SMABTP v. Statinor*, 22 March 1995, [1997] Rev. Arb. 550.
93. Cass. (1e civ.), *Peavey*, 6 February 2001, [2001] Rev. Arb. 765 (*'dans une chaîne homogène de contrats translatifs de marchandises, la clause d'arbitrage international se transmet avec l'action contractuelle, sauf preuve de l'ignorance raisonnable de l'existence de cette clause'*).

comprehensive, 'automatic' transfer under the 2007 *ABS* decision.[94] In conclusion, arbitral jurisdiction towards non-signatories is particularly delicate when it comes to assessing the implied consent in multilateral transactions. In addition, successors are regularly bound, although further discrepancies between national laws remain. Accordingly, arbitral jurisdiction will be heavily influenced by perceptions of the applicable law.

[2] Applicable Law

45. In general, there are several perspectives on the law applicable to jurisdictional questions:[95] under arbitration rules and laws, *arbitral tribunals* are under no obligation to follow a particular law other than the one chosen by the parties.[96] If anything, tribunals might contemplate on national private international law in order to anticipate eventual court reviews. Turning to the latter, *courts* may have to determine the applicable law when deciding on (i) a motion to stay court proceedings, compel arbitration or award damages for the breach of an arbitration agreement; (ii) set asides, e.g., under Article 34(2)(i)(a) Model Law[97]; or (iii) the recognition and enforcement of a foreign award under Article V(1)(a) NYC.[98] The applicable law might concern the parties' capacity to arbitrate, arbitrability as well as the formal, or substantive validity of the arbitration agreement. In any situation:

> there unquestionably circulate today an abundance of methodologies for identifying the law applicable to the agreement to arbitrate.[99]

46. This applies particularly to the effect on third parties where there is a range of potential characterizations and connecting factors. Whilst a thorough display of the relevant jurisprudence is impossible, an outline shall be provided. The US Court of Appeals for the Second Circuit applied the residual law of the third person as a form of conflictualist protection of this very party.[100] Moreover, arbitral tribunals applied the *lex causae* of the grounds for particular extended effects, i.e., the law applicable on agency, assignment and alter ego.[101] Furthermore, since third-party jurisdiction is effectively an issue of implied consent, German and Swiss law refers to the law of the

---

94. Cass. (1e civ.), *sté ABS et al. v. Amkor Technology*, 27 March 2007, [2007] Rev. Arb. 785 ('*dans une chaîne de contrats translatifs de propriété, la clause compromissoire est transmise de facon automatique en tant qu'accessore du droit d'action, lui-même accessoire du droit substantiel transmis, sans incidence du caractère homogène ou hétérogène de cette chaîne*').
95. Cf. Berger, *International Economic Arbitration* 304; Bermann, (2015) 381 Rec. des cours [142]; *Lew Mistelis and Kröll* 109.
96. Cf. Bermann, (2015) 381 Rec. des cours [151]; *Born* 579; Symeonides, (2016) 384 Rec. des cours 78. *See* Art. 36(1) HKIAC Rules; Art. 21(1) ICC Rules; Art. 31(1) SIAC Rules; Art. 35 (1) UNCITRAL Rules.
97. For the wording *see supra* Note 63.
98. For the wording *see supra* Note 64.
99. Bermann, (2015) 381 Rec. des cours [181].
100. *Sarhank Group v. Oracle Corp*, 404 F.3d 662 (2d Cir. 2005).
101. *ICC Case 5730*, (1990) 117 Clunet 1029; *ICC Case 10758*, Final Award, (2001) 128 (Clunet) 1171.

arbitration agreement's substantive validity.[102] Yet again, the resulting conflicts rule is in itself heavily debated. Whilst, e.g., Article V(1)(a) NYC provides for the law of the arbitral seat as the fallback option, the parties might be deemed to have impliedly chosen the law of the main contract to the (technically separable) arbitration clause contained therein. This is, e.g., the approach frequently adopted by English[103] and German[104] courts. US courts apply the *lex fori* revealing the concept that the arbitration agreement was nothing but a remedy to prevent litigation.[105] Finally, there are 'arbitration-specific' approaches preferring validation principles over complete bodies of law such as Article 178(2) Swiss Private International Law Act's (PILA) *in favorem validatis*[106] and French jurisprudence's transnational standards.[107] Comparable standards are also indicated by some US jurisprudence focusing only on the *lex fori*'s public policy.[108] An arbitration-specific approach privy to arbitral jurisdiction over parent companies and subsidiaries is the so-called group-of-companies jurisprudence of ICC tribunals and the Paris Court of Appeal, which facilitates a transnational *lex mercatoria* on implied consent.[109] The conclusion of this rapid overview on the issue of arbitral jurisdiction towards non-signatories is that the topic will regularly be exposed to a range of arguments both to the conflictualist determination as well as to the substantive application of the law.

---

102. TF, 19 August 2008, 4A_128/2008, [4.1.1]; BGH, [2014] SchiedsVZ 151, [20-21].
103. For example *International Tank & Pipe SAK v. Kuwait Aviation Fuelling Co. KSG*, [1975] QB 224 (CA); *Qatar Petroleum v. Shell International Petroleum*, [1983] 3 Lloyd's Rep. 35 (CA); *ABB Lummus Global Ltd v. Keppel Fels Ltd*, [1999] 2 Lloyd's Rep. 24; *Sonatrach Petroleum Corp. v. Ferrell International Ltd*, [2002] 1 All ER (Comm) 627; *Tonicstar Ltd v. American Home Assurance Co*, [2005] Lloyd's Rep. 32; *Svenska Petroleum Corp. v. Ferrell International Ltd*, [2002] 1 All ER 627 (Comm); *Svenska Petroleum Exploration AB v. Government of the Republic of Lithuania (No 2)*, [2005] EWHC 2437 (Comm). *Contra Dicey Morris and Collins* [16-018] and Rule 64 (1) (b). Yet, *see Sulamérica CIA Nacional de Seguros SA v. Enesa Engaharia*, [2012] EWCA Civ 638, [59] ('open question whether the law of the arbitration is the chosen law of the contract or the law of the arbitration seat').
104. For example, BGHZ 40, 320, [I.1]; BGH, [1976] NJW 1591, [IV.2b]; BGH, 3 May 2011, XI ZR 374/08, [38]; OLG Düsseldorf, [1996] RIW 239, 240 (obiter); OLG München, [2000] IPRspr No. 182b, [III.2d.aa] ('erstes Urteil'); BayObLG, [2004] SchiedsVZ 163, [II.3]; OLG Hamburg, 15 June 2009, 6 Sch 2/09, [22]; OLG Jena, 13 January 2011, 1 Sch 1/08, [B.II.1]; OLG München, 23 June 2017, 34 SchH3/16.
105. Cf. *Theofano Maritime Co. v. 9,55119 Long Tons of Chrome* Ore, 122 FSupp 853, 858 (DMd 1954); Restatement (Third) International Commercial Arbitration (Tentative Draft No. 4 2015), § 2-2.
106. '[T]he arbitration agreement shall be valid if it complies with the requirements of the law chosen by the parties or [...] the law applicable to the principal contract, or with Swiss law'.
107. Cass. (1e civ.), *Municipalité de Khoms El Mergeb v. sté Dalico*, 20 December 1993, [1994] Rev. Arb. 116 ('the existence and effectiveness of the arbitration agreement are to be assessed., subject to the mandatory rules of French law and international public policy, on the basis of the parties' common intention, there being no need to refer to any national law' - translation according to *Fouchard Gaillard and Goldman* [437]).
108. *See Rhône Méditerranée v. Achille Lauro*, 712 F.2d 50 (3d Cir. 1982) ('an agreement is null and void only (1) when it is subject to an internationally recognized defence such as duress, mistake, fraud or waiver, or (2) when it contravenes fundamental policies of the forum state'); *Ledee v. Ceramiche Ragno*, 684 F.2d 184 (1st Cir. 1982).
109. *See* Mayer, (1989) 217 Rec. des cours 407. On the jurisprudence *see supra* [41].

[B] Necessary Connection of Multiple Arbitration Agreements

47. Even if all parties to a multilateral transaction consented to arbitrate *in general*, a further obstacle arises in that all parties have to agree on a *particular* tribunal's jurisdiction. Above all, when several connected contracts exist, the arbitration clauses have to, at least impliedly, refer to each other.[110] Two cases reveal the delicacy of this standard.

48. As a first example, the French *Sofidif* case illustrates the gravity of distinct arbitral seats and distinct parties in connected contracts. The French Commissariat for Nuclear Energy (claimant 1) and the Iranian Organization for Atomic Energy (respondent) concluded an agreement on the peaceful development of nuclear energy and formed Sofidif (claimant 2), a company under French law which was supposed to carry out the nuclear developments in Iran. All disputes between these parties were to be settled by ICC arbitration in *Paris*. Sofidif then purchased Uranium from claimant 1's 100% subsidiary Eurodif (claimant 3) and agreed on ICC arbitration in *Geneva*. Eventually, in the course of the Iranian revolution, the respondent terminated the relationship and seized the Uranium development. Hence, the claimants initiated ICC arbitration in Paris. Although the respondent has never formed an arbitration agreement with Eurodif, and Eurodif only consented to arbitration in Geneva, the arbitral tribunal accepted jurisdiction in arguing that only multi-party arbitration could guarantee res judicata.[111] However, this reasoning was overruled, first in the Paris Court of Appeal's obiter dictum, then in the Supreme Court's and the Versailles Court of Appeal's *ratio decidendi*. The parallel arbitration clauses did not suffice to allow multi-party arbitration.[112]

49. Moreover, the *Adgas* case before the English Court of Appeal is a natural illustration for consensual thresholds even if two arbitration clauses do share the applicable law and the arbitral seat. This case concerned the construction of a plant producing liquefied natural gas in the Arabian Gulf. The Abu Dhabi employer contracted with the subsidiary of a large US construction enterprise. The latter chose a Japanese sub-contractor. Both contracts provided for arbitration in London and the applicability of English law. The employer initiated arbitration against the main contractor alleging that the gas tanks were defective. The main contractor alleged that any defects were the sub-contractor's responsibility and therefore sought to join the latter. However, the employer as well as the sub-contractor objected. Hence, the main

---

110. Fouchard, in *Multiparty Business Disputes* 63; *Schlosser* [560-562].

111. *ICC Case*, Arbitral Award, 25 April 1985, unpublished, reported by Gaillard, [1987] Rev. Arb. 283 ('*Au surplus, une sentence arbitrale rendue contre Sofidif à l'instance d'Eurodif ne serait vraisemblablement pas opposable aux présentes défenderesses qui, en l'absence d'un compromis arbitral les liant à Eurodif, ne peuvent pas être contraintes à participer à la procédure entre Eurodif et Sofidif. Sofidif est ainsi fondée à rechercher immédiatement et directement les défenderesses* [...].' The facts reported in this examination are significantly simplified.

112. CA Paris, *Sofidif*, 19 December 1986, [1987] Rev. Arb. 359; Cass. (1e civ.), *Sofidif*, 8 March 1988; CA Versailles, *Sofidif*, 7 March 1990, [1991] Rev. Arb. 326.

contractor initiated parallel arbitration against the sub-contractor demanding indemnification. The matter came before the Court of Appeal because in both arbitrations the parties were unable to agree on an arbitrator. In the judgment, the court considered itself unable to order consolidation for lack of consent[113] whilst Lord Denning (as he then was) plainly wished to act accordingly.[114]

[C] Procedural Difficulties, Particularly in Appointing the Arbitrators

50. Even if all parties have agreed on a particular tribunal's jurisdiction, the procedure of multi-party arbitration will comprise difficulties. Foremost, the arbitrator selection has caused arguments ever since the French *Dutco* decision. Therein, three parties were involved in a consortium agreement. One of them became the claimant suing the other two as defendants before an ICC tribunal. However, the two defendants were unable to consent on one party-appointed arbitrator. The ICC Court exercised its discretion under the former equivalent of Article 12(8) 2017 ICC Rules[115] and appointed one arbitrator for the defendants' side, yet allowed the claimant to nominate its arbitrator. The arbitral award was set aside on grounds of public policy.[116] The rationale behind this decision is *not* to allow 'non-neutral' arbitrators. Instead, it is a matter of equality between parties on both sides on influencing the tribunal's composition.[117] In other jurisdictions, the implementation of equality for the appointment of the arbitrators has been expressed by courts in Italy,[118] Switzerland[119] and in Germany where the Federal Court of Justice subjected arbitrations on shareholders' resolutions to all shareholders' equal opportunity to select the arbitrator.[120] The consequence of this restrictive jurisprudence is that joint parties can only be obligated to jointly nominate an arbitrator if they have fully identical interests.[121] Moreover, an '*agreement among a group of parties to jointly nominate an arbitrator*' might be admissible.[122] In

113. *Eastern Bechtel Corporation v. Chiyoda Chemical Engineering & Construction Company Ltd; Abu Dhabi Gas Liquefaction Co. Ltd v. Eastern Bechtel Corporation*, [1982] 2 Lloyd's Rep. 425, 427 per Watkins LJ (CA) ('There is no power in this court or any other court to do more upon an application such as this than to appoint an arbitrator or arbitrators.'). *See* on the court's pragmatic solution [76].
114. *Ibid.* ('[I]t is most undesirable that there should be inconsistent findings by two separate arbitrators on virtually the self same question, such as causation. It is very desirable that everything should be done to avoid such a circumstance.').
115. Article 10 (2) 1988 ICC Rules ('In the absence of such a joint nomination and where all parties are unable to agree to a method for the constitution of the Arbitral Tribunal, the Court may appoint each member of the Arbitral Tribunal and shall designate one of them to act as chairman.').
116. Cass. (1e civ.), *BKMI and Siemens v. Dutco*, 7 January 1992, (1992) Rev. Arb. 470.
117. *Fouchard Gaillard and Goldman* [792]; *Schlosser* [566-568].
118. Corte di Cassazione, *Coop Vigili Fuoco Borgotari v. Mariani*, 5 July 1995, (1995) I Foro pad 206.
119. ATF 107 Ia 155, *Esrig v. Theatergenossenschaft Bern*, 160-161.
120. *See infra* [234]. *See* on the transferability to non-corporate matters *Schlosser* [546]; Schwab, in *Liber Amicorum Habscheid* 290-293. *Contra* Berger, *International Economic Arbitration* 319-320.
121. Hanotiau, *Complex Arbitrations* [457].
122. Meier in Arroyo (ed.), *Arbitration in Switzerland* Ch. 13 [57]. *See also* TF, *République arabe d'Egypte v. Westland Helicopters Ltd et al*, 16 May 1983, [1984] ASA Bull. 203 on *ICC Case* 3879.

the absence of such an agreement and joint interests, the solution is to offer *no* party any influence on the tribunal's selection. For instance, the London Court of International Arbitration (LCIA), Stockholm Chamber of Commerce (SCC), Singapore International Arbitration Centre (SIAC) and German Institution for Arbitration (DIS) Rules stipulate that the institution nominates the *entire* tribunal.[123] The ICC, Hong Kong International Arbitration Centre (HKIAC) and Swiss Rules contain a discretionary provision equally allowing such practice.[124] Moreover, to illustrate the ample range of other solutions, in a US case, all three parties appointed one arbitrator each and those two jointly appointed two additional arbitrators.[125]

51. To enumerate further procedural problems even if the tribunal has been correctly established: parties might seek to *subsequently* join an additional party;[126] the collection of evidence might be complicated in particular where joint claimants or defendants disagree as to their presentation; confidentiality might be an issue if bilateral information shall be disclosed to all parties; finally, the more parties a proceeding includes, the more likely it becomes that the multi-party case scenario is exposed to personal substitutions. For example, in a recent ICC award, the claimant was the majority shareholder of a German company investing in Thailand.[127] Subsequent to initiating arbitration against the State of Thailand, the claimant sold its shares to a third party, who reserved the right to demand the claimant to terminate the arbitration. Although the third party finally exercised this right, the claimant continued with the arbitration. This caused a lengthy dispute about the enforcement in Germany. The court decided that the violation of the obligation to terminate arbitration towards a third party does not amount to a violation of international public policy under Article V(2)(b) NYC.[128] In conclusion, multi-party arbitration meets several obstacles: foremost the required consent of all parties to arbitration in general, the consent on the respective tribunal's jurisdiction in particular and the equal influence on the tribunal's appointment.

§1.02 MULTI-FORA DISPUTES AS AN IMMANENT ALTERNATIVE

52. If multi-party arbitration cannot be implemented, the multi-*party* relationship will turn into a 'multi-fora dispute'. This means that parallel proceedings comprising connected facts, legal issues and parties occur before different fora, i.e., before two arbitral tribunals or one arbitral tribunal and one court.[129] Certainly, multi-fora

123. Article 8(1) LCIA Rules; Art. 17(5) SCC Rules; Art. 12(2) SIAC Rules; s. 8(3) DIS Supp. Rules.
124. Article 8(2)(c) HKIAC Rules; Art. 8(5) Swiss Rules. *See* Smith, (2018) 39 J. Int'l Arb. 201. On the ICC Rules *see* Derains and Schwarz, *A Guide to the ICC Rules* 183.
125. *Companía Espanola de Petroleos v. Nereus Shipping*, 527 F.2d 966 (2d Cir. 1975). *See* on the case's outdated relevance for court-ordered consolidations *infra* at [70].
126. *See* Hanotiau, *Complex Arbitrations* [367-396] with case and rule references. *See infra*, [589].
127. Whilst the case concerned an investment arbitration, its legal reasoning is non-specific thereto.
128. BGH, [2017] NZG 227.
129. Schneider, (1990) 6 Arb. Int'l 101; Rubino-Samartano, *International Arbitration* 902-904. Cf. Nicklisch, (1994) 4 J. Int'l Arb. 57; Schaffstein, *Res Judicata* [0.02]; Shookman, (2010) 27 J. Int'l Arb. 362 ('closely related conflict before multiple adjudications'); Söderlund, *Investment Arbitration and the Energy Charter Treaty* 237 ('some communality of interests'); Wehland,

disputes are not a phenomenon privy to neither arbitration nor multi-party relationships. Instead, they can equally arise in international litigation and in bilateral relationships. Yet, multi-fora disputes in the arbitration context comprise increased probability to occur, distinct risks, and distinct principles to be addressed.[130] Moreover, with regard to arbitration's inherent restraints of party autonomy, multi-party relationships multiply the potential for multi-fora disputes.[131] The latter might even be called a *correlate* of multi-party relationships involving arbitration clauses. This raises the attention as to multi-fora disputes' content (*see* [A], *infra*) and detriments (*see* [B], *infra*).

[A] Content: Multi-Fora Disputes on the Substance and on Jurisdiction

53. Two contents of multi-fora disputes require distinction:[132] *first*, there might be a multiplication of disputes on the *substance*. For example, in a construction project such as in the Adgas case,[133] one issue (the gas tanks' deficiency) is brought before two tribunals (employer/main-contractor and main-/sub-contractor). *Second*, parallel disputes can concern the range of *jurisdictional*[134] issues provided by multilateral transactions. For example, in the previously mentioned Dallah case,[135] the non-signatory (Pakistan's Ministry of Defence) (i) objected to the tribunal's jurisdiction in the ICC arbitration, (ii) resisted recognition and enforcement in England, and (iii) applied for a set aside at the arbitral seat in Paris. The examination will adopt this distinction between substantive and jurisdictional multi-fora disputes. In fact, the two case scenarios provide ample differences. This primarily concerns the aspects of procedural tactics. Certainly, upon consent, any multi-fora dispute on the substance could be turned into a multi-arbitration. If a party refuses to consent, it is protected by the negative dimension of party autonomy. By contrast, tactics in creating jurisdictional multi-fora disputes do not only amount to passively exercising default situations, but actively seeking '*advantage from the absence of hierarchy and coordination among the various types of international tribunals*'.[136] Hence, it might even provide the danger for forum shopping.[137] Therefore, the following sections on pre-emptive Forum Coordination will distinguish between the two categories.

Multiple Proceedings in Investment Treaty Arbitration [1.20] ('substantially related parties and substantially identical requests for relief').

130. *See* Bermann, (2017) 381 Rec. des cours [275-277] ('Complex though parallel proceedings in litigation may be, their counterpart in international arbitration are even more complex. They are also more pervasive.').
131. Debourg, *Les contrariétés des décisions dans l'arbitrage international* [269].
132. *Ibid.*, [14]; Wehland, *Multiple Proceedings in Investment Arbitration* [1.07].
133. *See supra* [49].
134. *See* Park, (2007) 13 ICCA Congress Series 104 ('[T]he distinction between admissibility and jurisdiction might provide a helpful segue into a deeper analysis of jurisdictional challenges.').
135. *See supra* [41].
136. Douglas, (2003) 74 B.Y.I.L. 236.
137. *See* Bell, *Forum Shopping and Venue in Transnational Litigation* (2003); *Anchem Products Inc. v. British Columbia (Workers' Compensation Board)*, (1993) 102 DLR (4th) 96, [25] per Sopinka J. (SC Can) ('The business of litigation, like commerce itself, has become increasingly international.').

[B] Detriments

54. Multi-fora disputes create a welter of risks and detriments for both individuals and institutions. To cite the 2004 resolution of the Institut de Droit International, multi-fora disputes '*may lead to injustice, delay, increased expense and inconsistent decisions [and] should be discouraged.*'[138] The immediate practical impediment of multi-fora disputes, even before any parallel decision is rendered, is the waste of resources on related aspects.[139] This impedes both the private interests and, if one of the fora is a court, the public interests in efficiency.

55. Furthermore, the *potential* for contradicting decisions establishes impediments. On the one hand, multi-fora disputes with identical or substantially related claimants might significantly increase the latter's chances. Since already one arbitral award might suffice to obtain enforcement in other countries, claimants might receive '*two shots*'.[140] Correspondingly, in initial proceedings, they could also be motivated for tactics described by Emmanuel Gaillard as '*testing the water*'.[141] Vice versa, multi-fora disputes could also increase defendants' chances of success in specific situations. During the process, a multiplication might delay the dispute resolution, particularly where multiple bodies have been seized with jurisdictional issues.

56. After the process, the *existence* of contradicting decisions might deprive either party of its interests and unduly favour the opponent. For a *defendant*, a contradiction can be sufficient to bar enforcement of a successful arbitral award on grounds of irreconcilability.[142] If, however, irreconcilability is unsuccessful, the *claimant* might be favoured.[143] In addition and in a normative dimension, any contradiction on related issues might effectively deprive the parties of their individual right to consistency and fair justice.[144] Moreover, in non-monetary cases, defendants might be exposed to the impossibility to comply with all contradicting decisions if the contradicting decisions concern an action (e.g., the delivery of a unique good to two distinct claimants) or an omission (e.g., a non-delivery of merchandise on grounds of non-competition). Furthermore, parallel actions on a legal status might result in a so-called '*limping legal status*' described as '*the very antonym of the international harmony of solutions*'.[145]

---

138. Institut de Droit International, (2004) 70(II) Annuaire 252, [4].
139. *Redfern and Hunter* [2.212] ('When several parties are involved in a dispute, it is usually considered desirable that the issues should be dealt with in the same proceedings [...] this saves time and money.').
140. *See* Wälde, (2004) 5 J.W.I.T. 43 ('every rational person [...] will prefer two shots to one shot').
141. Gaillard, (2017) 32 ICSID Rev. 22-26.
142. *See infra* [155-168].
143. Cf. Bollée, in *Procédures parallèles et décisions contradictoires* 102.
144. Cf. Lowe, (1996) 8 African J. Int'l Comp. L. 48; Mantilla-Serrano, in *Procédures parallèles et décisions contradictoires* 36-39; *Poudret and Besson* [238].
145. Cf. Kegel and Schurig, *International Privatrecht* 140 ('*Hinkende Rechtsverhältnisse sind das Gegenteil von internationalem [...] Entscheidungseinklang.*') (translation of the author).

57. In addition, factual risks might also result if two disputes are not decided contrarily, but *correspondingly*, in that this might cause over-compensation or over-obligation. If one claimant successfully sues different defendants before different fora, he might be effectively compensated twice for the very identical claim. Vice versa, two claimants suing one defendant might be related. An example illustrating the relevance of over-obligation under national foreclosure law with an arbitration context is the *Sitco* case: Racoil had lost an arbitration against Deutsche Schachtbau- und Tiefbohrgesellschaft (DST). DST sought enforcement in England by means of a garnishee order[146] and was awarded Racoil's payment claims against Shell International Petroleum (Sitco) under an oil purchase contract. However, the Arabian State in which Rakoil has its seat, had successfully sued Sitco before its own courts establishing that the claims belonged not to Racoil but to the State on whose behalf Racoil acted. Hence, Sitco ran the risk to be obligated twice and thus successfully appealed against the garnishee order.[147]

58. A detriment of multi-fora disputes rather privy to selected arbitration laws is the potential inefficacy of arbitration agreements. E.g., in *Indian Organic Chemicals*, two arbitration agreements of the claimant with related companies had distinct arbitral seats, one in England, the other in India. As a result of this duplication, the High Court of Bombay eventually held that the Indian implementation of Article II(3) NYC did not bar the claimant's for multi-party *litigation* because the provision addressed merely '*an* agreement to arbitrate'.[148]

59. A final risk of multi-fora disputes arises for jurisdictional disputes. Here, *none* of the tribunals might accept jurisdiction. Then, the claimant's access to justice would be at stake (denial of justice). In a pure litigation scenario, this risk is less immanent, since it is a perhaps universal principle that defendants can be sued in their home State (*actor sequitar forum rei*), and the main risk therefore is that the home State might not provide for a fair trial as raised in US jurisprudence[149] and recent reports of the Institute de droit international.[150] In arbitration, such risk might be even more pertinent because of the exclusive nature of an arbitration clause, particularly in multi-party case scenarios with their inherent issues of non-signatories. For example, in ICC Case 6648 where the main contractor Y raised the loss of the sub-contractor Z ('name borrowing') against the principal X, the tribunal decided that Z was not a party to the arbitration agreement between X and Y under the applicable Malaysian (common) law. Hence, Z (represented by Y) was unable to bring its loss to arbitration.[151] If, hypothetically, Z

146. *See* Rose (ed.), *Blackstone's Civil Practice* [76.11] ('Third party debt orders - formerly called garnishee proceedings - have the effect of transforming a debt payable by a third party - the garnishee under the old terminology - to the judgment debtor into an obligation to pay the debt to the judgment creditor.').
147. *Shell International Petroleum Co. Ltd (Sitco) v. Deutsche Schachtbau- und Tiefbohrgesellschaft mbH (DST)*, [1988] 3 Weekly L. Rep. 1032 = (1989) XIV Y.C.A. 737 (HL).
148. *Indian Organic Chemicals Ltd v. Subsidiary 1 Subsidiary 2 and others*, (1979) IV Y.C.A. 271 (HC Bombay).
149. *See Kiobel v. Royal Dutch Petroleum Company*, 133 S Ct. 1659 (2013).
150. *See* Bucher, (2015) 372 Rec. des cours 13 et seqq.
151. *ICC Case 6648*, Interim Award, 1992, (1998) XXIII Y.C.A. 30.

eventually commenced litigation in X's home State, he bears the risk that the courts assess the arbitration agreement's personal scope differently, perhaps under a different law, and also decline jurisdiction.

Interim Conclusion

60. In conclusion, multilateral transactions are exposed to the risk of multi-fora disputes. Particularly, multi-party arbitration operates under strict boundaries. The practical impediments of multi-fora disputes such as waste of resources, disparate chances of success or deprivation of individual interests might affect the equality of the parties, the enforcement of individual rights and thereby flaw the entire dispute resolution process as well as the parties' right to justice. Therefore, legal systems need to consider measures of preventing multi-fora disputes. Such measures establish Forum Coordination instead. Yet, their operation has to be examined as to the reconciliation with the jurisdictional boundaries established.

§1.03 JURISDICTION UNDISPUTED: PARTY AUTONOMY AS BARRIER TO PRE-EMPTIVE COORDINATION

61. In light of the risks of multi-fora disputes, international arbitration is required to provide a framework for coordinating parallel fora. The following sections will address this framework assuming that multi-party arbitration was unavailable and that aspects of the *substance* are brought before multiple fora. It differentiates between third-party notice/intervention (*see* [A], *infra*), parallel arbitrations (*see* [B], *infra*) as well as parallel litigation and arbitration (*see* [C], *infra*).

[A] Third-Party Notice and Third-Party Intervention

62. The very first opportunity to prevent multi-fora disputes would be to expose a third party to the outcome of a dispute without rendering it a formal party. In litigation, there is ample opportunity for such 'third-party notices'. Courts, however, can generally exercise jurisdiction over the public in litigation. In arbitration, jurisdiction turns into the pivotal obstacle to third-party notices. Nearly all arbitration laws prohibit third-party notices in arbitration unless the third party is bound by the arbitration agreement.[152] The pivotal exception is US law. Whereas in a Delaware construction case, the sub-contractor was held not to be exposed to any vouching-in (third-party notice) in an

152. BGH, [1965] MDR 124; OLG Hamburg, [1950] MDR 295; Schlosser, in *Stein and Jonas* § 1042 [99]; Schwab and Walter, *Schiedsgerichtsbarkeit* Ch. 16 [18-19]; Meier in Arroyo (ed.), *Arbitration in Switzerland* Ch. 13 [40]; *Poudret and Besson* [241] with further references; *See Russell on Arbitration* [3-049] ('Judges have noted the benefits that could result from the abolition of the restriction preventing the joining of third parties and consolidation of arbitrations, but the draftsmen of the Arbitration Act 1996 decided that this would be too great an interference with the principle of party autonomy') with further references. *Contra* Berger and Kellerhals, *Arbitration in Switzerland* [580] ('an arbitration agreement between the third

arbitration context,[153] the US Court of Appeals for the Second Circuit extended the procedure towards non-signatories of an arbitration clause for efficiency purposes:[154]

> We are not convinced that the usual rule that a party will not be bound by arbitration absent its consent necessarily requires that a party consent before it may be vouched into an arbitration. Vouching is permitted in litigation for reasons of efficiency. The efficiencies [...] are as great in the case of maritime arbitration as in litigation. [...] We emphasize that we are dealing with an area in which arbitration is the common method by which disputes are resolved. [The indemnitors] are thus well aware that charter parties contain arbitration clauses [...]. One trial, whether before arbitrators or a court, is enough. Relitigation of disputes in several forums raises the costs of maritime transactions to all parties for no useful purpose and wastes of judicial resources as well.

63. The court has subsequently repeated this reasoning (also beyond maritime case scenarios).[155] The Fifth Circuit,[156] the Seventh Circuit,[157] the Eleventh Circuit[158] as well as several District and State Courts[159] applied this rule to judgments and awards alike whereas it has received few judicial critics.[160] In particular, a vast jurisprudence on suretyships[161] and insurances[162] affirms that judgments and awards alike bind sureties/insurers if they were served with notice and an opportunity to defend. Accordingly, US law is a pivotal exception on third-party notices.

64. A further aspect of third-party notices and arbitration that might raise discrepancies amongst national laws is the availability of third-party notices in court if the

party and the litigants is *not* an indispensable requirement [...]. Intervention and third-party notice are procedural instruments which aim at simplifying and expediting the resolution of disputes.').

153. *Lester Bldg Associates Inc. v. Davidson*, 514 A2d 1100, 1102-1103 (Del Ch. 1986).

154. *SCAC Transport (USA) Inc. v. SS Danaos*, 845 F.2d 1157, [6-9] (2d Cir. 1988).

155. *CH Sanders Co. Inc. v. BHAP Housing Development Fund Co. Ins*, 903 F.2d 114, 121 (2d Cir. 1990); *Fuerco Intern Steel Trading v. T Klaveness Shippings A/S*, 333 F.3d 838 (2d Cir. 2003). *See also* in this Circuit *Cargill Intern, SA v. Chilewich Intern Corp*, 1993 WL 535536 (S.D.N.Y. 1993).

156. *Universal American Barge Corp. v. J-Chem Inc*, 946 F.2d 1131, 1136-37 (5th Cir. 1991).

157. *Advanced Ground Systems Engineering Inc. v. RTW Industries Inc*, 388 F.3d 1036, 1042 (7th Cir. 2004) (Californian law).

158. *Drill South Inc. v. International Fidelity Ins. Co*, 234 F.2d 1232, 1235 (11th Cir. 2000).

159. *Pyro Energy Corp. v. Industria Azucarera Nacional*, 1989 WL 97940 (E.D. La 1989); *Odell Associates Inc. v. Alton Ochsner Medical Foundation*, 2002 WL 10465 (E.D. La 2002); *C&I Steel, LLC v. Travelers Cas and Sur Co. of America*, 876 NE2d 442, 448 Note 9 (Mass App Ct. 2007).

160. *US for Use of Pensacola Const Co. v. St Paul Fire and Marine Ins. Co*, 705 FSupp 306, 313 (WD La 1988) ('In *SCAC Transport* there was no significant federal interest in providing a judicial forum. When the party being vouched into warranty is a Miller Act surety, on the other hand, there is an important federal interest at stake.'). Critical on the application to non-maritime constellations *Commodity Trading Co. Ltd v. Connell Rice & Sugar Co. Inc*, 766 FSupp 138, 150 (S.D.N.Y. 1991).

161. *T & R Painting Contsr. v. St. Paul Fire & Marine*, 23 Call App 4th 738 (2d Dist 1994); *American Safety Cas Ins. Co. v. CG Mitchell Const* Inc. 601 SE2d 633, 639 (Va 2004); *Price v. RLI Ins. Co*, 914 So2d 1010, 1013 (Fla App 2005). *See* effectively *Board of Supervisors of Fairfax County v. Southern Cross Coal Corp*, 380 SE2d 636, 639 (Va 1989).

162. *Executive Risk Indem Inc. v. Jones*, 89 CalRptr3d 747, 756 (Call App 2009) ('distinct preclusion doctrine, which is more akin to the well-settled principles of contractual indemnity') with express reference to the compatibility with *Taylor v. Sturgell* 758. *See* on the latter case *infra* [206]. *See* on insurances further *infra* [270].

notified could rely on an arbitration clause against the party requesting the notice. Whilst the Italian *Corte di cassazione* had declared a third-party notice inoperable,[163] the opposite result was reached in a Belgian dispute where the re-seller applied for a third-party notice against the distributor, which was eventually considered in the indemnity arbitration under the ICC's auspices.[164] By contrast, an arbitral tribunal seated in France seized with indemnity claims between sub-contractors did not adhere to the liability shares stipulated in an earlier Paris judgment, although the Court extended jurisdiction over these sub-contractors. Yet, it should be read in this context that the Paris Court of Appeal eventually rejected a set aside,[165] and thereby retrospectively corrected the prior extension of its jurisdiction.[166]

65. Moreover, if the third party is not the opponent, but the applicant of a joinder, one might speak of third-party *intervention*. To cite a case example of a leading treatise:

> In a construction contract, A, the principal, starts an arbitration against B, the main contractor. May C, subcontractor, intervene in the proceedings [in order to prevent indemnity claims of B]?[167]

66. Generally, since an interventionist seeks to participate in the arbitration, the aforementioned requirements of consent apply. Hence, the interventionist and the original parties must have concluded an arbitration agreement or jointly agreed to the intervention.[168] However, *even if*, a third party has generally consented to the arbitration agreement underlying an ongoing arbitration, the standing to apply for a third-party intervention is *not* acknowledged under all arbitral rules. Whilst the HKIAC, SIAC and Swiss Rules expressly stipulate for third parties' standing to apply for their joinder,[169] others award only the arbitrating parties with the standing to apply for joinders.[170] In particular, upon the 2012 revision of the ICC Rules, the *Secretariat's Guide* stated that the *'Rules do not provide for [...] third-party intervention'*.[171] In conclusion, third-party notice and third-party intervention before arbitral tribunals comprise only limited efficacy since they require jurisdiction of the tribunal (except

163. Corte di Cassazione, *Heraues Kulzer GmbH v. Dellatorre Vera SpA*, 5 January 2007, (2008) XXXIII Y.C.A. 596. *See* for Germany: Schlosser, in *Stein and Jonas* § 1032 [47]. France (forum selection clauses): Cass, [2008] Rev. crit. DIP 108. *See also* CA Grenoble, (1996) Rev. Arb. 452.
164. *ICC Cases 2475 & 2762*, Award, (1974-1985) I ICC Collection 325.
165. CA Paris, *SNC Forézienne d'entreprise v. SAS Guintoli*, 17 March 2017, [2017] Rev. Arb. 1213.
166. Cf. Zajdela, [2017] Rev. Arb. 1223 (*'la Cour d'appel délimite en réalité la compétence des deux juridictions saisies successivement'*).
167. Hanotiau, *Complex Arbitrations* [362].
168. Cf. Art. 1045 (3) Dutch Code of Civil Procedure ('The intervention or joinder for the claim of indemnity may only be permitted by the arbitral tribunal, having heard the parties, if the third party accedes by agreement in writing between him and the parties to the arbitration agreement.'); Art. 1696 bis Belgian Judicial Code; Debourg, *Les contrariétés des décisions* [277-278]; Hanotiau, *Complex Arbitrations* [362]; *Russell on Arbitration* [3-049]; Schlosser, in *Stein and Jonas* § 1042 [92].
169. Article 27(9) HKIAC Rules; Art. 7(1) SIAC Rules; Art. 4(2) Swiss Rules.
170. *See* Art. 7(1) ICC Rules; Art. 22(1) LCIA Rules; Art. 13(1) SCC Rules; Art. 17(5) UNCITRAL Rules.
171. Fry Greenberg and Mazza, *The Secretariat's Guide to ICC Arbitration* [3.294].

under US law) and might be unavailable even if such jurisdiction were established (e.g., under the ICC Rules).

[B] Parallel Arbitrations

67. If multi-party arbitration and related concepts such as notice and intervention are unavailable, yet all parties to a multilateral transaction consented to arbitrate, parallel arbitrations will occur. Even in bilateral case scenarios, parallel arbitrations can arise, either because of dual-arbitration clauses without a 'fork-in-the-road' safeguard,[172] different versions of arbitration agreements as it has come before the Swiss Supreme Court in *Arthur Andersen*,[173] or distinctions as to the subject matter.[174] In such scenarios, there are two coordination tools that a tribunal or institution might consider: consolidation (*see* [1], *infra*) and lis pendens (*see* [2], *infra*). The cornerstone of their assessment is that arbitral tribunals are primarily obligated towards the parties of the underlying arbitration agreement to render an arbitral award and not towards third parties.[175] The implication of such obligation is that a discretionary handling of the tribunal in violation of the parties' agreement is prohibited and might render the arbitral award unenforceable under Article V(1)(d) NYC.[176] Moreover, it implies that each arbitrator should assist the parties in finding adequate solutions, sometimes requiring 'quite a bit of *Fingerspitzengefühl*'.[177]

---

172. For example: arbitration under *either* the auspices of the ICC with the arbitral seat in Paris or the HKIAC with the arbitral seat in Hong Kong. *See*, e.g., *Pantechniki SA Contractors & Engineers v. Republic of Albania*, ICSID Case ARB/07/21, Award, 30 July 2009, [50-64] (Paulsson); *H&H Enterprises Investments Inc. v. Arab Republic of Egypt*, ICSID Case ARB 09/15, Excerpts of Award, 6 May 2014 (Cremades P, Heiskanen and Gharavi).
173. TF, *Arther Andersen v. Andersen Consulting*, [2000] 3 ASA Bull. 546. For other examples *see ICC Case 3383*, 1979, (1974-1985) I ICC Collection 394 (during the hearing of the ICC arbitration where the Iranian party objected to jurisdiction on the grounds of incompatibility of Iranian Law with ICC arbitration, the parties concluded an ad hoc arbitration agreement); *ICC Case 5423*, 1987, (1986-1990) II ICC Collection 339.
174. *See* TF, 9 July 2014, Case 4A_90/2014, [2015] ASA Bull. 95 (contract of a football player provided for a split arbitration clause providing all contractual disputes, e.g., about premiums, to a sole arbitrator and all disputes about the player's desire to transfer to the association's settlement procedure).
175. Cf. *ICC Case 6840*, Arbitral Award, (1991-1995) III ICC Collection 468; Debourg, *Les contrariétés de décisions* [511, 590]; Hobér, (2013) 366 Rec. des cours, 247-248; Mayer, in *Liber Amicorum Reymond* 189. *See also ICC Case 10623*, Arbitral Award, 7 December 2001, (2003) 21 ASA Bull. 82, [128].
176. 'Recognition and enforcement of the award may be refused [...] only if [...] (d) The Composition of the arbitral authority or the arbitral procedure was not in accordance with the agreement of the parties, or, failing such agreement, was not in accordance with the law of the country where the arbitration took place'.
177. Hobér, (2013) 366 Rec. des cours 249.

[1] Limited Potential for Consolidation Without Consent

68. An immediate means of coordination would be the *consolidation*[178] of parallel arbitrations '*greatly reduc[ing] the risk of factual errors*'.[179] Certainly, any consolidation is desirable if all parties agree to it. If they do *not* agree, consolidation in violation of the parties' agreement stands against the inherent risk of the arbitral award's non-enforceability pursuant to Article V(1)(d) NYC[180] or a set aside under corresponding provisions.[181] In the absence of the parties' choice, there are two authorities that could potentially order a consolidation: the arbitral institution and the supervising courts. However, the powers of either of these authorities are very limited.

69. Institution- or tribunal-ordered consolidation inherently requires that the parallel arbitrations are conducted under the auspices of the very same arbitral institutions. Yet, even in this situation, only few arbitral rules provide the potential to consolidate proceedings between distinct parties arbitrating under distinct arbitration agreements. For instance, Article 10 ICC Rules requires either that distinct parties to parallel arbitration are all bound by the very same arbitration agreement (lit b)[182] or that the very same parties are arbitrating under two distinct arbitration agreements (lit c).[183] The ICC Court treats the same-parties requirement strictly.[184] Therefore, the statement that '*most of the consolidations that take place in ICC cases involve multiparty matters*'[185] has to be explained in that parties often agree on a consolidation. Correspondingly, Article 22(1)(x) 2014 LCIA Rules cannot overcome the same-parties requirement.[186] By contrast, other arbitral rules do in general allow for a consolidation of arbitrations between distinct parties and under formally distinct arbitration agreements. Yet, the consolidation potential remains restricted. Article 8(7)(c) SIAC Rules,[187] Article 15(1)(iii) SCC Rules and Article 28(1) HKIAC

178. The difference between consolidation and joinder is that the latter operates before a parallel arbitration has already been initiated. *See*, e.g., Art. 7, 10 a) c) ICC Rules.
179. Leboulanger, (1996) 13 J. Int'l Arb. 74.
180. 'The arbitral procedure was not in accordance with the agreement of the parties'.
181. *See*, e.g., Art. 34 (2)(a)(iv) UNCITRAL Model Law.
182. *See* CA Paris, *KIS France et al. v. sté Générale et al*, (1991) XVI Y.C.A. 145.
183. 'The Court may, at the request of a party, consolidate two or more arbitrations pending under the Rules into a single arbitration, where [...] (b) all of the claims in the arbitrations are made under the same arbitration agreement; or (c) the claims in the arbitrations are made under more than one arbitration agreement, the arbitrations are *between the same parties*, the disputes in the arbitrations arise in connection with the same legal relationship, and the Court finds the arbitration agreements to be compatible.' (emphasis added).
184. *See* Granier, in *Procédures parallèles et décisions contradictoires* 130; unpublished case reported by Whitesell, in *Multiple Party Actions in International Arbitration* [6.36].
185. Whitesell, in *Multiple Party Actions in International Arbitration* [6.27].
186. 'power [...] to order [...] the consolidation [...] between the same disputing parties [...]'.
187. 'After the constitution of any Tribunal in the arbitrations sought to be consolidated., a party may apply to the Tribunal to consolidate two or more arbitrations pending under these Rules into a single arbitration, provided that any of the following criteria is satisfied in respect of the arbitrations to be consolidated: [...] (c) the arbitration agreements are compatible, the same Tribunal has been constituted in each of the arbitrations or no Tribunal has been constituted in the other arbitration(s), and: (i) the disputes arise out of the same legal relationship(s); (ii) the

Rules[188] require '*compatible*' arbitration agreements. Compatibility requires identical arbitral seats, arbitration languages, arbitrator selection and applicable laws.[189] Whilst Article 4(1) Swiss Rules is even broader in that it allows consolidation regardless of the compatibility,[190] scholarship interprets the provision as requiring corresponding identities.[191]

70. The second alternative, i.e., court-ordered consolidation requires identical arbitral seats of the parallel arbitrations. Amongst the very few statutory grounds are the Hong Kong Arbitration Ordinance[192] and Article 1046(1) Dutch Code of Civil Procedure.[193] Yet, for third parties, section (3) of this very Article requires an accession to the arbitration agreement.[194] Against this background, the President of the District Court of Amsterdam ordered consolidation in a construction dispute with distinct, although consistent arbitration clauses and identical factual issues whilst rejecting consolidation against third parties.[195] Continuing on jurisprudence, US Circuit courts emphasize the boundaries of party autonomy and bar court-ordered consolidation under the Federal Arbitration Act (FAA).[196] It is only under State jurisdictions that the opportunity

disputes arise out of contracts consisting of a principal contract and its ancillary contract(s); or (iii) the disputes arise out of the same transaction or series of transactions'.

188. 'HKIAC shall have the power, at the request of a party and after consulting with the parties and any confirmed or appointed arbitrators, to consolidate two or more arbitrations pending under these Rules where: (a) the parties agree to consolidate; or (b) all of the claims in the arbitrations are made under the same arbitration agreement; or (c) the claims are made under more than one arbitration agreement, a common question of law or fact arises in all of the arbitrations, the rights to relief claimed are in respect of, or arise out of, the same transaction or a series of related transactions and the arbitration agreements are compatible'.
189. *See* Pair and Frankenstein, (2011) 25 Emory J. Int'l L. 1077; Smith (2018) 35 J. Int'l Arb. 199.
190. '[...] the Court may decide [...] that the new case shall be consolidated with the pending arbitral proceedings [...] where a Notice of Arbitration is submitted between parties that are not identical to the parties in the pending arbitral proceedings'.
191. Schramm in Arroyo (ed.), *Arbitration in Switzerland* Art. 4 Swiss Rules [12].
192. 2011 Hong Kong Arbitration Ordinance, Sch 2, s. 2: 'The court may consolidate proceedings or order them to be heard concurrently or consecutively if: (a) a common question of law or fact arises in both proceedings; (b) the disputes arise out of the same transaction or series of transactions; or (c) the court considers it desirable to do so for any other reason.' *See also Chun Wo Building Construction v. China Merchants Tower Co*, (2000) 2 HKC 255.
193. 'If arbitral proceedings have been commenced before an arbitral tribunal in the Netherlands concerning a subject matter which is connected with the subject matter of arbitral proceedings commenced before another arbitral tribunal in the Netherlands, any of the parties may, unless the parties have agreed otherwise, request the Provisional Relief Judge of the District Court in Amsterdam to order a consolidation of the proceedings'.
194. 'The joinder, intervention or joinder for the claim of indemnity may only be permitted by the arbitral tribunal, having heard the parties, if the third party accedes by agreement in writing between him and the parties to the arbitration agreement'.
195. Reported by Bitter, in *Multi-Party Actions in International Arbitration* [8.20].
196. *Weyerhaeuser Co. v. W Seas Shipping Co*, 743 F.2d 635 (9th Cir. 1984); *Del E Webb Constr v. Richardson Hosp Auth*, 823 F.2d 145 (5th Cir. 1987); *Protective Life Ins. Corp. v. Lincoln Nat'l Life Ins. Corp.*, 873 F.2d 281 (11th Cir. 1989); *Baesler v. Cont'l Grain Co*, 900 F.2d 1193 (8th Cir. 1990); Am. *Centennial Ins. Co. v. Nat'l Cas Co*, 951 F.2d 107 (6th Cir. 1991); *Gov't of United Kingdom of Great Britain & N Ireland v. Boeing Co*, 998 F.2d 68, 73-74 (2d Cir. 1993); *Philadelphia Reins Corp. v. Employers Ins. of Wausau*, 61 FAppx 816, 820 (3d Cir. 2003); *Lefkovitz v. Wagner*, 395 F.3d 773, 780 (7th Cir. 2005).

remains,[197] yet also only in bilateral case scenarios. If the court at the arbitral seat orders consolidation against a party's objection, it is debated whether Article V(1)(d) NYC bars enforcement abroad.[198] Particularly, the wording concerning the 'arbitral procedure' and the systematic protection against court intervention under Article II(3) NYC indicate a ground for non-enforcement. Yet, commentators state that the selection of the arbitral seat constitutes an implied approval of the *lex arbitri's* consolidation provisions.[199] In any case, none of them advocates on the situation of multiple parties. In conclusion, neither arbitral rules nor arbitration laws provide for comprehensive grounds to consolidate arbitrations between multiple parties against their express will, unless there is only one arbitration agreement, or potentially more, yet compatible agreements. In other words, consolidation requires that multi-party arbitration had been operable from the outset.

[2] Lis Pendens: Decline of Jurisdiction and Discretionary Stays

71. If parallel arbitrations remain unconsolidated, 'lis pendens' will come into play. Whilst the term originated as a civilist rule for priority in time, contemporary scholarship emphasizes:

> The concept of lis pendens does not denote a legal rule. Rather, it describes a factual situation of parallel proceedings relating to the same subject-matter proceeding concurrently in more than one court or tribunal.[200]

72. Before turning to its application in arbitration, this examination initially outlines the rules' origins in litigation revealing fundamental divides between common and civil law.[201]

73. At common law, courts generally enjoy broad discretion. Faced with connected disputes, they can either stay the proceedings, decline their jurisdictions (forum non conveniens, abuse of process) or restrain the parties from seizing other courts (anti-suit injunction).[202] Civil law differs in that the courts' discretion is limited in a many-fold

197. *See* s. 10(a) Uniform Arbitration Act ('upon [motion] of a party to an agreement to arbitrate or to an arbitration proceeding, the court may order consolidation of separate arbitration proceedings as to all or some of the claims if: (1) there are separate agreements to arbitrate or separate arbitration proceedings *between the same persons*'); California Code of Civil Procedure, § 1297.272; *New England Energy Inc. v. Keystone Shipping Co*, 855 F.2d 1 (1st Cir. 1988).
198. *See* Hascher, (1984) 1 J. Intl Arb. 127.
199. Austmann, (1990) 1 Am. Rev. Int'l 355; *Born* 2587-88; Chiu, (1990) 7 J. Int'l Arb. 72-73; Leboulanger, (1996) 13 J. Int'l Arb. 68-69; *Poudret and Besson* [249]; van den Berg, (1986) 2 Arb. Int'l 367 and (1987) 3 Arb. Int'l 259. *See also Karaha Bodas Co. v. Perusahaan Pertambangan Minyak*, 364 F.3d 274 (5th Cir. 2004); CA Paris, *Riverstone Ins. Ltd v. Liquidators of ICD*, 5 November 2009, 08/12816. *Contra* Jarvin, (1987) 3 Arb. Int'l 255.
200. McLachlan, *Lis Pendens in International Litigation* 461.
201. *See* generally *ILA Report on Declining and Referring Jurisdiction in International Litigation*; Fawcett (ed.), *Report to the XIVth Congress of the International Academy of Comparative Law* 27 et seqq.; McLachlan, *Lis Pendens in International Litigation*; Schlosser, (2000) 284 Rec. des cours 76-87; von Mehren, (295) Rec. des cours 341-369.
202. Cf. McLachlan, *Lis Pendens in International Litigation* 59-72 with further references.

manner. *First*, civil-law jurisdictions outside of Québec[203] and some South American states[204] are averse to anti-suit injunctions.[205] *Second*, civil law operates under the priority-in-time principle.[206] *Third*, under the original concept now referred to as 'true lis pendens', the subsequent court must stay its proceeding and, if the first tribunal accepts its jurisdiction, decline its jurisdiction if the cause of actions are identical,[207] e.g., under Article 29(1) Brussels Ibis Regulation.[208] In sharing the objective to prevent contradicting decisions,[209] this strict implementation might be considered the sister of res judicata.[210] Yet, it is sometimes overlooked - in scholarship as well as in practice - that civil law does acknowledge certain discretion. With the exception of German law,[211] courts enjoy discretion when it comes to disputes with distinct, albeit connected causes of action, e.g., under the French concept of *connexité*[212] or Article 30(1), (3) Brussels Ibis Regulation.[213] This might explain why e.g., the ALI/UNIDROIT principles

203. Cour supérieure du Québec (civ), *Lac d'amiante du Canada ltée*, 9 July 1999, REJB 1999-13747, J.E., 99 (implementation as a form of *astreinte*).
204. Tribunal de Justica Sao Paulo, *Enesa Engenharia ea v. Sulamérica Cia Nacional de Seguros ea*, [2014] Rev. Arb. 723, 759. *See* for other states Grigera Naón, in *Liber Amicorum Brinert* 335.
205. Within the EU, any anti-suit injunctions to the detriment of Member States are prohibited under ECJ, 2 October 2009, *West Tankers ('The Front Comor')*, C-185/07, EU:C:2009:69.
206. Cf. von Mehren, (2002) 295 Rec. des cours 345 with further references.
207. Cf. Cass. (1e civ.), *Miniera di Fragne*, 26 November 1974, (1975) Clunet 108; Art. 9 PILA; *ILA Final Report on Lis Pendens* 11-13; Fawcett (ed.), *Report to the XIVth Congress of the International Academy of Comparative Law* 27; Hobér, (2013) 366 Rec. des cours 144-152; Schack (1994) 58 RabelsZ 51-52.
208. '(1) [W]here proceedings involving the same cause of action and between the same parties are brought in the courts of different Member States, any court other than the court first seised shall of its own motion stay its proceedings until such time as the jurisdiction of the court first seised is established. [...] (3) Where the jurisdiction of the court first seised is established, any court other than the court first seised shall decline jurisdiction in favour of that court.' The corresponding predecessors of this provision were Art. 27(1) 2001 Brussels I Regulation and Art. 21 (1) 1978 Brussels Convention. *See* on the determination of the cause of action ECJ, 8 December 1987, *Gubisch*, 144/86, EU:C:1987:528, [14]; ECJ, 8 May 2003, *Gantner*, C-111/01, EU:C:2003:257, [32].
209. Cf. *Certain German Interests in Polish Upper Silesia*, Judgment, (1925) 6 PCIJ Rep. Ser. A 20.
210. McLachlan, *Lis Pendens in International Litigation* 22; Palsson, (1970) Scan Stud L. 68 ('where the *lis pendens* effect ceases, the *res judicata* effect commences.'); Voet, *Commentarius ad pandectus* 560. *Contra* Althammer, *Streitgegenstand und Interesse* 206-228 and 623. However, this scholarly contribution from Germany stems from a jurisdictional background in which there is no discretionary handling of related actions. Accordingly, there is a functional need to extend strict lis pendens in Germany.
211. Section 269 (3) ZPO focuses on the cause of action exclusively and s. 148 ZPO requires that a related actions would constitute res judicata, yee Greger, in *Zöller* § 148 [5].
212. Article 101 CPC (*'S'il existe entre des affaires portées devant deux juridictions distinctes un lien tel qu'il soit de l'intérêt d'une bonne justice de les faire instruire et juger ensemble, il peut être demandé à l'une de ces juridictions de se dessaisir et de renvoyer en l'état la connaissance de l'affaire à l'autre juridiction.'*).
213. 'For the purposes of this Article, actions are deemed to be related where they are so closely connected that it is expedient to hear and determine them together to avoid the risk of irreconcilable judgments resulting from separate proceedings.'

incorporate a general discretion under Article 2.5,[214] certainly supplemented by a non-binding inclination for priority in time in Article 2.6.[215]

74. In arbitration, lis pendens was long considered a *'non sujet par excellence'*.[216] Eventually, cases such as *Fomento*[217] and *West Tankers*[218] launched intensive discussions. Foremost, it is this examination's contention that a distinction is of the utmost importance: between the questions, whether a subsequent tribunal can be *obligated* to decline jurisdiction (strict lis pendens) and whether it might have the *discretionary power to stay* proceedings. The first question as to strict lis pendens has been affirmed in the previously mentioned *Arthur Anderson* case, where the Swiss Supreme Court decided that the second arbitral tribunal seized for an identical cause of action had to decline jurisdiction.[219] By contrast, scholarship emphasizes that both tribunals are obligated towards the parties to decide the dispute.[220] Either this concern, the influence of common-law traditions or the sheer desire for flexibility brings the focus to discretionary stays. Again, the anchor point is the arbitration agreement.[221] A tribunal faced with a motion to stay has to construe whether the arbitration agreement itself permits to postpone the decision. The majority opinion answers this question in the affirmative.[222] The opposing opinion raises the point that the parties' presumed agreement was in favour of a *quick* dispute resolution.[223] Preferably, secondary tribunals assess whether a suspension is in the interests of the parties based on several parameters of the primary proceedings: the information's importance, the dates of

214. 'Jurisdiction may be declined or the proceeding suspended when the court is manifestly inappropriate relative to another more appropriate court that could exercise jurisdiction.'
215. 'The court should decline jurisdiction or suspend the proceeding, when the dispute is previously pending in another court competent to exercise jurisdiction, unless it appears that the dispute will not be fairly, effectively, and expeditiously resolved in that forum.'
216. Schweizer and Guillod, in *Le juriste suisse face au droit et jugements étrangers* 71.
217. *See infra* [152].
218. *See infra* [88].
219. TF, *Arther Andersen v. Andersen Consulting*, [2000] 3 ASA Bull. 546.
220. Cf. Mayer, in *Liber Amicorum Claude Reymond* 193 and (2013) 4 J. Int Disp Settlement 407, [30]. Cf. Gaillard, (2017) 32 ICSID Review 28; Lew, in *Parallel State and Arbitral Procedures in International Arbitration* 311; Wehland, *Multiple Proceedings in Investment Arbitration* [4.86]. For ample support in investment jurisprudence *See SGS Société Générale de Surveillance SA v. Republic of the Philippines*, ICSID Case ARB/02/6 Decision on Jurisdiction, 29 January 2004, (2005) 8 ICSID Rep. 515 (El-Kosheri, Crawford and Crivellaro); *Reading & Bates v. Islamic Repub of Iran*, ITM 21-28-1, Interim Award, 9 June 1983, (1983) 2 Iran-US CTR 401 (ordering party to stay related ICC arbitration); *Fluor Corp. v. Islamic Repub of Iran*, ITM 62-333-1, Award, 7 August 1986, (1986) 11 Iran-US CTR 296.
221. *ICC Case 6840*, Arbitral Award, (1991-1996) III ICC Collection 468; Mayer, in *Liber Amicorum Reymond* 187; Debourg, *Les contrariétés de décisions* [511, 590] (forum-less tribunals).
222. *ILA Final Report on Lis Pendens* [4.48]; *Born* 3807; McLachlan, *Lis Pendens in International Litigation* 217.
223. Cf. Kaufmann-Kohler and Lévy, in *The Challenges of Insolvency Law Reform in the 21st Century* 269 ('[A] stay should be granted only in exceptional circumstances. [It] is contrary to one of the objectives of arbitration, which is to enable the reasonably speedy resolution of the dispute.').

initiation, the status of advancement,[224] and whether the arbitral award rendered during the stay might constitute res judicata.[225]

75. Whilst these considerations equally apply to bilateral case scenarios, multilateral case scenarios raise the question whether strict lis pendens and discretionary stays apply even in the absence of party identity in the parallel arbitrations. In international litigation, this has been most prominently brought before the Court of Justice of the European Union (ECJ): subsequent to a judgment upholding the strict same-parties requirement where several owners of a damaged maritime freight proceeded in parallel proceedings,[226] the ECJ established in *Drouot Assurances* that the same-parties requirement under Article 29(1) Brussels Ibis Regulation is met if distinct parties have identical interests and affirmed this for debtor and insurer.[227] Regardless of the applicable law, a transfer of this rationale to parallel arbitrations meets the significant concern that identical interests cannot override the rights under the arbitration agreement. Hence, if anything, the interests of related parties might be relevant for discretionary stays. This aspect is scarcely addressed in scholarship. As an exception, the ILA Report on Lis Pendens favours a liberal approach and states that '*arbitral efficiency and justice may dictate that one of the proceedings should be stayed pending the outcome of the other.*'[228] In conclusion, discretionary stays of parallel arbitrations appear permissible. There is some, yet limited authority, to suggest that such measures would be permissible in multi-party situations.

[3] Appointment of Identical Arbitrators

76. A final, very pragmatic means of coordinating parallel arbitrations has been chosen in the end by the previously mentioned *Adgas* judgment:[229] the courts supervising the arbitration in London appointed the identical arbitrator for both proceedings.[230] Correspondingly, when the ICC Court of International Arbitration is conferred with the power to appoint arbitrators in related proceedings, it may adopt

224. Cf. Lévy and Schlaepfer, (2001) Paris J. Int'l Arb. 22; Hobér, (2013) 366 Rec. des cours 255; Mayer, *Liber Amicorum Claude Reymond* 194. *See ICC Case 9787*, 1998, (2002) XXVII Y.C.A. 181.
225. Cf. Bermann, (2015) 381 Rec. des cours [306].
226. ECJ, 6 December 1994, *Tatry*, C-406/92, EU:C:1994:400, [35].
227. ECJ, 15 January 1998, *Drouot Assurances*, C-351/96, EU:C:1998:242, [11]. *See* on the application for contrasting interests BGH, 19 February 2013, VI ZR 45/12, [18]. *See* Briggs and Rees, *Civil Jurisdiction and Judgments* [2.231] ('reminiscent of [...] the common law of estoppel by res judicata').
228. *ILA Final Report on Lis Pendens* [4.49] ('In the situation of related claims between non-identical parties, the issue may be one of lis pendens (if the parties are so closely related that they are deemed identical), but it is again more likely to be an issue of case management. The Committee concluded that arbitral efficiency and justice may dictate that one of the proceedings should be stayed pending the outcome of the other.').
229. *See supra* [49].
230. *Abu Dhabi Gas Liquefaction Co. Ltd v. Eastern Bechtel Corporation*, [1982] 2 Lloyd's Rep. 425, 427 per Lord Denning (CA) ('It seems to me that there is ample power in the court to appoint in each arbitration the same arbitrator. It seems to me highly desirable that this should be done so as to avoid inconsistent findings.').

this practice.[231] Whilst this measure does technically *not* end a multi-fora dispute, it will frequently ensure that the (formally distinct) tribunals act consistently. In support of this informal measure of coordination, a party's objection was considered as a violation of good faith.[232] Moreover, the recent *Al Gobain* case under French law states that the dual appointment in parallel arbitrations does not trigger impartiality concerns.[233] Certainly, confidentiality needs to be guaranteed in that the arbitrator does not communicate findings of one arbitration against a party's interest to a third party involved in the parallel arbitration.[234] In their 2018 update, the HKIAC Rules provided for a specific Article 30.1 allowing tribunals that are identical in two related cases to suspend one of these cases.[235] Such solution can be a pragmatic means for coordinating parallel proceedings provided that the distinct parties do not exercise their fundamental right in appointing distinct arbitrators.

77. In conclusion, parallel arbitrations between distinct parties pose a welter of legal problems and no comprehensive means of pre-emptive Forum Coordination. If any, the most promising is the informal coordination of selecting identical arbitrators for parallel disputes.

[C] Parallel Litigation and Arbitration

78. In the scenario that not all parties to a multilateral transaction are bound to arbitrate, parallel litigation and arbitration need to be handled. At the outset, any coordination of the two fora seized by measure of the court is conclusively settled by Article II(3) NYC. It reads:

> The court of a Contracting State, when seized of an action in a matter in respect of which the parties have made an agreement [to arbitrate] shall [...] refer the parties to arbitration, unless it finds that the said agreement is [invalid].[236]

79. Certainly, it is debated whether this provision only applies if the arbitration agreement designates an arbitral seat outside of the court's jurisdiction. The corresponding opinion refers to an analogy to Article I(1) NYC,[237] the opposing opinion to

231. Cf. Fry Greenberg and Mazza, *The Secretariat's Guide to ICC Arbitration* [3.360]; Granier, in *Procédures parallèles et décisions contradictoires* 136; Greenberg Feris and Albanesi, in *Dossier of the ICC Institute of World Business Law – Multiparty Arbitration* 164.
232. Leboulanger, (1996) 13 J. Int'l Arb. 90-91.
233. Cass. (1e civ.), *Al Gobain c/ Crédit Foncier de France*, 2 December 2015, (2016) Rev. Arb. 525.
234. Cf. Winstanley, in *Multiple Party Actions in International Arbitration* [7.29].
235. 'The arbitral tribunal may, after consulting with the parties, conduct two or more arbitrations under the Rules at the same time, or one immediately after another, or suspend any of those arbitrations until after the determination of any other of them, where: (a) the same arbitral tribunal is constituted in each arbitration; and (b) a common question of law or fact arises in all the arbitrations'.
236. Article 8(1) UNCITRAL Model Law incorporates an almost identical wording.
237. *See Kaverit Steel and Crane v. Kone Corp*, 87 DLR (4th) 129 (CA Alberta 1992); TF, *Compagnie de Navigation et Transports SA v. MSC Shipping Company SA*, 16 January 1995; TF, 9 January 2008, 4A_436/2007; TF, 25 October 2011, 4A_270/2010; Poudret and Cottier, (1995) ASA Bull.

the rationale of establishing a harmonized legal framework.[238] Yet, many arbitration laws are identical, e.g., Article 8(1) UNCITRAL Model Law.[239]

80. Applying the provision's consequences on the arbitration agreement's negative effect, a court's hands are tied when there is fragmentated personal jurisdiction. Indeed, Article II(3) NYC exclusively confers preference upon arbitration *if* the third party is bound by the arbitration clause.[240] If the third party is *not* a party to the arbitration agreement, there is *de lege lata* no ground to terminate the litigation.[241] If the third party *is* a party to the arbitration agreement, there is no discretion for a court to exercise jurisdiction.[242] If the court violates this provision of public international law, it might even become liable for damages towards the applicant.[243] Correspondingly, the ILA observed:

> limited need to have a rule which determines which of two legitimate fora should proceed to determine the dispute, because the jurisdiction of the arbitral tribunal will trump the jurisdiction of any court.[244]

81. Turning to the arbitral tribunal's power to coordinate the parallel proceedings, its hands are equally as tied with fragmentated personal jurisdiction. It can neither *extend* jurisdiction over the non-signatory[245] nor *decline* its jurisdiction over the parties to the arbitration agreement.[246] Accordingly:

384; Sanders (ed.), *ICCA's Guide to the Interpretation of the 1958 New York Convention* 19; Wolff in Wolff (ed.), *New York Convention* 99-104. The wording of Art. I(1) NYC is: 'This Convention shall apply to the recognition and enforcement of arbitral *awards made in the territory of a State other than* the State where the recognition and enforcement of such awards are sought [...].' (emphasis added)

238. *See* CA Versailles, *sté Bomar Oil NV v. Entreprsie tunisienne d'activités pétrolières*, 23 January 1991 (aff'd Cass); *Gas Authority of India Ltd v. SPIE-CAPAG SA et al*, 15 October 1993, 1330IA 5206 (HC Delhi); *Fred Freudensprung v. Offshore Technical Services* Inc. *et al*, 03-20226 (5th Cir. 2004); Fouchard, (1990) Rev. Arb. 571; Minoli, in *Liber Amicorum Martin Domke* 203.
239. 'A court before which an action is brought in a matter which is the subject of an arbitration agreement shall [...] refer the parties to arbitration unless it finds that the agreement is null and void, inoperative or incapable of being performed.' *See UNCITRAL Digest on the Model Law* 33-35.
240. Cf. ATF 124 III 83.
241. Cf. *Gulf Canada Resources Ltd v. Arochem International Ltd*, (1992) 66 BCLR 113, CLOUT Case 31 (CABC); *Siderurgica Mendes Junior SA v. 'Icepearl' (The)*, 31 January 1996, CLOUT Case 178 (SCBC); *Born* 2569-71; Mayer, in *Liber Amicorum Reymond* 191. *See* UK Departmental Advisory Committee on Arbitration Law, *Report on the Arbitration Bill* [180] ('In our view, it would amount to a negation of the principle of party autonomy to give the tribunal or the court power to order consolidation or concurrent proceedings. Indeed, it would to our minds go far towards frustrating the agreement of the parties to have their own tribunal for their own disputes.').
242. Cf. *McCreary Tire & Rubber Co. v. CEAT SpA*, 501 F.2d 1032, 1036-37 (2d Cir. 1974); van den Berg, *The New York Convention* 135-137; *Schlosser* 304.
243. *See* Betancourt, (2017) 33 Arb. Int'l 233-245.
244. *ILA Final Report on Lis Pendens* at [1.9].
245. *See supra* [38-40].
246. *See supra* [67].

> there cannot be a situation of [true] lis pendens between court and arbitration proceedings but only a question of to which adjudicatory body jurisdiction properly belongs.[247]

82. The thus exclusively imaginable solution is that either the court or the arbitral tribunal temporarily stays their proceedings until the other rendered its decision.[248] Before courts, the assessment is influenced by the court's procedural *lex fori*. In this regard, there are several examples of stays in favour of related arbitrations in the US,[249] England[250] and Singapore,[251] notably all common law courts. Before tribunals, the discussion corresponds to the previously addressed assessment of stays in favour of parallel arbitrations:[252] For example, an arbitral tribunal in a maritime (indemnity) case stayed its proceedings in favour of a related litigation with different parties because it held it '*unreasonable and impractical [...] to assemble the high technical evidence [and] expect[ed] a wealth of such evidence will be presented in the California litigation.*'[253] As a consideration privy to parallel litigation and arbitration, the interests in favour of a stay might furthermore be overriding if a parallel dispute in non-arbitrable matters is pivotal for the relationship. For example, during an arbitration for patent infringement, it appears preferable to await the decision on the parallel invalidation suit in courts.[254] For these reasons, discretionary stays can apply between courts and tribunals. Yet, they are subject to a case-by-case assessment, and little debated in the absence of party identity.

Interim Conclusion

83. In conclusion, the consensual limits of multi-party arbitration have a prolonged effect on parallel proceedings. If multi-party arbitration is unavailable *because* some parties have not consented to arbitration in general, coordinative tools will equally be barred for jurisdictional reasons. An anomaly established under US jurisprudence is the concept of 'vouching in': a notice of arbitration to a stranger to the arbitration agreement, exposing him to the arbitral award's effects and thereby effectively undermining its lack of consent. If multi-party arbitration is unavailable, *although* all parties have in general consented to arbitration, yet in distinct arbitration agreements, consolidations are only possible under some arbitral rules (particularly HKIAC, SCC, SIAC, Swiss), yet require compatible clauses. By contrast, other rules such as the ICC

247. Söderlund, (2005) 22 J. Int'l Arb. 311. Cf. Bermann, (2015) 381 Rec. des cours [283-284]; *Born* 3794.
248. Cf. Hobér, (2013) 366 Rec. des cours 241.
249. *McCowan v. Sears Roebuck and Co*, 908 F.2d 1099, 1107 (2d Cir. 1990); *Hill Grimes and Canatxx Energy Ventures v. GE Power Systems et al*, 282 F.3d 343 (5th Cir. 2002).
250. *Mabey and Johnson Ltd v. Danos et al*, [2007] EWHC 1094 (Ch). See *McAlpine Construction v. Unex*, [1994] 38 Con LR 63 (CA) (rule acknowledged, yet now applied).
251. *Yee Hong Pte Ltd v. Tan Chye Hee Andrew and Ho Bee Development Pte Ltd*, published in Lawnet-Singapore Court Judgments (SGHC).
252. *See supra* [74-75].
253. *SMA Case 2065, Pacific Star Corporation (Voyage Charterer) v. Metal Transport Corporation of New York (Voyage Subcharterer)*, (1987) XII Y.C.A. 172.
254. Cf. CA Paris, 28 June 2008 referred to by Debourg, *Les contrariétés des décisions* [283].

Rules will not allow consolidation. Then, a pragmatic option is to appoint identical arbitrators for related disputes. Hence, multilateral transactions depend on a mosaic of forum-coordinative measures none of which is able to comprehensively overcome jurisdictional boundaries. Hence, arbitration might in fact expose multilateral transactions to the risks of multi-fora disputes. As noted by Mance LJ (as he then was), this is:

> well recognized – though the popularity of arbitration may indicate that this inability is not often inconvenient or that perceived advantages of arbitration [...] are seen as outweighing any inconvenience.[255]

§1.04 JURISDICTION DISPUTED: PARTY AUTONOMY'S SUSCEPTIBILITY TO FORUM COORDINATION

84. In contrast to multi-fora disputes about the substance, jurisdictional multi-fora disputes concern the very validity or effect of the arbitration agreement itself. They do not seek to out-balance the disputes' connection with party-autonomy considerations but concern adjudicatory hierarchy and prerogatives. In this regard, this preliminary section lays out why jurisdictional disputes can be aptly coordinated in *domestic* settings (*see* [A], *infra*), and it is the *international* dimension of arbitration that creates disorder (*see* [B], *infra*).

[A] Leitmotif of Vertical Jurisdictional Prerogatives in Domestic Settings

85. In domestic arbitration settings, jurisdictional disputes operate against two undisputed cornerstones. *At the beginning*, arbitral tribunals can determine their jurisdiction under the notion of competence-competence.[256] Whereas this is inevitable in litigation, arbitral tribunals' powers depend on positive formulations.[257] Yet effectively, they are subject to the *last word* of courts: if an arbitral tribunal unduly exceeded – or alternatively declined[258] – its jurisdiction, the arbitral award will regularly be set

255. *Sun Life Insurance Co. of Canada v. Lincoln National Life Insurance Co*, (2005) 1 Lloyd's Rep. 606, [68] per Mance LJ (CA). *See* on this case *infra* [270].
256. For example, Art. 16 Model Law ('The arbitral tribunal may rule on its own jurisdiction'); Art. 23 (1) UNCITRAL Rules; Art. 6(3) ICC Rules; Art. 23(1) LCIA Rules; Art. 25 SIAC Rules; Art. 21 Swiss Rules.
257. *See Sphere Drake Ins. Ltd v. All American Ins. Co*, 256 F.3d 587, 591 (7th Cir) ('Courts have jurisdiction to determine their jurisdiction not only out of necessity – how else would jurisidictional disputes be resolved? – but also because their authority depends on statutes rather than the parties' permission. Arbitrators lack a comparable authority to determine their own authority because there is a non-circular alternative – the judiciary [...].'); Bermann, (2015) 381 Rec. des cours [98-99].
258. England: L. *G Caltex Gas Co. Ltd v. National Petroleum Corporation & Anor*, (2001) EWCA Civ 788, [70-71] (obiter); *Monde Petroleum SA v. Westernzagros Ltd*, [2015] EWHC 67, [28] (Comm); France: Art. 1520(1) CPC. Germany: Kröll, (2004) 20 Arb. Int'l 56. Switzerland: Art. 190(2)(b) PILA. USA: § 10(a)(4) FAA. *See Born* 3211-12; Marchisio, *The Notion of Award* 102-4. *Contra* BGH, [2003] SchiedsVZ 39; *Poudret and Besson* 407.

aside.[259] US and German jurisprudence has even held arbitration clauses excluding jurisdictional court review invalid.[260] Hence, there is a vertical hierarchy between courts and tribunals.

86. The comparative divides concern the prerogatives of courts *before* set asides. Particularly, are they allowed to assess the arbitration clause (i) in declaratory actions, (ii) incidentally, in actions on the substance or (iii) in appeals to jurisdictional decisions of tribunals?[261] In this regard, there is a continuum of solutions. The Model Law,[262] China[263] and the FAA[264] always permit review. The opposite concept is the French principle of *negative* competence-competence, stipulating that courts must not rule on arbitral jurisdiction until an arbitral tribunal has rendered the award.[265] It is also applied in Panama,[266] Brazil[267] and Venezuela.[268] The concept prevents jurisdictional tactics whilst potentially delaying a final decision. Thus, other jurisdictions contain compromises. In Switzerland, the French approach applies to international arbitration. Moreover, under German law,[269] the European Convention[270] and the ILA Report,[271] courts can assess jurisdiction until arbitration is initiated. If, during the respective review, the arbitral tribunal renders an arbitral award, the German Federal Court of Justice recently decided that the review continues and binds the annulment procedures.[272] In conclusion, domestic arbitration laws provide for clear hierarchies. *After* an arbitral award has been issued, jurisdiction will always be reviewed in set-aside and enforcement procedures. The exclusive variations concern the status *before* an arbitral award has been issued.

---

259. Cf. Art. 34(2)(a)(i) Model Law; Art. 67(1)(a) English Arbitration Act; Art. 1520 No. 1 French CPC; Art. 190(2)(b) Swiss PILA; s. 10(4) FAA. *See* Cass. (com), *Southern Pacific Properties*, 6 January 1987, [1987] Rev. Arb. 489; *Major League Umpires Ass'n*, 357 F.3d 272 (3d Cir. 2004); Fouchard, (1999) Rev. Arb. 270; Racine, (2005) Rev. Arb. 684.
260. *Reisman Craig Park and Paulsson* 345-397.
261. *See* Bermann, (2012) 37 Yale J. Int'l L, 4-7.
262. Article 16 (3) ('[I]f the arbitral tribunal rules as a preliminary question that it has jurisdiction, any party may request, within thirty days after having received notice of that ruling, the court specified in article 6 to decide the matter, which decision shall be subject to no appeal; while such a request is pending, the arbitral tribunal may continue the arbitral proceedings and make an award.'). *See* Art. 8 UNCITRAL Model Law ('proceedings may nevertheless be commenced or continued and an award be made whilst the issue is pending before the court').
263. Tao, *Arbitration Law and Practice in China* [244].
264. Cf. Bermann, (2012) 37 Yale J. Int'l L, 28-47.
265. *Fouchard Gaillard and Goldman* 392-412.
266. Cf. Arrue Montenegro, (2014) Rev. Arb. 617.
267. Cf. Superior Tribunal de Justica, *Ferroatlântica SL v. Zeus Meneracao Ltda*, 29 June 2011, 17868 – BA (2011/0061155-6) reported by Debourg and Scheffer Da Silveira, (2014) Rev. Arb. 752.
268. Supreme Court of Venezuela, *Asistenza Astilleros de Venezuela CA v. Oceanlink Offshore III AS*, reported in *A Contribution by the ITA board of reporters*, Kluwer Arbitration.
269. Section 1032(2) ZPO ('*bis zur Bildung eines Schiedsgerichts*').
270. 'Where either party to an arbitration agreement has initiated arbitration proceedings before any resort is had to a court, courts of Contracting States subsequently asked to deal with the same subject-matter between the same parties or with the question whether the arbitration agreement was non-existent or null and void or had lapsed, shall stay their ruling on the arbitrator's jurisdiction until the arbitral award is made, unless they have good and substantial reasons to the contrary.'
271. *ILA Final Report on Lis Pendens* [4.20-4.46].
272. BGH, (2017) IPRax 614.

[B] Horizontalization of Jurisdictional Prerogatives in International Settings

87. In international case scenarios, the picture of clear hierarchies is instantly becoming blurred. The plurality of courts deciding on arbitral jurisdiction is *horizontalizing* the jurisdictional prerogatives. Generally, either court is fully competent to adjudicate on arbitral jurisdiction. (i) Courts that are supposed to exercise jurisdiction but for the arbitration agreement do not have to defer to foreign arbitral tribunals[273], nor to the seat's courts.[274] (ii) Courts at the arbitral seat deciding on, e.g., preliminary measures, or set asides can equally assess an arbitration agreement. (iii) Most importantly, courts at the place of recognition and enforcement undertake comprehensive, yet autonomous, jurisdictional review. In the case of an arbitral award, V(1)(a) NYC does not require the parties to seek any set aside first[275] and can even be examined whilst a set aside is pending.[276] In the case of a foreign judgment, national laws regard a violation of Article II(3) NYC as a ground for non-recognition.[277] The resulting range of competent courts might come to different results on jurisdiction in multilateral transactions as in *Dallah*.[278]

88. Moreover, pre-emptive and repressive protections of arbitration add additional voices within this polyphonic concert. From a *reactive* perspective, tribunals and courts might award damages for potential violations of an arbitration agreement.[279] From a *pre-emptive* perspective, anti-suit injunctions have significantly outgrown their origins in the parallel jurisdiction of equity and common law[280] and are now a tool of the

273. Article II(3) NYC does not establish any principle of *negative competence-competence* on such courts, *see* ATF 121 III 381; *Canada* No. *30 H&H Engine Service Ltd v. Volvo Penta of the Americas* Inc. *et al*, (2010) XXXV Y.C.A. 339 (SCBC). *Contra* arbitral jurisprudence *ICC Case 5103*, 1988, [1988] Clunet 1206; *ICC Case 6142*, 1990, [1990] Clunet 1039; *ICC Case 6709*, 1991, (1991-1995) III ICC Collection 435; *ICC Case 6000/6106*, unpublished, cited by the former; *ICC Case 6840*, 1991, (1991-1995) III ICC Collection 467.
274. Such pragmatic solution remained undeployed within the Brussels Ibis Regulation's recast. *See* for the proposals Hess Pfeiffer and Schlosser, *Heidelberg Report* [134] and the Commission's initial draft, COM(2010) 748 final, Art. 29(4).
275. Whilst *Svenska Petroleum Exploration AV v. Government of Lithuania and AB Geonafta*, [2005] EWHC 9 (Comm); reversed on other grounds [2006] EWVA Civ 1529 established that a party can only resist recognition and enforcement when it has previously attempted to annul the arbitral award, neither the wording of Art. V NYC nor efficiency considerations support this ratio, *see* Steeger, *Die Präklusion von Versagungsgründen* 267-274; Bermann, (2015) 381 Rec. des cours [732].
276. *See* Art. VI NYC ('If an application for the setting aside [...] has been made [...], the authority before which the award is sought to be relied upon *may, if it considers it proper*, adjourn the decision on the enforcement of the award [...].').
277. *See Poudret and Besson* [516].
278. *See supra* [41].
279. *See A v. B*, [2007] EWHC 54 per Colman J. (Comm); *Pipeline Services WA Pty Ltd v. ATCO Gas Australia Pty Ltd*, [2014] WASC 10. *See* on jurisdiction agreements Briggs and Rees, *Civil Jurisdiction and Judgments* [5.57-61].
280. Cf. *Barclays Bank plc v. Homan*, [1992] BCC 757, 762 per Hoffmann J. (CA); *Booth v. Leycester* (1837) 48 ER 430.

arbitral seat for restraining proceedings in violation of an arbitration agreement.[281] Whilst the existence of multiple parties is a strong inclination *against* issuing an anti-suit injunction,[282] the recent *Crescendo* judgment points out the possibility to overcome the threshold.[283] Certainly, until the Brussels/Lugano regime ceases to apply, English courts must not restrain litigation before European Union (EU) courts.[284] Yet, outside of the Brussels Regime, they remain possible and are likely to be recognized before civil-law courts.[285] In addition and without pre-emption of the Brussels Regime,[286] arbitral tribunals frequently issue anti-suit injunctions,[287] since this remedy is characterized as pure specific performance of the arbitration agreement.[288] These injunctions and damages awards will again be reviewed by a plurality of courts across jurisdictional frontiers. Moreover, several fora might be inclined to issue conflicting protective measures. For instance, in the *Sulamérica* case, one side successfully applied for an anti-suit injunction before the Commercial Court whilst the opposing party successfully applied for an injunction before the District Court in Sao Paulo holding the arbitration clause invalid.[289] Any of these decisions could be brought in recognition and enforcement proceedings before third-State courts. Additionally, the arbitral award and a judgment on the substance might be circulating. The clutter is thus accomplished.

89. Potentially, the clutter might be cleared by the application of forum-coordinative tools between courts. Foremost, it is widely known and heavily debated that some courts regard foreign courts' adjudications on the arbitration clause as susceptible to foreign judgment principles. For instance, they might reject on enforcement objection

281. Cf. *Starlight Shipping Co. v. Tai Ping Ins. Co. Ltd (Hubei Branch)*, (2008) 1 Lloyd's Rep. 230 (QB); *Paramedics Electro v. GE Medical Systems*, 369 F.3d 645 (2d Cir. 2004) (although the clause has already been deemed valid, thus incorporating a res judicata aspect); *Karaha Bodas Co, LLC v. Perusahaan ertambangan Minyak Dan Gas Bumi Negara*, 335 F.3d 357 (5th Cir. 2003).
282. *Bouygues Offshore SA v. Caspian Shipping Co*, [1998] 2 Lloyd's Rep. 461; *Donohue v. Armco*, [2002] 1 Lloyd's Rep. 425, [60-62]; *Noble Assurance v. Gerling-Konzern General Insurance*, [2007] EWHC 253 per Toulson LJ (Comm); *Verity Shipping v. NV Norexa*, [2008] EWHC 213; *Carlyle Capital Corporation v. Conway*, [2013] 2 Lloyd's Rep. 179.
283. *Crescendo Maritime Co. et al. v. Bank of Communications Company Ltd et al*, (2015) EWHC 3364 at [50-51] per Teare J. (Comm) ('I accept that the existence of claims against multiple parties, with the consequent risk of inconsistent finding, can amount to a strong reason not to issue an anti-suit injunction. [...] In the circumstances of this case it is, it seems to me, inappropriate and unjust for the [defendant] to rely upon a risk of inconsistent decisions when that risk arises from the [defendant's] own decision to allege fraud both in arbitration and in China [...].').
284. ECJ, 2 October 2009, *West Tankers ('The Front Comor')*, C-185/07, EU:C:2009:69.
285. Cf. Cass. (1e civ.), 14 October 2009, [2009] I Bull. civil No. 207; Kronke, in *Liber Amicorum Kaissis* 551-555.
286. *See* ECJ, 13 May 2015, *Gazprom*, C-536/13, EU:C:2015:316.
287. Cf. *ICC Case 10956*, Interlocutory Award, (2005) XXX Y.C.A. 66, [17]; *ICC Case 8887*, Award, (2000) 1 ICC Bulletin 91; *ICC Case 6998*, Final Award, (1996) XXI Y.C.A. 54; *ICC Case 3896*, Award, [1983] Clunet 917; *Société Generale de Surveillance SA v. Pakistan*, ICSID Case ARB/01/13, Procedural Order No. 2, 16 October 2002, [2005] ICISD Rep. 388 (Feliciano P, Thomas and Faurès).
288. *See ICC Case 8307*, Interim Award (Tercier) cited Gaillard, (2007) 13 ICCA Congress Series 256.
289. Tribunal de Justica Sao Paulo, *Enesa Engenharia ea v. Sulamérica Cia Nacional de Seguros ea*, [2014] Rev. Arb. 723, 759.

under Article V(1)(a) NYC if the courts at the arbitral seat have already rejected a set aside. Since such preclusion is a very manifestation of the doctrine of res judicata, it shall be reviewed at a later stage of the examination.[290] In any case, it can be proclaimed that the coordination is not comprehensive. Thus, there is the possibility of diverging jurisdictional assessments thereby increasing adjudications on the substance.

§1.05 INFERENCE: RES JUDICATA'S RESULTING CROSSROADS POSITION

90. The limited means of pre-emptive Forum Coordination in multilateral cross-border transactions result in a crossroads position of res judicata. In a literal sense, crossroads have two parameters. *First*, since reality does not operate on mono-pathways, they are inevitable. *Second*, they require important decisions. Both parameters apply to res judicata.

91. As to its inevitability, res judicata is a topic that is inherently triggered by all multilateral transactions, which have included an arbitration clause in some part of the transaction, but have not carefully tailored a multi-party regime and are subsequently unable to agree on the latter. Moreover, the uncertainties with regard to arbitral jurisdiction over non-signatories might allow multiple fora to affirm or reject such jurisdiction and thereby adjudicate on the substance. In all such scenarios, the necessary pre-emptive coordination of parallel multi-fora disputes has strong limits. Accordingly, as soon as one of the disputes has been terminated by means of a decision, parties in the parallel or in a subsequent procedure are likely to raise the decision's conclusive or preclusive effects on the substance in connected matters.

92. As to its importance, such argument on res judicata requires a delicate selection between two pivotal, albeit opposing objectives. *On the one hand*, res judicata would finally prevent the risks established by multi-fora disputes, particularly the existence of contradicting decision. Instead, it would establish Forum Coordination. *On the other hand*, the application of res judicata bears the inherent risk to undermine the very boundaries that have prevented pre-emptive coordination. Most importantly, those boundaries focused on the parties' consent and thereby safeguarded party autonomy. The resulting, potential antagony of res judicata and party autonomy is nothing less than what this examination perceives as the dichotomous framework against which the arbitral awards' third-party effects should be assessed.

290. *See infra* Chapter 9.

§1.06 CONCLUDING THESES

(1) Commercial transactions such as construction, industrial and maritime projects, M&A transactions or commodity purchases inherently constitute *multilateral* transactions. Moreover, many of arbitration's advantages such as the global enforceability serve as an incentive to include arbitration clauses in such transactions.[291]

(2) However, conducting arbitrations comprising all parties concerned, i.e., *multi*-party arbitrations, is subject to strict requirements: all parties' general consent to arbitration, identical or compatible arbitration clauses and equal influence on the arbitrators' selection. Otherwise, multi-party arbitration is inoperable.[292]

(3) Therefore, multilateral transactions comprise the default risk of multi-fora disputes often associated with caveats such as contradicting decisions, undue allocation of chances and inefficiency. Those risks serve as incentives for pre-emptive *Forum Coordination*, i.e., the prevention or coordination of parallel dispute resolution.[293]

(4) Third-party notice is inapplicable unless the notified consented to arbitration. A pivotal exception contains US jurisprudence permitting 'vouching in' regardless of the third party's consent to arbitration.[294]

(5) An informal tool particularly for the coordination of parallel arbitrations is the appointment of identical arbitrators. However, in multi-party case scenarios this might be impossible, when there is the right for party-appointed arbitrators.[295]

(6) Apart from this solution, the sole tool for coordinating parallel disputes in the absence of all parties' consent to arbitrate is a discretionary stay of proceedings. Yet, a stay of arbitration requires an interest of the parties in the stay outweighing the potential delay.[296]

(7) For these reasons, res judicata is likely to be raised and of pivotal importance if parties seek to apply for Forum Coordination in a multilateral transaction.

(8) However, res judicata also risks undermining the very boundaries imposed on pre-emptive Forum Coordination for multilateral transactions. These boundaries require consent and thereby safeguard arbitration's cornerstone: party autonomy.[297]

291. *See supra* [36-37].
292. *See supra* [36-51].
293. *See supra* [54-60].
294. *See supra* [62-65].
295. *See supra* [50, 76].
296. *See supra* [71-75, 78-83].
297. *See supra* [92].

CHAPTER 2

A Proceduralist Connotation of Arbitral Res Judicata under National Laws

93. This examination on the personal scope (*ratione personae*) of res judicata often presupposes the applicability of res judicata's other requirements. For instance, if a buyer has successfully claimed damages from a re-seller for non-conformity of the goods before an arbitral tribunal and the re-seller seeks indemnification against a producer, any argument as to the third-party effect of the arbitral award towards the producer will be in vain if the incidental adjudication on the non-conformity does not even fall under res judicata's operative scope (*ratione materiae*).

94. Therefore, this Chapter outlines the general operational aspects of arbitral res judicata. Many aspects of res judicata originate in litigation. Accordingly, procedural law is the outset of the examination (*see* §2.01, *infra*). Yet, whilst procedural consequences are generally deemed applicable to arbitral awards, some consequences and requirements are meeting significant concerns of party autonomy when it comes to arbitral awards (*see* §2.02, *infra*). Whilst these sections examined arbitral res judicata before the courts of the arbitral seat, it is furthermore necessary to outline the procedural framework for res judicata before foreign courts (*see* §2.03, *infra*) and before arbitral tribunals at the arbitral seat (*see* §2.04, *infra*). Moreover, a supplementary, yet indispensable dimension of res judicata in cross-border case scenarios is the relevance of res judicata for the assessment of conflicting decisions (*see* §2.05, *infra*). As an overall inference, the outline submits: *in arbitration, the doctrine of res judicata is generally perceived upon its proceduralist foundation* (*see* §2.06, *infra*). This will set the scene for the upcoming conflict with the *contractual* limits of pre-emptive Forum Coordination previously established.

95. As a final proclamation, the general operation of res judicata under national arbitration laws is by no means an issue privy to multi-party case scenarios. Moreover, it has already been reasonably covered by existing scholarship.[298] Therefore, it is *not* the focus of this examination. Instead, this Chapter is kept as brief as possible whilst still providing the necessary foundation for the upcoming multi-party problems as detailed as necessary.

§2.01 FOUNDATIONS OF RES JUDICATA IN CIVIL PROCEDURE

96. The doctrine of res judicata states: once a judgment has become final, duplicative claims shall be prevented, be it because the repetitive claim is regarded as proven, inadmissible or the subsequent court's jurisdiction suppressed.[299] Moreover, jurisdictions concur that preclusion does not merely cover dismissed claims, but also such that have been affirmed in order to prevent double compensation.[300] These rules apply generally independent of the first judgment's adequacy, thereby establishing a primacy of '*repose over correctness*'.[301] The prevention of duplicative claims is already applied under Roman law (*exceptio rei judicatae vel in judicium deductae*).[302] In national doctrines, it has distinct expressions: 'cause of action estoppel' at common law,[303] 'claim preclusion' (bar) in US law,[304] *materielle Rechtskraft* in Germany and *autorité (négative) de la chose jugée* in France.[305] Notably, the latter two terms are closely related to the German and French terms describing a judgment's finality (*formelle Rechtskraft, force de la chose jugée*). Perhaps, it stands against this background that the term 'res judicata' is occasionally understood as referring to a judgment's finality only.[306]

298. Reports on arbitral awards, often with incidental focus on judgments: *ILA Interim Report on Res Judicata* 41-54; *Born* 3747-67; Chanais, (2016) Rev. Arb. 3; Debourg, *Les contrariétés des décisions* 396-415; Erk-Kubat, *Parallel Proceedings in International Arbitration* 162-177; Hobér, (2015) 366 Rec. des cours 94 et seqq.; Lühmann, *Die Rechtskraft des Schiedsspruchs* 28-112; Schaffstein, *Res Judicata* [1.01-1.159] (judgments) and [4.14-4.121] (arbitral awards); Zajdela, *L'autorité de la chose jugée.* Reports on judgments: Germelmann, *Die Rechtskraft von Gerichtsentscheidungen* 8-257 (public law); Koch, *Unvereinbare Entscheidungen* 13-73; Landbrecht, *Teil-Sachentscheidungen und Ökonomie der Streitbeilegung* 73 et seqq., 137 et seqq. and 211 et seqq.; Peiffer, *Grenzüberschreitende Titelgeltung* 115-175; Otte, *Umfassende Streitentscheidung* 95-133; Spellenberg, in *Liber Amicorum Henckel* 841 et seqq.; Stapf, *Die Entwicklung der Rechtskraftlehre*; Stürner, in *Liber Amicorum Schütze* 913 et seqq.; van den Helden, *Finality in Litigation* 19-222; Zeuner and Koch, in *International Encyclopedia of Comparative Law.*
299. *See* on this distinction and its limited implications *ILA Interim Report on Res Judicata* 65.
300. Cf. Handley, *Res Judicata* [19.01] (former recovery); Restatement (Second) Judgments, § 17(1) ('If the judgment is in favor of the plaintiff, the claim is extinguished and merged in the judgment and a new claim may arise on the judgment.').
301. von Mehren, (1980) 167 Rec. des cours 21.
302. Ulpian, *Ad Legem Juliam et Papiam* 1, 5, 25 (addressing the status of a liberated person).
303. *Thoday v. Thoday*, [1964] P 181, 197 per Diplock LJ (CA). Cf. *Arnold v. National Westminster Bank plc*, [1991] 2 AC 93 (HL).
304. Restatement (Second) Judgments, § 19.
305. Article 480 CPC ('a judgment which decides in its operative part the whole or part of the main issue [...] will [...] become res judicata with regard to the dispute which it determines.'); Art. 1351 Cc ('The force of res judicata takes place only with respect to what was the subject matter of a judgment.').
306. *See* on the understanding of this examination *supra* [4].

97. Assuming that jurisdictions prevent duplicative claims, they equally concur on a conclusive effect. If a claim already decided is not re-litigated as such, but arises incidentally in a subsequent proceeding, it is regarded as conclusively adjudicated.[307] Only in France, the case scenario is still deemed controversial (*autorité positive de la chose jugée*), yet affirmed by the majority opinion.[308] From a comparative point of view, the French discussion often focuses on the distinct issue of preclusion's admissibility.[309]

98. For the upcoming application in arbitration, four specifications of the common outset of res judicata are necessary. They will partially reveal divides between the examined jurisdictions, thus illustrating the importance of private international law as well as the difficulties for uniform law: namely the conceptual nature of judgments (*see* [A], *infra*), the implemented interests (*see* [B], *infra*), the distinction to other judgment effects (*see* [C], *infra*) and, most importantly, the application of extended res judicata doctrines, e.g., to adjudicatory reasonings (*see* [D], *infra*).

[A] Judgments Within the Legal Order: Evidence, Substantive or Procedural Right?

99. As final and binding acts of the judiciary, judgments modify the legal order. However, amongst jurisdictions, the particular object of the modification is highly diverse. The differences illustrate res judicata's hybrid nature between procedural law (whose result it is) and substantive law (whose rights it addresses). Whilst the conceptual questions are sometimes deemed irrelevant,[310] the tension between procedural and substantive law is the continuous foundation upon which the upcoming international discussions on arbitral awards, the applicable law as well as requirements for third-party participations are built and therefore pivotal.

100. Civilist doctrines demonstrate the continuum of concepts. In France, the pioneers Jean Domat and Robert Joseph Pothiers regarded a judgment as a means of evidence,

307. BGH, [2003] NJW 3058, 3059 with further references (*Präjudizialität*); ATF 115 II 187, [E.3.b)]; *Yukos Capital SARL v. OJSC Rosneft Oil Company*, [2011] EWHC 1461, [53] (Comm); *P&O Nedlloyd BV v. Arab Metals Co. and others*, [2006] EWCA Civ 1717, [23-24]; *Arnold v. National Westminster Bank plc*, [1991] 2 AC 93, 105 (CA); *Blair v. Curran*, (1939) 62 CLR 464, 531-533 (HCA); Restatement (Second) Judgments, § 17(3).

308. Bollée, *Sentences arbitrales* [260-261]; Douchy-Oudot, in *JCl procédure civil* [2]; Héron and Le Bars, *Droit judiciaire privé* [365-367]; Sergaglini and Ortscheidt, *Droit de l'arbitrage* [465]; Tomasin, *Essai sur l'autorité de la chose jugée en matière civile* [239]. *See* Cass. (1e civ.), 4 January 1995, [1995] Bull. Civ I No. 7 (on maintenance and parenthood litigations); Cass. (1e civ.), 18 July 1995, [1995] Bull. civ I No. 330 (mentioned assessment of cause of action).

309. *See* Héron and Le Bars, *Droit judiciaire privé* [367] ('*la Cour de cassation fait obstacle à l'autorité positive de chose jugée, dans la mesure où c'est généralement dans les motifs de la décision*'); *ICC Case 13509*, Arbitral Award, (2008-2011) VI ICC Collection 739 ('*les droits de* common law *consacrent une telle autorité [positive] sous le nom d'*issue estoppel *ou* collateral estoppel').

310. *See*, e.g., Landbrecht, *Teil-Sachentscheidungen* 34 ('*nebensächlich*').

irrefutably deemed to state the truth.[311] As of the mid-twentieth century, scholarship extracts the doctrine of res judicata from the law of evidence. Instead, the judgment itself establishes a legal norm thereby inherently modifying the order of substantive rights – *force de vérité legale* (force of legal truth).[312] Progressive scholarship emphasizes the procedural function to prevent duplicative procedure.[313] Hence, res judicata were a genuine procedural obligation between the parties and the court preventing re-litigation (*ne bis in idem*).[314] Similarly, in Germany, the pioneer Friedrich Carl von Savigny regarded the doctrine of res judicata as an institute of substantive law, establishing a legal fiction.[315] Whilst it remained codified in the code of civil procedure,[316] jurisprudence followed a substantive concept previously,[317] but moved to the *ne bis in idem* characterization.[318] At *common law*, substantive and procedural rights were regarded jointly as writs.[319] This corresponds to the Roman *actio* concept.[320] Against this background and the import of res judicata from Roman law, English law shares the fundamental concept of Roman law: the claim merges into a decision.[321] The operational effect at common law is that the earlier decision can be introduced as a means of estoppel.[322] More directly, in the US, judgments are 'merging' the initial claim.[323] In conclusion, whereas civil law regards res judicata as a matter of the *judgment's* (substantive or procedural) authority, common law regards res judicata as a matter of the *claim's* adjudicated authority.[324]

311. Cf. Domat, *Les loix civile I* 251; *Oeuvres de Pothier II*, No. 888 284. Such evidentiary still exists for the related *force probante* establishing a judgment's authenticity, *see* Art. 457 CPC (*'le jugement a la force probante d'un acte authentique'*); Roland, *Chose jugée et tierce opposition* [117] (*'l 'autorité de la chose jugée n'est qu'un moyen de preuve, et n'est pas différente de la force probatoire du jugement '*).
312. Cf. Cass. (1e civ.), 24 October 2006, 04-18.819; Cass. (2e civ), 8 July 2010, 09-10.955; Douchy-Oudot, in *JCl procédure civil* Fasc 554 [3]; Guinchard Chainais and Ferrand, *Procédure civile* [1093].
313. Bléry, *L'efficacité substantielle des jugements civils* [180]; Héron and Le Bars, *Droit judiciaire privé* [349]; Tomasin, *Essai sur l'autorité de la chose jugée en matière civile* [343].
314. Mayer, in *Liber Amicorum Héron* [2].
315. Savigny, *System des heutigen römischen Rechts* 261-274.
316. *See* on the proposals to codify res judicata in the BGB, Thomale, (2018) 73 JZ 431-433.
317. For example RGZ 78, 389, 395.
318. BGH, [2004] NJW 1805, 1806 with further references.
319. Cf. Milsom, *Historical Foundations of the Common Law* 78-82.
320. *See* Althammer, *Streitgegenstand und Interesse* 12; Garnett, *Substance and Procedure in Private International Law* [2.03]; Mayer, in *Liber Amicorum Héron* [6].
321. *See Nelson v. Couch*, (1863) 15 CBNS 99, 108 per Willes J. *Mustill and Boyd* 27 ('new right of action, in substitution for the right on which [the original] claim was founded').
322. *Carl Zeiss Stiftung v. Rayner & Keeler Ltd (No 2)*, [1966] 2 All ER 536, 564 per Lord Guest (HL).
323. Restatement (Second) Judgments, § 24(1) ('judgment [...] extinguishes the plaintiff's claim pursuant to the rules of merger or bar [...]'); *In re Associated Vintage Group Inc*, 283 BR 549, 565 (9th Cir. 2002) ('[...] claim and issue preclusion follow from that fact of the judgment without reference to anyone's conduct'); Brenner, (1987) 7 N Ill U L. Rev. 146; Millar, (1940-1941) 35 Ill L. Rev. 46; Silberman and Stein, *Civil Procedure* 727.
324. *See* Chanais, (2016) Rev. Arb. 3 et seqq.

[B] Public and Private Interests Implemented by Res Judicata

101. Res judicata's content to preclude re-litigation irrespective of the first adjudication's correctness operates for a variety of procedural interests. Again, they are pivotal for eventual considerations on the transfer to arbitration law, private international law and uniform proposals. In conformity with two maxims from Roman law, it is regularly stated that res judicata promotes both public as well as private interests.[325] The public interest in res judicata arises because the latter prevents conflicting and duplicative decisions. It guarantees *consistency* instead. This consistency serves the public interest in a homogeneous and effective dispute resolution system.[326] Such efficacy conforms to the very *raison d'être* of a dispute resolution system,[327] hence serving the *rule of law.*[328] Furthermore, consistency and finality provide *legal certainty* for all members of a judicial system who can rely on previous decisions. Such legal certainty is a prerequisite for the adequate functioning of an economic society. Continuing on *efficiency*, a major aspect of res judicata and related doctrines of abuse of process is that they prevent the unnecessary expenses of judicial resources in duplicate proceedings.[329]

102. When it comes to the private interests in res judicata, they are highly intertwined with the public interests in res judicata. In particular, *consistency* serves the private trust in the finality of a dispute. Such trust is also worth protection under *fairness and due process* aspects such as to prevent undue burdens on the winning party.[330] Moreover, finality provides *legal certainty* to the individuals for future decisions.[331] In addition, in terms of *efficiency*, res judicata prevents the unnecessary expenses of additional resources for duplicate proceedings, e.g., on counsels, witnesses and

325. *Interest reipublicae ut sit finis litium* ('It is in the public interest that there should be an end to litigation'); *Nemo debet bis vecari pro una et eadem cause* ('No one should be proceeded against twice for the same cause'), mentioned by: *Arthur J. S Hall & Co. (a firm) v. Simons*, [2002] 1 AC 615, 701 per Lord Hoffmann (HL); *Born* 3733; Brown, *A Common Law of International Adjudication* 153; Hobér, (2011) 366 Rec. des cours 120.
326. *Dorion v. Roberge*, [1991] 1 SCR 374, [69] (SC Can) ('It is a social necessity of the first order that legal proceedings should not be started over and over again on the same matter. Stability in social relationships requires that decisions of the courts be observed in the same way as legislation.').
327. Cf. *Southern Pacific Railroad Company v. United States*, (1897) 168 U.S. 1, 49 ('demanded by the very object for which civil courts have been established').
328. Cf. *Application of the Convention on the Prevention and Punishment of the Crime of Genocide (Bosnia and Herzegovina v. Serbia and Montenegro)*, Preliminary Objections, Judgment, [1996] ICJ Rep. 595, [139] ('required by the nature of the judicial function'); ECtHR, *Kehaya et al. v. Bulgaria, App Nos. 47797/99 and 68698/01, Judgment, 12 January 2006 ('fundamental principle in democratic society whose disrespect by States may violate Art. 6 ECHR'); ATF 115 II 187, [E.3.b)]; BGHZ 38, 333, 336; The Ampthill Peerage, [1977] AC 547, 575-576 per Lord Simon of Glaisdale (HL); Andrews, English Civil Procedure [40.03]; Debourg, Les contrariétés des décisions [15]; Jarrosson, (2007) 8 Procédures No. 12, [34]; Shany, Regulating Jurisdictional Relations 143.*
329. *See* Barnett, *Res Judicata* [1.13] ('main object of the doctrine').
330. Cf. Bollée, [2007] Rev. Arb. 817; Hobér, in *Parallel State and Arbitral Procedures in International Arbitration* 247; Schaffstein, *Res Judicata* [4.05].
331. Wehland, *Multiple Proceedings in Investment Arbitration* [4.55] ('[T]he principle provides individuals with both the sword and the shield that are indispensable for obtaining legal security.').

administration fees. In conclusion, res judicata promotes both public as well as private interests of justice, consistency, legal certainty and efficiency.

[C] Distinction and Interrelation Between Res Judicata and other Judgment Effects

103. The final conceptual proclamation on res judicata concerns its distinction to other effects. This distinction will be of particular relevance for private international law. An initial line has to be drawn between res judicata and the doctrine of precedence. In fact, an application of stare decisis might render res judicata on legal questions unnecessary.[332] Notably, it is debated whether the doctrine of precedence should be characterized as substantive.[333]

104. Moreover, the preclusive and conclusive effect in subsequent proceedings should not be confused with the terminative effect on the instant proceedings. In particular, civil-law doctrine assesses the latter under related, yet distinct, terms (*formelle Rechtskraft, force de la chose jugée*).[334] An additional effect of a decision is the standing to seek enforcement. Whereas US doctrine regards res judicata as a form of enforcement,[335] civil-law doctrine emphasizes the conceptual distinction between res judicata and enforceability *(force exécutoire, Vollstreckbarkeit)*.[336] Whilst the two might share common requirements with regard to the finality of a judgment, [337] enforceability comprises additional requirements.[338]

105. For some proceedings, judgments do not require any enforcement, but are '*self-effectuating [...]. A divorce decree, or a judgment declaring a will to be void, for example, establishes legal 'facts' that are ends in themselves and need no follow up.*'[339] Commercial cases concern the liquidation of a corporation, for instance. In this regard, Germanic jurisdictions distinguish between suits for performance (*Leistungsklage*) and

332. Cf. Hobér, (2011) 366 Rec. des cours 118.
333. *Pro* Bermann, (2015) 381 Rec. des cours [561-565]; *Born* 3820-21; *Redfern and Hunter* 199. *Contra* Berger, (1992) 9 J. Int'l Arb. 15.
334. *See supra* [96]. *See also* Staes, in *JCl procédure civil* Fasc 500 [1] (*dessaisement*).
335. Restatement (Second) Judgments, § 84 comment a ('Enforcement of an award following an arbitration may involve two different kinds of sanction. One is enforcement of the award by execution or other judicial process. These sanctions are analogous to those used in enforcement of judicial judgments. As noted in the Introduction to this Restatement, problems of enforcement of judgments are beyond the scope of this Restatement. The other sanction by which a court can enforce an arbitration award is to refuse to entertain an action involving the same claim that was determined in the arbitration.').
336. Douchy-Oudot, in *JCl procédure civil* aFasc 554 [6]; Rosenberg Schwab and Gottwald, *Zivilprozessrecht* § 149 [4] ('*Die Vollstreckbarkeit [...] ist mit der Rechtskraft nicht identisch.*').
337. *See* Art. 336(1) Swiss Code of Civil Procedure illustrating this difference in the French version ('*Ein Entscheid ist vollstreckbar, wenn er (a) rechtskräftig ist*' – '*Une décision est exécutoire (a) lorsque'elle est entrée en force*'). France follows the Roman distinction between suits concerning financial rights and non-financial suits (*actions extrapatrimoniaux*), *see* Lobin and Desdevises, in *JCl procédure civil* Fasc 500-90 [40].
338. Schaffstein, *Res Judicata* [0.25]. *See* Rosenberg Gaul and Schilken, *Zwangsvollstreckungsrecht* § 6.I-II.1; Schilken, in *Festschrift für Friedhelm Gaul* 675.
339. *Zuckermann on Civil Procedure* [23.120].

suits for the modification of a legal status (*Gestaltungsklage*).[340] The latter comprise a genuine 'constitutive effect' (*Gestaltungswirkung*).[341] Functionally, this effect equally seeks to prevent inconsistent judgments and will therefore by covered by this examination's scope.

106. Finally, a judgment might comprise 'secondary effects' in that it triggers provisions under substantive law. Predominantly, this will be the case because the substantive provision explicitly mentions a judgment, e.g., a limitation period might be suspended by a judgment.[342] Moreover, decisions might also trigger substantive provisions' general requirements. In this regard, drawing the line between factual effects and the application of res judicata's boundaries might prove rather delicate. For instance, a judgment in favour of a patent owner against a distributor, prohibiting the latter from delivering a certain good to a customer might technically cause effects in the substantive relationship between distributor and customer, yet effectively trigger the latter's interest in the former litigation.[343] In conclusion, judgments trigger several effects. Whilst some can be clearly distinguished from res judicata, others are closely connected, particularly enforceability, constitutive and secondary effects.

[D] Three Comparative Divides on the Operational Limits of Res Judicata

107. Beyond res judicata's common ground to prevent duplicative claims,[344] the specific operational scope of res judicata differs substantially between jurisdictions. In summary, common law seeks to settle the entire legal relationship as far as possible whereas civil law focuses on the adjudicatory relief requested and seeks to uphold the subsequent judge's cognition power. The operational consequences concern three topics with fundamental discrepancies between common and civil law.

108. *First*, this concerns the identity of the dispute initially adjudicated with the subsequent dispute. Internationally, it is frequently agreed that there needs to be identity of *claim* and *cause of action*.[345] Whilst this is often displayed as an almost universal rule, the national meanings of these two terms are highly diverse. In fact, particularly the term 'cause of action' is the very paradigm for cross-jurisdictional misunderstandings on legal terms. The term can either be understood to refer to the facts exclusively (US), to the legal grounds (England, France) or to the request for relief for a certain set of facts (Germany). Preferably, comparative law should concentrate on the functional questions lying at the heart of these terms, i.e., whether (i) the request for relief and (ii) the legal grounds invoked are relevant for determining the scope of

340. For example, the Swiss Code of Civil Procedure provides two distinct provisions for these suits in Art. 84 (1) and Art. 87.
341. *See* Schlosser, *Gestalungsklagen und Gestaltungsurteile* 17 et seqq.
342. Rosenberg with Schwab and Gottwald, *Zivilprozessrecht* § 149 [6].
343. *See* further *infra* Chapter 7.
344. *See supra* [96-97].
345. *See ILA Recommendations* 85.

claim preclusion. This is rejected in US jurisdictions where claim and cause of action (in fact often used interchangeably) are regarded as purely factual.[346] For instance, the Second Restatement states that a claim:

> includes all rights […] with respect to all or any part of the transaction, or series of connected transactions, out of which the action arose.[347]

109. Consequently, claim preclusion comprises *all* losses suffered as a consequence of an event regardless of whether they have been brought before court or they have not.[348] By way of contrast, civil-law jurisdictions restrict res judicata to the relief requested and adjudicated in the dispositif. French law reaches this result in distinguishing the underlying facts (regarded as cause of action) from the relief requested (regarded as claim) under Article 1355 Cc.[349] Germanic jurisdictions reach this result in subjecting the cause of action (*Streitgegenstand*) to the relief requested determined on the basis of the facts.[350]

110. The discussion in France even went as far as whether res judicata could only operate between identical *legal grounds*. This would have necessitated that a judgment adjudicating a tort claim would not constitute res judicata for an eventual contract claim even though the monetary relief requested and the underlying facts were

346. Andrews, *English Civil Procedure* [40.12] ('a factual situation, the existence of which entitles one person to obtain from the court a remedy against another person. […] This concept has been much discussed in case law. It denotes the set of material facts, or core factual matrix, which support a recognized legal ground of claim.') with jurisprudence references; Spencer Bower and Handley, *Res Judicata* [4.86]. Cf. *Letang v. Cooper*, [1965] 1 QB 232, 242G-243A per LJ Diplock (CA).

347. Restatement (Second) Judgments, § 24(1-2). *Pro Petromanagement Corp. v. Acme-Thomas Joint Venture*, 835 F.2d 1329, 1335 (10th Cir. 1988); Casad and Clermont, *Res Judicata* 68 with further references. *Contra* Sinai, (2010-2011) 21 Duke J. Comp. & Int'l L. 364 ('no consensus has been reached'). Notably, the terms 'claim' and 'cause of action' are used interchangeably.

348. *International Union of Operating Engineers-Employers Constr Indus Pension, Welfare & Training Trust Funds v. Karr*, 994 F.2d 1426, 1429-39 (9th Cir. 1993); *Phillips/May Corp. v. US*, 524 F.3d 1264, 1271 (Fed Cir. 2008); *Duane Reade Inc. v. St Paul Fire and Marine Ins. Co*, 600 F.3d 190, 197-198 (2d Cir. 2010). For an arbitration case *see Brody v. Hankin*, 299 FSupp2d 454 (E.D. Penn. 2004). At common law, *see Conquer v. Boot*, (1928) 2 KB 336.

349. *See* Cass. (3e civ), 30 November 1964, [1964] Bull. Civ III No. 521; Brenner, *Les conceptions acutelles de l'autorité de la chose jugée* 228; Douchy-Oudot, in *JCl procédure civil* [107]. *Contra* Motulsky, [1968] Rec Dalloz 1 (*question ltigieuse*). The wording of Art. 1355 Cc is: '*L'autorité de la chose jugée n'a lieu qu'à l'égard de ce qui a fait l'objet du jugement. Il faut que la chose demandée soit la même; que la demande soit fondée sur la même cause; que la demande soit entre les mêmes parties.*' ('The res-judicata effect is restricted to a judgment's scope. This requires that the claimed object is the same; that the claim is based on the same grounds; that the claim is between the same parties […].').

350. Switzerland ATF 121 III 474, 474; ATF 128 III 191, [4.a]; ATF 136 III 345, *Atlético Madrid v. Benfica Lisbon*, 348; ATF 140 II 278, [3.3]. Germany: BGH, 17 March 2016, IX ZR 142/14, [17] with further references. *See* Althammer, *Streitgegenstand und Interesse* 1 ('With regard to the darth of relevant publications, any new treatise on the cause of action requires justification' – '*Jede neue Schrift zum Streitgegenstand begegnet angesichts der Fülle einschlägiger Literatur hohem Erwartungs- und Rechtsfertigungsdruck*').

identical.[351] This problem might be seen as a conceptual reflection of the fact that res judicata was long deemed to modify the order of substantive rights. In any case, the Supreme Court ended this discussion in its infamous *Cesareo* decision, notably by the court's plenary assembly. Establishing a 'duty of concentration' (*concentration des moyens et demandes*), it held that a claimant whose contractual salary claim was previously dismissed is barred from initiating a further lawsuit based on the identical facts, but on the legal ground of unjustified enrichment instead.[352] Common law would reach comparable results applying a narrow cause of action estoppel and then abuse of process (*see infra*, paragraph 116). Accordingly, the functional differences only concern the influence of the parties' request for relief and the decision's operative part on res judicata.

111. The *second* and perhaps one of the most critical issues when it comes to the comparison of domestic doctrines on res judicata addresses the relevance of adjudicatory reasonings. Its relevance for multilateral transactions has already been mentioned in the introductory case.[353] Again, there is a significant divide between civil and common law. At common law, the doctrine of 'issue estoppel' extends preclusion principles upon all essential elements upon which a judgment is built.[354] Certainly:

> the court must be satisfied after careful examination of all the circumstances that the issue present in the present claim is indeed the same issue as that which has been considered and decided in earlier proceedings.[355]

112. If it is satisfied, only exceptional circumstances will incline to re-examine previously adjudicated issues on a discretionary basis.[356] Correspondingly, US law contains the doctrine of 'issue preclusion'.[357] Notably, Swedish law is also favourable to broad preclusion. For example, in *Kurt Wilhelm v. Aktiebolaget Ragner J*, a purchaser previously ordered to pay the outstanding purchase price was precluded from claiming damages on the grounds of the goods' alleged non-conformity.[358] Moreover, the

351. *See* Cass. (1e civ.), 28 March 1995, [1995] Bull. civ I No. 139; Douchy-Oudot, in *JCl procédure civil* [167-85] with further references; Motulsky, [1968] Rec Dalloz 235; Mourre and Vagenheim, in *JCl procédure civile* Fasc 1067 [35-36]; Solus and Perrot, *Droit judicaire privé III* [71-73].
352. Cass. (ass plén), *Cesareo*, 7 July 2006, [2006] Bull. plén No. 8. *('Gilbert X ne pouvait être admis à contester l'identité de cause des deux demandes en invoquant un fondement juridique'). See* further Mayer, in *Liber amicorum Héron* [12-16]; Jarrosson, (2007) 8 Procédures No. 12 [41] using Motulsky's expression '*obligation de concentration des demandes*'.
353. *See supra* [93].
354. *Ihoysted v. Federal Com of Taxation*, (1921) 29 CLR 537, 561 per Higgins J. (HCA); *New Brunswick Rly Co. Ltd v. British and French Trust Corp. Ltd*, [1939] AC 1 (HL); *Jackson v. Goldsmith*, (1950) 81 CLR 448, 467-68 per Fullagar J. (HCA); *Thoday v. Thoday*, [1964] P 181, 197-98 (HL); *Carl Zeiss Stiftung v. Rayner & Keeler Ltd (No 2)*, [1967] 1 AC 853 (HL); *Mills v. Coopers*, [1967] 2 QB 459, 468-69 per Diplock; *Arnold v. National Westminster plc*, [1991] 2 AC 93 (HL); *Friend v. Civil Aviation Authority*, [2001] All ER 385, [42] per Chadwick LJ (CA). *Yukos Capital SARL v. OJSC Rosnet Oil Company*, [2011] EWHC 1461 (Comm), [53].
355. *Friend v. Civil Aviation Authority*, [2001] All ER 385, [42] per Chadwick LJ (CA).
356. *National Australia Bank Limited v. Sayed (No 4)*, [2015] NSWSC 420, [113].
357. Restatement (Second) Judgments, § 18(3).
358. Hobér, (2013) 366 Rec. des cours, 137.

ALI/UNIDROIT Principles are susceptible to issue preclusion in Article 28(3) when 'substantial injustice' needs to be avoided.[359]

113. By way of contrast, civil-law jurisdictions are averse to such concept,[360] an exception being the adjudication of counter-claims by virtue of set-offs.[361] Surprisingly, scholarly and jurisprudential justifications for this restriction on the objectives served by res judicata (justice, consistency, legal certainty and efficiency) are scarce. One opinion states that the abstract preclusion of legal issues might contravene litigation's mission to establish justice on the *individual* case only.[362] Another opinion emphasizes that issue preclusion is *in*efficient in that it motivates extended appeals when parties are merely dissatisfied with a reasoning and not the dispositif.[363] From a practical point of view, it should be noted that civil law compensates the strict rules on res judicata by broad possibilities for declaratory actions (*Feststellungsklage, action déclaratoire*).[364] Their requirement is a valid interest in the declaratory adjudication, e.g., because the issue is likely to rise in subsequent proceedings.[365] Accordingly, issue preclusions merely address the *default* situation *but for* a genuine declaratory application of any party.

114. Recently, the ECJ's *Gotheaer Versicherungen* judgment considered issue preclusion for cross-European judgments. The dispute between the claimant shippers and the defending transporter had been initially brought before the Antwerp Court of Appeal. It declined jurisdiction and referred to the Bill of Lading's forum-selection clause in favour of the courts of Iceland. Eventually, the claimants sued before German courts. The ECJ ruled that the Belgium judgment constituted res judicata on the forum selection's clause prerogative effect in favour of Iceland courts. It favoured:

359. 'The concept of issue preclusion, as to an issue of fact or application of law to facts, should be applied only to prevent substantial injustice.' This is seen as a restrictive treatment of issue preclusion in order to unburden tribunals from examining foreign law principles, *see* Stürner, (2005) 69 RabelsZ 251.
360. ATF 121 III 474, *Siegfried AG v. Wellcome Foundation Ltd*, 478; ATF 136 III 345, *Atlético Madrid v. Benfica Lisbon*, 348; Cass. (2e civ), 3 October 1984, [1984] Bull. civ II No. 140; Cass. (com), 15 July 1987, [1987] Bull. civ IV No. 182. *See* on French jurisprudence for reasons that *should have* been included in the operative part (*motifs décisoires*) CA Paris, *SA Thalès v. GIE Euromissile et al*, 18 November 2004, [2005] Clunet 382; Cass. (2e civ), 6 February 1965, [1965] Bull. Civ II No. 109; Cass. (com), 24 November 1965, [1965] Bull. Civ III No. 163; Cass. (2e civ); 8 May 1973, [1975] Bull. Civ II No. 163; Cass. (3e civ), 21 November 1974, [1974] Bull. civ III No. 432; Cass. (3e civ), 2 March 1976, [1976] Bull. Civ III No. 99.
361. Berger and Kellerhals, *Arbitration in Switzerland* [1654]; BGHZ 36, 316, 319. This decision applied s. 322 (2) ZPO beyond its wording ('*Entscheidung, dass die Gegenforderung nicht besteht*').
362. Althammer, *Streitgegenstand und Interesse* 35-104 ('*materielle Einzelfallgerechtigkeit*').
363. Héron and Le Bars, *Droit judiciaire privé* [349].
364. Cf. Landbrecht, *Teil-Sachentscheidungen* 334 ('*Wechselbeziehung*').
365. *See* s. 256(1),(2) ZPO; Zaug, [2017] ASA Bull. 330; Héron and Le Bars, *Droit judiciaire privé* [73-74]. In common law countries, such declaration has once been regarded unnecessary and inadmissible, but is now also codified in Rule 40.20 CPR in order to further shape the common law, *see Bank of Scotland v. A*, [2001] 1 WLR 751, 767 per Woolf CJ (HL); Burrows, in *English Private Law* [18.245]; Zamir and Woolf, *The Declaratory Judgment* [2.04] *Zuckermann* [22.15-19].

> a uniform application of European Union law [...] rather than [...] different national rules on res judicata. Moreover, the concept of res judicata under European Union law does not attach only to the operative part of the judgment [...].[366]

115. However, the majority commentary interprets the judgment to exclusively address *jurisdictional judgments*, so as to merely compensate for the Brussels Regulation's missing referral opportunity and thereby prevent negative jurisdictional conflicts.[367] This is supported by the attorney general's application.[368] More importantly, a later passage of the judgment supports this conclusion when narrowing down the ratio on '*a judgment by which a court of a Member State has declined jurisdiction on the basis of a jurisdiction clause [...].*'[369] Therefore, EU civil-law countries remain free to disregard issue preclusion on the substance.

116. A *third* and final major point of difference amongst the jurisdictions is the extent to which claims and arguments that were not, but *could have been*, raised earlier are precluded. In this regard, there are three case scenarios: (i) preclusion within a proceeding, e.g., if a party has waited until the last day in court before raising a point; (ii) preclusion in subsequent instances (appeal) or relief procedures (restitutions, anti-enforcement suits); (iii) preclusion in other, distinct proceedings. Due to the constraints of this thesis, the latter situation will be put under the magnifying glass. In the US, the transactional approach towards a cause of action already covers unraised claims,[370] yet not unraised *issues*.[371] At common law, the rule of *Henderson v. Henderson* allows to broadly strike out claims *and arguments* already available in other procedures.[372] This stands in line with the notion that common law has '*a longstanding preference for completeness in adjudication*'[373] and that a court should deal with '*as many aspects of the case as it can on the same occasion*'.[374] Notably, whilst *Henderson v. Henderson* originated as a genuine rule distinct from res judicata, it is now understood as an extended version of res judicata[375] because it equally serves public

366. ECJ, 15 November 2012, *Gothaer Allgemeine Versicherung*, C-456/11, EU:C:2012:719, [39].
367. Althammer and Tolani, (2014) ZZP Int 227; Bach, (2013) EuZW 58; Hess, in *Schlosser and Hess* Art. 36 [4]; Koops, (2018) IPRax 21; Nagel and Gottwald, *Internationales Zivilprozessrecht* [12.22]; Roth, (2014) IPRax 138.
368. ECJ, Opinion of AG Bot, 6 September 2012, *Gothaer Allgemeine Versicherung*, C-456/11, EU:C:2012:554, [93].
369. ECJ, 15 November 2012, *Gothaer Allgemeine Versicherung*, C-456/11, EU:C:2012:719, [40-41] (emphasis added).
370. *See supra* [108].
371. *See* Restatement (Second) Judgments, § 27 (Issue Preclusion – General Rule) comment e.
372. *Hendersvon v. Henderson*, (1843) 3 Hare 100, 115. Applied by *Port of Melbourne Authority v. Ashnun Pty Ltd*, [1981] 147 CLR 589 (HCA); *Asia Commercial Finance (M) v. Kawal Teliti Sdn Bhd*, [1995] 3 MLJ 189 (HC Malaysia); *Commissioner of Inland Revenue v. Bhanabhai*, [2007] 2 NZLR 478 (NZCA); *Goh Nellie v. Goh Lian Teck*, [2007] 1 SLR(R) 453 (SGHC); *China North Industries Investment Ltd v. Chum*, [2010] 5 HKLRD 1 (HKHC); *Fidelitas Shipping Co. Ltd v. V/O Sportchleb*, [1966] 1 QB 630.
373. *Zuckermann* [13.1].
374. CPR 1.4(2)(i).
375. *See Vervaeke v. Smith*, [1983] 1 AC 145, 157 per Lord Hailsham of St. Marylebone LC ('both a rule of public policy and an application of res judicata'); *Arnold v. National Westminster Bank*

and (though subsidiarily) private interests on finality and efficiency.[376] As to the functioning of abuse of process, a key difference to res judicata's outset is that it *extends the prerogative of the retrospective* tribunal in that the latter can go beyond the dispositif and exercise a discretionary assessment. By contrast, Germanic jurisdictions reject to apply abuse of process in subsequent proceedings, even in the scenario of undisclosed partial claims.[377] Preclusion is restricted to cases where the requests for reliefs are identical, but new facts that could have been raised earlier are raised.[378] Only in France it is now uncertain whether the *Cesareo* jurisprudence would apply on different claims and causes of action. On the one hand, the case itself concerned identical requests for monetary relief based on the same facts; on the other hand, it is aptly titled as 'concentration duty'.[379]

117. In summary, there is a general divide between common law and civil law with regard to res judicata's specific legal consequences, namely the relevance of (i) the dispositif, (ii) adjudicatory reasonings and (iii) non-adjudicated claims and arguments. Common law facilitates broad approaches in these three regards. By contrast, civil flaw focuses on the reliefs requested and excludes exceeding remedies of issue preclusion or abuse of process. Hence, it provides the subsequent judges with *extended* cognition power to comprehensively decide a dispute. As a final, functional remark, civil law's aversion to preclusion arguments corresponds to another aversion towards restricting the judge's cognition power. They allow their courts to 'know the law' (*iura novit curia*) and thus exceed the legal grounds brought forward by the parties as long as the court informs the latter.[380] By way of contrast, common law follows an adversarial approach. Courts are generally bound to merely decide what the parties have raised on the facts *and* on the law.[381] As with preclusion doctrines, their cognition power is restricted.

Plc (No 1), [1990] Ch. 573, 593 per Dillon LJ ('in *Fidelitas Shipping* this court applied the principles of *Henderson v. Henderson* to issue estoppel'); *Johnson v. Gore Wood & Co*, [2002] 2 AC 1 (HL) ('much in common'); *Virgin Atlantic Airways Ltd v. Zodiac Seats UK Ltd*, [2014] AC 160, [23-24] per Lord Sumption (UKSC); Rose (ed.), *Blackstone's Civil Procedure*, [4.4]; *Zuckermann* [25.77] ('[I]t may be too late to decouple the term [estoppel per rem judicatam] completely from abuse of process.'); Andrews, *English Civil Procedure* [40.60] ('the *Henderson* principle [...] can be regarded as an adjunct to *res judicata*').

376. *See De Crittenden v. Bayliss*, [2005] EWCA Civ 1425; *Barrow v. Bankside Members Agency Ltd*, [1996] 1 WLR 257 (CA).
377. BGHZ 151, 1, 3; BGHZ 135, 178; BGHZ 34, 340, 342 (obiter); ATF 125 III 8, [E.3b]; ATF 128 III 191, [E.4a].
378. Cf. Habscheid, (1952) 152 AcP 169-172; Rosenberg, (1950) 5 Süddt JZ 314-315; Landbrecht, *Teil-Sachentscheidungen* 40-45; Peiffer, *Grenzüberschreitende Titelgeltung* 281-316.
379. Cf. Mayer, in *Liber Amicorum Héron* [19]. *See* further Bollée note, (2006) Rev. crit. DIP 833, [7-8].
380. *See* Art. 16 CPC; s. 139(2) ZPO; ATF 89 II 336.
381. Mann, [1977] LQR 369 ('perhaps the most spectacular feature of English procedure is that the rule *curia novit legem* has never been and is not part of English law'). *See* for functional similarities ECJ, Opinion of AG Jacobs, 15 June 1995 *Van Schijndel*, C-430/93 and C-431/93, EU:C:1995:185, [34-35].

§2.02 RES JUDICATA OF ARBITRAL AWARDS AT THE ARBITRAL SEAT

118. Jurisdictions comprise a broad consensus that arbitral awards do constitute res judicata. Most expressly, § 1055 German Zivilprozessordnung (ZPO)[382] and Article 1484 French Code de procédure civile (CPC)[383] codify arbitral res judicata. Comparable rules can be found in other civil-law jurisdictions[384] and at common law.[385] Yet, these rules are less explicit on the specific requirements and effects of arbitral res judicata. Moreover, judgments' rules have not been tailored for arbitral awards. Such situation creates room '*to adapt the application of the principle of res judicata to the distinctive characteristics of arbitral proceedings*'.[386] In this spirit, a debate occurs often referring to arbitration theory's general tension between its *judicial function* and its *consensual foundation* (*see* [A], *infra*). Particularly, the tension stands at the heart of domestic discussions whether extended res judicata effects such as issue preclusion can apply to arbitral awards (*see* [B], *infra*). Moreover, an examination of res judicata's requirements (*see* [C], *infra*) and the operation of relief procedures (*see* [D], *infra*) reveal that arbitration's consensual nature demands to reshape litigation principles.

[A] Arbitral Awards Within the Legal Order: Equivalent to Judgments?

119. In litigation, res judicata builds upon the concept that judgments are acts of a State's judiciary. By contrast, arbitral awards are the result of private dispute resolution. Thus, specifying their effects requires addressing the general question whether

382. 'Amongst the parties, the arbitration award has the effect of a final and binding judgment handed down by a court.' ('*Der Schiedsspruch hat unter den Parteien die Wirkungen eines rechtskräftigen gerichtlichen Urteils.*').
383. 'The arbitral award, from the moment that it has been given, will become res judicata with respect to the dispute that it has determined'. ('*La sentence arbitrale a, dès qu'elle est rendue, l'autorité de la chose jugée relativement à la contestation qu'elle tranche*'.) This is similar to Art. 480 CPC for Judgments. For international arbitration, Art. 1506 (4) CPC declares Art. 1484 applicable.
384. Cf. s. 607 Austrian Code of Civil Procedure, Art. 1713(9) Belgian Judicial Code, Art. 1059(1) Dutch Code of Civil Procedure, Art. 43 Spanish Arbitration Act. Art. 387 Swiss ZPO (domestic arbitration). In *international* arbitration, where Art. 109 (1) PILA does not expressly address any res judicata effect and merely states that '[t]he award is final from its notification', it is the common opinion that the res judicata is nonetheless applicable, *see* ATF 117 II 166; Berger and Kellerhals, *Arbitration in Switzerland* [1631]; Kaufmann-Kohler and Rigozzi, *International Arbitration in Switzerland* [7.187]; Lalive Poudret and Reymond, *Le droit de arbitrage interne et international en Suisse* Art. 190 PILA [2].
385. Cf. *Doe d Davy v. Haddon*, (1783) 3 Doug KB 310; *Pitcher v. Rigby*, (1821) 9 Price 79; *Sybray v. White*, (1836) 150 E R 504; *Imperial Gas & Coke Co. v. Broadbent*, (1859) 7 HL Cas 600; *Cummings v. Heard*, (1869) LR 4 QB 669, 672; *Caledonian Railway Co. v. Turcan*, [1898] AC 256 (HL); *Siporex Trade SA v. Comdel Commodities Ltd*, [1986] 2 Lloyd's Rep. 223 (CA); *Noble Assurance Co. v. Gerling-Konzern General Insurance Co*, [2007] EWHC 253 (Comm). USA: Restatement (Second) Judgments, § 18.
386. Hobér, (2013) 366 Rec. des cours 141 referring to the Swedish Arbitration Act and its *travaux préparatoires*, *Aktiebolaget Skanska Cementgjuteriet v. Motoraktiobolaget i Karlstad*, [1953] NJA 751 and *Esselte AB v. Allmänna Pensionsfonden*, [1998] NJA 189.

arbitral awards can provide a judiciary-equivalent modification of the legal order. This question leads to the everlasting debate on the legal nature of awards and hence arbitration itself. Historically, and in line with the Roman concept,[387] arbitration was regarded as a purely private, *contractual* means of dispute resolution.[388] By contrast, contemporary doctrine acknowledges the *judicial* dimension of arbitration.[389] The predominant argument is the very capacity of arbitral awards to constitute res judicata.[390] Such judicial characterization is mostly invoked in order to stipulate that arbitration's standards of impartiality and due process have to conform to litigation standards.[391] Thereby, the characterization justifies State regulation on arbitration.[392] Moreover, it necessitates courts' support for arbitration agreements.[393] Yet effectively, in light of various codifications on specific topics, the debate has lost much of its delicacy in *domestic* settings.[394]

120. By contrast, *cross-border* settings contain many non- or inconclusively codified topics, e.g., the connecting factor for the arbitration agreement, the applicability of procedural law other than the seat's and the enforcement of annulled awards. Those issues are often addressed in conjunction with the underlying question of arbitration theory.[395] Whilst a comprehensive reflection of the debate, the range of theories and the implementations of particular issues would exceed this examination's constraints, the most important streams are displayed.

121. A first stream submits that arbitration is an entirely procedural mechanism. In an international dimension, this necessitates that arbitration is interwoven with the law of the arbitral seat. The arbitral tribunal were nothing but a part of the forum.[396]

---

387. D 4, 8, 2 (Ulpian) (*Ex compromisso placet exceptionem non nasci, sed poenae petitionem*); PS 5 5a, 1 (Paul) (*Ex compromisso autem iudex sumptus rem iudicatem non facit: sed si poena inter eos promissum sit, poena re in iudicium deducta ex stipulatu peti potest*). *See* Jarrosson, (2007) 8 Procédures No. 17 [2].
388. Cass. (req), 27 July 1937, JCP 1937 No. 449 ('*les sentences arbitrales qui ont pour base un compromis, font corps avec lui et participent de son caractère conventionnel*'); RGZ 116, 76; RGZ 117, 386. For Italien jurisprudence *see* Ricci, (2002) Rev. Arb. 857.
389. Cf. *Fouchard Gaillard and Goldman* [12-14]; *Mustill and Boyd* 42; *Schlosser* [40-53].
390. BGHZ 65, 59, 61-62 ('*Ein Schiedsgericht übt zwar keine öffentliche Gewalt aus, setzt keine Hoheitsakte. Schiedsgerichtsbarkeit ist gleichwohl materielle Rechtsprechung. Der Schiedsrichter ist wie der staatliche Richter zur Entscheidung eines Rechtsstreits berufen. (…) Der Schiedsspruch hat nach § 1040 ZP [a.F.] die Wirkungen eines rechtskräftigen gerichtlichen Urteils.*'); TF, 30 April 1991, [1992] ASA Bull. 259. *See* Lainé, (1899) Clunet 653 ('*Quelle est la mission donnée aux arbitres? C'est d'apprécier la valeur des prétentions respectives des parties […] et, cela fait, de décider suivant le droit […] c'est à dire […] de juger*'); Guldener, *Schweizerisches Zivilprozessrecht* 596; Ruede and Hadenfeldt, *Schiedsgerichtsrecht* 309.
391. Cf. *AT & T Corporation et al. v. Saudi Cable Company*, [2000] 2 Lloyd's Rep. 127 per Lord Woolf MR (CA); BGHZ 65, 59 (impartiality); BGHZ 180, 221, [21] (shareholder suits); ATF 97 I 488, *Associazione Calcio Bellinzona v. Komitee der Nationalliga des Schweiz. Fußballverbandes*, 489.
392. Cf. Bermann, (2015) 382 Rec. des cours [24] ('In its exercise of regulatory authority, the State may […] require all arbitral activity conducted on its territory to observe certain standards of minimal procedural fairness and to satisfy other criteria').
393. *Ibid.*, [24-29].
394. *Poudret and Besson* [11].
395. *See* Gaillard, *Legal Theory of International Arbitration* 1-4.
396. Goode, (2001) Arb. Int'l 19; *Poudret and Besson* [11]; Leurent, (1996) 12 Arb. Int'l 269; Reisman, *Systems of Control in International Adjudication and Arbitration* 113-120; Wagner,

122. The opposing, effectively predominant[397] stream seeks reconciliation with arbitration's private nature. Yet, given the range of judicial effects awarded to an arbitral award, it characterizes arbitration as a generally contractual means of dispute resolution upon which procedural effects are conferred ('hybrid theory'). Since a plurality of recognizing and enforcing jurisdictions confer effects on arbitration, the opinion concludes that arbitration is rooted in a plurality of legal orders.[398]

123. Taking this idea one step further, a third notion regards arbitration as detached from national legal orders and rooted within a *transnational* system of justice.[399] Particularly Emmanuel Gaillard has established the argument that arbitration disposes of its own legal sources and therefore of its own solutions. The solutions should not be based on genuine rules but rather developed as a concept of customary international law, thus a comparative approach.[400] Effectively, the doctrine has remained criticized outside of France.[401] An effective variation describes arbitration as an autonomous *social* institution independent of *legal* orders.[402]

124. Against this heavily debated background, this examination assumes that the issue of arbitral res judicata should not easily be answered by a reference to the judicial nature of arbitration. Not only is it '*tempting [...] to refer to precisely those conceptions of legal theory which are best suited to support his intended very argument.*'[403]

Prozessverträge 578-582. The perhaps most cited reference is Mann, in *Liber Amicorum Martin Domke* at 157 et seqq. Yet, he rejects any relevance of arbitration's nature and focuses on the seat's supervisory function, i.e. sovereignty aspects, 161-162 ('No other country other than that of the such has such complete and effective control over the arbitration tribunal. [...] Is not every activity occurring on the territory of a State necessarily subject to its jurisdiction? Is it not for such State to say whether and in what manner arbitrators are assimilated to judges and, like them, subject to the law?'). *See also* Petrochilos, *Procedural Law in International Arbitration* [2.04] ('one should be looking at the most appropriate *court* competent to supervise and assist the arbitral process').

397. *Lew Mistelis and Kröll* [5-26] ('the dominant world-wide theory').
398. Bermann, (2015) 381 Rec. des cours [269] ('centre of gravity in the pluralistic theory.'); Bollée, *Sentences arbitrales* [332]; *Redfern and Hunter* 29; Rubino-Samartano, *International Arbitration* 62; Solomon, *Die Verbindlichkeit von Schiedssprüchen* 333 ('*jurisdiktionelle Funktion des Schiedsgerichts [...] auf die vertragliche Vereinbarung der Parteien und deren Anerkennung durch eine bestimmte Rechtsordnung gestützt*'); von Mehren, *Limitations on Party Choice of the Governing Law* 19. Cf. Sauser Hall, *Annuaire de l'Institut de Droit International 44-I* 469.
399. Established by Goldman, (1963) 109 Rec. des cours 380 ('every investigation of a theory corresponding to the nature of international arbitration leads ineluctably to an autonomous, not a national, system' - translation according to von Mehren, *supra* 217).
400. Gaillard, *Legal Theory of International Arbitration* [50-61].
401. *See*, in addition to the references in Note 395 *Bank Mellat v. Helliniki Techniki*, [1984] 1 QB 291, 301 ('Despite suggestions to the contrary by some learned writers under other systems, our jurisprudence does not recognise the concept of arbitral procedure floating in the transnational firmament, unconnected with any municipal system of law.'); *Coppée Lavalin & Voest Alpine v. Ken-Ren Chemicals*, [1994] 2 All ER 449, 458 ('Transnationalism [...] cannot be the law of England.'); Schlosser, in *Stein and Jonas* vor § 1025 [6] ('*Der Versuch ist aber im luftleeren Raum geblieben. Welches materiell-rechtliche Substrat diese Rechtsordnung unterfüttern soll, bleibt völlig im Dunkeln.*').
402. Paulsson, (2011) 60 ICLQ 291 ('complex, three-dimensional form of pluralism, in which legal orders are not exclusively those of States and frequently overlap') and *The Idea of Arbitration* 45-50.
403. Gaillard, *Legal Theory of International Arbitration* [5].

Theoretical arguments on res judicata also risk to be circular: res judicata cannot be both, an *argument for* the judicial characterization of arbitration and a *consequence of* it. Instead, issues of res judicata should be answered by means of the underlying rationales as well as practical feasibility.

[B] Legal Consequences: Debate on Implemented Interests at Common Law

125. A major implementation of the conceptual foundation of arbitral awards is the discussion on the operative effect of arbitral res judicata beyond the *dispositive*. In civil-law jurisdictions, the availability of issue preclusion is swiftly rejected by a referral to the doctrine's procedural foundation.[404] For example, in a 2015 decision, the Swiss Federal Court reiterated that an arbitral award dealing with certain profits of a partnership for the years 2008/2009 constitutes no res judicata for any claims on the years 2010/2011 although the underlying legal arguments with regard to the percentage of the profits were identical.[405] Yet, notably, the cause of action is increasingly influenced by an arbitral award's reasonings. Particularly, arbitrators are under no obligation to formulate an operative part of their decision. Hence, sometimes it might be necessary that judges extract the operative part of a decision.[406]

126. At common law, the transferability of issue preclusion and abuse of process are subject to an intensive discussion focusing on the applicability of the procedural rationales of justice, consistency, legal certainty and efficiency.[407] Whilst their *private* dimension exists regardless of the chosen dispute resolution,[408] arguments are raised

404. France: Cass. (com), 9 January 1978, [1979] Rev. Arb. 478; Cass. (2e civ), 14 October 1987, [1988] Rev. Arb. 288; Cass. (2e civ), 28 October 1987, [1988] Rev. Arb. 149; Cass. (com), *INSERM v. Foundation Letten F Saugstad*, 26 January 2011, 09-10.198; CA Paris, *Melnik*, 26 September 2002, [2002] Rev. Arb. 1049; CA Paris, *sté Liv Hidravlika DOO v. SA Diebolt*, 28 February 2008, [2008] Rev. Arb. 712; CA Paris, 2 October 2012, [2013] Rev. Arb. 439. Germany: BGH, [2009] SchiedsVZ 181, [16-17]; OLG München, 14 January 2009, 34 Sch 02/09. Switzerland: Berger and Kellerhals, *Arbitration in Switzerland* [1640]. *See* on arbitrators' fees CA Paris, 19 December 1996, [1998] Rev. Arb. 121.
405. TF, 29 May 2015, 4A_633/2014, (2015) 33 ASA Bull. 599.
406. Cf. Jarrosson, (2007) 8 Procédures No. 12 [12]; Mayer, (2016) Rev. Arb. 96; Poncet and Mockler, *Liber Amicorum Craig* 312; Schlosser, in *Stein and Jonas* § 1055 [15-16]. *See* Cass. (2e civ), *Acquier v. Faure*, 25 March 1999, [1999] Rev. Arb. 312; CA Pau, *sté Carrefour proximité France v. SARL Falco et fils*, 22 February 2011, [2011] Rev. Arb. 287; Robert, *L'arbitrage* [207]. *See also* CA Paris, 17 October 1991, [1992] Rev. Arb. 672 (invalidity in cases of contradiction within the award).
407. Cf. Bermann, (2015) 381 Rec. des cours [539].
408. *See* Brekoulakis, *Third Parties in Arbitration* 243 ('While public concerns [...] are less relevant in the context of international arbitration than they are in national litigation, private considerations such as the need for commercial security resulting from the finality and repose of the dispute are critical for the interests and the expectations of the parties in international arbitration.'); Veeder, in *ICC Bulletin – Special Supplement* 73 ('Just as it would be absurd for parties to relitigate the same dispute time and again, like Sisyphus or the hero in Ground-Hog Day, would it not be equally absurd for parties to relitigate issues in a different arbitration where those same issues have already been decided in the reasons for an earlier award between the same parties?').

that there were no *public* interest in a homogenous system of arbitration and that duplicate arbitrations do not affect public resources.[409] Notably, US jurisprudence on arbitrability has a long-standing tradition on the unsuitability of arbitration to serve public interests.[410] Whilst some US jurisprudence leaned towards restrictions of res judicata,[411] the majority held in favour of issue preclusion[412] unless the claim itself was not arbitrable[413] or a collective labour matter.[414] The justifications for the transferal of claim and issue preclusion might vary. Some authors conclude that courts developed the habit without any justification.[415] More plastically, courts rejected the argument that arbitral awards should lack res judicata because the process lacked formal requirements and the arbitrators were frequently not to justify their decisions or not even lawyers.[416] Again, such points have been rejected in other discussions, most notably against broader arbitrability in international cases.[417] Amongst the Restatements, the Second Restatement on Judgments displays this jurisprudence,[418] whilst the recent Restatement on International Commercial Arbitration awards courts with:

> substantial discretion in deciding whether to grant issue preclusion based on a prior award [...] on a case-by-case-basis.[419]

409. *See* Shell, (1988) 35 UCLA L. Rev. 657-683.
410. *See Wilko v. Swan*, 74 S.Ct. 198 (1953); Kronstein, (1944) 54 Yale LJ 36 ('Business Arbitration - Instrument of Private Government'), distinguished for international arbitration in *Scherk v. Albert-Culver Co*, 94 S.Ct. 2449 (1974); *Mitsubishi Motors Corp. v. Soler Chrysler-Plymouth Inc*, 105 S.Ct. 3346 (1985).
411. *IDS Life Ins. Co. v. Royal Alliane Associates Inc*, 266 F.3d 645, 651 (7th Cir. 2001) ('Closed to *litigation*; not *necessarily* to arbitration. [...] Although res judicata and collateral estoppel usually attach to arbitration awards, they do so (if they do so) as a matter of contract rather than as a matter of law. The preclusive effect of the award is as much a creature of the arbitration contract as any other aspect of the legal-dispute machinery established by such a contract.').
412. *Greenblatt v. Drexel Burnham Lambert Inc*, 763 F.2d 1352, 1360 (11th Cir. 1985); *Sanders v. Washington Metropolitan Area Transit Auth*, 819 F.2d 1151, 1157 (DC Cir. 1987); *Manion v. Nagin*, 394 F.3d 1062, 1067 (8th Cir. 2005); *Freecharm Limited v. Atlas Wealth Holdings Corporation et al*, 2012 WL 6928136 (11th Cir. 2012).
413. Cf. *Dean Witter Reynolds Inc. v. Byrd*, 470 U.S. 213, 223 (1985). *See also NLRB v. Yellow Freight Systems Inc*, 930 F.2d 316 (3d Cir. 1991).
414. Cf. *General Committee of Adjustment et al. v. CSX RR Corp*, 893 F.2d 584, [10] (3d Cir. 1990).
415. G Sanders, (1992-1993) 24 L. Pol Int'l Business 102 ('less the result of any principled analysis of arbitral preclusion than of the largely irreflective extension of judicially fashioned preclusion doctrine to the arbitral context'); Shell, (1988) 35 UCLA L. Rev. 658-659 ('[...] courts rarely justify their decision to allow such preclusion. Many opinions imply simply that it is "fair" [...].').
416. *In re Khaligh*, 506 F.3d 956, 957 (9th Cir. 2008); *I Appel Corp. v. Katz*, 1999 WL 287370 (S.D.N.Y. 1999).
417. *See* the dissenting opinion by Douglas J. in *Scherk v. Albert-Culver Co*, 94 S.Ct. 2449, 2458-64 (1974).
418. Restatement (Second) Judgments, § 84(1) ('[A] valid and final award by arbitration has the same effects under the rules of res judicata, subject to the same exceptions and qualifications, as a judgment of a court.'). *See* comment c ('When the arbitration procedure leading to an award is very informal, the findings in the arbitration should not be carried over through issue preclusion to another action. [...] However, in the absence of such circumstances, there is good reason to treat the determination of the issues in an arbitration proceeding as conclusive in a subsequent proceeding, just as determinations of a court would be so treated.').
419. Restatement (Third) Int'l Comm Arbitration (TD 2), §§ 4-10.

127. A comparable discussion is occurring in England. Whilst issue estoppel undoubtedly applies to arbitral awards under the *Aegis* jurisprudence,[420] abuse of process is more delicate. The latter judgment opened the gate for discussion when it considered that abuse of process '*may fall on the other side of the line*'.[421] Some authors argue that abuse of process' public justifications (waste of judicial resources) are inapplicable in arbitration.[422] Moreover, they refer to the fact that arbitral tribunals have jurisdiction about nothing but the requests submitted.[423] Others affirm the applicability of abuse of process as long as the precluded arguments would have fallen under the general subject matter jurisdiction of the arbitrators.[424] In any case, the Commercial Court continuously affirmed the transferability of abuse of process to arbitration in bilateral situations.[425] A corresponding decision has been rendered in Singapore.[426] Notably though, the judgments do not affirm any public interests in arbitration.

128. To complete the picture, arguments against arbitration's public impact were named a key issue in the ILA Interim Report and rejected in the Final Report favouring issue preclusion and abuse of process.[427] Moreover in France, the Supreme Court transferred the *Cesareo* jurisprudence to domestic arbitral awards in 2008.[428] In international arbitration, however, both arbitral tribunals applying French law[429] and the Paris Court of Appeal[430] rejected this doctrine. Noteworthy, it is precisely for international arbitration that the French doctrine contains a discussion whether the arbitral tribunal should apply the law ex officio.[431] In conclusion, jurisdictions generally concur on the transfer of the respective doctrines of res judicata from judgments to

420. *Associated Electric and Gas Insurance Services Ltd v. European Reinsurance Co. of Zurich*, [2003] UKPC 11, [15] ('[An arbitral award] confer[s] a right which is enforceable by later pleading an issue estoppel').
421. *Ibid.*, [16]. For former jurisprudence *see Smith v. Johnson*, (1812) 15 East Rep. 213; *Dunn v. Murray*, (1829) 9 B & C 780, 788 (affirmative); *EE & Brian Smith (1928) Ltd v. Wheatsheaf Mills Ltd*, [1939] 2 KB 302 (dismissive).
422. Veeder, in *ICC Bulletin – Special Supplement* 75.
423. *Mustill and Boyd* 413.
424. *Russell on Arbitration* [6.176]; William and Tushingham, (2014) 26 SAoLJ 1036, [11].
425. *Dallal v. Bank Mellat*, [1986] 1 QB 441, 455; *Nomihold Securities Inc. v. Mobile Relesystems*, [2012] EWHC 130 (Comm); *OMV Petrom SA v. Glencore International AG*, [2014] EWHC 242 (Comm).
426. *Denmark Skibstekniske Konsulenter A/S I Likvidation v. Ultrapolis*, [2011] 4 SLR 997, [40] per Quentin Loh J. (SGHC).
427. *ILA Final Report on Res Judicata* [61] ('[T]here is a legitimate public interest in having an end to arbitration as well as an end to the supportive and corrective powers of domestic courts [...].').
428. Cass. (1e civ.), *sté G et A Distribution SARL v. sté Prodim SAS*, 8 May 2008, [2008] Rev. Arb. 461.
429. *See* Mayer, (2011) Paris J. Int'l Arb. 413; Radicati di Brozolo, in *ASA Special Series* 139-141, both citing unpublished awards.
430. CA Paris, *Somercom Sarl v. TND Gida Ve Temizlik Mad Dagtim AS Sarl*, 5 May 2011, [2011] Rev. Arb. 1093. *See* on a rejection of good faith principles prior to *Cesareo* CA Paris, *SA Thalès Air Défense v. GIE Euromissile*, 18 November 2004, [2006] Rev. crit. DIP 108 ('*Considérant que si la loyauté et la bonne foi procédurale dans l'arbitrage international imposent bien aux parties de faire connaître leurs demandes le plus tôt possible [...]*').
431. *See* Mourre and Vagenheim, in *JCl procédure civile* at Fasc 1067 [35-36].

arbitral awards. Meanwhile, especially the discussion in common-law countries shows that the transferal of res judicata's public rationales is yet to be conclusively discussed.

[C] Requirements

129. An arbitral award has to fulfil several requirements before it constitutes res judicata and thereby causes preclusion consequences. Particularly, arbitration laws require a certain finality (*see* [1], *infra*). Although arbitration laws, again, largely refer to proceduralist doctrines for the specifications, certain aspects show a particular influence of party autonomy that demands genuine rules. This observation holds particularly true when examining the inclusion of arbitral awards rendered upon the parties' settlement (*see* [2], *infra*) and the method how arbitral res judicata has to be invoked in subsequent litigation (*see* [3], *infra*). Accordingly, res judicata's requirements serve as an illustration that arbitration's distinct nature requires deviations from judgment principles when establishing the regime on arbitral res judicata.

[1] Necessary Finality on the Merits

130. In accordance with procedural law, arbitration laws generally require an arbitral award to be *final* in order to constitute res judicata. This includes partial awards[432] and excludes interim awards.[433] Moreover, it is often read that a decision must be 'on the merits' in order to be final. In this author's opinion, the requirement has limited impact. Foremost, jurisprudence from England,[434] France,[435] the US[436] and the

432. Cf. ATF 121 III 191; BGHZ 10, 325, 326; CA Prais, *Sardisud*, 7 July 1994, (1994) Rev. Arb. 391 (*'les décisions des arbitres qui tranchent d'une manière définitive, en tout ou partie, le litige qui leur a été soumis, que ce soit sur le fond, sur la cométence ou sur un moyen de procédure qui les conduit à mettre fin à l'instance'*); *Fidelitas Shipping Co. Ltd v. V/O Exportchleb*, [1965] 1 Lloyd's Rep. 213 (CA).
433. Berger and Kellerhals, *Arbitration in Switzerland* [1645].
434. Cf. *DSV Silo- und Verwaltungsgesellschaft mbH v. Owner of The Sennar and 13 other ships*, [1985] 1 WLR 490, 494 per Diplock LJ (HL) ('It is often said that the final judgment [...] must be "on the merits". The moral overtones which this expression tends to conjure up may make it misleading. What it means in the context of judgments delivered by courts of justice is that the court has held that it had jurisdiction to adjudicate on an issue raised [...] and that its judgment on that cause of action is one that cannot be varied, reopened or set aside by the court that delivered it or any other court of co-ordinate jurisdiction although it may be subject to appeal to a court of higher jurisdiction.'). *See Desert Sun Loan Corp. v. Hill*, [1996] 2 All ER 847 (CA); *Watt (formerly Carter) v. Raghib Ahsan*, [2007] UKHL 51. *See Christopher Brown Ltd v. Genossenschaft Oesterreichischer Waldbesitzer Holzwirtschaftsbetriebe GmbH*, [1954] 1 QB 8, 12-13 (QB); *Bon Groundwork Ltd v. Foster*, [2012] EWCA Civ 252 (excess of jurisdiction bars res judicata); *Christopher Brown Ltd v. Genossenschaft Oesterreichischer Waldbesitzer Holzwirtschaftsbetriebe GmbH*, [1954] 1 QB 8, 12-13 (QB); *Cameron v. Cole*, (1944) 68 CLR 571, 590-91 (HCA); *Isaacs v. Robertson*, [1985] AC 97, 102-03 (CA); *Strachan v. Gleaner Co. Ltd*, [2005] 1 WLR 3204, 3211-14 (PC) (superior courts are presumed to have jurisdiction); *Relfo Ltd v. Varsani*, [2009] EWHC 2297 (Ch); *Upendra Nath Bose v. Lall*, [1940] AIR 225 (PC).
435. Cass. (1e civ.), 8 June 1967, [1967] Bull. Civ I 1967 No. 216. For further jurisprudence *see* Douchy-Oudot, in *JCl procédure civil* [19].
436. Cf. *Costello v. United Sates*, 365 U.S. 265 (1961).

ECJ[437] demonstrate that adjudications on choice-of-court agreements can constitute res judicata. This inclines to also regard arbitral awards on jurisdictional issues as fulfilling the conceptual requirements of res judicata.[438] Certainly though, the jurisdictional award will be subject to the last word of annulments.[439]

131. Apart from this common outset, the specific point in time upon which an arbitral award is considered 'final' is exposed to comparative differences. Whereas procedural law can refer to the appeal period's expiry, arbitration law has to find genuine solutions. On a potential timeline, laws refer to the finalization of the arbitral award,[440] the communication to the parties,[441] the enforceability[442] or the incontestability of the confirmation/exequatur.[443] Given these differences amongst national laws, the drafters of the UNCITRAL Model Law were unable to find a compromise.[444]

132. A further aspect of finality is whether the arbitral award in itself constitutes res judicata or requires a prior confirmation by courts. Civil-law jurisdictions favour the former solution.[445] The FAA, however, comprises a heavy debate on the opportunity to seek court confirmation.[446] Since such confirmation 'merges' the award into a judgment,[447] and the Supreme Court stated that there was no obligation on behalf of federal

437. *See supra* [114].
438. Cf. *ILA Final Report on Res Judicata* [20]; Marchisio, *The Notion of Award* § 5.
439. *See supra* [85].
440. *See* England: *Russell on Arbitration* [6.65, 6.164] ('made' in distinction to 'published'). Italy: Art. 824 Italien Code of Civil Procedure (arbitrators' signatures).
441. France: Art. 1476, 480 CPC. Germany: RGZ 114, 165, 167; Schwab and Walther, *Schiedsgerichtsbarkeit* Ch. 22 [11].
442. Switzerland: ATF 117 Ia 166, [C.5a]; *Poudret and Besson* [475].
443. In the USA, this is accordingly a matter of the applicable law: *Pro Boston & Maine Corp. v. Chicago, Burlington and Quincy Railroad*, 258 FSupp 930, 933 (S.D.N.Y. 1966); *Ballweg v. City of Springfield*, 499 NE2d 1373, 1375 (Ill 1986); *In re Robinson*, 256 B.R. 482 at 488 (Bkrtcy SD Ohio 2000); *In re Bogdanovich*, 292 F.3d 104, 110 (2d Cir. 2002) (Cal Law); *Community State Bank v. Strong*, 651 F.3d 1241, 1266 (11th Cir. 2011) (Georgia Law). *Contra Ruyle v. Continental Oil Co*, 44 F.3d 837, 846 (10th Cir. 1994); *Khan v. Thorley*, FedAppx 978, 981 (10th Cir. 2001) (FAA); *DiSorbo v. Hoy*, 343 F.3d 172, 183 (2n Cir. 2003) (NY Law); *Collins v. DR Hortin Inc*, 505 F.3d 874, 882 (9th Cir. 2007) (res judicata of judgment in arbitration while appeal was pending); Restatement (Second) of Judgments, § 13.
444. *See* the discussion related to the rejection of the drafting group's proposal in Commission Report, A/40/17; Summary Record, A/CN.9/SR.328-329 333.
445. Germany: s. 1055 ZPO (for wording *see supra* Note 381). France: Cass. (2e civ), 7 June 1972, [1974] Rev. Arb. 91; Cass. (com), *Juillard v. Roy*, [1979] Rev. Arb. 478; overriding Cass, 8 March 1865, [1865] 1 DP 249; Cass. (com), 22 December 1959, [1960] Rev. Arb. 17. Switzerland: ATF 117 II 166 citing further jurisprudence; Berger and Kellerhals, *Arbitration in Switzerland* [1631] ('[Art. 190(1) PILA] implies that an award [...] has res judicata effects *without any additional court scrutiny*.'); Kaufmann-Kohler and Rigozzi, *International Arbitration in Switzerland* [7.187].
446. *See* s. 9 FAA ('If the parties in their agreement have agreed that a judgment of the court shall be entered upon the award made pursuant to the arbitration, and shall specify the court, then at any time within one year after the award is made any party to the arbitration may apply to the court so specified for an order confirming the award [...]. If no court is specified in the agreement of the parties, then such application may be made to the United States court in and for the district within which such award was made. [...]'.)
447. Cf. s. 13 FAA ('The judgment so entered shall have the same force and effect, in all respects, as, and be subject to all the provisions of law relating to, a judgment in an action; and it may be enforced as if it had been rendered in an action in the court in which it is entered.'); *Norris v.*

courts to award an unconfirmed arbitral award with preclusion effects equivalent to judgments,[448] some courts[449] and California law[450] have treated unconfirmed awards as nothing but contractual rights. By contrast, the Second Restatement,[451] the Ninth Circuit when applying California law[452] as well as other courts[453] held that the preclusion standards equally apply to unconfirmed awards. Accordingly, though jurisdiction differ on the specific point in time upon which arbitral awards constitute res judicata, they mostly concur on the independence from court confirmations.

[2] Res Judicata of Settlements: Consent Awards and Pure Settlements

133. The PCIJ once stated: '*the judicial settlement of international disputes [...] is simply an alternative to the direct and friendly settlement of such disputes [...].*'[454] Such bipolarity raises the question whether res judicata can also be awarded to settlements. Conceptually, judgments and settlements comprise distinct sources (normative act/reciprocal arrangement) and distinct functions (application of legal rules/avoidance of such application).[455] From a practical point of view, however, settlements and adversarial decisions are inherently intertwined, particularly from the perspective of a client instructing an attorney with the settlement of the dispute. Arbitration parties have a particular interest that settlements can be stipulated within an arbitral award: this elevates settlements into the NYC's scope.[456] Therefore, arbitral rules award ample authority to tribunals for rendering 'consent awards'. However,

Grosvenor Mktg Ltd, 803 F.2d 1281, 1285 (2d Cir. 1986) ('collateral estoppel applies to issues adjudicated in arbitration where the arbitration award has been entered as a judgment').

448. *McDonald v. City of West Branch, Michigan*, 104 S.Ct. 1799, [B] (1984) ('Because federal courts are not required by statute to give res judicata or collateral-estoppel effect to an unappealed arbitration award, any rule of preclusion would necessarily be judicially fashioned.').
449. *Gruntal & Co. Inc. v. Steinberg*, 854 F Supp 324, 337 (DNJ 1994) ('Absent judicial confirmation, an arbitration award will not result in a "final judgment" and cannot, therefore, have preclusive effect on subsequent litigation.'); *Shtab v. Greate Bay Hotel and Casino Inc*, 173 F Supp 2d 255, 261 (DNJ 2001). *See Florasynth Inc. v. Pickholz*, 750 F.2d 171, 176 (2d Cir. 1984) ('An unconfirmed award is a contract right that may be used as the basis for a cause of action.' – obiter).
450. §1287.6 California Code of Civil Procedure ('An award that has not been confirmed or vacated has the same force and effect as a contract in writing between the parties to the arbitration.').
451. Restatement (Second) Judgment's, § 84 (1) ('A valid and final award by arbitration has the same effects under the rules of res judicata [...] as a judgment of a court.').
452. *In re Khaligh*, 338 BR 817, 823 (9th Cir. 2005) ('Under California law, the unconfirmed award had merely the status of a contract in writing between the parties but it may still have res judicata effect').
453. *MACTEC Inc. v. Gorelick*, 427 F.3d 821, 832 (10th Cir. 2005); *City of Gainesville v. Island Creek Coal Sales Co*, 618 FSupp 513, 517 (ND Fla 1984), aff'd 771 F.2d 1495 (11th Cir. 1985); *Asahi Glass Co. v. Toledo Eng'g Co*, 505 FSupp2d 423, 430-431 (ND Ohio 2007).
454. *Free Zones of Upper Savoy and District of Gex* (*France v. Switzerland*), Order, (1929) 22 PCIJ Rep. Ser. A No. 22, 13.
455. Cf. Nouvel, [2007] 8-9 Procédures No. 18 [5-15].
456. Berger and Kellerhals, *Arbitration in Switzerland* [1541]; *Born* 3022; *Fouchard Gaillard and Goldman* [1366]; Newmark and Hill, (2000) 16 Arb. Int'l 84; *Russell on Arbitration* [6-027].

they,[457] national laws[458] and arbitral practice[459] do not force tribunals to correspond to parties' request for consent awards, particularly where the settlement would violate public policy.[460]

134. In procedural law, jurisdictions disagree whether a consent judgment constitutes res judicata. Whilst common law affirms this,[461] German law treats settlements as contractual rights only, even if they have been concluded in court.[462] French law has equated even contractual settlements with ordinary judgments until the 2016 *Code-civil* reform,[463] yet the revised Article 2052 Cc has an open wording and might thus create discussion.[464] In arbitration, Article 30(2) UNCITRAL Model Law contains the international guiding principle:

> Such an award [a consent award] has the same status and effect as any other award on the merits of the case[465]

457. *See*, e.g., Art. 33 ICC Rules ('the parties reach a settlement after the file has been transmitted to the arbitral tribunal in accordance with Article 16, the settlement shall be recorded in the form of an award made by consent of the parties, if so requested by the parties and if the arbitral tribunal agrees to do so.'); Art. 26 (9) LCIA Rules; Art. 34 (1) Swiss Rules.
458. *See* Art. 30(1) UNCITRAL Model Law ('If, during arbitral proceedings, the parties settle the dispute, the arbitral tribunal shall terminate the proceedings and, if requested by the parties and *not objected to by the arbitral tribunal,* record the settlement in the form of an arbitral award on agreed terms.'). Germany: s. 1053(1) ZPO. Common law: *Kiyue Co. v. Aquagen Int'l Pte Ltd*, [2003] 3 SLR 130 (SGHC); *Russell on Arbitration* [6-025]. Switzerland: Lazopoulos, in *Basler Kommentar* Art. 385 [26-31].
459. *See Iran v. USA*, 17 May 1982, DEC 8-A1-FT, 1 Iran-US CTR 144, 152-153 ('[arbitrators] should not attempt to review the reasonableness of the settlement in the place of the arbitrating parties'); *Born* 3025; Caron and Caplan, The UNCITRAL Arbitration Rules 785.
460. *Report of the Secretary-General*, 1985, UN Doc A/CN.9/264, Art. 30 [20] (consent award may be refused 'in case of suspected fraud, illicit or utterly unfair terms'). *See also ILC Draft on Arbitral Procedure*, UN Doc A/CN.4/59, Art. 22 comment (2), ('The use of the word "may" in article 22 is important, as it leaves the tribunal free to embody the settlement reached in an award or not. It is, in fact, necessary that the tribunal should be able to verify the legality and effective scope of the agreement. It cannot be compelled, even by an agreement between the parties to give binding force to an illegal or a purely fictitious settlement.'). *See* Holtzmann and Neuhaus, *A Guide to the UNCITRAL Model Law* 824.
461. *Haydock v. Goodier*, [1921] 2 KB 384 (CA); *Khan v. Golecha International Ltd*, [1980] 2 All ER 250 (CA); *Zurich Insurance Co. Plc v. Hayward*, [2011] EWCA Civ 641. *See Zuckermann on Civil Procedure* [25.97] ('relying on a consent judgment for an issue estoppel argument is not always straightforward because it may be difficult to determine precisely the issues that were essential and that were therefore determined by the consent order'). *See* on the relevance for abuse of process Fosket, *The Law and Practice of Compromise* 111. For US jurisdictions *see* the extensive case references of Shapiro, 91 ALR3d, 1170.
462. BGH, [1958] NJW 1970; BGH, [1983] NJW 996, 997 ('*keine der Rechtskraftwirkung ähnliche Wirkung*'); BGH, [2002] NJW 1503.
463. Article 2052 Cc (until 2016) ('Compromises have, between the parties, the authority of res judicata of a final judgment.' – Official translation).
464. '*La transaction fait obstacle à l'introduction ou à la poursuite entre les parties d'une action en justice ayant le même objet*'.
465. England: s. 51(3) 1996 Arbitration Act. France: Ortscheid and Seraglini, *Droit de l'arbitrage* [425]. Germany: s. 1053(2) ZPO. Switzerland: Berger and Kellerhals, *Arbitration in Switzerland* [1542-1548]. USA: *Mazza v. Dist Council of NY*, 2007 WL 2668116, [10] (EDNY).

135. In addition, French law contains a recent discussion whether settlements concluded by arbitration parties outside of arbitration proceedings comprise res judicata or relevance for irreconcilability rules.[466] Whilst both the French Supreme Court[467] and the ECJ[468] have rejected that settlements are relevant as a ground for denying recognition and enforcement to another decision, the 2013 *Planor Afrique* case raises doubts. In this case, an assignee of certain shares successfully sued its assignor (retaining certain shares) before a Burkina Faso court for having influenced a shareholders' resolution without the assignee. The French Supreme Court denied recognition and enforcement of this decision because the exequatur court had not examined potential preclusions by virtue of a certain Memorandum concluded in addition to the assignment and containing an arbitration clause.[469] The Memorandum was titled '*transaction*', the French equivalent for 'settlement'. Yet, it appears doubtful whether the court had fully reversed the previous jurisprudence. Alternative explanations might be that, *first*, the court had reversed the instance courts because they did not even mention the Memorandum. *Second*, the court might have referred to the Memorandum because it included an arbitration clause and thereby effectively undertook the (common[470]) review of the Burkina Faso court's jurisdiction.

136. In conclusion, arbitration law creates a particular interest of the parties to apply for consent awards when settlements have been reached. In contrast to pure settlements concluded by contract and consent judgments, consent awards undisputedly constitute res judicata.

[3] Arbitral Res Judicata as a Dispositive Right to be Invoked

137. Provided that res judicata's finality requirements are met, its invocation further illustrates the particular relevance of party autonomy for arbitral res judicata. When a party has not made any express statement on res judicata, procedural laws differ on the court's obligation to apply judgments' res judicata ex officio.[471] The perception might,

466. *See* on the interrelation between res judicata and irreconcilability *infra* [155-168].
467. Cass. (1e civ.), 11 February 1997, [1997] Clunet 1027. *Contra* CA Lyon, *SA Joubert Laurencin v. Viriani Ltd*, 15 September 1994, Juris-Data No. 1994-049090.
468. ECJ, 2 June 1994, *Solo Kleinmotoren*, C-414/92, EU:C:1994:221.
469. Cass. (1e civ.), *sté Emirates Telecommunications Corporation (Etisalat) v. sté Planor Afrique et al*, 28 March 2013, [2013] Rev. Arb. 411, 416 ('*le président du tribunal de grande instance retient que la sentence arbitrale rendue le 5 août 2009 a été annulée par un arrêt de la Cour commune de justice et d'arbitrage [...], l'existence d'une sentence possédant en France l'autorité de la chose jugée et contraire aux deux décisions burkinabées n'est pas établie; Attendu qu'en se déterminant ainsi, sans rechercher ainsi qu'il le lui était demandé, si la demande d'exequatur ne se heurtait pas à l'autorité de la chose jugée attachée à la transaction du 5 septembre 2007, le président du tribunal de grande instance n'a pas donné de base légale à sa décision*'). *See* Debourg, (2013) Rev. Arb. 425 ('*La confusion est donc à son comble.*').
470. *See infra* [147].
471. *Pro* BGHZ 82, 246, 247-248; *Boone v. Kurtz*, 617 F.2d 435, 436 (5th Cir. 1980) ('Dismissal by the court sua sponte on res judicata grounds [...] is permissible in the interest of judicial economy'). *Contra Morrison Rose & Partners v. Hillmann*, [1961] All ER 891 (CA); FRCP 8(c)(1); Cound et al, *Civil Procedure* 1223 ('preclusion may be waived unless it is claimed at an

but need not, relate on the perceptions towards *iura novit curia*.[472] For arbitral awards, the divide is vanishing in that arbitral res judicata is exclusively applied upon a party's request.[473] Switzerland remained the exception,[474] until the Federal Tribunal recently held that res judicata does not require an application ex officio before arbitral tribunals.[475]

138. Furthermore, the fact that arbitral res judicata will only be considered upon a party's request already necessitates that parties can jointly dispose of an arbitral award.[476] Even Swiss scholarship affirms this possibility.[477] In conclusion, the rules that arbitral awards' res judicata is not applied ex officio and can be disposed of by the parties' agreement reveals a restricted public interest in arbitral res judicata. Vice versa, the private interest in res judicata is strengthened. This interest is particularly prominent for the preferential treatment of 'consent awards'.

[D] Seeking Relief from Res Judicata

139. A final aspect of res judicata is the exposure to relief procedures. In litigation, the primary relief against judgments is the appeal. By contrast, it is frequently seen as one of arbitration's most significant advantages that parties opt out of the multi-instances system and settle for a 'one-stop shop' instead. In guaranteeing the primacy of the arbitration procedures, the primary relief against arbitral awards, i.e., the set aside does not allow any *révision auf fond*.[478] Instead, provisions such as Article 34(2) UNCITRAL Model Law allow a set aside only if the arbitration clause is invalid, it is not

early stage of the litigation'); Harnon, (1966) 1 Isr L. Rev. 547 ('undue emphasis on the private interest in the doctrine of res judicata.').

472. *See supra* [117].

473. France: CA Paris, *Omnium Marocain de Pèche*, 22 May 1997, 95/80231 (*'la règle de l'autorité de la chose jugée est d'intérêt privé et non d'ordre public'*); CA Paris, 9 September 2010, [2011] Rev. Arb. 97; Loquin, (2010) Rev. Arb. 229; Seraglini and Ortscheid, *Droit de l'arbitrage* [470]. Germany: BGH, [1958] NJW 950; Schlosser, in *Stein and Jonas* § 1055 [8]; Sweden: Svea Court of Appeal, *Czech Republic v. CME*, 15 May 2003, T 8735-01, (2013) 42 ILM 916; Hobér, (2013) 366 Rec. des cours 139.

474. TF, *République de Pologne v. Saar Papier Vertriebs GmbH et tribunal arbitral*, 20 September 2000, [2001] ASA Bulletin 487 [3b].

475. TF, 26 February 2015, No. 4A_374/2013, [4.3.1]. *See* on Swiss law's indifferential treatment of res judicata whether brought before court or before an arbitral tribunal *infra* [152].

476. *See* England: s. 58 1996 Arbitration Act (*'Unless otherwise agreed by the parties,* an award made by the tribunal pursuant to an arbitration agreement is final and binding both on the parties and on any persons claiming through or under them'). Germany: OLG Bremen, [1957] NJW 1035; BayObLGZ 1984, 45, 48; OLG Stuttgart, [2002] OLGR 2002, 166, [3]. USA: Restatement (Second) Judgments, § 84(4) ('If the terms of an agreement to arbitrate limit the binding effect of the award in another adjudication or arbitration proceeding, the extent to which the award has conclusive effect is determined in accordance with that limitation.'); *IDS Life Ins. Co. v. Royal Alliance Ass Inc*, 266 F.3d 645. 651 (7th Cir. 2001); *Anderson v. Beland*, 672 F.3d 113, 133 (2d Cir. 2011).

477. Girsberger, in *Basler Kommentar* Art. 387 [23] (*'lediglich ein Verzicht auf die aus ihm [dem Schiedsspruch] hervorgehenden Rechte'*); Stacher, in *Berner Kommentar* Art. 387 [3].

478. OLG München, [2011] SchiedsVZ 377; *United Mexican States v. Cargill Inc*, [2011] ONCA 622, [31]; *PT Perusahaan Gas Negara (Persero) TBK v. CRW Joint Operation*, [2010] SGHC 202, aff'd, [2011] SGCA 3; Cairo Court of Appeal, *March 2009*, 71/124; *Apa Ins. Co. Ltd v. Chrysanthus*

complied with, the tribunal violated due process or the award violates public policy.[479] These grounds are generally adjusted to Article V NYC.[480] Common-law jurisdictions contain particularities: section 69(1) 1996 Arbitration Act allows full appeals on question of English law as a default solution (which is regularly excluded by arbitral rules reference to 'final and binding'), and section 68(2) requires any set-aside grounds to be supplemented by 'substantial injustice' towards a party.[481] The FAA contains the non-codified ground of 'manifest disregard of the law' whose extent is heavily debated by opinions seeking to prevent any review on the merits.[482] Any arbitral res judicata will be invalidated if a set aside is successful. Beyond that common ground, jurisdictions differ on the question whether set-aside grounds can also be invoked *incidentally* against a party seeking to rely on an arbitral award's res judicata. Whilst German[483] and the majority of French[484] scholars seek to bar the incidental relevance, the Draft Third Restatement on Arbitration appears to allow incidental review.[485]

140. As an additional dimension of seeking relief, it should be noted that some grounds for relief might arise *after* an arbitral award has been rendered, e.g., a counter-claim. Particularly civil-law jurisdictions distinguish between cognition and execution competence thereby dealing with subsequent grounds for relief in genuine anti-enforcement suits.[486] If an anti-enforcement suit against an arbitral award raises an arbitrable matter, they have to be brought before the arbitral tribunal.[487] Whilst in litigation, it is generally understood that successful anti-enforcement suits hinder enforcement exclusively, and do not bar res judicata,[488] arbitral tribunals have the

---

Barnabas Okemo, M241 of 2005 (Nairobi HC); *Simbymanyo Estates Ltd v. Seyani Bros Co. (U) Ltd*, 555/2002 (Kampala HC 2004); Tribunal Supremo, 6 April 2004, ATS 4640/2004.

479. Implemented in s. 1059(2) ZPO. Article 190(2) PILA, Art. 1520 CPC, Art. 68(2) 1996 Arbitration Act and s. 10(a) FAA effectively and to a large degree contain comparable grounds.
480. Cf. *Report of UNCITRAL on the Work of its Eighteenth Session*, 3-21 June 1985, UN Doc A/40/17, [11-333].
481. *See Bulfracht (Cyprus) Ltd v. Boneset Shipping Co. Ltd (the Pamphilos)*, [2002] 2 Lloyd's Rep. 681.
482. Allegedly established in the case mainly concerning arbitrability, *Wilko v. Swan*, 74 S.Ct. 198, 187-188 (1953). *Crit Born* 3341-51; Restatement (Third) Int'l Comm Arbitration (TD 2), Rep's Memo (corresponding handling of vacatur/confirmation and recognition/enforcement).
483. Hausmann, in *Liber Amicorum Stoll* 594; Kröll in Böckstiegel et al. (eds), *Arbitration in Germany* s. 1059 ZPO [2]; *Schlosser* [906].
484. Cf. *Fouchard Gaillard and Goldman* [1567]; Audit Bollée and Callé, *Commerce International* [928].
485. Restatement (Third) Int'l Comm Arbitration (TD 2), § 4-9(a) ('A court precludes relitigation of a claim that was previously adjudicated in an international arbitral award to the extent that the party seeking preclusive effect demonstrates that the award is entitled to recognition under this Chapter'). *See* § 1-1 (r) ('international arbitral award is an arbitral award that, by virtue of its reasonable relation with one or more foreign States, is not a domestic award. The term includes Convention awards - both foreign awards and Convention awards made in the United States - and non-Convention awards').
486. *See* s. 767 ZPO, Art. 81(1) SchKG; Art. L. 311-12-1 C Org Jud. Notably, French law also allows to invoke subsequent set-off claims in appeal, *see* Art. 564 CPC.
487. CA Paris, 25 June 1982, [1983] Rev. Arb. 344; *Fouchard Gaillard and Goldman* [730]; Nelle, *Anspruch Titel und Vollstreckung* 222-223; Schlosser, in *Stein and Jonas* § 1029 [41]. CfAmeli, *La saisie-arrêt en DIP* [316] citing TGI Paris, 19 April 1984, unpublished.
488. ATF 120 Ia 82; Münzberg, in *Stein and Jonas* § 767 [2-6, 51]; Rosenberg Gaul and Schilken, *Zwangsvollstreckungsrecht* § 40.II.2; Vollkommer, in *Zöller* vo r§322 [72].

competence to suspend their own awards. In exercising such competence, a restriction might arise. For instance, § 767(2) ZPO excludes all defences of which the debtor had factual knowledge and availability in the initial proceedings.[489] Functionally, such exclusion is strongly related to abuse of process. The original concept as confirmed at common law precludes *claims*; § 767(2) ZPO precludes *defences*. Against this background, it might also be a valid position that French jurisprudence revises its previous opposition against such preclusion,[490] and extends the *Cesareo*'s rationale on 'concentrating the remedies' to 'concentrating the defences'. Accordingly, an arbitral award comprises res judicata as soon as it is rendered. Yet, it is exposed to relief possibilities. In this regard, procedural irregularities that occur *in* the proceedings are to be raised in set asides. Substantive defences arisen *after* the award has been rendered are covered by anti-enforcement suits before tribunals. Accordingly, the review of awards before courts is significantly more limited than the review of judgments. This also strengthens the perspective that private interests in arbitral awards outweigh public.

Interim Conclusion

141. In conclusion a descriptive overview over arbitral res judicata's requirements induces to infer that the public interest in arbitral res judicata comprises diminished relevance and that party autonomy may often demand adjustments of concepts established in civil procedure.

§2.03 RES JUDICATA OF FOREIGN ARBITRAL AWARDS

142. It is the prime advantage of arbitration over litigation that arbitral awards possess – almost – worldwide enforceability under the NYC. Conceptually, such *factual enforcement* is only one out of two means to confer efficacy upon foreign decisions. The second means is to *legally acknowledge* them, i.e., to apply res judicata.[491] Yet, in contrast to cross-jurisdictional enforcement, cross-jurisdictional res judicata cannot rely upon explicit uniform or national codifications. Undoubtedly tough, the rationales of justice, consistency, legal certainty and efficiency – potentially, the rule of comity[492] – do not only justify preclusive effects within a jurisdiction[493] but also across jurisdictional frontiers.[494] Accordingly, it is the task of tribunals and scholars to develop the framework necessary for handling arbitral res judicata in cross-border case scenarios. This comprises the delicate task to adjust foreign judgment with arbitration

489. *See* Herget, in *Zöller* § 767 [14], also mentioning the discussion whether this is an implementation of res judicata, genuine procedural concentration or a substantive preclusion rule.
490. *See* Cass. (com), 14 March 1972, [1972] Bull. civ IV No. 88; Cass. (comm.), *Judgment of* 12 January 1993, [1993] Bull. civ IV No. 4; Cass. (1e civ.), 11 April 1995, (1996) Rec Dalloz 121 (invalidity of contract); Glasson Tisser and Morel, *Traité théorique* 102-103.
491. Cf. Mayer and Heuzé, *Droit international privé* [372-377].
492. *Hilton v. Guyot*, 159 U.S. 113 (1895); Briggs, (2011) 354 Rec. des cours 149-150. *Crit Adams v. Cape plc*, [1990] Ch. 433.
493. *See supra* [101-102].
494. Cf. von Mehren, (1980) 167 Rec. des cours 34-35.

principles. The following passages outline this adjustment. Whilst the critical aspects of uniform and private international law will only be mentioned briefly (*see* [A], *infra*), the passages focus on the operative rules of national laws (*see* [B], *infra*).

[A] The NYC and the Applicable Law as Litmus Tests

143. The law of decisions' cross-border effects generally focuses on *recognition and enforcement*. Potentially, many of res judicata's uncertainties might be associated with its conceptual integration amongst these two terms. The most prominent examples concern uniform and private international law. Yet, since this examination's position towards these very perceptions will be of the essence for its solutions on awards' third-party effect, they will only be mentioned briefly in this Chapter on *national* laws and referred to eventual discussions.

144. The NYC's scope was long understood as relating to enforcement exclusively, thereby rendering 'recognition' a preliminary requirement for enforcement. By contrast, recent scholarship seeks to justify the pleas for uniform rules of res judicata by the argument that 'recognition' could be equated with res judicata. Yet, the specific content of uniform res judicata under the NYC remains to be developed in practice.[495]

145. The still predominant, traditional opinion leads to an exposure of res judicata to private international law. Such determination of the law applicable to res judicata mainly constitutes an antagony between two solutions originating from the handling of foreign judgments, namely the law of the decision's origin (*extension of effects*) and the subsequent *lex fori* (*equalization of effects*). In original litigation doctrine, the first view frequently raises that 'to recognize' means 'to extend effects'. The latter view relies on sovereignty in that exclusively each forum's law can establish binding effects within its jurisdiction. In arbitration, both positions are enhanced. The extension doctrine relies on the NYC's mandate for recognition, the equalization doctrine on the perception that arbitral awards had no judicial origin.[496]

[B] Operative Characteristics of Cross-Border Res Judicata

146. In addition to the pre-eminent discussions on cross-jurisdictional res judicata under uniform and private international law, *national* arbitration laws contain a range of – less-debated – operative aspects of cross-jurisdictional res judicata. These operative foundations need to be addressed in order to guarantee the practical feasibility and the substantive coherence of the eventual discussions. This concerns three aspects in particular. The *first* is the question whether a foreign arbitral award can be invoked as res judicata directly, or it requires preliminary proceedings known from enforcement. This refers primarily to exequatur procedures, i.e., declarations of enforceability

495. *Infra* Chapter 5.
496. *Infra* Chapter 6.

necessary for enforcing foreign arbitral awards in France[497] and Germany.[498] Even more strictly, US federal law demands a comprehensive confirmation suit, merging the foreign award into a domestic judgment and requiring personal jurisdiction over the award, the debtor or his property.[499] By contrast, enforcement can be applied for directly under Swiss law (where exequatur is optional)[500] and English law (where confirmations are optional).[501] For res judicata, *none* of the jurisdictions examined requires prior exequatur or confirmation procedures, neither for foreign judgments[502] nor for foreign arbitral awards.[503] This even applies when res judicata is the exclusive consequence of a decision, e.g., in procedures exclusively involving a legal status.[504] Instead, they allow to directly invoke the foreign arbitral award as preclusion ground in follow-up disputes. In civil-law doctrine, already the wording 'exequatur' ('let it be executed') indicates the limited relevance for res judicata.[505]

147. Res judicata's independence of prior recognition proceedings necessitates that a foreign arbitral award will be recognized incidentally when invoked as res judicata. This leads to the *second* aspect: cross-jurisdictional res judicata requires that the grounds for non-recognition, such as violations of jurisdiction or public policy, will also be examined incidentally.[506] For instance, in conformity with its *jurisprudence constante*, the Swiss Federal Tribunal has rejected an arbitral award of the Mexican

497. Article 1487 (1) CPC (domestic) and Art. 1516 (1) CPC. *Fouchard Gaillard and Goldman* [1575].
498. Section 1060 (2) ZPO ('*Der Antrag auf Vollstreckbarerklärung ist unter Aufhebung des Schiedsspruchs abzulehnen, wenn einer der in § 1059 Abs. 2 bezeichneten Aufhebungsgründe vorliegt.*').
499. *See Sonera Holding B.V. v. Cukurova Holding AS*, No. 12-4280-cv (2d Cir. 2014); Restatement (Third) Int'l Comm Arbitration (TD 1), § 5.19; *Yukos Capital SARL v. OAO Tomsknet VNK*, [2014] IEHC 115 (recognition was rejected because its sole purpose was to eventually rely on parallel entitlement).
500. Berger and Kellerhals, *Arbitration in Switzerland* (1989); *Poudret and Besson* [861].
501. s66(1) 1996 Arbitration Act (leave of the court or confirmation). *See Bremer Öltransport v. Drewry*, [1933] 1 KB 753 (CA); *Dicey Morris and Collins* [16.105].
502. France: CA Aix-en-Provence, 6 April 2000, [2001] Clunet 1130; Huet, in *JCl Droit International* Fasc 584-35 [65]; Cass. (1e civ.), *Hainard*, 3 March 1930, [1930] Clunet 981. *Contra* Cass. (civ), *Negrotto*, 10 March 1914, [1914] Rev. crit. DIP 449. In Germany, it was once debated whether foreign decisions modifying a legal relationship (*Gestaltungsurteile*) should be subjected to exequatur because they are 'self-executing', *see* Lakkis, *Gestaltungsakte im internationalen Rechtsverkehr* 392; Kronke, in *Soergel* Art. 38 Anh IV [141] with further references.
503. England: *Dicey Morris and Collins* [16.133]. France: Cass. (1e civ.), *sté Emirates Telecommunications Corporation (Etisalat) v. sté Planor Afrique et al*, 28 March 2013, [2013] Rev. Arb. 411, 416 ('*une décision peut être revêtue de l'autorité de la chose jugée même si elle n'est pas revêtue de l'exequatur*'); Art. 1516 CPC ('*La sentence arbitrale n'est susceptible d'exécution forcée qu'en vertu d'une ordonnance d'exequatur [...].*'); Art. 1514 CPC '*Les sentences arbitrales sont reconnues ou exécutées* [...]'; Debourg, (2013) Rev. Arb. 430; Jarrosson, (2008) 8 Procédures No. 12 [46]; Seraglini and Ortscheidt, *Droit de l'arbitrage* [921]. Germany: Kröll in Böckstiegel et al. (eds), *Arbitration in Germany* Intro ss 1060-1061 ZPO(4); *Schlosser* [906]. USA: Restatement (Third) Int'l Comm Arbitration (TD 1), § 5-5. Switzerland: TF, 14 February 2011, 4A_508/2010, [2012] ASA Bull. 108, [3.1].
504. Germany: Lakkis, *Gestaltungsakte im internationalen Rechtsverkehr* 392. On judgments *see* Kronke, in *Soergel* Art. 38 Anh IV [141] with further references.
505. Cf. *Poudret and Besson* [850].
506. England: *Dicey Morris and Collins* [16.117]. France: T com Nanterre, *Technip France*, 5 September 2001, [2002] Rev. Arb. 455; Audit Bollée and Callé, *Droit du commerce international* [928]; de Vareilles-Sommières, [2014] Clunet Doc No. 12 [8-9]. *See* Cour de cassation Belgique,

Football Association as res judicata because the claimants have not been awarded the right to be heard in the Mexican arbitration.[507] Such incidental review is a crucial difference to arbitral awards from the arbitral seat.[508] A *practical* justification might be: but for the possibility to incidentally examine the grounds for non-recognition, there would be the undesirable necessity to allow the forum a 'declarative non-preclusion suit'[509] as it is now discussed under the exequatur-free Brussels Ibis Regulation.[510]

148. The confluence of res judicata's and exequatur's requirements leads to the *third* aspect, their inter-relation. Swiss law holds that even though exequatur is not compulsory for res judicata, a successful exequatur relieves res judicata from the incidental review of non-recognition grounds.[511] At common law, the solution applies because the foreign arbitral award has been 'merged' into a domestic judgment.[512] Vice versa, where exequatur had been rejected, the French *Cour de cassation* stated that there was '*no arbitral award comprising res judicata effect in France*'.[513] At common law, the non-confirmation might comprise issue-preclusion effects towards subsequent non-recognition arguments.[514]

Interim Conclusion

149. In conclusion, national arbitration laws subject foreign arbitral awards to particular requirements in order to constitute res judicata in follow-up litigation. Particularly, the grounds for non-recognition will be examined incidentally. Whilst exequatur (admitting the award) or confirmation (merging the award) procedures are not compulsory, their result predetermines the availability of res judicata. The applicable law for res judicata's consequences is a major debate of uniform and private international law duly revisited in *Chapter 6*.

---

28 June 1979, [1981] Rev. crit. jur belge 332, 340. Germany: Kröll in Böckstiegel et al. (eds), *Arbitration in Germany* Intro s. 1060-61 ZPO [8-9]. Switzerland: TF, 14 February 2011, 4A_508/2010, [2012] ASA Bull. 108, [3.1]. USA: Restatement (Third) Int'l Comm Arbitration (TD 2), § 4-9(a) and § 4-10(a).

507. TF, 25 February 2015, 4A_374/2014, (2015) 33 ASA Bull. 576. *See* on the application of the New York Convention where the prior decision is a judgment ATF 124 III 83, *Compania Minera Condesa SA et al. v. BRGM-Pérou SAS et al*, [E.5.b]. Crit Berger and Kellerhals, *Arbitration in Switzerland* [1662] ('We consider, however, that it would be more appropriate to determine this issue by reference to PILS, Art. 7 and PILS, Art. 12.'). Now open aspect according to ATF 140 III 278, [E.3].

508. *See supra* [139].

509. *See Schlosser* [906].

510. *See* Althammer, in *Liber Amicorum Kaissis* 28.

511. Cf. TF, 25 February 2015, 4A_374/2014, (2015) 33 ASA Bull. 576.

512. Cf. Restatement (Third) Int'l Comm Arbitration (TD 2), § 4-1 (d).

513. (On the judgment's exequatur) Cass. (1e civ.), *sté Emirates Telecommunications Corporation (Etisalat) v. sté Planor Afrique et al*, 28 March 2013, [2013] Rev. Arb. 411, 416 ('*Attendu que [...] l'ordonnance d'exequatur de cette [OHADA] sentence ayant fait l'object d'un appel, l'existence d'une sentence possédant en France l'autorité de la chose jugée [...] n'est pas établié.*'). *See also* Jarrosson, (2008) 8 Procédures No. 12 [50] ('[...] *la reconnaissance de la sentence peut à tout le moins être utilisée pour la force probante qu'elle lui confère.*').

514. Cf. Restatement (Third) Int'l Comm Arbitration (TD 1), § 5-5.

§2.04 RES JUDICATA BEFORE ARBITRAL TRIBUNALS: A MATTER OF PUBLIC POLICY?

150. Whilst the preceding sections have focused on the case scenario that an arbitral award is invoked before courts, the inverse setting, i.e., that a prior decision is invoked as res judicata before arbitral tribunals, has recently turned into nothing but a high-profile topic of international scholarship. In particular, after the *ILA Report on Res Judicata* proposed that arbitral tribunals should not seek to determine an applicable national law and handle res judicata by means of transnational principles instead,[515] a range of publications discussed this proposal – mostly positive in terms of transnationalism, yet critical with regard to the ILA's limited range of proposals. Any further evaluation, theoretical discussion and practical examination will be presented in the Chapter dedicated to transnational law.[516] At this stage, the topic's dimension privy to *national* law is examined: can the application of res judicata by arbitrators be reviewed by the arbitral seat's courts? Notably, these review possibilities also explain why references to some national laws on arbitral res judicata in the comparative Chapters can increasingly facilitate judgments, namely set-aside judgments, whilst others cannot.

151. There is a fundamental divide amongst national jurisdictions on the review of res judicata by arbitrators. Some important arbitration jurisdictions allow parties to seek court review when an arbitral tribunal had neglected to apply the doctrine of res judicata. English law allows for a review of res judicata as part of the comprehensive appeal under section 69(1) Arbitration Act, which is excludable and regularly excluded (above all, by arbitral rules reference to 'final and binding' arbitral awards). Other countries do not know such *révision au fond* and have to examine set-side grounds. In this regard, it might be worth discussing whether res judicata restricts an arbitral tribunal's subject matter jurisdiction on a cause of action.[517] After all, the previous court or arbitral tribunal became *functus officio*. Yet, such discussion remains to gain prominence. It was *un*successfully raised before the Singapore Court of Appeal under the implementation of Article 34 (2)(c)UNCITRAL Model Law[518] and also rejected by the Paris Court of Appeal.[519]

152. Instead, the main discussion addresses whether res judicata forms part of procedural public policy. This assessment is particularly delicate since res judicata serves both private and public interests of justice, consistency, legal certainty and efficiency.[520] In this regard, it is the position of Swiss law that the public interests were overriding and that res judicata is part of procedural public policy. Hence, any arbitral

515. *ILA Final Report on Res Judicata* [21-26].
516. *Infra* Chapter 8.
517. *See* Hascher, in *Travaux comité français DIP* 28; Mayer, in *Liber Amicorum Reymond* 196-199; Mayer, (2016) Rev. Arb. 103; van den Berg, *New York Convention* 158.
518. *PT Asuransi Jasa Indonesia (Persero) v. Dexia Bank SA*, [2006] SGCA 41.
519. CA Paris, *Marriott Int'l Hotels Inc. v. JNAH Dev SA*, 9 September 2010, [2011] Rev. Arb. 970.
520. Cf. Zajdela, [2017] Rev. Arb. 1221.

award rendered in conflict with an earlier (Swiss or foreign) decision's res judicata will be set aside under Article 190(2) lit. e PILA. Established as an obiter dictum in the lis pendens case *Fomento,*[521] *Atlético Madrid v. Benfica Lisbon* rendered the rule a *ratio decidendi.*[522] Eventually, jurisprudence constantly reiterated that tribunals seated in Switzerland had to treat res judicata as a Swiss court would.[523] A corresponding application of public policy is also reported for Sweden[524] and New York.[525] For instance, in a 2007 dispute between Samsung and its headset licensor, the arbitral tribunal applied different royalty calculating methods for different periods in subsequent arbitrations. Although the arbitral tribunal explicitly '*ma[de] no decision regarding Period 2*', Samsung sought to rely on issue preclusion. The arbitral tribunal considered the argument and rejected it. In the set aside, the court dedicated five pages and independently established both the legal standard for issue preclusion (notably under New York law for an FAA award) and its application.[526]

153. By contrast, other countries are averse to reviewing res judicata by virtue of procedural public policy. For example, Singapore, which implemented the UNCITRAL Model Law, rejected the application of public policy to res judicata.[527] Equally, the Québec Supreme Court has rejected the argument.[528] Most consistently, French jurisprudence once reviewed tribunals' application of res judicata on public-policy grounds,[529] yet shifted the review stating that public policy forbids *nothing but*

521. ATF 127 III 279, *Fomento de Constucciones y Contratas SA v. Colon Container Terminal SA* [E.2.b.] ('It is contrary to public policy that there are within a given legal system two conflicting judicial decisions in the same action and between the same parties that are equally and simultaneously enforceable (*see* ATF 116 II 625 at 4a). In order to avoid such situation, there are basically two principles: litispendence and res judicata (ATF 114 II 183 at 2a and references therein). [...]. The principle of res judicata forbids a court to hear a case which has already been finally settled. [Res judicata] definitively excludes the jurisdiction of the second court.' – translation according to (2004) XXIX Y.C.A. 809, [6]).
522. ATF 136 III 345, *Atlético Madrid v. Benfica Lisbon,* [E.2.1] (*'Das Schiedsgericht verletzt den verfahrensrechtlichen ordre public, wenn es bei seinem Entscheid die materielle Rechtskraft eines früheren Entscheids unbeachtet lässt [...].Die Rechtskraftwirkung beschränkt sich auf das Urteilsdispositiv Die Urteilsbegründung wird davon nicht erfasst. Die Urteilserwägungen haben in einer anderen Streitsache keine bindende Wirkung, sind aber gegebenenfalls zur Klärung der Tragweite des Urteilsdispositivs beizuziehen.'*). Followed by TF, 2 September 2014, 4A_606/2013, [E.3].
523. ATF 140 III 278, [E.3.1]; TF, 2 September 2014, 4A_606/2013, [E.3]; TF, 16 October 2014, 4A_324/2014; TF, 25 February 2015, 4A_374/2014, (2015) 33 ASA Bull. 576; TF, 29 May 2015, 4A_633/2014, (2015) 33 ASA Bull. 599. *See* Berger and Kellerhals, *Arbitration in Switzerland* [1657-1664].
524. *Aktiebolaget Skanska Cementgjuteriet v. Motoraktiobolaget i Karlstad,* [1953] NJA 751; *Esselte AB v. Allmänna Pensionsfonden,* [1998] NJA 189; Hobér, (2013) 366 Rec. des cours 139.
525. *See Matter of Carp (Van Tassel),* 234 AD2d 715, 717 (3d Dep 1996); *Dibeneddeto v. Nationwide Associates Inc,* 297 AD2d 740 (2d Dep 2002); *Dokio Mar & Fire Ins. Co. v. Allstate Ins. Co,* 778 NYS2d 315 (2d Dep 2004).
526. *Interdigital Communications Corp. et al. v. Samsung Electronic Co. Ltd,* 528 FSupp2d 340, 354-359 (S.D.N.Y. 2007).
527. *PT Asuransi Jasa Indonesia (Persero) v. Dexia Bank SA,* (2006) SGCA 41, [8] ('Errors of law or fact, *per se,* did not engage the public policy of Singapore').
528. *Holding Tusculum BV v. Louis Dreyfus SAS,* [2008] QCCS 5904.
529. Cass. (1e civ.), *Hilmarton,* 10 June 1997, [1997] Rev. Arb. 376 (*'l'existence d'une décision francaise irrévocable portant sur le même objet entre les même parties faisait obstacle à toute reconnaissance en France de décision judiciaire ou arbitrale rendue à l'étranger incompatible*

irreconcilability.[530] Furthermore, in Germany, where the Federal Court of Justice has applied public policy to the application of res judicata by arbitral tribunals in its judgment of 11 October 2018 (I ZB 9/18), a progressive stream in scholarship seeks to merely apply public policy[531] when an arbitral tribunal has not even addressed the issue of res judicata.[532] This is also the solution of jurisprudence under section 10 FAA[533] that examined a 'manifest disregard of the law'.[534] This restriction stands against the rationale that the application of res judicata by a subsequent arbitral tribunal is regarded as an ordinary application of the law under the tribunal's prerogative. Hence, in order to prevent any *révision au fond*, set-aside courts should

---

avec elle'); CA Paris, 28 September 1979, [1980] Rev. Arb. 506. Cf. Cass. (1e civ.), *Putrabali*, 29 June 2007, [2007] Bull. civ I No. 251 ('*l'autorité de la chose jugée attachée à l'arrêt [...] faisant obstacle à l'exequatur de la [deuxième] sentence, inconciliable avec la première*').

530. CA Paris, *SA Sucres et denrées v. Scté Multitrade Cairo*, 10 March 2005, [2006] Rev. Arb. 456, 458 ('*Sucden fait valoir qu'une première sentence [...] engage Multigroup codébiteur solidaire, la chose jugée à l'égard de l'un des codébiteurs solidaires ayant autorité à l'égard de l'autre. [...] Mais considérant que Sucden ne démontre pas en quoi la sentence arbitrale [...] est inconciliable avec la sentence du 11 juillet 2002, exécutoire en France, condamnant AB à lui payer diverses sommes, notamment à titre de dommages-intérêts*'); CA Paris, *Papillon Group Corp. v. République Arabe de Syrie*, 26 March 2009, [2010] Rev. Arb. 525; CA Paris, *Marriott International Hotels*, 9 September 2010, [2011] Rev. Arb. 970 w Note Debourg 986 ('*L'affirmation est donc de principe: l'ordre public n'est pas atteint du seul fait de la violation de l'autorité de la chose jugée.*'); CA Paris, 17 January 2012, [2012] Rev. Arb. 569; CA Paris, 17 November 2011, [2011] Rev. Arb. 1104; CA Paris, *SNC Forézienne d'entreprise v. SAS Guintoli*, 17 March 2017, [2017] Rev. Arb. 1213, 1217 ('*sauf au cours d'une même instance*'). *Pro* Debourg, *Les contrariétés de décisions* [435]; Mayer, in *Liber Amicorum Reymond* 190.
531. *See* on the standard BGH, [2001] NJW 373 ('*ordre public wird durch die §§ 580 ff ZPO konkretisiert* [...].'); OLG Saarbrücken, 1 August 2000, 4 Sch 7/00, [B.II.]; OLG Stuttgart, 3 June 2003, 1 Sch 2/03, [II.2.a.]; BayObLG, [2004] SchiedsVZ 319, 320 (obiter); BT-Drucks 13/5273, 59. *See* s. 580 ZPO ('*Die Restitutionsklage findet statt [...] 7. Wenn die Partei a) ein in der Sache erlassenes, früher rechtskräftig gewordenes Urteil [...] auffindet oder zu benutzen in den Stand gesetzt wird [...].*').
532. Schlosser, in *ASA Special Series* 19; Schlosser, in *Stein and Jonas* [363] ('*Falls ein Schiedsrichter sich redlich um die Auslegung eines staatlichen Gerichtsurteils bemüht hat, besteht kein Grund, einen Verstoß gegen den deutschen ordre public schon immer dann anzunehmen, wenn die Interpretation nach Meinung des später mit dem Schiedsspruch befassten staatlichen Gerichts falsch ist.*'); Geimer, in *Zöller*, § 1059 [12]; Voit, in *Musielak and Voit* § 1059 [28]. *Contra* Gaul, in *Liber Amicorum Sandrock* 301-314; Münch, in *Münchener Kommentar* § 1059 [45]; Schwab and Walther, *Schiedsgerichtsbarkeit* Ch. 24 [51]; Schütze, in *Wieczorek and Schütze* [61, 69].
533. Res judicata of judgments: *Olick v. Dippel*, 93 FedAppx 386, 389-390 (3d Cir. 2004) (with explicit distinction to arbitrability); *Sutter v. Oxford Health Planc LLC*, 227 FedAppx 135, 138 (3d Cir. 2007); *Sherrock Bros Inc. v. Daimler Chrysler Motors Co., LLC*, 260 FedAppx 497, 499 (3d Cir. 2008); *Nicor Int'l Corp. v. El Paso Corp*, 292 FSupp2d 1357 (SD Fla 2003) ('the law in this circuit is that a res judicata defence is to be raised and decided by the arbitrator in the first instance; and that only if the arbitrator ignores the defence would it then be appropriate for the court to vacate an arbitration award'). Res judicata of arbitral awards: *Marshall v. Green Giant Co*, 942 F.2d 539, 550 (8th Cir. 1991); *Hudson v. ConAgra Poultry Co*, 484 F.3d 496, 504-505 (8th Cir. 2007) (although court would have come to the same conclusion on res judicata); *Beecham Biologicals, SA v. Biogen INC*, 1996 WL 209897 (S.D.N.Y.); *Duferco Int'l Steel Trading v. T Klaveness Shipping A/S*, 184 FSupp2d 271 (S.D.N.Y. 2002); *F Hoffmann-La Roche Ltd v. Qiagen Gaithersburg Inc*, 730 FSupp2d 318, 327-328 (S.D.N.Y. 2010).
534. *See supra* [139]. *See* for exceptions in labour matters *Aircraft Braking Sys Corp. v. Local 856 Int'l Union*, 97 F.3d 155, 159 (6th Cir. 1996) (not free to ignore); *John Morrell & Co. v. Local Union 304A of United Food & Commercial Workers*, 913 F.2d 544, 562-563 (8th Cir. 1990).

not review the application of res judicata.[535] Moreover, it is noteworthy that the *review* of res judicata under the FAA is accompanied by a discussion on another topic sharing the heart of the problem, the *prevention* of arbitral adjudications on res judicata by virtue of arbitrability. In applications to bar arbitration, some courts have fully awarded arbitral tribunals the competence to decide on matters of res judicata[536] whilst some have fully denied it,[537] others when the prior judgment was rendered by the very same court.[538]

154. In conclusion, amongst the examined set-aside jurisdictions, primarily Switzerland applies public policy when an arbitral tribunal failed to respect an earlier decision's res judicata. From a functional perspective, it should be noted that this apparently strict supervision in comparison to other jurisdictions might be compensated by two further observations. Primarily, although the Swiss Supreme Court obligates tribunals seated in Switzerland to fully apply res judicata *in general*, Swiss law has a rather restrictive position towards the extent of cross-border res judicata *in particular* because it merely upholds res judicata if both the law of decision's origin and the Swiss *lex fori* affirm it.[539] Moreover, it bars issue preclusion.[540] A further functional compensation is that other jurisdictions, which refuse to undertake annulments for violations of res judicata will more likely be confronted with set asides for irreconcilability.

§2.05 THE CONFLICT OF DECISIONS: INDISPENSABLE ANNEX TO RES JUDICATA

155. When a court or tribunal rejects res judicata and two decisions on related matters are in existence, the dispute is likely to continue as a matter of *conflicting decisions.*[541]

535. *Born* 3331 ('unclear why awards involving (mis)applications of rules of res judicata should be treated differently from awards involving other mistaken substantive rulings by a tribunal'). *See* G Sanders, (1992) 24 Georgetown Int'l L. J. 106; *Domke on Arbitration* [36.2].
536. *National Union Fire Ins. Co. v. Belco Petroleum Corp*, 88 F.3d 129, 135-136 (2d Cir. 1996) ('a component of the dispute on the merits [...] as much related to the merits as such affirmative defences as a time limit in the arbitration agreement or laches'); *Chrion Corp. v. Ortho Diagnostic System Inc*, 207 F.3d 1126, 1134 (9th Cir. 2000) ('we agree with the Second Circuit that a res judicata defence is a component of the merits of the dispute and is thus an arbitrable issue').
537. *Kelly v. Merrill Lynch Perce Fenner & Smith Inc*, 985 F.2d 1067 (11th Cir. 1993); *In re Y&A Group Sec Litig*, 38 F.3d 380 (8th Cir. 1994). Cf. *Domke on Arbitration* [36.2] with further references ('A majority of courts have held that it is for the court, rather than the arbitrator, to decide the res judicata effect of a prior court judgment.').
538. *John Hancock Mutual Life Insurance Co. v. Olick*, 151 F.3d 132 (3d Cir. 1998); Wong, (2005) 46 Santa Clara L. Rev. 51-67.
539. *See infra* [373].
540. *See supra* [113].
541. There are several alternative headings for the issue the examination decides against: *Incompatible* or *contradicting* decisions bear a rather strict connotation. By way of contrast, *inconsistent* decisions provide the room to rely on incidental reasonings. *Irreconcilable* decisions are intrinsically connected to the European and French concepts. Against this background, the thesis regards *conflicting* as the most neutral expression.

This topic is the last stage of Forum Coordination. Since it will thus constitute the immanent alternative when deciding against res judicata, it is outlined. Upon a proposal on a structure of the topic (*see* [A], *infra*), the examination reveals the widespread preference for priority in time and irreconcilability (*see* [B], *infra*), the latter term primarily being an implementation of res judicata's outset (*see* [C], *infra*).

[A] Case Scenarios, Conflict Criteria and Priority Criteria

156. The conflict of decisions faces a problem well known from cross-jurisdictional res judicata: neither arbitration treaties nor national statutes contain express rules.[542] Yet, '*common sense requires to take conflicting decisions into account*'.[543] This has to occur in three case scenarios. The *first* has already been touched upon in the recently mentioned scenario: the annulment court had to decide between the award and a prior decision invoked as an annulment ground. Moreover, there are the following other scenarios of conflicting decisions whose referral to res judicata requires due consideration. *Second*, in third states, a prior decision can be invoked as a ground against the recognition and enforcement of an arbitral award. *Third*, the arbitral award might not only be the target but also the means of defence when invoked against the recognition and enforcement of foreign judgments. Before addressing these case scenarios point-by-point, a structured analysis has to point out that any of these case scenarios has to decide on the same parameters: which requirements render two decisions conflicting (*conflict criteria*)? Pursuant to which criteria will one decision be awarded priority over the other (*priority criteria*)?

157. For instance, in the case scenario that a prior decision is invoked as an annulment ground, Swiss law has assumed a conflict in the case the prior decision's res judicata (i.e., on the cause of action under the Swiss *lex fori*) conflicts with *any* ratio decidendi of the arbitral award. By contrast, another conflict criterion known from foreign judgment principles is irreconcilability, the potentially most prominent example being Article 45(1) Brussels Ibis Regulation[544] and now Article 9(1) lit. f, g Hague Convention on Choice of Court Agreements.[545] For the latter, irreconcilability under the Brussels Regime might serve as a role model.[546]

542. The exception of Art. 45 Brussels Ibis Regulation will be promptly revisited.
543. Debourg, *Les contrariétés des décisions* [422] ('*le bon sens commande de tenir compte de l'existence d'une décision inconciliable*').
544. '[T]he recognition of a judgment shall be refused: [...] (c) if the judgment is irreconcilable with a judgment given between the same parties in the Member State addressed; (d) if the judgment is irreconcilable with an *earlier* judgment given in another Member State or in a third State *involving the same cause of action* and between the same parties, provided that the earlier judgment fulfills the conditions necessary for its recognition in the Member State addressed.' The Lugano Convention's equivalent is Art. 34 (1).
545. 'Recognition or enforcement may be refused if [...] (f) the judgment is inconsistent with a judgment given in the requested State in a dispute between the same parties; or (g) the judgment is inconsistent with an earlier judgment given in another State between the same parties on the same cause of action, provided that the earlier judgment [...]'.
546. *See* on the drafting history *Report on the Meeting of the Drafting Committee of the Hague Convention*, 18-20 April 2005, Prel Doc No. 28, [35].

158. If any conflict criterion applies, the applicable law has to decide on the *priority* criterion. The most well-known criterion is priority in time, i.e., the inefficacy of the latter decision. Yet, its application is by no means self-evident and exposed to alternatives. For instance, Article 45(1)(c) Brussels Ibis Regulation itself incorporates priority in territory. Another concept – unsuccessfully – invoked before the Spanish Supreme Court was priority in nature in that Article V(2)(b) NYC permitted the priority of judgments over arbitral awards, regardless of the date rendered.[547] Finally, US doctrine on inter-State case scenarios contains the last-in-time rule.[548] The justification is that the later proceeding provided the opportunity to rely on the earlier judgment's preclusive effect.[549]

[B] Widespread Application of Irreconcilability and Priority in Time

159. A jurisdiction-by-jurisdiction examination of the conflict and priority criteria for the conflict of decisions reveal tendencies towards priority in time and irreconcilability. Beginning with French law, it contains the most consistent and explicit regime. Taking up on the aforementioned case scenarios, irreconcilability with earlier decisions is, *first*, a violation of public policy necessary for annulling international arbitral awards rendered in France under Article 1520(5) CPC; *second*, a trigger for public policy against the recognition of foreign awards under Article 1525(4) CPC; and *third*, a trigger for public policy against the recognition of foreign judgments. As to the operation of priority in time, in the *Planor Afrique* case, where a court in Burkina Faso, an OHADA tribunal and an ICC tribunal adjudicated on the very same shareholders' resolution, the Paris Court of Appeal did not defer to the arbitral awards (receiving exequatur earlier), but a foreign judgment (rendered earlier).[550]

160. For foreign judgments, 328(1) No. 3 ZPO and Article 27(2)(c) PILA[551] equally stipulate the application of irreconcilability and priority in time. Correspondingly, common law contains ample precedence for the non-recognition of foreign decisions in violation of an earlier decision's cause of action.[552] By contrast, there is no authority to

547. Tribunal Supremo, *Fashion Robbon Co. Inc. v. Iberband SL*, (2005) XXX Y.C.A. 627, 629.

548. Restatement (Second) Judgments, § 15 ('When in two actions inconsistent final judgments are rendered., it is the later, not the earlier, judgment that is accorded conclusive effect in a third action under the rules of res judicata.'). *See* correspondingly Restatement (Second) Conflict of Laws, § 114.

549. Cf. *Robi v. Five Platters Inc*, 838 F.2d 318, 322-323; Casad and Clermont, *Res Judicata* 56; Ginsburg, (1968-1969) 82 Harv L. Rev. 831-832; Hay et al, *Conflict of Laws* 352; Smit, (1962) 9 UCLA L. Rev. 46.

550. CA Paris, 17 January 2012, [2012] Rev. Arb. 569; CA Paris, *SA Planor Afrique v. SA Atlantique Télécom*, 4 December 2012, [2013] Rev. Arb. 416. *See* on the later reversal *supra* [135].

551. 'That a lawsuit between the same parties and concerning the same causes of action had already been brought or decided in Switzerland or that the lawsuit had proceeded to judgment in a third State and that judgment can be recognized in Switzerland.'

552. *Vervaeke v. Smith*, [1983] 1 A.C. 145, 157 per Lord Hailsham of St. Marylebone LC (HL) (prior judgment from England); *ED&F Mann (Sugar) Ltd v. Yani Haryanto (No 2)*, [1991] 1 Lloyd's Rep. 429 (CA) (prior judgment on non-liability from England); *Showlag v. Mansour*, [1995] 1 AC 431 (PC) (prior judgment also foreign); *The Joanna V*, [2003] EWHC 1655 (Comm).

state that a latter decision will not be recognized if it is inconsistent with an earlier decision's incidental reasonings. In the US, some courts applied the last-in-time rule even when the prior judgment was foreign,[553] whereas a New York State Court rejected the last-in-time rule where the defendant had no opportunity to argue for the binding force of a prior Turkish judgment before Belgian courts.[554] In any case, the rule does not apply undisputedly in the context of foreign judgments.[555] Whilst the Third Restatement on Foreign Relations regards the issue to be at the discretion of courts,[556] the Uniform Act (adopted by states such as New York) favours *priority in time.*[557]

161. In contrast to the defence against foreign judgments, the defence against arbitral awards by virtue of prior decisions appears less debated amongst national laws outside of France. In Switzerland, it appears uncertain whether any failure of the foreign tribunal to apply res judicata renders the award unenforceable (as for set aside) or this will only be the case if the foreign arbitral award concerns the very same cause of action than the prior decision (as for foreign judgments). *Fomento*'s limited coverage implies the latter solution.[558] Common-law jurisdictions equally contain limited submissions. Given the limited English jurisprudence, scholarship proposes to apply foreign judgment principles comprehensively.[559] In the US, the matter remains unattended by the Draft Third Restatement on Arbitration. In *Coutina v. Marcus Trading*, the District Court of Connecticut examined a US judgment's entire preclusive effects as a ground against the recognition of a China International Economic and Trade Arbitration Commission (CIETAC) award, yet rejected the applicability.[560]

162. In any case, the primary framework for discussing defences against foreign arbitral awards should be the NYC. After all, Article V stipulates that only the grounds mentioned can hinder the recognition of a foreign award. In this regard, Italy's proposal to address conflicting decisions in the Convention was explicitly rejected during the

553. *Ackerman v. Ackerman*, 517 FSupp 614, 623-626 (S.D.N.Y.1981), aff'd 676 F.2d 898 (2d Cir. 1982). *See Derr v. Swerek*, 766 F.3d 430 (5th Cir. 2014) (subject matter were different).
554. *Byblos Bank Europe SA v. Syrketi*, 12 Misc3d 792, 798 (NYS2d 2006), aff'd as modified 837 NYS2d 54 (2007).
555. Restatement (Second) Conflict of Laws, § 114 Comment d ('It is uncertain whether the rule of this section will be applied to judgments rendered in a foreign nation.'). *See* on comity as the basis in contrast to the Full Faith and Credit Clause *Hilton v. Guyot*, 159 U.S. 113 (1895) with reference to Story, *Commentaries* § 28; Born and Rutledge, *International Civil Litigation in* U.S. *Courts* 1115.
556. Restatement (Third) Foreign Relations Comment g ('If a later foreign judgment otherwise entitled to recognition in a court in the United States conflicts with an earlier sister-State judgment, there is no principle requiring automatic preference for the sister-State judgment.').
557. *Uniform Money Judgments Recognition Act*, NYCPLR, s. 5304(b)(5). *See also In re Bruetman*, 259 BR 649, 670 (NDIll BrtcyCt 2001).
558. ATF 127 III 279, *Fomento de Constucciones y Contratas SA v. Colon Container Terminal SA* [E.2.b.] ('It is contrary to public policy that there are within a given legal system two conflicting judicial decisions *in the same action* and between the same parties that are equally and simultaneously enforceable.') *Contra* Berger and Kellerhals, *Arbitration in Switzerland* (2098) ('recognition and enforcement may be refused if the foreign award disregards the conclusive and preclusive effects of an earlier judgment or arbitral award').
559. *Dicey Morris and Collins* [16-123].
560. *Coutino Caro & Co. USA Inc. v. Marcus Trading Inc*, 2000 WL 435566 (D Conn).

drafting process.[561] Hence, again, nothing but the public-policy exception under Article V(2)(b) NYC might be facilitated. Whilst there is no authority to suggest that an award will be already unenforceable when it disregards an earlier decision's preclusive effects in its reasonings, the few statements submitted on this issue assume that foreign arbitral awards are unenforceable under Article V(2)(b) NYC when they are mutually exclusive to an earlier decision.[562] Yet, the leading case against the relevance of conflicting decisions under the Convention is *Tema Frugoli*. In this case, the Milan Court of Appeal enforced a CIETAC award for damages and rejected the argument that an earlier SCC award stipulating the debtor's non-liability could trigger the Italian implementation of Article V(2)(b) NYC.[563] Subsequently, the *Corte di cassazione* reversed this decision, yet merely because it held the arbitration clause to stipulate an implicit fork-in-the-road provision.[564]

163. As a final word on uniform law, there is a widespread debate whether Article 45(1) Brussels Ibis Regulation overrides national laws when an irreconcilable arbitral award is invoked against an EU judgment. Due to the provisions' wording ('judgments') and Article 1(2) lit. d Brussels Ibis Regulation,[565] some scholars state that European judgments can be recognized regardless of arbitral awards.[566] Other scholars advocate that the Brussels Ibis Regulation contained a *lacuna* for arbitral awards.[567] The final opinion favours an application of Article 45(1) BR *mutatis mutandis*.[568] It can

561. *Proposed Amendment to Draft NYC from Italia*, 29 May 1958, UN Doc E/Conf./26/L.38 ('add [to now Art. V]: [g] The arbitral award is incompatible with a judicial decision applying to the same parties and the same subject matter, rendered in the territory of the State where the award is relied upon.').
562. Cf. TF, 11 October 2011, 5A_427/2011, [2013] ASA Bull. 404, [7.2]; Russian Federal Arbitration Court - Northwestern District, *O & Y Investments Ltd v. OAO Bummash*, 10 December 2005, (2008) XXXIII Y.C.A. 687, [18] ('the existence within the territory of the Russian Federation of judicial acts of equal legal force that contain mutually exclusive holdings [...] would contradict [...] an inalienable part of public policy of the Russian Federation.'); Bollée, (2007) Rev. Arb. 817 (*'L'utilisation de l'exception d'ordre public [...] n'apparaît pas infondée.'*); Mankowski, (2014) SchiedsVZ 216. Otto and Elwan in Kronke et al. (eds), *Recognition and Enforcement* 393 citing Chinese Supreme People's Court, (2008) Min Si Ta Zi No. 11 and Chilenean Supreme Court, Rol 2087 (1999). Cf. Schlosser, in *Stein and Jonas* [363]. *Contra Born* 3681.
563. CA Milan, *Tema Frugoli SpA v. Hubei Space Quarry Industry Co. Ltd.*, 7 February 1999, (2001) XXVI Y.C.A. 807, [7] ('It can be [...] that the award at issue is at odds with the award rendered by the Stockholm arbitral tribunal, which was already recognized in Italy. This circumstance, however, does not hinder recognition of the CIETAC award, since it is not one of the grounds for refusing recognition listed in Art. 839 (4) nos 1 and 2(3) and in Art. 840 CCP') and Note 4 ('*Note General Editor*. Arts 839 and 840 CCP are considered implementing Art. III and v. of the New York Convention in Italy.').
564. Corte di Cassazione, *Tema Frugoli SpA, in liquidation v. Hubei Space Quarry Industry Co. Ltd*, 7 February 2001, (2007) XXXII Y.C.A. 390, [8].
565. 'This Regulation shall not apply to [...] arbitration'.
566. Assuming such construction, the Heidelberg Report on the Regulation's recast even stated that it were not preferable to defer to conflicting arbitral awards, *see* Hess, in *Heidelberg Report* [129] (potential deferral to annulment proceedings might delay the dispute). Notably, one of the Heidelberg Report's authors favours an extension of the provision to *domestic* arbitral awards, *see* Schlosser in Schlosser and Hess (eds), *Europäisches Zivilprozessrecht* Art. 45 EuGVVO [30].
567. Cf. Bollée, (2007) Rev. Arb. 808 [7]; Briggs and Rees, *Civil Jurisdiction and Judgments* [7.16].
568. Francq in Magnus and Mankowski (eds), *Brussels Ibis Regulation* Art. 45 [65a]; Kropholler and von Hein, *Europäisches Zivilprozessrecht* Art. 34 EuGVVO [60]; Lazic, (2012) 29 J. Int'l Arb. 21;

refer to Recital (12) BR,[569] the conflicting obligations under the NYC and Article 73(2) BR[570] as well the leading ECJ case *Hoffmann v. Krieg*[571] where the divorce judgment was equally outside the Regulation's scope. Yet, the French Supreme Court rejected a domestic arbitral award as a ground for irreconcilability under Article 34(1) lit. c Lugano Convention in *GAT Congo*.[572] Notably, it did not have to decide whether national law could apply. Hence, deferring to an earlier arbitral award under national law remains possible.[573]

164. As an overall conclusion on the conflict of decision in the arbitration context, two comparative tendencies can be summarized. *First*, out of two decisions it will usually be the earlier that enjoys priority, regardless of its origin, regardless of its nature as judgment or arbitral award. *Second*, the earlier decision will be perceived as overriding if it is irreconcilable. By contrast, there is only limited authority that the disregard of an earlier decision within the mere reasonings of the latter decision allows to hold the latter unenforceable.

[C] Irreconcilability as an Implementation of Res Judicata's Starting Point

165. The widespread referral to irreconcilability as the decisive criterion for a conflict of decisions inclines to specify its scope and its interaction with res judicata. For instance, French doctrine's distinction between the situation that an arbitral tribunal has *disregarded* res judicata, on the one hand, and that it has rendered an arbitral award *irreconcilable* with another decision, on the other,[574] begs the question whether the two situations truly are as distinct as they are sometimes displayed. This depends upon the definition of irreconcilability. Unfortunately though, it has been summarized:

> To date, the amount of jurisprudence is too weak in order to draw any definitive conclusion on the operation of irreconcilability in arbitration.[575]

Lew Mistelis and Kröll [19.77]; Mankowski, (2014) SchiedsVZ 216; Teixeira de Sousa and Hausmann in Simons and Hausmann (eds), *Unalex* Art. 34 [69]; van Houtte, (1997) 13 Arb. Int'l 90.

569. 'This Regulation should not apply to any action or ancillary proceedings relating to, in particular, the establishment of an arbitral tribunal, the powers of arbitrators, the conduct of an arbitration procedure or any other aspects of such a procedure, nor to any action or judgment concerning the annulment, review, appeal, recognition or enforcement of an arbitral award.' Defences *by virtue of* awards are missing.
570. 'This Regulation shall not affect the application of the 1958 New York Convention'.
571. ECJ, 4 February 1988, *Hoffmann*, C-145/86, EU:C:1988:61, [22] (emphasis added).
572. Cass. (1e civ.), 4 July 2007, [2007] Rev. Arb. 806.
573. Bollée, (2007) Rev. Arb. 817-820.
574. *See supra* [153].
575. Debourg, *Les contrariétés de décisions* [442] ('*Le vollume de la jurisprudence rendue en matière d'arbitrage est à ce jour trop faible pour en tirer des conclusions définitives.*').

166. This apparent vacuum and the origin of irreconcilability[576] incline to take a comparative look at the discussion under Article 45 lit. c Brussels Ibis Regulation. The leading ECJ case *Hoffman* defined irreconcilability autonomously as *'entail[ing] mutually exclusive legal consequences'*,[577] notably although the respective divorce and maintenance judgments had no conflicting dispositifs.[578] Beyond this outset, irreconcilability remains to be extensively addressed in jurisprudence. As noted by the *Heidelberg Report*:

> The sparse practice [...] may be explained by the fact that the provisions on pendency are generally respected.[579]

167. Most particularly, the ECJ and official reports remain yet to specify how to assess the 'mutual exclusiveness' of two monetary judgments.[580] The dispositifs do not suffice. Therefore, many authors advocate that the interpretation of 'mutual exclusive consequences' in the sense of *Hoffmann* can only occur by virtue of national res judicata doctrines.[581] Correspondingly, a prominent English textbook uses irreconcilability and res judicata conflicts as synonyms.[582]

168. The accessory nature of irreconcilability has also been expressed in arbitration scholarship, particularly by Pierre Mayer's persuasive *'tri-partite distinction'* of: (i) absolute conflicts (impossible in monetary matters), (ii) material conflicts of monetary decisions' dispositifs and (iii) intellectual conflicts of underlying reasons.[583] 'Absolute

576. Niboyet, (2012) Rev. Arb. 576 submits that the Brussels Regime served as French law's role model.
577. ECJ, 4 February 1988, *Hoffmann*, C-145/86, EU:C:1988:61, [22] (emphasis added).
578. *See* Schack, (1989) IPRax 141. Hence, the Attorney General advocated at [11] of its submission that factual irreconcilability might exceed res judicata.
579. Hess in Hess Pfeiffer and Schlosser, *Heidelberg Report* [563].
580. The *Jenard Report* provides the example that a judgment allowing damages is irreconcilable with another judgment declaring the contract invalid, *see Jenard Report* 45. For the jurisprudence in Member States on the Brussels I Regulation *see* Francq in Magnus and Mankowski (eds), *Brussels Ibis Regulation* Art. 45 [68].
581. Kropholler and von Hein, *Europäisches Zivilprozessrecht* Art. 34 [49]; Leible in Rauscher (ed.), *Europäisches Zivilprozess- und Kollisionsrecht* Art. 45 Brüssel Ia-VO [63]. Cf. Gottwald, in *Münchener Kommentar* Art. 34 EuGVVO [50] (*'Unvereinbarkeit besteht danach beim Widerspruch rechtskraftfähiger Entscheidungssätze und nur im Einzelfall auch bei besonders krassen Widersprüchen in den Entscheidungsgründen.'*); Hess in Schlosser and Hess (eds), *Europäisches Zivilprozessrecht* Art. 45 [31, 32]; Koch, *Unvereinbare Entscheidungen* 32-33. Althammer, *Streitgegenstand und Interesse* 650-691 with comprehensive references to other proposals.
582. *Ceshire North and Fawcett* 568-569.
583. Mayer, (2013) 4 J. Int Disp Settlement 407 [6-8] ('First there is what can be called an absolute conflict, meaning that the decisions cannot both be enforced: the enforcement of one of them makes it impossible to enforce the other one – physically impossible. It is to be noted that there can be no absolute conflict between two monetary decisions. If an award orders the Respondent to pay 500 as damages to the Claimant, and another award orders the same Respondent to pay 1000 to the same Claimant for the same cause, it is not impossible to enforce both awards. [...] However, in this example there is still a conflict, of a second kind, in that the operative parts of the decisions, the "orders" in the strict sense ("le dispositive"), are incompatible, materially incompatible: to enforce one is necessarily to ignore the other one, to deprive it of its object. [...] The third kind of conflict, by contrast, is purely intellectual. An intellectual conflict consists in the existence of two logically incompatible statements in the decisions (either in the dispositive part or in the reasoning).'). Adopted by Mantilla-Serrano, in

conflicts' can be determined on a purely factual basis in that it is *physically* impossible to enforce both decisions. Beyond them, material conflicts (triggering irreconcilability) need to be distinguished from intellectual conflicts (*not* triggering irreconcilability). Since, in monetary matters, the dispositif does not suffice, the cause of action is decisive. Thus again, material conflicts are *accessory* to res judicata's outset. They arise if a follow-up tribunal has not applied res judicata's outset in order to preclude a duplicative claim. This strengthens the above-mentioned position that irreconcilability has to refer to some applicable law for the cause of action.

169. To return to the main focus of this examination, two decisions might certainly cause conflicts even if rendered between distinct parties.[584] Unfortunately, however, the specific operation of irreconcilability in such multi-party scenarios is highly uncertain. Primarily, the aforementioned differentiation allows inferring that *absolute irreconcilability* is independent from party identity. Let us take the example that two arbitral awards, applied for by two distinct claimants, order the same respondent to deliver the very same unique good to each claimant. Here, it is factually impossible for the defendant to comply with both awards. They are irreconcilable although res judicata would undisputedly apply between the respective parties only. Therefore, irreconcilability can exceed a prior decision's res judicata. The assessment becomes more uncertain, however, when *material conflicts* of the decisions' (monetary) dispositifs are at stake. In European civil procedure, the ECJ's *Drouot* jurisprudence[585] inclines that distinct legal personalities could be overcome when the interests are identical. Outside of the Brussels regime, however, precedence is scarce. One scholarly observation inclines to understand irreconcilability broadly.[586] These concepts might, for instance, justify that an arbitral award rejecting a claim against a debtor and an eventual judgment affirming the creditor's claim against the surety were irreconcilable because the debtor might be obligated to reimburse the surety for complying with the judgment. Yet, the generally accessory nature of material conflicts and res judicata incline otherwise. There are reasonable grounds to argue: but for case scenarios of *absolute conflicts*, irreconcilability applies only where the prior decision's res judicata would have extended to the subsequent proceedings.

Procédures parallèles et décisions contradictoires 33. *See* on a comparable distinction under French judgment principles Debourg, *Les contrariétés des décisions* [67].

584. *See* Debourg, *Les contrariétés des décisions* [43] (*'il n'est pas indispensable que les litiges opposent des parties identiques pour fair craindre un risque de contrariété'*). *See supra* [52-53].

585. *See supra* [75].

586. Debourg, (2013) Rev. Arb. 426 (*'[…] il peut parfaitement y avoir inconciliabilité de décisions, alors même que les parties aux procédures diffèrent, ou encore que les demandes portent sur un objet ou reposent sur une cause différente. En définitive, l'inconciliabilité peut résulter de l'existence d'un simple lien de connexité entre deux procédures.'*).

§2.06 INFERENCES: A PROCEDURALIST FRAMEWORK OF FORUM COORDINATION

170. Res judicata is the primary means for sequential Forum Coordination in that a tribunal seized with a previously adjudicated dispute has to defer to the latter. Res judicata originates in litigation. In arbitration, many of its aspects are handled by a transfer of procedural rules. Most importantly, arbitral res judicata's consequences (e.g., the applicability of issue preclusion) and its safeguard through irreconcilability correspond to judgment principles. Therefore, one might describe arbitral res judicata as a *proceduralist means of Forum Coordination*. However, a welter of aspects has revealed that res judicata's operation in arbitration frequently demands genuine solutions, particularly with regard to its requirements, relief procedures and cross-border relevance. This strengthens the perspective that arbitral res judicata cannot always be handled by a swift referral to proceduralist doctrines. Particularly, res judicata cannot be both a reason for and a consequence of arbitration's juridicity. Instead, each topic has to be examined as to its susceptibility for procedural doctrines. For this examination's topic of arbitral awards' third-party effects, these inferences necessitate to take the rules on judgments' third-party effects as the outset in the following Chapter and then examine the transferability to arbitration in Part II.

§2.07 CONCLUDING THESES

(1) The doctrine of res judicata prevents duplicative claims. Furthermore, it bars the re-litigation of claims that arise as incidental matters in subsequent proceedings.[587]

(2) The divide between common and civil law concerns the extensions of the initial rule by virtue of (i) a cause of action detached from the initial relief requested, (ii) issue preclusion and (iii) preclusion of arguments not adjudicated (abuse of process). Common law seeks to *extend the effect* of litigation, civil law seeks to *focus the content* of litigation.[588]

(3) Jurisdictions concur that the doctrine of res judicata as established in procedural law equally applies to arbitral awards. As a justification, a blanket referral to arbitration's juridicity is insufficient. Not only is this juridicity highly problematic when it comes to *international* arbitration, the referral would also be circular in that res judicata cannot be both a justification for and a consequence of juridicity.[589]

(4) Accordingly, jurisdictions need to address the underlying interests. In litigation, res judicata is supported by both public and private interests of

587. *See supra* [96-97].
588. *See supra* [107-117].
589. *See supra* [118-124].

consistency, legal certainty and efficiency. In arbitration, the impact on public interests is scarcely debated.[590]

(5) When it comes to the requirements of res judicata, proceduralist rules undoubtedly receive modification in order to adjust the rules to party autonomy. Particularly, res judicata comprehensively extends to settlements and is at the parties' disposal.[591]

(6) When invoked before courts, foreign arbitral awards are subject to foreign judgment principles. Hence, res judicata does not require exequatur or confirmation. If undertaken nonetheless, they anticipate the incidental review of non-recognition grounds as it would otherwise occur when assessing the res judicata request.[592]

(7) The conflict of decisions is an indispensable annex to res judicata. Most rules concentrate on irreconcilability and award priority to earlier decisions. Particularly, Article V(2)(b) NYC mandates to deny recognition when the later decision is an arbitral award.[593]

(8) Whilst irreconcilability remains to be fully defined in jurisprudence, the major tendency in scholarship is to apply it *either* when it is factually impossible to implement two decisions on non-monetary claims, *or*, in monetary claims, when two decisions concern the same cause of action. Thus, the latter alternative sanctions that a tribunal failed to apply the outset of the doctrine of res judicata and allowed duplicative claims. In any case, irreconcilability of decisions rendered between distinct parties is scarcely specified.[594]

(9) In general, at the arbitral seat as well as in cross-border case scenarios, many aspects of res judicata in arbitration are handled by virtue of procedural doctrines. Yet, this transfer from civil procedure to arbitration is not self-sufficient but demands a case-by-case assessment of the underlying interests, rationales and practical concerns.[595]

590. *See supra* [125-128].
591. *See supra* [129-140].
592. *See supra* [143-149].
593. *See supra* [159-164].
594. *See supra* [165-168].
595. *See supra* [170].

CHAPTER 3

Judgments' Third-Party Effects as a Shift of the Participatory Burden

171. Although res judicata has in general created increasing comparative interest, its third-party scope has rather scarcely stood in the comparative spotlight. It is close to having not received any attention within comparative arbitration treatises.[596] Moreover, even in comparative *procedural* law, there is limited ground that the examination can build upon.[597] Such procedural foundation appears instantly necessary. Particularly, the previous Chapter has established that arbitration laws on res judicata heavily refer to proceduralist terminology, rationales and rules. Therefore, procedural law will reasonably lie at the heart of arbitration discussions on res judicata's third-party scope in the upcoming *Part II*. Accordingly, it constitutes the ambit of this Chapter.

172. Scholarship regularly refers to the comparative consensus that res judicata applies only between the formal parties to a process. In assessing the operation and invalidation of this *same-parties requirement*, the Chapter will contain two core submissions. Primarily, it understands res judicata's same-parties requirement as *a rule of due process* (*see* §3.01, *infra*). Therefore, it will take a functional perspective and extend its scope to every preclusive and conclusive effect impeding a third party's right to be heard, irrespective of whether national doctrine associates such effect with res judicata. Particularly, in a range of case scenarios, jurisdictions acknowledge *erga omnes* effects (*see* §3.02, *infra*). Moreover, in the particular case that a third party seeks to rely on a decision in its favour, common law affirms one-sided preclusion effects (*see* §3.03, *infra*). Effectively, it will only be in the remaining cases that arguments on res judicata's extension towards selected privies will arise. In this regard, the Chapter

596. *See* the exclusive exception with regard to German and U.S. law, Lühmann, *Die Rechtskraft des Schiedsspruchs* 113-183.

597. *See* Krause, *Urteilswirkungen gegenüber Dritten* (Germany, USA); Peiffer, *Grenzüberschreitende Titelgeltung* 176-280 (England, France, Germany); Zeuner and Koch, in *International Encyclopedia of Comparative Law*, 49-70.

predominantly outlines the functional criteria for handling complex transactions (*see* §3.04, *infra*).

173. The second core submission of this Chapter is that the extension of res judicata towards third parties is merely one out of several mosaics in assessing the exposure of multilateral transactions to litigation effects. Foremost, arguments about res judicata do frequently not even arise. Instead, parties can exercise ample coordinative opportunities for multi-party litigation. Vice versa, in the event that the third party would be exposed to a decision's outcome, procedural law awards the third party with comprehensive intervention possibilities. Therefore, this Chapter's functional inference from civil procedure is that *judgments' third-party effects merely shift the participatory burden* (*see* §3.05, *infra*).

§3.01 RES JUDICATA'S SAME-PARTIES REQUIREMENT

[A] A Rule of Due Process

174. From a comparative point of view, it is virtually undisputed that, in general, res judicata can exclusively apply when the parties to the previous and the subsequent proceedings are the same. In France, Article 1355 Civil Code establishes the triple identity test, i.e., of claim, cause of action and parties.[598] Correspondingly, in Germany, section 325(1) ZPO is commonly seen to refer to res judicata when it states that '*[t]he final judgment shall take effect for and against the parties [...].*'[599] Swiss jurisprudence equally subjects the non-codified doctrine of res judicata to the same-parties requirement.[600] This also holds true for Swedish[601] and Dutch[602] laws. In England, cause of action and issue estoppel are built upon common law's requirements of '*mutuality and privity*'.[603] Finally, the US Supreme Court expressed that:

> it is a principle of [...] jurisprudence that one is not bound by a judgment in personam in a litigation in which he is not designated as a party or to which he has not been made a party by service of process.[604]

598. '*L'autorité de la chose jugée n'a lieu qu'à l'égard de ce qui a fait l'objet du jugement. Il faut que la chose demandée soit la même; que la demande soit fondée sur la même cause; que la demande soit entre les mêmes parties.*' ('The res-judicata effect is restricted to a judgment's scope. This requires that the claimed object is the same; that the claim is based on the same grounds; that the claim is between the same parties [...].').
599. '*Das rechtskräftige Urteil wirkt für und gegen die Parteien* [...]'.
600. Cf. TF, 28 November 2013, 4A_545/2013, [E.2.2.2.] (rental contract) with further references.
601. Hobér, (2013) 366 Rec. des cours 136.
602. van den Velden, *Finality in Litigation* 105.
603. *Hunter v. Chief Constable of the West Midlands*, [1982] AC 529 (HL). *See* already *Penn. v. Lord Baltimore*, (1750) 1 Ves Sen 444 cited by Briggs, (2011) 354 Rec. des cours 128-129.
604. *Taylor v. Sturgell*, 128 S.Ct. 2161, 2166-67 (2008) citing *Hansberry v. Lee*, 311 U.S. 32, 40 (1940).

175. Less displayed than the rule's content is its rationale. It is particularly German scholarship,[605] US jurisprudence[606] and, very recently, the French Supreme Court[607] that elucidate the principle threatened by anything but a strict *inter partes* application of res judicata: the right to be heard (due process). In this regard, it is of the utmost importance to note that the right to be heard operates independently from the prior decision's adequacy and correctness. Instead, as a procedural guarantee, it secures the mere possibility to participate. A violation of due process is no violation of the right *for correct* decisions, but of the right *to influence* decisions. The factual interests protected by due-process considerations are plentiful: the third party might have provided additional factual or legal arguments against or in favour of a claim; the gathering of evidence might have lacked a certain expertise that the third party would have been able to provide; the parties might have agreed on certain settlements (or certain arbitrators) that the third party would have opposed. These means of influencing a decision are protected when national laws generally formulate the same-parties requirement for res judicata.

[B] An Incentive for Multi-Party Litigation and Third-Party Notices

176. From a practical perspective, parties considering to eventually invoke a decision towards third parties have an interest in preventing preclusion uncertainties. Therefore, they are well advised to join the third parties in the proceedings so as to undisputedly expose them to the decision's effects. The rules for admitting such plurality of parties have to balance the advantages for consistency against the disadvantages for the party facing numerous opponents:

> All systems therefore agree that plurality is permissible in certain cases only, where some form of connection exists between the various parties on either side.[608]

605. Calavros, *Urteilswirkungen zu Lasten Dritter*, 21-48; *Jauernig*, (1988) 101 ZZP 372; Lüke, *Die Beteiligung Dritter im Zivilprozeß* 94-98, 197-200; Marotzke, (1987) 100 ZZP 164; Schlosser, (1967) JZ 431; Wolf, (1971) JZ 405.
606. *Parklane Hosiery Co. Inc. v. Shore*, 99 S.Ct. 645, 649 (1979) ('It is a violation of due process for a judgment to be binding on a litigant who was not a party or a privy and therefore has never had an opportunity to be heard.'); *Martin v. Wilks*, 490 U.S. 755 (1989) ('part of our deep-rooted historic tradition that everyone should have his own day in court'); *General Foods Corp. v. Massachusetts Dept of Public Health*, 648 F.2d 784, 792 (1st Cir. 1981) ('The due process clauses of the Fifth and Fourteenth Amendments protect a non-party from being bound by an *in personam* judgment unless in the underlying litigation he had directly or vicariously a full and fair opportunity to present evidence and argument').
607. Cass. (com), 5 May 2015, 14-16.644 (reference to Art. 6 EHRC). In scholarship *see* Boyer, (1951) 49 RTD civ 163; Douchy-Oudot, in *JCl procédure civil* Fasc 554 [131] (*'cette vérité est une 'vérité judiciaire' [...] on peut penser aussi que la vérité eût été différente si un tiers avait apporté des éléments d'information que le juge a ignorés'*).
608. Cohn, in *International Encyclopedia of Comparative Law XVI* [5-128].

177. Whilst, historically, there was certain scepticism towards exposing parties to multiple opponents at common law,[609] contemporary procedural laws comprehensively allow the joinder of claimants and defendants. The necessary form of connection is generally affirmed when the obligations or the legal rights of the dispute in question have some factual ties to more than one party.[610]

178. Subsidiarily, parties frequently consider exposing the third party to the litigation's outcome by virtue of third-party notices which, in return, enable the third party to participate as an intervener. Effectively, they are the prime tool for preventing inconsistent decisions in indemnity matters. In Germanic jurisdictions, they are known as *Streitverkündung* ('notice of dispute'). The resulting *Interventionswirkung* ('interventionist preclusion') is regarded as distinct to res judicata in national doctrine. Particularly, it is more extensive in that it precludes the third party from re-litigating *any issues* previously adjudicated unless the former party had insufficiently presented the arguments.[611] From a functional perspective, this might be seen as the one case scenario where German law in fact does acknowledge issue preclusion. French law both exceeds and restricts this concept by virtue of its two-fold mechanism. On the one hand, Articles 334-338 CPC allow a debtor to instantly claim indemnity within the very same proceeding from a third person (*appel en garantie*). If restricted to preclusion purposes, Article 331(2) CPC equally includes the third party as formal party to the dispute, yet being only exposed to res judicata (*appel en declaration de jugement commun*). English law also provides for defendants' opportunity to raise indemnity claims against 'additional parties'.[612] In addition, judges may at any time notify third persons in estate, trust and property disputes under Civil Procedure Rules (CPR), 19.8A(2-8.) thereby causing preclusion consequences.[613] Covering all concepts, US procedural law allows not only to raise claims against third parties turned into 'impleaders' (third-party practice[614]), but to serve any indemnitor with notice. At US common law,[615] such notice necessitates that a judgment binds the notified as a non-party (vouching in).[616]

609. *See* Hazard Leubsdorf and Bassett, *Civil Procedure* 236-241.
610. England: Art. 19.2(2) CPR ('if (a) it is desirable to add the new party [...] (b) there is an issue [...] connected to the matters in dispute [...]'); France: Cass. (comm.), 29 November 1949, [1950] Rec Dalloz 73 (criteria of *connexité*). Germany: ss 59, 60 ZPO (*Streitgenossenschaft*). Switzerland: Art. 71(1) ZPO ('*gleichartige Tatsachen oder Rechtsgründe*'). USA: Rule 20(a)(1), (2) FRCP ('any question of law or fact common to all plaintiffs [defendants] will arise in the action').
611. Germany: ss 74, 68 ZPO. Switzerland: Art. 77-80 ZPO.
612. *See* Rule 20(5-13) CPR.
613. CPR 19.8A(6) ('If a person served with notice of a claim does not acknowledge service of the notice he will be bound by any judgment given in the claim as if he were a party.').
614. *See* Rule 14(1) FRCP ('A defending party may, as third-party plaintiff, serve a summons and complaint on a nonparty who is or may be liable to it for all or part of the claim against it.').
615. For statutory provisions *see* Neiderman, (2003-2004) 23 J. L. & Com 1.
616. *See* § 57 Restatement (Second) Judgments ('[W]hen one person (the indemnitor) has an obligation to indemnify another (the indemnitee) for a liability of the indemnitee to a third person, and an action is brought by the injured person against the indemnitee and the indemnitor is given reasonable notice of the action and an opportunity to assume or participate in its defence, a judgment for the injured person has the following effects on the indemnitor in a subsequent action by the indemnitee for indemnification: (a) The indemnitor is estopped

179. In conclusion, broad possibilities of multi-party litigation compensate res judicata's strict application *inter partes*. Cases of connected liability such as guarantees, sureties and collaterals can be handled by joining multiple defendants. Cases of indemnity, either amongst connected debtors or along chains of contracts are adhered to by adjusted multi-party litigations. The latter allows either issue preclusion in Germanic jurisdictions (*Interventionswirkung*), the possibility for direct indemnity claims in France (*appel en garantie*) or both at common law. As a final, functional remark, the broader range of possibilities at common law might further reflect the latter's tendency to concentrate as much aspects as possible within the very same proceedings.[617]

§3.02 ERGA OMNES EFFECTS OF DECISIONS

180. Before the application and extension of the same-parties requirement in specific case scenarios is revisited, it is pivotal to note that the general *inter partes* standard is by no means as comprehensive as it frequently appears. Instead, there are several case scenarios where decisions do not even require a sufficiently close relationship of an actual and a third party in order to affect the latter. Here, jurisdictions acknowledge a certain range of effects erga omnes. Such comprehensive effect is instantly necessary when a legal status is being adjudicated upon. This general result is achieved throughout all jurisdictions examined. However, the differences amongst the conceptual pathways towards these results are striking (*see* [A], *infra*). Beyond legal status, jurisdictions are rather reluctant to acknowledge *erga omnes* effects, the standalone exception being French law's concept of *opposabilité* (*see* [B], *infra*). In any of these *erga omnes* effects, the discussion about due process, i.e. the functional heart of preclusion problems is displaced, from the *effect of* to the *participation in* litigation (*see* [C], *infra*).

[A] Adjudications on Legal Status: Res Judicata In Rem and Constitutive Effects

181. When a marriage is being dissolved, parenthood established or a corporation liquidated, a comprehensive efficacy erga omnes is required. For instance, it would be particularly burdensome for a person A if she or he were regarded as divorced towards person B, yet still regarded as married towards person C. Moreover, this would heavily impede the legal community's interest in consistency and reliability. Therefore,

from disputing the existence and extent of the indemnitee's liability to the injured person; and (b) The indemnitor is precluded from relitigating issues determined in the action against the indemnitee if: (i) the indemnitor defended the action against the indemnitee; or (ii) the indemnitee defended the action with due diligence and reasonable prudence.').

617. *See supra* [116].

jurisdictions generally concur that adjudications on such legal status[618] are not exposed to res judicata's same-parties requirement. Yet, there are substantial differences as to the conceptual implementation as well as to the actions covered by such *erga omnes* effects.

182. Common law distinguishes between personal judgments (in personam), on the one hand and judgments determining the status of a person, on the other. The latter are binding on everybody.[619] Moreover, common law acknowledges the distinct treatment of judgments determining the legal status of objects (in rem), for instance the determination of certain property. Such judgments equally operate against *'the whole world'*.[620] This very distinction between effects in personam and in rem already originated in Roman law where the *actio* could operate in these two manners.[621] In US doctrine, the genuine *erga omnes* effect of certain types of judgment was once titled *'legislative effect'* by Holmes J[622] and now addressed as *'transformational effect'* of judgments in scholarship.[623] Such classification comprises the exclusive impact that judgments' effects are not restricted to the same-parties requirement.[624] This is particularly stated in the Second Restatement containing two special rules for judgments in rem[625] and judgments determining personal status.[626] It is pivotal though that the efficacy erga omnes affects nothing but the main adjudication such as the divorce itself or the determination of ownership. That is, issue preclusion does not operate beyond the formal parties to the lawsuit.[627]

183. Germanic jurisdictions share common law's outset to distinguish between suits requesting a certain performance by a respondent (*Leistungsklage* – performance suit)

618. *See*, e.g., *Zeuner and Koch*, in *International Encyclopedia of Comparative Law XVI* [9.146] ('the very purpose of litigation [...] and is expressly mentioned in the judgment').
619. *Ampthill Peerage*, [1977] AC 547 (HL); Zuckerman, in *Halsbury's Laws of England XI* [1191-1195].
620. *Lazarus-Barlow v. Regent Estates Co. Ltd*, [1949] KB 465 (CA). Cf. Barnett, *Res Judicata* [3.35].
621. *See* Zimmermann, *The Law of Obligations* 7.
622. *Brigham v. Fayerweather*, 5 NE 265, 266 (Mass 1866).
623. Hazard Leubsdorf and Bassett, *Civil Procedure* 646.
624. *Ibid.*, 647.
625. Restatement (Second) Judgments, § 30(1) ('A valid and final judgment in an action based only on jurisdiction to determine interests in a thing is conclusive as to those interests with regard to all persons, if the judgment purports to have that effect [...]').
626. Cf. Restatement (Second) Judgments, § 31(2) ('A judgment in an action whose purpose is to determine or change a person's status is conclusive with respect to that status upon all other persons, with the following qualifications: (a) If a person has, under applicable law, an interest in such status such that he is entitled to contest its existence, the judgment is not conclusive upon him unless he was afforded an opportunity to be a party to the action; (b) When a statute, rule of court, or provision of the judgment itself limits the effect of the judgment with respect to other persons, the effect of the judgment is limited accordingly; (c) As against a person who is not entitled to contest the existence of the status, the judgment is not accorded effect to the extent it would result in unjust effect on that person's own status, rights, or obligations.'). *See Di Donato v. Di Donado*, 40 A2d 892, 894-895 (Pa Super Ct. 1945) ('An annulment establishes the invalidity of a marriage finally and certainly [...] generally and for every purpose'); *Cecil v. Cecil*, 356 P2d 279, 280 (Utah 1960). *See* for collateral attacks *Johnson v. Muelberger*, 340 U.S. 581, 587-588 (1951); *Cook v. Cook*, 342 U.S. 126, 127-128 (1951).
627. Restatement (Second) Judgments, § 30(3) ('conclusive between parties, in accordance with the rules of issue preclusion') and corresponding wording in § 31(3).

and suits establishing, modifying or terminating a certain legal status (*Gestaltungsklage* - constitutive suit). As at common law, judgments from the latter category are binding towards everybody.[628] However, there are two pivotal distinctions. Effectively, constitutive suits can exclusively cover a *person*'s status. Applications beyond family law concern the existence of a corporation (section 61 GmbHG), the validity of shareholders' resolutions (section 247 AktG) and the entitlement for a certificate of inheritance (section 2353 BGB). By contrast, although property rights certainly exist erga omnes in substantive law, ownership in property cannot be exercised in constitutive suits. With the exception of adjudications in enforcement and insolvency proceedings,[629] it will always be incidentally examined in performance suits against a certain defendant, e.g., for the return of property, the omission of interferences or the disgorgement of profits. Whilst the functional reason for this restrictive actionability of property in Germanic jurisdictions might be beyond this thesis' constraints, it should be mentioned that German substantive law compensates this shortcoming by other protections of property, most importantly the protection through the severability and abstract relationship of sales and transfer contracts as well as the protection of bona fide purchasers enhanced by evidence assumptions (section 1006 BGB).

184. The more fundamental distinction between Anglo-American and Germanic jurisdictions is that constitutive judgments raise certain effects in addition to res judicata. In Germany and Switzerland, res judicata can merely cover the cause of action, i.e., the *right to* a constitutive judgment. Hence, when the right to a constitutive judgment is re-litigated, e.g., after an unsuccessful constitutive suit or within a disgorgement claim, res judicata is applicable. However, when the *modified status itself* is re-litigated, it will be a genuine *Gestaltungswirkung* (constitutive effect) that precludes the objections to the constitutive judgment.[630] From this examination's functional point of view, such classification under national law constitutes no obstacle for jointly examining constitutive effects under German law and res judicata under other laws. Even scholars supporting the category of constitutive effects concede that this opinion is not predominant on the international level and that, more importantly, res judicata and constitutive effects have *'one important aspect in common [...] the prevention of inconsistent judgments'*.[631] This holds particularly true when re-stating the very reasons why certain modifications of the legal order (e.g., divorces) are subject to the courts' powers and others (e.g., contract terminations) are subject to the parties' will: court reservations guarantee public supervision and legal certainty.[632] With the latter rationale, constitutive effects precisely enforce what is functionally seen to be the

628. Rosenberg Schwab and Gottwald, *Zivilprozessrecht* [156.5]; Weber, in *Basler Kommentar* Art. 87[7].
629. Such adjudications have no constitutive effect, yet bind all creditors, s. 183(1) InsO; s. 856(4) ZPO.
630. Rosenberg Schwab and Gottwald, *Zivilrpozessrecht* [91.16]; Schlosser, *Gestaltungsklagen und Gestaltungsurteile*; *Zeuner and Koch*, in *International Encyclopedia of Comparative Law XVI* [9.146-48].
631. *Zeuner and Koch*, in *International Encyclopedia of Comparative Law XVI* [9.149].
632. Cf. Schlosser, *Gestaltungsklagen und Gestaltungsurteile* 32. *See* Basedow, *Die Anerkennung von Auslandsscheidungen*, 7 et seqq.

cornerstone of res judicata.[633] In conclusion, jurisdictions concur that certain suits modifying a legal status need to preclude the re-litigation of this status erga omnes.

[B] The French Doctrine of *opposabilité*

185. Under French law, res judicata (*autorité de la chose jugée*) was discussed to comprise *autorité absolue* (absolute preclusion) in certain cases.[634] Yet, the implementation of status adjudications occurs distinctively, and potentially more boldly. Though heavily discussed, French doctrine acknowledges an effect titled *opposabilité* (effectiveness). Whilst there are still concessions that *'the concept constitutes hardly more than a guiding principle'*,[635] it essentially stipulates: the modification of the legal order established within a judgment's dispositif can be invoked against and by everybody.[636] Potentially, this doctrine might build upon the understanding that judgments immediately modify the legal order of substantive rights.[637] From a functional perspective, *opposabilité* applies in no less than three scenarios.

186. *First*, the doctrine of *opposabilité* is French law's vehicle in order to guarantee that the establishment, modification or termination of a legal status by a court operates erga omnes. Then, it will overlap with the previously mentioned constitutive effect or res judicata in rem. *Second*, the doctrine exceeds legal status. It applies in all situations where the consequences established by the judgment become incidentally relevant, even if a judgment is only supposed to adjudicate private obligations. Primarily, this allows to handle scenarios where other jurisdictions averse to this doctrine can only speak of 'factual effects', namely when the obligations imposed by a judgment trigger certain provision of substantive law. Such provision can either explicitly depend upon a prior decision such as suspension of limitation periods, or only comprise a broad ground for legal consequences that is regarded as triggered by a prior decision such as impossibility, hardship or force majeure.[638] To a certain degree, the distinction between such factual effects and the *third* application is blurring. The doctrine of opposabilité also applies in case scenarios where other jurisdictions examine the requirements for an application of res judicata. For instance, decisions between a

633. *See supra* [101].
634. Cf. Lobin and Desdevises, in *JCl procédure civil* Fasc 500-90 [41].
635. Bollée, (2015) Rev. Arb. 702 (*'la notion d'opposabilité n'exprime guère plus qu'une idée directrice'*).
636. Boyer, [1951] RTD civ 163; Duclos, *L'opposabilité*; Héron and Le Bars, *Droit judiciaire privé* [361]; Loquin, in *JCl procédure civile* Fasc 1042 [38] (*'Ce qui est opposable aux tiers, c'est seulement la situation juridique créée par le jugement ou la sentence. [...] Il [l'effet] figure dans le dispositif de celle-ci.'*); Roland, *Chose jugée et tierce opposition*.
637. *See* Bollée, [2015] Rev. Arb. 703 (*'pour quelle mystérieuse raison le droit devrait-il par principe ignorer une norme dont il a lui-même permis la naissance?'*); Jarrosson, [2007] 8 Procédures No. 12 [34]; Goutal, (1988) Rev. Arb. 439.
638. *Infra* Chapter 7.

debtor and a creditor can be invoked against and by a guarantor as a fact.[639] A functionally comparable exposure was once proposed by German scholarship as *Drittwirkung* (third-party exposure),[640] yet explicitly rejected by the Federal Court of Justice for sureties and sub-tenants as an impermissible application of res judicata *ultra partes*.[641] In addition, the French *Cour de cassation* has even held the prior reasonings susceptible to *opposabilité*, in a case scenario where common-law courts would have most probably applied issue preclusion.[642] In conclusion, the French doctrine of *opposabilité* (i) guarantees the efficacy of status adjudications erga omnes, (ii) allows that substantive law can stipulate further consequences for obligations imposed on or claims conferred to parties by a judgment despite their nature *inter partes* and (iii) applies in certain case scenarios that are perceived as applications of res judicata in other jurisdictions.

[C] Participation Possibilities as Due-Process Assessments

187. As a procedural guarantee, the principle of due process operates independently from the content of the procedure. It applies in traditional suits exercising monetary claims as well as in matters involving legal status. Since the latter cause *erga omnes* effects, other procedural means need to secure the adequate possibility for a third party to exercise its right to be heard. In this regard, national procedural law contains a sheer welter of mechanisms. The following, necessarily brief outline of national procedural law duly differentiates between protections exercised during the procedure causing the *erga omnes* effect (*pre-emptive protections*) and protections exercised subsequent to it (*retroactive protections*).

188. To commence with pre-emptive protections: the most effective way is to mandatorily turn certain parties into formal parties. Such approach is, for instance, exercised under Federal Rules of Civil Procedure (FRCP) 19(a)(2) which requires the court to join certain parties whose '*absence may as a practical matter impair or impede the person's ability to protect the interest*'.[643] Whilst plaintiff autonomy is the outset and provides the opportunity to restrict a lawsuit against one out of several joint debtors, factors which need to be outweighed are the interest of the absent party and society's interest

639. Cf. Cass. (2e civ), 14 January 1999, [1999] Bull. civ II No. 63 (*assureur subrogé*); CA Paris, 4 January 1960, [1960] Rev. Arb. 122; CA Paris, 21 May 1964, [1964] Rec Dalloz 602; Loquin, [1994] Rev. Arb. 248.
640. Cf. Rosenberg Schwab and Gottwald, *Zivilprozessrecht*, § 156 [35-36] ('*Aufgrund der Drittwirkung könne der Dritte [...] nicht behaupten, der erste Prozess sei zwischen den seinerzeitigen Parteien unrichtig entschieden worden. [...] Das Urteil zwischen Dritten ist [...] als Faktum zu beachten; dieses Faktum verändert nicht die objektive Beweislast zwischen den neuen Prozessparteien. Drittwirkungen sind mithin nicht als allgemeine prozessuale Wirkung, sondern nur aufgrund materiellrechtlicher Abhängigkeit anzuerkennen.*'); Schwab, (1964) 77 ZZP 124 et seqq.
641. BGH, [1996] NJW 395, 396; BGH, [1998] NJW 2972, 2973; BGH, [2010] NJW 2208.
642. *See infra* [238].
643. Established in conformity with *Provident Tradesmens Bank v. Patterson*, 390 U.S. 102 (1968).

in avoiding multiple litigation.[644] These interests demand to, for instance, join parties potentially claiming title to an action in rem.[645] In England and Wales, Rule 19.2(2)(a) CPR provides that everybody will be joined who is necessarily affected by the issues in dispute. A rule comparable in function, yet distinct in subject matter, can be observed under German law. Since property matters do not fall under constitutive suits, the main applicability is family law: section 7(2) No. 1 FamFG[646] obligates the family court to include all persons *directly affected* by the proceedings.[647] Moreover, the act contains another, technically distinct, yet equally protective rule. Under section 26 FamFG, courts need to establish the facts upon their own motion.[648]

189. If a court is not obligated to include a certain party upon its own motion, the relationship between judicial *erga omnes* effects and the right to be heard has been comprehensively assessed within a leading case before the German Constitutional Court. The case concerned the liquidation of a *GmbH* (private limited company) that occurred without the participation of a shareholder. The court ruled that third parties whose interests might be immediately affected by a constitutive effect either need to be notified of the proceedings or at least awarded an opportunity for appeal.[649] The former solution secures that third parties exercise their right for voluntary participation and has now become obligatory.[650]

190. The latter opportunity, i.e., the right to appeals brings the examination to retroactive protections. Appeal mechanisms compensating judicial *erga omnes* effects are widely known. In France, judgments' *opposabilité* necessitates such protection of third parties. In this regard, Article 582 CPC establishes the possibility for every person whose interest is affected by a decision's dispositif to appeal to the decisions by means of the *tierce opposition* (third-party appeal). Such third-party appeal includes a review on the merits of the case.[651]

191. Anglo-American's relief mechanisms are narrower in that they usually require a *direct* effect on the interests, but wider in that they do not require a review of the merits. In England, Rule 40.9 CPR provides that anybody '*who is not a party but who is directly affected by a judgment or order may apply to have the judgment or order set aside or*

644. Hazard Leubsdorf and Bassett, *Civil Procedure* 286.
645. Cf. *McShan v. Sherrill*, 283 F.2d 462 (9th Cir. 1960).
646. *Familienverfahrensgesetz* (Act on Proceedings in Family Matters and in Matters of Non-contentious Jurisdiction).
647. '*Als Beteiligte sind hinzuzuziehen […] diejenigen, deren Recht durch das Verfahren unmittelbar betroffen wird* […]'.
648. '*Das Gericht hat von Amts wegen die zur Feststellung der entscheidungserheblichen Tatsachen erforderlichen Ermittlungen durchzuführen*'.
649. *See* BVerfGE 60, 7; Pika, (2018) 118 ZZP 234.
650. Section 75(2) GmbHG referring to s. 246(4) AktG.
651. '*La tierce opposition tend à faire rétracter ou réformer un jugement au profit du tiers qui l'attaque. Elle remet en question relativement à son auteur les points jugés qu'elle critique, pour qu'il soit à nouveau statué en fait et en droit*'.

varied.' In this regard, property interests trigger the standing to seek a set aside.[652] Another example concerns estate matters.[653] In US law, the Second Restatement allows a:

> declaration that the judgment is ineffective [...] when: (1) the existence of the judgment jeopardizes a protectable interest of his; and (2) The character of his interest warrants his being given relief forthwith rather than on a future occasion.

192. Again, applications include property interests.[654] In conclusion, national procedural laws provide for a multi-tiered regime of participation guarantees in proceedings causing *erga omnes* effects. Effectively, it is not the fact that *erga omnes* effects exist, but the question whether a third party can exercise such participation possibilities that settle due-process interests. In some scenarios, laws contain *mandatory participation* provisions, for instance in family matters. In other scenarios, there are mere *participation possibilities* implemented through notifications, for instance in corporate matters. Moreover, national laws might contain wide relief procedures, for instance, as a compensation against the French *opposabilité* or common law's judgments in rem. If such compensations are not applicable to a third person, then the right to be heard will be determinatively regarded as subordinate. E.g., a creditor has no participation guarantee in divorce proceedings merely because the marital status might affect the debtors at his disposal. In such scenarios, the public interest in stability overrides the individual interest in participation.

§3.03 NON-MUTUAL PRECLUSIONS IN FAVOUR OF THIRD PARTIES AT COMMON LAW

193. A further invalidation of res judicata's *inter partes* principle concerns non-mutual preclusion. This term describes that whilst a judgment cannot by invoked *against* third parties third parties can rely on it *in their favour*. In this regard, common law facilitates the rule of *Henderson v. Henderson* (abuse of process) in order to allow parties to strike out a claim or certain arguments, which the claimant had previously lost against *another* party in another proceeding.[655] Conceptually, it is now well established that the rule's consequence overlaps with the traditional doctrine of res judicata in that both institutes seek to prevent re-litigation for public rationales.[656] The remaining difference

652. Cf. *Hepworth Group Ltd v. Stockley*, [2006] EWHC 3626 (Ch); *White Book* [40.9.1].
653. *Zuckermann* [23.36].
654. Restatement (Second) Judgments, § 76 comment a.
655. Cf. *Yat Tung Investment Co. Ltd v. Dao Heng Bank Ltd*, [1999] 1 WLR 1482 (CA); *Ashmore v. British Coal Corp*, [1990] 2 QB 338 (CA); *Asher v. Secretary of State for the Environment*, [1974] Ch. 208.
656. *Virgin Atlantic Ltd v. Zodiac Seats UK Ltd*, [2014] AC 160, [23-24] per Lord Sumption (UKSC).

is the standard applied:[657] whereas estoppel per rem judicatem builds upon well-defined rules, abuse of process operates under a discretionary, now *'merit-based'*[658] approach involving a number of factors. The leading decision *Aldi Stores* pointed out:

> [T]he fact that the defendants to the original action and to this action are different is a powerful factor in the application of the broad-merits based judgment.[659]

194. In a corresponding manner, the US doctrine of non-mutual issue preclusion (collateral estoppel, *Bernhard* rule) allows even a '*complete stranger*' to rely on a prior decision.[660] Both offensive (third party in former is a claimant in subsequent proceedings)[661] and defensive (third party in former is a *defendant* in subsequent proceedings)[662] non-mutual issue preclusion exist. The relevant issue must be identical to a prior issue, must have been necessary to a prior judgment and the opponent must have had full and fair opportunity to air the relevant evidence.[663] In the latter regard, there is a certain discretion of the subsequent court. Therefore, the Second Restatement offers an extensive set of criteria for the assessment. For instance, joint creditors[664] and third-party beneficiaries[665] are exposed to collateral estoppel. Yet, a general exception applies when the third party expressly refused to join the proceedings.[666]

---

657. *Zuckerman* [25.75-76] ('considerable overlap [...] distinction between rules and discretion').
658. *Gleeson v. Wippell*, [1977] 1 WLR 510, 515 per Sir Megarry V-C (HL). *See* generally *Johnson v. Gore Wood*, [2002] 2 AC 1 (HL); *Bradford & Bingley Building Society v. Seddon*, [1999] 1 WLR 1482 ('the task of the court [is] to draw the balance between the competing claims of one party to put his case before the court and of the other not to be unjustly hounded given the earlier history of the matter').
659. *Aldi Stores Ltd v. WSP Group plc*, [2007] EWCA Civ 1260, [10] per Thomas LJ. Applied in *Clutterbuck v. Cleghorn*, [2017] EWCA Civ 137.
660. Cf. *Parklane Hosiery Co. v. Shore*, 439 U.S. 322, 327-328 (1979); *Georgia-Pacific et al. v. Four-U-Packaging Inc*, No. 11-4394 (6th Cir. 2012); Restatement (Second) Judgments, § 29.
661. *See Bernhard v. Bank of America Nat Trust & Sav Ass'n*, 19 Sal2d 807 (Cal); Currie, (1957) 281 Stan L. Rev. 281 et seqq.
662. *See Parklane Hosiery Co. v. Shore*, 439 U.S. 322, [C] (1979) ('We have concluded that the preferable approach for dealing with these problems in the federal courts is not to preclude the use of offensive collateral estoppel, but to grant trial courts broad discretion to determine when it should be applied. The general rule should be that in cases where a plaintiff could easily have joined in the earlier action [...] a trial judge should not allow the use of offensive collateral estoppel.').
663. Cf. *French v. Jinright & Ryan*, 735 F.2d 435, 436 (11th Cir. 1984).
664. *Ibid.*, § 52, 56.
665. Restatement (Second) Judgments, § 56.
666. Restatement (Second) Judgments, § 29 ('The circumstances to which considerations should be given include those enumerated in § 28 and also whether: (1) Treating the issue as conclusively determined would be incompatible with an applicable scheme of administering the remedies in the actions involved; (2) The forum in the second action affords the party against whom preclusion is asserted procedural opportunities in the presentation and determination of the issue that were not available in the first action and could likely result in the issue being differently determined; (3) The person seeking to invoke favorable preclusion, or to avoid unfavorable preclusion, could have effected joinder in the first action between himself and his present adversary; (4) The determination relied on as preclusive was itself inconsistent with another determination of the same issue; (5) The prior determination may have been affected by relationships among the parties to the first action that are not present in the subsequent action, or apparently was based on a compromise verdict or finding; (6) Treating the issue as conclusively determined may complicate determination of issues in the subsequent action or

195. The need for common-law courts' discretion results out of the underlying interests. Taking res judicata's primary rationale of due process, the rule appears justifiable. The party exposed to non-mutual preclusion did in fact submit on the precluded aspects before court. The opposing, pivotal interest is equality: a third party to the prior proceeding is able to rely on a prior judgment although such third party would not be exposed to any detriments arising out of the decision. Equality even caused US authors to describe the equivalent US rule as *'[p]erhaps the most controversial development in preclusion law in the last century'*.[667] Moreover, scholars point out that a party *'is unlikely to invest anything like the same resources that he would invest if the same issue arose in a high value claim on the multi-track.'*[668] Yet, it stands against the protection of resources, the stability of the legal order and individual fairness that the Court of Appeal continuously holds:

> Mutuality may be a necessary component of issue estoppel, but it is not a requirement of the doctrine of abuse of process. [669]

196. By contrast, German scholarship rejects non-mutual preclusion for equality purposes.[670] This also induced the Svea Court of Appeal to uphold the second *CMS* award.[671] From a functional perspective though, it should be noted that German law allows providers of accessory securities to rely on judgments favourable to the main creditor, whilst they are generally not exposed to judgments rendered in favour of the creditor.[672] This is, e.g., equally the case in Greece.[673] In conclusion, common and civil law jurisdictions differ significantly in the evaluation of procedural res judicata effects *in favour* of third parties. Whilst common law allows such under the rationales of consistency and efficiency, civil law rejects them under considerations of equality of weapons. Yet, both worlds acknowledge exceptions: common law restricts the rule under discretionary standards; civil law extends the rule for certain collaterals.

---

prejudice the interests of another party thereto; (7) The issue is one of law and treating it as conclusively determined would inappropriately foreclose opportunity for obtaining reconsideration of the legal rule upon which it was based; (8) Other compelling circumstances make it appropriate that the party be permitted to relitigate the issue.').

667. Silberman and Stein, *Civil Procedure* 793.
668. *Zuckerman* [25.67].
669. *Kotonou v. National Westminster Bank plc*, [2015] EWCA Civ 1106, [59]. *See* on the mentioned rationales *Aldi Stores Ltd v. WSP Group plc*, [2007] EWCA Civ 1260, [16-31] per Thomas LJ.
670. Gottwald Rosenberg and Schwab, *Zivilprozessrecht* § 156 [37]; Otte, *Umfassende Streitentscheidung* 71; Schack, [1988] NJW 872; Stucken, *Einseitige Rechtskraftwirkung von Urteilen im deutschen Zivilprozess* 40.
671. Svea Court of Appeal, *Czech Republic v. CME*, T 8735-01, 15 May 2003, 42 ILM (2003) 919, 966. *See* on investment arbitration further *infra*, [545-552].
672. BGH, [1970] NJW 279; BGH, [2006] NJW-RR 1628, [11] (obiter).
673. Article 328, 896 Greek Code of Civil Procedure.

§3.04 TURNING THIRD PARTIES INTO EFFECTIVE PARTIES: PRIVY DOCTRINES

197. In the scenario that neither an *erga omnes* effect nor a non-mutual preclusion can be applied for, the specific operation of res judicata's same-parties requirement comes into play. Some third parties to the proceedings might be deemed so close to the litigating parties that they fall under res judicata's same-parties requirement. In other words, their connection to one of the litigants allows to regard the third party's interest in influencing the decision as neglectable. In this regard, the examination chooses the common-law term 'privy' to summarize these situations. A primary application and the regular focus of comparative scholarship[674] concern 'substitutions', i.e., the situation that a third party intentionally replaces the formal party *during* the proceedings (disclosed representation) or *after the* proceedings (succession). Such scenarios require extending res judicata (*see* [A], *infra*).

198. The application of res judicata in complex transactions involving multiple parties is more controversial. Not only do jurisdictions contain unsettled scenarios, they also comprise several divides and they differ on the relationship between substantive and procedural law (*see* [B], *infra*). Upon the outline of the deductible principles, the examination returns to the previously mentioned interaction between res judicata and intervention possibilities. In particular, it will submit that jurisdictions contain ample basis for privies to join as party or intervener (*see* [C], *infra*).

[A] Substitutions (Disclosed Representation and Succession)

199. In order to guarantee the continuity of adjudicatory effects, it is rather uncontroversial that anybody who succeeds to a former party by virtue of inheritance, corporate transformation or a transfer of particular contracts, receivables or property, should be exposed to res judicata. Otherwise, parties could easily dispose of the binding effects of litigation. In Germany, such rule is codified jointly with the very same-parties requirement of res judicata.[675] In Switzerland[676] and France[677] it is developed in jurisprudence. At common law, it is well established that cause of action and issue

674. *See* the references from Note 596.

675. Section 325(1) ZPO ('A judgment that has entered into force shall take effect for and against the parties to the dispute and the persons who have become successors after the matter has become pending.').

676. ATF 93 II 329, [E.3.b]; ATF 125 III 8, [E.3]; TF, 28 November 2013, 4A_545/2013, [3.2.1.] ('*L'effet inter partes de l'autorité de la chose jugée s'étend aux successeurs à titre universel des parties*'). Zingg, in *Berner Kommentar* Art. 59 ZPO [136].

677. Cass. (1e civ.), 5 November 1962, [1962] Bull. civ I No. 460; Cass. (1e civ.), 10 March 1969, [1969] Bull. civ I No. 105; Cass. (3e civ), 30 May 1969, [1969] Bull. civ III No. 436; Héron and Le Bars, *Droit judiciaire privé* [359].

estoppel do not only apply towards deemed parties,[678] but additionally to the detriment as well as to the benefit of so-called 'privies'. There are privies in blood, title, or interest.[679] The two former categories cover the situations of inheritances and transfer of property.[680] Successors to claims and contracts are regarded as privies in interest.[681] The US Supreme Court expressly exposed assignees to res judicata.[682] Universal successors are not mentioned, albeit affirmed in scholarship.[683] The Second Restatement mentions them as well as successors to property.[684] The latter case scenario raises the follow-up issue whether bona fide purchasers should be protected. If such issue is addressed in national law, it is affirmed.[685]

200. The further, albeit related case scenario concerns disclosed representations, for instance by virtue of proxies, estate or bankruptcy administration.[686] In this regard, national laws have to decide whether (i) the representing party and (ii) the represented party are bound to res judicata. Either way, a phrase within Article 1355 Cc's triple-identity test constitutes the basis for French doctrine. The rule states that res judicata requires '*the claim to be raised between the same parties, in the same capacity*'.[687] On the one hand, this allows that some formal parties in fact representing others will not be exposed to res judicata when eventually litigating in their own name. For instance, the Supreme Court rejected res judicata if the party first represented a corporation as its CEO and then litigated in his own name.[688] On the other hand, the reference to the parties' capacity allowed French doctrine to develop the rule that res judicata is extended in cases of *répresentation*.[689] Correspondingly, Germanic doctrines unanimously apply res judicata to extend res judicata towards the represented where the law itself or the represented permitted a representation by another in its own name (*Prozessstandschaft* – action on another's behalf).[690] Moreover, the US Supreme Court held that statutory schemes rendering a certain administrator the formal party to a

678. Barnett, *Res Judicata* [3.17] ('those who intervene and take part in the proceedings; those who insist on being added as a party and obtain an order to this effect; such as principal or employer; who direct one another, such as a servant or agent, to pursue litigation on their behalf').
679. *Carl Zeiss Stiftung v. Rayner de Keeler Ltd*, [1967] 1 AC 853, 910 and 936 per Guest LJ (HL).
680. Cf. *Bishop of Salisbury v. Phillips*, (1704) 90 ER 927; Handley, (2011) 127 LQR 90.
681. *Powell v. Wilshire*, [2005] QB 117, [25] per Latham LJ (CA) ('where title to goods is in dispute [...] a person claiming title is privy to the interests of those through whom he claims that title for the purposes of the operation of the doctrine of estoppel per rem judicatam but only if the title he claims was acquired after the date of the judgment.'); *Rohan v. Singh*, [2017] EWHC 176 (Ch); Handley, *Res Judicata* 147. Cf. *ILA Interim Report on Res Judicata*, 44, 48 and 52.
682. *Taylor v. Sturgell*, 128 S.Ct. 2161, 2164 (2008). Cf. *Small Business Admin v. Taubman*, 459 F.2d 991, 992 (9th Cir. 1972); *European American Bank v. Royal Aloha Vacation Club*, 704 FSupp 1233, 1245 (S.D.N.Y. 1989).
683. Wright and Miller, *Federal Practice & Procedure* § 4462.
684. Restatement (Second) Judgments, §§ 43, 55.
685. *See* s. 325(2) ZPO; Restatement (Second) Judgments, § 43 Reporter's Note.
686. Zeuner and Koch, in *International Encyclopedia of Comparative Law XVI* [9.108].
687. '*entre les mêmes parties, et formée par elles et contre elles en la même qualité*'.
688. Cf. Cass. (1e civ.), 7 January 1976, Bull. civ 1977 I No. 7.
689. Héron and Le Bars, *Droit judiciaire privé* [360] (Art. 1355 CC's wording: party 'quality').
690. Germany: Rosenberg Schwab and Gottwald, *Zivilprozessrecht* [156.20]. Switzerland: Habscheid, *Zivilprozessrecht* [509]; Zingg, in *Berner Kommentar* Art. 59 [139].

proceeding do not pre-empt the represented from being exposed to res judicata.[691] Finally, common law establishes that represented beneficiaries are privies in interest to the litigating trustee.[692]

201. The mentioned statutory representation regimes in estate or bankruptcy matters might regularly concern non-arbitrable matters. Moreover, even voluntary representation on another's behalf might face significant obstacles in arbitration, most importantly the necessary consent of the opponent. Therefore, the examination refrains from further comparisons of specific cases of representation. Instead, it concludes that national procedural law contains ample opportunities to extend res judicata towards successors and represented. Both scenarios share the functional basis that res judicata is (often) not merely extended, but rather *re-allocated*.

[B] Complex Substantive Relationships

202. In strong contrast to the general rule on res judicata, commercial reality and thereby substantive relationships operate multilaterally. Regularly, entire webs of interdependent relationships exist, for instance, involving insurances, corporate groups or collaterals. This raises the question whether res judicata can not only be re-allocated but will instantly apply between more than the formal parties to the procedures, in particular where they have not explicitly consented to being represented by a litigating party. In this regard, the constraints of this Chapter outside of arbitration law require foregoing an extensive case-by-case enumeration. Such will occur within the upcoming Chapter. Instead, the following paragraphs outline two opposing tendencies of national jurisdictions, i.e., one reconciliation predominantly undertaken under substantive law and one undertaken under procedural discretion.

203. The first tendency can be found within Germanic jurisdictions containing the constant reiteration that res judicata's same-parties requirement is indispensable beyond successions and representations. Particularly, res judicata cannot be extended against sub-tenants,[693] co-obligors[694] and sureties.[695] Yet, German jurisprudence has applied provisions of substantive law to affirm preclusive effects towards partnership

691. *Taylor v. Sturgell*, 128 S.Ct. 2161, 2164 (2008) citing further jurisprudence.
692. Cf. *Churchill & Sim v. Goddard*, [1937] 1 KB 92, 103 (CA); *Gleeson v. J. Wippell & Co. Ltd* [1977] 1 WLR 510 (Ch); *Young v. Murphy*, [1996] 1 VR 279, 285-287 (SCV).
693. Germany: BGH, [1996] NJW 395, 396; BGH, [2010] NJW 2208. Switzerland: ATF 93 II 329, [E.3.b].
694. Germany: s. 425(2) BGB. Switzerland: Guldener, *Zivilprozessrecht* 371; S Zingg, in *Berner Kommentar* Art. 59 [139].
695. BGH, [1998] NJW 2972, 2973; BGH, [2016] NJW 3158, [20-21] ('*Dementsprechend hat vorliegend die rechtskräftige Verurteilung der Hauptschuldnerin zur Folge, dass dieser die Einrede der Verjährung nicht mehr iSd § 768 I 1 BGB 'zusteht' und sie daher auch der Bürge nicht mehr geltend machen kann. [...] Entgegen der Auffassung der Revision ist dieses Ergebnis nicht Folge einer Rechtskrafterstreckung nach § 325 ZPO einer den Hauptschuldner verurteilenden Entscheidung zu Lasten des Bürgen.*').

members,[696] in leasing case scenarios,[697] in certain insurance case scenarios[698] and *in favour* of sureties.[699] In light of the restrictive wording of § 325(1) ZPO and the resulting justification on the basis of the substantive obligations, it is often submitted that such third-party preclusions were *not* cases of res judicata, but results of substantive law. Hence, such preclusions were not to be applied ex officio. This has been expressly affirmed by the Federal Court of Justice in leasing case scenarios and mentioned for insurance case scenarios[700] as well as sureties.[701] These statements can refer to § 69 ZPO, allowing an intervention of anybody exposed to res judicata '*under the rules of civil law*'.[702]

204. By contrast to such case-by-case analysis of substantive law, English and French laws contain a general invalidation of res judicata's same-parties requirement. Effectively, this allows third-party preclusions in cases where Germanic jurisdictions would reject them. Conceptually, such procedural standard largely pre-empts discussions on the relevance of substantive law. In France, res judicata can be extended under the concept of *répresentation*. In light of the already existing *opposabilité*, the most important implementation of extended res judicata is that the *tierce opposition* is barred,[703] provided that there was no fraudulent conduct to the third party's detriment.[704] Whilst the standard of *répresentation* had initially been developed for successions and disclosed representation, it provides certain discretion. Most critically, it also applies in situations where the actual party is deemed to have parallel economic interests to a third party.[705] In litigations, this has been, for instance, affirmed for joint debtors[706] and guarantors.[707]

205. This discretionary concept appears even exceedingly at common law where the application of res judicata towards privies in interest is allowed if there is a '*sufficient*

696. BGH, [2006] NZG 459, 460.
697. BGHZ 114, 57, 62 (to the detriment of leasor); OLG München, (1993) NJW-RR 123 (in favour).
698. *See* BGH, [1993] NJW 68, 69; s. 124(1) VVG.
699. BGH, [1970] NJW 279; BGH, [2006] NJW-RR 1628, [11] (obiter).
700. Zeuner and Koch, in *International Encyclopedia of Comparative Law XVI* [9.116] ('*the very purpose of the substantive contractual relation between insurer and the insured*').
701. Habersack, in *Münchener Kommentar zum BGB*; § 768 [11] Schack, [1988] NJW 870. *See* BGH [1970] NJW 279; Zeuner and Koch, in *International Encyclopedia of Comparative Law XVI* [9.137].
702. '*Insofern nach den Vorschriften des bürgerlichen Rechts die Rechtskraft der in dem Hauptprozess erlassenen Entscheidung auf das Rechtsverhältnis des Nebenintervenienten zu dem Gegner von Wirksamkeit ist, gilt der Nebenintervenient im Sinne des § 61 als Streitgenosse der Hauptpartei.*'
703. Cf. Goudal, [1988] Rev. Arb. 289. This is subject to the exception of fraud, *see* Cass. (1e civ.), 14 February 1990, [1990] Bull. civ I No. 42; Cass. (1e civ.); 10 December 1991, (1991) Bull. civ I No. 348.
704. Cass. (1e civ.), 14 February 1990, [1990] Bull. Civ No. 42, 31; Cass. (1e civ.); 10 December 1991, [1991] Bull. civ I No. 348.
705. Douchy-Oudot, in *JCl procédure civil* [143]. Cf. Héron and Le Bars, *Droit judiciaire privé* [360].
706. Cass. (com), 18 October 1982, [1982] Bull. civ IV No316; Cass. (1e civ.), 14 February 1990, [1990] Bull. civ I No. 42; Cass. (com), 30 October 2007, [2007] Bull. civ IV No. 229; Cass. (com), 25 November 2008, 08-14.583.
707. Cass. (1e civ.), 12 March 1974, [1974] Bull. civ I No. 83; Cass. (2e civ), 17 November 1977, [1978] Rec Dalloz 413; Cass. (1e civ.), 14 February 1990, [1990] Bull. Civ I No. 42, 31; Cass. (com), 27 September 2011, 10-21.686; Cass. (com), 16 October 2012, 11-22.062.

degree of identification between the parties'.[708] The resulting fact-based analysis has created '*a dearth of authority*'.[709] Yet, most authorities have rejected to regard third parties as privies in interest. In general, courts across the Commonwealth continuously affirm that the interest has to exceed a mere financial interest.[710] Upon this foundation, privy relationships have been, e.g., rejected for indemnification agreements,[711] sureties,[712] licensing relationships[713] and sister companies.[714] The most relevant case scenario where res judicata was extended was a solidary obligation in tort.[715]

206. Finally, the application of res judicata's same-parties requirement is applied most elaborately and yet most widely in US jurisdictions. Traditionally, they referred to privy assessments[716] regarded as:

> merely a word used to say that the relationship between one who is a party on the record and another is close enough to include the other within the res judicata. Privity connotes those so connected in law with a party to the judgment as to have such an identity of interest that the party to the judgment represented the same legal right.[717]

207. In the 2008 leading case *Taylor v. Sturgell*, the Supreme Court specified this standard and admitted no less than six exceptions.[718] In this regard, two exceptions open the floodgate for case-by-case discretion, namely extension by virtue of substantive relationships and 'effective control'. The former category has received extensive consideration, for instance in the Second Restatement.[719] Whilst it in the end causes no

---

708. Barnett, *Res Judicata* [3.22].
709. *Ibid.*
710. *Shiels v. Blakeley*, [1986] 2 NZLR 262, 268; *Parakou Shipping Pte ltd v. Jinhui Shipping and Transportation Ltd*, [2011] 2 HKLRD 1, [102-103]; *Effem Foods Pty Ltd v. Trawl Industries of Australia Pty Ltd*, (1993) 43 FCR 510.
711. *Gleeson v. J. Wippell & Co. Ltd*, [1977] 1 WLR 510 per Megarry VC (Ch). Approved by *Johnson v. Gore Wood & Co*, [2002] 2 AC 1, 32 per Bingham LJ (HL); *Secretary of State for Business, Innovation and Skills v. Potiwal*, [2012] EWHC 3723 (Ch).
712. Cf. *Bain v. Copper*, (1841) 8 M&W 751, 754 per Parke J.
713. *Mecklermedia Corp. v. DC Congress GmbH*, [1998] Ch. 40.
714. *Resolution Chemicals Ltd v. H Lundbeck A/S*, [2013] EWHC 739 (Pat).
715. *House of Spring Gardens Ltd v. Waite*, [1991] 1 QB 241 per Stuart-Smith LJ (CA); approved of by *Powell v. Wiltshire*, [2004] EWCA Civ 534 per Letham LJ; recognised by *Thomas and Agnes Carvel Foundation v. Carvel*, [2007] EWHC 1314 per Lewison J. (Ch).
716. Cf. *Parklane Hosiery Co. Inc. v. Shore*, 99 S.Ct. 645, 649 (1979).
717. *Anchor Glass Container Corp. v. Buschmeier*, 426 F.3d 872, 879 (7th Cir. 2005) with references.
718. *Taylor v. Sturgell*, 128 S.Ct. 2161, 2164 (2008) ('The rule against nonparty preclusion is subject to exceptions, grouped for present purposes into six categories. First, a person who agrees to be bound by the determination of issues in an action between others is bound in accordance with the agreement's terms. Second, nonparty preclusion may be based on a pre-existing substantive legal relationship between the person to be bound and a party to the judgment, e.g., assignee and assignor. Third, "in certain limited circumstances," a nonparty may be bound by a judgment because she was "adequately represented by someone with the same interests who [wa]s a party" to the suit. Fourth, a nonparty is bound by a judgment if she "assume[d] control" over the litigation in which that judgment was rendered. Fifth, a party bound by a judgment may not avoid its preclusive force by relitigating through a proxy. [...] Sixth, a special statutory scheme otherwise consistent with due process – e.g., bankruptcy proceedings – may "expressly foreclos[e] successive litigation by nonlitigants".').
719. *See* Restatement (Second) Judgments, §§ 43-57.

consequences unknown to other jurisdictions, the additional ground of 'effective control' has proven pivotal for corporate case scenarios.[720] Applying federal law, claim and issue preclusion have been applied towards 100% shareholding companies whose board of directors authorized the subsidiary's suit[721] and towards sister companies.[722] Such extension of res judicata beyond corporate personalities appears less likely under the other jurisdictions examined.

208. As a summary of this outline, there is a conceptual and an effective conclusion. *Conceptually*, some jurisdictions seek to handle complex substantive relationships by analysing whether substantive law *itself* demands third-party preclusion. By contrast to this approach from Germany, English and French laws have established broad discretion standards. Notably though, the immanent relevance for res judicata's application ex officio is limited, because English and French laws do not acknowledge it.[723] US law tends towards the latter approach without pre-empting further preclusions under substantive law, e.g., '*[t]o the extent required by the law of suretyship*'.[724] *Effectively*, critical categories where some jurisdictions do acknowledge a third-party preclusion that others would not are: solidary obligations (unknown in Germany), guarantees (only in France and US) as well as exceptional corporate control (only in US).

[C] Participation Possibilities as a Necessary Consequence of Preclusion Exposure

209. It is this examination's utmost contention that there is another side of the coin of privyship in multilateral transactions. It is already known from *erga omnes* effects: the possibility to join the very litigation triggering res judicata. In this regard, civil law is favourable to a broad opportunity for third-party intervention. In distinguishing between interventions where the intervener raises a claim for himself (*intervention principale*) and interventions where the intervener merely seeks to support the main party (*intervention accessoire*), French law allows interventions of third parties exposed to res judicata. In the latter case, Article 330(2) CPC requires that the intervener has '*an interest in protecting its rights through the support*'.[725] In this regard, the significant threat of being exposed to res judicata will reasonably justify the mentioned

720. Cf. Wright and Miller, *Federal Practice and Procedure* § 4460. Previously, the topic had also been addressed with regard to representation, *see* most recently *Hallinan v. Republic Bank & Trust Co*, 2007 WL 39302 (S.D.N.Y. 2007) which is potentially outdated after the Supreme Court's 2008 judgment.
721. *Astron Indus Associates Inc. v. Chrysler Motors Corp*, 405 F.2d 958 (5th Cir. 1968); *Mars Inc. v. Nippon Conlux Kabushiki-Kaisha*, 58 F.3d 616, 619 (Fed Cir. 1995); *Griswold v. County of Hillsborough*, 598 F.3d 1289, 1293 (11th Cir. 2010).
722. *Gulf Power Co. v. FCC*, 669 F.3d 320 (DC Cir. 2012) basing the decisions on two ratios, the third party's capacity as intervenor to the first proceedings as well as the corporate relationship.
723. *See supra* [137].
724. Restatement (Second) Judgments § 50(1)(b).
725. '*Elle [l'intervention accessoire] est recevable si son auteur a intérêt, pour la conservation de ses droits, à soutenir cette partie*'.

interest. It is precisely the same solution that applies under German law. Section 66 ZPO subjects the voluntary third-party intervention to the requirement that the intervener has a '*legal interest [...] in supporting a party*'.[726] Again, it is undisputed that everybody eventually exposed to res judicata has such legal interest,[727] particularly since § 69 ZPO addresses this very situation and declares the intervener to be a joint party.[728]

210. At common law, the matter of third-party intervention is more delicate. On the one hand, common law largely acknowledges it in matters of public relevance. This is functionally necessary since common law does not distinguish between civil and administrative litigation.[729] On the other hand, common law's focus on enforcing a claimant's remedy and regarding him as the '*master of the suit*' necessitates an aversion against third-party interventions.[730] Now, such aversion has vanished. English law allows any '*person who wishes to become a party*' (Rule 19.4(2)(b) CPR) to apply for such measure. The court's necessary[731] permission will be assessed under Rule 19.2(2) CPR. Either it must be desirable to join the third party in order to resolve all the matters in dispute or a critical issue involves the third party.[732] This provides ample ground to assume that the exposure of privies is a matter connected with the parties. Vice versa, it was held that an insurer could not claim to be joined when the process between the victim and the tortfeaser will not be conclusive on the insurer's liability.[733] In US federal law, it is equally the subject matter of the requests by the intervener that determine whether they are allowed to join. Under Rule 24(b)(1)(B) FRCP the '*claim or defence [has to] share with the main action a common question of law or fact*'. There is valid ground to additionally request an interest of the third party.[734] Given the relevance of due process in preclusion matters, there has been no objection towards the application on privies. In conclusion, parties exposed to res judicata can assert their right to be heard by initiating interventions.

---

726. '*Wer ein rechtliches Interesse daran hat, dass in einem zwischen anderen Personen anhängigen Rechtsstreit die eine Partei obsiege, kann dieser Partei zum Zwecke ihrer Unterstützung beitreten*'.
727. Althammer, in *Zöller* § 66 [11] with further references.
728. '*Insofern nach den Vorschriften des bürgerlichen Rechts die Rechtskraft der in dem Hauptprozess erlassenen Entscheidung auf das Rechtsverhältnis des Nebenintervenienten zu dem Gegner von Wirksamkeit ist, gilt der Nebenintervenient im Sinne des § 61 als Streitgenosse der Hauptpartei*'.
729. Cohn, in *International Encyclopedia of Comparative Law XVI* [5.186].
730. Hazard Jr Leubsdorf and Bassett, *Civil Procedure* 296 ('For the most part, the notion that third person might invite themselves into lawsuits between others ran counter to the Anglo-American notion that the plaintiff was the master of the suit.').
731. Rule 19.4(1) CPR ('The court's permission is required to remove, add or substitute a party [...].').
732. 'The court may order a person to be added as a new party if (a) it is desirable to add the new party so that the court can resolve all the matters in dispute in the proceedings; or (there is an issue involving the new party and an existing party which is connected to the matters in dispute in the proceedings, and it is desirable to add the new party so that the court can resolve that issue.').
733. *XYZ v. Various Companis sub nom PIP Breast Implant Litigation*, [2014] EWHC 4056 (QB).
734. Cf. Shapiro, (1968) 81 Harv L. R 721.

§3.05 FUNCTIONAL INFERENCES

[A] Res Judicata as a Shift of the Participatory Burden

211. The primary submission of this thesis is that res judicata should not be examined independently. Instead, comprehensive functional evaluations have to go beyond the legal institute examined and reveal the connections to related institutes.[735] For example, a comparative examination on the law of unjustified enrichment has to take into account necessities under property law and the potential principles of separation and abstraction.[736] Likewise, examinations on the *burden* of proof in procedural law cannot occur without the *means* of proof, i.e., the availability of document production and discovery.[737] In the same spirit, an examination on res judicata should be undertaken conjointly with intervention possibilities.

212. If a lawsuit between two parties would not comprise res judicata towards third parties, possibilities *for the parties* to join such third parties or apply for third-party notice compensate the parties. Vice versa, when res judicata is extended, *third parties* are compensated either pre-emptively (by the right to participate) or retroactively (through appeal mechanisms such as the French *tierce opposition*). Accordingly, the interests of the formal parties (consistency, legal certainty, efficiency) and the third party (due process) will not be undermined completely. The formal parties can always secure comprehensive effects. The third party will regularly be awarded with an opportunity to be heard. Hence, the exclusive question to be decided is: who bears the burden to exercise its right? Therefore, in this examination's contention, a judgment's third-party effect primarily regulates the *participatory burden*.

[B] Criteria for the Shift: Accessory to Substantive Law or Procedural Discretion?

213. When categorizing the cases where the participatory burden is shifted by virtue of a judgment's third-party effect, this examination submits to undertake a functional analysis by virtue of the underlying interests. In this regard, it can be stated that jurisdictions regularly balance consistency, legal certainty and efficiency (supporting res judicata), on the one hand, and due process (restricting res judicata), on the other. In some case, the balancing will be in favour of the former because it is deemed of overriding significance, e.g., for legal status. In other cases, the interests in res judicata are overriding because due process is subordinate in light of the parties' proximity, for instance in successions, disclosed representations or (if admitted) 'effective control' within corporate groups.

735. Cf. Basedow, (2016) 71 JZ 269; Kischel, *Rechtsvergleichung* 93-97; Michaels, in *The Oxford Handbook of Comparative Law* 339; Zweigert and Kötz, *An Introduction to Comparative Law* 34.
736. *See* Häcker, *Consequences of Impaired Consent Transfers* 25.
737. *See* IBA Rules on the Taking of Evidence in International Commercial Arbitration 5.

214. The litmus test appears in how to handle complex substantive relationship. In this regard, the examination reveals a two-fold distinction of the solutions available. On the one hand, particularly German-speaking authors submitted that some preclusion effects should be functionally regarded as effects under substantive law and were therefore distinct to the above-mentioned categories.[738] However, the substantive/procedural categorization cannot undermine due process, regularly a constitutional guarantee. Hence, also complex substantive relationships need to be justified from a due-process view. Thus, res judicata by virtue of substantive relationships should be understood as a *procedural reception of* substantive law. On the other hand, the broad discretionary assessments under French, English and US law only consider the substantive relationship as one out of several means for a case-by-case assessment. Here, the substantive relationship will equally be the ambit of a procedural reception, albeit not an automatic reception. Instead, the existence of a certain relationship is only one out of several aspects in addition to the specific knowledge and influence potentials in a certain case. Therefore, it is submitted that a functional differentiation of judgments' third-party effects should not differentiate between substantive and procedural effects, but between *automatic* and *discretionary* receptions of substantive relationships under procedural law.

[C] Transferability of the Shift: The Emissive Constraints of Arbitral Jurisdiction

215. Part I has revealed a fundamental dichotomy against which arbitral awards' third-party effects need to be evaluated. In civil procedure, such third-party effects are nothing but a shift of the participatory burden. If a third-party effect does *not* exist, the litigating party can regularly join or notify a third party. If a third-party effect *does* exist, the third party will regularly be able to intervene. In arbitration, however, such intrinsic connection to broad participation possibilities is inoperable. As established in *Chapter 1*, any participatory measure is subject to the jurisdictional constraints of arbitral tribunals. Yet, *Chapter 2* has established that the effects of arbitral awards will generally be assessed upon their proceduralist foundations. The resulting dichotomy between proceduralist res judicata and contractual jurisdictional standards will be the ambit of Part II.

§3.06 CONCLUDING THESES

(1) Generally, res judicata applies between the same parties to a dispute. This transnational rule is an implementation of the principle of due process.

738. Peiffer, *Grenzüberschreitende Titelgeltung* 234-236; Zeuner and Koch, in *International Encyclopedia of Comparative Law XVI* [9.137-41].

Correspondingly, any exception to the same-parties rule must be justified under due-process rationales.[739]

(2) Res judicata's same-parties requirement is suspended for adjudications on legal status. The interests in consistency and legal certainty demand *erga omnes* effects. In return, due-process interests demand to allow certain participation possibilities. This interaction appears even exceedingly in France where any judgment will be awarded effectiveness (*opposabilité*) erga omnes thereby allowing third-party appeals (*tierce opposition*).[740]

(3) Res judicata's same-parties requirement is furthermore suspended for non-mutual preclusions at common law. Due process is *not* at stake. Moreover, efficiency justifies that a party cannot re-raise unsuccessful arguments against other parties. Yet, it violates equality. Therefore, civil law regards such principle as generally not preferable.[741]

(4) Across jurisdictions, res judicata will regularly be extended towards successors and in scenarios of disclosed, statutorily mandated or voluntary representation. In these scenarios, the third parties' right to be heard appears fulfilled.[742]

(5) By contrast, national assessments of complex substantive relationships differ significantly. It will heavily depend on the applicable law whether e.g., co-obligors, guarantors, sureties, subsidiaries or parent companies will be exposed to res judicata.[743]

(6) In addition, jurisdictions also comprise a conceptual antagony: some jurisdictions seek to handle the scenarios and the necessary balancing of the procedural interests by allowing a comprehensive, discretionary assessment focusing on the third party's proximity thereby its interest in due process. By contrast, others instantly refer the substantive position.[744]

(7) In any case, third parties will regularly be compensated for their exposure to res judicata by intervention possibilities. Vice versa, the formal parties are compensated for restricted res judicata effects by joinder and notice possibilities. Hence, res judicata's extension towards third parties should be regarded as *a shift of the participatory burden.*[745]

739. *See supra* [174-175].
740. *See supra* [180-192].
741. *See supra* [193-196].
742. *See supra* [199-201].
743. *See supra* [202-208].
744. *See supra* [213-214].
745. *See supra* [209-212].

PART II
A Reconciliatory Regime on Arbitral Awards' Third-Party Effects

216. Part II is dedicated to the assessment of arbitral awards' third-party effects and, in this capacity, reconciles the dichotomy between proceduralist res judicata standards and contractual jurisdiction revealed in Part I. In particular, it will submit that the applicable standards result out of a hybrid transmission from both the rules for judgments' third-party effects *and* arbitration *agreements'* third-party effects. For this purpose, *Chapter 4* will undertake a comparative overview of national arbitration laws revealing that such hybrid solution is increasingly receiving due attention nationally. This sets the scene for the proposals on *international* awards before courts. *Chapter 5* will examine the overriding uniform law submitting that Article V(1)(a) NYC can and should be interpreted as subjecting foreign arbitral awards' third-party effects to jurisdictional boundaries. As to the further requirements, *Chapter 6* examines the applicable law and generally favours the *lex fori*, albeit under certain modifications. Moreover, *Chapter 7* addresses the largely unshaped topic of the factual effects of arbitral awards. Turning from the effects before courts to the effects before arbitral tribunals, *Chapter 8* will consider the increasingly preferred application of transnational principles feasible and seek to close the existing gap on third-party effects. Finally, *Chapter 9* will mention the application of the said regime concerning decisions on the substance, to decisions about arbitral jurisdiction itself.

CHAPTER 4

Third-Party Effects of Arbitral Awards under National Arbitration Laws

217. Thebasis for the specific examination of international arbitral awards' third-party effects is an exploration of the topic under national arbitration laws. It has not occurred yet.[746] Such comparative foundation realizes three main objectives. *First*, it highlights the differences amongst national jurisdictions and thereby the delicacy of a decision as to the applicable law. *Second*, it reiterates the functional perspective already adapted within the previous Chapter: the discussion should include preclusive effects which might be deemed technically distinct to res judicata under national laws, yet functionally related, e.g., *opposabilité* or abuse of process. *Third*, the domestic solutions provide potential options to be eventually discussed for international case scenarios. This 'toolbox' aspect has been immanent to comparative law ever since Ernst Rabel provided the ground for the UN Convention on Contracts for the International Sale of Goods (CISG).[747]

218. When commencing with the general standards applicable to arbitral awards' third-party effects in subsequent litigation, the outset is the very dichotomy that Part I has established as a framework to this entire examination. On the one hand, arbitration's judicial nature and the understanding that res judicata issues are due-process issues incline a transferal of the solutions established in civil procedure. On the other hand, there is one pivotal difference between courts and arbitral tribunals: arbitral tribunals can exclusively extend jurisdiction over third parties when they have consented to arbitrate. With a view to the inherent connection of pre-emptive coordination and subsequent preclusion, this inclines to reconcile the third-party effects of arbitral *awards* and arbitration *agreements* (*see* §4.01, *infra*).

746. *See* on the exclusive exception, a comparison of German and US law Lühmann, *Die Rechtskraft des Schiedsspruchs* 113-183. Moreover, selected aspects of national laws on arbitral awards' third-party effect are mentioned in Brekoulakis, *Third Parties in Arbitration* [10.13-10.30]; Schaffstein, *Res Judicata* [4.29-4.31, 4.47].

747. Rabel, *Recht des Warenkaufs*.

219. After outlining the possibility for preclusion agreements (*see* §4.02, *infra*), the Chapter turns to the default rules revealing an increasing number of national authorities that arbitral awards' third-party effects should *not* exceed the previous tribunal's jurisdictional boundaries. This holds true for inter-omnes effects (*see* §4.03, *infra*), for non-mutual preclusion (*see* §4.04, *infra*) and for extensions of res judicata under privy doctrines (*see* §4.05, *infra*). Therefore, the Chapter summarizes an emerging convergence, yet enumerates the divergences, which will raise arguments on the level of private international and uniform law (*see* §4.06, *infra*). As a final proclamatory remark, the overview will be descriptive in nature. It does not seek to *contribute to*, but merely to *describe and compare*, the discussions under national laws.

§4.01 ANTAGONY OF POTENTIAL LEGAL STANDARDS

220. In conformity with the general rule in litigation, arbitration laws subject res judicata to the same-parties requirement. In France, Article 1484 CPC[748] refers to Article 1355 Cc and its triple-identity test.[749] More expressly, in Germany, § 1055 ZPO states that an arbitral award is res judicata '*amongst the parties*'. Swiss jurisprudence and scholarship equally apply a same-parties requirement under Article 190 PILA.[750] Common law also states that an arbitral award causes preclusions between the parties only.[751] When considering the exceptions to this standard, a conceptual perspective is faced with two – potentially opposing – alternatives: either to apply the standards developed for judgments (*see* [A], *infra*) or to (additionally) apply the standards developed for the third-party effect of arbitration *agreements* (*see* [B], *infra*).

[A] Due Process as an Indication for Arbitral and Procedural Confluence

221. There are several inclinations for transferring the rules on judgments' third-party effects to arbitral awards. Primarily, one might raise arbitration's juridicity. On this basis, jurisdictions frequently state that the general operation of res judicata for arbitral awards equals the operation for judgments.[752] This juridicity is also the very reason why some national statements directed at arbitral awards' third-party effects comprehensively refer to the standards developed for judgments.[753] However, it has already been elaborated that such justification bears the risk of circularity since res judicata

748. '*La sentence arbitrale a, dès qu'elle est rendue, l'autorité de la chose jugée relativement à la contestation qu'elle tranche*'. This wording corresponds to Art. 480 CPC for Judgments.
749. On Art. 1355 Cc *see supra* [174].
750. Cf. ATF 140 III, 278, [E.4.2.1.]; TF, 28 November 2013, 4A_545/2013, [E.2.2.2.] (rental contract) with further references; Berger and Kellerhals, *Arbitration in Switzerland* [1507]; Girsberger, in *Basler Kommentar* Art. 387 [14]; Stacher, in *Berner Kommentar* Art. 387 [49].
751. *Sacor Maritima SA v. Repsol Petroleo SA*, [1998] 1 Lloyd's Rep. 518 per Mance J. (Comm); Restatement (Third) Int'l Comm Arbitration (TD 2), § 4-9 and § 4-10.
752. *See supra* [125-128].
753. *See* Bosch, *Die Rechtskraft des Schiedsspruchs* 122-140; Wagner, in *Die Beteiligung Dritter an Schiedsverfahren* 13-41. Cf. Schlosser, in *Stein and Jonas* § 1055 [30-31]; Schwab and Walther, *Schiedsgerichtsbarkeit* Ch. 21 [2]; Seraglini and Ortscheid, *Droit de l'arbitrage* [468].

cannot be both a *reason for* and a *consequence of* arbitration's juridicity.[754] Moreover and more plastically, other areas such as the point in time upon which res judicata operates, the possibility for 'consent awards' and disposals of res judicata have already illustrated that juridicity is by no means the final word when it comes to arbitral res judicata.[755] Therefore, each proceduralist res judicata principle requires a careful analysis as to its underlying rationales before being transferred to arbitration.

222. The fundamental rationale demanding res judicata's same-parties requirement is: due process. Vice versa, in cases where res judicata is extended to third parties, due process requires intervention possibilities or that national laws deem third parties' interest in due process as subordinate.[756] Such understanding that res judicata issues are due-process issues provides a persuasive inclination to apply procedural rules to arbitral awards. Due process is a cornerstone not only of litigation but also of arbitration. For instance, Article 18 UNCITRAL Model Law states that '*each party shall be given a full opportunity of presenting his case*'. Courts have held this provision mandatory[757] and any violation is a set-aside ground under Article 34 (2)(a)(ii) Model Law.[758] Under the Model-Law implementation of Germany's Arbitration Act, it has been held that the corresponding provision is even merely declarative, since the constitutional due-process guarantee applied directly to arbitration.[759] Amongst non-Model-Law jurisdictions, the French Supreme Court recently held Article 6(1) Convention for the Protection of Human Rights and Fundamental Freedoms (ECHR)[760] to be applicable in the arbitration context, notably in a res judicata case.[761] Moreover, section 10 (c) FAA stipulates due-process violations to be a ground for vacation. In consequence, res judicata's due-process rationale is a persuasive inclination for transferring judgments' third-party effects to awards.

[B] Conjecture: Party Autonomy as Additional Consideration in Arbitration

223. The transfer of judgment principles to arbitral awards meets one fundamental obstacle: party autonomy. As the very cornerstone of arbitration,[762] party autonomy

754. *See supra* [124].
755. *See supra* [129-141].
756. *See supra* [174-210].
757. *See UNCITRAL Digest on Model Law* Art. 34(2)(a)(ii) citing six common and civil law decisions.
758. 'An arbitral award may be set aside [...] if [...] the party making the application was [...] unable to present his case.'
759. BGHZ 31, 43; BGHZ 85, 288, 291-293; BGH, [1986] JZ 401, 403; BGH, (1992) NJW 2299, [2.a)]; OLG Köln, 26 November 2012, 9 Sch 20/02; OLG Celle, 20 November 2003, 8 Sch 02/03; OLG Köln, 6 July 2012, 19 Sch 8/11, [II.2.b)bb)]; Schlosser, in *Stein and Jonas*, § 1042 [37].
760. 'In the determination of his civil rights and obligations [...], everyone is entitled to a fair and public hearing within a reasonable time by an independent and impartial tribunal established by law [...]'.
761. *See infra* [261]. *Corresp* Jarrosson, [1989] Rev. Arb. 573; Schlosser, in *Stein and Jonas* § 1042 [34].
762. *See Dell Computer Corp. v. Union des consommateurs*, [2007] 2 SCR 801, [52] ('Arbitration is a creature that owes its existence to the parties alone'); *AT&T Techs Inc. v. Commen's Workers*

limits personal jurisdiction of arbitral tribunals in order to protect each individual's right to his natural judge. In bilateral discussions about res judicata's extent, this jurisdictional limitation is regularly indecisive in that both parties agreed to arbitration.[763] In litigation discussions about res judicata's third-party extent, this jurisdictional limitation is equally indecisive because courts conform to a public mission and can thus exercise jurisdiction over everybody. *'By contrast, when an arbitration agreement is inapplicable, arbitral jurisdiction altogether ceases to exist.'*[764] But for a third party's consent, an arbitral tribunal cannot exercise any adjudicatory power (*see* Chapter 1, *supra*). Yet, an arbitral award's third-party effect would effectively expose a third party to an arbitral adjudication. This inclines to *not* only determine arbitral awards' third-party effects under judgment principles but additionally require the arbitration *agreement*'s third-party effect.

224. Such additional requirement is inclined not only by conceptual considerations but also by practical feasibility. In particular, in *Chapter 3*, it has been revealed that judgment principles on third-party effects operate under the general assumption that broad joinder and intervention possibilities are available. However, as examined in *Chapter 1*, the jurisdictional limits of arbitral tribunals generally prevent joinders and interventions. Given the intrinsic connection of the pre-emptive measures to res judicata, it appears practical to state: if jurisdiction bars joinders and interventions of third parties, it should equally bar awards' third-party effects.

225. National authorities are increasingly recognizing the inherent connection between jurisdiction and arbitral awards' third-party effects. In scholarship, the general reconciliation of third-party res judicata and third-party jurisdiction remains yet to be subjected to extensive examinations. Yet, there are initial remarks. In England, *Redfern and Hunter* concluded that arbitral tribunals' limited personal jurisdiction inclines a strict *inter partes* application of res judicata.[765] In the US, the Tentative Draft of the Third Restatement on International Commercial Arbitration states:

---

of Am., 475 U.S. 643, 648-649 (1986) ('[A]rbitration is a matter of contract and a party cannot be required to submit to arbitration any dispute which he has not agreed so to submit.'); D 4, 8, 32 § 21 (*arbiter nihil extra compromissum facere potest* – 'The arbitrator can do nothing beyond the agreement to arbitrate.'); Bermann, (2015) 381 Rec. des cours [13-22]; Rubino-Samartano, *International Arbitration* 56.

763. *See* for an exception when an arbitral tribunal has limited subject matter jurisdiction Trib com Paris, *Fougerolle v. Procofrance*, 4 September 1990, unpublished, mentioned in Nelle, *Anspruch Titel und Vollstreckung* 52 (restitution claims were not precluded by an award dealing with contractual claims).

764. Bermann, (2015) 381 Rec. des cours [85] ('In private international law generally, a finding that a particular court lacks personal or subject matter jurisdiction does not mean that the underlying claim cannot be judicially adjudicated. [...] By contrast, when an arbitration agreement is inapplicable, arbitral jurisdiction altogether ceases to exist.').

765. *Redfern and Hunter* [9.182-84] ('An arbitral tribunal has no power to make orders or to give directions against someone who is not a party to the arbitration agreement [...]. It follows that an award can neither directly confer rights nor impose obligations upon a person who is not a party to the arbitration agreement. [...] The award would not be res judicata in any subsequent claim against that third party [...].').

> In the arbitration context, [the] inquiry into the identity of the parties is often, though not always, closely linked to the questions of whether the party resisting recognition, and hence claim preclusion, is bound by the arbitration agreement.[766]

226. In France, a recent observation has noted the tension between arbitral tribunals' limited jurisdiction, on the one hand, and an arbitral award's *opposabilité*, on the other.[767] In Germany, recent opinions submit that the arbitration agreement predetermines res judicata's subjective boundaries.[768] In Switzerland, an *obiter* of the Federal Tribunal on party identity for the sake of res judicata examines whether '*signatories of the arbitration clause*' participated in both proceedings.[769]

227. Moreover, in the specific scenario of consent awards, there is increasing authority to restrict the application of third-party preclusion. Consent awards constitute res judicata under national arbitration laws.[770] Since the privity of contract demands that there be no contractual effect to the detriment of third parties, two techniques are proposed in order to limit consent awards' third-party effects otherwise possible under procedural standards. The UNCITRAL Case Digest on the Model Law states that an arbitral tribunal could reject to issue a consent award if '*third parties' interest are affected.*'[771] Alternatively, one might allow to issue consent awards, yet limit their effect towards third parties as proposed in Model-Law scholarship[772] and by Gary Born's plea for '*particular scrutiny*' under the NYC.[773]

---

766. Restatement (Third) Int'l Comm Arbitration (TD 2), § 4-9 Comment f (for claim preclusion). On issue preclusion *see* § 4-10 Reporter's Notes [d.ii.] ('relatively obvious point that non-parties to the original arbitration cannot be precluded by findings of the tribunal, since they presumably did not consent to arbitral jurisdiction in the first place').

767. Bollée, (2015) Rev. Arb. 699 ('*Comme on a pu l'observer, une décision judiciaire reflète déjà 'une situation pathologique latente ou patente qui la rend, de ce fait, particulièrement suspecte aux yeux des personnes qui n'ont pas participé à l'instance'. Cependant, cette dimension est dans une certaine mesure contrebalancée par l'origine publique du jugement, qui est propre à rassurer les tiers – dans la mesure, du moins, où l'appareil judiciaire dont il émane présente lui-même des garanties suffisantes. Une sentence, au contraire, n'est pas l'œuvre de magistrats en lesquels la société a placé une confiance particulière; elle émane de personnes privées qui, en général, ne doivent leur investiture qu'à la volonté des parties à l'arbitrage. L'aura qui s'attache au souverain et à la justice administrée en son nom n'est donc pas là pour légitimer un rayonnement minimum de la décision, au-delà du cercle des parties qui avaient par avance consenti à s'y soumettre.*').

768. Münch, in *Münchener Kommentar* § 1055 ZPO [22]; Pika, (2018) 131 ZZP 235-243.

769. ATF 140 III, 278, [E.4.2.1.] ('*[O]n peut sérieusement se demander si [...] une approche moins formaliste de la notion d'identité des parties ne serait pas souhaitable [...] sans attacher trop d'importance au critère formel de la seule participation des signataires de la convention d'arbitrage à l'un et l'autre procès.*' – 'worth investigating whether a less formalistic approach concerning the parties' identity would be preferable [...] without holding to the formal criteria of participation of the signatories of the arbitration clause in the one or the other proceedings.' – translation of Swiss Arbitration Decisions).

770. *See supra* [133-136].

771. *UNCITRAL Case Digest* 125. *See also* the statement *Russell on Arbitration* [6-025].

772. *See* Geimer, in *Die Beteiligung Dritter an Schiedsverfahren* 86; Schlosser, in *Stein and Jonas* § 1053 [17]; Voit, in *Musielak and Voit* § 1053 [5]; Schwab and Walther, *Schiedsgerichtsbarkeit* Ch. 23 [8].

773. *Born* 3026-27 ('[G]reat care should be taken in recognition and enforcement of consent awards insofar as third party rights are arguably affected. In general, an award will only have preclusive effects on the parties to the arbitration. There may be unusual circumstances,

228. In conclusion, an arbitral award's third-party effect under national laws will *not* be swiftly referred to judgment principles. Instead, conceptual and practical considerations incline to examine whether the underlying arbitration *agreement*'s third-party effect is additionally required. This conjecture lies at the heart of the subsequent comparative survey.

§4.02 PRECLUSION AGREEMENTS IN MULTILATERAL TRANSACTIONS

229. Before turning to the default rules on arbitral awards' third-party effect, the potential for party agreements requires attention. With a view to the commercial interests in preventing conflicting decisions, parties to multilateral transactions might seek to prevent any conflict by virtue of extended preclusions. In particular, they might stipulate that arbitral awards take effect not only between two parties to an arbitration but also between all members of the transactions. For example, in an M&A transaction, the parties could ascertain that any arbitral determinations as to the target company's quality and status are binding between the purchaser, seller, guarantor and financer alike. Conceptually, there appear several parameters pursuant to which the efficacy of such preclusion agreements demands assessment: (i) Has the agreement been concluded prior to or after the arbitration causing the preclusion? (ii) Has the preclusion agreement been included into the arbitration clause or stipulated within the main contract? (iii) Has the preclusion agreement been formed by all parties to a transaction or have two parties agreed to regard arbitral awards between other parties as binding for them?

230. Effectively, most of the few scholarly submissions on extended preclusion agreements concentrate on the latter case scenario where two parties contractually agreed to accept adjudications in related matters albeit between different parties as binding. An example for such scenario is that a contractor and a sub-contractor agree to regard any adjudication between the principal and the contractor as binding in indemnity matters. Most authors submit that such preclusion agreements are valid and binding in subsequent disputes.[774] Whilst the New York Court of Appeal merely regarded such stipulation as a '*directive as to how the [subsequent] dispute shall be resolved*',[775] the Federal Court of Appeal for the 11th Circuit emphasized the valid and binding nature of such agreement, since such:

however, where a consent award is alleged to affect third parties; in these circumstances, recognition of the award under international arbitration conventions and/or arbitration statutes should be subject to particular scrutiny.').

774. Hwang and Chan, (2001) 10 ICCA Congress Series 164; *Mustill and Boyd* 365; *Russell on Arbitration* [6.183] with reference to *Jackson v. Henderson, Craig & Co*, (1916) 115 LT 36; *Co-operative Wholesale Society Ltd v. Birse Construction Ltd*, (1997) TLR 454 (CA); Schlosser, in *Stein and Jonas* § 1055 [14]. Cf. Harris Planteros and Tecks, *The Arbitration Act 1996* 280; Tweeddale and Tweeddale, *Arbitration of Commercial Disputes* [30.18].

775. *HRH Const Corp. v. Bethlehem Steel Corp*, 384 NE2d 1289 (NY 1978).

> type of provision is not unusual in the construction industry and [it] believe[d] enforcement of the provision in the present dispute [was] not manifestly unfair or unreasonable.[776]

231. The favourable position towards preclusion agreements is even further strengthened by their general acknowledgement in civil procedure. The Swiss Federal Court held in a succession case that:

> an exception to the same-parties requirement applies only [...], if the persons which are part of the relationship in dispute, but have not been included in the prior proceedings, declared in advance to be bound by the decision.[777]

232. In US civil procedure, preclusion agreements are mentioned as one of the six categories in *Taylor v. Sturgell*[778] and under the Second Restatement,[779] notably stressing that *'[n]o such agreement should be inferred except upon the plainest circumstances'*.[780] In Germany, persuasive scholarship even submits that preclusion agreements do not merely produce contractual effect but extend the public force of res judicata, which applies ex officio because the interests restricting res judicata (due process) are at the disposal of the parties.[781]

233. Turning from agreements *extending* preclusion to the role of arbitration agreements as a *restriction* of preclusion, a rather undiscussed feature is confidentiality. In particular, some scholarly statements consider that confidentiality might be an obstacle to an arbitral award being invoked towards third parties;[782] others regard preclusion interests as a justification for foregoing confidentiality.[783] Preferably, confidentiality comprises no relevance in the subsequent proceedings, since it is no obligation towards the third party.[784] In conclusion, multilateral transactions can prevent inconsistency by virtue of extended preclusion agreements.

---

776. *Cecil v. Morris Mechanical*, 735 F.2d 437, 438 (11th Cir. 1984).
777. ATF 89 II 429, 435 (*'Eine Ausnahme von der Regel, dass ein Urteil nur die Prozessparteien bindet, gilt [...] nur dann, wenn die am streitigen Rechtsverhältnis mitbeteiligten, aber nicht in den Prozess einbezogenen Personen zum voraus erklärt haben, das Urteil gegen sich gelten lassen zu wollen*').
778. *Taylor v. Sturgell*, 128 S.Ct. 2161, 2164 (2008) ('a person who agrees to be bound by the determination of issues in an action between others is bound in accordance with the agreement's terms').
779. Restatement (Second) Judgments, § 40 ('A person who agrees to be bound by the determination if issues in an action between others is bound in accordance with the terms of the agreement').
780. *Ibid.* Comment b.
781. *See* Wagner, *Prozessverträge* 725-726 with further references to the opposing opinion.
782. *See* Woolhouse, (2004) 7 Int'l Arb. L. R 150-156; *ILA Final Report on Res Judicata* [13] ('confidentiality of awards may have an impact on res judicata issues, but that this was less likely in further proceedings between the same parties').
783. *Russell on Arbitration* [6-185] ('It is qualified, however, when disclosure is reasonably necessary to establish or protect a party's legal rights as against a third party by founding a cause of action or a defence to a claim. In these circumstances disclosure of the award, including any reasons given, will not be a breach of the duty of confidentiality').
784. *See infra* [557].

§4.03 ERGA OMNES EFFECTS OF ARBITRAL AWARDS

[A] Arbitral Awards in Issues of Status

234. All jurisdictions concur that judgments' determinations on legal statues operate erga omnes.[785] Turning to the arbitration context, a large number of status suits are not arbitrable such as family, estate or liquidation matters.[786] Functionally comparable, common law bars 'arbitrations in rem'. Arbitrations in maritime matters are actions in personam, since the *res* (the ship) cannot consent to arbitration.[787] Moreover, modifications of *inter partes* relationships, such as a resolution of a contract by the arbitral tribunal, do not raise any concerns of *erga omnes* effects. Against this background, only two scenarios in particular merit the assessment of legal status by arbitral tribunals and the exposure of third parties to such adjudication.

235. The primary case scenario concerns internal corporate disputes, e.g., about shareholders' resolutions. Many jurisdictions regard them as arbitrable.[788] The decision might affect all shareholders and officers regardless of their participation in the dispute as e.g., under German law.[789] Against this background, the Federal Court of Justice decided that arbitration agreements within a corporation's articles of association about actions contesting the validity of a shareholders' resolution are valid if: all shareholders are notified about a nullity arbitration so that they are able to join the proceedings and all shareholders are treated equally when selecting the arbitrator.[790] Eventually, the court considered the standards to apply '*in principle*' to partnerships.[791] Moreover, the jurisprudence has induced the DIS to draft the *Supplementary Rules for*

785. *See supra* [181-184].
786. *Born* 1028.
787. *See The 'Engedi'*, [2010] SGHC 95; *Kuo Fen Ching v. Dauphin Offshore Engineering & Trading Pte Ltd*, [1999] 2 SLR(R) 793.
788. *See* Austria: OGH, 19 April 2012, 6Ob42/12p. England: *Fulham Football Club (1987) Ltd v. Richards*, [2011] EWCA Civ 855, [28] ('there is no express provision in either the [English Arbitration Act, 1996 or the English Companies Act, 2006] which excludes arbitration as a possible means of determining disputes of this kind'). Netherlands: Hoge Raad, *Silver Lining Fin v. Perstorp Waspik*, 26 November 2010, [2011] NJ 55. USA: *JSC Surgutneftegaz v. President & Fellows of Harvard College*, 2005 WL 1863676 [4] (S.D.N.Y. 2005) ('The FAA does not carve out disputes relating to the internal affairs of corporations as an exception to the general enforceability of arbitration agreements').
789. § 248(1) AktG ('If the resolution has been declared null and void by a judgment that is final and not subject to appeal, such judgment shall be binding on all shareholders and the members of the management board and the supervisory board, even if such persons were not parties to the action').
790. BGHZ 180, 221, [20]. *See* Duve and Wimalasena in Böckstiegel et al. (eds), *Arbitration in Germany* [17-47] with further references on the jurisprudential, legislative and scholarly history.
791. BGH, [2017] SchiedsVZ 194.

Corporate Law Disputes containing provisions for notice, participation, parallel proceedings and the tribunal's selection.[792] Accordingly, this illustrates the intrinsic connection of res judicata and participation possibilities.

236. Other situations determining the legal status erga omnes can be observed in sports arbitration. For instance, disqualifications of athletes necessarily affect third parties such as the athletes' employers. To provide an example arising out of an incident that occurred during the 2014 World Cup in Brazil: subsequent to biting Giorgio Chiellini, the Uruguayan player Luis Suárez received a four-month ban by FIFA. Having just hired Luis Suaréz, the FC Barcelona applied for an appeal before the Court of Arbitration for Sport (CAS). The latter generally affirmed the FC Barcelona's standing to seek appeal because – although the FC Barcelona was a third party to the FIFA's sanction and did not even participate in the World Cup – the sanction would also bind the club.[793] This affirms the mechanism revealed in *Chapter 3*. If arbitrations can create *erga omnes* effects, the intrinsic connection to participation possibilities has to be upheld. If an affected third party has consented to arbitration, the arbitral process needs to guarantee certain participation or appeal mechanisms.

[B] *Opposabilité* in French Arbitration Law

237. Under French law, every judgment comprises *opposabilité* erga omnes. That is, the primary consequence of the adjudication, e.g., the obligation of a debtor, can be invoked by and against third parties incidentally, e.g., for sureties. Third parties are compensated by their ability to apply for a *tierce opposition* (third-party appeal).[794] Generally, both doctrines apply in arbitration. However, the scope of their application triggers delicate discussions.

238. Concerning the scope of an arbitral award's *opposabilité*, the delineation between the primary consequence of an adjudication and merely incidental reasonings has recently caused attention. Whilst such delineation has already been criticized in procedural law,[795] arbitration discussions are particularly prominent. In the 2007 *Prodim* judgment, a franchisor sold its business to a third party without adhering to a

792. *See* in particular Art. 8(3) ('Where claimant's or respondent's side do not reach an agreement within the time limit of s. 8.2, the DIS Appointing Committee nominates two arbitrators upon request of the claimant, respondent or intervenor pursuant to s. 13.2 DIS-Arbitration Rules.').

793. CAS Case 2014/A/3665-3667, *L. Suarez, FC Barcelona et al. v. FIFA*, Arbitral Award, 2 December 2014, [47] ('In the view of the Panel it is a fact that the ban of the Player on any football-related activity and from visiting any stadium for four months does burden the Club [FC Barcelona] in its own direct interests to work with the Player [...] and to include him in the new season's team. Therefore, [...] the Panel finds that the Club is sufficiently affected by the Appealed Decision and that the Club has a interest of financial and sporting nature at stake').

794. *See supra* [186, 190].

795. *See* Héron and Le Bars, *Droit judiciaire privé* [361] ('*[I]l arrive fréquemment que la Cour de cassation confonde l'opposabilité de l'effet substantiel d'un jugement et son autorité de chose jugée. Ceci est regrettable, car la portée et la valeur des arrêts qu'elle rend s'en trouvent sensiblement altérées. Parler à tort d'autorité de chose jugée ne peut que renforcer la confusion qui règne dèjà en doctrine comme dans la pratique, sur cette délicate notion.*').

preference option within the franchising contract. The franchisee successfully claimed damages before an arbitral tribunal under the contract. Subsequently, he sued the third party for inducing a breach of contract and invoked the arbitral award as conclusively establishing the purchase's unlawfulness. The *Cour de cassation* applied the arbitral award's *opposabilité* on this unlawfulness against the third party.[796] Vice versa, in a subsequent *Prodim* case, it was stated that the incidental quantification of damages within an arbitral award could be relied upon by third parties to an arbitration.[797] Subsequent jurisprudence – mainly from the same case history – applied *opposabilité* in a corresponding manner.[798] Scholarship heavily criticizes this application of *opposabilité*, since it would not refer to the legal situation created by an arbitral award's operative force (franchisor obligated towards franchisee), but facilitated its reasonings instead (franchisor breached the contract).[799] Recently, the *Cour de cassation* might have returned to the restrictive outset of the *opposabilité*: a 2016 judgment concerned two parallel disputes each initiated against *France Telecom*, yet brought by distinct claimants. One claimant was unsuccessful in arbitration. France Telecom raised this arbitral award in the litigation against the other. The court denied any *opposabilité*.[800] It remains yet to be established whether this constitutes an entire deviation of the previously wide concept. Alternatively, the decisions might be reconciled in that the recent decision concerns a situation of distinct factual causes of action (i.e., two separate contracts) whereas the previous *Prodim* decisions concerned a comparable cause of action in that both disputes focused on the joint action of the franchisor and the purchaser.

239. In any case, the other side of the *opposabilité* coin, the *tierce opposition* (third-party appeal) raises a further issue: for domestic arbitral awards, Article 1501 CPC admits a third-party appeal before courts.[801] Hence, both the third party's right to be heard and to a natural judge are protected. Notably, this stands in contrast to Belgian law, where the wording of Article 1122 Judicial Code on the *tierce opposition* applied only to judgments. The Constitutional Court of Belgium held this situation unconstitutional[802] and Belgian practice now admits the *tierce opposition* against arbitral awards.[803] In France, where domestic arbitral awards are explicitly addressed, the CPC contains no comparable provision for *international* arbitral awards rendered in France.

796. Cass. (com), *sté Prodim et al. v. sté Distribution Casino*, 23 January 2007, [2007] Rev. Arb. 2007, 769.
797. Cass. (com), *sté ITM entreprises et al. v. sté Prodim et al*, 2 December 2008, [2009] Rev. Arb. 326.
798. Cass. (com), *G et A Distribution SARL v. Prodim SAS*, [2008] Rev. Arb. 46; Cass. (com), 26 May 2009, 08-11.588; CA Paris, *Prodim SAS v. G et A Distribution SARL*, [2010] Rev. Arb. 345; Cass. (1e civ.), 12 April 2012, 11-14.123.
799. Cf. Mayer, (2009) Rev. Arb. 332 ('*détournement de la notion d'opposabilité*'); Jarrosson, (2007) 8 Procédures No. 12 [49]; Loquin, in *JCl procédure civile* Fasc 1042 [41].
800. Cass. (com), 2 February 2016, 14-23.921, [2016] Rev. Arb. 812.
801. '*La sentence arbitrale peut être frappée de tierce opposition devant la juridiction qui eût été compétente à défaut d'arbitrage, sous réserve des dispositions du premier alinéa de l'article 588*'.
802. Constitutional Court of Belgium, 16 February 2017, 21/2017, [2018] Rev. Arb. 253.
803. *See* Court of First Instance of Brussels, 29 January 2016 and 12 April 2018, 2014/480/A and 2015/6305/A, [2018] Rev. Arb. 195.

Instead, Article 1518 CPC states that an international arbitral award can exclusively be reviewed in set-aside proceedings.[804] This indicates that the third-party appeal is unavailable. Yet, an application of *opposabilité* without such review would threaten the said interests of third parties. As preservation, two solutions appear possible: either *opposabilité* is considered inapplicable on international arbitral awards or the *tierce opposition* is opened.[805] The latter solution has recently gained persuasive support in scholarship.[806] In conclusion, *opposabilité* and the *tierce opposition* equally apply to arbitral awards, albeit the extent of either of them remains to be conclusively settled in jurisprudence and scholarship.

§4.04 ARBITRAL AWARDS AS GROUND FOR NON-MUTUAL PRECLUSION AT COMMON LAW

240. Non-mutual preclusion (abuse of process or *Henderson* rule in England; collateral estoppel or *Bernhard* rule in US) prevents a claimant or defendant from raising those claims or arguments that have been already unsuccessfully raised in former proceedings. The party relying on such doctrine in the subsequent proceedings need not have been a party to the former. Hence, a third party that would not have been exposed to detrimental results of former proceedings can rely on results in his favour. This raises concerns of equality, the very rationale that prevents civil-law jurisdictions from applying the rule. Yet, at common law, interests of consistency and particularly public resources are considered overriding.[807] When an arbitral award gives rise to non-mutual preclusion in subsequent litigation, both sides of the balancing need to be adjusted thereby raising the obstacles against non-mutual preclusion. *First*, with regard to public resources, it needs to be mentioned that the first dispute, i.e., the arbitration has not consumed any public resources. Hence, the question needs to be specified in that not a *double*, but a *single*, expense of public resources were prevented. Certainly though, such argument arises irrespectively of multilateral applications and has already been invoked against the existing application of abuse of process in bilateral case scenarios.[808] This brings the proclamation to the *second* and more significant difference between judgments and arbitral awards as a basis for non-mutual preclusion. The concerns of equality are significantly enhanced by virtue of multilateral transactions' exposure to jurisdictional fragmentation. In particular, if the third party is no party to the arbitration agreement, there is no opportunity to join the third party to

804. '*La sentence rendue en France en matière d'arbitrage international ne peut faire l'objet que d'un recours en annulation*'.

805. Cf. *Fouchard Gaillard and Goldman* [1598] ('the privity of the arbitration agreement and of the res judicata effect of the arbitrators' decision suffices to protect third parties from any negative impact which they consider the award might have'); Jarrosson, (2007) 8 Procédures No. 12 [49] ('*La question mérite peut-être un réexamen, ne serait-ce que parce que le tiers, lui, n'a pas voulu l'arbitrage.*').

806. Bollée, (2015) Rev. Arb. 695, [25-42]; Bollée, (2018) Rev. Arb. 148-152; Callé, (2016) Rev. Arb. 85-90.

807. *See supra* [193-196].

808. *See supra* [127].

the arbitration.[809] In other words: although a party to an arbitration had no opportunity whatsoever to bring the third party in the proceedings, it bears the risk to be subsequently exposed to non-mutual preclusion against that very third party before courts.

241. It is this very disruption that lies at the heart of current discussions at common law: whereas in Hong Kong, an arbitral award was applied as a ground for abuse of process in favour of a third party in 2011,[810] English law has long been missing precedence. Foremost, abuse of process was *not* relied upon in *Sun Life Assurance*.[811] In 2012, the Commercial Court considered non-mutual preclusion inapplicable.[812] In 2013, however, it applied abuse of process to the detriment of an insured against an insurer.[813]

242. In 2017, the Court of Appeal rendered the judgment in the leading case *Michael Wilson & Partners v. Sinclair* reversing a 2012 judgment of the Commercial Court:[814] a former employee of Michael Wilson & Partners (MWP) acquired certain shares ('Max Shares') as trustee for a former client of MWP. In an arbitration between MWP and the former employee for breach of fiduciary duty, the tribunal held the acquisition of shares lawful. Eventually, MWP sued the former client for damages, which invoked the arbitral award as precluding MWP for raising an allegedly unlawful acquisition of the shares. In his 2012 judgment, Teare J. affirmed the general applicability of abuse of process in favour of third parties in arbitration, but set a high threshold:

> Arbitrations are private and consensual and non-parties cannot, in the absence of consent, be joined or be affected by the decisions of the arbitral tribunal. [...] The Max action is therefore the only means by which MWP can bring its claim against Mr Sinclair.[815]

243. In other words, Teare J. took into account the jurisdictional fragmentation that abuse of process threatens to disregard when applied to arbitral awards. He then continued by balancing this dimension against other factors and concluded that there

809. *See supra* [38].
810. *Parakou Shipping Pte ltd v. Jinhui Shipping and Transportation Ltd*, (2011) 2 HKLRD 1.
811. Cf. *Sun Life Assurance Company of Canada et al. v. The Lincoln National Life Insurance Company*, [2004] EWCA Civ 1660, [54, 63] per Mance LJ; emphasised in *Michael Wilson and Partners Ltd v. Sinclair et al*, [2017] EWCA Civ 3, [52] ('It is equally clear that no argument was advanced [in *Sun Life Assurance*] on the basis of abuse of process.'). *Dadourian Group International v. Simms* is equally in applicable, *see Michael Wilson & Partners Ltd v. Sinclair et al*, [2012] EWHC 2560, [50] (Comm).
812. *Nomihold Securities Inc. v. Mobile Relesystems Finance SA*, (2012) EWHC 130 (Comm), [42-43] ('[W]here the previous dispute was determined in arbitration, the principle of Henderson v. Henderson has a narrower application than where it was determined in court proceedings. The consensual nature of arbitration means that a tribunal determines disputes referred to it by the parties. It is because of this [...] that the principle of Henderson v. Henderson applies in relation to previous arbitrations only if all parties to subsequent litigation (or their privies) have also been parties to the earlier [...].').
813. *Arts & Antiques Ltd v. Richards*, [2013] EWHC 3361, [40] per Hamblen J. (Comm).
814. The five-years gap comprised other disputes with regard to the costs of the previous arbitration, *see Michael Wilson & Partners Ltd v. Sinclair et al*, [2017] EWCA Civ 55 with further references.
815. *Michael Wilson & Partners Ltd v. Sinclair et al*, [2012] EWHC 2560, [50 and 59] (Comm).

were '*special circumstances*' implying an abuse of the court.[816] The Court of Appeal reversed the judgment's holding on the special circumstances and thus even further raised the standard for abuse of process.[817] Simon LJ explicitly formulated a '*high threshold*' to apply:[818] '*[I]t will probably be a rare case, and perhaps a very rare case, where court proceedings against a non-party to an arbitration can be said to be an abuse of process.*'[819] He stressed that mutuality lied at the heart of the analysis[820] and reiterated that '*the tribunal did not have jurisdiction to adjudicate on the claims in a way that bound MWP in relation to a non-party.*'[821] Finally, he stated that the former arbitration's parties could request to be treated *fair*.[822] In conclusion, although arbitral awards can generally give rise to non-mutual preclusion on a case-by-case basis ('merit-based approach' and fairness), there is a strong presumption *against* any favourable third-party effect when arbitral jurisdiction is limited. Otherwise, there would be disruptions with the opponent's lack of opportunity for joinders, third-party notices or consolidation. Vice versa, there is reasonable ground for abuse of process where the third party was bound to arbitrate, but was not joined.

244. In the US, there is less criticism of non-mutual preclusion in arbitration. For instance, in a 2006 case before the 10th Circuit, a distributor that previously lost in an arbitration against a steel manufacturer for antitrust damages was unable to bring the corresponding damages claim against the collaborators of the alleged antitrust violation.[823] Correspondingly, the 3rd Circuit precluded a claimant from suing a transferee of property under Pennsylvanian law after an arbitral tribunal had already dismissed a similar claim against the transferor for breach of fiduciary.[824] Further judgments applied the concept without raising any equality or jurisdiction concerns.[825] In scholarship, it has been submitted that an arbitration clause might be construed in that the parties '*may also have implicitly bargained for application of collateral estoppel*'.[826]

816. *Ibid.*, [67].
817. *See Michael Wilson & Partners Ltd v. Sinclair et al*, [2017] EWCA Civ 3, [67-97] per Simon LJ.
818. *Ibid.*, [87].
819. *Ibid.*, [68].
820. *Ibid.*, [90].
821. *Ibid.*, [97].
822. *Ibid.*, [99].
823. *B-S Steel of Kansas Inc. v. Texas Industries Inc*, 439 F.3d 653 (10th Cir. 2006).
824. *Witkowski v. Welch*, 173 F.3d 192, 201 (3d Cir. 1999) ('The issues got to arbitration, confirmed by extensive testimony [...] the ultimate and controlling issues have been decided').
825. Defensive: *Ritchie v. Landau*, 475 F.2d 151, 154 (2d Cir. 1973); *Norris v. Grosvenor Marketing Ltd*, 803 F.2d 1281, 1285-1287 (2d Cir. 1986) (New York law); *Wellons Inc. v. T.E. Ibberson Co*, 869 F.2d 1166, 1168-72 (8th Cir. 1986) (federal law); *Mandich v. Watters*, 970 F.2d 462, 465-467 (8th Cir. 1992) (Minnesota law); *Murray v. Dominick Corp. of Canada, Ltd*, 631 FSupp 534, 536-538 (S.D.N.Y. 1986) (New York law); *Ray v. Continental Western Ins. Co*, 920 FSupp 1094, 1097-98 (DNev 1996) (Nevada law); *Aufderhar v. Data Dispatch Inc*, 452 N.W.2d 648, 652-653 (Minn 1990) (Minnesota law); *Western Indus. and Environmental Services Inc. v. Kaldveer Associates Inc*, 887 P2d 1048, 1051-1052 (Idaho 1994) (Idaho law); *Riverdale Development Co, LLC v. Ruffin Bldg. Systems Inc*, 146 SW3d 852, 860 (Ark 2004) (Arkansas law). Offensive: *Cities Service Co. v. Gulf Oil Corp*, 980 P.2d 116, 125-126 (Okla 1999); *Fireman's Fund Ins. Co. v. Cunningham Lindsey Claims Management Inc*, 2005 WL 1522783 (EDNY 2005) (obiter); *In re Neopharm* Inc. *Sec Lit*, 2007 WL 625533 (NDIll 2007) (New York law and federal law); *Tankersley v. Lynch*, 2012 WL 683384 (EDMich 2012) (Michigan and federal law).
826. Shell, (1987-1988) 35 UCLA L. Rev. 668.

However, such reasoning appears problematic in that the party eventually relying on collateral estoppel is a third party to the arbitration clause's bargain. In this spirit, other authors criticize the application of collateral estoppel to arbitral awards.[827] They can rely on jurisprudence from California and Utah. In *Vandenberg*, the California Supreme Court rejected non-mutual preclusion under explicit reference to the limited scope of the arbitration agreement.[828] The Supreme Court of Utah held that if arbitration were to comprehensively cause non-mutual preclusion, it would have to meet more formal requirements, which would endanger its informal characteristics.[829] Most recently, the Draft Third Restatement on International Commercial Arbitration states that:

> non-mutual offensive use of issue preclusion in international arbitrations is generally not appropriate. It is axiomatic that arbitration jurisdiction is based on, and limited by, the consent of the parties.[830]

245. Accordingly, in conformity with English jurisprudence, there is considerable US authority that non-mutual preclusion should not exceed the previous tribunal's personal jurisdiction.

§4.05 ARBITRAL AWARDS' INTER PARTES EFFECTS TOWARDS PRIVIES

246. When neither *erga omnes* effects nor non-mutual preclusions are applicable, the argument arises whether res judicata can still apply towards a third party under exceptional circumstances. In civil procedure, this is possible when a third party has a sufficiently close relationship to the former dispute's parties, either evidenced by a certain substantive relationship as such are a broad discretionary assessment.[831] In arbitration, it has already been mentioned that the ILA refrained from proposing any uniform solutions because there were '*too many different situations in relation to the question whether a party, by virtue of assignment, succession, close relationship or otherwise, is bound [...] that these issues are left to the applicable law.*'[832] However, when examining national arbitration laws, a rather unsettled situation can be disclosed. Whilst the effects of arbitral awards towards successors (*see* [A], *infra*) and represented (*see* [B], *infra*) are little debated, the assessment of complex transactions bears problems as to conflicting third-party standards for judgments and arbitration *agreements* (*see* [C], *infra*).

827. Hall (2005-2006) Ark L. Rev. 929; Luehmann, *Die Rechtskraft des Schiedsspruchs* 181; G Sanders, (1992) 24 Law & Policy Int'L Bus 119-120. Cf. Cromwell, (2000) J. Disp Res 425.
828. *Vandenberg v. Superior Court*, 982 P2d 229, 242 (Cal 1999).
829. *Buckner v. Kennard*, 99 P3d 842, 850 (Utah 2004).
830. Restatement (Third) Int'l Comm Arbitration (TD No. 2 2012), § 4-10, Reporter's Notes d (ii).
831. *See supra* [197-214].
832. *ILA Final Report on Res Judicata* [47].

[A] Successions

[1] Successions Occurring after an Arbitral Award Is Rendered

247. The previous outlines have stated that both judgments as well as arbitration agreements are generally effective towards universal or individual successors.[833] In light of such convergent standards, arbitral awards equally affect successors.[834] Potentially, this might be uncontroversial. However, at a second glance, successions in fact *do* comprise potentially conflicting standards, namely when the arbitration agreement can*not* be invoked towards the successors. This might be the case for (i) transfer of property (except under French law), (ii) assignments in general (exceptional jurisprudence in Russia and Italy), (iii) assignments when the assignee has explicitly rejected to be bound to arbitrate (except under French law).[835]

248. The resulting tension between proceduralist and arbitration-agreement standards have caused particular attention in German scholarship, potentially because of the Federal Court of Justice's *obiter* where it considered that an '*arbitral award [...] exclusively constitutes res judicata as between the parties of the arbitration agreement and does not affect successors.*' [836] Notably though, this *obiter* had been rendered before the court held assignees bound to arbitrate.[837] This might explain why the Higher Regional Courts Karlsruhe and Munich recently rendered precisely opposing *obiter.*[838] Scholarship remains divided. Some authors reject res judicata's extension by reference to the arbitration agreement's limited scope,[839] whilst the majority refers to arbitration's judicial nature and seeks to apply judgment standards.[840] The author has recently taken the latter opinion's position, yet *not* by virtue of the 'blanket' juridicity argument, but by considering the third party's interest in party autonomy subordinate. Instead, the exclusively decisive interest of a third party against being bound by an arbitral award is a potential *bona fide* interest. Whether a *bona fide* acquisition can occur without being bound by res judicata is a matter addressed by judgment principles. [841] Therefore, it is concluded that arbitral awards generally bind successors,

833. *See supra* [41-44, 199].
834. Switzerland: Girsberger, in *Basler Kommentar* Art. 387 [14]. USA: Restatement (Third) Int' Comm Arbitration (TD 2), § 4-9 comment f.
835. *See supra* [41-44].
836. BGHZ 64, 122, 123 ('*Dies muss erst Recht für einen rechtskräftigen Schiedsspruch gelten, der nur zwischen den Parteien des Schiedsvertrags wie ein rechtskräftiges Urteil wirkt und dem nicht die Wirkung auf Rechtsnachfolger nach § 325 ZPO zukommt*').
837. *See* BGHZ 71, 162; BGHZ 77, 32; BGH, [1979] MDR 382; BGH, [1979] NJW 2567; BGH, [1998] NJW 371; BGH, [2000] NJW 2346.
838. OLG Karlsruhe, [2015] SchiedsVZ 145, 148; OLG München, 15 April 2015, 34 Sch 7/15, [2015] BeckRS 9570, [11-12].
839. Additional requirement: Schütze, in *Wieczorek and Schütze,* § 1055 [19]; Spohnheimer, *Gestaltungsfreiheit* 27. Sole requirement: Münch, in *Münchener Kommentar* § 1055 [21-22].
840. Bosch, *Rechtskraft und Rechtshängigkeit im Schiedsverfahren* 141; Geimer, in *Zöller* § 1055 [7]; Loritz, (1993) 100 ZZP 13-17; Schlosser, in *Stein and Jonas* § 1055 [31]; Schwab and Walther, *Scheidsgerichtsbarkeit* Ch. 21 [3]; Wagner, in *Die Beteiligung Dritter am Schiedsverfahren.*
841. Pika, (2018) 131 ZZP 243-245.

although there might be diverging submissions under national laws when the latter is not bound to arbitrate.

[2] *Successions Occurring During the Arbitration*

249. In contrast to the unproblematic successions after the arbitration, the problem becomes more delicate when the succession occurred *during* arbitral proceedings. Under German law, it is regarded as preferable to transfer the solutions for judgments pursuant to which any successor, assignee or acquirer of property will be bound towards a decision when the succession has occurred during the proceedings (§ 265(2) ZPO).[842] This exposure of the third party then justifies awarding the third party with intervention possibilities.[843] Moreover, the Draft Third Restatement also states that:

> if there is an assignment during the pendency of the arbitration [...] a third party may be treated as the 'same party' so that a grant of preclusive effect for or against that party may be appropriate on a subsequent action.[844]

250. In this spirit, the tribunal in *ICC Case 13509* which applied standards inspired by French law noted that an assignee acquiring a claim during a prior arbitration, acquired 'uncertain' rights. However, it rejected any third-party effect of the ongoing arbitration even though the assignee had been invited to join. Instead, the tribunal held that the assignee had a legitimate interest in appointing its own arbitrator.[845]

[B] Disclosed Representation and Class Arbitrations in Particular

251. The extension of res judicata in cases where a representative has acted as a formal party, yet on another's behalf has drawn only limited, generally favourable attention. This is the case in Germanic jurisdictions.[846] In particular, since they regard an insolvency administrator bound by a previous arbitration agreement,[847] unless the dispute concerns insolvency-specific rights,[848] there are no statements objecting to the effect on the administered company.[849] In the US, courts considered heirs and

842. Schlosser, in *Stein and Jonas*, § 1055 [33]; Wagner, *Die Beteiligung Dritter an Schiedsverfahren* 27.
843. Pika, (2018) 131 ZZP 246.
844. Restatement (Third) Int' Comm Arbitration (TD 2), § 4-9 comment f.
845. *ICC Case 13509*, Arbitral Award, (2008-2011) VI ICC Collection 739 ('*Le cessionnaire succède à la situation juridique du cédant, telle que'elle existe à l'instant de la cession. Si, à cet instant, l'étendue des droits du cédant était incertaine, la même incertitude affecte les droit du cessionnaire [...]*'). *See infra*, [588].
846. *See* Berger and Kellerhals, *Arbitration in Switzerland* [1652]; Pfeiffer, (2017) SchiedsVZ 139-140.
847. *See* in general BGH, [2011] SchiedsVZ 281, [14]; BGH, [2017] NJW 488; ATF 136 III 107, *Atlético Madrid v. Benfica Lisbon*, 108-109; Kaufmann-Kohler and Rigozzi, *International Arbitration in Switzerland* [3.165] with further references.
848. *See* BGHZ 179, 304, [9]; *Poudret and Besson* [290].
849. *See* Pika, (2018) 131 ZZP 247-248.

beneficiaries under a legacy bound to the arbitration where they had been represented by the administrator.[850] In France, the Supreme Court applied the representation standard where a claim had been assigned prior to the arbitration and decided against representation.[851] Beyond compulsory representation, the scenario of arbitral awards applied for by voluntary representatives has even drawn less attention. Potentially, arbitration proceedings rarely involve voluntary representation, since it requires the opponent's consent in order to protect his interest in efficient dispute resolution and confidentiality.[852]

252. The topic that has created by far the most attention with regard to res judicata towards represented parties is the FAA's relation to class actions. In a class action, claimants represent an entire group of equally affected individuals, which are all exposed to res judicata.[853] The important rationale of this rule is *not* a protection of the defendant, but the claimants: private individuals affected by tort or consumer violation might otherwise be deterred from litigation, either because the small amount of the claims does not justify the expenses or the complexity of the case and therefore the initial costs are too burdensome for a private citizen. Therefore, class actions are considered a cornerstone of US procedure's guarantee to enforce individuals' rights. Against this background, the interaction of class actions and arbitration comprises two problems for the purpose of this examination:[854] *first*, the transfer of the class action as such to arbitration has been subject to extensive jurisprudence. Under State laws, some judgments declared class arbitrations inadmissible[855] whilst the corresponding rule in California[856] has now been replaced by their general possibility.[857] Under federal law, class arbitrations are generally admissible[858] when the parties consented to it.[859] However, the much-debated issue is the threshold of consent. Federal courts required explicit stipulation.[860] By contrast, in *Oxford Health*, the Supreme Court found no excess of arbitral authority where the arbitration agreement was silent on the admissibility of class arbitrations and the tribunal justified implied consent.[861]

850. *O'Keefe v. Merrill Lynch & Co*, 84 P.3d 613, 619 (Kann App 2004).
851. Cf. Cass. (2e civ), *sté Ampafrance v. Wasteels et autres*, 14 October 1987, [1988] Rev. Arb. 288.
852. *See* Pika, (2018) 131 ZZP 247.
853. *Taylor v. Sturgell*, 128 S.Ct. 2161, 2165-2175 (2008), discussed *supra* [206].
854. *See* Strong, *Class, Mass and Collective Arbitration* 205-227 with extensive references.
855. *Med Ctr Cars Inc. v. Smith*, 727 So2d 9 (Ala 1998); *Stein v. Geonerco Inc*, 105 WashApp 41 (2001); *Steinberg v. Prudential-Bache Sec Inc*, 12 Del J. Corp. 371, 380 (Del Ch. 1986) (ordering class arbitration was impermissibly 'rewriting the contract').
856. *Vernon v. Drexel Burnham & Co. Inc*, 52 CalApp3d 706, 716 (Cal Ct. App 1975); *NW Civic Ass'n Inc. v. Cates*, 241 Ga 39 (1978).
857. *Keating v. Super Ct*, 167 CalRptr 481, 490 (Cal Ct. App 1980), aff'd, 31 Cal3d 584, 610-612 (Cal S.Ct. 1982); *Sanders v. Kinko's Inc*, 99 CalApp4th 1106, 1113-14 (Cal Ct. App 2002).
858. *Green Tree Fin Corp. v. Bazzle*, 539 U.S. 444 (2003).
859. *Stolt-Nielsen SA v. AnimalFeeds Int'l Corp*, 559 U.S. 662, 130 S.Ct. 1758, [B] (2010) ('parties concurred that they had reached no agreement on that issue').
860. *Champ v. Siegel Trading Co*,55 F.3d 269, 275 (7th Cir. 1995); *Gammaro v. Thorp Consumer Discount Co*, 828 FSupp 673, 674 (D Minn 1993).
861. *Oxford Health Plans LLC v. Sutter*, 133 S.Ct. 2064, 2070 (2013) ('In Stolt-Nielsen, the arbitrators did not construe the parties' contract, and did not identify any agreement authorizing class proceedings. [...] Here, the arbitrator did construe the contract and did find an agreement to permit class arbitration. So to overturn his decision, we would have to rely on a finding that he

253. The *second* question relates to the inverse situation being how to treat class-action *waivers* within bilateral arbitration clauses. Since this topic is not instantly related to the extension of arbitral preclusion towards third parties, but rather concerns the validity of arbitration agreements, it is mentioned but briefly. California's restrictive jurisprudence[862] is inapplicable under the FAA.[863] Hence, class-action waivers are possible. In conclusion, class arbitrations are the pre-eminent application of res judicata towards represented. Whilst other case scenarios remain little debated under national laws, it is regularly affirmed that an arbitral award constitutes res judicata towards represented third parties when the latter has (at least impliedly) consented to the underlying arbitration agreement.

[C] Complex Substantive Relationships

254. At the very outset, the Chapter has labelled the application of res judicata towards third parties as torn between judgment and arbitration-agreement standards.[864] For *erga omnes* effects and non-mutual preclusions, the contrasts of broad procedural preclusions and the privity of arbitration agreements was self-evident. By contrast, for complex substantive relationships, judgments and arbitration agreements share a common outset in that they do *not* affect third parties. However, the difference between judgment and arbitration-agreement regimes comes down to the *means* of assessing the exception. Civil procedure either facilitated the substantive relationships as such are a discretionary assessment to influence the proceedings.[865] By contrast, the regime for arbitration agreements focuses on nothing but the third party's consent to arbitration.[866] The delicate delineation between these standards is examined for particular scenarios. In each of the following, the examination will adopt a three-step method. It will, *first*, structure the factual claims covered by the scenario, *second*, outline the standards for arbitration agreements and judgments in order to then, *third*, focus on the operation of arbitral awards.

misapprehended the parties' intent. But §10(a)(4) bars that course: It permits courts to vacate an arbitral decision only when the arbitrator strayed from his delegated task of interpreting a contract, not when he performed that task poorly. Stolt-Nielsen and this case thus fall on opposite sides of the line that §10(a)(4) draws to delimit judicial review of arbitral decisions.').

862. *Discover Bank v. Superior Court*, 113 P3d 1100, 1110 (Cal 2005) relating to a 'waiver found in a consumer contract of adhesion in a setting in which disputes between the contracting parties (i.) predictably involve small amounts of damages and (ii.) when it is alleged that the party with the superior bargaining power has carried out a scheme to deliberately cheat large numbers of consumers out of individually small sums of money [...]'.

863. *AT&T Mobility LLC v. Concepcion et al*, 563 U.S. 333, 131 S.Ct. 1740, 1750-51 (2011); *DIRECTV Inc. v. Amy Imburgia et al*, 136 S.Ct. 463 (2015). *See* the Note of Pika and Trippel, [2016] SchiedsVZ 291.

864. *See supra* [220-225].

865. *See supra* [40].

866. *See supra* [202-214].

[1] Co-obligors

255. The most immanent connection of a third party to one of the prior arbitration's parties is that it shares the (alleged) obligation in question. In order to speak of *solidary obligations*, a specific connection of the joint debtors has to arise, e.g., from the very same contract, explicitly related contracts or a jointly committed tort. Moreover, both debtors must be instantly and fully liable towards the creditor.[867] By contrast, purely parallel obligations have to be distinguished. For instance, the mere fact that two distinct customers purchase comparable steel from a producer does not create any privyship between them. In this regard, it has been held that privyship would not even result if both customers in the end submit claims that (because of the comparability of the questions at hand) were heard by the identical CIETAC tribunal.[868]

256. In general, there are three scenarios in which an arbitral award's effect towards a solidary debtor that has not been part of the prior arbitration becomes relevant. *Primarily*, the creditor might seek repetitive satisfaction, first from one co-obligor, then from the other, because the first co-obligor was unable to undertake the very payments it was ordered to undertake by the arbitral tribunal. The *second* scenario modifies the repetitive claim in that the creditor lost the prior arbitration. If the creditor had succeeded in the arbitration and had in fact received payment, a *third* case scenario is that the opponent might seek (partial) indemnification from its co-debtor. In the latter case, res judicata will certainly operate if both debtors have already been part to the prior arbitration. As the Swiss Federal Tribunal had to reiterate, neither the fact that indemnification actions require the parties to change roles nor the fact that some parties to the former dispute (creditor) are no longer included prevents the fulfilment of res judicata's same-parties requirement.[869]

257. If the co-obligor has not been included in the prior arbitration, either scenario raises concerns as to potentially contrasting procedural and consensual standards. The exposure of the solidary debtor to the *arbitration agreement* depends on nothing but his consent to an arbitration clause. Such consent might be implied on a case-by-case assessment where a third party interfered with another's contractual rights.[870] Furthermore, in an indemnification suit, this consent can be expressed towards either the other debtor or the original creditor.[871] Under most national laws, *judgments* have an equally restrictive application towards solidary debtors. This is established in Germanic

867. Meier, in *Max Planck Encyclopedia of European Private Law* 'Solidary Obligations'.
868. *Coutino Caro & Co. USA Inc. v. Marcus Trading Inc*, 2000 WL 435566, 9 (D Conn).
869. ATF 140 III, 278, [E.4.2.1.].
870. *See Hughes Masonry v. Greater Clark County School Bldg*, 659 F.2d 836 (7th Cir. 1981); *McBro Planning Development v. Triangle Electrical Construction*, 741 F2 342 (11th Cir. 1984).
871. *See* on the *cessio legis* France: Cass. (1e civ.), *Orri v. Lubrifants Elf Aquitaine*, 11 June 1991; CA Paris, 11 January 1990, [1992] Rev. Arb. 95. Switzerland Berger and Kellerhals, *Arbitration in Switzerland* [577]. Cf. TF, 18 December 2001, 4P.126/2001, (2002) ASA Bull. 482, [2.e.aa]; ATF 129 III 727, 735 (obiter with further references). *See* on the deviating approach for forum-selection clauses ATF 105 II 229, *Hafinag AG v. Modernbau Klier und Rabe KG*, 232.

jurisdictions[872] and under the Second Restatement, which states that judgments to the detriment of one co-obligors preclude neither his objections[873] nor relieve him from his obligation.[874] By contrast, English law contains more liberal statements. In *House of Spring Gardens* one of several joint tortfeasors was precluded from arguing that a foreign judgment has been obtained by fraud on the grounds that this defence has already been unsuccessfully in a set aside in Ireland.[875] In addition, there is scholarly support for the proposition that '*an award against a person who is jointly liable with someone who is not a party [...] may have the effect of discharging the third party's liability.*'[876] However, more specific precedence that a co-obligor could be regarded a privy for the purpose of arbitral awards is missing. In particular, *House of Spring Gardens* might be distinguished on the facts since the joint tortfeasors were all joined defendants in the original lawsuit abroad (prior to the set aside). Accordingly, the co-obligor had reasonable knowledge about the dispute. The situation might be very different in arbitration if the co-obligor is not even bound to arbitrate.

258. The procedural law that is most favourable towards res judicata amongst co-obligors stems from France.[877] Corresponding to French judgment principles, the Paris Court of Appeal held a joint buyer under a sales contract that has not been a party to the preceding arbitration as represented by the co-buyer and thus exposed to res judicata.[878] However, in this case, no argument was raised to the potentially limited scope of the arbitration agreement. Instead, it was included in the jointly concluded contract. Accordingly, there are no jurisprudential affirmations of holding third parties with parallel interests as represented even though they have not been bound by the arbitration agreement. Certainly, the doctrine of *opposabilité* might comprehensively extend the efficacy of arbitral awards amongst joint debtors as it has been established in *Prodim*. However, only an extension of res judicata will additionally pre-empt the co-obligor from raising a *tierce opposition*.[879] In conclusion, there are only limited grounds under national laws to assume that an arbitral award can be invoked towards a co-obligor, particularly when the latter is not bound under the arbitration clause. Notably though, in case scenarios where the co-obligor raises the arbitral award in his *favour*, the distinct discussion on non-mutual preclusion (*see* [240-245], *supra*) arises.

872. Germany: s. 425(2) BGB. Switzerland: Guldener, *Zivilprozessrecht* 371; S Zingg, in *Berner Kommentar* Art. 59 [139].
873. Restatement (Second) Judgments, § 49 ('A judgment against one person liable for a loss does not terminate a claim that the injured party may have against another person who may be liable therefore.') and comment b ('A judgment against one obligor under a contract does not terminate the claim against another obligor under the contract.').
874. Restatement (Second) Judgments, § 50(1) ('A satisfaction or release of the judgment, or covenant not to execute upon it, or other agreement terminating in whole or in part the judgment debtor's obligation, does not discharge the liability of any of the other persons liable.').
875. *House of Spring Gardens Ltd v. Waite (No 2)*, [1991] 1 QB 241.
876. *Mustill and Boyd* 365.
877. *See supra* [204].
878. CA Paris, *SA Sucres et denrées v. Scté Multitrade Cairo*, 10 March 2005, (2006) Rev. Arb. 456.
879. *See supra* [204].

[2] Collaterals, Suretyships and Guarantees

259. The effects of arbitral awards towards third parties that provided securities have caused increasing attention, particularly with regard to (independent) guarantees and (accessory) sureties. Both types have in common that a third party secures a main debt. Whilst the security need not operate subsidiarily towards the creditor, it regularly provides for full indemnification towards the debtor.[880] Metaphorically, the difference to solidary obligations is that the guarantor/surety does not stand *next to but one step behind* the main debtor. Yet, the factual case scenarios for res judicata remain identical to solidary obligations (*see* [255-258], *supra*). There can be sequential claims by the creditor and indemnity claims by the guarantor/surety against the main debtor.

260. To take the outset of arbitral jurisdiction, all jurisdictions concur that the relevant guarantee or surety in itself does not imply an obligation to arbitrate. Instead, it needs to be examined whether the guarantor/surety also consented to arbitration.[881] For instance, the necessary case-by-case assessments of arbitration clauses have caused a welter of US jurisprudence both binding guarantors[882] and rejecting their obligation to arbitrate.[883] However, in procedural law, some jurisdictions consider guarantors bound by judgments. This discrepancy has recently been triggered by the discussion on arbitral awards.

261. In France, guarantors faced with a claim already affirmed against the main debtor are exposed not only to judgments' *opposabilité* but also res judicata. Hence, they

880. *See* Drobnig, in *Max Planck Encyclopedia of European Private Law* 'Guarantee, Independent' and 'Suretyship (Modern Law)'.

881. France: Cass. (com), 20 December 1982, [1984] Rev. Arb. 477; Loquin, (1994) Rev. Arb. 235 [26]. Switzerland: ATF 134 III 565, 569; TF, 19 August 2008, 4A_128/2008, [4.2.1] Kaufmann-Kohler and Rigozzi, *International Arbitration in Switzerland* [3.172].

882. *Maxum Found Inc. v. Salus Corp*, 779 F.2d 974 (4th Cir. 1985); *Exchange Mut Ins. Co. v. Haskell Co*, 742 F.2d 274 (6th Cir. 1984); *Son Shipping Co. v. De Fosse & Tanghe*, 199 F.2d 687, 688 (2d Cir. 1952); *Dev Bank of Philippines v. Chemtex Fibers Inc*, 617 FSupp 55 (S.D.N.Y. 1985) (guarantor of loan agreement, that also signed loan agreement, bound by arbitration clause in that agreement); *Banque de Paris et des Pays-Bas v. Amoco Oil Co.*, 573 FSupp 1464 (S.D.N.Y. 1983); *Hidrocarburos y Derivados, CA v. Lemos*, 453 FSupp 160 (S.D.N.Y. 1977); *Midland Tar Distilleries Inc. v. M/T Lotus*, 362 FSupp 1311, 1313 (S.D.N.Y. 1973); *Lowry & Co. v. SS Le Moyne D'Iberville*, 253 FSupp 396, 398 (S.D.N.Y. 1966). *Frederick v. United States*, 385 F.2d 481, 485 (5th Cir. 1967); *Reymond Int'l Builders Inc. v. First Indem of Am. Ins. Co*, 516 A.2d 620, 622 (NJ 1986); *George v. Hartford Accident and Indem Co*, 404 S.E.2d 1, 3 (NC Ct. App 1991).

883. *Bridas SAPIC*, 345 F3d, 357 ('typically a guarantor cannot be compelled to arbitrate on the basis of an arbitration clause in a contract to which it is not a party'); *Asplundh Tree Expert Co. v. Bates*, 71 F.3d 592, 595 (6th Cir. 1995) ('as a general rule, a guarantor who is not a signatory to a contract containing an arbitration clause is not bound by the arbitration clause'); *Proshred Holdings Ltd v. Conestoga Document*, 2002 WL 1067328, *3 (ND Ill) ('guarantors for the performance of a contract are bound by the arbitration clause in that contract only when they expressly agree to the obligation to arbitrate') (quoting *Grundstad v. Ritt*, 106 F.3d 201, 204 (7th Cir. 1997).

cannot initiate any third-party appeal against the arbitral award.[884] When an arbitral award has been rendered between the main debtor and the creditor, its *opposabilité* certainly extends towards guarantors and sureties.[885] With regard to res judicata, some authors sought to restrict it,[886] whilst the Commercial Court Nanterre impliedly considered a foreign ICC award to constitute res judicata against the surety.[887] In 2015, the *Cour de cassation* prominently took the position to distinguish judgments from arbitral awards. It held that a surety is not bound by an arbitral award's res judicata when it has not consented to the underlying arbitration clause. The proceduralist rules could not apply when the '*surety has not accepted arbitral jurisdiction [...] and could not have intervened in the arbitration*'.[888]

262. In the US, former jurisprudence considered arbitral awards rendered against main debtors as 'prima facie evidence' against the guarantors.[889] Others expressly considered guarantors to be bound by an arbitral award's preclusion effects.[890] In any case, much practical need to rely on privy doctrines is prevented by US law's opportunity for non-mutual preclusion (on behalf of the guarantor) and vouching in (on behalf of the creditor).[891] In this regard, English law appears more restrictive. In general, non-mutual preclusion cannot exceed arbitral jurisdiction.[892] Moreover, when the creditor invokes an arbitral award against the guarantor, arbitral scholarship submits:

> If it is intended that an award against the principal debtor will bind the guarantor then the guarantee should contain express provision to that effect. Failure to include that provision may make the award unenforceable against that third party.[893]

---

884. For example, Cass. (1e civ.), 14 February 1990, [1990] Bull. civ I No. 42; T com Nanterre, *Technip France*, 5 September 2001, [2002] Rev. Arb. 455; CA Paris, 21 May 1964, [1964] Rec Dalloz 602; CA Paris, 4 January 1960, [1960] Rev. Arb. 122. *See* implicitly Cass. (2e civ), 23 November 2000, 98-13394.
885. CA Paris, 4 January 1960, [1960] Rev. Arb. 122; CA Paris, 21 May 1964, [1964] Rec Dalloz 602; T com Nanterre, *Technip France*, 5 September 2001, [2002] Rev. Arb. 455 Loquin, [1994] Rev. Arb. 235 248; Goutal, (1988) Rev. Arb. 439. *See* Chambreuil, (1991) Rev. Arb. 33.
886. *See* Loquin, (1994) Rev. Arb. 235 [32-36] favouring a restrictive approach.
887. T com Nanterre, *Technip France*, 5 September 2001, [2002] Rev. Arb. 455.
888. Cass. (com), 5 May 2015, No. 14-16.644 ('*Alors que le principe jurisprudentiel de la représentation mutuelle des co-obligés solidaires qui interdit à la caution de former une tierce opposition contre la décision rendue dans l'instance opposant le débiteur principal et le créancier ne peut être appliqué à une sentence arbitrale dès lors que la caution n'a pas accepté la compétence d'une juridiction arbitrale en l'absence de signature de la convention d'arbitrage et ne peut intervenir volontairement à l'instance à défaut d'accord des parties.*').
889. *Sauer v. Detroit Fidelity & Surety Co*, 237 Mich 697, 702 (1927); *Kent Probate Judge v. American Employers Insurance Co*, 283 Mich 328, 334-335 (1938); *Madawick Contracting v. Travelers Insurance Company*, 307 NY 111 (1954); *PR Post Corporation v. Maryland Casualty Company*, 68 MichApp 182 (1976); *Deposit Parsons & Whittemore Contractors*, 48 NY 2d 127 (1979).
890. *T&R Painting Constr v. St Paul Fire & Marine*, 23 Cal. App 4th 739 (2d Dist 1994). *See Kelly v. Vons Companies*, 67 Cal. App 4th 1329, 1338 (2d Dist 1998).
891. *See supra* [62, 244].
892. *See supra* [242].
893. *Russell on Arbitration* [3-015] referring to *In Re Kitchin Ex p Young*, (1881) 17 ChD 669; *Bruns v. Colocotroonis (The Vasso)*, [1979] 2 Lloyd's Rep. 412. Cf. *Hayter v. Nelson and Home Insurance*, [1990] 2 Lloyd's Rep. 265.

263. Effects to the detriment of sureties and guarantors will be equally difficult in Germanic jurisdictions rejecting the extension of res judicata in procedural law.[894] Yet, when an arbitral award *dismissed* the creditor's claims against the main debtor, scholarship affirms the applicability of non-mutual preclusion in favour of the surety.[895] By contrast, the author has submitted that this rule should be restricted to those cases where the surety has consented to the arbitration agreement in order to focus on the creditor's opportunity to sue both opponents.[896]

264. In conclusion, most national laws provide limited authorities to argue that an arbitral award rendered against the main debtor can be invoked in subsequent proceedings to the detriment of the guarantor/surety. In addition, indemnity matters between guarantor/surety and main debtor have caused limited attention. Primarily, if a guarantor/surety satisfies the main debtor pursuant to an arbitral award, a potentially automatic assignment of the claim against the main debtor cannot establish res judicata, since the receivable of the creditor against the main debtor was not adjudicated upon. Hence, the restrictive privy assessments are likely to apply unless the guarantee/surety regime is deemed to include an implied preclusion agreement.

[3] Third-Party Beneficiaries

265. If parties stipulated for claims in favour of third parties, the effects of judgments, arbitration agreements and therefore arbitral awards are exposed to differentiating assessments. To begin with the jurisdictional basis of tribunals, common law is generally favourable to binding the third-party beneficiary to arbitrate. In England, section 8 1999 Contract Act extends arbitration clauses to third-party beneficiaries.[897] In the US, jurisprudence reached similar results.[898] By contrast, civil-law jurisdictions are more hostile. In Switzerland, jurisprudence has only affirmed that the third party has the *option* to rely on the arbitration clause,[899] but did not address the situation whether there is an obligation to arbitrate. Scholarship from Switzerland and Germany supports the third-party beneficiary's duty to arbitrate since the contract could create nothing but advantages for the third party.[900] By contrast, the *Cour de cassation* has

894. *See supra* [203].
895. Bosch, *Rechtskraft und Rechtshängigkeit im Schiedsverfahren* 143-144; Lühmann, *Die Rechtskraft des Schiedsspruchs* 150; Wagner, in *Die Beteiligung Dritter am Schiedsverfahren* 35.
896. Pika, (2018) 131 ZZP 250-251.
897. '[T]he third party shall be treated for the purposes of the Act as a party to the arbitration agreement as regards disputes between himself and the promisor relating to the enforcement of the substantive term by the third party'; *Nisshin Shipping Co. Ltd v. Cleaves & Co*, [2003] EWHC 2602 (Comm).
898. *Spear, Leeds & Kellogg v. Cent. Life Assur. Co.*, 85 F.3d 21, 27 (2d Cir. 1997); *Fink v. Carlson*, 856 F.2d 44, 46 n.3 (8th Cir. 1988) ('Of course, if the third party beneficiary seeks to enforce the contract, he will be bound by the contract's limitations.').
899. TF, 19 April 2011, 4A_44/2011, [2012] ASA Bull. 659, 666-669; TF, 8 March 2012, [2012] ASA Bull. 647, [3, 30]; Kaufmann-Kohler and Rigozzi, *International Arbitration in Switzerland* [3.168].
900. *Poudret and Besson* [289]; Schlosser, in *Stein and Jonas*, § 1029[70]; *Schwab and Walter* Ch. 7[36].

facilitated the principle of privity of contracts and denied that any third-party beneficiary could be bound to arbitrate unless it consented to do so.[901] An option for the third-party beneficiary remains.[902]

266. For judgments, explicit statements are even more critical. For instance, the German Federal Court of Justice rejected that a third-party beneficiary is exposed to res judicata when a judgment was rendered between the debtor and the promisor.[903] The same result is favoured under the Second Restatement.[904] By contrast, for *arbitral awards*, the Fifth Circuit took a different position in *Nauru*. In this case, the claimant (Nauru) hired the respondent (Drago Interests) for developing purchased land. In exchange, Nauru issued a promissory note to a third party, Drago Trustee. After disputes about the development's costs and profitability arose, an arbitral award against the respondent stipulated that Nauru had no liability under the promissory note. The respondent applied for annulment arguing that the dispute could not have reasonably been decided without Drago Trustee. The court rejected the argument holding:

> As effective third-party beneficiar[y] [Drage Trustee] may be precluded from relitigating the issue of breach of the Development Agreement in any subsequent proceeding and may be bound by the panel's finding of non-liability on Nauru's part.[905]

267. In conclusion, the effects of arbitral awards towards third-party beneficiaries remain unsettled. Whilst express US precedence affirms them, arbitration-agreement (France) and judgment principles (Germany) oppose them.

[4] Chains of Contracts

268. It has been stated in the very *Introduction* to this examination that chains of contracts are inherently exposed to the risks of multi-fora disputes and therefore in particular need of Forum Coordination. However, it appears highly doubtful whether any of the examined jurisdictions would expose a third party to an arbitral award's res judicata in indemnity claims. In particular, neither judgment nor arbitration-agreement standards allow to extend the effect towards sub-contractors or purchasers. For instance, English law provides that indemnification is no grounds for assuming a privy

901. Cass, *Bisutti*, [1987] Rev. Arb. 139. *Contra ICC Case 9762*, Final Award, 2001, (2004) XXIX Y.C.A. 26, 40 ('It is generally accepted that if a third party is bound by the same obligations stipulated by a party to a contract and this contract contains an arbitration clause or, in relation to it, an arbitration agreement exists, such a third party is also bound by the arbitration clause, or arbitration agreement, even if it did not sign it.'); Jarrosson, in *ASA Special Series* [36-37].
902. Goutal, (1987) Rev. Arb. 145.
903. BGH, [1952] NJW 178.
904. Restatement (Second) Judgments, § 56(1) ('A judgment for or against the promisee in an action between him and the promisor does not preclude an action by the beneficiary on the obligation to him unless at the time the judgment was rendered the promisee had power to discharge the obligation.').
905. *Nauru Phosphate Royalties Inc. v. Drago Daic Interests Inc*, 138 F.3d 160, 166 (5th Cir. 1998).

relationship.[906] Moreover, in civil-law jurisdictions, even if res judicata could in general be extended to a sub-contractor or along chains of sales contract, an operative issue of res judicata arises. The cause of action, decisive for res judicata merely concerns the obligation, not incidental issues relevant for indemnity matters such as the goods', the construction's or the rented property's conformity.[907] This restriction with regard to incidental reasonings would also bar the application of the French *opposabilité* towards e.g., sub-contractors.[908] Moreover, it has to be mentioned that French contract law contains the genuine *action directe*, i.e., direct payment claims of, e.g., a sub-contractor against a principal or a landlord against the sub-tenant. In this regard, the third party can exercise the payment claim of the actual creditor in his own name. Whilst this provides no modification for indemnity matters, it necessitates that chains of contracts raise the above-mentioned questions of res judicata against and amongst co-obligors and towards third-party beneficiaries. In conclusion, national jurisdictions contain only limited grounds to extend an arbitral award's res judicata in chains of contracts.

[5] Insurances

269. Generally, the effects of dispute resolutions towards insurers require due distinction of the scenarios that, *first*, the insured debtor lost the primary dispute and seeks indemnification from the insurer eventually, *second*, the creditor initiated repetitive disputes against the insured debtor and against the insurer eventually as well as, *third*, the insurer reimbursed one party (either creditor or insured debtors) and seeks indemnification from the other. From a jurisdictional perspective, the effects of arbitration agreements appear settled. Disputes between the insured and the insurer are governed by the insurance contract and its potential dispute resolution clause. In indemnification procedures against the opponent, the insurer is generally bound by an arbitration clause between the parties under the principle of subrogation.[909] By contrast, the effects of decisions heavily depend on the applicable insurance law. Whilst French scholarship submits to regard an insurer as represented by the insured in prior disputes,[910] German law states in section 124(1) VVG that proceedings between

906. *Gleeson v. J. Wippell & Co. Ltd* [1977] 1 WLR 510 per Megarry VC (Ch). Approved of by *Johnson v. Gore Wood & Co*, [2002] 2 AC 1, 32 per Bingham LJ (HL); *Secretary of State for Business, Innovation and Skills v. Potiwal*, [2012] EWHC 3723 (Ch).

907. *See supra* [108-114].

908. Cass. (com), 2 February 2016, 14-23.921, [2016] Rev. Arb. 812. *See* further *supra* [238].

909. England: *Schifffahrtsgesellschaft Detlev von Appen v. Voest Alpine Intertrading et al*, [1997] Lloyd's Rep. 279; *West Tankers Inc. v. Ras Riunione Adriatica di Sicurta* (*'The Front Comor'*), [2005] 2 Lloyd's Rep. 257, 264 (QB). France: CA Paris, 13 November 1992, [1993] Rev. Arb. 632. Switzerland: KG Geneva, 16 October 1987, [1987] ASA Bull. 269, 273; Kaufmann-Kohler and Rigozzi, *International Arbitration in Switzerland* [3.164]. US: *Allianz Global Risk* U.S. Ins. Co. *v. General Electric Co*, 2012 WL 689957, *1 (9th Cir) ('The subrogated [non-signatory] insurer stands in the shoes of its insured., and is entitled to its contractual rights and remedies').

910. Jarrosson, [2007] 8 Procédures No. 12 [37] with reference to litigation case: Cass. (2e civ), 14 January 1999, [1999] Bull. civ II No. 63. *See* in litigation Tomasin 84.

the main parties can only cause beneficial, not detrimental, preclusion towards the insurer. Yet, jurisprudence established that the insurer is bound in indemnification proceedings initiated by the insured under substantive insurance law.[911] Notably, this is another manifestation for the *contractual* cognizance of adjudications. Correspondingly, in California, an insured was able to rely on an arbitral award against its insurer under the contract in order to establish a recoverable loss.[912]

270. The most extensive assessment of arbitral awards' effects towards insurers and the application of procedural privy doctrines occurred by the English Court of Appeal in *Sun Life Assurances*: Sun Life had commenced arbitration against Cigna claiming reimbursement for accidents under a reinsurance contract. The first arbitral tribunal stated that the accidents would generally fall under the reinsurance contract's scope. Yet, it held the reinsurance contract avoided for misrepresentation. Subsequently, Sun Life initiated a second arbitration against the later respondent (Lincoln) with whom it had also concluded a reinsurance agreement. It was undisputed that this agreement obligated Lincoln to reimburse Sun Life for the relevant accidents if the accidents would still not have fallen under the scope of the agreement between Sun Life and Cigna. Therefore, the decisive issue was whether that scope has been conclusively settled in the first arbitration. Since the first arbitral tribunal mainly relied on the avoidance, the second tribunal considered the elaboration on the reinsurance contract's scope merely an *obiter*, hence issue estoppel inapplicable. The Court of Appeal affirmed this reasoning.[913] Since issue estoppel was not even applicable, the question whether Lincoln (as Sun Life's reinsurer) would have been a privy to the first arbitration was indecisive. Yet, the court addressed this matter *obiter*. Strikingly, Mance LJ's speech lays out that privy doctrines should not apply as comprehensively in arbitration as they do in litigation because they are not accompanied by pre-emptive means of forum coordination such as joinders and consolidation.[914] Hence, there is

911. BGH, [1993] NJW 68, 69. *See* for arbitral awards Pika, (2018) 131 ZZP 253-254.
912. *Executive Risk Indem Inc. v. Jones*, Cal. Rptr 3d 747 (Cal Ct. App 2009).
913. *Sun Life Assurance Company of Canada et al. v. The Lincoln National Life Insurance Company*, [2004] EWCA Civ 1660, [64-69] per Mance LJ.
914. *Ibid.*, [68] ('[M]ore fundamentally, the solution for which [the appellant] contends appears to me to overlook or obscure important differences between arbitration and litigation. In the context of litigation, problems of potentially conflicting judgments arrived at between different parties to the same overall complex of disputes are met by provisions for joinder of parties or proceedings or for trial together, if necessary on a mandatory basis using the courts' compulsive powers. Even in circumstances in which there has been no such joinder, and where neither res judicata nor issue estoppel has any application, the court may intervene to prevent abuse of its process. All this is facilitated by the public nature of litigation, the public interest in the efficient administration of justice and the courts' coercive powers. [...] Arbitration is in contrast a consensual, private affair between the particular parties to a particular arbitration agreement. The resulting inability to enforce the solutions of joinder of parties or proceedings in arbitration, or to try connected arbitrations together other than by consent, is well-recognised – though the popularity of arbitration may indicate that this inability is not often inconvenient or that perceived advantages of arbitration, including confidentiality and privacy are seen as outweighing any inconvenience. [...] The arbitrators in each arbitration are appointed to decide the disputes in that arbitration between the particular parties to that arbitration. The privacy and confidentiality attaching to arbitration underline this; and, even if they do not lead to non-parties remaining ignorant of an earlier arbitration award, they are

authority that reinsurers, which have not consented to a prior tribunal's jurisdiction, are no privies to arbitral proceedings at common law. Such restrictive treatment might serve as a paradigm for a reconciliation of res judicata and jurisdiction. In conclusion, the third-party effects of arbitral awards in insurance case scenarios are intrinsically connected to the legal concept facilitated: jurisdictions which consider decisions' third-party effect an implied term under the insurance contract, such as Germany and US laws, are likely to affirm them for arbitral awards. By contrast, the discretionary privy assessment at common law duly adheres to the jurisdictional constraints of the prior arbitration and is therefore restrictive.

[6] Corporate Liability

271. Given the ample opportunities for shelf companies, creditors who have already obtained an arbitral award against their debtor might seek to hold the latter's shareholders liable, either because the very debtor is a partnership providing full liability or because the creditor sees potential for piercing the corporate veil. In such scenario, res judicata would relieve the creditor from re-establishing the main debt and enable him to focus on the shareholder's liability. In addition to this case scenario, preclusion arguments can also arise when the parties themselves formulated the ability to invoke counter-claims of related companies. For instance, in *Sinochem*, the contract in dispute stated: '[I]n the event [that] any party shall [...] default in the payment [...] the other party shall have the right to set-off, counterclaim or withhold payment in respect of any default by the non-performing party *or any affiliates* of the non-performing party under this agreement or any other agreement between the parties *or their affiliates*.'[915] Potentially, claims by such affiliates have already been adjudicated upon so that preclusion arguments arise.

272. A scenario causing increased attention with regard to res judicata concerns partnerships. In Germany, for instance, § 129 Handelsgesetzbuch (HGB) stipulates that a judgment against a partnership (*offene Handelsgesellschaft*) is *not* enforceable towards the partner, but constitutes res judicata towards them.[916] Such distinction between enforceability and res judicata is also known to Austrian law, which is why the English High Court once rejected to enforce an Austrian judgment against a partner.[917] Comparable to the scope of res judicata, German jurisprudence affirms that

calculated to lead to difficulties in obtaining access, and about the scope of any access, to material relating to that award.').

915. *Sinochem Int'l Oil (London) Co. v. Mobil Sales & Supply Corp*, [2000] 1 Eng Rep. 758 (QB) (emphasis added).

916. *See*, e.g., s. 129 HGB: '*(1) Wird ein Gesellschafter wegen einer Verbindlichkeit der Gesellschaft in Anspruch genommen, so kann er Einwendungen, die nicht in seiner Person begründet sind, nur insoweit geltend machen, als sie von der Gesellschaft erhoben werden können. [...] (4) Aus einem gegen die Gesellschaft gerichteten vollstreckbaren Schuldtitel findet die Zwangsvollstreckung gegen die Gesellschafter nicht statt.*' *See also* § 727 ZPO which does not contain applications on the partners.

917. *Blohn v. Desser*, [1962] 2 QB 116.

partners are also bound by the partnerships' arbitration clauses.[918] Given the thus converging extension of judgments and arbitration agreements, arbitral awards will equally constitute res judicata towards partners. Recently, a decision of the Higher Regional Court Karlsruhe caused uncertainty, since it rejected to enforce an ICC award rendered in Switzerland in favour of a Turkish sub-contractor against a German-Qatari joint venture for a construction project in Qatar. The court reasoned that under both German and Swiss laws an arbitral award was *'res judicata between the arbitrating parties only'*.[919] However, in rejecting the appeal *against the enforcement decision*, the Federal Court of Justice highlighted that such problems of enforceability do not necessarily bar res judicata.[920]

273. Moving from partnerships to corporations with limited liability, most jurisdictions are generally very restrictive towards lifting the corporate veil: in substantive law, German jurisprudence now rejects *any* liability of private limited companies' shareholders and has created the concept of pure *interior liability*.[921] In jurisdictional matters, Swiss jurisprudence required particular abuse of corporate rights in order to hold a shareholding company bound by an arbitration clause.[922] For judgments, English law states that controlling shareholders are no privies.[923] By contrast, US law contains the most extensive precedence not only for piercing the corporate veil in substantive law but also for extensions of claim and issue preclusion in procedural law.[924] Also for arbitral awards, there is remarkable precedence: arbitral awards have been held to have preclusive effects against the president and managing director of an undercapitalized party to a charter contract[925] and towards a subsidiary who provided the arbitrating parent company with a loan and directed the parent company's negotiations in the underlying transaction.[926] In a labour matter, the Southern District of New York was confronted with requests by employees to facilitate an arbitral award rendered against the (defunct) employer in order to grant enforcement against the employer's shareholders on grounds of alter ego. Noting that the claimants were barred

918. BGH, [1991] NJW-RR 423, 424 (obiter, *Partenreederei*); BayObLG, [2004] SchiedsVZ 45, 46 (KG); OLG Köln, 23 September 2010, 19 SchH 15/10, [51] (GbR).
919. OLG Kalrsruhe, [2015] SchiedsVZ 145, 148 (*'Von der materiellen Rechtskraft werden die Parteien und ihre Rechtsnachfolger gebunden'*).
920. BGH, [2015] SchiedsVZ 139 (*'Die Befürchtung der Antragstellerin, dies habe negative präjudizielle Folgen für eine zukünftige Leistungs- oder Feststellungsklage gegen die Antragsgegnerinnen, vermag der Senat nicht zu teilen. Denn da der Inhalt des Beschlusses und damit der Umfang seiner Rechtskraft erforderlichenfalls auch unter Heranziehung der Entscheidungsgründe zu bestimmen ist, kann hier aus der Nichtanerkennung nicht abgeleitet werden, dass es der Antragstellerin in einem solchen Verfahren verwehrt wäre, sich auf die von ihr insoweit behauptete materielle Rechtslage nach katarischem Recht zu berufen.'*).
921. BGHZ 173, 246.
922. TF, 29 January 1996, 4P.330&332/1994, [1996] ASA Bull. 496, [6b, 14]; Beger and Kellerhals, *Arbitration in Switzerland*, [573-574]; Müller in Arroyo (ed.), *Arbitration in Switzerland*, Art. 178 PILA [67-69].
923. *Baratok Ltd v. Epiette Ltd*, [1998] 1 BCLC 282 (CA).
924. *See supra* [206].
925. *Eagle Transport Ltd Inc. v. O'Connor*, 470 FSupp 731, 733-734 (S.D.N.Y. 1979).
926. *Anchor Glass Container Corp. v. Buschmeier*, 426 F.3d 872, 879-880 (7th Cir. 2005).

from raising a duplicative claim against the employer's shareholder,[927] the court regarded the alter-ego requirements as met.[928] Furthermore, in *Carte Blanche*, a franchisee successfully sued the franchisor for payment before an arbitral tribunal. Eventually, the District Court confirmed the arbitral award and the Second Circuit then granted the franchisee's request to have it enforced against the franchisor's parent company.[929]

274. The jurisdictional dimension of the issue, i.e., whether the arbitration agreement was equally extended, did not receive any consideration in those cases. By contrast, *In re Kaplan* before the Third Circuit is the leading case for a different assessment: Mr Kaplan has been the sole shareholder and managing Director of a stock corporation (MKI). The latter agreed with a clearing firm (First Options) to forward tax refunds. Subsequent to substantial deficits of MKI, the clearing firm closed the corporation's commercial account and initiated arbitration against MKI and Mr Kaplan claiming the tax refunds and damages. MKI invoked claims arising out of the commercial account's closure by the clearing firm. The arbitral award was rendered in the clearing firm's favour, and it rejected any counter-claims. Furthermore, the tribunal extended its jurisdiction to Mr Kaplan as a non-signatory to the arbitration agreement on grounds of the alter-ego doctrine (piercing the corporate veil). For this reason and *to this extent*, the arbitral award was vacated. This conclusion on jurisdiction was in the meantime confirmed by the Supreme Court.[930] Against MKI, the arbitral award was confirmed. In the subsequent bankruptcy proceedings, Mr Kaplan objected to the clearing firm's claims once again raising the alleged counter-claims. The clearing firm invoked the arbitral award (technically the confirming judgment) towards Mr Kaplan who was, after the partial set-aside, a third party to the award. The court rejected the preclusion on the grounds of the jurisdictional aspect. It explicitly placed the consensual standards developed for the extension of arbitration over the procedural standards developed for the extension of judgments towards third parties.[931] In conclusion, whilst partners may be exposed to arbitral awards and there is also precedence exposing corporations'

927. Cf. *Feithshans v. Kahn*, 2006 WL 2714706, [IV.A.] (S.D.N.Y. 2006) ('[P]laintiffs can only have one recovery for a single wrong [...]. Naming new defendants in this action does not help plaintiffs because res judicata 'operates to preclude claims, rather than particular configurations of parties.').
928. *Ibid.*, [IV.B.].
929. *Carte Blanche (Singapore) Pte Ltd v. Diners Club International Inc*, 2 F.3d 24 (2d Cir. 1993).
930. *First Options of Chicago Inc. v. Kaplan*, 514 U.S. 938, 947 (1995).
931. *In re Kaplan*, 143 F.3d 807, 815-816 (3d Cir. 1998) ('Generally applicable res judicata rules must sometimes be adapted to fit the arbitration context. Moreover, we believe that First Options' argument is inconsistent with the rule that the scope of the obligation to arbitrate – and to accept arbitral decisions – is defined by contract. An arbitration agreement may limit its preclusive effects. Where, as in this case, a corporation agrees to arbitration but the corporation's principal and sole shareholder withholds such consent, we presume, in the absence of any contractual provision addressing the issue of res judicata in so many words, that the parties agreed that the principal and sole shareholder, who would necessarily control the corporation's participation in any arbitration proceeding or litigation, would not be bound by any arbitral award or judgment based on the theory that he or she controlled the relevant proceeding. Any other rule would render essentially meaningless the principal and sole shareholder's withholding of consent to be bound personally by the arbitral award or judgment.').

shareholders, the latter concept has been opposed by the Third Circuit demanding an adjustment of preclusion and jurisdictional rules.

§4.06 FUNCTIONAL INFERENCES

275. In general, national laws acknowledge arbitral awards' third-party effects only restrictively. In particular, the due-process rule developed in civil procedure applies: decisions are only preclusive and conclusive between the parties. Moreover, the examination establishes three functional inferences from this survey.

[A] The Emerging Reconciliation of Arbitral Res Judicata and Jurisdiction

276. At its beginning, the Chapter had expressed the conjecture that the proceduralist res judicata principles demand further restriction in arbitration. Considering the specific jurisprudence on *erga omnes* effects, non-mutual preclusion and res judicata against privies, one can summarize many authorities for this general statement. In particular, the English Court of Appeal in *Michael Wilson* on non-mutual preclusion[932] and *Sun Life Assurances* on privy relationships in insurance case scenarios,[933] the Third Circuit on res judicata against shareholders[934] and the Cour de cassation's 2015 surety decision[935] refuse to apply the well-established standards from civil procedure to scenarios where the third party is *not* bound to arbitrate. Yet, there remain other areas where third-party effects exist regardless of the prior jurisdiction; e.g., the *opposabilité* in France or specific privy scenarios in the US.

[B] Irrelevance of Intervention Possibilities under Arbitral Rules?

277. At the Chapter's beginning and in jurisprudence the main rationale to assess arbitral awards' third-party effects by virtue of judgment principles *and* the arbitration agreement's scope was to guarantee that res judicata and intervention possibilities could go hand-in-hand. For instance, as expressed in *Michael Wilson* an arbitrating party should not be exposed to non-mutual preclusion to a third party's benefit if it had not joined this third party.[936] Regularly, the applicability of the arbitration agreement towards a third party guarantees joinder possibilities.[937] Yet, there is a specific case scenario where even the arbitration agreement's third-party effect might not guarantee an adequate interaction of res judicata and intervention possibilities: when third-party

932. *See supra* [242].
933. *See supra* [270].
934. *See supra* [274].
935. *See supra* [261].
936. *See supra* [242].
937. *See supra* [36].

intervention is unavailable under the arbitral rules. In civil procedure, third parties that will be exposed to res judicata as privies can regularly apply for such intervention.[938] In arbitration, however, some arbitral rules such as the ICC Rules do *not* allow third-party intervention even if jurisdiction would otherwise exist.[939] Apparently, it remains yet to be discussed whether such restriction under arbitral rules comprises any relevance for the application of arbitral res judicata. In particular, it might be a valid argument that if a third party can by no means intervene in an arbitral process, it should not be exposed to res judicata even if it were a privy under judgment principles and consented to arbitration in general. The limited discussion is even more striking, since vice versa the increasing adjustments of arbitral rules to multi-party arbitration in the past two decades have not be facilitated as an argument for the applicability of proceduralist res judicata doctrines neither.

[C] Comparative Divides and Litmus Tests for Cross-Border Case Scenarios

278. In light of this comparative survey, a final inference is drawn as to those national doctrines, which are most likely to cause discussions in cross-border case scenarios. Certainly, since the instant issue is at the crossroads of legal topics as complex as: (i) the procedural doctrine of res judicata, (ii) the third-party effect of arbitration agreements and (iii) substantive provisions on, e.g., sureties, insurances or corporate liability, national laws will frequently differ in details. On top of that, three doctrines appeared as particular exceptional: *first*, French law's *opposabilité*, i.e., the effectiveness of arbitral awards erga omnes compensated by third-party appeals before courts is unknown to other jurisdictions. *Second*, common law's application of non-mutual preclusion (if the third party relying on the award consented to the arbitration agreement) is unknown to civil-law jurisdictions. *Third*, some US jurisdictions contained the most extensive privy doctrines allowing for effects against third-party beneficiaries, guarantors and controlling shareholders. Such effects would be ineffective in other jurisdictions. Any of these tropics will cause particular attention as to the solutions to cross-border case scenarios under uniform, private international and transnational law.

§4.07 CONCLUDING THESES

(1) The determination of the rules on arbitral awards' third-party effects illustrates the dichotomy of Forum Coordination for multilateral transactions: on the one hand, the application of due process in arbitration indicates the application of judgment principles to arbitral awards. On the other hand,

938. *See supra* [209210].
939. *See supra* [65].

party autonomy and the restriction of pre-emptive tools indicate the relevance of arbitration-*agreement* standards towards third parties.[940]

(2) In general, national laws contain no general rule for arbitral awards' third-party effects.[941]

(3) Parties to multilateral transactions can generally conclude preclusion agreements.[942]

(4) Under certain circumstances, arbitral awards can comprise *erga omnes* effects. Yet, party autonomy demands that affected parties either consented to the arbitration clause or that they are awarded the opportunity for third-party appeals before courts.[943]

(5) Generally, arbitral awards can create non-mutual preclusions at common law. However, authorities such as the *Michael Wilson* judgment formulate a '*high threshold*', particularly that the third party must have consented to arbitration.[944]

(6) Generally, arbitral awards create preclusive effects towards successors.[945]

(7) Although some matters might be non-arbitrable, disclosed representations and class arbitrations can generally bind a third party to an arbitral award's res judicata.[946]

(8) In complex substantive relationships such as solidary obligations, guarantees, sureties or insurances, arbitral awards will only affect third parties under exceptional circumstances. Already judgment principles have been restrictive. Moreover, issue preclusion might be inapplicable, and the arbitration *agreement* not binding the third party.[947]

(9) The examination of the authorities under national laws on selected third-party effects of arbitral awards allows to state that there is reasonable authority for the submission that: in general, arbitral awards' third-party effects will not exceed the underlying arbitration *agreement*'s third-party effect.[948]

940. *See supra* [220-225].
941. *Ibid.*
942. *See supra* [229-233].
943. *See supra* [234-239].
944. *See supra* [240-244].
945. *See supra* [247-248].
946. *See supra* [251-253].
947. *See supra* [254-270].
948. *See supra* [275-276].

CHAPTER 5
Third-Party Effects of Arbitral Awards under the New York Convention

279. Uniform arbitration law has long been considered indecisive for the topic of res judicata. By far the most important uniform instrument in international arbitration is the NYC. Upon the initiative by the ICC,[949] it overcame the preceding 1927 Geneva Convention's weaknesses (double-exequatur and burden of proof)[950] and is now considered the primary reason for arbitration's pole position in dispute resolution.[951] Certainly, the NYC does not explicitly address the topic of res judicata. Yet, its relation to res judicata has recently gained increasing scholarly attention (*see* §5.01, *infra*). To cite a preeminent treatise's observation on res judicata in international arbitration:

> Remarkably little attention has been devoted by national courts or commentators to the role of international arbitration conventions. [...] [I]t would be surprising if both the parties' arbitration agreement and the [New York] Convention's provisions guaranteeing the binding character of awards were entirely silent concerning such matters.[952]

280. In this regard, the Chapter takes the general position that – even though it might be desirable – the Convention does *not yet* provide any comprehensively uniform regime on res judicata. Primarily, the Convention's rules on 'recognition' concern merely *one out of several aspects* of international res judicata. Thus, whilst res judicata can be examined under the grounds set forth in Article V NYC, its specific requirements and consequences are regularly to be determined under national laws (*see* §5.02, *infra*).

949. *ICC Draft of NYC*, 1953, reprinted (1998) 9 ICC Bull. 35.
950. Cf. *UNCITRAL Guide to NYC* Art. III [8] ('pro-enforcement bias') with further references.
951. Cf. Di Pietro and Platte, *Enforcement of International Arbitration Awards* 11; Kronke in Kronke et al. (eds), *Recognition and Enforcement of Arbitral Awards* 3; Liebscher in Wolff (ed.), *New York Convention* Prelims [1, 17, 20]; McLachlan, *Lis Pendens in International Litigation* 189; Rubins and Kinsella, *International Investment* 352; van den Berg, *New York Convention* 1.
952. Born, 3741-3742.

281. Turning to res judicata's third-party scope, it is the Chapter's core and genuine contention that Article V(1)(a) NYC comprises a pivotal preliminary requirement, i.e., the third party's consent to arbitration. It is methodologically possible and practically preferable to state: Article V(1)(a) NYC demands that no third party is exposed res judicata except it is bound by the arbitration agreement. Consequently, the Chapter proposes a hybrid assessment examining personal jurisdiction and the otherwise applicable law as conjoint requirements (*see* §5.03, *infra*). Finally, the Chapter examines the Convention's mandate for extended preclusion agreements as they might be preferable for parties to multilateral transactions (*see* §5.04, *infra*).

§5.01 STATUS QUO OF THE DISCUSSION ON RES JUDICATA UNDER THE NYC

282. The current, steadily increasing discussion on the NYC's relevance for the operation of res judicata constitutes the outset of this Chapter. Within the respective opinions, the consequences for arbitral awards' third-party effects will be mentioned.

283. An initial opinion notes that the Convention's guarantee for recognition under Article III constitutes a '*general principle that arbitral awards have res judicata effect*'.[953] Such reading has also been applied in a 2009 case before the US District Court for the Southern District of New York.[954] However, the statements refrain from addressing the effects of any general principle on res judicata's specific problems, e.g., the admissibility of issue preclusion. Potentially, one might construe the Convention as a minimum guarantee.[955] Yet, such minimum guarantee would beg the question as to its content. Perhaps issue preclusion, as a concept rejected in many civil-law jurisdictions,[956] would not fall under the minimum guarantee. But to provide another example: would the Convention prohibit that res judicata exclusively applied if the prior dispositif and the subsequent request for relief are entirely identical?

284. Amongst more specific statements on the NYC's application to res judicata, a restrictive opinion denies any interrelation: the Convention were to affect enforcement exclusively whilst excluding res judicata entirely.[957] Notably, the proponent of this opinion additionally proposes a broad third-party effect of arbitral awards detached

953. Schaffstein, *Res Judicata* [4.107, 5.68]. *Corresp* Kaufmann-Kohler and Rigozzi, *International Arbitration in Switzerland* [8.230].

954. *American Express Bank Ltd v. Banco Espanol de Crédito SA*, 597 FSupp2d 394, 403 (S.D.N.Y. 2009) ('Though the convention does not expressly speak to the res judicata effect of an international arbitral award [...] it reflects the principle that until it is successfully challenged., an arbitral award presumptively establishes the rights and liabilities of the parties to the arbitration.'). In this case, the Convention was applied as one out of three grounds, i.e., in addition to contract and New York law, in order to justify an award's res judicata. *See also Gulf Petro Trading Company Inc. et al. v. Nigerian National Petroleum Corporation et al*, 7 January 2008, 06-40713 (5th Cir).

955. *See* Scherer in Wolff (ed.), *New York Convention* Art. III ('absurd to conclude that the NYC left Contracting States free to accord arbitral awards no, or only very limited., preclusive effect').

956. *See supra* [113].

957. Brekoulakis, *Third Parties in Arbitration* [9.07].

from any applicable law. Since courts are less likely to entirely forego treaty and national law, this proposal will be further revisited in the context of res judicata before arbitral tribunals.[958]

285. In the opposite manner, other proposals confirm the NYC's relevance for res judicata. There are two thematic anchors reappearing within these opinions, i.e., that the Convention seeks to implement (i) the recognition of arbitral awards and (ii) the parties' intentions. Yet, they differ as to the degree of uniformity: most drastically, one opinion promotes comprehensive uniform requirements. On the basis of Article III NYC and the preference for the parties' intention in finality, courts and scholars were able to develop a uniform standard that '*must be elaborated over time*'.[959] As to the uniform standard's content, the proposal favours broad preclusion in similarity to common-law concepts.[960] Apart from this consideration, the opinion has not been accompanied by specific rules yet, particularly in third-party matters.

286. A further opinion concurs that the Convention requires preference for the parties' intention in res judicata. Accordingly, the NYC required Member States' courts to respect the parties' agreements on res judicata's scope.[961] In contrast to the aforementioned opinion, it rejects the idea that international standards apply as a blanket construction of the parties' intention. Instead, an implied agreement on res judicata constitutes the minimum threshold. If such cannot be inferred, national law applies to res judicata.[962] With regard to the operation towards third parties, the opinion argues that the referral to the parties' expectations necessitates that res judicata could exclusively operate between the parties to the arbitration agreement.[963]

287. Moreover, the Draft Third Restatement on International Arbitration and its Chief Rapporteur's General Course at the Hague Academy[964] take a differentiated approach.

958. *Ibid.*, [11.38] ('Admittedly, this suggestion may be difficult to apply in practice, particularly by national courts, which are normally bound by the conflict of laws rules of the lex fori [...]. However, it should be less problematic for arbitral tribunals [...].'). *See infra* Chapter 8.
959. *Born* 3741-42. *Corresp* Radicati di Brozolo, in *ASA Special Series* 8-9. Cf. Scherer in Wolff (ed.), *New York Convention* Art. III [9] ('The rules regarding res judicata [...] must be determined either (i) by reference to a national law [...] or, alternatively, (ii) by reference to international standards.').
960. *Born* 3742 ('Indeed., a substantial argument can be made that presumptively broader preclusion rules are required., as between the parties, for international arbitral awards than for national court judgments. [...] More controversially, principles of preclusion mandated by the New York Convention should generally prevent parties from relitigating a dispute that has been resolved by an award - regardless of whether particular claims arising out of that dispute were or were not asserted in earlier arbitral proceedings. So long as claims were within the scope of the parties' arbitration agreement, and were related to affirmative claims that the party asserted., a party should not be permitted to hold back claims for relitigation in subsequent proceedings: permitting this to occur contradicts the parties' objective of a speedy, final resolution of their disputes in a single forum, and instead rewards, and thereby encourages, technical pleadings and multiplicitous dispute resolution proceedings.').
961. Lühmann, *Die Rechtskraft des Schiedsspruchs* 323.
962. *Ibid.*, 326 ('*soweit [...] kein Rückschluss auf den mutmaßlichen Parteiwillen möglich ist [...] besteht [...] kein Anlass, auf allgemeine transnationale Rechtsgrundsätze zurückzugreifen*').
963. *Ibid.*, 330, 341.
964. Bermann, (2015) 381 Rec. des cours [544-557].

They propose that a foreign arbitral award comprises res judicata if it (i) meets the requirements for recognition under the Convention, (ii) meets the requirements for res judicata under the applicable national law (*lex fori*) and (iii) is not opposed by the parties' intentions.[965] To take up on the latter requirement, the proposal stipulates a primacy of the parties' intentions because although it only mentions these intentions as a *restriction* of preclusion,[966] the Tentative Draft generally applies US law, i.e., the law containing the broadest preclusion rules. As to its application, courts enjoy substantial discretion and are invited to take into account the parties' home jurisdictions, the industry practices, the arbitral record and the arbitral seat.[967] With regard to the application of res judicata towards third parties, the Tentative Draft contains considerations, albeit under US law exclusively.[968] As to the NYC's uniform criteria, the Tentative Draft expresses that they are only one limb of cross-jurisdictional res judicata. From a comparative point of view, this idea conforms to the mechanisms within national laws.[969] Whilst jurisprudence is scarce, this impact is also supported by an English *obiter*: an award of the Iran-US Claims Tribunal[970] was invoked to preclude the re-litigation of a damages claim. Whereas it was undisputed that the respective criteria under English law were met, the efficacy of the award was disputed, because the NYC was inapplicable. The court remarked that the Convention would have solved *this* matter.[971]

288. In conclusion, there are several streams with regard to the relationship between the NYC and res judicata. In this regard, the streams might be summarized in addressing three functional issues: (i) Is the NYC entirely restricted to enforcement or does cross-jurisdictional res judicata fall under its scope? (ii) If it does, does the NYC contain any rules on res judicata beyond its express provisions on 'recognition'? (iii) If it does not, does the NYC at least mandate to consider express party agreements on preclusion standards as binding?

965. Restatement (Third) Int'l Comm Arb. (TD No. 2 2012), § 4-9: 'A court precludes relitigation of a claim that was previously adjudicated in an international arbitral award to the extent that the party seeking preclusive effect demonstrates that the award: (a) is entitled to recognition under this Chapter; (b) involves the same parties and the same claim as required by the law of the court in which claim preclusion is sought; and (c) barring relitigation of the claim is consistent with the arbitration agreement and the reasonable expectations of the parties.' On issue preclusion, § 4-10 contains a comparable provision, substituting the terms 'same parties and same claim' for 'requirements for issue preclusion' in requirement (b).
966. *See* in this regard Lühmann, *Die Rechtskraft des Schiedsspruchs* 318 ('*Der Vorschlag im Restatement [...] greift zu kurz*').
967. Restatement (Third) Int'l Comm Arb. (TD No. 2 2012), § 4-9 comment c (claim preclusion), § 4-10 comment d.iii (issue preclusion).
968. *Ibid.*
969. *See supra* [147].
970. *Mark Dallal v. Islamic Republic of Iran, Bank Mellat*, IUSCT Case 149, Arbitral Award, 10 June 1983, 53-149-1, (1983) 3 Iran-USCTR 10.
971. *Mark Dallal v. Bank Mellat*, (1986) XI Y.C.A. 547, [6] per Hobhouse J. (Comm) ('the New York Convention [...] would have avoided arguments of the type which I am now having to consider.').

§5.02 PROPOSED PERSPECTIVE ON RES JUDICATA IN GENERAL (ARTICLE III NYC)

289. The examination has to proclaim its perspective on res judicata under the NYC in general before it will proceed to third-party effects in particular. Therefore, it examines whether the Convention applies to res judicata at all and if it does, whether it contains any rule beyond its explicit wording.[972] In this regard, it adheres to its sincere *de lege lata* perspective.[973] Hence, it applies the construction methods affirmed by the majority opinion:[974] the NYC requires an autonomous interpretation, constitutes treaty law and as such is to be interpreted under the Vienna Convention,[975] i.e., by facilitating the wording, context, rationale[976] and drafting history.[977]

290. Seeking to apply the NYC to res judicata by virtue of its wording, the outset is the Convention's silence as to this very term. Accordingly, the proximate resort might be to regard res judicata as comprised by 'recognition and enforcement' found within the title, the obligation under Article III[978] and the grounds in Article V.[979] Initially, it might be undisputed that 'enforcement' comprises no relevance for any res judicata effect since they are distinct effects.[980] Hence, the term 'recognition' is decisive. In fact, there appear three potential constructions of 'recognition' favouring distinct opinions. *First*, the opinion pursuant to which the Convention had no relevance for res judicata at all[981] would have to regard 'recognition' as a preliminary requirement for enforcement exclusively. Within the wording, it would stress the word 'recognition *and* enforcement' as establishing a joint process. *Second*, the very opposite reading of 'recognition' might be possible in that it is the alternative to enforcement and to be equated with res

972. For the third matter of preclusion agreements *see infra* [351-362].
973. *See supra* [20].
974. *UNCITRAL Report on NYC*, 2008, UN Doc A/CN.9/656, [36] ('*significant number*' of Member States); Liebscher, in R Wolff (ed.), *New York Convention* Prelims [76]; M Paulsson, *The 1958 New York Convention in Action* 43-52; van den Berg, *The New York Convention*, Introduction [4]. *See* on uniform commercial law in general Goode Kronke and McKendrick, *Transnational Commercial Law* [21.06] ('by now solid *acquis* in this respect').
975. In Member States to the Vienna Convention *and* in non-Member States, because the Vienna Convention can be regarded as customary public international law, *see Malaysian Historical Salvors SDN BHD v. The Government of Malaysia*, ICSID Case ARB/05/10, Decision on Annulment of 16 April 2009, [56] (Schwebel P, Shahabuddeen, Tomka).
976. *See* Art. 31(1) ('A treaty shall be interpreted in good faith in accordance with the ordinary meaning to be given to the terms of the treaty in their context and in the light of its object and purpose').
977. Art. 32 ('Recourse may be had to supplementary means of interpretation, including the preparatory work of the treaty and the circumstances of its conclusion.').
978. In full: 'Each Contracting State shall recognize arbitral awards as binding and enforce them in accordance with the rules of procedure of the territory where the award is relied upon, under the conditions laid down in the following articles. There shall not be imposed substantially more onerous conditions or higher fees or charges on the recognition or enforcement of arbitral awards to which this Convention applies than are imposed on the recognition or enforcement of domestic arbitral awards'.
979. 'Recognition and enforcement of the award may be refused [...]'.
980. *See supra* [104, 142-149].
981. *See supra* [284].

judicata. Such reading is inclined by scholarly statements considering isolated recognition a '*defensive process*'.[982] *Third*, it might be possible to regard 'recognition' as a preliminary step in establishing the efficacy of an award, either for the purpose of enforcement or res judicata. Such construction finds support amongst scholarly statements carefully laying out that recognition is not in itself a defensive process but occurs *in order to establish* the defence.[983] In this regard, the examination does not regard the second and third reading as mutually exclusive. Particularly, the equation of 'recognition' and res judicata by no means instantly results in an entire uniform regime of res judicata. Instead, it might be possible to see all preclusion aspects not regulated within the Convention as *lacunas*, a regular setting for uniform law.[984] Therefore, the issue to be solved is whether the Convention has any ambition to establish preclusion consequences, and if yes, beyond its wording.

291. To elaborate in this regard on the drafting history, the preceding Geneva Convention spoke of 'recognition *or* enforcement' in its Articles 2[985] and 3[986] thereby indicating that there are other relevant scenarios of recognition beyond enforcement. Certainly, this finding can go either way. It could serve as an argument *e contrario* illustrating that the NYC took a different approach, or for a historical interpretation in confluence with the Geneva Convention. In any case, during the drafting process of the NYC, res judicata has not been mentioned as an independent consequence of arbitral awards, only in its sense of 'finality' as a requirement for enforcement.[987] This has been different during the drafting of the Model Law, notably also drafted by UNCITRAL and intended as a supplement to the Convention: comparable to Article III NYC, Article 35 Model Laws states that arbitral awards will be '*recognized as binding*'. According to a note by the secretariat to the 1984 Working Group session, this terminology is intended to '*help to convey the idea of res judicata, without using that term which is not known*

982. *See Dicey Morris and Collins* Rule 66(1); *Lew Mistelis and Kröll* [26.10-11]; Kronke in Kronke et al. (eds), *Recognition and Enforcement of Arbitral Awards* 7; Liebscher in Wolff (ed.), *New York Convention* Prelims [23]; *Redfern and Hunter* [11.23]; van den Berg, *New York Convention* 244.
983. Cf. Berger and Kellerhals, *Arbitration in Switzerland* [2111] ('recognition [...] is a preliminary question [...] where a party invokes [res judicata]'); *Fouchard Gaillard and Goldman* [1667] ('[...] recognition may be requested where the party relying on an award merely wishes it to have a negative effect. In such a case, it is not easy to distinguish between recognition and the res judicata effect of arbitral awards. The difficulties with this terminology might have been avoided if care had been taken to draw a clear distinction between exequatur [...] and the enforcement of the award.'); Poncet and Mockler, *Liber Amicorum Craig* 317 ('Where a party to an arbitration seeks to invoke res judicata to bar a successive claim [...] the award must first pass the test of *recognition*' – emphasis in original) *Poudret and Besson* [850] ('recognition [...] can be raised preliminarily [...] in the context of [...] a res judicata plea').
984. *See*, e.g., Art. 7(2) CISG ('Questions concerning matters governed by this Convention which are not expressly settled in it are to be settled in conformity with the general principles on which it is based or, in the absence of such principles, in conformity with the law applicable by virtue of the rules of private international law.'); Art. 5(2) Capetown Convention.
985. '[T]he competent authority of the country where recognition or enforcement of the award is sought can, if it think fit, postpone such recognition or enforcement'.
986. '[T]he Court may, if it thinks fit, either refuse recognition or enforcement of the award'.
987. *See Proposed Amendment to Draft NYC from Delegation of Yugoslavia*, 5 June 1958, UN Doc E/CONF.26/L.55 ('This convention shall apply only to arbitral awards which acquired the force of res judicata and became final after the entry into force of the Convention').

in all legal systems although the concept seems to be commonly shared'.[988] Another statement refers to the automatic character of recognition[989] which was in contrast with the majority opinion pursuant to which res judicata needs to be *invoked*. Accordingly, the drafting history contains only limited support for the NYC's relevance for res judicata at all.

292. If it is regarded as permitted to undertake the autonomous interpretation by means of comparative considerations,[990] it should be noted that national laws comprise considerable comparative differences on res judicata's operation.[991] This indicates a high threshold for the Convention to establish any uniform preclusion consequences. Moreover, it has been examined that national laws consider 'recognition' as the pure establishment of cross-jurisdictional efficacy. It can either occur in exequatur proceedings or incidentally when an arbitral award is invoked as a preclusion ground. In the latter case, res judicata requires an examination of the grounds for non-recognition *and* the applicable preclusion law.[992] A very illustrative example of the interaction between recognition under the Convention and the means for invoking an award can be found in section 101(1) English Arbitration Act which differentiates:

> A New York Convention award shall be recognized as binding on the persons as between whom it was made, and may accordingly be relied on by those persons by way of defence, set-off or otherwise in any legal proceedings in England and Wales or Northern Ireland.

293. In other words, recognition only enables to rely on national preclusion rules. Hence, a comparative interpretation favours the construction that 'recognition' in the sense of Article III NYC is not to be equated with res judicata. Instead, it could only be one step in establishing cross-jurisdictional res judicata.

294. As to the context of the Convention, the opinion in favour of uniformity refers to the conceptual interaction of res judicata and arbitration *agreements*.[993] Such arbitration agreements are inherently protected by the Convention fulfilling the core purpose to promote both arbitral awards and arbitration agreements.[994] Particularly, Article

---

988. *Composite draft text of a model law on international commercial arbitration*, 1984, UN Doc A/CN.9/WG.II/WP50, [27].
989. *Report of the Working Group on International Contract Practices*, 1984 UN Doc A/CN.9/246, 146 ('Recognition is an abstract legal effect which could obtain automatically without necessarily being requested by a party.').
990. *See* Gebauer, (2000) 5 Unif L. Rev. 687 ('comparative law [...] can be qualified as systematic arguments').
991. *Supra* Chapters 2-4.
992. *See supra* [147]. *See* for the comparable technique in international litigation Jayme, (1995) Rec. des cours 259 ('dialogue' of international legal sources).
993. *Born* 3744.
994. *See Scherk v. Alberto-Culver Co.*, 417 U.S. 506, 520 (1974) ('The goal of the Convention [...] was to encourage the recognition and enforcement of commercial arbitration agreements in international contracts and to unify the standards by which agreements to arbitrate are observed [...].'); BGHZ 187, 126, [8] = (2011) XXXVI Y.C.A. 282 ('The Convention was meant to make the enforcement of arbitration agreements easier internationally.'); *Redfern and Hunter* [2.07].

II(1) stipulates the obligation to 'recognize' arbitration agreements.[995] Yet, Article II(1) NYC does not establish any uniform regime neither. It protects nothing but the cross-border efficacy of arbitration agreements. The particular requirements for arbitration agreements' validity are governed by national law.[996] To turn to another interaction, the opinion in favour of uniformity invoked the NYC's rationale to prevent multiple proceedings.[997] Certainly, this also constitutes a major rationale of res judicata.[998] Yet, apart from Article II(3) NYC,[999] the Convention does not even mention parallel proceedings neither. A further and perhaps more instant step in examining the Convention's context is to draw attention to the limited regulation of enforcement. In particular, Article III NYC exclusively regulates the *general* obligation of Member States to enforce foreign arbitral awards. It leaves several aspects unregulated, such as the formal steps in obtaining enforcement (e.g., the necessity of executionary certificates) and the substantive scope of the possibility for enforcement (e.g., protection of personal assets, enforceability against successors). Accordingly, the Convention's context further strengthens the position that the Convention has some relevance for res judicata, albeit refers certain aspects to national law.

295. Continuing on practical feasibility, a uniform operation of res judicata would be largely thwarted by the fact that many aspects related to the operation of res judicata are undoubtedly excluded from the NYC, e.g., the validity of the arbitration agreement, the arbitral procedure and most importantly the point in time upon which an arbitral award can be considered 'binding' in the sense of Article V(1)I NYC.[1000] Accordingly, it appears disrupted to assess the binding nature of the arbitral award and the arbitral procedure *under national law* and the consequences of res judicata entirely *under uniform law*. In addition, a uniform operation would stand in contrast not only to the applicability of national law on preclusion requirements but also to preclusion

995. 'Each Contracting State shall recognize an agreement in writing under which the parties undertake to submit to arbitration all or any differences which have arisen or which may arise between them in respect of a defined legal relationship, whether contractual or not, concerning a subject matter capable of settlement by arbitration'.
996. *See supra* [45].
997. *Born* 3743.
998. *See supra* [101-102].
999. *See* on its operation as a matter of lis pendens *supra* [71-75]. For parallel reviews *see* Art. VI.
1000. CA Paris, *Compagnie de Saint-Gobain-Pont-à-Mousson v. The Fertilizer Corp. of India*, 10 May 1971, [1971] Rev. Arb. 108; CA Napoli, (1979) IV Y.C.A. 275, 276; *Fertilizer Corp. of India v. IDI Management Inc*, 517 F Supp 948 (SD Ohio 1981); ATF 108 Ib 85, *Joseph Müller AG v. Sigal Bergesen*, [5]; TF, *Denysiana SA v. Jassica SA*, 14 March 1984; KG Zürich, (2004) XXIX Y.C.A. 819, 828; OLG Düsseldorf, 19 January 2005, I-26 Sch 5/03; Tribunal Supremo, (2006) XXXI Y.C.A. 846, 851; OLG Celle, (2007) XXXII Y.C.A. 322, 325; *Pactrans Air & Sea Inc. v. China National Chartering Corp. et al*, (ND Florida 2010); Bermann, (2015) 381 Rec. des cours [714]; *Fouchard Gaillard and Goldman* [1680-1682]; Darwazeh in Kronke et al. (eds), *Recognition and Enforcement of Foreign Arbitral Awards* 312-313. *Contra Diag Human Se v. Czech Republic*, [2014] EWHC 1639 (comm.) ('binding [...] must of course be given an autonomous meaning'); El Hakim, (1989) 6 J. Int'l Arb. 161-170; Schmidt, *Typologie von Schiedssprüchen* 49. *See* already the Geneva Convention ('That the award become *final* in the country in which it is made, in the sense that it will not be considered as such if it is open to opposition, to appeal or pourvoi en cassation or if it is proven that any proceedings for the purpose of contesting the validity of the award are pending.' – emphasis added).

consequences for foreign judgments. This has been described as a potential trigger for the international *dis*harmony of solutions in Member States resulting out of '*two different res judicata systems: one under forum law for foreign judgments and another under international law for international awards*'.[1001] Accordingly, from a practical point, uniform res judicata consequences would not fully achieve uniformity in any case.

296. As to the Convention's rationales, the opinion in favour of uniformity refers to the rationale to promote arbitration.[1002] Since arbitral awards are the utmost implementation of arbitral authority, this opposes the position that the Convention had no relevance whatsoever for res judicata. Yet, beyond this, another aspect is that the Convention seeks to advance the efficient dispute settlement and establish legal certainty. In this regard, a practical aspect requiring due consideration is the currently unsettled discussion on cross-jurisdictional res judicata. In particular, there are only a few statements as to the preclusion consequences developed under the Convention.[1003] This might be undesirable, yet significantly opposes uniform standards.

297. As a final aspect, to assume that a general intention of parties to resolve disputes permits any inferences on a legal topic as complex as res judicata appears rather presumptive. Even if this was possible, several specific aspects would oppose this proposal. *First*, res judicata comprises considerable comparative differences. Accordingly, it appears rather unlikely that, e.g., parties from jurisdictions with strict preclusion rules have the general intention to apply broad preclusion rules in a common-law sense. *Second*, broad preclusion rules frequently result in inflated arguments during the arbitration. By contrast, narrow res judicata is an incentive for focused submissions.[1004] This opposes a general intention in favour of broad preclusion rules.[1005] More importantly, *third*, from a perspective of practical feasibility, it has to be borne in mind that the operation of res judicata is intertwined with the procedural tools available: e.g., it has been shown that civil-law jurisdictions frequently compensate strict cause-of-action preclusion by allowing declaratory suits. Accordingly, it appears preferable to adjust res judicata to the procedural tools available and not to apply international standards irrespective of them.

298. Therefore, applying the Convention's text, drafting history, context and rationales, the examination submits that the Convention generally applies to res judicata in that. *First*, Article III NYC obligates Member States to treat arbitral awards and judgments correspondingly and, *second*, the grounds under Article V NYC can be invoked against res judicata. Exceeding uniform rules on res judicata's scope might be desirable but do *not* exist. Applied to the wording, this means that 'recognition' is *either* a preliminary requirement of cross-jurisdictional res judicata *or*, if 'recognition' can be equated with res judicata, preclusion consequences remain a *lacuna*.

1001. Bermann, (2015) 381 Rec. des cours [555].
1002. *Born* 3742.
1003. *See supra* [285].
1004. *See supra* [113].
1005. Lühman, *Die Rechtskraft des Schiedsspruchs* 320.

§5.03 LEGAL STANDARD FOR THIRD-PARTY EFFECTS OF ARBITRAL AWARDS BEFORE FOREIGN COURTS

299. Given this examination's inclination that nothing but the Convention's recognition mechanism applies to res judicata, two non-recognition grounds demand particular consideration. If, in the future, scholarship on res judicata under the Convention advances a transnational regime of arbitral res judicata under the NYC, the considerations under Article V NYC can equally apply. Initially, one might ask whether third-party effects might violate due process under Article V(1)(b) NYC. Yet, this ground appears inapplicable (*see* [A], *infra*). This draws the attention to Article V(1)(a) NYC and its mandate to deny recognition for jurisdictional deficiencies. In this regard, it is this examination's core and genuine contention that Article V(1)(a) NYC can and should be applied to res judicata necessitating that a third party cannot be exposed to res judicata unless it was subject to the tribunal's general personal jurisdiction (*see* [B], *infra*). Whilst these submissions address the traditional setting that an arbitral award fully constitutes res judicata towards third parties, i.e., also to their detriment, the examination eventually analyses the assessment of non-mutual preclusion *in favour* of third parties and equally advocates that nothing but an application of Article V(1)(a) NYC is preferable (*see* [C], *infra*). This jurisdictional reconciliation under Article V(1)(a) NYC applies irrespective of more liberal *lex fori* under Article VII NYC (*see* [D], *infra*). Finally, application of the standard to *factual effects* requires a specification of the latter and thus occurs in Chapter 7.

[A] Infeasibility of Due Process for Uniform Standards (Article V(1)(b) NYC)

300. Res judicata issues are due-process issues.[1006] Hence, it appears worth investigating whether awards' third-party effects are non-recognizable for violation of *due process*[1007] under Article V(1)(b) NYC. This provision covers two grounds, i.e., the opponent '(i.) *was not given proper notice* [...] (ii.) *or was otherwise unable to present his case*'. The latter alternative was unknown to the Geneva Convention and had been inserted at the penultimate session of the New York Conference.[1008] It is one of the '*most frequently invoked grounds for non-recognition*'.[1009]

301. Initially, the broad wording[1010] of Article V(1)(b) NYC might appear sufficiently wide for developing boundaries against third-party effects. Moreover, it might be argued: if res judicata could not even operate against a party who received *insufficient*

1006. *See supra* [175].
1007. Notably, *Born 2577* proposes to avoid the term 'due process' under the NYC because of its domestic connotations and facilitate 'procedural fairness' instead.
1008. *See NY Conference –Twenty-Third Meeting*, 9 June 1958, UN Doc E/CONF.26/SR.23.
1009. Scherer in Wolff (ed.), *New York Convention* Art. V [130].
1010. *See* crit. on this broad wording Submission of the Austrian delegation in *Comments by Governments on Draft NYC*, 31 January 1956, UN Doc E/2822, Annex 1, 20.

notices or submission, then it should not operate against a third party, receiving *no* notice or submission possibility *a fortiori*. Yet, four fundamental considerations oppose that Article V(1)(b) NYC could be facilitated for uniform or minimum standards with regard to arbitral awards' third-party effects.

302. The initial consideration against applying Article V(1)(b) NYC to awards' third-party effects is its rationale. Such is to sanction serious procedural irregularities, which violate minimum standards of procedural justice. The main examples where the provision served against the recognition of arbitral awards concern unequal treatment, short time limits, dismissal of evidence, denial of oral submissions and rejection of comment possibilities.[1011] Whilst these aspects all concern the *arbitral process itself*, an objection against a third-party effect concerns the consequences of an award prima facie rendered in regular proceedings. Hence, the rationale accorded to Article V(1)(b) NYC in jurisprudence does not appear to be at stake.

303. To shift the angle on this aspect: res judicata issues are due-process issues *from the perspective of the subsequent tribunal*. The preclusion of claims and arguments by virtue of res judicata restricts the right to be heard in the subsequent proceedings. By contrast, Article V(1)(b) NYC sanctions due-process violations in the *previous* arbitration. Accordingly, the general rationale against third-party res judicata is not incorporated in Article V(1)(b) NYC.

304. Moreover, it has to be noted that the capacity of Article V(1)(b) NYC to establish uniform notions of procedural fairness is rather limited. Whilst an autonomous interpretation is advocated in scholarship,[1012] recognition courts regularly apply their *lex fori* in order to specify the threshold for due process.[1013] Notably, a comparable antagony between transnational and national standards can also be observed for public policy under Article V(2)(b) NYC.[1014] In any case, the concepts are certainly intertwined when transnational concepts use national notions as inspirations on the one hand, and national courts distinguish between due process in national and international cases on the other. Therefore, Albert Jan van den Berg regarded the question:

> rather academic and [...] a matter of taste. In addition, the question whether a violation of due process is present is, in most cases, largely a question of fact.[1015]

305. Yet, the discussion shows a certain reluctance against deducing extensive uniform grounds from Article V(1)(b) NYC. This reluctance should be particularly triggered by res judicata and its application towards third parties. Under what criteria

1011. *UNCITRAL Guide to NYC* Art. V(1)(b) [31-36] with further case references.
1012. *Born* 3504; *Fouchard Gaillard and Goldman* [1696]; Scherer in Wolff (ed.), *New York Convention* Art. V [141].
1013. *See* the extensive enumerations of more than 20 cases from France, Germany, Switzerland, the USA and other Member States by Scherer in Wolff (ed.), *New York Convention* Art. V [139].
1014. Cf. Bermann, (2015) 381 Rec. des cours [478-480]; Gaillard, *Legal Theory of International Arbitration* [115-123]; Lalive, (1987) 3 ICCA Congress Series 261; Lew, *Applicable Law in International Commercial Arbitration* 201 ('increasingly interpreted [...] from a non-national, a-national or transnational standard'). *See* crit. ATF 120 II 155, *Westland Helicopters*.
1015. van den Berg, *The New York Convention* 298.

should a uniform standard under the Convention decide whether due process is adhered to because of a certain proximity of the third parties to the arbitrating parties or the factual possibility to take notice of the arbitration? In this regard, this thesis submits that Article V(1)(b) NYC is simply too brief in order to adequately regulate the welter of case scenarios in multilateral transactions and overcome the necessary threshold in order to override national law by virtue of treaty law. This holds particularly true given the range of uncertainties under national arbitration (and procedural) laws itself.[1016] Creating new uncertainties under uniform law should not be the preferred means to rectify them.

306. Therefore, in light of the focus of Article V(1)(b) NYC on procedural irregularities, the focus of res judicata on due process in the subsequent proceedings, the focus of national courts on national law and the large uncertainty associated with an opposite solution, it is submitted that Article V(1)(b) NYC should not be facilitated to establish any genuinely uniform requirements for arbitral awards' third-party effects in cross-border case scenarios.

[B] The Case for a Uniform Jurisdictional Requirement (Article V(1)(a) NYC)

307. Before an arbitral award is rendered, Article V(1)(a) NYC[1017] and its set-aside equivalents in national arbitration laws[1018] subject multiparty relationships to consensual jurisdiction. But for the consent of all parties involved, neither multiparty arbitration nor tools such as third-party notice or consolidation are admissible. To cite the wording of Article V(1)(a): '*Recognition ... of the award may be refused ... if ... the [arbitration] agreement referred to in article II ... is not valid.*' In the following paragraphs, it will be submitted that this very boundary to arbitral authority over third parties equally applies to the third-party effects of arbitral awards. Unless the third party is a successor, it should only be exposed to arbitral res judicata under the condition that it consented to the arbitration agreement. Otherwise, the third party can invoke the non-recognition ground under Article V(1)(a) NYC against an award's third-party effect. After the proposed standard is further specified (*see* [1], *infra*), the examination submits that the argument in favour of Article V(1)(a) NYC is essentially an argument in favour of party autonomy (*see* [2], *infra*). Yet, it submits that the application of Article V(1)(a) NYC is not only demanded by legal theory but more importantly by practical feasibility. Only a reconciliation of jurisdiction and res judicata can guarantee a consistent, certain, efficient and therefore fair regime of Forum Coordination (*see* [3], *infra*). This very rationale justifies to subject one aspect of res

1016. *See supra* [237-274].

1017. 'Recognition [...] of the award may be refused., at the request of the party against whom it is invoked., only if [...] the agreement referred to in article II [...] is not valid [...]'.

1018. For example Art. 34(2)(a)(i) UNCITRAL Model Law. *Corresp* Art. 67(1)(a) English Arbitration Act; Art. 1520 No. 1 French CPC; Art. 190(2)(b) Swiss PILA; s. 10(4) FAA.

judicata in multilateral transactions to a uniform requirement whilst other aspects may remain under the auspices of national law (*see* [4], *infra*).

[1] Introduction of the Hybrid Standard

308. This examination advocates a hybrid standard in determining international arbitral awards' third-party effects in follow-up litigation. In a *first step*, the uniform rule under Article V(1)(a) NYC demands to assess whether the prior third party has consented to the arbitration agreement establishing the former arbitral tribunal's jurisdiction. If it did, the *second step* examines whether res judicata can apply towards the third party although it has not participated in the arbitration. Since the examination has previously submitted that the Convention contains no uniform rules beyond its recognition regime and that Article V(1)(b) NYC cannot establish any uniform regime of res judicata, the second step has to be undertaken under national law whose determination will be adhered to in the upcoming Chapter.

309. To illustrate this submission by virtue of case examples: (i) If a creditor who has already successfully obtained an international arbitral award against the debtor which has defaulted in payment eventually sues the debtor's shareholders before courts, he will seek to submit on corporate-veil piercing. In addition, he will invoke that the main debt is established under the arbitral award, e.g., by relying on US jurisprudence.[1019] In this regard, Article V(1)(a) NYC demands that the debtor's main obligation can exclusively be invoked towards the shareholders, if the arbitration agreement could have equally been extended. (ii) The same mechanism applies if the creditor seeks to subsequently hold the solidary debtor liable and seeks to establish the main debt, e.g., by relying on French law.[1020] Again, Article V(1)(a) NYC demands as a preliminary requirement that the solidary debtor consented to the arbitration agreement. This applies irrespective of whether the creditor seeks to invoke the actual French doctrine of res judicata (*autorité de la chose jugée*) or the wide *opposabilité*. In particular, the fact that an *opposabilité* can be compensated by a *tierce opposition* does not render Article V(1)(a) NYC inapplicable. Not only is the applicability of the *tierce opposition* on international arbitral awards rendered in France debated.[1021] Article V NYC is independent from the review at the seat.[1022] (iii) By contrast, when the third party is a successor to a party and not bound to the arbitration clause, e.g., because the third party merely purchased the good in dispute or it was assigned the claim in dispute and explicitly rejected to join the arbitration agreement,[1023] the examination takes the position that Article V(1)(a) NYC can still be regarded as complied with.[1024]

1019. *See supra* [273].
1020. *See supra* [237, 258].
1021. *See supra* [239].
1022. *See supra* [87].
1023. *See supra* [43].
1024. *See infra* [319, 327].

310. An instant inference from the proposal is that arbitral awards will be very unlikely invoked before courts. *Either* the third party is *not* bound by the arbitration agreement necessitating that Article V(1)(a) NYC bars recognition and thereby res judicata, *or* the third party *is* bound to arbitrate. In such case, Article II(3) NYC obligates the courts to refer the parties to an arbitral tribunal. Yet, several exceptional circumstances might allow that the arbitration agreement is generally applied towards the third party *and* that the court can exercise jurisdiction. For instance, the arbitration agreement might be (i) limited in the subject matter, (ii) time limited or (iii) merely optional, i.e., not derogating courts.

311. In such situations, the proposed standard demands further elaboration on its operation. Primarily, one might ask whether the standard for arbitral awards' *third-party* effects has any effects on res judicata between the *actual* parties to the dispute. Most drastically, if the above-mentioned creditor was unsuccessful in introducing the arbitral award as res judicata in the follow-up dispute against the debtor's parent company or surety, the debtor itself might eventually seek to resist enforcement arguing that the arbitral award had already been denied recognition. Yet, there is no obstacle for the arbitral award. The recognition rejection in favour of the third party operates as any judgment would and therefore only applies *inter partes*.[1025] Moreover, the Convention mandates that recognition and enforcement between the formal parties can occur independently from recognition against third parties. This can be inferred from Article V(1)(c) NYC's rule of severability.[1026] Whilst severability raised some concern in the drafting process of the Convention,[1027] the provision is now regarded as displaying a '*general, underlying principle of the Convention*'.[1028] This particularly applies in multiparty situations. In the scenario that an arbitral tribunal rendered an award against multiple parties and some of those parties did not consent to arbitral jurisdiction, Article V(1)(a) NYC only bars recognition and enforcement against the latter and not against the parties who did consent to jurisdiction.[1029] The same reading should apply to res judicata. Hence, the application of Article V(1)(a) NYC to arbitral awards' third-party effects bears no consequence for res judicata between the actual parties.

1025. Cf. *supra* [174].

1026. 'Recognition and enforcement of the award may be refused [...] if [...] The award [...] contains decisions on matter beyond the scope of the submission to arbitration, provided that, if the decisions on matters submitted to arbitration can be separated from those not so submitted., that part of the award which contains decisions on matters submitted to arbitration may be recognized and enforced'.

1027. *Comment by France on* Art. *4 Draft NYC*, 13 April 1956, E/2822/Corr.1 ('an arbitral award constitutes an organic whole').

1028. Borris and Hennecke in Wolff (ed.), *New York Convention* Art. V [258].

1029. *FIAT SpA v. The Ministry of Finane and Planning of the Republic of Suriname et al*, (1998) XXIII Y.C.A. 880, [7-9] (S.D.N.Y. 1989); *UNCITRAL Guide to NYC* Art. V(1)(c) [32]. Cf. *Poudret and Besson* [955] ('if the party applying for recognition and enforcement invokes the award against two parties and one of the parties can prove that it did not have legal capacity or that it was not validly represented., the enforcement judge should admit the request against the other').

312. Moreover, one might ask whether Article V(1)(a) NYC also applies when the otherwise applicable national law regards the award's third-party effect as a matter of substantive law. For instance, this is the case for certain national laws on sureties or insurances.[1030] It is submitted that Article V(1)(a) NYC should be interpreted autonomously. Thus, it is irrelevant how national law embeds a third-party effect. Instead, it is exclusively decisive whether such third-party effect on an arbitral award conclusively establishes the requirements under national laws and thereby precludes counterarguments, e.g., on the limitation of the main debt. Hence, the proposed standard is equally applicable to third-party effects under substantive surety or insurance law.

313. By slight way of contrast, in some case scenarios, an arbitral award will not conclusively preclude potential arguments on substantive law's requirements. Instead, the arbitral award's *existence* itself might *trigger* a requirement. For instance, an arbitral adjudication on legal status, e.g., a shareholders' resolution might trigger legal incapacity for corporate transactions. In addition and strongly related, substantive law might consider certain 'factual effects' of arbitral awards, e.g., in damages calculations or hardship provision. As extensively addressed in Chapter 7, Article V(1)(a) NYC again demands autonomous interpretation and thus applies in such scenarios albeit raises distinct concerns of irreconcilabilities.

314. A further inquiry raised by the standard concerns the burden of proof. Generally, an autonomous interpretation of the wording of Article V NYC ('refused *at the request of*') demands that the party resisting recognition bears the burden to prove the arbitration agreement's invalidity, respectively inapplicability.[1031] However, Article V(1)(a) NYC generally addresses the situation that an arbitral tribunal has already affirmed its jurisdiction and the party resisting recognition unsuccessfully objected to it in the arbitration. By contrast, when res judicata is invoked towards a stranger to the proceedings, there is no such prima facie affirmation. Instead, the res judicata request will be the first instance where the arbitration agreement's applicability towards the third party will be examined. Therefore, it appears preferable to burden the party relying on res judicata with the burden to prove the arbitration agreement's third-party effect.[1032]

315. The final introductory remark on Article V(1)(a) NYC acknowledges: given that this examination has adopted the position that the Convention leaves res judicata largely unaddressed[1033] and given the to-date limited submissions on the interaction of Article V(1)(a) NYC and res judicata, this examination's submission certainly comprises a rethinking nature. Therefore, it will revisit potential counterarguments

---

1030. *See supra* [259-278].

1031. *UNCITRAL Guide to NYC* Art. V(1)(a) [44]; Tribunal Supremo, *Cominco France S.A. v. Soquiber SL*, 24 March 1982, (1983) VIII Y.C.A. 408, 409 ('clearly affirmed in the introductory sentence of Art. V para 1'); Corte di Casazione, *Trans World Film SpA v. Film Polski Import and Export of Films*, 22 February 1992, (1993) XVIII Y.C.A. 433, 436; Bermann, (2015) 381 Rec. des cours [712]; Kröll, (2004) 117 ZZP 364-367; Scherer in Wolff (ed.), *New York Convention* 216-217.

1032. Cf. Lühmann, *Die Rechtskraft des Schiedsspruchs* 339.

1033. *See supra* [289-298].

promptly.[1034] At the outset, the status quo of a commercial-law treaty should not result in accomplished facts. Rather, transnational commercial law is exposed to the salient danger of '*fossilization [...] through putting in place hard law conventions*'.[1035] Hence, it should be the task of scholarship and jurisprudence to participate in the evolution of – often brief – uniform treaties. Moreover, the option to subject awards' third-party effects to jurisdictional boundaries has not remained entirely overlooked in scholarship. One author infers this solution from his general perspective that the arbitral award's recognition essentially constitutes a recognition of the underlying arbitration agreement.[1036] Furthermore, the Draft Third Restatement considered the assessment of the arbitration *agreement*'s and the arbitral *award*'s third-party effects '*often, though not always, closely linked*' and additionally mentions that:

> a court ordinarily need not undertake a separate analysis of that issue [res judicata] if it has made an affirmative finding in the recognition context that the party resisting preclusion is bound by the arbitration agreement.[1037]

316. Against this background, the following paragraphs illustrate that the application of Article V(1)(a) NYC on arbitral awards' third-party effects is methodologically possible under the wording, context and rationales of the NYC as well as practically preferable.

[2] The Conceptual Starting Point: Party Autonomy

317. Facilitating the above-mentioned tools for interpreting the Convention,[1038] the wording of Article V(1)(a) NYC should constitute the outset of the instant argument. At plain sight, its formulation '*not valid*' does not appear to be triggered, since the very arbitral award initially resulted from a valid arbitration agreement between two parties and is only invoked towards a third party which has potentially no party to the said prima facie valid agreement. However, the wording of Article V(1)(a) NYC is not tailored for third-party case scenarios at all. A literal interpretation of the provision would allow to even recognize arbitral awards where the tribunal assumed jurisdiction over a third party which has not consented to the (otherwise valid) arbitration agreement. In order to prevent such unintended application, there is a widespread consensus that Article V(1)(a) NYC's passage '*not valid*' is interpreted as 'not binding

1034. *See infra* [329-334].
1035. Goode Kronke and McKendrick, *Transnational Commercial Law* [21.20].
1036. Lühmann, *Die Rechtskraft des Schiedsspruchs* 330 ('*Folge der hier vertretenen vertraglichen Anerkennungstheorie ist, [...] auch in Bezug auf einen Dritten zu verlangen, dass dieser an die ursprüngliche Schiedsvereinbarung gebunden ist.*').
1037. Restatement (Third) Int'l Comm Arbitration (TD 2), § 4-9 comment f.
1038. *See supra* [289].

towards the party resisting recognition'.[1039] If this is the reading commonly undertaken, and recognition is seen as a preliminary requirement of res judicata,[1040] it is a blunt application of Article V(1)(a) NYC on res judicata, which results in the instantly proposed standard of res judicata.

318. This reading is further supported by the Convention's rationales. The rationale inherent to Article V(1)(a) NYC is to guarantee the rule of party autonomy. In a *positive* sense, party autonomy is the very reason for arbitration's existence. The latter is a '*matter of contract*'[1041] which '*owes its existence*'[1042] to an act of party autonomy. In a *negative* sense, only an act of party autonomy can justify a '*waiver of the right to state-administered justice*'[1043] or a '*partial renunciation*'[1044] of the right to be heard before court. This very rationale is at stake when a third party is exposed to an arbitral award's preclusive effects. Although it has not consented to the adjudicatory authority of an arbitral tribunal and has not renounced its right to its natural judge, res judicata exposes a third party as if it had consented accordingly. Therefore, this examination's submission to apply Article V(1)(a) NYC on res judicata and require consent to arbitrate for exposure to res judicata is a submission safeguarding party autonomy.

319. This very mandate for party autonomy already induces to differentiate between multilateral relationships on the one hand and sequential relationships, i.e., successions on the other. When a third party succeeds to a formal party to the arbitration after the award is rendered, its interest in party autonomy is not triggered. Indeed, at the time of the arbitration, the third party has not had any relationship with the parties or the subject matter yet. When acquiring the rights or obligations in dispute, only a specific bona fide interest of the third party is at stake. Yet, this interest is not protected by Article V(1)(a) NYC. Therefore, it is up to national law to decide whether the bona fide interest of the third party justifies to exempt it from res judicata. Moreover, the other form of substitution, i.e., disclosed representations will not pose any problems, since the represented must have regularly consented to arbitration.

320. Finally, the general interaction of party autonomy and res judicata could certainly motivate a by far more intensive legal-theory elaboration. Particularly, any submission on party autonomy in the context of res judicata will always touch upon conceptions of the contractual foundation of arbitration and the normative quality of arbitral

1039. *See supra* [40]. *See Dallah Real Estate and Tourism Holding Co. v. Ministry of Religious Affairs, Government of Pakistan*, [2010] UKSC 46, [77].

1040. Established *supra* [147, 298].

1041. *AT&T Techs Inc. v. Commen's Workers of Am.*, 475 U.S. 643, 648-649 (1986) ('[A]rbitration is a matter of contract and a party cannot be required to submit to arbitration any dispute which he has not agreed so to submit.').

1042. *Dell Computer Corp. v. Union des consommateurs*, [2007] 2 SCR 801, [52] ('Arbitration is a creature that owes its existence to the parties alone') (SC Can).

1043. Petrochilos, *Procedural Law in International Arbitration* [4.11].

1044. ECtHR, *X v. Germany*, App. No. 1197/61, (1962) 5 *Yearbook of the European Convention on Human Rights* 88, 96 ('amounting legally to partial renunciation of those rights defined by Article 6').

awards.[1045] Certainly, in national arbitration doctrine, this conceptual argument has already been invoked against the application of proceduralist preclusion doctrine.[1046] However, this concerns general doctrines of issue preclusion and abuse of process as they can equally arise in bilateral relationships. One might invoke that these aspects of the 'to what extent' of res judicata rather refer to arbitration's *judicial* nature, whereas the 'against whom' increasingly touches upon the *contractual* foundation. In any case, it is this examination's contention that the eternal discussion on arbitration's contractual foundation and judicial nature should not be the resort for the very specific discussion on the interaction between jurisdiction and preclusion. Therefore, the examinations refrain from further submissions in this regard and regard party autonomy as nothing but the teleological outset of the argument. Instead, it will continue on practical matters.

[3] The Practical Target: Consistent Forum Coordination

321. The core of this examination's submission in favour of the application of Article V(1)(a) NYC exceeds the mere protection of party autonomy. Instead, it touches upon the very framework of Forum Coordination. As established in *Chapter 1*, the scope of the arbitration agreement is the anchor for pre-emptive measures of Forum Coordination in multilateral transactions. But for a third party's consent, neither joinders nor consolidations or lis pendens measures are permitted. Instead, jurisdictional fragmentation necessitates that disputes in multilateral relationships proceed as multi-fora disputes.[1047] It is this examination's submission that such rule of *pre-emptive* Forum Coordination should equally apply to res judicata, which is nothing but *sequential* Forum Coordination. Such adjustment is a matter of procedural fairness, of the very interests protected by res judicata and, most importantly, mandated by the NYC's context in that Article II(3) NYC acknowledges the decisive role of arbitration agreements.

322. Moreover, Chapter 3 has revealed that judgments' third-party effects are nothing but a shift of the participatory burden. Without res judicata, the formal parties can join the third party. With res judicata, the third party can intervene in or appeal to the process.[1048] The instant proposal transfers this interaction to international arbitral awards. Again, the Convention's context provides a basis. By virtue of Article V(1)(a) NYC, the questions whether a third party can be joined to or intervene in the arbitration are regulated by the Convention. Hence, there is a strong contextual inclination to extend this decisive role of the arbitration agreement to res judicata.

323. Notably, the interaction of intervention possibilities and res judicata has already been upheld in the exclusive examination containing an extensive argument on res

1045. *See*, e.g., Bollée, *Sentences arbitrales* [332]; Solomon, *Verbindlichkeit von Schiedssprüchen* 319-334.
1046. *See supra* [126-128].
1047. *Supra* Chapter 1.
1048. *See supra* [211-212].

judicata in multiparty case scenarios: certainly, Stavros Brekoulakis favours a broad third-party effect of arbitral awards mostly focusing on the commercial proximity of the parties and regards the Convention as generally inapplicable.[1049] Yet, he does favour consistency between pre-emptive and sequential Forum Coordination, only from a very liberal perspective on jurisdiction. His proposal has been submitted through a perspective that seeks to equip arbitral tribunals with liberal, court-equivalent jurisdictional power.[1050] Whilst such concept does not prevail *de lege lata*,[1051] his scholarship reveals the need to conjointly discuss the scope of arbitration agreements and an arbitral award's third-party effect.

324. To continue on the functional interaction between intervention possibilities and res judicata, it is not only a technical matter but also a matter of procedural fairness, a rationale immanent to the Convention. Procedural fairness demands that a third party will only be exposed to a dispute's outcome if it had opportunity to intervene in the process. The sheer referral of the matter to national laws of res judicata, which are often determined by proceduralist concepts, risks to undermine this very opportunity.

325. Moreover, the interaction of pre-emptive and sequential Forum Coordination allows a further argument on the application of Article V(1)(a) NYC. If a joinder to initiate arbitration already depends on standards of party autonomy, the exposure to the *result* of this very arbitration, without any opportunity to influence it, should depend on party autonomy *a fortiori*. Particularly, the private interests protected by Article V(1)(a) NYC are even more concerned where the detrimental result has already been established. In this regard, one might invoke that the third party could be invited to join an arbitral process and has voluntarily rejected its consent to arbitrate. Yet, this very *rejection of* arbitration is just as much protected by (the negative dimension of) party autonomy and therefore Article V(1)(a) NYC as the *consent to* arbitration.

326. The very rejection of a third party to join an arbitration brings the argument to focus on possible incentives for multilateral transactions. If, for instance, a creditor initiated arbitration against the debtor, the debtor's surety is not party to the arbitration agreement and it is uncertain, whether a potential arbitral award would preclude the debtor's surety from re-litigating the main debt in a follow-up dispute, the creditor and the surety might both consider an application for joinder. Notably, only the consent of *both* can permit such joinder. In this regard, either party will be likely to consent to a joinder when it is optimistic for the outcome. By contrast, when it fears a detrimental arbitral award, it will seek to keep the arbitration bilateral so as to receive the possibility to re-litigate the main debt in follow-up disputes. Given the negative dimension of party autonomy, it has to be taken as a matter of fact that each party always enjoys the right *not* to consent to an extension of the arbitration agreement. Hence, the decisive issue is how to set the best incentive for the parties in exercising this consent. In this regard, the examination submits that there is no 'best incentive' to

1049. Brekoulakis, *Third Parties in Arbitration* Ch. 9-10; Brekoulakis, (2005) 16 Am. Rev. Int'l Arb. 199.
1050. Brekoulakis, *Third Parties in Arbitration* [7.43-7.45].
1051. *See supra* [40].

decide on the joinder. Instead, the joinder's decision will always be motivated by the success prospectus. However, what *can* be established is *legal certainty*. Indeed, by virtue of an application of Article V(1)(a) NYC on res judicata, the parties can rest assured that a non-consent to arbitration will not only influence the joinder but also be decisive for the follow-up question of res judicata.

327. The established arguments on Article II(3) NYC, procedural fairness, adequate incentives and legal certainty furthermore inclines to differ between multilateral relationships and successions. When a third party succeeds to a formal party without joining the arbitration agreement, the said interests are not triggered. If, at the time of the arbitration, the third party had no relationship to the parties or the subject matter, there are no procedural interests of the third party at stake, no uncertainty and no potential for incentives. Moreover, Article V(1)(a) NYC safeguards a third party's interest in having a *future* dispute decided by its natural judge. By contrast, when an arbitral award has already been rendered, the consequences of *past* arbitral adjudication are clearly defined. Therefore, the third party's interest against the arbitration agreement does not pre-empt res judicata. Further incentives for a reconciliation of res judicata and jurisdiction, particularly the adjustment for the purpose of Forum Coordination, do not apply neither. Moreover, courts have held successors even bound by waivers against annulments.[1052]

328. In conclusion, it is only for multilateral relationships that this examination regards the application of Article V(1)(a) NYC to third-party res judicata as a practically preferable and methodologically possible interpretation of the Convention. Such measure establishes consistency with other means of pre-emptive Forum Coordination in multilateral relationships as they are largely determined by the NYC. It provides the parties with procedural fairness and legal certainty. Potentially, one might invoke that this submission restricts the effectiveness of arbitral awards. Yet, this examination submits the very opposite. It is an incentive for the parties to contemplate on multiparty arbitration clauses or preclusion agreements and thereby implement what is the very ambit of the idea of arbitration: their proper intention.[1053]

[4] *The Consequence: A Necessarily Differentiated Regime of Res Judicata*

329. The proposal to assess arbitral awards' third-party effects by virtue of a uniform, jurisdictional requirement under Article V(1)(a) NYC might raise opposition in that this proposal covers merely one mosaic of the welter of issues associated with res judicata in international arbitration. Indeed, this examination refrains from fully regulating res judicata in total, or even its third-party extent. Instead, its *hybrid assessment* demands to assess the third party's consent to arbitral jurisdiction under Article V(1)(a) NYC[1054]

1052. TF, 9 December 2011, 4A_631/2011, [2012] ASA Bull. 383, 386-391.
1053. *See infra* Chapter 10.
1054. *See supra* [307-315].

and its proximity to the parties and subject matter of the dispute under the applicable national law.[1055] Yet, potential objections to this differentiation between uniform and national res judicata rules can be met.

330. The primary differentiation is of *internal* nature: the uniform rule under Article V(1)(a) NYC coexists with the range of other issues of res judicata, e.g., the admissibility of issue preclusion. Notably though, but for indemnity case scenarios, it is frequently the adjudicated claim itself and not an incidental adjudication that is invoked against a third party, e.g., against and amongst sureties, guarantors, solidaransfeees and groups of companies.[1056] For indemnity case scenarios, the examination takes the position that the interaction of uniform and national law is demanded, since the Convention *de lege lata* permits nothing but an application of Article V NYC on res judicata. This submission to differentiate between subjective and objective aspects of res judicata gains further support from a look on the underlying interests. In fact, arguments as to a wide cause of action, the admissibility of issue preclusion and of abuse of process are effective arguments between *focused* and *concentrated* litigation.[1057] Whilst concentration serves the individual legal security and the public as well as private dimension of efficiency, focused litigation can equally serve efficiency and individual fairness.[1058] By contrast, discussions as to third-party extensions amount to a careful balancing of consistency, legal certainty and efficiency against the right to be heard, equality and, in the case of arbitration, party autonomy.[1059] Hence, it is feasible to submit a proposal on the latter aspect without any ambition to additionally settle res judicata's general operative issues.

331. Moreover, a *relational differentiation* between res judicata and enforcement in multilateral case scenarios might be feared. Particularly, Article III NYC lays out nothing but the enforcement guarantee and Article IV NYC individual formal aspects for enforcement whereas specific enforcement requirements are referred to national law. This also concerns the standing to seek enforcement against, e.g., successors[1060] or shareholders.[1061] In addition to such formal enforcement, multiparty case scenarios might equally allow *effective* enforcements, i.e., by virtue of set-off. Notably, the

1055. *See supra* [289-306].
1056. *See supra* [254-274].
1057. *See supra* [117].
1058. Cf. Althammer, *Streitgegenstand und Interesse* 506-507 (*'Der Anspruch des Klägers auf effektiven Rechtsschutz würde [...] beeinträchtigt, wenn durch die Konzentration auf ein Verfahren die Geltendmachung weiterer materieller Rechte in erheblichem Umfang ausgeschlossen würde. [...] Insoweit ist der intendierte Individualrechtschutz im Verhältnis zum Wunsch nach umfassender Streitbereinigung stärker zu gewichten. [...] Im Übrigen brächte eine erweiterte Präklusion eine Aufblähung und Ausdehnung des laufenden Rechtsstreits durch die Parteien mit sich.'*); Mayer, in *Liber Amicorum Héron* 487 (*'[L]a notion de cause [...] se réfère non à l'ensemble concret de faits et des règles de droit qui avaent été invoqués dans la première procédure, mais a une réalité plus vague et plus large, elle implique une certaine déchéance du droit d'agir en justice.'*).
1059. *See supra* [175, 221-228].
1060. *See* CA Milan, *Milloil SpA v. De Agostini & Germani*, (1998) XXIII Y.C.A. 727; OLG Hamburg, (2000) XXV Y.C.A. 641.
1061. *See FR8 Singapore Pte Ltd v. Albacore Marine Corp*, (2011) XXXVI Y.C.A. 403 (S.D.N.Y.); s. 129(4) HGB.

German Federal Court of Justice permitted set-offs even in recognition proceedings.[1062] A potentially detrimental delay of the proceedings[1063] was prevented if exequatur courts could make a partial judgment on the exequatur and another, later, on the set-off.[1064] In any case, the standing to apply for a set-off even in the absence of party identity will equally be a matter of national law. However, as to the conclusive establishment of this claim, Article V(1)(a) NYC can equally apply.

332. In addition, the proposed application of Article V(1)(a) NYC does not cause a *sequential differentiation* neither. This refers to the next step in the sequence after a res judicata problem, i.e., the handling of potentially irreconcilable decisions. Indeed, when two decisions have been rendered between distinct parties, the situation is uncertain and there is scholarly support that irreconcilability operates independently and more broadly than res judicata. From such perspective, the instant proposal might increase the application of irreconcilability. However, in general, irreconcilability has to facilitate res judicata notions when monetary decisions are concerned.[1065] The decisive exception concerns the so-called absolute contradictions, i.e., the situation that one person cannot physically comply with one arbitral award and another decision. This might for instance concern two orders to deliver one unique good to distinct persons. Yet, in order to prevent such irreconcilability, the applicable *substantive* law will regularly adhere to previous adjudications as a factor relieving the debtor from its delivery obligation. Hence, the issue rather is whether such application of decisions *as a fact* can occur irrespective of Article V(1)(a) NYC. This issue demands the framework of factual effects and will be revisited.[1066]

333. Furthermore, the submission to apply Article V(1)(a) NYC on arbitral res judicata towards third parties threatens to cause a *conceptual differentiation* between foreign arbitral awards and foreign judgments. Such differentiation always causes the fear for internal disharmony.[1067] Yet, in general, foreign-judgment principles are by no means averse to but rather embrace a jurisdictional review of the foreign court rendering the judgment.[1068] Particularly the recognition of judgments where a third party has been joined might be subjected to jurisdictional review.[1069] Moreover, when a party seeks to

1062. BGH, [2010] SchiedsVZ 330, [10]; OLG Stuttgart, 18 April 2013, 1 Sch 7/12; reversing KG Berlin, 18 January 2010, 20 Sch 9/09; BayObLG, [2000] NJW 1170, 1171.
1063. *See* Kröll, in *Liber Amicorum Schütze* 311-319.
1064. Schlosser, in *Stein and Jonas* § 1063 [10] (‘*Über diesen muss nicht gleichzeitig mit der Entscheidung, den Schiedsspruch für vollstreckbar zu erklären, befunden werden. [...] Andernfalls könnte sich der Schuldner [...] einen ungerechtfertigten Suspensiveffekt verschaffen.*’).
1065. *See supra* [168].
1066. *See infra* Chapter 7.
1067. *See* in general Bermann, (2015) 381 Rec. des cours [549-554].
1068. *See* von Mehren, (1980) 167 Rec. des cours 39 (‘Procedural review [of foreign judgents] can also take the form of imposing jurisdictional requirements. Such requirements test the fairness of proceedings [...]. Compliance with appropriate standards of adjudicatory jurisdiction thus serves what can be referred to as a ‘hallmark’ function by evidencing that the State of origin shows fairness and good judgment generally in its handling of litigation.’). *See* for the fundamental rules amongst national laws *Sirdar Gurdyal Singh v. The Rajah of Faridkote*, [1894] AC 670 (PC); BGHZ 52, 30, 37-39; BGHZ 124, 237; Kegel and Schurig, *Internationales Privatrecht* 1062; Mayer and Heuzé, *Droit international privé* [367].
1069. *See* BGH, [1970] NJW 387 (indemnity claim of defendant against third party).

object to judgment recognition in that it *relies* on an arbitration agreement overlooked by the foreign court, courts have held that Article II(1) NYC, as part of the national jurisdiction's public policy, bars recognition.[1070] Certainly, these jurisdictional reviews all re-examine the foreign court's jurisdiction *over the formal parties to the foreign litigation* and not necessarily imply that it would be examined whether a third party exposed to res judicata *would have been* subject to the foreign court's adjudicatory power. In this regard, at least the most immanent fear for inconsistency between foreign awards and foreign judgment principles, namely when an arbitral award is confirmed and thus recognized as judgment at common law,[1071] can equally be met. Indeed, scholarship submits that the recognition of such confirmation judgments can equally be rejected if the underlying award violates Article V(1)(a) NYC.[1072] Hence, the instant proposal would not be trumped by common law's parallel entitlement. If, otherwise, there remains a distinction between the efficacy of arbitral awards and foreign judgments towards third parties, then this is required by the specific nature of arbitral awards as a result of privately established justice.

334. Finally, the proposal to apply Article V(1)(a) NYC on res judicata might demand *conflictualist differentiation*. It supplements already complex discussions about the law applicable to res judicata in that the law applicable to the arbitration agreement is additionally relevant. Yet, the potential fear for conflictualist discussions should not pre-empt the application of a prima facie preferable rule. Moreover, the plurality of relevant applicable laws can be adhered to by means of adequate methods of private international law as they will be examined in Chapter 7. Therefore, the range of differentiations caused by a uniform boundary to third-party res judicata and other aspects of arbitral awards are not pre-empting the applicability of Article V(1)(a) NYC. Instead, reconciling arbitral jurisdiction and arbitral res judicata is adhering to party autonomy, Forum Coordination, fairness and practicable feasibility.

[C] Transfer of the Established Argument to Non-mutual Preclusion

335. Given the prominence of non-mutual preclusion at common law, the examination has to address whether the requirements established on arbitral awards to the *detriment* of third parties also apply if third parties seek to invoke an arbitral award in their *favour*. This very issue has recently arisen in a post-LCIA litigation before German courts: a Cypriote corporation controlled by a Russian Senator claims damages from a major German energy supplier for non-realization of a joint venture. The main argument is whether a 'preliminary agreement' signed and negotiated by the defendant's former managing director obligates the defendant to realize the joint venture. Under the 'preliminary agreement', an LCIA tribunal seated in London had jurisdiction. It rejected the claim on the substance. Subsequently, the Cypriote corporation brought the claim before German courts against *both*, the energy supplier and its former

1070. *See* ATF 124 III 83, [E.5b].
1071. *See infra* [605].
1072. Bermann, (2015) 381 Rec. des cours [742]; *Dicey Morris and Collins* [16-165].

managing director personally. The latter, as a third party to the prior dispute, invoked the arbitral award against the claimant. The German district court rejected this defence holding that the former managing director was not a privy under English law, that abuse of process would not be recognizable in Germany *and* that the NYC does not allow to apply res judicata towards non-signatories of the arbitration agreement.[1073] The appeal is pending.

336. The admissibility of non-mutual preclusion under the NYC, which was briefly mentioned in the recent case, demands an adjusted assessment of Article V NYC. To set the scene, it is now the very third party to the arbitration, which seeks to invoke the arbitral award. In opposition, it is a former party to the arbitration against whom the award is invoked and which objects to such preclusion. These roles are of the utmost importance, because Article V NYC's recognition grounds operate upon '*the request of the party against whom [the award] is invoked*'. Hence, it will now be the very former party to the arbitration, which invokes Article V NYC. Therefore, it needs to be examined whether preclusive effects in favour of a third party violate the former party's right to be heard under Article V(1)(b) NYC (*see* [1], *infra*) and whether the former party can rely on Article V(1)(a) NYC although it did consent to arbitration (*see* [2], *infra*).

[1] Infeasibility of Article V(1)(b) NYC for Uniform Standards

337. When assessing whether the NYC contains any rule on non-mutual preclusion, it is of the essence that the shift of the parties' roles implies a shift of the rationales at stake. The admissibility of non-mutual preclusion is *not* a traditional matter of due process. Instead, it is a matter of equality. The third party seeks to enjoy the benefits of a decision, although it would not be exposed to its detriments. To invert this problem, the former party to the dispute risks losing against a third party against whom its success might not have been conclusive.[1074] Therefore, a uniform rule of the NYC on non-mutual preclusion would be a rule on equality.

1073. LG Essen, 24 March 2015, 12 O 37/12, [2015] Beck-Online 07614, [II.] ('*Die Kammer hat Zweifel daran, ob der Beklagte zu 2) nach englischem Prozessrecht als privy (of Interest) oder aus Sec. 58 des Arbitration Act oder aus dem Gesichtspunkt des abuse of process von der Bindungswirkung des Schiedsspruchs erfasst wäre. […] Soweit in dem Gutachten I1 (Seite 63) eine Bindung aus Sec. 58 i. V. m. Sec. 82 Abs. 2 Arbitration Act abgeleitet wird und auf seine Stellung als Vorstandsvorsitzender sowie als an dem Verhandlungsabbruch beteiligte Person abgehoben wird, dürfte dies wohl mangels einer ausdrücklichen oder funktionsäquivalenten Entsprechung im deutschen Recht einer Anerkennung nicht zugänglich sein. Gleiches gilt auch hinsichtlich einer Begründung einer Bindungswirkung nach englischem Recht über abuse of process. […]Letztlich kann dies indes auf sich beruhen, da bei Annahme einer schiedsgerichtlichen Entscheidung, die sich auch auf den Beklagten zu 2) erstreckte, jedenfalls von einem Anerkennungshindernis gem. Art. V Abs. 1 lit. c, Abs. 2 lit. b UNÖ auszugehen ist. Die Schiedsvereinbarung erstreckt sich in personaler Hinsicht zunächst auf die vertragsschließenden Parteien, zu denen der Beklagte zu 2) nicht gehört.*').

1074. *See supra* [196].

338. Amongst the relevant grounds of Article V NYC, the principle of equality is not explicitly addressed. This stands in strong contrast to national arbitration laws and Article 18 UNCITRAL Model Law. Yet, the former Supreme Court of Hong Kong has applied equality under Article V(1)(b) NYC.[1075] Correspondingly, scholarship points out that:

> the principle of equal treatment [...] is a part of the NYC and, in particular, of Article V(1)(b)'s due process requirement. [...] Even though there are surprisingly few authorities addressing the issue, the guarantee of equal treatment logically stems from the core idea of procedural fairness itself.[1076]

339. However,ransferalral of the above-introduced rationales also inclines *not* to facilitate this provision in order to establish a general rule for or against non-mutual preclusion. Primarily, it is also with regard to equality that Article V(1)(b) NYC is concerned with the arbitral process itself. Yet, an arbitral award giving rise to non-mutual preclusion might have originated from an entirely regular procedure. In addition, also with regard to equality, Article V(1)(b) NYC equally depends on domestic notions of procedural justice. For the specific case of non-mutual preclusion, this becomes most delicate because of the divide between common and civil law. The former generally allows non-mutual preclusion, and the latter rejects it.[1077] Hence, facilitating an unwritten ground for non-recognition in order to pre-empt one of those two positions, appears unpreferable. Instead, non-mutual preclusion generally remains a matter of national law.

[2] Adjusted Rationales Favouring the Application of Article V(1)(a) NYC

340. When a former party to the arbitration requests not to recognize the foreign arbitral award as a ground for non-mutual preclusion in favour of a third party, the setting for Article V(1)(a) NYC differs fundamentally from the previously affirmed situation. In the latter, a third party could demand that without consent to arbitration, there can be no exposure to arbitral res judicata (*see* [308-316], *supra*). In the instant situation, the party objecting to res judicata did consent to arbitration. It was both a party to the arbitration agreement and a party to the arbitral procedure. Therefore, the issue is whether a party can request to refuse recognition because it has not consented to arbitrate *with the third party now relying on the award.* In this regard, the examination will adopt the previously undertaken interpretation of the wording, context and rationale of Article V(1)(a) NYC with regard to party autonomy and Forum Coordination.

1075. *Paklito Investment Ltd v. Klockner East Asia Ltd,* (1994) XIX Y.C.A. 664, 671 (SCHK).
1076. Scherer in Wolff (ed.), *New York Convention* Art. V [171]. *Corresp Born* 3520; *Redfern and Hunter* [11.73].
1077. *See supra* [193-196].

341. To start from the wording, it has previously been established that Article V(1)(a) NYC's referral to invalidity must be read as 'the arbitration agreement is inapplicable towards the party resisting recognition'.[1078] When a third party itself seeks to rely on the arbitral award against a party to the arbitration agreement, this reading is not triggered.

342. Moving to the inherent rationale of party autonomy, the party now exposed to non-mutual preclusion has generally consented to be exposed to an arbitral award. In a positive manner, it has conferred adjudicatory competence upon the arbitral tribunal. In a negative sense it has renounced its right to a natural judge. In addition, there is also a particular personal element to party autonomy in that consent to arbitrate is consent to arbitrate *with a specific opponent*, because arbitration agreements are concluded in order to establish a swift and confidential dispute resolution. Yet, the interest of the party exposed to res judicata in arbitrating with a particular partner is complied with since the party now relying on non-mutual preclusion remained a stranger to the arbitration. Therefore, also in a conceptual manner, there is a certain threshold for regarding non-mutual preclusion as a violation of party autonomy.

343. This threshold appears to be met by applying the above-mentioned implementations of Forum Coordination:[1079] initially, the dimension of procedural fairness is concerned, albeit in a different manner. Whilst the party exposed to res judicata did have an opportunity to influence the arbitration, it had no opportunity to influence any adjudication towards the third party itself. As a stranger to the arbitration agreement, the third party could always have objected to arbitral jurisdiction. Accordingly, the general concerns of equality that non-mutual preclusion triggers are even *enhanced* when a third party has not consented to arbitration.

344. Following up on the interaction of non-mutual preclusion and pre-emptive Forum Coordination: at common law, non-mutual preclusion interacts with the opportunity to join a third party to the initial litigation. Since, in arbitration, this very interaction is generally disrupted, the Court of Appeal sets a high threshold for arbitral awards to constitute a ground for abuse of process in favour of third parties. Moreover, persuasive jurisprudence, scholarship and the Draft Third Restatement in the US seek to restrict non-mutual preclusion.[1080] Accordingly, an interpretation of Article V(1)(a) NYC as an anchor of Forum Coordination in multilateral transactions demands to reconcile preclusion and jurisdiction no matter whether the third party is exposed to or seeks to rely on res judicata.

345. This inclination becomes even more compelling when focusing on the otherwise resulting incentives and uncertainties. In this regard, the NYC needs to be interpreted as a medium for promoting the usage of arbitration agreements and a guarantor of legal certainty:[1081] without the application of Article V(1)(a) NYC, it would depend on the

1078. *See supra* [40].
1079. *See supra* [321-328].
1080. *See supra* [240-244].
1081. *See supra* [294-296].

applicable law, hence on the forum of the follow-up dispute whether an arbitral award triggers non-mutual preclusion. If such forum facilitates an arbitral award as a ground for non-mutual preclusion, the third party will have no incentive whatsoever to agree on arbitration. Already without the consent, the third party can enjoy the benefits of the arbitral award without risking to be exposed to a detrimental result. Certainly, in international scenarios, it is more practical to assume that the follow-up dispute might be brought before a variety of fora. Yet, this further triggers legal certainty. If the admissibility of non-mutual preclusion depends entirely on private international law, there are strong incentives for either party to decide on a favourable forum for the follow-up dispute. Particularly the third party might be inclined to apply for a negative declaration of liability before courts applying non-mutual preclusion. Therefore, the effective promotion of arbitration agreements and the mandate for legal certainty also favour an application of Article V(1)(a) NYC on non-mutual preclusion.

346. In conclusion, since the Convention's mandates for consistent Forum Coordination, procedural justice and legal certainty are at stake, it is submitted that an arbitral award should only give rise to non-mutual preclusion if (i) the third party relying on the award has consented to the arbitration agreement and (ii) the otherwise applicable national law allows for non-mutual preclusion. As to the first, uniform requirement, the examination notes the discretionary nature of Article V(1)(a) NYC (*'may be refused'*). Therefore, as elaborated by the English Court of Appeals in *Michael Wilson* on English law,[1082] courts retain a certain discretionary power to apply non-mutual preclusion in order to prevent serious injustices.

[D] Irrelevance of More Liberal *Lex Fori* (Article VII NYC)

347. If, for instance, an arbitral award is invoked against a party's surety before the courts of a jurisdiction which applies its *lex fori* to arbitral res judicata and the *lex fori* state that arbitral res judicata extends to parties' sureties even though they might not have consented to arbitrate, the issue arises whether this rule of res judicata pre-empts the proposed application of Article V(1)(a) NYC. In particular, Article VII(1) Alt. 2 NYC provides that the Convention:

> shall not [...] deprive any interested party of any right he may have to avail himself of an arbitral award in the manner and to the extent allowed by the law or the treaties of the country where such award is relied upon.

348. In other words, the provision establishes what Jan Albert van den Berg titled the *'more-favourable-right provision'*.[1083] Historically, a more-favourable-right provision had already been included in Article 5 Geneva Convention. As elaborated in UNCITRAL's 2006 recommendation, Article VII NYC has the rationale to *'enable the*

1082. *See supra* [240-244].
1083. van den Berg, *The New York Convention* 81.

enforcement of foreign arbitral awards to the greatest extent'.[1084] Nowadays, by far the most prominent application certainly is the French *Hilmarton/Putrabali* jurisprudence with regard to the enforcement of annulled awards.[1085] Moreover, the provision is applied '*mutatis mutandis*' when the forum law is more favourable with regard to the validity of an arbitration agreement.[1086] Another general implementation is section 104 English Arbitration Act providing that a party may choose between enforcement under the Convention and enforcement at common law.[1087] Whilst at plain sight, the provision might also open the gate for the forum's more extensive preclusion law, the examination submits that one essential feature of Article VII NYC demands to hold otherwise and that Article V(1)(a) NYC should bar third-party effects irrespective of the *lex fori*.

349. The provision defers to forum law where the latter does not *contain* a ground comparable to Article V NYC. By contrast, it does not apply where the forum law does contain such a ground but merely *applies* it more liberally. Whilst the specific scope of Article VII NYC in this respect has not triggered extensive scholarship, one treatise summarizes that the provision '*has very limited role in the states which have closely followed the provisions of Article V in their domestic law* [...]'.[1088] For instance, Article VII NYC has not even been invoked for the delicate topic of jurisdiction over non-signatories as a ground to disregard the constraints established under Article V(1)(a) NYC. Methodologically, the restriction of Article VII NYC to situations where the forum law does not contain a ground comparable to Article V is necessary because, otherwise, Article VII NYC would flaw the uniform interpretation of Article V NYC in two respects. Indeed, courts applying Article V NYC could always facilitate Article VII NYC for non-autonomous applications. Moreover, the foreign authorities referred to as persuasive guidelines under an autonomous interpretation could always be rejected by stating that they constituted an implementation of Article VII. Hence, the very idea of a uniform interpretation of Article V NYC demands not to apply Article VII NYC when the *lex fori* contain a ground identical to Article NYC. Since Article V(1)(a) NYC is a ground common to most national laws, Article VII NYC does not pre-empt the proposed jurisdictional boundary to arbitral awards' third-party effects.

Interim Conclusion

350. In summary, the examination proposes that the Convention does *not* mandate a comprehensive, uniform regime of res judicata. Therefore, in general, the examination proposes to determine arbitral awards' third-party effects under national law. Yet, the

1084. *UNCITRAL Recommendation on* Art. *II, VII NYC*, Recital No. 7.
1085. *See infra* [604].
1086. *UNCITRAL Recommendation on* Art. *II, VII NYC*, Recommendation No. 2; Quinke in Wolff (ed.), *New York Convention* Art. VII[45]. Cf. BGH, 21 September 2005, (2006) XXXI Y.C.A. 679, 681; Schlosser, in *Stein and Jones* [378]; van den Berg, *The New York Convention* 86-87.
1087. 'Nothing in the preceding provisions of this Part affects any right to rely upon or enforce a New York Convention award at common law or under section 66'.
1088. *Poudret and Besson* [888].

examination proposes an *additional, uniform requirement for foreign arbitral awards' third-party effects in subsequent litigation deducted from Article V(1)(a) NYC.*

351. The proposed uniform requirement is: *an award's third-party effect requires that the third party consented to the underlying arbitration agreement.* If a comprehensive res judicata regime under the Convention evolves in the future, it applies *a fortiori*. The requirement equally applies to non-mutual preclusion and factual effects (the latter will be revisited in *Chapter 7*). By contrast, since successors had no opportunity to consent to arbitration, the requirement is unnecessary.

§5.04 PRECLUSION AGREEMENTS (ARTICLE II(1) NYC)

352. Several opinions sought to take the position that even if the Convention does not contain any default provisions on res judicata, its overall character and Article II(1) will mandate at least a uniform rule pursuant to which express party agreements on extended res judicata enjoy preference.[1089] Such preclusion agreements might avoid the re-litigation of complex factual or legal issues and could be particularly feasible in multi-party case scenarios. For instance, all parties to a construction project (principal, contractor, subcontractor) could agree that – to provide a formulation – 'any arbitral award rendered between two of the signing parties, including its reasonings, will be preclusive and conclusive in subsequent disputes between any of the parties irrespective of whether the parties in the previous and subsequent dispute are identical'. Such clause might be added to (i) the arbitration clause in a multilateral contract, (ii) another clause in the contract or (iii) an isolated multilateral clause standing next to bilateral contracts. In any case, several factors render such comprehensive preclusion clauses unlikely to come before courts. Yet, when confronted with the general (hypothetical) question, several factors speak in favour of the Convention's protection for such clauses (*see* [A], *infra*). The situation is more delicate in one situation, which is in fact likely to come before court, namely when preclusion agreements have merely been concluded between two out of several parties to a situation. Here, the relevance touches upon the waivability of Article V(1)(a) NYC (*see* [B], *infra*).

[A] Multilateral Preclusion Agreements

353. At the outset, it has to be borne in mind that the applicability of the Convention to *multilateral* preclusion agreements is very unlikely to come before courts. Particularly, if all parties to a multilateral transaction agree on preclusion arrangements, they will regularly also agree on arbitration. Primarily and in strong contrast to the default situation, this can provide the grounds for multi-party arbitration pre-empting any preclusion arguments.[1090] Even if multi-party arbitration is not applied for and subsequent disputes between distinct parties to the multilateral transactions arise, Article

1089. *See supra* [282-287].
1090. *See supra* [36-51].

II(3) NYC will always obligate the courts to decline jurisdiction, unless the arbitration agreement is limited in subject matter, time or exclusiveness.

354. If courts in the latter situations do have to analyse whether the Convention protects preclusion agreements, an interpretation is faced with the narrow wording of Article II(1). It protects agreements where the parties *'undertake to submit to arbitration [...] differences'*.[1091] At plain sight, this wording does not broadly cover all agreements 'in relation to arbitration'. Instead, it merely covers the establishment of arbitral jurisdiction. However, such jurisdiction allows tribunals to conduct the proceedings and to render a final and binding arbitral award. Hence, it is not excluded to interpret Article II(1) NYC in that courts do not only have to respect the jurisdiction of tribunals but also the arbitral proceedings and the arbitral award.

355. With a view to the context of the provision, it is evident that the Convention regulates arbitral awards in other provisions. This well corresponds to the Convention's historical focus on arbitral awards. The drafts of the ICC in 1953[1092] and the UN Committee in 1955[1093] were directed at arbitral awards only. Article II NYC was merely added during the final three-week conference in New York.[1094] This increased prominence of arbitral awards could go either way in interpreting Article II(1) NYC. On the one hand, one could raise the distinct scope of the provisions and the distinct treatments of arbitration agreements and arbitral awards. On the other hand, it appears feasible to state that the Convention's focus on arbitral awards even increases the relevance for party agreements on preclusion consequences.

356. A comparative perspective would support the latter view. In fact, amongst national laws, preclusion agreements are exposed to little opposition.[1095] What is more, national arbitration laws as well as the Model Law stipulate the binding nature of 'consent awards'.[1096] This allows for a transferred argument in favour of preclusion agreements, particularly in multi-party case scenarios: if the parties involved can join a third party to the procedure and form a settlement stipulated within a consent award that the arbitral award shall equally be preclusive and conclusive towards the third parties, then it should be reasonably possible to form such an agreement in anticipation of the procedure, i.e., in the arbitration agreement.

1091. 'Each Contracting State shall recognize an agreement in writing under which the parties undertake to submit to arbitration all or any differences which have arisen or which may arise between them in respect of a defined legal relationship, whether contractual or not, concerning a subject matter capable of settlement by arbitration'.

1092. *ICC Draft NYC*, 1953, reprinted (1998) 9 ICC Bull. 32.

1093. *Report of the Committee on the Enforcement of International Arbitral Awards & Draft NYC*, 28 March 1955, UN Doc E/2704, [18-19].

1094. *See* in particular the first discussions after proposals by Sweden and Poland in *NY Conference – 9th Meeting*, 26 May 1958, UN Doc E/CONF.26/SR.9, 3-13 and the adoption of the working group's proposal in *NY Conference – 21st Meeting*, 5 June 1958, UN Doc E/CONF.26/SR.21, 21.

1095. *See supra* [230].

1096. *See supra* [134].

357. Such solution would also be mandated by the Convention's rationales to promote arbitration, the swift settlement of international disputes and legal certainty to parties of international commercial transactions. Avoiding the welter of issues associated with res judicata's operation towards third parties by virtue of an anticipated preclusion agreement in the arbitration clause promotes these interests. Moreover, this examination notes that its proposal in favour of an extended application of Article V(1)(a) NYC on res judicata should by no means overregulate and thereby interfere with cross-border commerce.[1097] Therefore, there is reasonable ground to assume that such preclusion agreements are protected by the Convention.

358. However, the general protection of explicit preclusion agreements does not pre-empt problems with less explicit, potentially implied preclusion agreements. For instance, transactions might provide ample arguments that certain provisions of a contract should be construed as impliedly establishing the extended preclusion of an arbitral award. Vice versa, it might be argued that a preclusion arrangement outside of the arbitration clause was not meant to have the comprehensive effect under the Convention. In this regard, instant legal issues are the necessary threshold of consent and the relevant burden as well as the *standard* of proof. Here, the silent Convention does not appear as any ground for uniform rules. Instead, the matters are governed by national law. The instant question in this regard is whether this should be the law governing the arbitral award's res judicata or the arbitration agreement. This issue will be revisited in *Chapter 6* on private international law.

[B] Bilateral Preclusion Anticipation: *Lacuna* of the NYC

359. A slight modification of the above-mentioned scenario is practically more relevant and legally more challenging: instead of a multilateral preclusion agreement, the scenario assumes that only *two out of several* parties to a multilateral transaction agree on preclusions. To follow up on the above-mentioned scenario, this might be the case, when a sub-contractor agrees with the contractor to regard any arbitral award rendered between the principal and contractor as binding in indemnity matters. If, in addition, the contractor and the sub-contractor do *not* agree on arbitration but rather conclude a forum-selection clause, this is the preeminent scenario, where a follow-up dispute *does* come before courts and the Convention's relevance for the preclusion agreement demands examination.

360. It is submitted that the Convention should not be interpreted as protecting preclusion agreements between parties who have not subjected their own disputes to arbitration. Foremost, when one of the parties of the *subsequent* dispute has not consented to the arbitration agreement underlying the *former* dispute, the intrinsic connection between the arbitration clause and the preclusion arrangement is disrupted. The agreement on preclusion is formally distinct to the agreement protected by Article II(1) NYC.

1097. *See* in general Kronke, in *Liber Amicorum Geimer* 398.

361. Instead of a protection, the issue under the Convention rather is whether it even *bars* the preclusion agreement. This issue arises under the assumption that the above-mentioned standard of Article V(1)(a) NYC generally applies to res judicata. Under this standard, the party agreeing to the preclusion (above, the sub-contractor) would otherwise *not* be exposed to res judicata. Hence, the preclusion agreement would effectively be a waiver of Article V(1)(a) NYC. Generally, the waivability of Article V NYC has caused broad discussion. Whilst national jurisprudence is divided[1098] and some authors[1099] as well as the Draft Third Restatement on International Commercial Arbitration[1100] deem such waivers invalid, the European Court of Human Rights (examining Article 6 ECHR) affirmed at least the waiver of set-aside opportunities under Article 192 Swiss PILA.[1101] In particular, the different wordings of Article V(1) ('at the request of the party') and Article V(2) ('if the competent authority finds') support the waivability. However, there is a crucial difference between the classic discussion and the instant waivability of Article V(1)(a) NYC. Generally, the party waiving its objections under Article V agrees to arbitrate. By contrast, in the instant case, the third party does not even agree to arbitrate. Accordingly, the threshold for allowing the waiver is raised.

362. Yet, the thesis strongly submits that the parties' interest in legal certainty, finality and efficiency justifies foregoing the protection under Article V(1)(a) NYC. If a commercial party voluntarily agrees to expose itself to the results of arbitration proceedings conducted between other parties, it will not require any increased protection. Instead, the interest in favour of preclusion agreements, particularly the circumvention of the welter of complex legal issues associated with res judicata, is persuasive. Moreover, the Convention's rationales in promoting arbitration, efficiency and particularly party autonomy demand not to restrict the latter. Therefore, a preclusion agreement concluded by at least one party that did not consent to the former dispute's arbitration clause is not deemed inoperative under Article V(1)(a) NYC. However, it does not fall under the protection of Article II(1) NYC neither. Hence, it will be governed by national law further raising the focus on private international law.[1102]

Interim Conclusion

363. To conclude on preclusion agreements, multilateral, explicit agreements for extended preclusion in multi-party relationships irrespective of party identity should be

1098. *See Born* 3440-3442.
1099. Borris and Hannecke in Wolff (ed.), *New York Convention* 263.
1100. Restatement (Third) Int'l Comm Arbitration (TD 2), § 4-24 (a) (Parties may not by agreement reduce or eliminate the grounds for vacating or denying confirmation of a US Convention award or for denying recognition or enforcement of a foreign Convention award.' Yet *see* § 4-25 (a) ('a party may at any time waive its right to invoke an objection that would justify a court vacating or denying confirmation, recognition, or enforcement'). *See* Bermann, (2015) 381 Rec. des cours [723] ('There is simply very little to suggest that anything like an international standard has emerged').
1101. ECtHR, *Noureddine Tabbanne v. Switzerland*, 1 March 2016, 41069/12.
1102. *See infra* [420-421].

protected by Article II(1) NYC. However, with a view to the establishment of arbitral jurisdiction, the protection is unlikely to be raised in court. Instead, it is more likely when a preclusion party has *not* consented to arbitration. Such situation should be governed by national law as it will be designated in *Chapter 6*.

§5.05 CONCLUDING THESES

(1) Whilst the NYC has long been considered irrelevant for arbitral res judicata, an emerging debate addresses whether (i) res judicata falls under the NYC's scope, (ii) if it does, whether the NYC contains any rules beyond its explicit enforcement regime and (iii), in any case, whether it protects preclusion agreements.[1103]

(2) The wording, context, drafting history and rationales of the NYC incline to hold that (i) its scope on 'recognition' generally does cover res judicata, albeit (ii) the NYC does *not* allow to apply anything but its explicit provisions in Articles II, III, V. Yet, if the consensus on a transnational regime advances, the following theses apply correspondingly.[1104]

(3) Although res judicata issues are due-process issues, Article V(1)(b) NYC is of no relevance to res judicata's third-party scope, because it focuses on the procedural regularity of the previous arbitral proceedings itself.[1105]

(4) By contrast, it is the examination's core and genuine contention that Article V(1)(a) NYC should be applied to arbitral awards' third-party effects. This necessitates a *hybrid standard*: under Article V(1)(a) NYC, the third party will only be bound to res judicata if it agreed to the underlying arbitration agreement. The other requirements are governed by national law.[1106]

(5) This proposal is a proposal on implementing party autonomy. Moreover, it is a proposal on practical feasibility in that the reconciliation of jurisdiction and preclusion reflects res judicata's role as *sequential Forum Coordination*. Indeed, pre-emptive Forum Coordination is already restricted by party autonomy. Hence, procedural fairness, legal certainty and the context of Article II(3), V(1)(a) NYC incline to extend the decisive role of party autonomy in multi-party case scenarios to sequential Forum Coordination, i.e., res judicata.[1107]

(6) These considerations do not only apply to res judicata invoked *against* third parties but also to non-mutual preclusion invoked *by* third parties.[1108]

1103. *See supra* [282-288].
1104. *See supra* [289-298].
1105. *See supra* [300-306].
1106. *See supra* [308-315].
1107. *See supra* [317-334].
1108. *See supra* [340-346].

(7) Article II(1) NYC obligates courts to uphold preclusion agreements concluded by all signatories to a multilateral arbitration clause. Yet, national law governs the threshold for consent and the agreements' interpretation.[1109]

(8) By contrast, the NYC is inapplicable where two parties do *not* agree on arbitration but conclude a bilateral preclusion agreement with regard to an arbitration between (partially) different parties on related matters. For instance, when a sub-contractor agrees to regard arbitral awards rendered between the contractor and the principal binding in indemnity proceedings. Neither does Article II(1) NYC protect such agreements nor does Article V(1)(a) NYC bar them. Instead, national law applies.[1110]

1109. *See supra* [347-349].
1110. *See supra* [358-362].

CHAPTER 6

Third-Party Effects of Arbitral Awards in Private International Law

364. The previous elaborations on the comparative and uniform framework of res judicata illustrate the immanent need to examine private international law. Indeed, to date, uniform principles deducted from the NYC do not govern the consequences of foreign arbitral res judicata before courts. Even if one follows the previous proposal to apply Article V(1)(a) NYC:[1111] when the third party was a stranger to the arbitration proceedings, yet consented to the arbitration *agreement*, national law will govern the further requirements. Moreover, those arbitral tribunals, which are sceptical towards transnational techniques examined in *Chapter 8*, will also apply private international law.[1112]

365. The applicable law turns particularly delicate since the comparative overview has revealed fundamental divides amongst national arbitration laws. To illustrate some by virtue of the Introduction's construction case:[1113] when a principal seeks to invoke an arbitral award against the contractor's parent company, US law will provide the most promising recourse. When a contractor seeks indemnity from its sub-contractor, only French law's *opposabilité* might overcome the same-parties requirement. When a principal has unsuccessfully arbitrated against the contractor and then sues the principal, common law might preclude him to do so.[1114]

366. Certainly, the law applicable to res judicata is a true classic of private international law (*see* §6.01, *infra*). Yet, in this examination's perspective, the present debate inclines to be enhanced, both doctrinally and - in particular - practically (*see* §6.02, *infra*). Upon its basis, the examination proposes the solutions for the specific categories of an arbitral award's third-party effect (*see* §6.03, *infra*). Finally, the examination

1111. *See supra* [307-350].
1112. *See infra* [481-486].
1113. *See supra* [2].
1114. *See supra* [278].

mentions ancillary aspects, i.e., preclusion agreements and damages for the non-compliance with an arbitral award (*see* §6.04, *infra*).

367. As a final proclamation, this Chapter maintains the examination's comparative contention. That is, it will jointly assess several jurisdictions. At the same time, it certainly acknowledges the general *national* character of private international law and the resulting need for differentiations. Yet, res judicata's third-party dimension remains rather unexplored within national doctrines and thus requires a recourse to fundamental methodologies. Since these very methodologies have become increasingly transnational, the genuine proposals within this Chapter can be read as recommendations irrespective of the relevant forum.

§6.01 STATUS QUO: THE LAW APPLICABLE TO RES JUDICATA AS A MATTER OF TERRITORIALITY

368. The law applicable to res judicata is one of the most classic issues of private international law. Already for foreign judgments, it is heavily debated. For arbitral awards, the discussion aggravates in light of the additional argument on whether proceduralist solutions are transferable. Thereby, the issue turns into a practical litmus test for arbitration's judicial function (inclining proceduralist solutions) and its consensual foundation (inclining adjustments).[1115] Vice versa, the predominant emphasis of arbitration's consensual foundation requires private international law to reconsider the line drawn between choice of law (the conflict of *laws*) and international procedural law (the conflict of *jurisdictions*). For these reasons, res judicata is a paradigm for arbitration's and private international law's roles as '*mutual prisms*'.[1116]

369. A preliminary aspect of res judicata's handling in private international law has largely vanished from the argumentative stage: its characterization (classification). Given that res judicata was once even perceived as an institute of substantive law,[1117] the argument that res judicata should be assessed under the law of the (former or subsequent) dispute's substance appears not far-fetched. Yet, there are no submissions in this regard. Indeed, in *AEGIS*, the Privy Council only mentioned the complex nature of issue estoppel.[1118] Moreover, US jurisprudence certainly contains several statements

1115. *See supra* [119-124].

1116. *See* Bermann, (2015) 381 Rec. des cours 41 [1] ('[G]iven arbitration's international character and its core mission of resolving disputes between private parties, arbitration may fairly be regarded as the quintessential private international law endeavour. [...] In a very real sense, the two fields serve as mutual prisms.').

1117. *See supra* [100].

1118. *Associated Electric and Gas Insurance Services Ltd v. European Reinsurance Company of Zurich*, [2003] 1 WLR 1041, 1048 (PC) ('The award has conferred upon them a right which is enforceable by later pleading an issue estoppel. It is a species of the enforcement of the rights given by the award just as much as would be a cause of action estoppel. It is true that estoppels can be described as rules of evidence or as rules of public policy [...] but that is to look at how estoppels are given effect to, not at what is the nature of the private law right which the estoppel recognises and protects.').

allocating the issue of res judicata in arbitration to the substance.[1119] However, these statements do not address the applicable law. Instead, they concern arbitrability and are submitted in order to protect arbitral tribunals' jurisdiction.[1120] Scholarship only mentions that such solution was possible or preferred by others.[1121] For example, whilst a preliminary publication of the ILA's Rapporteur proceeded accordingly,[1122] the ILA Interim Report states that '*[t]he law governing the parties' relationship appears not to be relevant*'.[1123] In the same spirit, it has been elaborated that the substantive characterization is in conflict with res judicata's function serving both the legitimacy of the original tribunal and the resources and consistency of the subsequent jurisdiction since the jurisdiction to which the law of the merits is subjected has no inherent legislative interest in guaranteeing a decision's finality.[1124]

370. Therefore, the classic debate about the law applicable to res judicata mainly constitutes an antagony between two solutions originating from foreign judgment principles: the law of the decision's origin (doctrine of 'extension of effects') and the subsequent *lex fori* (doctrine of 'equalization of effects'). In arbitration, the extension doctrine is translated in that the origin was the law of the arbitral seat. Generally, the discussion on the law applicable to res judicata's consequences does not differentiate between the general, operative issues of res judicata (cause of action, issue preclusion, examination ex officio) and the particular question whether a third party is exposed.

371. Noteworthy, the origin/*lex fori* discussion is no struggle on the adequate connecting factor. Instead, the method of recognition applies thereby illustrating the pluralism of private-international-law methodologies.[1125] Whether the recognition method demands that a forum applies foreign preclusion standards is, in essence, a matter of territoriality and sovereignty. Indeed, to assess a decision's effects by virtue of foreign law means to fully refer to foreign judicial authority and to restrict the own adjudicatory competence thereupon. Some authors invoke that this is the very meaning

1119. *National Union Fire Ins. Co. v. Belco Petroleum Corp*, 88 F.3d 129, 135-136 (2d Cir. 1996) ('a component of the dispute on the merits').
1120. *See supra* [153]. *See, e.g.*, *Chrion Corp. v. Ortho Diagnostic System Inc*, 207 F.3d 126, 1134 (9th Cir. 2000) ('a res judicata defence is a component of the merits of the dispute and *is thus an arbitrable issue*'); *PenneCom BV v. Merrill Lynch & Co. Inc*, 2003 WL 21512216, 5 (S.D.N.Y. 2003), rev'd on other grounds, 372 F.3d 488 (2d Cir. 2005); *Anchor Glass Container Corp. v. Buschmeier*, 426 F.3d 872, 877 (7th Cir. 2005) ('Anchor argued in its briefs that the district court erred in holding that Pennsylvania law governed the res judicata analysis and contended that the law of the forum state, Indiana, applied. At oral argument, however, Anchor *explicitly withdrew its objection.*').
1121. Cf. Mayer, in *Liber amicorum Reymond* 184; Seraglini, (2016) Rev. Arb. 60. For judgments, however, *see* Basedow, *Materielles Recht und Prozessrecht*; Inboyet-Hoegy, *L'action en justice* [473]; Peiffer, *Grenzüberschreitende Titelgeltung* [117] ('*ggf. Wirkungsbegrenzung nach der* lex causae').
1122. Sheppard, in *Parallel State and Arbitral Procedures* 230 ('It may be that the lex contractus has also to be considered.').
1123. *ILA Interim Report on Res Judicata* 65.
1124. Bermann, (2015) 381 Rec. des cours [534].
1125. *See* Batiffol, (1973) 139 Rec. des cours 75 (Title: '*Le pluralisme des méthodes en droit international privé*'); Symeonides, (2016) 384 Rec. des cours 348 ('When pluralism is voluntary rather than forced or accidental it is called *eclecticism*, and eclecticism is the dominant feature of Private International Law.'); Weller, (2017) RabelsZ 770-779.

of the term 'recognition'.[1126] Methodologically, one could add that the opposing assessment of a foreign decision's effects under the *lex fori* facilitates not the method of *recognition*, but of *substitution* in that a foreign legal act merely triggers domestic norms.

372. To turn from the conceptional framework to the outcomes under national doctrines: against the background of territoriality as the '*the first great idea*'[1127] of the common law of private international law, the English *lex fori* determine the boundaries of res judicata and abuse of process.[1128] For foreign arbitral awards, scholarship assumes the same solution.[1129] Appellate jurisprudence remains to be rendered.[1130] Moreover, whereas there is no homogeneous jurisprudence on foreign judgments,[1131] US courts faced with arbitral awards rendered abroad or in another State regularly applied their *lex fori* on the issue of res judicata.[1132] This is also the proposal of the Draft Third Restatement.[1133] French doctrine on foreign judgments remains divided.[1134]

1126. *See infra* [378].

1127. Briggs, *Private International Law in English Courts* [1.10].

1128. *Carls Zeiss Stiftung v. Rayner & Keeler Ltd (No 2)*, [1967] 1 AC 853 (HL); *Dicey Morris and Collins* [14.032]; Barnett, *Res Judicata* [7.09]; Harder, (2013) 62 ICLQ 441.

1129. Briggs, *Private International Law in English Courts* [14.90]; *Ceshire North and Fawett* 667; *Dicey Morris and Collins* [16-108].

1130. *Good Challenger Navegante SA v. Metalexportimport SA (The Good Challenge)*, (2003) EWCA Civ 1668 is inapplicable, since it concerned issue estoppel in a case where a Romanian Court has refused to enforce an arbitral award rendered by '*London Arbitrators*'.

1131. *US v. Kashamu*, 656 F.3d 679, 683 (7th Cir. 2011) ('no consensus'); *King v. Cessna Aircraft Co.*, 2010 WL 5253526, 6 (SFFla 2010) ('Cases [...] are in considerable conflict.'); Hay Weintraub and Borchers, *Conflict of Laws* 347 ('relatively unexplored by the courts'). *See* Brand, (1991) 67 Notre Dame L. Rev. 253; Kulzer, (1966) 16 Buff L. Rev. 84; Silberman and Stein, *Civil Procedure* 841; Smit, (1962) 9 UCLA L. Rev. 44; von Mehren and Trautman, (1968) 81 Harv L. Rev. 1691.

1132. *Overseas Motors Inc. v. Import Motors Limited Inc*, 375 FSupp 499, 510 (E.D. Mich. 1974) (applying federal law without argument), aff'd 519 F.2d 119 (6th Cir. 1975); *Schattner v. Girard Inc*, 668 F.2d 1366, 1368 (DC Cir. 1981) (applying federal law without discussion); *Bhd of Mainz of Way Employees v. Burlington NRR Co*, 24 F.3d 937 (7th Cir. 1994); *Hydra-Pro Dutch Harbor Inc. v. Scanmar AS*, 2010 WL 3730183 (WDWash 2010); *Pirito v. Penn. Engineering World Holdings*, 833 FSupp2d 455, 473 (EDPa 2011); *Gordon v. Softech Intern Inc*, 828 FSupp2d 665, [26] (obiter) (S.D.N.Y. 2011); *Guard-Life Corp. v. S Parker Hardware Mfg Corp*, 406 NE2d 445, 452 (NY 1980). *Contra Lynne Carol Fashions Inc. v. Cranston Print Works Co*, 453 F.2d 117, 118 (3d Cir. 1972) (New York law on arbitral award by tribunal seated in New York).

1133. Restatement (Third) Int'l Comm Arbitration (TD 2), § 4-9 comment d ('An award is entitled to claim preclusive effect the award if [...] (ii) there is an identity of claims and parties, as required by the forum law [...]') and, § 4-10 comment d (correspondingly for issue preclusion.).

1134. Lex fori: Cass. (1e civ.), 11 January 1972, [1972] Bull. civ I No. 14; Cass. (1e civ.), 14 January 1975, [1975] Bull. civ I No. 12; Audit, [2007] 8-9 Procédures No. 16 [22] (law of origin restricted by lex fori); Bollée, *Sentences arbitrales* [347]; Huet, in *JCl droit international* Fasc 582-30 [30] (lex fori on preclusive effect), [14] (law of the substance on conclusive effects); Francescakis and Lucas, in *Encyclopédie Dalloz Droit international* [61]; Péroz, *La réception des jugements étrangers* [243]. *See Fouchard Gaillard and Goldman* [1419] ('[Art. 1476 CPC] is primarily directed at the French courts, [...] concerns the functioning of the French judicial system.'; Extension of effects: Cass. (1e civ.), 19 March 1974, [1974] Bull. civ I No. 90; Cass. (1e civ.), 21 May 1997, [1998] Rev. crit. DIP 306; Bartin, *Principes de droit international privé* 595; Mayer and Heuzé, *Droit international privé* [420].

For arbitral awards, scholarship summarized the issue as an 'uncertain' problem.[1135]

373. The concept foregoing the *lex fori* and referring to the law of the decision's origin applies under inter-jurisdictional systems, most importantly the Brussels Regime[1136] and the US Full Faith and Credit Clause.[1137] Where they are inapplicable, it is also the solution preferred under section 7(1) Uniform Foreign Money Judgments Act (adopted, e.g., in New York),[1138] the Third Restatement on Foreign Relations[1139] and German law.[1140] In Germany, appellate jurisprudence on foreign arbitral awards remains to be rendered[1141] and scholarship remains divided.[1142]

374. In any case, it needs to be mentioned, that German law restricts foreign res judicata rules if they are functionally unknown to German law ('controlled takeover of effects'). Whilst issue preclusion might be admitted because German law knows declarative actions, interventionist effects and preclusion of set-off claims, third-party

1135. Mayer, in *Liber Amicorum Reymond* 187 (*'l'incertitude règne'*); Seraglini, (2016) Rev. Arb. 51 [15-27] (*'désignation incertaine'* - sub-heading).
1136. ECJ, 4 February 1988, *Hoffmann*, C-145/86, EU:C:1988:61, [10] ('Recognition must have the result of conferring on judgments the authority and effectiveness accorded to them in the State in which they were given') with reference to *Jenard Report* 42-43; ECJ, 15 November 2012, *Gothaer Allgemeine Versicherung*, C-456/11, EU:C:2012:719; BGH, [2008] FamRZ 400; Kropholler and von Hein, *Europäisches Zivilprozessrecht* vor Art. 33 [11]; Teixeira de Sousa and Hausmann, in *Unalex* Art. 33 [20]. *Contra* Briggs and Rees, *Civil Jurisdiction and Judgments* [7.26] ('nothing to prevent an English court applying its own principles of issue estoppel to conclusions reached and expressed by a [EU] court').
1137. Cf. *Riley v. New York Trust Co*, 315 U.S. 343, 350 (1942); *Magnolia Petroleum Co. v. Hunt*, 320 U.S. 430, 439-440 per Stone CJ (1943); *General Foods Corp. v. Massachusetts Dept of Public Health*, 648 F.2d 784 (1st Cir. 1981); Restatement (Second) Conflict of Laws, § 94. *See* 28 USC §1738 ('[R]ecords and judicial proceedings or copies thereof, so authenticated., shall have the same full faith and credit in every court within the United States and its Territories and Possessions as they have by law or usage in the courts of such State, Territory or Possession from which they are taken.'); Art. IV(1) U.S. Constitution; Restatement (Second) Judgments, §18; Restatement (Second) Conflict of Laws, §§93-121.
1138. '[T]he foreign-country judgment is conclusive between the parties to the same extent as the judgment of a sister state entitled to full faith and credit in this state would be conclusive'. *See* Hay, in *Festschrift Geimer* 325 et seqq.
1139. Restatement (Third) Foreign Relations, § 481 comment c ('[A] foreign country judgment should ordinarily have no greater effect than it has in the country in which it was rendered. [...] However, no rule prevents a court in the United States from giving greater preclusive effect to a judgment in a foreign state that would be given in the courts of that state.').
1140. BGHZ 118, 312; OLG Köln, [2010] FamRZ 1590; Geimer, *Internationales Zivilprozessrecht* [2776]; Kegel and Schurig, *Internationales Privatrecht* 1061 (*'Eine ausländische Entscheidung anerkennen heißt: man beurteilt ihre Wirkungen nach dem Recht des ausländischen Gerichtsstaats.')*. Nagel and Gottwald, *Internationales Zivilprozessrecht* [12.112]; Schlosser, (2000) 284 Rec. des cours 41-42; von Hoffmann and Thorn, *Internationales Privatrecht* [3.154]. *Contra* Kronke, in *Soergel* Art. 38 [Anh 141]; Schack, *Internationales Zivilverfahrensrecht* [886].
1141. The issue is left open by OLG Karlsruhe, [2015] SchiedsVZ 145; LG Essen, 24 March 2015, 12 O 37/12, [2015] Beck-Online 07614, *see supra* [336].
1142. Judgment principles transferable: Adolphsen, in *Münchener Kommentar* Art. III NYC [2]; Geimer, *Internationales Zivilprozessrecht* [3879]; von Schlabrenndorff and Sessler in Böckstiegel et al. (eds), *Arbitration in Germany* s. 1055 [30]; Schlosser, in *Stein and Jonas* [123]; Schuetze, *Schiedsgericht und Schiedsverfahren* [258, 538]; Stürner, in *Liber Amicorum Schütze* 581. Lex fori: Note 1146.

effects are more delicate: class actions and non-mutual preclusion will be barred.[1143] Such restrictive framework is even more generally and more drastically established in Switzerland. The Federal Tribunal continuously holds that foreign arbitral awards exclusively constitute res judicata if the specific consequences are known to both, the arbitral seat *and* the subsequent (Swiss) *lex fori*.[1144]

375. With a view to the limited amount of appellate jurisprudence on *arbitral* res judicata outside of Switzerland, scholarship gains particular relevance. Amongst international scholars, there is almost a consensus against the seat's law and in favour of the *lex fori*. It builds upon the now predominant assumption that arbitration is not a judicial process inherently embedded into its seat's jurisdiction, but a dispute resolution of *private nature* serving *judicial functions*.[1145] The contractual origin of the arbitral process flaws the doctrine of extension of effects, as (even if a judicial act could create extra-judicial effects) there is no judicial origin an arbitral award's effect could be *extended* from. Some authors mainly invoke this thought against the lex arbitri.[1146] Others state that only the *lex fori* could transpose an award into the legal order.[1147]

376. In summary, the law applicable to arbitral res judicata has only scarcely been addressed in appellate jurisprudence. Yet, the general tendency is to apply the *lex fori*, either because the *lex fori* already govern foreign judgment principles (at common law), only the *lex fori* can transpose the arbitral award from its contractual foundation into the legal order (in international scholarship) or the arbitral seat's law is restricted by the *lex fori* (in Switzerland).

§6.02 PROPOSED PERSPECTIVE: BETWEEN CONFLICTUALIST METHODOLOGIES AND PRAGMATISM

377. For handling the law applicable to awards' third-party effects in particular, the examination has to proclaim its perspective on the law applicable to res judicata in general. Since neither Article III NYC (*see* [A], *infra*) nor a territorialist conception of international arbitration (*see* [B], *infra*) demands the application of the arbitral seat's law, the examination adapts the current majority opinion in favour of the *lex fori*. Yet,

1143. Cf. Krause, *Urteilswirkungen gegenüber Dritten* 244 et seqq.; Nagel and Gottwald, *Internationales Zivilprozessrecht* [12.124]; Peiffer, *Grenzüberschreitende Titelgeltung* [480].

1144. TF, 14 February 2011, 4A_508/2010, [E.3.3] ('The force of res judicata of a foreign arbitral award may [...] produce effect in Switzerland only insofar as provided by the procedural law of the State in which the arbitral award was rendered. Conversely, such force of res judicata cannot exceed the force of res judicata of an identical decision rendered by an arbitral tribunal with the seat in Switzerland.' – translation according to Berger and Kellerhals, *Arbitration in Switzerland* [1659]); TF, 25 May 2014, 4A_633/2014, [2015] ASA Bull. 642, [3.2.3].

1145. *See supra* [119-124].

1146. Brekoulakis, (2005) 16 Am. Rev. Int'l Arb; Hascher, in *Travaux du comité français DIP* 25-28; Mayer, in *Liber Amicorum Reymond* 189; Radicati di Brozolo, in *ASA Special Series* 8.

1147. Cf. Berman, (2015) 381 Rec. des cours [366]; Bosch, *Rechtskraft und Rechtshängigkeit im Schiedsverfahren* 191; Klement, *Rechtskraft des Schiedsspruchs* [II.2.a)bb)(3)]; Solomon, *Die Verbindlichkeit von Schiedssprüchen* 319-334. *Corresp* Bollée, *Sentences arbitrales* [347] (submission on foreign arbitral awards corresponds to submission on foreign judgments).

it submits that this opinion should not be the destination, but a *point of departure* for further contemplating on the applicable law (*see* [C], *infra*). In particular, practical feasibility sets strong incentives to respect that some aspects in intrinsic connection to res judicata are subject to foreign law (*see* [D], *infra*).

[A] Irrelevance of Article III NYC

378. Amongst the few authorities that seek to apply to seat's law to arbitral res judicata, some referred to Article III NYC: in obligating the signatories to 'recognize' arbitral awards, it were to demand such solution.[1148] Evidently, this argument corresponds to the rather uncontroversial reading of the Brussels/Lugano Regime where the obligation to 'recognize' other Member States' judgment is the basis for the extension doctrine.[1149] However, it is this examination's contention that the opposing opinion in favour of the *lex fori* is justified when it effectively overlooks Article III NYC. In this regard, the above-mentioned methodology for interpreting the NYC as a treaty apply.[1150]

379. The wording of Article III NYC differs from the Brussels Ibis Regulation in two respects. The latter dedicates an entire section on the recognition effect of judgments before addressing enforcement.[1151] By contrast, Article III NYC contains only one provision and even mentions national law. It obligates signatories to:

> recognize arbitral awards as binding and enforce them in accordance with the rules of procedure of their territory.

380. To continue on the drafting history, res judicata's consequences have not been addressed during the NYC's drafting process.[1152] This becomes even more compelling when focusing on the background of the NYC: it is a worldwide Convention. It has 159 Member States and consequently covers many diverging notions of res judicata. By contrast, even the Lugano Convention only obligates thirty-one Member States.[1153] A consensus of thirty-one Member States to apply each other's preclusion rules is significantly easier to infer then a consensus of 159 members.

381. Moreover, it has been submitted that the particular context of recognition is to establish the cross-jurisdictional efficacy of an arbitral award.[1154] Thereby, recognition overcomes an arbitral award's foreign nature. This does by no means necessitate any particular preclusion law once the arbitral award is treated as a domestic award.

1148. *See* Schlosser, in *Stein and Jonas* [123]; Adolphsen, in *Münchener Kommentar* Art. III NYC [2].
1149. *Supra* [1136].
1150. *See supra* [289].
1151. Articles 36-38 Brussels Ibis Regulation. The predecessor also contained a distinct section.
1152. *See supra* [291].
1153. As of 1 March 2019.
1154. *See supra* [146-149, 289-298].

382. Most importantly, the very rationales of the Brussels Ibis Regulation and the NYC differ substantially. The former is an instrument on judicial cooperation in that the signatories themselves profit from *mutual* recognition of judgments rendered by courts, i.e., public institutions of Member States. This inherently triggers the justification to apply each other's preclusion rules. By contrast, the NYC does not set out mutual obligations and is not concerned with public acts of other Member States. Therefore, the obligated Member States do not instantly profit. Instead, arbitration parties profit from the Member States' obligations. States benefit only indirectly in that arbitration reduces the costs for its judiciary and increases the efficiency of its markets. Therefore, under its wording, drafting history, context and rationale, Article III NYC does not impose any obligation to apply the seat's preclusion law.

[B] Irrelevance of Territorialist Perceptions of International Arbitration

383. Assuming that, in general, res judicata is not to be characterized as a matter of substantive law, the examination has to proclaim its general point of view on the bipolar discussion between the doctrines of extension (arbitral seat) and equalization (*lex fori*) of effects. From a purely practical point of view, the latter is predominant across jurisdictions.[1155] Yet, the examination will not only adapt the equalization doctrine for such opportunistic reason. It also proclaims that the extension doctrine begs conceptual support.

384. As a point of departure, it can*not* be based on Article III NYC.[1156] Therefore, the main argument in its favour remains that the extension doctrine is generally preferable in international civil procedure *and* that arbitral awards were to be equated to foreign judgments since they intrinsically originated from the arbitral seat. The latter point is nothing less than a severe manifestation of a territorialist notion of international arbitration.[1157] However, to apply the *lex arbitri* to res judicata because of a territorialist notion of international arbitration bears severe deficiencies. Foremost, the overwhelming opinion infers that arbitration's *hybrid* nature transcends it from the arbitral seat's legal order.[1158] Even if one generally favours a territorialist conception, the fact that the arbitral award is integrated into the arbitral seat's legal order does by no means require that the recognition State has to restrict its own legal order in preclusion terms. A simple example is English law comprising significant scholarly and jurisprudential statements in favour of a territorialist notion of international arbitration,[1159] yet still subjecting an arbitral award's res judicata to the *lex fori* for the sake of its own

1155. *See supra* [367-375].
1156. *See supra* [377-380].
1157. *See supra* [372-374].
1158. *See supra* [122].
1159. *See* Goode, (2001) 17 Arb. Int'l 19; Mann, in *Liber Amicorum Martin Domke* 157. *See Bank Mellat v. Helliniki Techniki*, (1984) 1 QB 291, 301 ('our jurisprudence does not recognise the concept of arbitral procedure floating in the transnational firmament, unconnected with any municipal system of law.'); *Coppée Lavalin & Voest Alpine v. Ken-Ren Chemicals*, (1994) 2 All ER 449, 458 ('Transnationalism [...] cannot be the law of England.'); Petrochilos, *Procedural*

territoriality.[1160] Moreover, the presumption that an arbitral award originates from a certain legal order does not explain why it is equivalent to a judgment. For instance, the German Federal Court of Justice (notably, the jurisdiction where most proponents of the extension theory originate from) constantly emphasizes that arbitration constitutes *'effective judicature'*.[1161] Finally, the examination reiterates a concern: it might be circular to state that res judicata is both, a *reason for* and a *consequence of* arbitration's juridicity.[1162] Therefore, even if foreign judgment principles allowed the extension doctrine and even if one follows a territorialist notion of international arbitration, the examination concurs with the majority that the arbitral seat exercises no claim to have its law applied.

385. In this regard, an alleged shift from conflictualist to law-and-economics arguments focusing on the reduction of transaction costs,[1163] legal certainty,[1164] the correction of market failures[1165] as well as the competition between legal orders[1166] would not change the outcome. The facilitation of such private and public interests is the very bipolar framework of contemporary private international law.[1167] Moreover, it is the very framework against which res judicata operates.[1168] Accordingly, '*once the economic models are translated into doctrines, they look similar [...] reach the same result, and they face the same problems.*'[1169] Therefore, law-and-economics arguments do not incline the law of the arbitral seat neither.

[C] The *Lex Fori* as the Starting Point: From Legal Theory to Practical Feasibility

386. Turning from the arbitral seat to the subsequent forum, it *does* exercise a certain claim to have its law applied. Particularly, res judicata's functions remain the heart of the assessment. Indeed, res judicata advances consistency, certainty and efficiency, all intrinsic interests of the subsequent forum.[1170] On top of that, res judicata restricts the

Law in International Arbitration [2.04] ('one should be looking at the most appropriate *court* competent to supervise and assist the arbitral process.').

1160. *See* Briggs, *Private International Law in English Courts* [14.90]; *Ceshire North and Fawett* 667; *Dicey Morris and Collins* [16-108].

1161. *See* BGHZ 51, 255, 258; BGHZ 54, 392, 395; BGHZ 65, 59, 61-62 ('*materielle Rechtsprechung*'); BGHZ 98, 32, 36; BGHZ 98, 70, 72. The Third Senate recently adopted the formulation *Rechtsprechung im weiteren Sinne* (jurisprudence in the broader sense), *see* BGHZ 159, 207, 212; BGHZ 162, 9, 16.

1162. *See supra* [124].

1163. *See* Basedow, in *An Economic Analysis of Private International Law* 61-63.

1164. *See* Guzmann, (2002) 90 Geo L. J. 894; O'Hara and Ribstein, (2000) 67 Univ Chic L. Rev. 1152.

1165. *See* Kirchner, in *An Economic Analysis of Private International Law* 50; Cooter and Ulen, *Law and Economics* 43-45; Schaefer and Ott, *Lehrbuch der oekonomischen Analyse* 109.

1166. *See* Romano, (1985) 1 J. L. Econ & Organiz 233-265; Kieninger, *Wettbewerb der Privatrechtsordnungen*; Muir Watt, (2004) 307 Rec. des cours 25 [20]; O'Hara and Ribstein, (2000) 67 Univ Chic L. Rev. 1190-1191.

1167. *See* Basedow, *The Law of Open Societies* [21].

1168. *See supra* [101-102].

1169. Michaels, (2008) 71 Law & Contemp Probs 103. *Corresp* Ruehl, *Statut und Effizienz* 252.

1170. *See supra* [101-102].

subsequent parties' right to be heard[1171] and therefore the subsequent forum's procedural guarantees. As a consequence, the *lex fori* should be the centre of gravity when assessing a foreign award's res judicata.

387. Nonetheless, the examination takes the position that practical, non-theoretical aspects could still motivate the *lex fori* to restrict its scope. In general, private international law – even when it refers to foreign laws – is always *'part of the forum'*.[1172] In the absence of treaty obligations, a forum *can* always apply its own law.[1173] Yet, in some case scenarios, certain aspects motivate to designate foreign law. Such motivated decisions remain a manifestation of territoriality.[1174] The only issue to be decided is: when *should* forum law refer to foreign law? There is no difference in the instant question. Due to territoriality and the non-demanding claim of the arbitral seat, the forum is by no means obligated to comply with foreign res judicata rules. Yet, the question remains whether there are further considerations motivating a forum to do so.

388. Before the examination focuses on practical considerations in this regard, it mentions a final doctrinal aspect even further inclining to depart from the theoretical discussion on foreign judgment principles' transferral: the contractual foundation of arbitration does not only conceptually bar the extension doctrine, it might even bar the procedural recognition method as such. Indeed, since arbitral awards are no acts of a public judiciary, but originate from private agreements, arbitral awards do not necessitate the application of the conflict of *jurisdictions*, but of the conflict of *laws*.[1175] Particularly, it would be generally permissible to treat the recognition of awards as a recognition of, e.g., contracts. Against this background, only practical reasons incline to apply judgment principles.[1176] In conclusion, the law applicable to arbitral res judicata should not be assessed under purely doctrinal considerations, but focus on practical aspects and thereby implement a core rationale of private international law: pragmatism.[1177]

1171. *See supra* [175].
1172. Bogdan, *Private International Law as Component of the Law of the Forum* 25-46. *See* Schinkels, *Normsatzstruktur des IPR* 79-114; Story, *Commentaries on the Conflict of Laws* [25].
1173. *Dicey Morris and Collins* [1.006]. *Contra* progressive opinions such as Jayme, *Rechtsvergleichung und kulturelle Identität* 12-13; Mills, *The Confluence of Public and Private International Law* 71-113; Weller, (2017) 81 RabelsZ 760-770.
1174. Cf. Mayer, (2007) 327 Rec. des cours [93] (*'lorsqu'il [le for] énonce ses règles de conflict de lois et celles relatives à la reconnaissance des jugements étrangers, il ne prétend pas délimiter la compétence législative ou juridictionelle des Etats étrangers, mais seulement indiquer quel usage ses organes devront faire de certains éléments des ordre juridique étrangers'*).
1175. *See* in general on the differentiation Bucher, *La dimension sociale du droit international prive* [4].
1176. Bollée, *Sentences arbitrales* [332].
1177. *See* Briggs, *Private International Law in English Courts* [1.16] ('No doubt there are those who will say that pragmatism is not a principle. Too bad: a principle it most certainly is. Pragmatism makes a powerful, if unstated., contribution to the force that drives [...] private international law.').

[D] Practical Criteria for Determining the Law Applicable to Res Judicata

389. The following passages establish general *practical* criteria that could motivate the *lex fori* to defer to foreign preclusion law. These criteria will be revisited for the specific categories of awards' third-party effects. The primary practical guideline for unsettled arbitration issues should be to promote the parties' opportunities for managing litigation risks through party autonomy. In this regard, some authors submitted that the parties' choice of the arbitral seat is regularly not undertaken against res judicata considerations.[1178] Yet, this could equally be invoked against the choice of the substantive law or the law of the arbitration agreement. Foremost, party autonomy would have no inclination in favour of the *lex fori* at all. Accordingly, from a party-autonomy perspective, the only question is whether any of these regimes might come at least close to res judicata considerations. In this regard, the arbitral seat might be the most relevant. Arbitral seats are regularly selected by the degree to which they protect and respect arbitration. This appears at least connected to the efficacy of arbitral awards.

390. In addition to party autonomy, the major aspect influencing the applicable law should be to guarantee the coherent cross-jurisdictional circulation of arbitral awards. In this regard, the considerations are many-fold. An instant aspect is a classic conflictualist dualism, namely between *international and internal harmony of solutions*. The latter favours the *lex fori* in that foreign and national decisions are treated alike. By contrast, the former rationale opposes the *lex fori* in that an arbitral award might comprise different preclusions in different fora. Implying that any jurisdiction applies the same preclusion standards. However, the international harmony of solutions is certainly difficult to realize in practice. Therefore, three other aspects might be of relevance that equally focus on the coherent assessment of arbitral awards.

391. First, one might raise *individual coherence*, i.e., the rationale that all aspects relating to an arbitral award's efficacy are treated under the same law. In this regard, even supporters of the lex arbitri concede that enforceability requirements belong to the *lex fori* exclusively.[1179] Given the functional interrelation between enforcement and res judicata, this opposes the lex arbitri. Another aspect of an award's efficacy is governed by the lex arbitri, namely the question whether an arbitral award is final under Article V(1)(e) NYC.[1180] A further matter of individual coherence is to assess res judicata's consequences under one consistent legal order.

392. An additional aspect is understood as *functional coherence*, namely a conflict regime's referral to the fact that practically, arbitration serves judicial functions for the parties as much as litigation. Correspondingly, it has been submitted in scholarship that '*it seems more important that national legal systems deploy res judicata in a*

1178. Bermann, (2015) 381 Rec. des cours [533]; Radicati di Brozolo, in *ASA Special Series* 6.
1179. *See*, e.g., *Schlosser* [901].
1180. *See supra* [295].

consistent and coherent manner as between prior judgments and prior awards than that they all agree on a common judicial standard'.[1181] Such statement is even more valuable in light of the fact that many jurisdictions allow for the recognition of confirmation or exequatur judgments.[1182] This further strengthens the *lex fori*.

393. The final aspect that is going to lie at the heart of the subsequent assessments is *procedural coherence*, i.e., that res judicata's scope is adjusted to procedural mechanisms. Already in bilateral case scenarios, civil-law jurisdictions compensate strict cause-of-action preclusion with additional procedural tools such as declaratory actions. In multilateral case scenario, the interaction of res judicata and intervention possibilities inclines to regard third-party effects as a *shift of the participatory burden*. In arbitration, such procedures are not necessarily provided by the lex arbitri. The parties might choose otherwise.[1183] Most importantly, the arbitral rules regularly determine procedural aspects. Therefore it is important, not to overlook these connections when applying res judicata.

Interim Conclusion

394. In summary, the international tendency is to subject an arbitral award's res judicata to the subsequent forum's law. With a view to the descriptive nature of this Chapter, such solution is acknowledged. With a view to this examination's conceptual ambition, it is even supported since there are no binding doctrinal justifications for applying the law of the arbitral seat. Instead, res judicata's function to advance forum interests and restrict procedural guarantees of the forum supports the *lex fori*. Nonetheless, it is submitted that not only doctrinal but also more tangible considerations such as party autonomy, procedural fairness and above all individual, procedural and functional coherence should guide the discussion on the applicable law. With regard to res judicata's third-party scope, they might restrict the *lex fori*. In the following passage, this is examined for the specific comparative categories.

§6.03 THE LAW APPLICABLE TO FOREIGN ARBITRAL AWARDS' THIRD-PARTY EFFECTS

395. The subsequent assessment facilitates the functional categories of arbitral awards' third-party effects, as they have been revealed in the comparative Chapters: *erga omnes* effects (*see* [A], *infra*), non-mutual preclusion (*see* [B], *infra*) and privy extensions by virtue of substitutions (*see* [C], *infra*) or complex substantive relationships (*see* [D], *infra*).

396. For any of the categories, the method in reaching the solutions will be identical. *In a first step*, the examination facilitates the above-mentioned rationales of party

1181. Bermann, (2015) 381 Rec. des cours [556].
1182. *See infra* [605].
1183. Cf. Mayer, in *Liber Amicorum Reymond* 187.

autonomy, procedural fairness and coherence in order to submit which law *should* govern the respective third-party effect. The core submission will be that conflictualist fairness considerations demand to adjust the law applicable to awards' third-party effects with the law applicable to arbitral interventions mechanisms and personal jurisdiction. Otherwise, private international law would risk exposing a third party to an arbitral award that had no opportunity to participate in the arbitration and therefore violates due process. *In a second step*, the examination will address how this solution can be reached *lege artis* in conformity with the established private-international-law methods of the examined jurisdictions. The latter step will generally pre-suppose the primacy of the *lex fori*, but also mention other approaches.

[A] *Erga Omnes* Effects: Cumulative Application of Arbitral Seat's Law and *Lex Fori*

[1] Legal Status

397. There is an inherent interest to award some decisions with full efficacy and relieve their preclusive effects from res judicata's same-parties requirements. Those decisions particularly concern legal status. For instance, it is universally acknowledged that the dissolution of a marriage or the liquidation of a company by a court operate erga omnes. Arbitration settings for issues of status particularly concern corporate (shareholders' resolutions) and sports (athlete suspensions) disputes.[1184] To provide an example on the decisive law applicable to arbitral awards' status adjudication: a German corporation sold its business to a US purchaser by virtue of an asset deal. The APA included a New York Jurisdiction clause. As it was necessary under the articles of association, the seller's shareholders' resolution agreed on the sale. Afterwards, one shareholder successfully initiated an arbitration in Germany against the shareholder resolution.[1185] As a consequence of the arbitral award, the seller allegedly lacked the capacity to agree on the asset deal. When sued for specific performance by the purchaser in New York, the seller invokes the arbitral award as conclusively establishing his incapacity as an obstacle to the performance claim (and potentially as origin of damages). When confronted with the binding force of the arbitral award with regard to the seller's capacity, the purchaser might invoke that the arbitral award should not constitute res judicata towards him.[1186]

398. In such scenarios, the outset should be that issues of status trigger extraordinary interests in consistency. These interests equally apply to cross-border case scenarios. Hence, it is preferable to guarantee the efficacy of legal status regardless of jurisdictional boundaries and avoid any 'limping legal status'. However, this does not instantly necessitate applying the law of the decision's origin. Instead, the *lex fori* can equally guarantee the cross-jurisdictional efficacy of legal status provided that the *lex fori* will

1184. *See supra* [181-184, 234-236].
1185. *See supra* [235].
1186. For additional aspects of such award's *factual effect see infra* Chapter 7.

be applied in a manner that adheres to the foreign adjudication. For instance, even though German law might award an arbitral award with a *Gestaltungswirkung* (constitutive effect) that is unknown to common law, English courts can *transpose* an award on a German corporation's shareholders' resolutions as *in-rem* effect.

399. In some case scenarios, the *lex fori* might not only meet the origin's legal-status effects but even *exceed* them. For the sake of consistency, this is to be avoided. Instead, the *lex fori* should only apply *when* the invoked status effect exists in its origin. This can be well reconciled with foreign judgment principles. Countries following the extension doctrine also apply it in status matter.[1187] Jurisdictions preferring the *lex fori* such as England state that the foreign judgment must '*operate* in rem *within the jurisdiction of the rendering State*'.[1188]

400. Another aspect that needs to be taken into account is that *erga omnes* effects might endanger a third party's right to be heard. Therefore, the law has to assess whether a third party meets a certain threshold of proximity to the legal status in order to exercise (perhaps mandatory) intervention possibilities.[1189] Against this comparative background, it is submitted that procedural fairness and procedural coherence demand: the applicable law should not disrupt the intrinsic connection of status effects and intervention necessities. Hence, it should be decisive which law determines intervention necessities. Effectively, it was the law of the arbitral award's origin that governed the intervention standing of third parties. Yet, this law exercised *its* due-process notion. Potentially, the subsequent forum might have distinct due-process notions. Given that due process is inherent to each jurisdiction, it appears well justified to apply the *lex fori* on that matter. For these reasons, practical concerns of party autonomy, procedural fairness and coherence do not pre-empt the *lex fori* from governing a potential *erga omnes* effect of an arbitral award. Therefore the examination proposes the following three-tiered assessments of status effects established by foreign arbitral awards. (i) The *lex fori* has to preliminarily assess whether the said *erga omnes* effect exists at the origin. (ii) If it exists, it has to examine whether it contains a rule which might be triggered by the foreign decisions (*substitution*) or can translate the foreign effect into an effect under the *lex fori* (*transposition*).[1190] (iii) Finally, the *lex fori* review whether they would have permitted the third party's intervention possibilities in the foreign status arbitration.

401. To illustrate the resulting mechanism by virtue the case example on the arbitral award holding the German corporate seller incapable of concluding the asset purchase agreement with the buyer and the latter claiming specific performance in New York: (i) the invoked effect generally exists at the arbitral seat and (ii) the constitutive effect unknown to common law can be transposed into a res judicata effect (in rem). Hence, the decisive aspect is (iii) whether New York law requires a shareholder arbitration to

1187. Geimer, *Internationales Zivilprozessrecht* [2813]; Nagel and Gottwald, *Internationales Zivilprozessrecht* [12.124].
1188. Barnett, *Res Judicata* [3.39] referring to *Castrique v. Imrie*, (1879) LR 4 HL 414, 429-430.
1189. *See supra* [93-99, 119-120].
1190. *See* on substitution and transposition Lewald, (1939) 69 Rec. des cours 5 et seqq.

provide the company's contract partners with intervention possibilities. If this is not the case, the seller can rely on the arbitral award. As a final remark, foreign arbitral awards' *erga omnes* effect does not only raise questions of the applicable law but also of lis pendens. For instance, during the said litigations in New York and Hamburg, the alleged arbitral award might be reviewed at the courts of the arbitral seat. Given that no status effect should exceed the effects at the arbitral seat, it is highly preferably to defer to such review. Moreover, once the award is annulled, the need for consistent legal status reinforces other arguments for applying Article V(1)(e) NYC and deny recognition. [1191]

[2] *Opposabilité*

402. Moreover, it is examined how to handle the *opposabilité* in cross-border case scenario.[1192] For instance, when transposing the 2007 *Prodim* decision to an international setting where only the arbitral or the subsequent forum is in France, will the doctrine still expose the third party to the tribunal's adjudication on the collusion between the franchisor and the third party? In this regard, it has already been mentioned, that there are statements characterizing the *opposabilité* as an institute of substantive law.[1193] Yet, the consideration of procedural coherence is overwhelming: *opposabilité* is always compensated by the *tierce opposition*. Thereby, due process and party autonomy are guaranteed in that the relevant award can still be brought before court. By applying the *opposabilité* to awards across jurisdictional borders only because the award's substance is governed by French law, this coexistence risks to be utterly disrupted. Instead, the law governing such alleged effect has to guarantee intervention necessities. Hence, the *opposabilité* should be characterized as a procedural effect.

403. Therefore, when an arbitral award from France is invoked abroad, the previous approach to *erga omnes* effect should apply:[1194] in some case scenarios, the *opposabilité* can be transposed into *in-rem* or constitutive effects. In others, the subsequent *lex fori* would not acknowledge any broad third-party effect. Then, *opposabilité* will be inapplicable. If it is known to a (potentially francophone) jurisdiction, then it should adhere to the result of the *tierce opposition* at the arbitral seat. In the situation that the subsequent forum is France, French law should either refrain from applying the *opposabilité* when a comparable efficacy abroad does not exist or also allow the *tierce opposition* for foreign arbitral awards, which are recognized in France. In 2017, the Paris District Court had chosen the latter option and held an exequatur decision recognizing a foreign award susceptible to the *tierce opposition*.[1195] As a consequence, in the adjusted *Prodim* example, the fact that the subsequent forum is Germany,

1191. *See infra* [604].
1192. *See supra* [185-186, 237-239].
1193. *See supra* [368-416].
1194. *See supra* [381-385, 394-398].
1195. TGI Paris, 25 April 2017, [2017] Rev. Arb. 1064.

England, Switzerland or the USA renders the *opposabilité* inapplicable. Vice versa, if the arbitral award between the franchisor and the franchisee has been rendered outside of France, the French courts should preferably allow the *opposabilité* and the *tierce opposition* conjointly as it was confirmed in the Paris judgment.

[B] Non-mutual Preclusion: *Lex Fori*

404. The law applicable to non-mutual preclusion on the basis of foreign arbitral awards appears less complex than *erga omnes* effects. It is submitted that no practical considerations oppose the treatment at common law pursuant to which abuse of process – as a rule preventing the waste of judicial resources – applies when English courts are the forum of the subsequent dispute:[1196] individual and functional coherence indicate the application of classic proceduralist solutions from private international law. Moreover, procedural coherence and procedural fairness are not at stake, since common law evaluates the previous participation possibilities.[1197] There is no reason to suppose that common law would not examine this requirement if the preceding arbitration had been conducted abroad. This illustrates that careful rules on a legal issue's substance sometimes prevent conflictualist discussions and thereby the interwoven nature of the two fields. Vice versa, no practical concerns incline civil-law jurisdictions to apply non-mutual preclusion and thereby forego their equality restrictions. As a consequence, in the above-mentioned *LCIA case example* on the energy joint venture,[1198] the objection of abuse of process raised by the former managing director is governed by the *lex fori*, i.e., German law that does not acknowledge non-mutual preclusion.

[C] Privy Extensions in Substitutions: *Lex Fori*

405. Arbitral awards' third-party effects towards successors and explicitly represented are as universally acknowledged as the necessity of *erga omnes* effects.[1199] Comparative differences for the treatment of arbitral awards concern the effect of arbitral awards towards those successors that do not join the arbitration agreement and towards bona fide successors. Article V(1)(a) NYC does not apply as an overriding requirement.[1200] In addition, arbitration laws might deviate on the admission of voluntary representation in arbitration, although this will then already be a problem of the arbitral proceedings. More importantly with regard to res judicata, the effects of arbitral award in the insolvency context and in class arbitrations might deviate. In such situations, the law applicable to res judicata's extension will be of the utmost interest.

1196. *See supra* [193-195, 240-244].
1197. *See supra* [123-125].
1198. *See supra* [336].
1199. *See supra* [199-201, 247-253].
1200. *See supra* [308-309].

406. For successions, procedural coherence is irrelevant, since the successor only succeeds after the award is rendered and could not intervene in the arbitration. Instead, individual coherence and procedural fairness indicate the *lex fori*. Potentially, the law of the succession's substance might differ, particularly with regard to bona fide acquisitions. Yet, bona fide aspects will regularly be *incidental questions* (preliminary question). If, for instance, an assignee brings a claim under an English contract before German courts and the debtor invokes an arbitral award rendered against the assignor, the German *lex fori* generally extend res judicata, yet § 325 ZPO refers to bona fide acquisitions, which will then be assessed at common law.[1201] Moreover, the validity of the succession itself will equally be an incidental question. If, for instance, an award rendered in England is invoked against an assignee before Swiss courts, res judicata could in general be extended (both at common law and under Swiss law). If the assignee invokes the assignment's invalidity, it depends on the law governing the assignment.

407. The perspective shifts when disclosed representations need to be assessed. When a class-arbitration award is invoked abroad, the applicable law will effectively be the *lex fori*, since class-actions are inherently connected with due-process notions and trigger public policy in those countries whose procedural law does not contain them.[1202] Accordingly, a class-arbitration award from the USA will not constitute res judicata towards class members before European courts. Moreover, when an arbitral award's effect in the context of insolvency is relevant, the interest of individual and functional coherence is overriding, thereby mandating the application of the *lex fori*. Hence, when for instance an arbitral award from London rendered against the administered is invoked against the insolvency administrator or in the actual dissolution proceedings, it will be the *lex fori* handling the applicability of res judicata.

[D] Privy Extensions in Complex Substantive Relationships

408. The most delicate case scenario concerns awards' third-party effects towards third parties that are contractually connected to a party. Practically, the matter is of paramount importance, since parties are regularly connected to, e.g., guarantors, sureties, insurers or parent companies. Legally, the applicable law is pivotal, because some jurisdictions open the door for discretionary assessments (privies in interest, effective control, *répresentation*) that adhere to all aspects of an individual scenario, whereas others strictly adhere to res judicata's same-parties requirement (particularly

1201. '(1) A judgment that has entered into force shall take effect for and against the parties to the dispute and the persons who have become successors in title of the parties after the matter has become pending, or who have obtained possession of the disputed object such that one of the parties or its successor in title has become constructive possessor. (2) The stipulations of civil law benefiting parties deriving rights from a person who is not a beneficiary in this regard shall apply mutatis mutandis'.

1202. *See* Krause, *Urteilswirkungen gegenüber Dritten im US-amerikanischen Zivilprozessrecht* 244 et seqq.; Nagel and Gottwald, *Internationales Zivilprozessrecht* [12.124].

Germanic jurisdiction). To provide a case example: if the above-mentioned construction example[1203] involved an arbitration seated in Geneva and a subsequent litigation in New York against the parent company, it will be decisive whether the strict Swiss standard or the lenient standard under New York, respectively federal law applies. In this regard, the examination submits that the availability and operation of discretionary privy assessments are generally governed by the *lex fori* (*see* [1], *infra*). However, the overwhelming consideration of *procedural coherence* might necessitate considering foreign law applicable to, e.g., the arbitration agreement or the intervention possibilities as *fact* when exercising the discretionary assessments (*see* [2], *infra*). Finally, the examination adheres to a further comparative divide in that jurisdictions sometimes allow res judicata's extension under substantive law directly.[1204] This raises a preliminary matter almost vanished from res judicata discussions: characterization (*see* [3], *infra*).

[1] The Lex Fori as the Starting Point for Discretionary Privy Assessments

409. The comparative assessment has revealed that particularly English (privies in interest), French (*représentation*) and US laws (effective control) contain extensions of res judicata that are the result of the alleged communality of procedural interests of the third party and an actual party. They are founded upon a rule that contains discretionary elements in that it evaluates all aspects of the individual scenario on a case-by-case assessment.[1205] The above-established practical criteria of party autonomy and coherence for determining the law applicable to res judicata[1206] are manifold when it comes to the law applicable to such assessments.

410. To commence with party autonomy: the general inclination in favour of the arbitral seat does *not* comprise any demanding rationale with regard to the effects towards third parties. Particularly, the third party does not necessarily have consented to the arbitral seat. Hence, the issue turns from a promotion of party autonomy into an issue of procedural fairness in that the third party has an interest in not being exposed to unforeseeable preclusion standards. In this regard, the *lex causae* might be more foreseeable for the third party. Notably though, the very argument that the *lex causae* is a necessary protection of a third-party's interests when exposed to arbitration has already been *un*successfully advanced for the law applicable to the arbitration *agreement*.[1207] Instead, it might be preferable to state that procedural fairness and a protection of the third party's interest necessitate the *lex fori*. The very reason is that the third party is subject to the subsequent court's adjudicatory jurisdiction. In

1203. *See supra* [2, 181].
1204. *See supra* [202-214, 254-274].
1205. *See supra* [204-206].
1206. *See supra* [386-391].
1207. *See* BGH, [2014] SchiedsVZ 151, [21].

particular, jurisdictional rules are the very implementation of procedural fairness.[1208] Therefore, party autonomy and procedural fairness do not oppose the application of the *lex fori* to arbitral awards' third-party effects, but demand it.

411. Continuing on party autonomy, this examination submits that it is a persuasive argument *against* cumulatively applying the *lex fori and* the arbitral seat's law as preferred in Swiss jurisprudence. In contrast to status decisions, the examination submits that the forum has no inherent interest against exceeding the arbitral seat's preclusion standards. Instead, such cumulative application would necessitate that arbitral res judicata might fall short of judgment principles. However, by agreeing on arbitration, the parties exercised their very intention for a more efficient and more effective (world-wide recognition under the NYC) dispute resolution.

412. As to individual coherence, it inclines the *lex fori*, albeit non-demanding. Whilst the *lex fori* decide about enforcement matters, in third-party case scenarios, preclusion and enforcement standards might differ as it is illustrated by § 129 HGB exposing partnership members to res judicata, yet preventing the direct enforcement against them.[1209] Moreover, individual coherence triggers the adjustment of res judicata's third-party scope (*against whom?*) with its objective scope (*which part?*). In indemnity matters, one might invoke that it were infeasible to distinguish one from the other. Otherwise, a third party might be potentially bound by the arbitral award, yet the reasonings would not even be relevant. However, at a closer look, there is no significant risk of *depeçages* since such situation would in fact not be infeasible. Instead, the admissibility of issue preclusion concerns different interests at stake than the admissibility of the third-party scope. Whereas the latter is an assessment of due process, the former is less immanently connected with due process. Instead, jurisdictions admitting only narrow cause of action estoppel and barring issue preclusion, such as Germanic and francophone jurisdictions, seek to protect the foreseeability of the adjudication and prevent unnecessary arguments in favour of a streamlined procedure.[1210] Therefore, it would appear admissible to differentiate amongst res judicata's objective and subjective boundaries.

413. What is of the utmost importance is *procedural coherence*. Decisions' third-party effects are highly intertwined with intervention possibilities. Without res judicata, the actual parties have to seek a third-party notice in order to extend the decision's preclusive effect. With res judicata, the third party can seek to intervene in order to influence the decision it will be exposed to. Hence, res judicata only shifts the participatory burden.[1211] Therefore the law governing the arbitration agreement and the law governing intervention procedures demand additional adherence to. However, those aspects might all be governed by distinct laws. The arbitration agreement and the arbitral procedure might, but need not be governed by the law of the arbitral seat. Moreover, intervention possibilities are regularly subject to the arbitral rules, which

1208. *See* Pfeiffer, *Internationale Zuständigkeit und prozessuale Gerechtigkeit* 199-287.
1209. *See supra* [272].
1210. *See supra* [113].
1211. *See supra* [211-212].

might sometimes *not* allow for third-party intervention, e.g., the ICC Rules. Accordingly, taking the law of the arbitral seat as the starting point would be equally dissatisfying.

414. In conclusion, since *no* law has the capacity to adhere to all aspects of the necessary interest assessment, since the *lex fori* are the centre of gravity for res judicata assessments and since third-party effects inherently trigger due-process notions of the forum, the examination generally concurs that the *lex fori* should govern res judicata's extension. Therefore, when a party invokes res judicata towards a third party because the latter's interests were represented, the legal standard of the extension (privy in interest, effective control, *représentation*) depends on the forum where the extension is invoked. If such standard does not exist, for instance before Swiss or German courts, than a discretionary privy assessment should be *un*available.

[2] The Implementation of Procedural Coherence: Foreign Law as Fact

415. When *applying* the *lex fori*'s discretionary privy standard, it is additionally submitted that foreign laws on, e.g., the arbitration agreement, the arbitral procedure and the substantive relationship should not be deemed irrelevant. They influence the parties' subjective expectations and objective participation possibilities. The proposed solution is to consider them under the *lex fori*'s test *as facts*. This means, that in the comprehensive assessment of the third party's position as, e.g., a privy in interest, it should not be assumed *that* it had a certain position as, e.g., a parent company or a co-obligor. Instead, it should be assessed whether this position as parent company or co-obligor (i) would or would not result in an exposure to res judicata under the law governing the substantive relationship, (ii) would or would not result in an exposure to the arbitration agreement and (iii) would or would not enable the third party to intervene under the law of the arbitral procedure. To illustrate this proposition: a German seller and an English purchaser agreed on arbitration in Switzerland. The purchaser's debt was guaranteed by an English bank agreeing on German guarantee law. After a successful arbitration, the seller sued the English bank before the Commercial Court and invoked the Swiss arbitral award as precluding the bank from objecting to the goods' conformity. (i) Primarily, the court should examine Article V(1)(a) NYC and inquire whether the Bank agreed on arbitration. (ii) If this is the case, or this examination's proposal to apply Article V(1)(a) NYC is rejected, the court will assess whether the English bank was a privy in interest to the English purchaser. Thereby, it should consider whether Swiss arbitration law would have allowed the bank to intervene and that the German law governing the guarantee does generally not provide for res judicata extensions to the guarantor's detriment. Hence, there is a high threshold for the privy assessment to be rebutted.

416. A further implementation of this proposal is the limited force of precedence. Indeed, when, e.g., a guarantor has previously been considered a privy in interest in a domestic case, the decision should not constitute stare decisis in another case scenario involving foreign elements.

417. As a doctrinal foundation for this submission, it might be feasible to refer to the emerging theory that foreign laws can be considered as *data*. The notion to consider foreign laws as facts when applying the *lex fori* originated in US scholarship.[1212] It has received particular consideration in German doctrine emphasizing that foreign law can be considered at both levels, the *determination* as well as the *application* of the law.[1213] Moreover, French scholarship has emergently been susceptible to the interpretation of certain foreign laws as facts.[1214] In addition, although not named as a particular doctrine, common law has treated foreign and penal laws as facts, since their application as laws are prohibited. For instance, this allowed implementing foreign embargo laws for the invalidity of contracts.[1215] In this regard, one might invoke that such concepts are generally discussed for matters of *substantive* law. By contrast, the instant proposal is that also *procedural* law has to adhere to foreign elements. Nonetheless, there are two justifications.

418. Primarily, the differentiation between procedural and substantive law is highly delicate and often purely fictitious when with regard to arbitral awards.[1216]

419. More importantly, the rationale underlying the facilitation of foreign laws as facts in substantive law applies correspondingly in the instant case. Applying foreign laws as facts softens the harsh referral of complex situations to the *lex fori*. In this regard, the application compensates for the broad nature of the referral and the unavailability of a more differentiated regime of the conflict of laws. This is also the case in the instant situation. Third-party effects of arbitral awards justify the *lex fori*'s general standard on due-process protections, yet are intertwined with the arbitration agreement, the substantive relationship and the arbitral procedure. Therefore, the discretionary assessment under, e.g., English, French and US laws should respect when such elements are governed by foreign laws.

[3] A Substantive Characterization of Accessory Third-Party Effects?

420. The final aspect of arbitral awards' third-party effects in private international law brings the examination back to a preliminary matter handled at this Chapter's outset: generally, res judicata is *not* characterized as an institute of substantive law and

1212. Currie, (1958) 58 Colu L. Rev. 964; Ehrenzweig, (1966) 16 Buff L. Rev. 55.
1213. *See* Jayme, in *Liber Amicorum Ehrenzweig* 35 et seqq.; Jayme, (2014) 375 Rec. des cours 27; Mansel, *Personalstatut Staatsangehörigkeit und Effektivität* 49-50; Maultzsch, in *BeckOGK* Art. 17 Rom II [4]; Pfeiffer, in *Liber Amicorum Schurig* 234 ('*kollisionsrechtliches Element der Verweisung [...] innewohn[end]*'); Weller, *Die Grenze der Vertragstreue von (Krisen-)Staaten* 47-50; Weller, (2014) IPRax 231; Weller, (2017) 81 RabelsZ 775-780. *Contra* Schurig, *Kollisionsnorm und Sachrecht* 313; von Hein, in *Münchener Kommentar* Einleitung IPR [271].
1214. *See* Fohrer-Dedeutwaerder, *La prise en considération des normes étrangères* [103-104, 116-145]; Kinsch, *Le fait du prince étranger* 347-364.
1215. *See* Briggs, *Private International Law in English Courts* [3.195] with case references.
1216. *See supra* [374, 385].

therefore, the law governing the dispute's substance regularly considered indecisive.[1217] Yet, the arguments in favour of res judicata's substantive characterization might be reinforced for third-party effects. Particularly, some jurisdictions understand particular third-party effects *not* as institutes of procedural law, but of substantive law, e.g., the effects towards sureties, insurers or leasees.[1218] For instance, in the case example mentioned *supra* [415], the purchaser might argue that the English bank should be bound by the arbitral award, because of the guarantee contract *itself*. Given the *lex fori*'s primacy for characterization in general,[1219] jurisdictions which understand the relevant third-party effect as a substantive institute in their national law might be inclined to characterize such third-party effects as substantive matters. This necessitates to revisit the preliminary topic of characterization. Since, in general, the conflictualist line to be drawn between substantive and procedural law begs comprehensive guidelines[1220] and amounts to a case-by-case assessment instead,[1221] the examination will largely focus on the specific scenario.

421. In scholarship, express statements as to the characterization of arbitral awards' third-party effects are scarce. For foreign judgments, only one publication considers the decisive criteria and proposes to distinguish whether the third-party effects '*originate from the judicial authority itself*' or were a mere '*reaction of substantive law to the decision*'. A third-party effect originated from the judicial authority when the judge either decided in knowledge about the effects on the third party or would not have decided differently if he had known about a third-party effect.[1222] This is affirmed for most third-party effects.[1223] Yet, when res judicata is extended within complex substantive relationships, the author prefers the law governing the substance. As examples, he mentions solidary obligations (characterized as procedural, but then referred to the *lex causae*)[1224] and sureties (characterized as substantive).[1225] It is submitted that such proposal comprises two deficiencies. *First*, the judge's knowledge

1217. *See supra* [368].

1218. *See supra* [214].

1219. Est'd by Bartin, (1927) Clunet 225 et seqq.; Kahn, (1891) 30 Jhering's Jb 1 et seqq. *See* now BGHZ 29, 137; *Dicey Morris and Collins* [2.011-14]; Bogdan, *Private International Law as a Component of the Law of the Forum* 183 with further references.

1220. *See* Basedow, in *Materielles Recht und Prozessrecht* 140 ('*Diese Thesen [zur Qualifikation] begegnen dem Einwand, dass für die Abgrenzung von materiellem Recht und Prozessrecht nicht einmal ein Kriterium genannt wird.*').

1221. Garnett, *Substance and Procedure in Private International Law* [2.04].

1222. Peiffer, *Grenzüberschreitende Titelgeltung* [443-446] ('*Es lässt sich damit die These aufstellen, dass mit ausländischen Urteilen all diejenigen Effekte importiert werden sollen, die ihre eignetlich Geltungswurzelung in der richterlichen Entscheidung haben. […] Eine Drittwirkung hat – um konkreter zu werden – einerseits dann ihre Geltungswurtel in der richterlichen Tätigkeit, wenn der Richter wissentlich mit Wirkung gegenüber dem Dritten entschieden hat [oder] wenn der Richter auch bei Kenntnis von Person und Position des Drittbetroffenen nicht anders entschieden hätte […]. Lässt sich demgegenüber in einem Entscheidungseffekt kein bzw. nur ein sehr geringer Rückbezug zum richterlichen Tätigwerden feststellen, handelt es sich um eine Regelung, die die materielle Rechtslage an den Richterspruch anpasst, diesem gewissermaßen nur Rechnung trägt*').

1223. *Ibid.*, [447-452].

1224. *Ibid.*, [97-118; 463-466; 516-18].

1225. *Ibid.*, [453].

about the third party is purely fictitious. For instance, when only one out of two co-obligees is sued, there is no necessity that the judge knows about the other co-obligee, particularly for parallel contracts. *Second*, the knowledge can be influenced by the parties. For instance, when a debtor is sued, the creditor might likely present a contract which is also signed by a surety. To develop this example one step further: a creditor might raise that the debtor could likely claim indemnity from a sub-contractor and thereby make the sub-contractor's liability known to the court.

422. Therefore, *if* one seeks to establish criteria under which decisions' third-party effects can be characterized as substantive effects, it might be preferable to propose another distinction. This distinction could facilitate the *functional source* of the third-party effect invoked, as it is in general permitted when characterizing legal institutes.[1226] If, for instance, a surety objects to the main creditor's claim on the ground that the main debt were invalid and the creditor invokes that the main debtor had already been held liable by an arbitral tribunal, it would be decisive whether the surety's alleged exposure should result out of its surety position *as such* or out of a broad discretionary assessment (privies in interest, effective control, *répresentation*). The former third-party effect would result out of the mere existence of a surety, leasing or insurance contract (*contract determined*) and the latter of the subsequent forum's assessment of due process and common interests in the individual case (*judge determined*). Therefore, the latter effect would be characterized as a matter of procedural law, i.e., the *lex fori*, the former third-party effect could be characterized as a matter of substantive law. The connection of this substantive exposure should than be made to the law governing the *third party's* relation, e.g., the law of surety. By contrast, it should not be the *lex causae* of the main debt against which the surety objects. Although, but for an arbitral award, these objections would be assessed under the law governing the main debt (incidental question), the surety's interests demand otherwise.

423. In any case, the decisive question remains *if* such distinction between substantive and procedural third-party effects is doctrinally possible and practically preferable. One might invoke that the third-party effect would be a default solution but for a (restrictive) preclusion agreement, thus justifiable as a contractual effect. However, this would not justify the primacy of the *lex causae* over the otherwise applicable lex res judicata. In particular, any preclusion agreement could also be governed by the law governing res judicata. Instead, a differentiated characterization of substantive and procedural third-party effects might establish a plurality of options for a party that seeks to rely on preclusion rules. For instance, even though the guarantee in the Swiss example was considered insufficient under English privy doctrines, the purchaser can still seek preclusion under the guarantee's law. It appears *not* preferable that private international law allows parallel means for achieving the very same functional objective: a conclusive effect. Therefore, the examination submits that arbitral awards' third-party effects should *not* be characterized as substantive law even though national

1226. *See* Briggs, *Private International Law in English Courts* [3.55-3.59]; Bogdan, (2010) 348 Rec. des cours 134-156; von Hein, in *Münchener Kommentar BGB* Einl IPR [112].

laws on insurances, leasing or guarantee might understand the effect accordingly. Instead, if a decision is facilitated to be preclusive or conclusive for legal or factual arguments, it should be regarded as a matter of res judicata, therefore of the *lex fori*, potentially under adjustments to foreign laws.[1227]

Interim Conclusion

424. As an overall conclusion, this examination submits that the *lex fori* should be the outset for res judicata matters, since res judicata restrict due process. Yet, considerations of party autonomy, procedural fairness and coherence might demand adjustments of the *lex fori*. This concerns two case scenarios in particular. For *erga omnes* effects, the *lex fori* should preliminarily assess whether the said effect exists at the origin, translate that effect into the *lex fori* and examine whether the arbitral seat's due-process guarantees conform to the forum's notions. For extensions in complex substantive relationships, discretionary privy assessments should adhere to the foreign elements of the underlying transactions, the arbitral procedure and the arbitration agreement. Accordingly, the extension of arbitral res judicata towards third party turns into a paradigm for the contemporary private-international-law methods. That is, the topic originates from the recognition method, the *lex fori* are generally designated but then potentially adhered to by means of synthetic methods. As a final remark, it is this examination's contention that such differentiation does not trigger the immanent criticism to the very subject of private international law: over-complicating matters. Instead, the differentiation is the necessary in order to guarantee consistency, practical feasibility and fairness for multilateral transactions.

§6.04 ANCILLARY MATTERS OF PARTICULAR RELEVANCE TO THIRD-PARTY CASE SCENARIOS

[A] Preclusion Agreements

425. The primary conflictualist topic in intrinsic connection to res judicata is the handling of preclusion agreements. Particularly, the examination has adopted the position that preclusion agreements between the – potentially multiple – parties to an arbitration agreement have to be considered before courts, since they are protected by the NYC. Yet, neither the formation nor the interpretation of such agreements can be governed by the silent NYC.[1228] Hence, it will be necessary to refer to a national law. In this regard, the conceptual protection by Article II(1) NYC as well as the effective connection with the arbitration agreement incline to subject such aspects to the law of the arbitration agreement. In the unorthodox case that the preclusion agreement is multilateral, yet the arbitration agreements are numerous and bilateral, the closest

1227. *See* on the constellation that the arbitral award itself *triggers* a requirement under substantive law *infra*, Chapter 7.
1228. *See supra* [358-362].

connection of the preclusion agreement should be established by referring to the legal order that comprehensively governs decisive aspects towards all parties: the arbitration agreement, subsidiarily the arbitral seat, subsidiarily the substantive law, subsidiarily the domicile/habitual residence, subsidiarily another closest connection. In any case, it has already been mentioned that multilateral preclusion agreements will regularly be accompanied by multilateral arbitration agreements, which prevents the dispute to be brought before court.[1229]

426. What is more likely to come before courts is that a bilateral preclusion agreement has been formed with regard to a dispute between different parties. For instance, a sub-contract might contain a clause that all arbitral awards rendered between the principal and the contractor will be preclusive and conclusive towards the sub-contractor in the indemnity litigation between the contractor and the sub-contractor. Both the interpretation and particularly the efficacy of this agreement demand an assessment of the applicable law, since the NYC is inapplicable.[1230] Regularly, an overriding explicit choice of the law applicable to such preclusion agreements will be missing. The resulting conflictualist assessment bears a certain proximity to those case scenarios where the sheer existence of a certain relationship, for instance, a guarantee is interpreted as a ground for res judicata extensions. Even if such extensions can be perceived as default preclusion extensions, they should be governed by the law of res judicata.[1231] This provides a certain inclination to also apply this law to *explicit* preclusion agreements. Otherwise the applicable conflict-of-laws rule would need to differentiate between implied and explicit preclusion agreements, which appears over-complex. Moreover, the preclusion agreement has the effect to restrict the right to be heard before the subsequent courts. Therefore, in the case example, the efficacy of the preclusion agreement depends on the *lex fori*.

[B] Damages for Non-compliance with an Arbitral Award

427. When addressing an arbitral award's efficacy, there are means beyond enforcement and res judicata. There is also the opportunity to enforce an arbitral award substantively. Since '*[e]very submission to arbitration contains an implied promise by each party to abide by the award of the arbitrator and to perform his award*',[1232] it is possible to claim damages from an award debtor for non-compliance.[1233] Certainly, this would require a further procedure causing additional expenses. Therefore, it is an often impractical means of implementing the obligations under an arbitral award. Yet, there might be situations motivating such claims. For instance, the law applicable to damages claims towards third parties for non-compliance with arbitral awards has been observed as a relevant option where the third party would be exposed to the

1229. *See supra* [352-357].
1230. *See supra* [358-362].
1231. *See supra* [415-419].
1232. *Mustill and Boyd* 360.
1233. Cf. *Redfern and Hunter* [11.14].

opposabilité. Eventual damages claims for the intervention with the obligations under the arbitral awards were characterized as non-contractual and therefore assessed under Article 4(1) Rome II Regulation, i.e., under the law where the damages has occurred.[1234]

428. At the outset, it might be feasible to distinguish the case scenarios. Where one of the arbitral parties eventually sues the other for non-compliance, the damages claim will be governed by the law of the arbitration agreement. In European civil-law countries, the solution will occur outside the Rome I Regulation (Article 1(2) lit. e) and have difficulties with the Rome II Regulation's inapplicability on *voluntary* commitments. In third-party case scenarios it appears therefore necessary to differentiate whether the third party is bound by the arbitration agreement or is not. In the former case, damages claims should equally be governed by the law of the arbitration agreement. Only if the third party is *not* bound to arbitrate, the Rome II Regulation will be applicable. This might be the case, if a third party to an arbitration colludes with the respondent in preventing the performance of the obligations formulated under the arbitral award. If the Rome II Regulation were applicable, it appears preferable to localize the damage at the arbitral seat since it is more foreseeable than the law of the arbitration agreement to the tortfeasor (the former third party) and as much selected by the victim (the former claimant) as the arbitration agreement. The thus applicable tort law of the arbitral seat has to assess whether the third party was even bound by the arbitral award's res judicata. This is an incidental (preliminary) question assessed under the *lex fori*.

§6.05 CONCLUDING THESES

(1) The law applicable to arbitral awards' third-party effects has not received extensive scholarly attention yet. As to the general discussion on res judicata in civil procedure, foreign judgment principles are divided between the law of the decision's origin (*extension of effects*) and the subsequent *lex fori* (*equalisation of effects*). In arbitration, the former solution is translated in that the origin is the arbitral seat.[1235]

(2) The majority of explicit scholarly and jurisprudential statements on the law applicable to res judicata prefer the *lex fori*. This examination notes and promotes the rejection of the extension doctrine, since res judicata restricts due process. Yet, the *lex fori* should be taken as the outset for further inquiring whether considerations of practical feasibility, foremost party autonomy, procedural fairness as well as individual, functional and procedural coherence incline to consider foreign law for particular issues.[1236]

1234. Bollée, (2015) Rev. Arb. 695, [20, 24].
1235. *See supra* [367-375].
1236. *See supra* [377-391].

(3) For effects of arbitrations on legal status, these considerations necessitate to adjust the *lex fori* in that (i) the status modification has to exist at the arbitral seat, (ii) should be translated as closely as possible into the *lex fori* (substitution, subsidiarily transposition), yet (iii) reviewed under the *lex fori*'s due-process guarantee.[1237]

(4) For the *opposabilité*, the interaction with the *tierce opposition* is of paramount importance. If the *lex fori* acknowledge neither concept, the *opposabilité* will be unavailable. If the *lex fori* do acknowledge both concepts, e.g., in France, foreign arbitral awards should only trigger both, *opposabilité* and the potential for third-party appeals.[1238]

(5) Non-mutual preclusions such as the doctrine of *Henderson v. Henderson* or *collateral estoppel* are to be assessed under the *lex fori*. In this regard, the forum's comprehensive assessment of participation possibilities can adhere to foreign elements.[1239]

(6) Res judicata by virtue of successions as well as disclosed representations is to be assessed under the *lex fori*. The potential validity of the successions or the admissibility of the representation in the proceedings will be incidental questions.[1240]

(7) Arbitral awards' third-party effects within complex substantive relationships should equally be assessed under the *lex fori*. In particular, it appears unpreferable to distinguish between procedural and substantive third-party effects.[1241]

(8) If the *lex fori* allow for a comprehensive case-by-case assessment such as the English privy-in-interest doctrine, effective control in the USA or *réprésentation* in France, the assessment should respect whether the arbitration agreement, the arbitral procedure or the substantive relationships was governed by a foreign (preclusion friendly/unfriendly) law and therefore created subjective expectations and objectives intervention criteria.[1242]

(9) Preclusion agreements concluded by the parties to an arbitration agreement are governed by the law applicable to that agreement. If the parties to the preclusion agreement are not identical to the parties concluding the arbitration agreement, e.g., in sub-contracts, the *lex fori* govern the interpretation and efficacy of the preclusion agreement.[1243]

(10) The law governing damages for intervention with an arbitral award will be the law of the arbitration agreement. If the third party is no party to the latter, it is the law of the arbitral seat. The third party's exposure to res judicata will then be an incidental question.[1244]

1237. *See supra* [394-398].
1238. *See supra* [399-400].
1239. *See supra* [401].
1240. *See supra* [402-404].
1241. *See supra* [415-419].
1242. *See supra* [406-412].
1243. *See supra* [420-421].
1244. *See supra* [422-423].

CHAPTER 7

The Unshaped Factual Effect of Arbitral Awards

429. The preceding Chapters were based on and examined the exceptions to the transnationally acknowledged rule that res judicata operates *inter partes*. In functional terms, they have handled the degree to which an arbitral award's preclusive and conclusive effects extend to third parties in follow-up litigation. Now, it is examined whether arbitral awards can also cause factual effects in follow-up litigation. This means that they do *not preclude an argument or claim as already adjudicated* when it arises in follow-up proceedings. Instead, the mere *existence* of the arbitral award will be a fact to be taken into account.

430. To provide an example: if the Swiss producer A licensed the French distributor B with the right to distribute certain products in the EU exclusively and B sells those products to a US customer C, an arbitral award requested by A against B, ordering the latter not to sell the products outside of the EU might be a fact relevant to follow-up litigation initiated by C against A for specific performance. The arbitral award rendered in favour of B will not preclude C from any arguments or claims. Instead, the mere *existence* of the award might constitute an obstacle for C's claim for specific performance. Yet, such referral to an arbitral award still begs the inherent question whether it impermissibly extends the effects of arbitration to third parties. After all, the principles of due process and party autonomy necessitate the privity of arbitration.

431. The Chapter will initially provide exemplifying gateways under national and uniform laws that might allow applying arbitral awards as facts, e.g., objective impossibility or hardship (*see* §7.01, *infra*). Turning to national arbitration laws, arbitral awards' factual effects remain largely unexplored, an exception being the French *opposabilité* (*see* §7.02, *infra*). This unexplored status necessitates that this Chapter will largely exercise a discovering mandate.

432. As a first step in this regard, it draws inferences from related topics. In particular, substantive law might also apply judgments, foreign norms or contracts as facts (*see*

§7.03, *infra*). Thereupon, the examination focuses on the cross-border dimension of arbitral awards' factual effects. In particular, it mentions the applicability and operation of recognition boundaries under Article V NYC including the proposal from *Chapter 5* pursuant to which no third-party effect should exceed the personal effects of the underlying arbitration agreement (*see* §7.04, *infra*). If recognition is no obstacle or the arbitral award is invoked in a purely domestic setting, national laws will decide about factual effects' admissibility. In this regard, the Chapter can merely propose selected guidelines. It will submit that the admissibility of awards' factual effects should be handled by balancing the interests against third-party effects on the one hand, i.e., party autonomy and due process, against concerns of irreconcilability on the other (*see* §7.05, *infra*).

§7.01 GATEWAYS FOR DECISIONS' FACTUAL EFFECTS IN COMPARATIVE AND UNIFORM LAW

433. The first step in assessing the factual effect of arbitral awards is to enumerate selected provisions from national laws and uniform instruments, which allow such application. In this regard, the thesis' constraints do not allow a comprehensive assessment of all relevant provisions across the examined jurisdictions. Therefore, the following paragraphs merely illustrate some normative examples in order to specify this discussion.

434. As to the first category, it has already been mentioned that the initial case example on the distribution might prevent third parties' claims for specific performance. Certainly, the availability of specific performance constitutes a major conceptual divide between common and civil law.[1245] Yet, with a view to, on the one hand, equity's susceptibility for specific performance once real property or unique goods are involved and, on the other, parties' preference for damages if such goods are not at stake, the functional divide is diminished.[1246] *If*, in general, the purchaser can exercise a claim for specific performance, the fact that the seller is restrained from the delivery by virtue of a binding adjudication might bar specific performance for reasons of *objective impossibility*. Such ground is generally acknowledged in, e.g., England,[1247] France,[1248] Germany[1249] and *'all major domestic systems'*.[1250] From a functional perspective, the objective impossibility's effect on the primary obligation is closely related to (i) its additional effect on subsidiary damages (force majeure) and (ii) the

1245. *See* Weller, *Die Vertragstreue* 399-404.

1246. *See* Zweigert and Kötz, *An Introduction to Comparative Law* 470-486.

1247. England: s. 7 1979 Sale of Goods Act ('Where there is an agreement to sell specific goods and subsequently the goods, without any fault on the part of the seller or buyer, perish before the risk passes to the buyer, the agreement is avoided.').

1248. *See* France: Art. 1148 Cc (*'Il n'y a lieu à aucuns dommages et intérêts lorsque, par suite d'une force majeure ou d'un cas fortuit, le débiteur a été empêché de donner ou de faire ce à quoi il était obligé, ou a fait ce qui lui était interdit.'*).

1249. Gemany: s. 275(1) BGB (*'Der Anspruch auf Leistung ist ausgeschlossen, soweit diese für den Schuldner oder für jedermann unmöglich ist.'*).

1250. Schelhass in Vogenauer (ed.), *PICC – Commentary* Art. 7.2.2[18].

effect of subjective hardship.[1251] For instance, in uniform law, the wording[1252] and context[1253] of Article 79(1) CISG[1254] cover only the destiny of damages claims after potential impediments. This renders the exception of impossibility to specific performance (Article 46 CISG) heavily debated.[1255] The UNIDROIT PICC – which are particularly relevant to arbitral tribunals, both as chosen law of contract and as interpretative tools of national laws[1256] – differentiate between the effect of impossibility on specific performance (Article 7.2.2(a)[1257]), the effect on damages and force majeure (Article 7.1.7(1)[1258]) and subjective hardship (Article 6.2.3(1)[1259]). All such grounds might be raised when one party to a sales contract was ordered by an arbitral tribunal *not* to deliver the goods.

435. Another topic where the arbitral award might be taken into account as a fact is the *quantification of damages* in chains of contracts. To modify the above-mentioned distribution scenario as an example: when the French distributor B was ordered to pay damages for deficient products to a German customer D by an arbitral tribunal, B might seek indemnity from the producer A. If the producer's breach of contract has been affirmed, national contract laws will regularly provide for damages in that it is possible to claim the loss suffered.[1260] Under the CISG for instance, damages are calculated in that they are '*a sum equal to the loss […] suffered […] as a consequence of the breach*'.[1261] Another uniform instrument, the PICC explicitly refers the calculation method to the principle of '*full compensation*'.[1262] Against this background, the

1251. Schwenzer, in *Schlechtriem and Schwenzer* Art. 79[4].
1252. 'A party is not liable for a failure to perform any of his obligations if he proves that the failure was due to an impediment beyond his control […]'.
1253. *See* in particular Art. 79(5) CISG ('Nothing in this article prevents either party from exercising any right other than to claim damages under this Convention.').
1254. 'A party is not liable for a failure to perform any of his obligations if he proves that the failure was due to an impediment beyond his control and that he could not reasonably be expected to have taken the impediment into account at the time of the conclusion of the contract or to have avoided or overcome it, or its consequences'.
1255. *See* Atamer in Kröll et al. (eds), *CISG – Commentary* Art. 79[16-21, 29-34].
1256. *See* Scherer in Vogenauer (ed.), *Commentary on the PICC* 110 et seqq.
1257. 'Where a party who owes an obligation other than one to pay money does not perform, the other party may require performance, unless (a) performance is impossible in law or in fact […]'.
1258. 'Non-performance by a party is excused if that party proves that the non-performance was due to an impediment beyond its control and that it could not reasonably be expected to have taken the impediment into account at the time of the conclusion of the contract or to have avoided or overcome it or its consequences'.
1259. 'In case of hardship the disadvantaged party is entitled to request renegotiations. The request shall be made without undue delay and shall indicate the grounds on which it is based'.
1260. *See* France: Art. 1231-2 Cc ('*Les dommages et intérêts dus au créancier sont, en général, de la perte qu'il a faite* […]'. Germany: § 249(1) BGB ('A person who is liable in damages must restore the position that would exist if the circumstance obliging him to pay damages had not occurred.'). USA: § 2-715(2) UCC ('Consequential damages resulting from the seller's breach include (a) any loss resulting from general or particular requirements and needs […].').
1261. Article 74. *See* on the calculation in general *CISG Advisory Council Opinion* No. 6.
1262. Article 7.4.2 (1) PICC ('The aggrieved party is entitled to full compensation for harm sustained as a result of the non-performance. Such harm includes both any loss which it suffered and any gain of which it was deprived […].').

question arises whether the mere existence of an arbitral award can establish recoverable loss of B in the case example. Alternatively, one might prefer that the subsequent court will review the damages quantification and only allow reimbursement against A of those claims that B *should have been* exposed to against D.

436. A further case scenario where the arbitral award might be a fact to third parties' detriment shifts the focus to property interests and the *discretion for interim measures*. To further modify the case example: the Swiss producer A sold goods to the French distributor B. The parties agreed on arbitration in Brussels. Moreover, A has retained the property in the goods until he received payment. B was uncertain whether the agreement with A allowed the re-sale to non-European countries (where A is not protected by the Lugano Convention) until A received payment. Yet, B needed liquidity and thus sold the good to the Chinese customer E under a contract containing a CIETAC arbitration clause. Eventually, B was reluctant to deliver the goods. Upon request by E, the CIETAC tribunal ordered B to deliver the goods to E. Even if the delivery would not affect A's property right, it would certainly affect its factual interests, since it will be financially burdensome for A to realize the property right against E in China. Hence, when A is of the opinion that it will not receive payment from B and B is still in possession of the goods, A might decide to directly sue B for the return and conjointly apply for an injunction before the arbitral tribunal. The tribunal seated in Belgium – a Model Law jurisdiction[1263] – might duly consider Article 17A(1)(a) UNCITRAL Model Law. The provision allows a discretionary assessment by balancing the potential harm to either party.[1264] Therefore, B might invoke the arbitral award in favour of E as a ground impeding A's injunctive and thus property interest. As a final remark in this regard, if the goods were, e.g., railway rolling stock and the Cape Town Convention applied, chargees such as A would increasingly benefit from legal certainty. Indeed, Article 29(3) lit. a prevents any bona fide acquisition upon registration. Article 14(1), (4) guarantee A's remedies. Article 43(3) guarantees the option for interim court relief regardless of arbitration clauses. Before courts such relief might also be extendable towards E.[1265]

437. To distinguish the three mentioned scenarios on impossibility, damages calculations and interim measures from another case scenario where the examination already mentioned provisions of substantive law with regard to the extended effects of decisions towards third parties. Some jurisdictions might facilitate the relevant law on surety, guarantees or leasing contracts in order to expose third parties to an arbitral

---

1263. *See* Art. 1691 Belgian Judicial Code ('Without prejudice to the powers accorded to the courts and tribunals by virtue of article 1683, and unless otherwise agreed by the parties, the arbitral tribunal may order any interim or conservatory measures *it deems necessary*.') (emphasis added).

1264. 'The party requesting an interim measure [...] shall satisfy the arbitral tribunal that: (a) Harm not adequately reparable by an award of damages is likely to result if the measure is not ordered., and *such harm substantially outweighs the harm that is likely to result to the party against whom the measure is directed* if the measure is granted.' (emphasis added)

1265. *See* FRCP 65(d)(2) ('The order binds only the following who receive actual notice of it by personal service or otherwise: (C) other persons who are in active concert or participation'). *See Eli Lilly v. Gottstein*, 617 F.3d 186 (2d Cir. 2010).

award in case scenarios of connected/accessory liability and indemnity matters.[1266] However, the difference is that this substantive law is regularly not *stipulating further consequence for the pure existence of obligations imposed or claims conferred by an arbitral award*. Instead, the arbitral award is facilitated in order to preclude the, e.g., surety or guarantor from objecting to the main debt's validity or enforceability. Therefore, such third-party effects functionally correspond to res judicata and exceed mere factual effects. Only if the applicable law or the contract states that the guarantor becomes liable once the creditor obtains a judgment against the debtor, the decision's effect towards the guarantor is a factual effect. Under such circumstances the effect of the arbitral award will not fall under the preceding but this *Chapter*'s scope.

Interim Conclusion

438. In conclusion, arbitral awards provide ample potential to be considered as facts to the detriment of third parties when (i) applying impossibility, force majeure or hardship provisions, (ii) quantifying damages in indemnity proceedings and (iii) undertaking discretionary assessments for interim relief. These situations significantly differ from the classic extensions of res judicata under substantive law towards, e.g., sureties or leasees in that they do not preclude arguments but instead implement the mere existence of an arbitral award.

§7.02 STATUS QUO: LIMITED EXPLORATION OF FACTUAL EFFECTS IN NATIONAL DOCTRINE

439. Amongst arbitration jurisdictions, the exclusive law that can swiftly handle factual effects of arbitral awards is French law. It contains the standalone rule that the existence of arbitral awards can be invoked by and towards everybody. In compensation, third parties can apply for a *tierce opposition* (third-party appeal) before courts. Whilst this is the doctrine's outset, further developments of the doctrine of *opposabilité* might be functionally more related to matters of issue preclusions such as in *Prodim*.[1267] By contrast, other arbitration laws do not address such factual effect. Instead, they focus on arbitral res judicata exclusively operating *inter partes*. Hence, they have to address the problem where to draw the line between impermissible effects *ultra partes* and potentially admissible factual effects.

440. In this regard, initial authorities can be found at common law. *The Sargasso* is a leading case where an arbitral award served as a fact with regard to the quantification of damages flowing from a breach.[1268] Moreover, in an obiter dictum, an arbitral award was equated to a contract and therefore as a fact that a third party could rely on when

1266. *See supra* [259-278].
1267. *See supra* [237-239].
1268. *Stargas SpA v. Petredec (The Sargasso)*, [1994] 1 Lloyd's Rep. 412 (Comm).

seeking to establish a breach committed by one of the arbitrating parties.[1269] Moreover, *Redfern and Hunter* comprise a narrow view on res judicata and mentions *indirect* effects of arbitral awards in addition.[1270] Most elaborately – although a judgment cannot constitute any means of evidence for criminal convictions[1271] – Longmore LJ considered an arbitral award as:

> evidence [...] though [...] not necessarily conclusive evidence. It may be a 'fact in the world'.[1272]

441. Yet, there is no precedence with regard to drawing the line between issue estoppel or abuse of process on the one hand and a merely factual (or indirect) effect on the other. Accordingly, drawing such line will be a task of further jurisprudence or scholarship.

§7.03 INFERENCES FROM OTHER NORMS' FACTUAL EFFECTS

442. With a view to the limited exploration of awards' factual effects under national laws, the examination proposes an *inductive* approach in that it attempts to draw inferences from related topics. Particularly, awards are by no means the only norms that bear the potential to be applied as facts. Instead, other judicial, legislative and private norms might equally establish facts to the detriment of third parties. Yet again, a comprehensive assessment of this topic will well exceed the instant examination on arbitration. Thus, the following paragraphs merely illustrate the connection of the topics and focus on inferences for arbitral awards.

1269. *George Moundreas & Co. SA v. Navimpex Centrala Navale*, [1985] 2 Lloyd's 515, 520 per Saville J. (Comm) ('It seems to me that where the rights or obligations of the parties to a contract are determined by the contractual machinery of arbitration under that contract there is something to be said for the view that the result that the arbitrators reach can (in the absence of special circumstances) be treated in effect as part of the contract and thus established by third parties in the same way as any contract can be proved.'). The relevant claim was by Moundreas for breach by Navimpex of a commission agreement relating to a separate shipbuilding contract between Navimpex as builders and Solway Maritime Ltd as buyers. Mounreas invoked that the shipbuilding contract had been affirmed in an arbitration between Navimpex and Solway. But Moundreas also presented evidence and proved the breach independently.

1270. *Redfern and Hunter* [9.184] ('Nonetheless, an award may often have a significant indirect effect on persons who were not parties to the arbitration. For example, a third party may be affected by an award where one person is jointly liable with another who is a party to the arbitration. The award would not be res judicata in any subsequent claim against that third party, but it should be of persuasive significance in that a tribunal is likely to consider the findings of the earlier award to inform its own findings. Conversely, it is possible that an award (even if unsatisfied) against one of the persons who was jointly liable would have the effect of discharging the third party's liability. Finally, where an award orders performance (for example in relation to the delivery of property by one of the parties), it is doubtful whether it is effective if the property concerned is temporarily in the hands of a third party under a licence.').

1271. Cf. s. 11 1968 Civil Evidence Act; *Hollington v. F Hewthorn & Co. Ltd*, [1943] All ER 35.

1272. *Sun Life Assurance Company of Canada et al. v. The Lincoln National Life Insurance Company*, [2004] EWCA Civ 1660, [84].

[A] Judgments as Facts: Issues of Status as the Explored Point of Departure

443. To commence with the most proximate topic, courts seized with the previously mentioned case examples might equally refer to a judgment. Yet, the factual effects of judgments and the line to be drawn to impermissible res judicata *ultra partes* also remain to be generally discussed. But for French law's *opposabilité*,[1273] procedural laws do not contain a comprehensive doctrine and particularly no comprehensive third-party appeal, as it would be required by due process. In Germanic jurisdictions, it is acknowledged that judgments can trigger substantive provisions' requirements *if they mention a judgment as a requirement*, e.g., the suspension of limitation periods.[1274] By contrast, factual effects under substantive provisions containing general, broad requirements such as hardship, loss or urgency are not addressed.

444. The one situation where jurisdictions *do* address the capacity of judgments to create legal situations that can be invoked towards and by everybody is where the judgment modifies a legal status. Common law perceives judgments that concern personal or property status as operating in rem. Germanic jurisdictions award a *Gestaltungswirkung* (constitutive effect) to judgments that modify a person's legal status. Correspondingly, both jurisdictions award some third parties with participation possibilities whilst other third parties are perceived as too remote to rely on their right to be heard.[1275] These case scenarios are closely related to the exemplified case scenarios for factual effects. Just as much as the *existence* of a judgment or an arbitral award might bar specific performance, the existence of a judgment in rem might be facilitated in order to consider one of the parties to a follow-up litigation as, e.g., liquidated. The intrinsic connection is illustrated by French law, which does *not* differentiate between factual effects and status effects. *Opposabilité* covers both. Notably the very term *opposabilité* is facilitated in francophone Swiss jurisprudence to describe the constitutive effects of judgments in issues of status.[1276] Against this background, it should preferably be discussed (i) whether and to which degree status and factual effects differ from a functional point of view and (ii) whether the doctrine on status effects allows any inferences for factual effects.

445. Primarily, *in-rem* (at common law) or constitutive effects (in Germanic jurisdictions) operate erga omnes because of a particular nature of the prior litigation. From a common-law point of view, it does not merely concern a claim against a certain debtor in personam. In Germanic terms, the cause of action would not be a request for performance (*Leistungsklage*). By contrast, the said factual effects under impossibility, damages or interim-measure provisions might result out of prior decisions in personam or stipulating performances. Hence, the said decisions lack a certain justification for

1273. *See supra* [185].
1274. *See supra* [106].
1275. *See supra* [181-192].
1276. *See* ATF 140 II 278, [4.2.1] (*'le principe de la relativité subjective de la chose jugée [...] est sous réserve des jugements constitutifs (Gestaltungsurteile), lesquels sont opposables aux tiers.'*).

erga omnes effects in that the prior judge has only adjudicated against specific defendants. This inclines the following inference: if status adjudications are subjected to due process, then the factual effects of decisions in personam should be subjected to third party's due process *a fortiori*. Hence, it should be examined whether due process demands adequate intervention possibilities for third parties against factual effects, as it is the case under French law. If they are not guaranteed, e.g., since a third-party appeal known from French law is unavailable, factual effects might be barred.

446. Moreover, it should be noted that status effects comprise a double nature. Sometimes it is *not only the existence* of a certain decision that is invoked. Instead, status adjudications might also *preclude* counter arguments. In particular, Germanic jurisdictions acknowledge this double-nature of status decisions in that the constitutive effect only concerns the status as such and res judicata additionally precludes re-litigation of the *right to have the status modified*. If, for instance, a judgment in rem clarifies the ownership in certain property, it will not only be the existence of the judgment that is relevant in follow-up litigation. Rather, the judgment might preclude a third party from objecting to the ownership on grounds of, e.g., bona fide acquisitions. Hence, when precluding arguments, status effects might sometimes affect a third party more directly in its own rights. This now opposes the transfer of the above-mentioned due-process constraints. In conclusion, it should be noted that judgments' status effects are largely, though not always, related to factual effects. Since the law on status effects focused on due process and the corresponding intervention possibilities, arbitral awards' factual effects might be equally restricted in cases where a third party should have the standing to influence a decision.

[B] Foreign Judgments as Facts: Exposed to Recognition Review?

447. When a foreign judgment establishes a factual effect, the application of foreign judgment principles has received attention in civil-law scholarship. In Germany, for instance, § 328(1) No. 1 ZPO applies *mutatis mutandis*, if a *foreign* judgment suspends the statute of limitation. Thus, the most important recognition boundary applies in that a foreign judgment can only suspend limitation periods when the foreign court had jurisdiction.[1277] Methodologically, however, it should be noted that the relevant limitation norm *itself* mentions a judgment as a requirement (*substitution*).[1278] Therefore, it is uncertain, whether the jurisdictional review would also apply if a foreign judgment, e.g., establishes force majeure under § 313(1) BGB.[1279]

448. The jurisdiction with a more general and more intense discussion on the factual effects of foreign judgments is yet again France. Already discovered by Étienne

1277. *See* Geimer, *Internationales Zivilprozessrecht* [2827-2832]; Gottwald, in *Münchener Kommentar* § 328 [180-182].

1278. *See* Basedow, in *Materielles Recht und Prozessrecht* 148-149 (with regard to s. 136 BGB).

1279. 'If circumstances which became the basis of a contract have significantly changed since the contract was entered into and if the parties would not have entered into the contract or would have entered into it with different contents if they had foreseen this change [...]'.

Bartin,[1280] it is now widely acknowledged that foreign judgments can establish factual effects either where the French norm refers to a judgment or is a blanket norm such as force majeure.[1281] In contrast to recognition, such scenarios were not to extend the normative force of the judgment.[1282] With regard to the potential review of such factual effects, the *Cour de cassation* reiterated in 2005 that the '*factual effect of a foreign judgment in France is independent from its verification in recognition or exequatur procedures*'.[1283] In this dispute the appellant to an order freezing a ship situated in the port of Marseille relied upon a judgment from Gibraltar stipulating his ownership (*vente judicaire*). In order to apply *opposabilité*,[1284] the court regarded the stipulation of ownership by the Gibraltar court as a factual effect and undertook no jurisdictional review of the judgment. As a comparative remark, the effect of the Gibraltar judgment would have been understood as res judicata at common law (in rem)[1285] and as a *Gestaltungswirkung* (constitutive effect) in Germany. There, a recognition review would apply.[1286] Thus, jurisdictions differ on the application of foreign judgment principles to judgments' factual effects. For arbitral awards, this allows the inference that the application of recognition reviews demands elaboration.

[C] Foreign Law as Facts: Exposed to Public-Policy Review

449. Turning from individual to abstract norms, substantive law could also provide the potential to apply foreign *laws* as facts. In particular, restrictive foreign laws on export trade can trigger objective impossibility, force majeure or hardship.[1287] For instance, in a very recent case before the Higher Regional Court Frankfurt, an airline from Kuwait refused to transport a passenger from Israel. Even though German law governed the contract (Article 5(2) Rome I Regulation), the airline relied on Kuwait law threatening criminal sanctions for the transport of Israeli passengers. The court facilitated such norm as a ground for objective impossibility.[1288] Yet, as to the review of such laws, it is increasingly submitted that *if* foreign laws can be facilitated as facts,

1280. Bartin, (1924) Clunet 857.
1281. Fohrer-Dedeurwaerder, *La prise en considération des normes étrangères* [300]; Mayer and Heuzé, *Droit international prive* [472-473].
1282. Mayer and Heuzé, *Droit international privé* [475].
1283. Cass. (com), *Sté Coopérative du Lamanage des Parts de Marseille et du Golfe des Fos v. Sté Cruise Invest One*, 4 October 2005, (2006) 96 Rev. crit. DIP 405 ('*Un jugement étranger produit en France des effets en tant que fait juridique, indépendamment d'une vérification de sa régularité internationale par une procédure de reconnaissance ou d'exequatur*') (translation of the author).
1284. *See* the crit. Note Muir-Watt. (2006) 96 Rev. crit. DIP 410 ('*la qualification du jugement de Gibraltar de simple fair juridique permet à la Cour de cassation de conclure que le changement de propriétaire [...] était opposable au créancier saisissant.*').
1285. *See Castrique v. Imrie*, (1879) LR 4 HL 414, 429.
1286. *See* on constitutive effects Peiffer, *Grenzüberschreitende Titelgeltung* 265-270.
1287. *See supra* [414].
1288. OLG Frankfurt, 25 September 2018, 16 U 209/17; LG Frankfurt, 26 November 2017, 2-24 O 37/17, [41].

they need to conform to the forum's public policy.[1289] In this regard, the court did not regard an embargo against certain *citizens* as a public-policy violation.[1290] Yet, it was not examined whether the embargo might be an effective discrimination of passengers of Jewish religion, which would then trigger public policy as an obstacle to such discrimination.

450. Returning to the inferences for decisions' factual effects: the public-policy review of foreign laws' factual effects induces to review foreign *decisions* accordingly. Foremost, the consideration of foreign *laws* and foreign *decisions* as facts are intrinsically connected.[1291] Moreover, one might state that foreign laws as acts of the foreign legislative, i.e., the supreme sovereign authority of a country, have even more imperative force to be applied as facts than foreign decisions. Potentially, one might object that foreign decisions as individual norms have a more specific claim to be applied as facts. Yet, at least for arbitral awards, this appears insufficient, since awards have a private origin. If even *public* laws are reviewed on public-policy grounds, *private* arbitral awards should be reviewed *a fortiori*.

[D] Contracts as Facts: The Privity of Contract as a Threshold Matter

451. The general rule that effects only extend *inter partes* is by no means privy to arbitration or procedural law. Instead, the law of contracts also stipulates that third parties cannot be exposed to detrimental effects without their consent (privity of contracts, *effet relatif du contrat, Relativität der Schuldverhältnisse*).[1292] Accordingly, the restrictive efficacy of individual norms might be described as a cornerstone of private law in its entirety. In this regard, the operation of the privity of contracts comprises particular relevance for potential transfers to arbitral awards, since the latter are built upon contractual foundation.[1293]

452. The privity of contract does certainly not pre-empt *all* effects of contracts on third parties. Instead, many indirect third-party effects are unavoidable in the contemporary society.[1294] To provide an example:[1295] an employer concludes an economically detrimental deal. The detriments might prevent the employer from paying the salaries to its employees or even require the employer to terminate some employment contracts. Accordingly, the contract between the employer and the business partner did result in a significant detriment towards third parties. Yet, the employer has not colluded with the business partner but simply exercised bad business judgment. Consequently, it might not be too bold to state that no law would hold the deal invalid

1289. Fohrer-Dedeurwaerder, *La prise en considération des normes étrangères* [695]; Weller, (2014) IPRax 232.
1290. LG Frankfurt, 26 November 2017, 2-24 O 37/17, [48].
1291. *See* Fohrer-Dedeurwaerder, *La prise en considération des normes étrangères* [2].
1292. England: *Winterbottom v. Wright*, (1842) 10 M&W 109. France: Art. 1199 Cc. Germany: BVerfG, [1987] NJW 827, 828. Italy: Art. 1372(2) Cc.
1293. *See supra* [119-124].
1294. *See* Habersack, *Vertragsfreiheit und Drittinteressen* 5 et seqq.
1295. Inspired by Bollée, (2015) Rev. Arb. 696.

for violation of the privity of contract. It might equally be realistic to assume that no law would allow the employees requesting a court to hold the termination of the employment contracts invalid to have the situation assessed but for the economically detrimental deal. This illustrates that the privity of contract requires a certain *threshold* for contractual third-party effects to be considered relevant.

453. Naturally, the threshold will assess whether the third party's, in the instant case the employees', interest in party autonomy demands that they are not exposed to the contract's result. Yet, as for judgments, the specific line to be drawn between remote factual effects that do not concern party autonomy and such that do trigger the privity of contract remains largely unexplored. Yet again, the exception is French law stating that the existence of contracts can be invoked by and towards third parties,[1296] as long as it does not establish obligations thereto.[1297]

Interim Conclusion

454. In conclusion, the brief survey of other norms' factual effects has revealed that, *first*, factual effects of domestic norms (judgments and contracts) regularly focus on a certain threshold. If a third party can be regarded as affected in its own rights, it is necessary that it had the standing to influence the norm. Below such threshold, *erga omnes* effects are possible. *Second*, factual effects of foreign norms (judgments and laws) are possible but might not pre-empt the very review that is exercised for the traditional referral to such foreign norms under recognition and designation methods. In particular, jurisdictional and public-policy reviews might apply. Hence, for international awards, these norms' factual effects allow the inference that international arbitration doctrine examines whether, *first*, the recognition regime for foreign arbitral awards, i.e., the NYC equally applies to foreign awards' factual effects and, *second*, the law applicable to an award's factual effect might establish a threshold for due process and party autonomy as the decisive rationales against arbitral awards' third-party effects.

§7.04 INTERNATIONAL ARBITRAL AWARDS' FACTUAL EFFECTS AND THE EXPOSURE TO ARTICLE V NYC

455. As the overriding uniform regime, the NYC demands primary adherence when an international arbitral award establishes a factual effect in follow-up litigations outside of the seat. In particular, the party opposed to the factual effect might submit that Article V NYC applies, stating that '*[r]ecognition [...] of the award may be refused*'. This question is primarily examined for the previously established requirement under Article V(1)(a) NYC pursuant to which an arbitral *award*'s third-party effect must not exceed the underlying arbitration *agreement*'s third-party effect (*see* [A], *infra*). In

1296. Article 1200 Cc ('*Les tiers doivent respecter la situation juridique créée par le contrat. Ils peuvent s'en prévaloir notamment pour apporter la preuve d'un fait*'.
1297. Article 1199 CC ('*Le contrat ne crée d'obligations qu'entre les parties.*').

addition, it is examined whether third parties might invoke the other grounds under Article V NYC such as violations of the arbitral procedure or public policy (*see* [B], *infra*). If such examination of Article V NYC is required under a uniform interpretation, national courts of signatory states are obligated to exercise this review. As treaty law, the NYC overrides national laws or at least requires interpreting national substantive laws in conformity with the NYC. If the factual effect occurs under a treaty, e.g., Article 79(1) CISG, the NYC, as *lex specialis* treaty,[1298] enjoys preference.

[A] Personal Jurisdiction as a Limit to Factual Effects

[1] The Threshold for Applying Article V(1)(a) NYC

456. In *Chapter 6*, the examination has submitted that Article V(1)(a) NYC can and should be interpreted as preventing any third-party effect of an arbitral award against such third parties that have not consented to the arbitral tribunal's personal jurisdiction over them. This instantly raises the issue whether such strict boundary of awards' third-party effects equally applies when the arbitral award is not invoked as res judicata but as a fact. Again, the above-mentioned methods for interpreting Article V(1)(a) NYC determine the solution.[1299]

457. As to the wording, Article V(1)(a) NYC allows to refuse 'recognition'. This term describes the cross-jurisdictional efficacy of arbitral awards.[1300] From a comparative point of view, it has been mentioned that French law merely regards the *immediate* implementation of a decision's consequences as recognition.[1301] Moreover, from the absence of discussions under other jurisdictions, one might infer that the consideration of decisions as facts is not considered a matter of recognition However, this does not pre-empt the autonomous interpretation of the Convention, particularly in light of arbitration's distinct features. From a contextual perspective, there are scholarly submissions that the court can refrain from enforcement '*in appropriate cases take[ing] into consideration the effects of the award on non-parties*'.[1302] This indicates that the Convention permits an extensive interpretation exposed to indirect consequences.

1298. *See* in general ITLOS, *Southern Bluefin Tuna* (*Australia v. Japan, New Zealand v. Japan*), Award on Jurisdiction, 4 August 2000, (2006) XXIII UN Rep. Int Arb. Awards 1, [123] ('The [*lex-specialis*] principle is, in truth, a general principle of law recognized in all legal systems, and it was cited as an example of such in the drafting of Article 38 of the Statute of the Permanent Court of International Justice. It follows that if the lex specialis contains dispute settlement provisions applicable to its content, the lex specialis prevails over any dispute settlement provision in the lex generalis.').

1299. *See supra* [289].

1300. *See supra* [140, 298].

1301. *See supra* [442-443].

1302. Cf. Hwang and Chan, (2001) 10 ICCA Congress Series 164 ('In principle, the mere fact of non-parties' rights being affected should not impinge on enforceability under the Convention if the grounds for refusing enforcement under the Convention are not satisfied. This is because the grounds under the Convention for refusing enforcement are exhaustive. However, where a ground for refusal is made out, there is no reason why the enforcement court, in the exercise

458. With a view to the undemanding nature of other interpretation tools, the examination submits that the rationale underlying Article V(1)(a) NYC should govern the assessment. In general, the provision safeguards party autonomy as the very cornerstone of arbitration. When concerned with arbitral awards' third-party effect, it prevents that a third party who has not renounced its right to a natural judge on a matter and who had not had any opportunity to influence the arbitration is exposed the arbitration's results. It is submitted that this rationale to safeguard participation possibilities should decide whether an arbitral award's factual effect is exposed to the jurisdictional constraints under Article V(1)(a) NYC. Hence, if the award's factual effect concerns any interest of the third party, which it should have been able to protect by virtue of participation possibilities, party autonomy demands that a factual effect towards non-signatories to the arbitration agreement will generally be impermissible.

459. The delicate question is how to determine whether the third party should have been able to protect its interests by virtue of participation. Effectively an interest to participate only exists when there is a possibility to submit on the relevant issues. This standing to submit depends on the subject matter in question and a third party's relationship to this subject matter. Therefore, it is submitted that the threshold for Article V(1)(a) NYC as a jurisdictional barrier to awards' third-party effects applies if *the prior third party had the standing to submit on the prior subject matter*. Substantive law will be one factor when assessing this standing.

460. To apply this test on the four scenarios mentioned above:[1303] (i) The arbitration about B's right to sell the products in certain countries concerns a subject matter (the products) immediately connected to C in that C has the contractual right to receive them. Hence, C might potentially raise a claim against A not to interfere with this right. Accordingly, Article V(1)(a) NYC is at stake. (ii) An arbitration about B's liability towards D does not immediately result in an obligation of A. Privy to an assignment to D, A's liability is a matter of its contractual relationship to B exclusively. Yet, A's liability for the subject matter (the deficient goods) could also be raised by B. Hence the subject matter is again connected to A. (iii) The arbitral award rendered in favour of E did concern a subject matter immediately connected to A, since the latter is the owner of the good in dispute. (iv) In the scenario where the employer has concluded an economically detrimental deal and then seeks to rely on the contract's alleged invalidity, the business partner might initiate arbitration. Here, the subject matter would have *no* connection to the employee. But for such remote case scenarios, it is submitted that a teleological interpretation of Article V(1)(a) NYC necessitates a wide application with regard to factual effects.

---

of its residual powers to enforce, may not in appropriate cases take into consideration the effects of the award on non-parties.').

1303. *See supra* [425, 430, 431, 447].

[2] *Admissibility of Factual Effects Re-examining the Arbitral Award*

461. The application of Article V(1)(a) NYC to arbitral awards' factual effect necessitates that a third party must not be exposed to results it was unable to influence. Yet, a lenient standard for arbitral awards' factual effects might guarantee that the third party can still exercise an opportunity to effectively review the arbitral award and, e.g., invoke that the arbitral award has been rendered incorrectly or that the party relying on it has omitted to raise certain arguments. Particularly, in scenario (ii) the law on damages calculations regularly allows for tools, which enable a review of certain aspects of the arbitration. For instance, the institute of *mitigation* as it is, e.g., codified in Article 77 CISG[1304] would bar to invoke an arbitral award, which the party seeking the indemnity has caused through inadequate arguments. Notably, this requires that the indemnity debtor can review the submissions of the indemnity creditor in the arbitration. Moreover, the applicable law might allow undertaking damages calculation in general on a discretionary basis.[1305] Such broad comparative assessment is also allowed for the interim measure under Article 17A UNCITRAL Model Law in example (ii). It allows facilitating the arbitral award as merely one out of several aspects and considering additional submission of the indemnity debtor in this regard. Therefore, the examination submits that Article V(1)(a) NYC does not prevent arbitral awards factual effects, if the content of the arbitral award can still be reviewed in accordance with the third party's submission under the applicable law. Vice versa, Article V(1)(a) NYC necessitates that the *lex causae* guarantee such review possibilities.

[3] *Admissibility of Factual Effects Preventing Absolute Irreconcilabilities*

462. If an arbitral award's factual effect concerns a subject matter meeting a certain threshold of connection to the third party and if the factual effect occurs *automatically*, i.e., without any review, Article V(1)(a) NYC generally opposes the factual effect. This will be the case in example (i) from this Chapter's introduction (*see* [430], *supra*). The arbitral award *as such* triggers objective impossibility. Hence, nothing but a focus on a discretionary non-application of Article V(1)(a) NYC might allow such effect. For recognition courts, it is possible to disregard Article V(1)(a) NYC on a discretionary basis, since Article V(1) NYC states that recognition '*may* be refused'.

463. In this regard, the exclusive consideration justifying foregoing the jurisdictional protection established under Article V(1)(a) NYC might be to prevent irreconcilabilities. Particularly, the prevention of irreconcilabilities can be regarded as an inherent

1304. 'A party who relies on a breach of contract must take such measures as are reasonable in the circumstances to mitigate the loss, including loss of profit, resulting from the breach. If he fails to take such measures, the party in breach may claim a reduction in the damages in the amount by which the loss should have been mitigated'.
1305. *See*, e.g., § 287 ZPO.

mandate of any uniform regime on the cross-border recognition of decisions. Moreover, the Convention itself allows applying irreconcilability as a ground against recognizing arbitral awards.[1306] Therefore, it is submitted that the discretion under Article V(1)(a) NYC might allow awards' factual effects when they are necessary to implement the forum's overriding interest against irreconcilabilities.

464. In this regard, the above-mentioned survey has submitted that irreconcilability is generally a prolongation of res judicata. Therefore, in many instances, there will be no irreconcilability if there are no conflicting res judicata. Yet, *absolute irreconcilabilities* can arise when it is *factually impossible* to comply with two decisions:[1307] An arbitral award ordering B to deliver to C will expose B to the dilemma that it can impossibly comply with both, the order in favour of A *not* to deliver and the order in favour of B. Comparable dilemmas might arise, when one party is ordered by two tribunals to deliver a unique good, albeit to different claimants each. In such circumstances, objective impossibility or hardship prevents absolute irreconcilabilities.

465. In exercising the discretion under Article V(1)(a) NYC, a balancing of several criteria appears preferable, namely whether (i) the forum will likely be exposed to irreconcilable requests for enforcement, (ii) the third party is adequately compensated for the factual effect (e.g., through damages), (iii) the third party exposed to impossibility ought to have been aware of the previous dispute, (iv) the dispute in arbitration has been initiated earlier than court proceedings and (v) the third party to the arbitration would have no standing under the *lex fori* to intervene in a comparable preceding dispute before courts. Applied to initial case scenario where B sold certain goods to C although an arbitral award in favour of A restrained B from doing so. The forum might likely be exposed to irreconcilable enforcement requests, C will be compensated by virtue of damages and the arbitration has been initiated earlier. Hence, it might be justifiable to apply impossibility and affirm the arbitral award's factual effect even though C was no party to the arbitration agreement and Article V(1)(a) NYC generally applicable.

[4] Admissibility of Factual Effects Implementing a Status Adjudication

466. The wide application of Article V(1)(a) NYC to arbitral awards' factual effects necessitates a final matter where a restriction needs to be discussed. Potentially, the arbitral award invoked concerns a matter of legal status. To provide an example: a German corporation sold its business to a US purchaser by virtue of an asset deal. The APA included a New York Jurisdiction clause. Necessary under the articles of association, the seller's shareholders' resolution agreed on the sale. Afterwards, one shareholder successfully initiated an arbitration in Germany against the shareholders' resolution.[1308] As a consequence of the arbitral award, the seller allegedly lacked the

1306. *See supra* [161].
1307. *See supra* [166].
1308. *See supra* [235].

capacity to agree on the asset deal. When sued for specific performance by the purchaser in New York, the seller invokes the arbitral award as conclusively establishing his incapacity as an obstacle to the performance claim (and potentially as an origin of damages). When confronted with the binding force of the arbitral award with regard to the seller's capacity, the purchaser might invoke that the arbitral award should not constitute res judicata towards him. This raises the question whether Article V(1)(a) NYC applies thereby barring any effects of the arbitral award towards business partner.

467. In this regard several aspects necessitate that Article V(1)(a) NYC does not bar the factual effect. Foremost, the subject matter, i.e., the shareholders' resolution could not have been influenced by the business partner. Moreover, the interaction of res judicata and intervention possibilities can be turned into a persuasive consideration *against* the application of Article V(1)(a) NYC in issues of status. The adequate guarantee of intervention possibilities is already adhered to by the rules governing the arbitration agreement. Indeed, but for such guarantee, arbitration agreements in issues of status will be invalid.[1309] Vice versa, if they are valid, intervention possibilities can be deemed as adequately adhered to. The delicate step in this regard is that the adequate guarantee of intervention possibilities by the arbitration clause is assessed under *national* law whilst Article V(1)(a) NYC applies as a *uniform* guarantee of intervention possibilities. Yet, this very uniform guarantee always refers to national law in that the law applicable to the arbitration agreement determines the effect on non-signatories.[1310] Therefore, Article V(1)(a) NYC should *not* be applied when the arbitral award comprises an *erga omnes* effect at the arbitral seat and the arbitration agreement as such is valid. Hence, in the case example, the arbitral award can be invoked if the corporate arbitration clause is valid under German law.

Interim Conclusion

468. As an interim conclusion, the jurisdictional boundary under Article V(1)(a) NYC is generally at stake when an arbitral award comprises a factual effect towards third parties before foreign courts. Yet, in many case scenarios, Article V(1)(a) NYC will, in the end, not bar the factual effect, particularly if, *first*, the third party could not have submitted on the subject matter, *second*, the substantive law applied by the court allowed for adequate review mechanisms or, *third*, was necessary to prevent absolute irreconcilabilities. Nonetheless, Article V(1)(a) NYC obligates the court to examine whether a factual effect conforms to these criteria.

[B] Other Non-recognition Grounds as Limits to Factual Effects

469. Whilst Article V(1)(a) NYC has triggered the specific question, whether the NYC's particular rules on awards' third-party effects extend to factual effects, Article V

1309. *See supra* [235].
1310. *See supra* [45-46].

NYC bears the further potential to invoke other non-recognition grounds. This triggers the legal issue functionally equivalent to the above-mentioned discussion under foreign-judgment principles: whether the factual effect is a form of recognition. Again, the examination submits to examine the specific rationale of the specific non-recognition ground.

470. In this regard, both the structure of the two sections of Article V and the subject matters of the individual grounds allow a distinction, namely between recognition grounds protecting *individual* interests and recognition grounds exercised for *normative* reasons. The grounds of due process (section 1 lit. b), excess of subject matter jurisdiction (section 1 lit. c) and irregularities of the arbitral procedure (section 1 lit. d) inherently protect the arbitral parties themselves. By contrast, the referral to set asides (section 1 lit. e), inarbitrability (section 2 lit. a) and public policy (section 2 lit. b) do not only protect the arbitral parties. For the latter two grounds, this is already illustrated by the fact that Article V(2) NYC does not contain the dispositive passage of section 1 ('*at the request of the party against whom it is invoked*'). Therefore, annulment, inarbitrability and public policy comprehensively prevent the cross-border efficacy of arbitral awards. For uniform grounds under the Convention, there should be no difference between situations where the arbitral award is formally invoked under national res judicata and enforcement provisions or factually invoked under other provisions. Therefore, the normative grounds for non-recognition under Article V(1)I, (2)(a) and (b) NYC *can* be invoked against requests for factual effects.

Interim Conclusion

471. In conclusion, the examination submits that the NYC establishes boundaries on foreign arbitral awards' factual effects. That is, an arbitral award can only trigger objective impossibility or constitute a recoverable loss towards third parties if the arbitral award conforms to recognition requirements such as public policy, *and* the third party can adequately apply for a review of the arbitral award or the factual effect is demanded by considerations of irreconcilability. Therefore, the substantive law providing for the arbitral award's factual effect has to be interpreted accordingly in examining these criteria under the overriding NYC.

§7.05 ARBITRAL AWARDS' FACTUAL EFFECTS UNDER NATIONAL ARBITRATION LAWS

[A] The Law Applicable to Arbitral Awards' Factual Effects

472. When recognition is no obstacle to an arbitral award's factual effect (because the award is invoked before courts of the arbitral seat *or* the assessment under Article V NYC allowed the effect), national law will determine the admissibility of a factual effect. In this regard, a preliminary matter concerns the applicable law. At the outset, a prior decision's factual effect is prima facie a matter of the *lex causae*, hence substantive law. For instance, for an English court considering a decision as damages quantification at common law, the latter will also govern the admissibility of such factual effect. The same holds true if a German court applies a foreign decision as a ground for legal impossibility under section 275(1) BGB.[1311]

473. The matter turns more delicate when the *lex causae* and the *lex fori* differ. For instance, the foreign law applicable to a contract might contain more extensive opportunities for decisions' factual effects than the *lex fori* do. For example, English law might be applied before a court of another jurisdiction whose *lex fori* explicitly state that in indemnity matters, the loss suffered needs to be re-examined even though it has been adjudicated upon by another tribunal. In such scenario, the court would have to decide whether the *lex fori* override the English *lex causae*'s potential for factual effects. The solution might be to apply the *lex causae* and then public policy as a vehicle for the forum's due-process considerations.

474. The other case scenario in which the law governing the admissibility of factual consideration is delicate is when the applicable law is a uniform instrument. The latter are usually limited in scope. For instance, in its Article 7(2), the CISG states that national law governs all *lacunas*.[1312] Therefore, when a judgment is invoked as an impediment beyond anybody's control under Article 79(1) CISG, one might argue that the applicability of res judicata's same-parties requirement is beyond the limited scope of the CISG. The decision will remain a matter of each particular instrument. For the case of the CISG, one might invoke that the instrument is not aimed at procedural interests such as due process. Yet, it seems preferable to regard Article 79 CISG as a comprehensive balancing of the parties' performance interest and particularly as a compensation for strict liability (Article 74 CISG). These considerations support the construction that Article 79(1) CISG *itself* allows to apply a decision as an impediment. Moreover, for uncertainties under uniform law, one might facilitate more specific instruments. This might be the NYC whose recognition regime has the capacity to apply correspondingly.

Interim Conclusion

475. In conclusion, factual effects' admissibility is a matter of the law including the very provision that stipulates for a factual effect. Hence, the matter is extracted from private international law's traditional recognition and designation methods.

1311. 'A claim for performance is excluded to the extent that performance is impossible for the obligor or for any other person'.

1312. 'Questions concerning matters governed by this Convention which are not expressly settled in it are to be settled in conformity with the general principles on which it is based or, in the absence of such principles, in conformity with the law applicable by virtue of the rules of private international law'.

[B] Potential Considerations: Party Autonomy, Due Process and Irreconcilability

476. Given the unexplored status of arbitral awards' factual effects, this examination proposes some considerations that could be adopted under national arbitration laws that do *not* contain any doctrine as comprehensive as French law's *opposabilité*. The examination maintains its perspective that distinct national laws demand distinct assessments.[1313] In particular, the considerations on decisions' factual effects might be heavily susceptible to domestic jurisprudence and scholarship. Hence, the examination can have *no* ambition to provide conclusive proposals under several national laws in parallel. Instead, it merely proposes some functional considerations that might be applied in view of the cornerstones of arbitration and res judicata as revealed in the previous Chapters.

477. It is submitted that the applicable law should examine whether res judicata's same-parties requirement, i.e., the rule that an arbitral award takes no effect beyond the same parties bars factual effects towards third parties. Preferably, this assessment should be undertaken by applying the rationales underlying res judicata's same-parties requirement: due process and party autonomy.[1314] Hence, an arbitral award should only be applied as a fact against a former third party, if the latter has no standing to insist on its right to be heard and party autonomy. As it can be inferred from other factual effects' relation to due process (judgments' status effects) and party autonomy (contracts' reflexive effects), the standing depends on the threshold.

478. Elaborating on party autonomy: if the privity of contracts stipulates that as of a certain threshold factual effects turn into - generally non-permissive - detrimental third-party effects, arbitration will also have to undertake such assessment. To return to the above-mentioned case example on the employer.[1315] If the economically detrimental deal is potentially invalid or avoidable for a misunderstanding between the parties, and an arbitral tribunal has to decide on the contract's validity, the factual effect of the contract and the arbitral award's factual effect will go hand-in-hand. The arbitral award will be a fact to be invoked against the employees. For determining the necessary threshold, the solution under national laws should correspond to the assessment of party autonomy under the NYC, namely that party autonomy is a persuasive inclination to apply res judicata's same-parties requirement if *the third party exposed to the factual effect (i) would have had a standing to submit on the arbitration's subject matter and (ii) a review of the award is not guaranteed by the substantive provision's discretion.*[1316]

479. Moreover, due process as the foundation of all *inter partes* effects is of the essence. In particular, under French law and its *opposabilité*, due process mandates

1313. *See supra* [27].
1314. *See* on these rationales *supra* [175, 221-228].
1315. *See supra* [447].
1316. *See supra* [453, 456].

third-party appeals. When such appeals are unavailable under other laws, yet the third party's right to be heard is affected by an award's factual effect, there is a persuasive inclination *e contrario* to bar the effect.

480. Turning from the rationales *against* factual effects to the rationales *promoting* them, the examination submits that practical reasons might sometimes necessitate awards' factual effects. Indeed, the latter might prevent *absolute irreconcilabilities*. This is particularly the case for impossibility or hardship provisions. In this regard, the examination has proposed a discretionary assessment for allowing impossibility or hardship by virtue of arbitral awards even though party autonomy and due process oppose it. Modified by a forum's due-process notions, these balancing criteria might equally apply under national laws: whether (i) the forum will likely be exposed to irreconcilable requests for enforcement, (ii) the third party is adequately compensated for the factual effect (e.g., through damages), (iii) the third party exposed to impossibility ought to have been aware of the previous dispute, (iv) the dispute in arbitration has been initiated earlier than court proceedings and (v) the third party to the arbitration would have no standing under the *lex fori* to intervene in a comparable preceding dispute before courts. In conclusion, the admissibility of arbitral awards' factual effects under national laws should thus amount to an assessment of party as well as due process and, if these interests are at stake a balancing against the forum's interest to prevent irreconcilabilities.

§7.06 CONCLUDING THESES

(1) Arbitral awards might not only preclude third parties' arguments in follow-up litigation. In addition, the very *existence* of a claim conferred to or an obligation imposed on a party by a prior arbitral award might be raised in follow-up litigation. This might affect prior third parties. For instance, an award might impede a third party's claim for specific performance or quantify a third party's obligation to indemnify.[1317]

(2) But for French law which comprehensively provides for arbitral awards' *opposabilité* and compensates third parties with the *tierce opposition* before courts, arbitration laws contain no comprehensive rule whether factual effects are permissible or barred for the very rationales that restrict res judicata: due process and party autonomy.[1318]

(3) Factual effects are no topic privy to arbitration. Instead, laws, judgments and contracts can equally comprise factual effects. Whilst a comprehensive elaboration of this technique is evolving, it can be inferred that the applicability of recognition barriers (foreign judgments), public policy (foreign laws) and a certain threshold to distinguish impermissible, direct third-party effects

1317. *See supra* [424-433].
1318. *See supra* [434-435].

from indirect third-party effects (judgments and contracts) needs to be considered for arbitral awards.[1319]

(4) Article V(1)(a) NYC exclusively permits a foreign arbitral award's factual effect if (i) the third party exposed to the factual effect would have had no standing to submit on the subject matter, or (ii) the follow-up dispute adequately considers the third party's objections against the arbitral award, or (iii) the factual effect is necessary for preventing absolute irreconcilability. Moreover, a foreign arbitral award cannot trigger factual effects when it was annulled, concerned a non-arbitrable matter or violated public policy. In this regard, Article V NYC constitutes specific treaty law and thus overrides contract laws.[1320]

(5) The further permissibility of arbitral awards' factual effects is a matter of the law governing the provision, which is potentially susceptible to factual effects and the *lex fori*'s due-process notions. The resulting assessment should focus on the prior third party's interests of due process and party autonomy.[1321]

1319. *See supra* [437-449].
1320. *See supra* [450-466].
1321. *See supra* [467-475].

CHAPTER 8

Transnational Res Judicata and Third-Party Effects Before Arbitral Tribunals

481. So far, the examination has focused on the effects of arbitral awards before courts. Now, the examination shifts the perspective from the re-*litigation* to the re-*arbitration* of matters. It assesses the standards applied to res judicata - both, of arbitral awards and of judgments - when brought before international arbitral tribunals. A traditional, ultimately territorialist conception of international commercial arbitration might not even regard it necessary to distinguish between the application of res judicata before courts and before arbitral tribunals, let alone dedicate an entire Chapter to the latter. As effective part of the seat's judiciary, arbitral tribunals were to adopt court approaches. Yet, even irrespective of the immanent discussion on territoriality and juridicity, arbitral jurisprudence and scholarship increasingly seek to determine res judicata by means of transnational standards (*see* §8.01, *infra*).

482. In general, the examination takes the perspective that by applying res judicata, an arbitral tribunal restricts its adjudicatory mandate established by the parties. Accordingly, the law applicable to res judicata has to conform to the parties' intention. Since the parties' classic choices of the seat and the applicable law should not be understood as choices of the law applicable to res judicata, practical reasons incline this examination to consider a transnational approach towards res judicata before international arbitral tribunals feasible. The transnational principles should be developed by means of comparative law (*see* §8.02, *infra*).

483. Assuming that an arbitral tribunal decides to apply transnational principles, the Chapter will focus on one of the existing gaps amongst transnational principles of res judicata before arbitral tribunals. It will examine *whether an arbitral tribunal can reject a party's request or argument by referring to prior judgments or arbitral awards if an arbitrating party was a third party to the prior proceedings*. In essence, it will be submitted: but for any preclusion agreement, the two interests lying at the heart of this entire examination should govern the assessment, i.e., party autonomy and due process. Hence, a third-party effect should exclusively be affirmed, if the said third party to the prior proceedings could and should have participated therein. Moreover, the Chapter seeks to also subject factual effects to these criteria and, in addition, takes a position *against* the application of non-mutual preclusion before arbitral tribunals (*see* §8.03, *infra*). Upon these considerations, the Chapter will apply the proposed principles to a range of illustrative case scenarios (*see* §8.04, *infra*). It will conclude by summarizing the transnational principles on third-party effects before international arbitral tribunals (*see* §8.05, *infra*).

§8.01 STATUS QUO OF THE DISCUSSION ON RES JUDICATA BEFORE ARBITRAL TRIBUNALS

484. The currently eminent debate between transnational and conflictualist proposals towards the assessment of res judicata before international arbitral tribunals constitutes the outset of this Chapter (*see* [A], *infra*). In this regard, it is this examination's perception that any upcoming discussion on the preferability of transnational res judicata requires a proclamation as to the specific solutions proposed. Otherwise, the discussion risks to be undertaken in a practical vacuum. Therefore, the examination will proceed with specific case decisions and proposals on transnational res judicata examining issue preclusion (*see* [B], *infra*), abuse of process (*see* [C], *infra*), res judicata's finality requirement (*see* [D], *infra*) as well as the focus of this examination: third-party effects (*see* [E], *infra*). In this regard, a two-fold restriction is necessary. *First*, this examination's purpose to handle *third*-party effects necessitates limiting the outline of res judicata's general operational aspects. *Second*, every analysis of arbitral jurisprudence has to face the immanent obstacle that most awards in international commercial arbitration remain un-published and are confidential. Even if arbitral awards are published, this will regularly occur only after a certain delay and often partially. Therefore, it might be impossible to provide a true reflection of the tendencies in arbitral jurisprudence as a whole. Instead, arbitral awards will rather be individual sources of inspiration and practical means of illustrations for a scholarly analysis.

[A] General Antagony Between Transnational and Conflictualist Approaches

485. Res judicata before arbitral tribunals currently raises a salient discussion between national and transnational law. Such discussion reveals an antagony paradigmatic for international arbitration's multi-tiered governance setting. *Primarily*, arbitral tribunals enjoy full authority to decide all issues raised. In addition, courts operate as *secondary* – in many instances determinative – authorities once they can review decisions under jurisdictional, due-process or public-policy grounds. For the instant topic, the two authorities' perspectives differ. On the one hand, arbitral jurisprudence and scholarship increasingly seek to determine res judicata by means of *transnational* standards (*see* [1], *infra*). By contrast, courts supervising these decisions in set-aside or recognition proceedings apply *national* law (*see* [2], *infra*).

[1] Primary Perspective: Arbitral Jurisprudence and Scholarship

486. When faced with res judicata issues, some arbitral tribunals have applied national law. Whilst most of them could build upon an agreement of the parties or a limited international character of the case,[1322] other tribunals explicitly decided to adopt the approach taken at the arbitral seat.[1323] By way of contrast, many arbitrators and arbitration scholars seek to handle res judicata differently. Whereas some '*arbitrators state their need to rely on principles of national law [as] lip service to a traditional conception*'[1324] and adjust the applicable law, others fundamentally oppose the above-mentioned 'conflictualist approach'. Instead of determining an applicable national law, they prefer to handle res judicata under a 'substantive approach', i.e., genuine solutions frequently characterized as 'transnational'.[1325] The most widely discussed and often criticized proponent might be the *ILA Report on Res Judicata.*[1326] The methodological nature of such comparative approach should be initially put under the magnifying glass.

1322. *ICC Cases 2475 & 2762*, Award, (1974-1985) I ICC Collection 325, 328 (first and second arbitration seated in France, contract under Belgian law); *ICC Case 6293*, Award, 1990, cited by Hascher in *Travaux du comité français DIP* 20 (parties submitted on New York law exclusively); *ICC Case 7438*, Award, 1994, cited by Hascher in *Travaux du comité français DIP* 19 (first and second arbitration seated in Zurich); *ICC Case 8023*, Award, 1995, cited by Hascher in *Travaux du comité français DIP* 21 (all aspects of case in France); *ICC Case 10027*, Award, 2000, cited by Hascher in *Travaux du comité français DIP 20* (party agreement); *ICC Case 13254*, Award, 2011, unpublished, reported by Radicati di Brozolo, in *ASA Special Series* 14-15 (party agreement). No. indications about the background of the cases and potential arguments of the applicable are reported for: *ICC Case 3540*, Award, cited by Hascher in *Travaux du comité français DIP* 18; *ICC Case 4279*, cited by Mayer, in *Liber Amicorum Reymond* 188.

1323. *ICC Case 5901*, Award, cited by Grigera Naón, (2001) 289 Rec. des cours 169 (French lex arbitri on Swiss award); *ICC Case 10574*, Award, 2000, cited by Grigera Naón, (2001) 289 Rec. des cours 171 (English lex arbitri on US judgment); ICC Case (Wirth P, Kellerhals, Kaufmann-Kohler), 2 April 2002, (2003) 21 ASA Bull. 810, [16].

1324. Radicadi di Brozolo, in *ASA Special Series* 10-11.

1325. *ICC Case 3267*, Final Award, (1987) XII Y.C.A. 87; *ICC Case 4126*, Partial Award, (1974-1985) I ICC Collection 511, 513-514; *ICC Case 5835*, 1992, cited by Hascher in *Travaux du comité français DIP* 19; *ICC Case 6233*, 1992, (1991-1995) III ICC Collection 332; *ICC Case 6363*, Arbitral Award, 1991, (1992) XVII Y.C.A. 185; *ICC Case 9800*, 2000, (2001-2007) v. ICC Collection 659; *ICC Case 12226*, Award, 2004, unpublished, cited by the commentator to ICC Case 9800, 667; *ICC Case 13133*, Final Award, (2010) XXXV Y.C.A. 129, [36-39]; *ICC Case 13509*, Arbitral Award, (2008-2011) VI ICC Collection 739; Berman, (2015) 381 Rec. des cours [535]; *Born* 3776; Hanotiau, *Complex Arbitrations* 239-256; Hascher in *Travaux du comité français DIP* 25-26; Mayer, in *Liber Amicorum Reymond* 187; Mayer, (2016) Rev. Arb. 101; Radicati di Brozolo, in *ASA Special Series* 1; Schaffstein, *Res Judicata* [6.214]; Seraglini, (2016) Rev. Arb. 66-75; Yaffe, (2017) 34 J. Int'l Arb. 824.

1326. *ILA Final Report on Res Judicata* [23-28].

487. In general, the shift from private international law to genuine solutions of international disputes well pre-dates the rise of international arbitration. Already in ancient Rome, the *praetor peregrinus*:

> directly disposed of the merits of the dispute by constructing and applying a new substantive rule drawn from the laws of the involved states.[1327]

488. In contemporary legal culture, the technique to circumvent private international law by means of transnational law is manifold. It comprises actual uniform law established under treaties such as the NYC or the CISG. In addition it covers implemented model laws, particularly by UNCITRAL as well as non-binding texts developed under the auspices of institutions such as the International Law Commission (ILC), UNIDROIT or the IBA. Such soft law might be seen as an implementation of the traditional *lex mercatoria* idea,[1328] once established in order to handle a-national fact patterns and contracts between privates and States.[1329] Whilst the examination has no ambition to conclusively establish any legal theory of transnational law, the instant plurality of instruments inclines the examination to set out the conceptual characteristics of transnational res judicata. This is taken alongside two parameters, namely *origin* and *consistency* of the alleged transnational concept.

489. The immanent critic any submission on transnational res judicata is exposed to is the *legal origin* of the solutions. An allegedly transnational approach runs the risk of operating outside any legal sources and purelyadopting what has been summarized as '*ad hoc solutions*',[1330] i.e., the discretionary handling of res judicata. For instance, some awards handling res judicata have not cited any legal source.[1331] Another tribunal referred to a transnational approach, yet facilitated French law as '*source of inspiration*'[1332] thereby raising the critics that the solution was '*not necessarily the reflection of generally recognized rules but of the French vision of what such rules are or should be.*'[1333] The widely acknowledged rectification of the lack of legal sources is to determine transnational res judicata on the basis of comparative observations. For instance, the tribunal in ICC Case 5835 developed its solutions by reconciling Swiss law

1327. Symeonides, (2016) 384 Rec. des cours 65 with further references.
1328. *See* Drobnig, in *75 Jahre Max Planck Institut für Privatrecht* 745 ('soft law is [...] formulation of rules of law which, to the extent that it touches upon areas of commercial law, is called *lex mercatoria*').
1329. *See* von Hoffmann, in *Liber Amicorum Kegel* 217-223.
1330. Schaffstein, *Res Judicata* [5.07].
1331. *ICC Case 3267*, Final Award, (1987) XII Y.C.A. 87, 88 ('none of the parties did require the application of any particular system of law, nor did they rely on any specific provision of any municipal system'); *ICC Case 6363*, Arbitral Award, 1991, (1992) XVII Y.C.A. 185; *ICC Case 6233*, 1992, (1991-1995) III ICC Collection 332; *ICC Case 9800*, 2000, (2001-2007) v. ICC Collection 659, 664-5; *ICC Case 13133*, Final Award, (2010) XXXV Y.C.A. 129, [36-39].
1332. *ICC Case 13509*, Arbitral Award, (2008-2011) VI ICC Collection 739.
1333. Radicati di Brozolo, in *ASA Special Series* 16.

(agreed as procedure) and Italian law (agreed as seat).[1334] Another tribunal justified its solution for res judicata by referring to the:

> good procedural order in an important number of countries including those of the European Community.[1335]

490. In scholarship, close to all publications, which contain more than mere statements in favour of transnationality and address specific problems use comparative law either for proclamatory reports[1336] or justifications of the proposals.[1337]

491. The aspect more delicate than the comparative origin of transnational res judicata is its *coherence and norm quality*. Undisputedly, transnational res judicata maintains an evolving status. Hence, no source can go beyond merely persuasive rules of law, 'principles', or – to facilitate the term of the ILA's proposal – 'Recommendations'.[1338] Whilst rule-based law supposes a binding nature both in terms of normative force and in terms of specific content, principles are:

> without exception suppletive (dispositive) law, they are more general and abstract and they are flexible in that they are open to judicial interpretation and adaptation according to the circumstances a court or tribunal may deem appropriate to take into account.[1339]

492. However, in contrast to other soft laws of UNIDROIT, the ILC and the IBA, the ILA Recommendations lack an aspect that is often raised by legal theorists in order to underline the quality of transnational instruments as *law*. Indeed, they are yet to be cited in jurisprudence.[1340] Hence, one author has recently proposed that arbitral tribunals should increasingly examine previous arbitral awards and judgments rendered by international tribunals in order to evolve a system comparable to common law.[1341] In conclusion, it is an emerging perception that arbitral tribunals should apply transnational, comparative-inspired principles to res judicata.

1334. *ICC Case 5835*, Award, 1992, cited by Hascher in *Travaux du comité français DIP* 19. *See also* the adjustment of the French lex arbitri with Swiss and transnational practice in *ICC Case 5901*, Award, 1989, cited by Grigera Naón, (2001) 289 Rec. des cours 169.
1335. *ICC Case 4126*, Partial Award, (1974-1985) I ICC Collection 511, 513-514 (translation of the author).
1336. *ILA Interim Report*; Schaffstein, *Res Judicata* [2.01 et seqq].
1337. *Born* 3776 (relying on NYC and construing it by virtue of comparative law); Radicati di Brozolo, in *ASA Special Series*; Mayer, in *Liber Amicorum Reymond* 187.
1338. Cf. Schaffstein, *Res Judicata* [6.01] ('Given the lack of a universal res judicata doctrine and the uncertainty existing in international commercial arbitration law and practice as to how to deal with res judicata issues, a codification of transnational res judicata rules appears premature.').
1339. Kronke, in *Liber Amicorum von Hoffmann* 1007.
1340. For explicit rejections *see ICC Case 13808*, Award, 2008, unpublished, reported by Radicati di Brozolo, in *ASA Special Series* 2-3 and 13-14.
1341. Yaffe, (2017) 34 J. Int'l Arb. 824 et seqq. *See* for critics *infra* [540-548].

[2] Secondary Perspective: Supervisory Courts

493. It has already been outlined that Swiss courts annul arbitral awards for violations of procedural public policy when the arbitral tribunal failed to respect an earlier decision's res judicata in the manner a Swiss court would have. By contrast, other jurisdictions are more averse to reviewing the non-application of res judicata as long as the arbitral tribunal has not entirely neglected the issue. Yet, they effectively review the outset of the doctrine of res judicata, i.e., the prevention of duplicative claims in that awards can be set aside when they are *irreconcilable* with a prior decision.[1342]

494. If a tribunal has decided to apply the doctrine of res judicata not in a more *restrictive* (non-application) but a more *extensive* (over-application) manner than the arbitral seat's law provides for, the party affected by the preclusion might equally seek a set aside. For example, an arbitral tribunal seated in Switzerland might have decided to apply issue estoppel or abuse of process, stipulated in English law, but unknown to Swiss law. Whilst the Barcelona Court of Appeal has annulled an award which affirmed issue estoppel,[1343] the law in many jurisdictions that consider res judicata's *non*-application a violation of procedural public policy is uncertain. The Swiss Federal Tribunal, for instance, '*never had the opportunity to decide the opposite scenario*'.[1344]

495. In anticipation of future jurisprudence, the underlying interests in favour of res judicata, i.e., consistency, legal certainty and efficiency are *not* violated by on over-application of res judicata. They are *promoted*. Moreover, Swiss jurisprudence applies procedural public policy in order to avoid irreconcilable decisions. This risk only arises from the non-application of res judicata, not its over-application.[1345] Hence, the current public-policy jurisprudence on res judicata's non-application should have limited implications for its *over*-application.

496. Instead, the discussion should address whether set-aside grounds can sanction that the party exposed to res judicata could *not* exercise its right to have an argument decided. In England, this would constitute a set-aside ground under Article 68(2)(d) 1996 Arbitration Act obligating tribunals to '*deal with all issues that were put to it*'. By contrast, the Swiss Article 190(2)(c) PILA covers the failure '*to rule on a claim*' which is not at stake when merely a certain argument is excluded by virtue of issue preclusion. The French Article 1520(3) CPC contains a broad ground for violations of the arbitrators' mandate that has been submitted to be at stake.[1346] However, the French rationale against applying public policy to res judicata, i.e., to preventbsen-ce*ion au fond* can be deemed to extend to this case scenario. Accordingly, Swiss, French and Model law jurisdictions would have to concentrate on due process.

1342. *See supra* [150-154].
1343. CA Barcelona, *Win Petrol v. Total Espana*, 1 September 2009, [2010] Paris J. Int'l Arb. 538.
1344. Berger, (2015) ASA Bull. 656.
1345. Schaffstein, *Res Judicata* [6.88].
1346. Hascher, in *Travaux comité français DIP* 29 with reference to CA Paris, *Gouvernement de l'Etat du Qatar v. Crighton Ltd*, [1996] Rev. Arb. 428, which addresses several arbitral awards rendered in the course of *one* proceedings.

Particularly, national procedural laws precisely stipulated the strict boundaries of res judicata towards third parties in order to protect due process.[1347] In bilateral scenarios, by contrast, the party affected by res judicata was able to appear in both the previous and the subsequent proceedings. In this regard, there are only a few statements: in Switzerland, one persuasive authority affirms that Swiss law allowed the set aside of an arbitral award facilitating issue preclusion, since it would amount to '*a denial of the right of access to justice and, as such, in a violation of the right to a fair trial*'.[1348] In Germany, this has been rendered a *ratio decidendi*: on 11 October 2018 (Case I ZB 9/18), the Federal Court of Justice annulled an arbitral award for violation of due process, because the Germany-seated tribunal had applied res judicata not only to an earlier arbitral award's operative part but also to its reasonings.

497. In conclusion, domestic jurisdictions differ as to their review on arbitrators' decisions on issues of res judicata. Whilst Swiss courts fully review the non-application of res judicata by arbitrators, others contain limitations and controversies. Moreover, in the examined jurisdictions there is limited authority for stating that an *over*-application of res judicata would be reviewable under annulment grounds such as public policy or due process.

[B] Transnational Divide on Issue Preclusion

498. If a transnational approach towards res judicata before arbitral tribunals *were* permissible, the most salient antagony between civil and common law, and thus a litmus test for transnational principles concerns the admissibility of issue preclusion, i.e., the extension of res judicata to adjudicatory reasonings.[1349] Effectively, arbitral jurisprudence and scholarship reveal a comparable divide, although in no significant connection to the arbitrators' background. The often cited reference in favour of issue preclusion under transnational law is ICC Case 3267 holding that:

> it would be unfair to both parties to depart in a final award from the views held in the previous award, to the extent they were necessary for the disposition of certain issues.[1350]

499. However, this very case could address a partial award rendered within the very same proceedings. Hence, the incentive against contradictions was overriding. If concerned with the application of issue preclusion between *different* arbitral tribunals, specific precedence is scarce. In fact, many arbitral awards - under both national and non-national standards - took the cause of action as the outset for res judicata.[1351] In

1347. *See supra* [175, 222].
1348. Berger, (2015) ASA Bull. 657.
1349. *See supra* [111-114].
1350. *ICC Case 3267*, Final Award, (1987) XII Y.C.A. 87, 89.
1351. *ICC Case 7438*, Award, 1994, cited by Hascher in *Travaux du comité français DIP* 22 (Swiss law); *ICC Case 8023*, Award, 1995, cited by Hascher in *Travaux du comité français DIP* 23 (French law); *ICC Case 9800*, 2000, (2001-2007) v. ICC Collection 659, 664-5 (no referral to

this spirit, the arbitral tribunal in *ICC Case 7061* involving four parallel and sequential proceedings concluded that there '*can be no issue estoppel*', yet that a prior arbitral award between the parties '*provides a helpful analysis of the common factual background*'. Accordingly, the arbitrators:

> have born its finding and conclusions in mind, whilst taking care to reach [their] own conclusions.[1352]

500. A more recent arbitral award against issue preclusion is *ICC Case 13509*:[1353] it concerned a joint venture contract (French law, ICC arbitration in Paris). One party unsuccessfully sued the other alleging that the distribution in certain countries constituted a violation of the contract. The successor of the former claimant then again sued the respondent for the distribution of the products in other countries. The respondent invoked the first arbitral award's holding that the contract provided no stipulations as to any non-competition obligation.[1354] Applying 'transnational law inspired by French law', the tribunal assessed the preferability of issue preclusion by balancing the underlying interests. It considered the principle of efficiency as a support for issue preclusion whilst the tribunal's duty towards the subsequent parties exclusively and the previous parties' potential satisfaction with the dispositif in opposition.[1355] It then rejected issue preclusion, however, it facilitated a citation of Pierre Mayer and considered the interpretation of the contract res judicata. Functionally, this is a solution comparable to res judicata of declarative suits in Germanic jurisdictions[1356] and therefore not infringing civil law's aversion towards issue preclusion.

501. In scholarship, the position is divided. The ILA favours the position of common law, as principles of issue preclusion:

> for reasons of procedural efficiency and finality seem acceptable on a worldwide basis notwithstanding the fact that they are yet unknown in civil law jurisdictions.[1357]

502. Gary Born – who arrives at transnational principles through the NYC, equally regarded as binding for tribunals – submits correspondingly.[1358] Moreover, Principle 5

particular law, however, arbitral seat and contract law French); *ICC Case 13133*, Final Award, (2010) XXXV Y.C.A. 129, [36-39] (no referral to particular law).

1352. *ICC Case 7061*, unpublished, cited by Hanotiau, *Complex Arbitrations* [551].
1353. *ICC Case 13509*, Arbitral Award, (2008-2011) VI ICC Collection 739.
1354. *Ibid.* ('*ne contiennet aucune stipulation ayant pour effet de restreindre la production, la vente, la commercialisation ou l'usage*').
1355. *Ibid.*, 741 ('*Cela se traduirait par un coût en termes de temps et d'argent, et risquerait de déboucher sur une contradiction entre les solutions retenues par les deux sentences. En sens inverse on peut fair valoir, en premier lieu que le second tribunal arbitral, spécialement investi d'une mission par les parties, doit jouir de la même libérte […] en second lieu, qu'une partie pourrait avoir décidé de ne pas former de recours contre une décision parce qu'elle se satisfaisait du dspositif de celle-ci […]*').
1356. *See supra* [113].
1357. *ILA Final Report on Res Judicata* [56].
1358. *Born* 3776, 3771.

at the conclusion of Silja Schaffstein's treatise favours issue preclusion[1359] unless the '*preliminary issue [...] constitutes the main issue in the arbitration*',[1360] because of the interest in finality, the increase of efficiency and the limited risks of due process when both international parties received legal counsel.[1361] By way of contrast, George A Bermann stresses that issue preclusion remains unknown to many procedural laws and is even debated amongst common-law scholars. Moreover, the *previous* arbitration's subject matter concerned the claim exclusively.[1362] In addition, Pierre Mayer raises that issue preclusion might cause follow-up disputes on its requirements and that issue preclusion might contravene the jurisdiction conferred upon the *subsequent* tribunal by the parties.[1363] In line with this, one might add that civil law, by restricting issue preclusion, upholds the subsequent court's cognition power[1364] and that an arbitration agreement even increases the need to uphold an arbitral tribunal's cognition power. In conclusion, the discussion on issue preclusion reflects the divide known from procedural law. Efficiency and consistency are advocated in favour of issue preclusion, whilst opponents refer to the need for focused dispute resolutions and the cognition power of the subsequent tribunal. There is no consensus.

[C] Transnational Reluctance Towards Abuse of Process

503. A divide comparable to issue preclusion exists regarding abuse of process, i.e., the preclusion of claims or arguments that have not, but could have been raised in the earlier procedure.[1365] Again, the divides extend to transnational res judicata. The ILA regards abuse of process as an '*acceptable compromise regarding the private and public interests at stake*'[1366] provided that arbitrators retain discretion for counsel tactics, particularly with regard to the following aspects:

> Costs, psychological influences, relational elements, cross-cultural considerations, persuasiveness, political constraints.[1367]

1359. Schaffstein, *Res Judicata* [Principle 5, pre 6.236] ('Unless the parties agree otherwise, a national court judgment has conclusive and preclusive effects in the arbitral proceedings as to: determinations and relief contained in its dispositive part *as well as in the reasoning necessary thereto; issues of fact or law which have actually been arbitrated and determined by it, provided any such determination was essential or fundamental to the dispositive part of the national court judgment*.', emphasis added) and [pre 6.246] for prior awards.
1360. *Ibid.*, [6.236, 6.246].
1361. Schaffstein, *Res Judicata* [6.78-6.79].
1362. Bermann, (2015) 381 Rec. des cours [539-540].
1363. Mayer, in *Liber Amicorum Reymond* 198-200; Mayer, (2016) Rev. Arb. 105.
1364. *See supra* [117].
1365. *See supra* [116].
1366. *ILA Final Report on Res Judicata* [62].
1367. *ILA Final Report on Res Judicata* [60].

504. This discretionary proposal has gained support from Luca Radicati di Brozolo.[1368] Silja Schaffstein illustrates concerns of *ultra petita*[1369] yet favours preclusion by virtue of abuse of process:

> provided that the raising of any such new claim, cause of action or new issue of fact or law amounts to procedural unfairness or abuse.[1370]

505. Finally, Dominique Hascher favours that the parties are obligated to concentrate their arguments.[1371] Although submitted before the *Cesareo* judgment, it should be noted, that the said duty compensates previous French doctrine restricting res judicata to the same legal grounds.[1372]

506. The status quo in arbitral jurisprudence is rather restrictive towards abuse of process. The tribunal in *ICC Case 5901* applied French law (of the seat) in adjustment with Swiss law (of the first award) and refused to preclude any claims that have not, but could have been raised by virtue of set-off in the previous arbitration.[1373] Correspondingly, the tribunal in *ICC Case 13254* was unpersuaded that there was a '*desirable and [...] progressively emerging*' principle of concentration and turned to the arbitration agreement. Although it affirmed the principles of finality and efficiency, they did not demand extended preclusion rules.[1374]

507. Finally, in *ICC Case 13808*, an arbitral tribunal awarded damages for breach of contract without addressing arguments of EU competition law, since the parties have not raised such. Due to the failure to apply EU competition law, one party applied for set aside which was rejected by the Paris Court of Appeal.[1375] *Obiter*, the court remarked that the undecided nullity of the contract does not fall under the award's res judicata and could therefore still be raised by the defendant in a subsequent arbitration. In the unpublished second arbitral award, the tribunal stressed its (retrospective) prerogative,[1376] yet concurred that the issue of nullity in itself could very well still be raised. Given the French background of the case, the tribunal mainly relied on French law and rejected transnational arguments on the ILA Recommendations and the UNIDROIT/ALI Principles. However, it rejected the claim for restitution since this would overturn the first arbitral award constituting res judicata.[1377] In conclusion, the availability of abuse of process amongst transnational approaches to res judicata is perceived critically.

1368. Radicati di Brozolo, in *ASA Special Series* 20-22 ('options set out in the ILA's Recommendations are on balance well considered').
1369. Schaffstein, *Res Judicata* [6.93-6.97].
1370. *Ibid.*, [Principle 6, pre 6.237] and [pre 6.246] for prior awards.
1371. Hascher, in *Travaux du comité français DIP* 26.
1372. *See supra* [110].
1373. *ICC Case 5901*, Award, 1989, cited by Grigera Naón, (2001) 289 Rec. des cours 169, 170.
1374. *ICC Case 13254*, Award, 2011, unpublished, reported by Radicati di Brozolo, in *ASA Special Series* 14-15.
1375. CA Paris, *Thalès Air Défense v. Euromissile*, 18 November 2004, [2005] Rev. Arb. 751.
1376. *See supra* [116-117].
1377. *ICC Case 13808*, Award, 2008, unpublished, cited by Radicati di Brozolo, in *ASA Special Series* 2-3 and 13-14.

[D] Transnational Uncertainty on Res Judicata's Requirements

508. Turning from res judicata's consequences to its requirements, the statements on transnational principles become very scarce. The ILA regards res judicata as an aspect that needs to be invoked by parties and not applied ex officio,[1378] yet can build upon a comparative consensus in this regard.[1379] Moreover, there is a common agreement that public international law's requirement pursuant to which res judicata can only operate within 'the same legal order' is no obstacle for commercial arbitration operating in parallel to litigation.[1380] Other aspects are more delicate such as the point in time upon which res judicata commences and the relevance of remaining appeal possibilities. Amongst transnational proposals, some authorities state that the finality of an arbitral award remains a matter of the seat's law,[1381] whilst Silja Schaffstein submits that tribunals should develop a transnational notion of finality and proposes the moment when the arbitral award '*is rendered and not (or no longer) subject to appeal on the merits*'.[1382] Notably, this submission invokes that such uniform criteria applied under Article V(1)(e) NYC, although the majority jurisprudence interprets the provision otherwise. It refers to the seat's law.[1383]

509. Another little debated aspect of finality are default decisions. For example, when the SCC dismissed the counterclaims in Case 24/2002 after the deadline for payment had expired, the tribunal mentioned *obiter* that the counterclaim would *not* fall under res judicata eventually.[1384] Whereas the commentators mentioned the potential applicability of abuse of process under English law,[1385] Gary Born sees:

> no reason that an otherwise valid award should be denied preclusive effect because it is a default award.[1386]

510. A further delicate aspect of the transnational discussion concerns the question whether arbitral tribunals can reject res judicata for reasons of irregularity, e.g., jurisdictional, due-process or public-policy deficiencies of the prior arbitration. This touches upon the question whether arbitral tribunals can apply the grounds under Article V NYC to reject recognition. Certainly, the NYC *binds* only states and thereby courts. Yet, this does not settle the aspect whether arbitral tribunal *can* refer to the NYC. The question is a genuine issue of res judicata, since arbitral tribunals will

---

1378. *ILA Final Report on Res Judicata* [66-67].
1379. *See supra* [137].
1380. *ILA Final Report on Res Judicata* [35]; Hobér, (2013) 366 Rec. des cours 264; Schaffstein, *Res Judicata* [5.66]; Shany, *Regulating Jurisdictional Relations* 126.
1381. *ILA Final Report on Res Judicata* [18] ('the law of the place of arbitration of the prior award by and large will govern the question whether determinations in the prior award [...] may qualify for conclusive and preclusive effects'); Bermann, (2015) 381 Rec. des cours [528].
1382. Schaffstein, *Res Judicata* [6.156].
1383. *See supra* [295].
1384. *SCC* Case 24/2002, Arbitral Award, 2003, Bond and Linn Bergman (eds), [2004-2009] SCC Arbitral Awards 127.
1385. *Ibid.*, 139-153.
1386. *Born* 3773.

certainly not be requested to enforce prior awards. Whilst the applicability of Article V NYC against res judicata requests for arbitral tribunals has been specifically rejected in *ICC Case 3383*,[1387] there are also more general statements pursuant to which there were:

> no sound reason why an international arbitral award's entitlement to recognition should vary as between the two settings.[1388]

511. In this spirit, the scholarly majority submits that a prior arbitral award can only constitute res judicata if it can be recognized at the subsequent arbitral seat.[1389] Moreover, corresponding submissions also state that res judicata of prior *court judgments* before arbitral tribunals requires that they can be recognized at the arbitral seat.[1390]

Interim Conclusion

512. In conclusion, taking together the previous overview on issue preclusion, abuse of process and finality, there are in fact very *few* specific aspects of res judicata currently governed by a transnational consensus. Therefore, a submission in favour of transnational principles risks being *Pyrrhic victory* for the sake of certainty and foreseeability.

[E] Transnational Detection of Third-Party Effects

[1] Res Judicata's Same-Parties Requirement, Privies and Opposabilité

513. There is only a hand full of statements on potential transnational standards for the question whether and to what degree arbitral tribunals can apply res judicata when the parties before the tribunal are not identical to the prior proceedings. To commence with jurisprudence, amongst the published ICC cases, four awards addressed this case scenario. Two built upon francophone perceptions, addressed individual aspects of third-party preclusion and particularly mentioned the application of the French doctrine of *opposabilité*.[1391] The other two comprise the potential to be facilitated for a general transnational standard.

1387. *ICC Case 3383*, Award, 1979, (1974-1985) I ICC Collection 394.
1388. Bermann, (2015) 381 Rec. des cours [525].
1389. *ILA Recommendations* No. 3.1; Schaffstein, *Res Judicata* [6.219-6.221]. *Accord*, under Swiss law, Berger and Kellerhals, *Arbitration in Switzerland* [1664]. *Contra* Mayer, (2016) Rev. 101-102.
1390. Schaffstein, *Res Judicata* [6.126-6.134]; Söderlund, (2005) J. Int'L arb 305 (jurisdiction). *Accord*, under Swiss law, ATF 140 III 278, [E.3.2.]; Berger and Kellerhals, *Arbitration in Switzerland* [1661-1663].
1391. *ICC Case 8023*, Award, 1995, cited by Hascher in *Travaux du comité français DIP* 21-22, *see infra* [589]; *ICC Case 13509*, Arbitral Award, (2008-2011) VI ICC Collection 739, *infra* [586].

514. *ICC Case 4126* involved a European contractor's claim against an African principal to have a bank guarantee returned. Such guarantee for the principal's potential damages claims had been issued at the outset of a construction project. Delicately, the guarantee operated independently from potential objections of the contractor. After disputes about the building arose, the contractor sought to prevent that the principal facilitated the guarantee and exposed the contractor to indemnity claims by the bank. IThe contractor *un*successfully applied for interim relief against his bank in court. In the ICC arbitration against the principal, the contractor applied for a return of the guarantee in exchange for a new guarantee for claims under potential award obligations. The tribunal seated in Amsterdam rejected this application and referred to the court decision, notably even though the latter was merely an interim order. Since the contractor was no party to the litigation, the tribunal acknowledged that '*a strict application of the principle ne bis in idem does not apply.*' However, it held that:

> the rules of good procedural order in an important number of countries including those of the European Community do not prevent any less a party to an arbitration from availing itself for a request that is essentially identical.[1392]

515. Accordingly, the decision might be interpreted in favour of a rationale softening res judicata's same-parties requirement when there is 'essential identity' of claims.

516. In *ICC Case 6363* a main contractor (and licensor) claimed licensing fees from a sub-contractor (and licensee) of a sewage treatment installation in the Middle East. The respondent invoked that the claimant had previously assigned its payment claims and that the assignee had already unsuccessfully claimed the licensing fees before local courts. Even though the arbitral tribunal seated in Geneva held the assignment ineffective, the respondent invoked the prior judgment as res judicata on the licensing fees as such. The tribunal decided on res judicata without any reference to a particular national law. Although it was undisputed that the claimant knew about the litigation, was advisor to the assignee, communicated with the assignee and even used the term 'we' towards the respondent, the arbitral tribunal rejected res judicata. Res judicata could only apply between the same parties and the claimant and the assignee were separate legal personalities.[1393] Thus, the case comprises the rationale that res judicata

1392. *ICC Case 4126*, Partial Award, (1974-1985) I ICC Collection 511, 513-514 – translation according to Schwartz, in *Conservatory and Provisional Measures in International Arbitration* 57).

1393. *ICC Case 6363*, Arbitral Award, 1991, (1992) XVII Y.C.A. 185, [40-41] ('[A]ll of [the] aspects of the agreement are consistent with the separate legal and factual personalities of the claimant and the ME company. [...] The fact that the claimant wanted the Korean company and the ME company to resolve their dispute amicably and even used "we" to refer to itself and the ME company, to whom it thought it had transferred the right, does not make it a party in the case in the CSCD. Nor does the fact that it gave advice to the ME company make it a party, especially in the light of Art. 6 of the 1980 Agreement. Its role as advisor to the ME company with regard to the latter's efforts to collect from the Korean company is consistent with its obligations under the 1980 Agreement. It is not unusual for advisers to refer collectively to themselves and their principal as "we", particularly when they are negotiating on behalf of their principals with third parties. [...] Indeed., the ME company's suit in the

operates between the parties only. Yet, the sheer fact that it addressed the involvement of the licensor in the litigation implies that the same-parties requirement does not need to focus on the formal roles of parties only. Instead, as in ICC Case 4126, the arbitral award indicates that it is permissible to treat some third parties as effective parties. Whilst ICC Case 4126 referred to the claim, ICC Case 6363 focused on the third party's relationship with the formal parties. This corresponds to the two functional criteria from comparative civil procedure, i.e., the prior third party's proximity to either the former parties or the former subject matter.[1394]

517. Turning from arbitral jurisprudence to arbitral scholarship, the standards for transnational res judicata towards prior third parties remain almost unaddressed. Foremost, the ILA labelled the problem as too complex and thus excluded it from its Report.[1395] Amongst the three scholars who do mention the delicate topic of res judicata's operation towards third parties in a transnational context, Pierre Mayer submits that the same-parties requirement prevails. Moreover, he submits that the doctrine of *opposabilité* should apply towards third parties as long as there is no fraudulent action.[1396] In both regards, the treatise of Silja Schaffstein concurs. The treatise's principles formulate that res judicata could, in general, exclusively apply between the parties to the prior proceedings.[1397] The very reason is the application of due process.[1398] For exceptions, the treatise favours '*the common law-style 'privity of interest' test*'.[1399] In addition, every third party:

CSCD failed precisely because it was separate from the claimant/Dutch company and, as a result, could not rely on a contractual right with regard to the system.').

1394. *See supra* [213-214].

1395. *ILA Final Report on Res Judicata* [41, 46-49] ('The Recommendations maintain the traditional triple identity test, i.e., identity of the claims, of the causes of action and of the parties. [...] [They] refrain from formulating new rules in relation to the requirement of the identity of the parties. First, they do not forumulate a requirement as to mutuality [...]. Second, [they] also refrain from formulating definitions as to the notion of parties. [...] There are too many different situations in relation to the question whether a party, by virtue of assignment, succession, close relationship or otherwise, is bound [...] that these issues are left to the applicable law. [...] The Committee notes that, in practise, important and delicate problems arise in relation to the identity of the parties, particularly in relation to groups of companies and BIT arbitrations. These issues are, however, too complex to deal with in [this Report]. [...] Moreover, different countries have different methods and theories for identification of third parites [...] (eg alter ago, agency, protection of legitimate expectations). Furthermore, the most important application of identification questions is in the field of piercing the veil of corporations and raises fundamental issues of international corporate law [...] which [...] deserved better and more elaborate treatment elsewhere.').

1396. Mayer, in *Liber Amicorum Reymond* 200.

1397. Schaffstein, *Res Judicata* [Principle 1.4.4, pre 6.245] and [Principle 2.3.4, pre 6.244].

1398. *Ibid.*, [6.212] ('[...] a related third party [...] did not have an opportunity to express its opinion on the factual and legal issues decided in the prior award. Hence, a related third party should not generally be bound by the factual and legal determinations made in a prior award between other parties.').

1399. *Ibid.*, [6.120] ('In this respect, a reference to the common law-style "privity of interest" test may be appropriate to assess the "sameness" between the parties [...]. The test would be met where the parties are either formally identical or so closely related to represent virtually the same interests [...]. However, international commercial arbitral tribunals must be careful not do unduly restrict the right of access to justice and the right to be heard of a party with

> may have to respect the legal situation created by the prior award [...] invoking the concept known in French law as 'opposabilité aux tiers'.[1400]

[2] *The Proposal of Stavros L. Brekoulakis*

518. The currently most extensive proposal on prior decisions' third-party effects before arbitral tribunals has been submitted by Stavros L. Brekoulakis.[1401] Whilst the proposal generally addresses the effects of arbitral awards irrespective of whether they are invoked in follow-up litigation or in follow-up arbitration, the latter case scenario is the focus.[1402] Upon a brief comparative examination that exceptions to res judicata's same-parties requirement were inherent to national procedural laws when there is a communality of interests,[1403] the author observes that the traditional treatment of arbitral res judicata towards third parties was neither '*satisfactory nor suitable for the needs and purposes of international arbitration*'.[1404] Instead, it '*creates the risk of inconsistent, if not conflicting, determinations and decisions. More importantly, it creates a sense of injustice for both parties and third parties in arbitration.*'[1405] Above all, other mechanisms such as joinders or consolidations were often unavailable.[1406]

519. Therefore the author proposes a genuine 'third-party effect'. In the proposal, the term is not used in the functional meaning that the instant examination has adopted (summarizing res judicata against privies, non-mutual preclusion and factual effects).[1407] Instead, the:

> third-party effect of an arbitral award suggested here [by Stavros L Brekoulakis] has a different scope from that of the res judicata effect, and therefore the two effects should be clearly distinguished. Res judicata mainly covers the claims or cause of action adjudicated in previous arbitration proceedings. [...] By contrast, the suggested third-party effect is limited only to a limited number of relevant issues. [...] It follows that the suggested third-party effect does not actually bind the third party on the award. It is rather an adverse effect or prejudice vis-à-vis third parties.[1408]

---

different interests [...].'). Whilst the said reference concerns res judicata of judgments, the standard equally applies to arbitral awards, *see* [6.210].

1400. *Ibid.*, [6.213].
1401. Established in Brekoulakis, (2005) 16 Am. Rev. Int'l Arb. 199 et seqq., extended in Brekoulakis, *Third Parties in Arbitration* [9.01-10.70].
1402. Brekoulakis, *Third Parties in Arbitration* [11.38] ('Admittedly, this suggestion may be difficult to apply in practice, particularly by national courts, which are normally bound by the conflict of laws rules of the lex fori [...]. However, it should be less problematic for arbitral tribunals [...].').
1403. *Ibid.*, [9.12-9.14].
1404. *Ibid.*, [9.15].
1405. *Ibid.*, [9.19].
1406. *Ibid.*, [9.20-9.25].
1407. *See supra* [6-7].
1408. Brekoulakis, *Third Parties in Arbitration* [10.31, 10.32, 10.36].

520. In granting such 'third-party effects', tribunals enjoyed discretion and should consider (i) the legal and factual overlap of two arbitrations, (ii) whether the prior third party was invited to join the prior arbitration and (iii) whether the prior third party is a victim of collusion between the former parties.[1409] Whilst the author acknowledges that res judicata's same-parties requirement is often associated with due process, the second criteria guaranteed the third party's opportunity to be heard in the prior arbitration.[1410] Finally, when a third party seeks to rely on an arbitral award in its favour and the opponent thus '*had a full day in court*', due process is not at stake, hence the 'third-party effect' was even more preferable.[1411]

521. Whilst the proposal has been expressly rejected by other scholars examining res judicata,[1412] it is this examination's contention that, before any conclusion could be drawn, three core ideas of that treatise should be differentiated. *First*, the proposal has a preference for non-mutual preclusion in the sense of common law's (judgment) principles. *Second*, detrimental third-party effects should be '*in particular*'[1413] admitted when the third party had been invited to join the arbitration. Such proposal is less revolutionary in terms of res judicata. Instead, it is an effective implementation of the tool of third-party notice as it is known in the USA (*vouching in*), and it is rejected elsewhere for jurisdictional reasons.[1414] The *third* proposal is the most significant: even in the absence of joinder invitations, a '*legal and factual overlap*' which '*will usually be the case when at least one of the parties in the first arbitration has a contractual relationship or otherwise a strong substantive nexus with one of the parties*'[1415] suffices to establish a 'third-party effect'. Explicit examples are guarantees, groups of companies, insurances and construction projects.

522. Until the examination will comment on these three ideas in its own specific proposals,[1416] an accessory aspect to the proposal needs to be highlighted. This aspect is intertwined with the proposed 'third-party effect' and softens potential considerations against it. The author not only supports broad effects of arbitral awards. He also supports broad *jurisdictional powers* of arbitral tribunals foregoing consensual constraints. In fact, the more extensive part of the treatise submits: instead of consensual standards, arbitral tribunals should apply jurisdictional standards fully equivalent to those of court adjudication.[1417] Particularly, the jurisdiction over third parties is

1409. *Ibid.*, [10.45-10.56].
1410. *Ibid.*, [10.60-10.70].
1411. *Ibid.*, [10.58-10.59].
1412. *Lühmann*, Die Rechtskraft des Schiedsspruchs 342-344; Schaffstein, *Res Judicata* [6.212].
1413. Brekoulakis, *Third Parties in Arbitration* [10.67].
1414. *See supra* [62].
1415. Brekoulakis, *Third Parties in Arbitration* [10.45].
1416. *See infra* [564-565, 575-578].
1417. Brekoulakis, *Third Parties in Arbitration* [7.43-7.45] ('If a valid arbitration exists between the two original parties, the tribunal 'comes into life' as a legitimate adjudicatory forum [...]. [A]ssuming that the dispute between the two parties in arbitration happens to involve a claim by or against a third party, the tribunal will need to determine whether the third-party claim is in effect part of the main dispute upon which the tribunal has exclusive jurisdiction. [...] If the tribunal finds that the rights and obligations of the parties are dependent and concomitant

regarded as ancillary to the substantive rights affected.[1418] In order to effectively realize such substantive rights, due process demanded such jurisdictional approach.[1419] With regard to the potential boundaries of court review, Article V(1)(a) NYC were only to apply to the undue *establishment* of jurisdiction and not to the *extension* of an already established jurisdiction.[1420] Finally, from a policy view, such standard would prevent multi-fora disputes and, to facilitate the terms of the instant examination, guarantee Forum Coordination.[1421] In any case, the proposal notes its own status *de lege ferenda*.[1422]

523. In conclusion, the existing submissions on a transnational operation of res judicata towards third parties are assessable. Two arbitral awards and arbitral scholars each mention that the same-parties requirement should be the outset, that certain third parties might be equated to third parties and that there might be factual effects (*opposabilité*). An additional opinion seeks to effectively forego the same-parties requirement and favours not only non-mutual preclusion but also detrimental preclusion towards third parties that are contractually connected to the formal parties. It would also confer broad jurisdictional powers upon arbitral tribunals.

§8.02 FEASIBILITY OF TRANSNATIONAL RES JUDICATA

524. This examination adopts the general perspective that any issue of res judicata before arbitral tribunals should be assessed under one particular legal source: the arbitral tribunal's obligation towards the parties *before it* to fully adjudicate upon their requests. Accordingly, it depends upon the parties' (reasonably presumed) intentions when establishing this obligation, whether restrictions to it by virtue of res judicata should be assessed under national or transnational law (*see* [A], *infra*). On the basis of this perception, the following passages will submit that the annulment review as it is, e.g., exercised by the Swiss Federal Tribunal has *no* persuasive inclination on arbitral tribunals (*see* [B], *infra*). This opens the door for a comprehensive assessment of practical considerations that in balance render a transnational approach towards res judicata by international arbitral tribunals feasible (*see* [C], *infra*), unless the case before the arbitral tribunal can be perceived as a national scenario (*see* [D], *infra*). The transnational principles should be developed by means of comparative law. By contrast, principles from public international law, particularly from international investment arbitration should not be applied in commercial arbitration (*see* [E], *infra*).

with the rights and obligations of the third party, and that the third party is effectively part of the main dispute, then the tribunal will have the power to hear the third-party claim.').

1418. *Ibid.*, [7.39].
1419. *Ibid.*, [8.08].
1420. *Ibid.*, [8.25-8.27]. (Such extension could exclusively violate Art. V (1) lit. *c* New York Convention. In this regard, the supervisory courts can supervise the degree to which the claims were interwoven.)
1421. *Ibid.*, [8.31-8.42].
1422. Cf. *ibid.*, [7.71] ('Of course, courts and tribunals still remain under the influence of the prevailing contractual approach and the non-signatory theories.'). *See also* the modified proposal in Brekoulakis, (2017) 8 J. Int'l Disp Settlement 620 ('dispute-based test').

[A] Res Judicata as a Restriction of an Arbitral Tribunal's Obligation to Adjudicate

525. The very cornerstone of this examination's understanding of res judicata before arbitral tribunals is that it concerns but one legal regime: the arbitral tribunal's obligation towards the parties to adjudicate the requests.[1423] In general, arbitrators differ from court judges. Whereas courts render justice in public service, arbitrators operate in private service. In other words, whereas court judges are bound to the public, arbitrators are bound to the parties. Therefore, any decision by an arbitral tribunal has to conform to the parties' agreement. Moreover, the *law applied by* an arbitral tribunal has to conform to the parties' agreement. As a manifestation, arbitral rules[1424] and arbitration laws[1425] generally stipulate that the arbitral tribunal shall apply the (rules of) law agreed by the parties and, subsidiarily, the law it deems appropriate or has the closest connection. In addition, most arbitral rules explicitly stipulate that an interpretation of the contract has priority. This allows the application of soft law, transnational principles, or the contract as the exclusive source, unless significant concerns of procedural justice and public policy demand to apply a certain national law.[1426] This framework allows a three-fold inference for the application of res judicata by arbitral tribunals. *First*, since arbitral tribunals are in general obligated to decide requests and res judicata restricts this cognition duty, res judicata should only be applied when it is in conformity with the parties' intention. *Second*, since arbitral tribunals are in general obligated to primarily apply the parties' agreement to a dispute, res judicata constitutes a deviation, since the tribunal applies a different norm, i.e., the prior decision. Therefore, res judicata should only be applied when it is in conformity with the parties' agreement. *Third*, against the framework for generally determining the applicable law, arbitral tribunals should decide res judicata primarily pursuant to the parties' choice of law. Since explicit choices of the law applicable to res judicata will scarcely occur, the primary task is to assess whether any traditional choice (i.e., of the law of the substance and the arbitral seat) has any inclination for the law applicable to res judicata. If this is not the case, arbitral tribunals should apply the law that has the closest connection or is the most appropriate as per the parties' intentions.

[B] Limited Impact of Court Supervision at the Arbitral Seat

526. Even though arbitral tribunals are primarily obligated towards the parties, the parties' interest in an effective arbitral award inclines tribunals to assess whether their

1423. Mayer, in *Liber Amicorum Reymond* 189. *Corresp* Schaffstein, *Res Judicata* [5.74].

1424. Article 36(1) HKIAC Rules; Art. 21(1) ICC Rules; Art. 31(1) ICDR Rules; Art. 22(3) LCIA Rules; Art. 27(1) SCC Rules Art. 31(1) SIAC Rules; Art. 33(1) Swiss Rules; Art. 35 (1) UNCITRAL Rules; Art. 61(1) WIPO Rules.

1425. Article 46(1) English Arbitration Act; Art. 1511 French CPC; Art. 187(1) Swiss PILA; Art. 28 UNCITRAL Model Law.

1426. Mayer, (2013) Rev. Arb. 339 [4-9]; Mayer, (1989) 217 Rec. des cours 393-405.

decision would be upheld by a set-aside court.[1427] Such set-aside review of res judicata decisions could incline arbitral tribunals to apply national laws to res judicata. For instance, the distinguished arbitrators in an ICC case interpreted the Federal Tribunal's jurisprudence in inferring that:

> it is settled law by now that an arbitral tribunal sitting in an international arbitration in Switzerland must apply the same rules as would a Swiss court in matter of res judicata.[1428]

527. As to scholarship, even proponents of transnational res judicata express a certain awareness of potential tensions with court supervision. The ILA did not submit its transnational proposal in rebutting incentives set by a potential set-aside review. Instead, the ILA Report also submits that courts should not apply public policy.[1429] Another transnational proponent expresses that:

> to protect the efficacy of their award, arbitral tribunals should take account of the law of the arbitral seat. Ignoring this law may prove imprudent in practice as it may lead to the setting aside of the award.[1430]

528. It is submitted that arbitral tribunals should certainly not ignore the law of the arbitral seat. Effectively, however, the supervision of set-aside courts at the arbitral seat will regularly *not* be any obstacle towards the application of transnational principles. Instead, set aside and recognition exclusively demands *specific results*. An arbitrator does not necessarily have to apply *national* law in order to reach a certain result that will prevail in set aside or recognition proceedings. It can also achieve such results by means of transnational law.[1431] As to the results reached, they will only under very limited circumstances be dismissed by supervisory courts.

529. Foremost, many arbitral seats will only annul an arbitral award when the arbitrators have entirely ignored the issue of res judicata or rendered an arbitral award that is irreconcilable with a prior decision.[1432] In this regard, it has been shown that irreconcilability is primarily a vehicle to implement res judicata's outset, i.e., the preclusion of duplicative claims. Such review will be no obstacle to transnational principles on res judicata's consequences, since *no* submission states that arbitrator should entirely disregard res judicata and permit duplicative claims. Even if an arbitral seat regards res judicata as part of public policy such as Switzerland, the implications are limited. Notably, a non-application will only be assumed when both, the prior

1427. Mayer, (2013) Rev. Arb. 339 [15-18]. Cf. Mayer, (1989) 217 Rec. des cours 407.
1428. ICC Case, No. not indicated, 2 April 2002, (2003) 21 ASA Bull. 810, [16] (Wirth P, Kellerhals, Kaufmann-Kohler) ('it is settled law by now that an arbitral tribunal sitting in an international arbitration in Switzerland must apply the same rules as would a Swiss court in matter of res judicata.').
1429. *ILA Final Report on Res Judicata* [69].
1430. Schaffstein, *Res Judicata* [6.15].
1431. Mayer, (1989) 217 Rec. des cours 407.
1432. *See supra* [150-154].

decision's forum and Switzerland would acknowledge res judicata.[1433] This excludes issue preclusion. Instead, it reduces the non-application of res judicata to scenarios (i) where the identical claim is raised (ii) or the prior decision's cause of action had arisen as an incidental issue in the subsequent arbitration and the tribunal rejected a conclusive effect of the prior decision. The latter aspect is thus the exclusive surplus of the Swiss jurisprudence on public policy compared to irreconcilability. Yet again, there is no transnational submission that arbitral tribunals should disregard a prior adjudication on a claim when it arises incidentally in subsequent arbitration.

530. Instead, the issues at the heart of the discussion are whether a transnational concept of res judicata can be facilitated to implement broader notions on res judicata's operative (issue preclusion, abuse of process) and subjective (privy doctrine, *opposabilité*) scope. In this regard, there is no appellate authority that Swiss law would prohibit such *over-application* of res judicata under public-policy rationales. Moreover, there is no binding authority that due process could be invoked as a set-aside ground against extended applications of res judicata outside of Germany.[1434] Hence, arbitral tribunals could only estimate the supervision at the arbitral seat. Even if the arbitral seat's courts were likely to annul an arbitral award facilitating extensive res judicata doctrines, the parties might still seek to have the annulled award recognized abroad, potentially because Article V(1)(e) NYC should not apply, since a set aside for an over-application of res judicata might merely be understood as a 'Local Standard Annulment'.[1435]

531. A final aspect worth considering is that in many arbitration settings, the specific supervision of res judicata by the arbitral seat's courts might be uncertain, because (i) the very extent of such supervision is debated (e.g., in Switzerland on res judicata's over-application), (ii) the applicable law is debated (e.g., in Germany[1436]) and (iii) even under the applicable law, the content of this very law is debated (e.g., on abuse of process at common law[1437] or third-party effects, particularly in France and the USA[1438]). Therefore, it might be unfeasible to adopt the approach that courts at the arbitral seat would adopt towards res judicata. In conclusion, the fact that some arbitral seats have annulled arbitral awards for violation of res judicata should not have any determinative force against the general application of transnational principles of res judicata.

1433. *See supra* [373].
1434. *See supra* [489-491].
1435. *See infra* [609].
1436. *See supra* [372].
1437. *See supra* [127].
1438. *See supra* [238, 244, 262].

[C] The Case for Transnational Principles Established Through Comparative Law

532. Assuming that an arbitral award rendered by a tribunal seated in country A is invoked before another arbitral tribunal seated in country B (*see* [525], *supra*), it is this examination's contention that the decision between a conflictualist and a transnational approach towards res judicata should be an assessment of the general intentions of the parties to the arbitration in country B. In this regard, the examination submits that an assessment of the parties' choice of law, their reasonable expectations, foreseeability, legal theory and, most importantly, practical feasibility incline to regard the application of transnational standards as a feasible option for tribunals. Whilst the examination commences with the feasibility for res judicata *of* prior arbitral awards *before* other arbitral tribunals, most of the arguments apply correspondingly when a prior judgment is invoked.

533. At the outset, arbitration parties regularly do decide on the applicable law and the arbitral seat. In this regard, empirical surveys show that parties carefully select these laws.[1439] Hence, these decisions might incline a tribunal to apply such law to res judicata. However, none of these choices comprises a demanding inclination with regard to res judicata. A substantive choice of law would exclusively be relevant if res judicata were to be characterized as a substantive mechanism, which is largely rejected.[1440] Choices of procedural law appear less frequently in practice and arbitral rules contain generally no statements as to res judicata.[1441] Hence, it can only be the choice of the arbitral seat that might be decisive. Particularly, one might argue that parties carefully select arbitral seats with regard to their supervision and protection of arbitration proceedings. Thus, one might argue that this very arbitral seat of the subsequent arbitration should also decide how to determine the lex res judicata. However, the counterargument against a binding force of the arbitral seat comprises a certain connotation against territorialist perceptions of arbitration. Since the arbitral tribunal deciding on res judicata were no part of the seat's judiciary, the idea of the *lex fori* would be flawed.[1442] More practically, one might oppose any obligation of the tribunal to apply 'its' *lex fori* in that an arbitral tribunal does not have 'one' *lex fori*, but instead might apply a certain law on the arbitration agreement, another on the arbitral procedure and those might differ from the arbitral seat.[1443] Amongst them, one might even go as far as stating the parties did not have *any* expectation as to a certain national law on arbitral res judicata, since these national laws have not been tailored for arbitration, let alone *international* arbitration. Whilst, in general, there is ample

1439. *2010 Queen Mary Arbitration Survey* 7. *See* on choice of law in sales contracts in general Meira Moser, (2017) 8 J. Int'l Disp Settlement 250 et seqq.
1440. *See supra* [369, 418].
1441. *See supra* [11].
1442. Radicadi di Brozolo, in *ASA Special Series* 10.
1443. Mayer, in *Liber Amicorum Reymond* 188.

authority that the consequences of arbitral res judicata equal judgments' res judicata,[1444] the application towards third parties receives genuine perceptions.[1445] However, one can still argue that parties particularly chose arbitration to leave national fora. Thus, they might have no intention to subject themselves to the preclusion rules of an arbitral seat.[1446] Therefore, the choice of law undertaken by the parties to the subsequent arbitration indicates no particular law to be applicable to res judicata.

534. Turning from the previous to the former arbitral seat, it has already been established that there is no comprehensive justification, neither from a doctrinal nor a practical perspective, to apply the law of the former tribunal's seat to res judicata.[1447] This applies *a fortiori* before arbitral tribunals, which are not obligated towards the public, but only towards the subsequent parties (*see* [525], *supra*). Since these parties might differ from the previous, the seat's law should be indecisive. In particular, although it might be considered efficient that every subsequent tribunal applies the law of the former arbitral seat to res judicata, efficiency considerations by arbitrators risk to contravene the fact that the arbitrators are primarily obligated to provide nobody but the parties with justice.[1448]

535. The argument most comprehensively raised in favour of transnationality yet again facilitates the parties' expectations and builds upon foreseeability: the content of national laws on res judicata were too uncertain, both in terms of private international law and in terms of the substance.[1449] Hence, transnational law were more foreseeable than conflict of laws, more consistent between tribunals and more familiar to the parties.[1450] Admittedly, the current status quo of transnational res judicata's specific content is far from being well defined.[1451] Foremost, the ILA's proposal does not address specific issues such as third-party effects, finality, it takes no '*position regarding claim preclusion in relation to claims related to the same transaction or connected transactions*'[1452] and it generally excludes the issue of res judicata of prior judgments.[1453] In addition, evolving transnational principles through a 'common law' of arbitral jurisprudence are practically almost impossible, since most awards remain *un*published. Yet, the evolving discussion on transnational res judicata evidenced by

1444. *See supra* [118-128].
1445. *See supra* [276].
1446. Bermann, (2015) 381 Rec. des cours [533].
1447. *See supra* [377-383].
1448. *See* Mayer, (2013) Rev. Arb. 339 [19]. *See* on efficiency considerations by arbitrators in general Harney, (2012) Rev. Arb. 757.
1449. *ILA Final Report on Res Judicata* [27]; Debourg, *Les contrariétés de décisions* [506]; Mayer, in *Liber Amicorum Reymond* 188; Radicati di Brozolo, in *ASA Special Series* 4-5; Schaffstein, *Res Judicata* [5.23]. Cf. Bermann, (2015) 381 Rec. des cours [532, 537].
1450. Cf. *Born* 3742-43; Brekoulakis, *Third Parties in Arbitration* [11.29]; Hascher, in *Travaux du comité français DIP* 25; Mayer, in in *Liber Amicorum Reymond* 190 et seqq.; Jarrosson, (2007) 8-9 Procédures No. 12 [B.1.a], Radicati di Brozolo, in *ASA Special Series* 143 et seqq.; Schaffstein, *Res Judicata* [5.33]; Stier, (2004) 15 Am. Rev. Int'l Arb. 325.
1451. *See supra* [506].
1452. *ILA Final Report on Res Judicata* [55].
1453. Although tailored for arbitral awards, *see* on res judicata of judgments in arbitration *ILA Final Report on Res Judicata* [11] ('arbitrators may [...] take the Recommendations into consideration').

the increasing submissions might rectify the uncertainty. Moreover, one might rectify uncertainty in that a transnational method of res judicata goes beyond pure arbitral discretion or acts of *amiable compositeurs*. Instead, transnational res judicata facilitates a *comparative* method.[1454]

536. Moreover, a practical interest is to have res judicata treated simultaneously before courts and before arbitral tribunals. Vice versa, a proponent of transnational res judicata indicates the preferability of transnational standards before courts, because:

> Ideally the effects [...] of an international arbitral award should remain the same, regardless of whether they are considered by a State court or by another arbitral tribunal.[1455]

537. However, *de lege lata*, comprehensive standards under the NYC do not exist. Therefore, courts will regularly apply their *lex fori* to arbitral res judicata.[1456] Yet, this does not imply the application of national law before arbitral tribunals. Instead, this necessitates that the effects of res judicata will always differ before different fora. This flaws the idea of an award to be always treated the same.

538. Another practical aspect in favour of transnationality is that, in general, uniformity is perceived as one of arbitration's major advantages over litigation.[1457] In this regard, applying dissimilar res judicata rules from national procedural laws might create '*questionable outcomes when dealing with arbitration and with its effects, that should ideally always be assessed in the same way*'.[1458] Moreover, uniformity through soft laws is closely related to avoiding complexity. Particularly, there is a certain scholarly reluctance to over-formalize arbitration, because complexity equates arbitration with litigation and parties wanted to precisely escape litigation.[1459] This favours transnational principles of res judicata in that they provide a uniform core, yet allow tribunals to seek fair results for individual cases.[1460]

539. A final practical aspect of particular importance to this examination is the intrinsic interaction of res judicata - as sequential Forum Coordination - with other proceduals tools such as declarative requests, joinder and consolidation, which are *pre-emptive* Forum Coordination.[1461] National standards of res judicata presuppose that all these aspects were governed by the very same law. However, in an international setting, this will not be the case. Particularly, the law of the arbitration agreement and the law of the procedure might differ, or the arbitral rules might contain

1454. *See supra* [481-486].
1455. Radicati di Brozolo, in *ASA Special Series* 8.
1456. *See supra* [371-391].
1457. Cf. Bermann, (2015) 381 Rec. des cours [42].
1458. Radicati di Brozolo, in *ASA Special Series* 6.
1459. *See*, e.g., Fouchard, *L'arbitrage Commercial International* [258]; Lalive, (1994) 1-2 Rev. Suisse DIE 13 ('*processualisation*'); Oppetit, (1994) Clunet 818 ('*juridictionnalisation*'). Cf. Kaufmann-Kohler, (2010) 1 J. Int'l Disp Settlement 1.
1460. Radicati di Brozolo, in *ASA Special Series 38* 18; Schaffstein, *Res Judicata* [5.07-5.08]. Cf. Park, (2003) 19 Arb. Int'l 281.
1461. Noted by Zaugg, (2017) ASA Bull. 330.

specific rules. Therefore, the determination of *one* legal order governing res judicata in international case scenarios is exposed to the inherent risk of disruptions. It is for this reason that the instant examination has, e.g., submitted that the *lex fori* refer to certain aspects that are governed by foreign laws.[1462] Outside of courts, arbitral tribunals should facilitate their liberty in establishing transnational standards that adhere to the previous, often transnational, procedure or comprises the discretion to adhere to national procedural tools. Therefore, the flexible interaction with procedural tools, significant concerns of the parties' expectations as well as the legal nature of international arbitral tribunals render it feasible to apply transnational law on the topic of res judicata before arbitral tribunals.

540. The rationales in favour of a transnational assessment of res judicata equally apply when the prior decision is not an arbitral award, but a judgment rendered outside of the arbitral seat. In particular, since the decisive perspective has to focus on the general *intentions of the parties to the subsequent arbitration*, they remain largely untouched. The subsequent arbitral seat remains to have an indecisive claim on regulating res judicata. More importantly, considerations of foreseeability and flexibility apply correspondingly. A differentiated assessment is required with regard to the role of the prior forum. In particular, courts *do* originate from a legal order establishing certain res judicata rules. More practically, the prior forum also regulated the interaction of res judicata and intervention possibilities. However, the overriding practical concern *against* applying the law of the prior forum is that this approach is by no means prevailing amongst foreign-judgment principles. Instead, common-law jurisdictions and a significant opinion in France prefer the *lex fori*. Moreover, even Germanic jurisdictions restrict the extension of foreign decisions' effects.[1463] Against this background, there appears no reason why arbitral parties would expose themselves more comprehensively to the prior judgment's law before tribunals than they would before courts. Therefore, it is also feasible to assess prior judgments' res judicata by virtue of transnational principles.

[D] The Threshold Between National and Transnational Case Scenarios

541. Undoubtedly, the parties' intention as well as the legal authority of arbitrators to apply transnational standards would not apply in purely national settings. When an arbitral tribunal seated in London in a dispute between two Englishmen has to assess res judicata with regard to a prior judgment of the Commercial Court, it will most likely be English law that governs the question of res judicata but for any contrary agreement of the parties. Yet, the litmus test is where to draw the line between such scenarios and *inter*national scenarios. In particular, from a normative element, the establishment of transnational principles for res judicata will be largely thwarted if national laws will

1462. *See supra* [412-414].
1463. *See supra* [371-373].

prevail as soon as more than one element of an individual case is located within one jurisdiction. As to drawing the line, two case scenarios demand particular elaboration.

542. Primarily, it might be worth discussing whether a joint origin of the parties to the arbitration justifies to apply their residual law or at least to adjust the transnational standards. For instance, when two parties from country A conducted a first arbitration in England and a second arbitration in France, the tribunal might be inclined to inquire whether the res judicata rules of country A would not be more appropriate than transnational standards. Yet, several concerns oppose such general priority of the parties' common background. At the outset, the parties deliberately decided in favour of international arbitration despite their common background. From a practical perspective, motives might be the relevance of foreign law for the contract or the relationship of the transaction at hand with other international transactions. Hence, the mere common background does not pre-empt the interest in international solutions. Moreover, the parties' background has no relationship to prior intervention possibilities. Albeit it might remain necessary to adhere to individual cases and individual parties' expectations. There should thus be a high threshold against undermining transnational principles for the parties' common origin.

543. The second, more delicate case scenario is that the arbitral tribunal deciding on res judicata has its arbitral seat in the very jurisdiction where the prior judgment was rendered or the prior arbitral tribunal had its seat. Particularly, Pierre Mayer, who generally favours transnational res judicata, submits that it should *not* apply, if the prior and the subsequent tribunal have an identical arbitral seat.[1464] *A fortiori*, one can infer that an arbitral tribunal should assess res judicata of a prior judgment rendered at the arbitral seat under the seat's law. However, this solution bears the consequence that follow-up disputes at the same arbitral seat might be decided differently than follow-up disputes at other arbitral seats. Therefore, it is difficult to assume a *general* intention of arbitration parties to have national law applied. Moreover, the concerns of flexibility and foreseeability as to the *content* of res judicata and *against* exceptions to a transnational regime (*see* [532-540], *supra*) apply correspondingly. However, it might conform to the intention of the *particular* parties to have a dispute decided under the law of the arbitral seat, when there are no such parallel follow-up disputes. Coming from the parties' intention, one might facilitate the circumstances that the parties' continuously selected some forum for their disputes. The decision will be a matter of individual cases. Yet, it is submitted that arbitral tribunal should yet again set a high threshold against the invalidation of transnational principles.

544. In any case, the idea that the parties expressed their intention through the continuous application of the arbitral seat's law is flawed when the prior and the subsequent dispute comprises distinct parties. Here, the issue is more straightforward: do the parties to an international arbitration expect a prior arbitral award's third-party effect to be assessed under transnational standards when it originates from another arbitral seat and under the arbitral seat's law when it originates from the latter? In this

1464. Mayer, (2016) Rev. Arb. 104.

regard, it is submitted that the intrinsic intention of parties to have third-party effects assessed simultaneously opposes this consideration. Therefore, the law of the arbitral seat might prevail in bilateral situations, yet not regarding third-party effects. Hence, to return to the example, when an arbitral tribunal seated in London has to assess the third-party effect of a prior judgment of the Commercial Court, it might still apply transnational standards, if the arbitration is otherwise international, e.g., regarding the parties and/or the contract.

[E] Privity as an Obstacle to the Application of *Investment* Arbitration Principles

545. Recently, one of the proponents of the movement towards transnational res judicata has taken the argument one step further. Upon acknowledging the recent lack of specific proposals on res judicata's application, Nathan Yaffe submitted:

> [T]ribunals could look to [...] ICSID and ICJ case law on res judicata, to develop a sui generis transnational preclusion standard for international arbitration.[1465]

546. In terms of the consequences of such transmissions, the author provides the example of the *Apotex* award on the application of res judicata towards privies in interest.[1466] In fact, the operation of res judicata's operation beyond the same-parties requirement has triggered significant discussions in international investment arbitration. Upon its outline, this examination will address its lack of transferability to international *commercial* arbitration.

547. International investment law has to deal with the immanent problem that legally distinct, yet commercially related investors repetitively sue a certain host State for the very same alleged fact pattern, potentially under different BITs or multilateral treaties. The situation becomes even more delicate, since shareholders are in themselves regularly regarded as investors under BITs.[1467] For avoiding multiple proceedings,

1465. Yaffe, (2017) 34 J. Int'L Arb. 795.

1466. *Ibid.*, 826-829. *Apotex Holdings Inv v. United States of America*, ICSID Case ARB/(AF)/12/1, Award, 2014, (Veeder P, Crook and Rowley).

1467. *See SCC* Case 24/2007, *Renta 4 SVSA et al. v. Russian Federation*, Decision on Preliminary Measures, 20 March 2009, [142]; *M Total SA v. Argentine Republic*, ICSID Case ARB/04/01, Decision on Liability, 27 December 2010, [198] (Sacerdoti P, Alvarez and Marcano); *Suezz, Sociedad General de Aguas de Barcelona SA et al. v. Republic of Arguentina*, ICSID Case ARB/03/17, Jurisdictional Decision, 16 May 2006, [51] (Salacuse P, Kaufmann-Kohler and Nikken); *Pan Mexican Energy LLC and BP Argentina Exploration Company v. Argentine Republic*, ICSID Cases ARB/03/13 and ARB/04/8, Preliminary Decision, 27 July 2006, [219] (Caflisch P, Stern and van den Berg); *Sempra Energy International v. Argentine Republic*, ICSID Case ARB/02/16, Jurisdictional Decision, 11 May 2005, [91] (Orrega Vicuna P, Lalonde and Morelli Rico); *Wena Hotels Ltd v. Arab Republic of Egypt*, ICSID Case ARB/98/4, Award, 8 December 2000, (2002) 41 ILM 896, [197] (Leigh P, Fadlallah and Wallace Jr); Wu, (2010) 6 Asian Int'l Arb. J. 134.

strict triple-identity tests - particularly with regard to party identity - render lis pendens and res judicata ineffective.[1468]

548. Such problem is often associated with the *CME/Lauder* case history, described by one author as the '*ultimate fiasco in investment arbitration*'.[1469] In this case, an investor and its main shareholder sued the host State Czech Republic on the very same facts and alleged violations of common BIT standards, albeit in distinct UNCITRAL proceedings under distinct BITs.[1470] In the end - notably after the Czech Republic refused to have the two cases consolidated - one tribunal rejected the majority of the claims,[1471] whilst the other affirmed them[1472] and awarded almost USD 270 million in damages.[1473] The Svea Court of Appeal Stockholm rejected to annul the later award.[1474] To avoid such inconsistencies and the one-sided benefits for corporate investors, the arbitral tribunals in *Grnyberg v. Grenada* as well as *Apotex v. USA* held that prior arbitral awards rendered against investor companies were preclusive towards the companies' controlling shareholders.[1475] Whilst many scholars labelled the resulting principle as a privy doctrine for res judicata in investment arbitration,[1476] another stream in scholarship reaches the same result through an international doctrine of abuse of process.[1477] As more recent jurisprudence highlights, however, generalizations might be hazardous. Instead, any preclusion will heavily depend upon a situation's fact pattern. The tribunal in *Eskosol v. Italy* rejected any res judicata effect of an award rendered against Blusun, Eskosol's 80% subsidiary and also considered that Italy, as the respondent in both arbitrations, was reluctant to disclose the earlier award against Eskosol.[1478] The tribunal in *Orascom TMT v. Algeria*, by contrast, did

1468. Ben Hamida, in *Procédures parallèles et décisions contradictoires* 20-21 ('*paralyser le fonctionnement des mécanismes de res judicata et litispendance, encourageant ainsi la multiplication du contentieux*'); Mantilla-Serrano, in *Procédures parallèles et décisions contradictoires* 36.

1469. Reinisch, in *International Law between Universalism and Fragmentation* 116. Notably, the author acted as legal expert in the *CME* case.

1470. Certainly, it is noteworthy that it was the responding Czech Republic who opposed any means of consolidation and insisted on Lauder discontinuing one of proceedings.

1471. *Lauder v. Czech Republic*, UNCITRAL, Award, 3 September 2001 (Briner P, Cutler and Klein).

1472. *CME Czech Republic BV v. Czech Republic*, UNCITRAL, Partial Award, 13 September 2001 (Kühn P, Schwebel and Hándl), [624].

1473. *CME Czech Republic BV v. Czech Republic*, UNCITRAL, Final Award, 14 March 2003 (Kühn P, Schwebel and Brownlie) [650].

1474. Svea Court of Appeal, *Czech Republic v. CME*, 15 May 2003, T 8735-01, (2003) 42 ILM 919, 966.

1475. *Grynberg v. Grenada*, ICSID Case ARB/10/6, Award, 2010, (Rowley P, Nottingham and Tercier); *Apotex Holdings Inv v. United States of America*, ICSID Case ARB/(AF)/12/1, Award, 2014, (Veeder P, Crook and Rowley).

1476. Douglas, *The International Law of Investment Claims* [577]; McLachlan Shore and Weininger, *International Investment Arbitration* [4.189-90]; Rubins, [2003] Stockholm Arb. Rep. 210; *CME Czech Republic BV v. Czech Republic*, UNCITRAL Case, Legal Opinion Prepared by Schreuer and Reinisch, 20 June 2002, [37].

1477. Wehland, *Multiple Proceedings in Investment Treaty Arbitration* [7.44-7.51]. *See* generally on abuse of process in investment arbitration Gaillard, (2017) 32 ICSID Rev. 27-36.

1478. *Eskosol S.p.A. in liquidazione v. Italian Republic*, ICSID Case ARB/15/50, Decision on Respondent's Application under Rule 41(5), 20 March 2017 (Kalicki P, Santiago Tawil and Stern), paras 168-169 ('For its part, Italy claims reluctance to share the *Blusun* award with Eskosol, on the grounds that so doing might be considered a breach of its confidentiality obligations to the *Blusun* claimants. At the very least, this suggests Italy has some doubts that Eskosol and Blusun must properly be considered the same party. In these circumstances,

conclude that a previously initiated – and settled – arbitration by a related company rendered the claim inadmissible. Yet, it specifically emphasized that this was '*the result of the peculiar facts of the case*'[1479] and observed accordingly for the outcome of *CME/Lauder*.[1480]

549. Irrespective of the doctrinal label and the requirements of any third-party effect of investment awards, this examination submits that international investment jurisprudence precluding shareholders from repetitive claims can*not* be facilitated for the determination of prior awards' third-party effects in international *commercial* arbitration. In general, the two worlds of international arbitration regularly comprise distinct legal bases (private arbitration clauses in contracts/beneficial arbitration provisions in treaties), subject matters (contract law/public international law) and causes for multiple proceedings (limited jurisdiction/plurality of competent fora).[1481] In short: whereas privity is the very cornerstone of international commercial arbitration, investment proceedings are '*arbitration without privity*'.[1482] Corresponding differences have already been facilitated to explain why investment tribunals facilitate precedence as persuasive authorities whilst commercial arbitral tribunals are more averse.[1483] For awards' third-party effect, in particular, this conceptual divide necessitates significant obstacles for transferring investment precedence to commercial arbitration.

550. Foremost, the said investment jurisprudence is not transferrable to commercial arbitration because of the grave differences in terms of jurisdiction. *De lege lata*, arbitral tribunals cannot exercise jurisdiction over commercially related companies to the arbitration parties but for (implied) consent.[1484] By contrast, the very shareholders that were exposed to investment awards' preclusive effects could have relied on the BIT and thus jointly sued the defendant State. In fact, the wide preclusion is the very compensation for these broad jurisdictional benefits of investors:

> The tribunals in these cases [...] apply the doctrine of res judicata [...] to those persons who are in privity of interest with them [...] on the basis that since, in the context of investment arbitration, a shareholder is entitled to pursue a claim for

---

Tribunal would have difficulty concluding – and certainly cannot find it 'manifest' – that Blusun and Eskosol effectively were the same party [...].').

1479. *Orascom TMT Investments S.à r.l. v. People's Democratic Republic of Algeria*, ICSID Case ARB/12/35, Award, 31 May 2017 (Kaufmann-Kohler P, van den Berg and Stern), para. 546.

1480. *Ibid.*, para. 547 ('*CME v. Czech Republic* and *Lauder v. Czech Republic* [...] should be placed in the context of their procedural history, in which the respondent hat refused several offers to consolidate or otherwise coordinate proceedings.').

1481. *See* in general McLachlan Shore and Weininger, *International Investment Arbitration* [4.05, 4.12, 4.39]; Hobér, (2013) 366 Rec. des cours 112. *See ILA Final Report on Res Judicata* [17] ('The Committee understands that the ILA Committee on Law of Foreign Investment is studying res judicata of BIT awards.').

1482. Paulsson, (1995) 10 ICSID Rev. 232 (article title).

1483. *See* Kaufmann-Kohler, (2007) 23 Arb. Int'l 372 et seqq. *Accord ICC Case 7061*, unpublished, quoted by Hanotiau, *Complex Arbitrations* [253]. On FIDIC *see* Berger, (1992) 9(4) J. Int'l Arb. 20.

1484. *See supra* [40].

> investments that are indirectly held through a corporation, it must also be subject to defences that would be available against the corporation.[1485]

551. Hence, investment arbitration builds upon a nexus of jurisdictional potentials and preclusion realities. In commercial arbitration, such nexus is disrupted. Therefore, the investment rationales need to be strongly distinguished.

552. Even in the scenario that a third party to a commercial arbitration has generally consented to arbitration and could thus have joined the proceedings, significant differences to the investment jurisprudence remain. The latter concerned the situation that the alleged privy (i) had corporate control of the claimant, (ii) was effectively a co-obligee in that it could have jointly initiated an investment claim and (iii) both the actual claimant and the privy were third-party beneficiaries of the claims and the arbitration agreement. This coexistence of corporate relationship, contractual obligations and beneficial origin will one irregularly appear in commercial arbitration. Hence, the case scenarios can be severely distinguished on the facts. In consequence, investment jurisprudence is inapplicable to commercial arbitration.

Interim Conclusion

553. In conclusion, this examination submits that arbitral tribunals should primarily handle res judicata in conformity with the intentions of the parties before it. In the absence of specific intentions, considerations of practical feasibility allow an application of transnational principles. In particular, since set asides will exclusively review the *results* reached, and the results reached through transnational principles can conform to common set-aside standards, there is no persuasion to apply the arbitral seat's law. The thus admissible transnational principles before arbitral tribunals should be developed by means of comparative law in that the common ground of national arbitration law and, subsidiarily, procedural laws should be established. By contrast, jurisprudence applying public international law, in particular, international investment law is generally *not* transferrable to international commercial arbitration. The resulting transnational standards should only be substituted, if the case's national elements meet a high threshold.

§8.03 TRANSNATIONAL PRINCIPLES ON DECISIONS' THIRD-PARTY EFFECTS

554. In general, this examination considers the application of transnational principles on res judicata before international arbitral tribunals feasible. Given that any regime of transnational principles will be exclusively feasible if its content is sufficiently discussed,[1486] the following passages seek to contribute to the emerging specification of transnational principles on res judicata. In this regard, the examination has no

1485. McLachlan Shore and Weininger, *International Investment Arbitration* [4.193].
1486. *See supra* [530].

ambition to comprehensively take a standpoint vis-á-vis all operational aspects of res judicata. Instead, the focus of this examination is: *when and under which requirements can a prior decision be invoked as preclusive or conclusive by or against a party to an arbitration proceeding that was no formal party to the prior proceeding?* Certainly, the answer might not necessarily determine res judicata before arbitral awards, since the latter might additionally raise general operative issues, such as the admissibility of issue preclusion in indemnity settings. Yet, the thesis' constraints effectively require excluding such operative issues. Moreover, the separate analysis of the matter is doctrinally feasible, since the issue of res judicata's third-party dimension ('against whom?') will often involve the uncontroversial adjudication of the cause of action and, even if it does not, triggers rationales distinct to general operative issues ('what and under which requirements?').[1487]

555. Transnational res judicata principles can only be general in nature and should not be established *de novo*, but rather facilitate comparative law in that they seek a common, and potentially the best ground amongst national laws.[1488] Therefore, the following sections will be largely built upon the preceding Chapters' comparative observations. This indicates to adapt res judicata's same-parties requirement as a transnational principle (*see* [A], *infra*). The litmustest concerns its exceptions. In this regard, the heart of the proposal is to assess the exposure of privies to res judicata under a multi-tiered test adhering to preclusion agreements, due process, prior jurisdiction and irreconcilability concerns (*see* [B], *infra*). Moreover, it is submitted that non-mutual preclusion should be generally inapplicable (*see* [C], *infra*). Whilst these submissions have assessed an *extension* of res judicata, certain effects might be perceived as creating *erga omnes* (in rem, *Gestaltungswirkung*) or factual effects (*opposabilité*) under national laws. In this regard, a preliminary submission is that decisions rendered on a legal status should be respected by arbitral tribunals (*see* [D], *infra*). As to further factual effects before arbitral tribunals, the examination submits that they require a balancing of party autonomy, due process and irreconcilability (*see* [E], *infra*). Finally, the topic of awards' third-party effects raises an ancillary aspect: the preclusion *within* an arbitration towards parties that have been third parties at the arbitration's outset and become parties during the arbitration (*see* [F], *infra*). The resulting principles will be proclaimed at the outset of each section and collectively displayed at the end of this Chapter.

[A] Res Judicata's Same-Parties Requirement as a Transnational Principle

> In general, an arbitral tribunal should exclusively preclude any party's request or argument under referral to a judgment or arbitral award rendered in prior proceedings (res judicata), if all parties have also been parties therein or succeeded to a party thereto.

1487. *Surpa* [330].
1488. *See supra* [486].

556. It is submitted that any solution on third-party case scenarios should primarily interpret the reasonable expectations of the subsequent arbitrating parties.[1489] In this examination's view, the heart of such reasonable expectation is the common ground of national – procedural and arbitration – laws:[1490] generally, res judicata requires that the parties to the prior and the subsequent proceedings are the same. This outset is equally acknowledged amongst transnational proposals.[1491] Moreover, this common ground exists in order to safeguard a party's right to be heard which is necessary as any preclusion towards non-participants is a restriction of this very right.[1492] Since the right to be heard is universally acknowledged in arbitration laws,[1493] it might be deemed a transnational cornerstone of arbitration. Accordingly, for the parties' expectations raised by the national laws' convergence and for the due-process rationale, the same-parties requirement should be the outset of transnational principles on res judicata before arbitral tribunals.

557. Res judicata's same-parties requirement does not necessitate that claimant A in the prior proceedings also needs to be the claimant in the subsequent proceedings, and that B needs to be the respondent in both proceedings. Instead, the roles might be inverted. Moreover, the parties to the subsequent arbitration might only have been *some* of the parties to the prior proceedings.[1494] In other words, the test comes down to whether all parties participated in the prior proceedings. Finally, res judicata should apply towards parties succeeding to a party after the prior decision is rendered, since such rule is equally acknowledged amongst national laws.[1495]

[B] The Test for Preclusive and Conclusive Effects Against Privies

558. Taking the same-parties requirement as the outset might be rather uncontroversial. Instead, the source of controversies and thereby the very objective of this examination is to provide a framework on how to handle the exceptions to the same-parties requirement. In this regard, the examination proposes the following test on the facilitation of a prior decision as a ground for preclusive or conclusive effect in subsequent arbitrations towards a party that was a third party to the prior proceedings. If the test is met, such third party will be described as 'privy' even though this does not indicate any application of common law. The test is as follows:

(1) Can res judicata affect the prior third party because there is a preclusion agreement?

1489. *See supra* [520].
1490. *See supra* [174, 220].
1491. *See supra* [508-514].
1492. *See supra* [175].
1493. *See supra* [222].
1494. *See supra* [174, 220].
1495. *See supra* [199, 248]. *Accordingly ICC Case 13509*, Arbitral Award, (2008-2011) VI ICC Collection 739.

(2) If it does not, can res judicata be justified under comparative due-process principles?
(3) If comparative due-process principles justify a third-party effect, should res judicata be excluded, because res judicata is based on a prior arbitral award and the third party to the prior arbitration has *not* consented to the prior tribunal's jurisdiction?
(4) If either requirement opposes an extension of res judicata to the prior third party, can res judicata be justified for overriding interests such as the prevention of irreconcilabilities?

[1] Priority of Preclusion Agreements

> A party that was no party to the prior proceedings and did not succeed to a party thereto (prior third party) should only be exposed to or be able to rely on res judicata, if an agreement concluded between the parties stipulates accordingly; or [...]

559. The first step in assessing the admissibility of res judicata towards a party that was a third party to the prior dispute might be as uncontroversial as the same-parties requirement itself. Preclusion agreements concluded between the parties before the subsequent tribunal should enjoy preference. The uncontroversial nature of arbitral tribunals' referral to preclusion agreements might derive from the fact that preclusion agreements are largely unopposed before courts.[1496] Foremost, the Draft Third Restatement on International Commercial Arbitration expresses that the parties' intention could restrict the (before US courts generally wide) preclusion rules determined under the subsequent court's *lex fori*.[1497] Correspondingly, scholarly submissions that do address the matter imply that preclusion agreements are a primary source for the arbitral tribunal's decision.[1498]

560. To address the very reason why arbitral tribunals' referral to preclusion agreements is preferable: since arbitral tribunals are primarily obligated to conform to the arbitrating parties' agreements,[1499] preclusion agreements are a binding normative source. This applies particularly when the preclusion agreement has been concluded retrospectively, e.g., in terms of reference. This also applies to anticipated preclusion agreements, e.g., in the contract underlying the arbitral dispute. In the latter regard, for the arbitral tribunal faced with the issue of res judicata, the binding force of the parties' agreement does not depend on whether the preclusion agreement has been concluded between all parties of the former dispute (multilateral preclusion agreement) or

1496. *See supra* [229-233].
1497. *See supra* [287].
1498. Cf. Radicati di Brozolo, in *ASA Special Series* 22 ('considerable scope for the parties to address the matter in their arbitration agreements or in the terms of reference'); Schaffstein, *Res Judicata* [Principle 5, pre 6.247] ('Unless the parties agree otherwise [...]').
1499. *See supra* [520].

between the subsequent parties only (bilateral preclusion agreement). The latter case scenario might, e.g., arise, when a contractor and a sub-contractor agree that 'any judgment or award rendered between the contractor and the principal will be final and binding, also in disputes between the contractor and the sub-contractor' (*see* [352-362, 425-426], *supra*).

561. Whilst the referral to explicit preclusion agreements is thus highly inclined, difficulties for arbitral tribunals might arise if the preclusion agreement is less explicit and provides room for arguments. Potentially this might occur in two situations: *first*, tribunals might have to interpret an agreement when the extent of the preclusion is not expressly indicated. For instance, a clause might read 'any judgment or award rendered between the contractor and the principal has to be *respected* in disputes between the contractor and the sub-contractor'. *Second*, arbitral tribunals might have to interpret the very consent of the party exposed to extended preclusion when the source ('any *dispute* [...] has to be respected') or the participants ('any judgment or award rendered *in relation to the subject matter of this contract* will be final and binding also in disputes between the contractor and the sub-contractor') to the prior proceedings are not properly indicated unequivocally. In such situations, the sub-contractor might invoke that any unspecified renouncement of its right to be heard (effectively protected by res judicata's same-parties requirement) should be impermissible. With regard to such issues, this examination submits that arbitral tribunals will have to primarily interpret the true intent of the parties. Hence, they can take recourse to the technique applied to the most immanent and most frequent tasks of arbitral tribunals. In this regard, they can either facilitate national law, transnational standards, or - more practically - primarily adhere to the facts.[1500]

562. As a final remark, the examination notes that scholarship mentions confidentiality as a potential restriction for invoking an arbitral award before other tribunals.[1501] However, it is submitted that an agreement on confidentiality will *not* constitute any impediment on the potential for res judicata before other tribunals. (i) When the parties in the prior and the subsequent arbitration are the same, the disclosure of the prior arbitral award will not render it non-confidential. The parties participated in the prior proceedings. The arbitrators in the subsequent proceedings are the only additional persons to whom the award is disclosed. Yet, they can be equally obligated to keep this disclosure confidential. (ii) When only one party participated in the prior proceedings and its opponent in the subsequent proceedings was a third-party to the prior proceedings, the duty of confidentiality only covers the *prior*, not the *subsequent* proceedings. The subsequent parties have not concluded any confidentiality agreement with regard to the prior proceedings. The prior parties have. But this does not bind the *subsequent* tribunal. Instead, a disclosure of the arbitral award might merely

1500. *See supra* [520].
1501. Hascher, in *Travaux du comité français DIP* 39; Jarrosson, (2007) 8-9 *Procédures* No. 12 [B.1.b]; *Redfern and Hunter* [1.113]; Schaffstein, *Res Judicata* [5.89] ('Where the parties in the second arbitration are not the same as those in the first arbitration, the confidentiality of the first arbitration *could* make it impossible for the second tribunal to take the first arbitration into account, even though both arbitrations are closely interrelated.').

expose the disclosing party to claims from its prior opponent. (iii) Finally when the subsequent parties differ from the prior parties, yet did conclude a confidentiality agreement with regard to the prior dispute (e.g., in a multilateral arbitration agreement), confidentiality will be conformed as in scenario (i) in that the multilateral agreement will likely provide the prior third party with relevant information. In conclusion, confidentiality is no factor in determining the third-party extent of res judicata and explicit as well as implied preclusion agreement between the subsequent parties should be adhered to by the subsequent arbitral tribunal.

[2] *Due Process' High Threshold*

> A [...] prior third party should only be exposed to or be able to rely on res judicata, if [...] or considering the prior tribunal's jurisdiction as well as *the prior third party's legal relationship and effective actions*, the prior third party could and *should* have participated in the prior procedure *in order to exercise its right to be heard*; or [...]

563. Regularly, there will be no preclusion agreement between the parties. This brings arbitral tribunals to the default standard applied to res judicata's third-party scope. Under national laws, the exceptions to res judicata's same-parties requirement are perceived as restrictions of a prior third party's right to be heard.[1502] Effectively, this restriction necessitates that the prior third party had the burden to participate in the prior proceedings in order to exercise its defensive interests.[1503] Against this comparative background, an arbitral tribunal should apply the functional criteria revealed in comparative law, namely whether the prior third party's legal relationship or effective actions allow to regard its right to be heard as subordinate.[1504] Effectively, the assessment will often come down to case-by-case assessments, as they will be duly revisited.[1505] Yet, in general, due process necessitates a very high threshold.

564. It is the utmost contention of this examination that the threshold applies equally to claim preclusion and issue preclusion (if the latter effect is deemed admissible by a tribunal). Accordingly, the examination will *not* adopt the scholarly proposal pursuant to which a genuine 'third-party effect' of a prior arbitral award's reasonings could operate independently from and more leniently ('legal and factual overlap') than res judicata.[1506] This is for several reasons: *first, the distinction* between claim preclusion's and issue preclusion's personal scope severely contradicts the comparative background of res judicata. From a civil-law perspective, issue preclusion is already rejected. Even if issue preclusion were perceived as preferable by transnational perceptions,[1507] the expectations of parties from a civil-law background would be even

1502. *See supra* [175].
1503. *See supra* [211-212].
1504. *See supra* [213-214].
1505. *See infra* [590-598].
1506. Brekoulakis, *Third Parties in Arbitration, supra* [514].
1507. *See supra* [493-496].

more impeded if issue preclusion exceeded claim preclusion's *inter partes* operations. From a common-law perspective, the same-parties requirement equally applies to claim and issue preclusion.[1508] *Second, the result of* the distinction, i.e., to apply issue preclusion when there is a 'legal and factual overlap' is more lenient than *any* of the national laws examined. The parties' general expectation that serves as the normative justification for any transnational principle might not support a transnational rule, which exceeds any national law. In particular, the counter argument that arbitration parties had a particular interest in efficiency cannot override the inclination for due-process rationales. Instead, parties' interest to extend res judicata should require at least an implied agreement. By contrast, the general submission to arbitration should not be interpreted as a renouncement of fundamental procedural guarantees. *Third*, the proposal should be read in conjunction with its author's other proposal in favour of arbitral tribunals' non-consensual jurisdictional competences. In particular, only such jurisdiction renders it consistent to examine whether the third party has been invited to join. *De lege lata*, however, arbitral jurisdiction rests upon consent.[1509] Thus, third parties can legitimately reject to be joined.

565. *Fourth* and finally, the authorities provided by the proposal have each affirmed a (non-technically speaking) third-party effect, yet are highly divergent and have not applied a doctrine as broad as the one proposed:[1510] the French *Prodim* decision applied the doctrine of *opposabilité* in a scenario functionally comparable to issue preclusion. Yet, the decision has been heavily criticized and potentially reversed in *France Telecom*.[1511] More importantly, *opposabilité*'s outset is the obligation imposed on or a claim conferred to a party by prior decisions. To facilitate the doctrine in order to state that issue preclusion can be more leniently invoked than such obligation is the very inversion of the doctrine of *opposabilité*. The US decisions *Executim Risk Indem* and *Navimpex* affirmed the effects of vouching-in. However, such measure is not acknowledged under other arbitration laws and unknown to arbitral rules.[1512] In particular, in contrast to the proposal's additional argument, consent remains the very cornerstone of arbitral jurisdiction. Amongst English judgments, *The Sargasso* did not concern issue preclusion. Instead, the arbitral award had a factual effect in influencing damages calculations.[1513] To conclude, Mance LJ's *obiter* in *Sunlife Assurances* does not support, but indeed questions the entire applicability of litigation's privy principles in arbitration.[1514] Therefore, the proposal that an award's reasoning could create a genuine 'third-party effect' when there is legal or factual overlap is perceived as unpreferable. Yet, from a policy perspective, the examination supports the proposal's

1508. *See supra* [174, 220]. *See* Restatement (Second) Judgments, § 27 ('between the parties'); Restatement (Third) Int'l Comm Arb. (TD Draft No. 2), § 4-10 comment a ('another adjudicatory body has already decided that issue in an earlier adjudication between the same parties').
1509. *See supra* [40, 517].
1510. *See* Brekoulakis, *Third Parties in Arbitration* [10.13-10.30].
1511. *See supra* [238].
1512. *See supra* [62].
1513. *See supra* [435].
1514. *See supra* [270].

interaction of jurisdiction and preclusion. However, as long as arbitral jurisdiction depends on consent, it is up to the parties to explicitly provide for multiparty arbitration or preclusion agreements.

[3] No Third-Party Effect Without Third-Party Jurisdiction

> A [...] prior third party should only be exposed to or be able to rely on res judicata, if [...] or considerung *the prior tribunal's jurisdiction* as well as the prior third party's legal relationship and effective actions, the prior third party *could* and should have participated in the prior procedure in order to exercise its right to be heard; or [...]

566. With regard to the third-party effect of international arbitral awards *before courts*, the examination has previously submitted: under a doctrinally possible and practically preferable application of Article V(1)(a) NYC, a third party to a prior arbitration cannot be exposed to res judicata but for its consent to the underlying arbitration agreement.[1515] Such argument inclines to assess whether the submission applies before arbitral tribunals.

567. Initially, one might equate this issue to a pure issue of the NYC's application before arbitral tribunals. Certainly, the Convention itself only binds its signatories, i.e., States, thereby courts. Yet, whether the Convention has an indirect effect on the recognition before arbitral tribunals, has not been settled. Potentially, the limited jurisprudence stems from the fact, that arbitral tribunals cannot enforce prior arbitral awards. Thus, they will only 'recognize' them in the course of a res judicata decision. In this regard, there is authority to state that although tribunals are not *bound* to the NYC, they *can* refer to it.[1516]

568. When referring to the primarily relevant intention of the parties to the subsequent arbitration, the above-mentioned rationales in favour of the extended application of Article V(1)(a) NYC apply correspondingly before arbitral tribunals. Foremost, there is a reasonable interest of parties not to be exposed to an arbitral award that could not have been influenced for the lack of jurisdiction. Such lack of jurisdiction bars pre-emptive measures of Forum Coordination such as joinders, consolidation and lis pendens,[1517] and should therefore be adhered to for res judicata, which is *sequential* Forum Coordination. Moreover, but for a reconciliation of jurisdiction and res judicata, the latter's functional role as a *shift of the participatory burden*[1518] would be undermined. Therefore, it conforms to the parties' reasonable intention to subject res judicata to a jurisdictional boundary in third-party case scenarios.

1515. *See supra* [307-334].
1516. *See supra* [510].
1517. *Supra* Chapter 1.
1518. *Supra* Chapter 3.

569. As to the application of the jurisdictional boundary, the third party to the prior arbitration generally *did* consent to arbitration, since it is now a party to the subsequent arbitration. Yet, the prior tribunal could only have exercised jurisdiction over all relevant parties if the prior arbitration agreement and the arbitration agreement of the subsequent parties were compatible with regard to the seat, the arbitral rules and the applicable law.[1519] These constraints equally apply to consolidations.[1520] Therefore, the subsequent tribunal should not apply a third-party effect, if the prior and the instant arbitration agreement are incompatible.

570. Moreover, the examination submits that transnational principles of res judicata should acknowledge that any preclusion against third parties is originally conceptualized as a procedural *shift of the participatory* burden. Particularly, third parties exposed to a judgment's res judicata can regularly join or intervene in litigation.[1521] In arbitration, by contrast, some arbitral rules such as the ICC Rules do *not* allow third-party interventions, not even if the third party is bound by the underlying arbitration agreement.[1522] It is submitted that the availability of third-party intervention should constitute one aspect for the tribunal's discretionary assessment.

571. In addition, the submission in favour of a jurisdictional boundary of res judicata towards third parties raises the follow-up question whether such boundary should also be applied towards *judgments'* res judicata before subsequent arbitral tribunals. For instance, when an insured invokes a judgment rendered in favour of a creditor and claims indemnity from the insurer, the latter might invoke that it agreed on arbitration only and therefore could not have been joined to a litigation with the insured. Certainly, under Article II(3) NYC, an exclusive arbitration agreement prevents litigation between the parties to the agreement. However, there is limited authority that this derogative force also applies when one of the arbitral parties is joined to an otherwise on-going litigation with multiple parties before courts.[1523] Therefore, the third party will have often been able to exercise participatory opportunities. Hence, the jurisdictional restriction of res judicata is only applied for prior arbitral awards.

[4] Overriding Preclusion Consideration: The Non-sujet of Irreconcilability

> In addition, a [...] prior third party should only be exposed to or be able to rely on res judicata, if [...] or specific precedence necessitates such measure in order to prevent a set aside.

572. The exposure of all adjudications to the strict boundaries of third-party res judicata might create situations in which an arbitral tribunal would risk inconsistencies

1519. *See supra* [47-49].
1520. *See supra* [68-70].
1521. *Supra* [209-210].
1522. *See supra* [65].
1523. *See supra* [64].

with prior adjudications. Such inconsistencies might be sanctioned by supervisory courts. Hence, it will be necessary for arbitral tribunals to inquire whether a rejection of the preclusive effect *and* an eventual adjudicatory result opposing the prior adjudication will incline the competent court to annul the award. If this is the case, an arbitral tribunal has the discretion to apply res judicata. In general, the examination has submitted that this framework does regularly not pre-empt the application of transnational principles to a prior decision rendered between the same parties.[1524] The constraints established by set-aside reviews might differ with regard to decisions' third-party effects. In any case, the effect on tribunals should be limited.

573. An award could be set aside for disregard of res judicata in jurisdictions equating res judicata with procedural public policy such as Switzerlandand Germany whose laws comprise the strictest notions on decisions' third-party effects. It will be equally inapplicable, if eventual transnational principles are inapplicable, particularly in guarantee or sub-contractor scenarios. Moreover, Swiss law contains no submissions against the proposed jurisdictional restriction of awards' third-party effects, but in fact an *obiter* of the Federal Tribunal in its support.[1525]

574. In other jurisdictions, the main ground to annul the eventual arbitral award is irreconcilability.[1526] However, the topic of irreconcilability in international arbitration remains a particular *non-sujet* with regard to its application in multiparty case scenarios. Since, in general, irreconcilability can be regarded as accessory to res judicata's outset, there is a certain inclination that res judicata's personal boundaries also determine irreconcilability's personal boundaries, unless it is *physically* impossible to enforce two decisions. Yet, it is not impossible that irreconcilability is a broader notion that might exist between two decisions with different parties even though the first decision's res judicata would not extend to the third party thereto. In any case, there are no specific authorities that annulled an arbitral award for irreconcilability with earlier decisions rendered between different parties.[1527] Therefore, any anticipation of the set-aside review on grounds of irreconcilability will often amount to a speculation of the solutions preferred by courts. In this regard, it is submitted that an arbitral tribunal should only forego the aforementioned boundaries established in order to safeguard its adjudicatory mandate, party autonomy and due process, if there is precedence that a set-aside court would apply irreconcilability even though a prior decision has been rendered between distinct parties. Such precedence should stem from the arbitral seat and concern highly comparable complex substantive relationships. By contrast, the mere formulation of a broad standard (e.g., 'communality of interests') and its application in a specific scenario (e.g., against insurers) does not specifically predetermine other scenarios such as guarantees or leasing case scenarios would equally meet the test. Therefore, it is submitted that the arbitral tribunal should only exercise its discretion in deferring to *specific* precedence and not to speculation.

1524. *See supra* [526-531].
1525. *See supra* [225].
1526. *See supra* [150-154].
1527. *See supra* [168-169].

[C] The Case Against Non-mutual Preclusion Before Arbitral Tribunals

> In addition, a [...] prior third party should only be exposed to *or be able to rely on* res judicata, if [...].

575. A delicate question is how to handle non-mutual preclusion to the benefit of an arbitration party that was no party to the prior proceedings. One scholarly submission favours non-mutual preclusion before arbitral tribunals, yet only as far as a prior award's reasonings are concerned.[1528] In general, the examination maintains the perspective that the former third party's ability to rely on non-mutual preclusion is not a matter of due process, but of equality. Particularly, equality is triggered because non-mutual preclusion exposes the party to the prior proceedings to the risk of losing against more parties than it could have succeeded. For this reason, civil-law jurisdictions reject non-mutual preclusion. Yet, common-law jurisdictions favour such rule for the rationale of efficiency and against the overall functional tendency of *concentrating* as many issues as possible in one instance.[1529]

576. If the prior decision is an arbitral award, the prior third party could not have been joined to the prior arbitration, unless the arbitration agreements are compatible. In line with precedence from England, the emerging opinion in US doctrine and the previous submissions under the NYC,[1530] such jurisdictional boundaries bar non-mutual preclusion.

577. If jurisdiction would not have been an obstacle to joining the prior third party, it is submitted that four considerations fundamentally oppose a transnational application of non-mutual preclusion. *First*, since non-mutual preclusion is unknown outside the common law, there is a significant inclination that parties from a civil-law background do not expect such preclusion. Potentially, non-mutual preclusion is a particularly relevant ground for the matter whether it should at least be allowed when both parties and the arbitral seat are located in a common-law jurisdiction. However, the litmus test is where to draw the line: is it sufficient if only one party and the arbitral seat are located in common-law jurisdictions? Would be sufficient if both parties, but not the arbitral seat are located in a common-law jurisdictions? In this regard, the examination proposes a restrictive handling. Otherwise, any foreseeability for the parties provided by transnational standards would be flawed.[1531]

578. *Second*, non-mutual preclusion primarily operates in order to establish efficiency. TEfficiency certainly is a general intention of international arbitration parties. However, non-mutual preclusion has a strong connotation to save public, and not private resources.[1532] *Third*, any establishment of non-mutual preclusion effectively advances

1528. Brekoulakis, *Third Parties in Arbitration*; *see supra* [520].
1529. *See supra* [193-196].
1530. *See supra* [240-244, 340-346].
1531. *See supra* [541-544].
1532. *See supra* [193].

issue concentration before the prior tribunal. However, international arbitration settings are the very antonym to issue concentration. Instead, party autonomy is an inherent restriction to any adjudication *ultra petita*. *Fourth*, even if the arbitration agreements were compatible or the prior decision was a judgment, arbitral tribunals are mandated to decide the parties' requests.[1533] By contrast, they are not mandated to promote further rationales such as the concentration of disputes in one instance. Therefore, it is submitted that non-mutual preclusion should not constitute any transnational principle.

[D] The Necessity to Refer to Prior Status Decisions

> An arbitral tribunal should refer to any prior judgment or arbitral award establishing, modifying or terminating a person's or an object's legal status.

579. It is submitted that arbitral tribunals should refer to prior decisions that adjudicated a legal status and operate erga omnes. For example, when a defendant to a damages claim for patent infringement raises a court judgment applied for by another party against the claimant in the arbitration and declaring the patent invalid, there is a strong inclination to follow the court judgment.[1534] Another example might be when an arbitration concerns a dispute about property and this very property has been the object of a court suit in rem. Examples where a legal status might have been adjudicated by an arbitral tribunal concern corporate and sport matters.[1535] Sport sanctions, for instance, should be referred to in follow-up arbitration.

580. In such situations, there is a three-fold inclination to do so. *First*, issues of status increase the parties' interest in cross-jurisdictional consistency. *Second*, since courts exercise the competence to establish, modify or terminate a legal status for public rationales, these rationales might trigger an arbitral seat's public policy and therefore justify a set aside in violation of the status adjudication. *Third*, issues of status, particularly in IP and property disputes often demand extensive evidence gathering. Therefore, the examination submits that, in general, arbitral tribunals should refer to adjudications on a legal status. The general rule begs the question whether it applies even if though the prior decision has violated fundamental rules of jurisdiction, due process or public policy. However, this is a general matter of the question whether arbitral tribunals should apply recognition standards to prior decisions.[1536]

1533. *See supra* [525].
1534. Inspired by Debourg, *Les contrariétés des décisions*. *See* ATF 121 III 474, *Siegfried AG v. Wellcome Foundation Ltd*; CA Paris, 28 June 2008, reported by Debourg.
1535. *See supra* [234-236]. For an example of a shareholders' resolution in follow-up disputes *see supra* [466].
1536. *See supra* [510].

[E] The Factual Effect of Prior Decisions Before Arbitral Tribunals

[1] Functional Delineation Between Preclusive and Factual Effects

> *Any obligation imposed on and any claim conferred to a party by a prior decision* can necessitate further consequences under the otherwise applicable law (factual effect). [...]

581. Selected scholarly statements on transnational res judicata remark that prior decisions could not only constitute res judicata but additionally comprise *opposabilité* vis-à-vis third parties.[1537] The term *opposabilité* originates from French doctrine and has a three-fold meaning in that it (i) guarantees the efficacy of status adjudications erga omnes, (ii) allows that substantive law can stipulate further consequences for obligations imposed on and claims conferred to parties by a judgment despite their nature *inter partes* and (iii) applies in certain case scenarios that are functionally perceived as res judicata in other jurisdictions.[1538] Whereas the first of these case scenarios has already been adhered to, the delineation of the second and the third case scenario demands an analysis.

582. It has been established in *Chapter 7* that prior decisions can comprise 'factual effects' in that they trigger further consequences under the law applicable to the substance. These factual effects need not operate *inter partes*. Instead, a practical example is that a party to an arbitration requests that it should be relieved from delivering a unique good contracted for since an earlier decision has already imposed the obligation to deliver the unique good to another party. The distinction between such factual effects and res judicata is: the former are established under the law of the substance in that it stipulates further consequences for the obligations imposed and claims conferred by a prior decision. The latter, by contrast, allows to reject an otherwise justified claim, request or argument purely by referring to an earlier decision. In other words: whereas factual effects merely concern the prior decision's *existence*, res judicata is preclusive in nature.[1539] Sometimes, however, the distinctions might be delicate. For a guarantee, for instance, both can be applicable. If the applicable law or the contract state that the guarantor becomes liable once the creditor obtains a judgment against the debtor, the decision's effect towards the guarantor is a factual effect. If there is no such provision, the guarantor becomes liable when the main debtor is liable. If the guarantor then objects that the main debt is time-barred, yet the creditor refers to a judgment rendered against the debtor, the decision's effect towards the guarantor will be preclusive, thus res judicata.

583. This distinction necessitates that the assessment of factual effects before arbitral tribunals should be narrower than the scope of the French doctrine of *opposabilité*, which is sometimes applied so as to preclude requests and arguments in follow-up

1537. Mayer, in *Liber Amicorum Reymond* 200; Schaffstein, *Res Judicata* [6.213].
1538. *See supra* [186].
1539. *See supra* [437].

litigation. In particular, the additionally discussed French topic of res judicata (*autorité de la chose jugée*) has the primary impact that it excludes the co-obligor's or surety's *tierce opposition* (third-party appeal.),[1540] a mechanism largely unknown to other arbitration laws. If thus, in an international setting, the decisive role of res judicata should prevail, but there is regularly no third-party appeal available, it can only be before the arbitral tribunal that res judicata governs whether a prior third party can be exposed. Therefore, the examination submits that an assessment distinct to res judicata might be necessary if the law applicable to the substance stipulates further consequences for the existence of obligations or claims established by a prior decision.

[2] Assessment of Due Process, Party Autonomy and Irreconcilability

A prior third party should only be exposed to or be able to rely on a factual effect, if

an agreement concluded between the parties stipulates accordingly; or

the prior third party could have participated in the prior proceedings; or

it had no reasonable standing to submit on the prior subject matter; or

the otherwise applicable law allows to invoke the prior decision's inaccuracy; or

specific precedence necessitates such measure in order to prevent a set aside.

584. Factual effects can be invoked against an arbitrating party that was a third party to the prior proceedings. For instance, a prior decision might (i) serve as a trigger of impossibility, hardship or force majeure, (ii) stipulate loss to be recoverable against the third party, (iii) bar interim measures, (iv) be stipulated as a trigger for indemnification. Admittedly, awards' factual effects have received limited attention in national doctrine.[1541] Therefore, transnational principles risk to be developed in a scholarly vacuum. In addition, by regularly agreeing on the contract, on the generally applicable law, the parties themselves establish the potential factual effect, which then overrides any legitimacy of transnational principles. If the admissibility of a factual effect under such contractual provision or applicable law is uncertain, it is preferable to assess due process, party autonomy and irreconcilability.[1542]

585. In addition, factual effects necessitate examining recognition boundaries to the prior decision such as jurisdiction, due process and public policy.[1543] Moreover, if the prior decision is an arbitral award, the examination has proposed a multi-tiered assessment before courts under Article V(1)(a) NYC.[1544] Corresponding to the assessment of the prior tribunal's jurisdiction for res judicata,[1545] the examination also submits to extend such jurisdictional assessment to factual effects. Party autonomy

1540. *See supra* [188, 204, 239].
1541. *See supra* [433-440].
1542. *See supra* [476-480].
1543. *See supra* [510].
1544. *See supra* [451-460].
1545. *See supra* [561-566].

demands to restrict the factual effect if the third party had a legal standing to submit on the subject matter, yet was barred for jurisdictional or procedural reasons from doing so and cannot raise the relevant objections. However, a factual effect might be justified in order to prevent absolute irreconcilabilities in that a party cannot physically comply with both the prior and the eventual arbitral award. The discretionary assessment should focus on (i) the likelihood of absolute irreconcilability, (ii) the compensation, (iii) the prior third party's awareness about the dispute and (iv) the dates of initiation.

[F] Preclusion Towards Joining Parties

> An arbitral tribunal should exclusively reject any joined party's request or argument by referring to earlier stages of the arbitral proceedings, if that party succeeded to another party thereto, or would be exposed to res judicata under Principle 2.

586. A topic related to the third-party effects of prior decisions, yet comprising an increased procedural connotation, is the question whether arbitral tribunals can expose parties that have been third parties to the arbitration at the outset, yet became parties during the arbitrations to findings established in the earlier course of the very arbitration, i.e., partial awards, procedural orders or evidence collected. In particular, for partial awards courts,[1546] scholars[1547] and the sole arbitrator in *ICC Case 3267*[1548] state that arbitral tribunals have to fully conform to all findings stipulated in a partial award by them. Yet, the question remains whether this is also necessary when a third party joins the arbitration. In particular, the joining party's right to be heard might demand a re-assessment. Such issue arises when a third party succeeded to a party's legal position (*see* [1], *infra*) or was joined otherwise during the arbitration (*see* [2], *infra*).

[1] Successions During the Arbitration

587. Amongst transnational proposals on res judicata, the consequences of a succession occurring *during* the arbitration, most importantly an assignment, are not examined. If the successor is not bound by the arbitration agreement, there will be no problem. The arbitration continues without the successor or is discontinued and it will be up to the courts to decide whether the successor is bound by arbitral res judicata. However, assignees usually join the arbitration agreement.[1549] When the opposing

1546. ATF 128 III 191, [4.a]; CA Paris, *SNC Forézienne d'entreprise v. SAS Guintoli*, 17 March 2017, [2017] Rev. Arb. 1213, 1217 (*'l'autorité de chose jugée n'est pas d'ordre public sauf au cours d'une même instance'*).

1547. Mayer, in *Liber Amicorum Reymond* 200; Mayer, (2016) Rev. Arb. 98.

1548. *ICC Case 3267*, Arbitral Award, 1984, (1987) XII Y.C.A. 87 *'the binding effect of its [the tribunal's] first award is not limited tot the contents of the order thereof [...] but that it extends to the legal reasons'*).

1549. *See supra* [41-44].

party applies for a joinder of the assignee or even a substitution, arbitral tribunals are generally faced with three options: (a) they could reject any alteration of the parties, render an arbitral award against the assignor and leave it up to a subsequent arbitral tribunal to decide on the preclusive effect; (b) they could join the successor or even substitute the assignor and thus render an arbitral award against the successor who will then be bound by the award's res judicata; (c) the arbitral tribunal could terminate the proceedings against the assignor and initiate new proceedings against the successor. Certainly, any of these steps requires a request by a party. In essence, the examination submits that the admissibility of scenario (a) is decisive. If a third-party effect is possible, the successor will decide to join. If it is impossible, the opposing party will regularly decide to reset the proceedings. Therefore, it is necessary to examine whether successors such as assignees are bound by an arbitral award's res judicata when the succession occurs during the proceedings.

588. As previously mentioned, whilst German scholarship and the Draft Third Restatement affirm an applicability of res judicata, because a successor acquires an 'arbitrated' right, the tribunal in *ICC Case 13509* rejected it by reasoning that a successor has an interest in its own arbitrator.[1550] In essence, these rationales illustrate the opposing consideration to be assessed by potential follow-up tribunals: should a successor to an arbitrated right be treated as a subsequent successor, because the rights and liabilities were already uncertain, or should he be treated as a successor who succeeded prior to the arbitration and thus has the standing to appoint its own arbitrator? It is submitted that the former standpoint is preferable. In particular, it should not make any difference to the due-process interest of the successor whether he is exposed to the entire results of an arbitration, i.e., the arbitral award, or only parts of this arbitration when he joined. Indeed, the exclusively decisive aspect is, that in addition to this exposure, the successor could only arbitrate and be adjudicated by a tribunal he did not select. Yet again, just as the successor is exposed to the predecessor's selection when the arbitral award has already been rendered, he should be exposed to this selection when the arbitration is on-going. In particular for assignees, they can adequately assess the arbitrators' quality before deciding to acquire the receivable. Therefore, it appears preferable that a follow-up tribunal would affirm res judicata. Hence, a third party should be able to join the arbitration *upon its or the opponent's request*.

[2] Joinders During the Arbitration in Complex Substantive Relationships

589. If a bilateral arbitration involves a complex substantive relationship (e.g., involving guarantors or sureties) and others *did* consent to the arbitration agreement, either party might apply for a joinder after certain steps in the arbitration have been undertaken, e.g., evidence gathered and evaluated. In particular, whereas under Article 7(1) ICC Rules, a joinder during the arbitration can exclusively occur upon

1550. *See supra* [249].

consent of all parties involved,[1551] '*[t]here is no temporal restriction on a party's request for joinder under the Swiss, LCIA, SIAC, HKIAC or UNCITRAL Rules*'.[1552] Yet, it is for the arbitral tribunal to decide whether a joinder during the arbitration necessitates a re-assessment of requests and evidence, or whether the joining party can be fully exposed to the previous finding. In this regard, it is submitted that the potential privy standards should be decisive. If the joining party would even be exposed to the entire arbitral award as a third party, it should be exposed to prior evidence, procedural orders or partial awards *a fortiori*. Moreover, corresponding to the above-mentioned succession argument (*see* [588], *supra*), the privy position necessitates that the joining party has no right to modify the tribunal's composition. If, however, the joining party is no privy, the interests of joining parties in influencing the evidence and selecting an arbitrator comprise significant weight and will therefore generally oppose an exposure to prior results. Therefore, when a partial award has been rendered, a tribunal would find itself in a dilemma to either disregard this award and thereby risk the final award's set aside[1553] or expose the joining party to results it could not influence and thereby put the award's efficacy at risk as well. Accordingly, there might be a certain inclination to reject the joinder. If no partial award has been rendered, it is preferable to grant the joining party the right to oppose the findings which might also be discretionary criteria *against* even allowing the joinder. In conclusion, the privy standards established for the effects of arbitral awards should equally be decisive for the matter whether joining parties can be exposed to prior results of the arbitration.

§8.04 ILLUSTRATION BY VIRTUE OF SPECIFIC SCENARIOS

590. To conclude, the proposed transnational principles are applied to a range of exemplified scenarios. Since the principles generally operate transnationally, the case examples will not name specific jurisdictions. Instead, it can be presumed that the parties' origin and the arbitral seat are in distinct jurisdictions. If the applicable substantive law becomes relevant, the examples will maintain their transnational spirit and mention solutions under uniform instruments. Moreover, since the applications comprehensively facilitate the observations and proposals from the proceedings Chapters, the case applications will not provide any cross-references. As a final proclamation, the following principles have no ambition to be carved in stone. Instead, the manifold aspects to be taken into consideration (proximity of third party, jurisdiction, intervention possibilities, irreconcilability concerns) render it highly preferable that arbitral tribunals retain the mandate to adapt the principles on a case-by-case basis.

1551. 'No additional party may be joined after the confirmation or appointment of any arbitrator, unless all parties, including the additional party, otherwise agree'.

1552. Smith, (2018) 35 J. Int'l Arb. 195.

1553. *See* ATF 128 III 191, [4.a]; CA Paris, *SNC Forézienne d'entreprise v. SAS Guintoli*, 17 March 2017, [2017] Rev. Arb. 1213, 1217 ('*l'autorité de chose jugée n'est pas d'ordre public sauf au cours d'une même instance*').

[A] Successions

> X purchases a machine from Y. In invoking that the machine were deficient, X refuses payment. Y initiates arbitration. During the arbitration, Y assigns its payment claim to Z who had no knowledge about the ongoing arbitration. After X has succeeded in the first arbitration, Z initiates arbitration and claims the purchase price.

591. If a party to an arbitration invokes the conclusive or preclusive effect of a prior decision rendered against party to whom the party now exposed to res judicata succeeded, the latter will generally be exposed to res judicata. In particular, it is an almost universal rule of procedural and arbitration law that both universal (inheritance, corporate transformations) and individual (assignments, transfer of contracts or property) successions can occur only conjointly with the obligations already adjudicated. Furthermore, it is submitted that successors are equally bound when the succession occurred during the arbitral award. Therefore, the arbitral tribunal should preclude Z's claim unless Z can successfully rely on a bona fide acquisition of the receivable. This depends on the law governing the assignment. Yet, assignments are regularly insusceptible to bona fide acquisitions, for instance under the Ottawa Convention.

[B] Multiple Actions by Creditor Against Co-obligors

> A joint venture of the separate legal entities X and Y is mandated by Z to construct a sewage plant by Z. Z concludes distinct contracts with X and Y, albeit containing identical arbitration agreements and identical obligations to be fully liable for the construction as a whole. Eventually, Z successfully claims damages from X before an arbitral tribunal for deficiencies of the plant. Since X defaults in payment, Z initiates arbitration against Y and invokes that the latter is precluded from objecting to the obligation.

592. If a creditor sues one out of several co-obligors and alleges that the debt or some of its requirements have already been confirmed in a prior decision rendered against another co-obligor, the primary assessment is whether the co-obligor has agreed to be bound by any decisions rendered against the other co-obligor. In the absence of specific indications for such agreement, it should not be presumed. Hence, res judicata additionally requires that both co-obligors could have been sued before the same tribunal. Since X and Y signed fully identical arbitration clauses, this requirement is met. Accordingly, the delicate aspect is whether co-obligors should be regarded as privies. Germanic jurisdictions and the Second Restatement contain restrictive rules whilst French judgment principles are more liberal. Against this background, the examination submits that, in general, co-obligors should *not* be exposed to third-party effects. Instead, it can be regarded as an adequate burden for the creditor to be exposed to restrictive res judicata effects since the creditor has full possibility to join all co-obligors as joint defendants in an arbitration. Finally, the potential set-aside review on grounds of irreconcilability should not incline res judicata, since a rejection of Z's claim against Y will not deprive him of the benefits from the award against X and Y's potential indemnity obligation against X already existed. Accordingly, the arbitral tribunal should not apply res judicata towards Y.

[C] Multiple Actions by Creditor Against Debtor and Surety/Guarantor

> The bank B guaranteed all payment obligations of the joint venture mentioned in scenario (B.). The guarantee contains an arbitration agreement identical to the contracts with X and Y. It provides that 'payment under the guarantee can only be refused if it is ascertained that neither X nor Y are obligated to undertake the payment'. Moreover, the applicable law includes a passage comparable to Article 19(2)(b) UN Guarantee Convention, pursuant to which 'the guarantor has a right to withold payment [...] if the underlying obligation of the principal/applicant has been declared invalid by a court or arbitral tribunal [...].' Since X has defaulted in payment after an arbitral tribunal awarded damages to Z, Z sues B which invokes the construction's conformity.

593. If a creditor has obtained a prior decision against the debtor and seeks to invoke the conclusively settled main debt in follow-up arbitration against a surety or guarantor, the relevant surety or guarantee contract has to be interpreted primarily. In the instant case, the passage 'ascertained' could imply that it has to be extraordinarily likely that neither X nor Y is liable. However, even if such interpretation were preferable, the interpretation should not go as far as facilitating a prior arbitral award against such likelihood. This would amount to an effective preclusion agreement preferably requiring more specific indications. This brings the arbitral tribunal to the default test whether B can still invoke that X should not be liable under the proper application of the law and the facts. Primarily, it is necessary that the arbitral tribunal rendering the award against X could have exercised jurisdiction against B. Given the identical arbitration agreements, this can be presumed. Hence, it will be decisive whether B as a guarantor can be perceived as a privy. In particular, whilst French and the majority of US jurisprudence affirm this, Germanic jurisdictions and English jurisdictions are more sceptical. In confluence with solidary debts, the examination submits that this divide should be an inclination against a privy affirmation. In particular, a creditor can be burdened to join the guarantor. Therefore, the exclusive and most important aspect is to interpret whether the guarantee itself includes a (potentially implied) preclusion agreement. Finally, the applicable law might allow a factual effect in that an arbitral award might immediately trigger the guarantor's liability. However, the instant law exclusively affirms the situation vice versa. But for explicit provisions, the tribunal should not apply factual effects. Thus, the arbitral tribunal should *not* preclude B's requests.

[D] Multiple Actions by Creditor Against Corporate Group Members

X licensed the corporation Y to use a certain, patented chemical formula for its production. The licensing agreement contained an arbitration agreement. After Y had defaulted in payment, X terminated the license and obtained an arbitral award restraining Y from further exploiting a license. Since Y has continued using the chemical formula, X initiates further arbitration against Y and its 100 per-cent shareholder Z for damages. Z invokes that even if it were liable, X's termination should have required prior notice.[1554]

594. If a creditor has obtained a decision against a corporation and seeks to hold a shareholder or member of the corporate group liable, arbitral tribunals should generally take a restrictive approach. In particular, international investment principles on lenient preclusion standards towards shareholders are *in*applicable. Unless the prior decision is invoked against a partnership member that is personally liable for the partnership's debts, primarily US law allows a discretionary assessment of 'effective control'. The relevant doctrine would equally lift the 'jurisdictional veil' in that the shareholders could have also been joined by the prior tribunal. The latter standard should also apply to factual effects, e.g., if the applicable law permits damages for violations of obligations imposed by an arbitral award. For instance, in the original *ICC Case 8023* the arbitral tribunal applied the *opposabilité* against the member of an economic interest grouping under French law (*groupement d'intérêt économique*) which it considered to be bound by the arbitration agreement. If, in the instant case, the arbitral tribunal assumes jurisdiction over Z, it can equally refer to a factual effect of the prior decision and assume that Y was obligated *not* to use the formula when assessing Z's liability.

[E] Multiple Actions by Promisee and Third-Party Beneficiary Against Promisor

X provides and maintains a medical treatment room to the hospital Z. It was agreed that the purchasing price could be paid to and claimed by the parent company of X, namely Y. Upon dissatisfaction with the treatment room, Z terminates the contract and refuses payment. X initiated arbitration against Z. The arbitral tribunal held the termination valid and refused the payment claim. Eventually, Y initiates arbitration against Z.

595. If a promisee has unsuccessfully sued the promisor, the third-party beneficiary subsequently initiates arbitration against the debtor and the arbitral tribunal affirms jurisdiction over the third-party beneficiary, the decisive aspect is whether promisor and third-party beneficiary should be considered as privies. Again, national laws differ. As an inclination in favour of a privy assessment, a restrictive operation of res judicata

1554. Inspired by *ICC Case 8023*, Award, 1995, cited by Hascher in *Travaux du comité français DIP* 21.

would incline every promisor sued by a promisee to join the third-party beneficiary. However, under some national arbitration laws, a third-party beneficiary has no 'obligation' to arbitrate. Instead, it might merely have an 'option'. This creates a dilemma: either an obligation to arbitrate is effectively conferred upon the third-party beneficiary by exposing him to res judicata, or the promisor has no opportunity to defend itself against both opponents simultaneously. Given that the third-party beneficiary can enjoy nothing but benefits from the contract and the arbitration whilst the promisor risks multiple proceedings, it is submitted that an exposure of the third-party beneficiary is preferable. Moreover, this might also be inclined by an irreconcilability perspective, since a successful claim of the third-party beneficiary would intrinsically deprive the promisor of the benefits obtained from the prior decision. Therefore, Y's claim should be precluded.

[F] Multiple Actions by Financial Leasee Against Supplier and Lessor

> In scenario (A.), Y insistent on instant payment. Since X was unable to provide full payment, yet instantly required the machine, the commercial leasing bank Z purchased the machine and concluded a financial leasing agreement with X. Upon dissatisfaction with the machine, X directly and successfully sues Y in court as it is e.g. provided by Article 7(1, 2) UNIDROIT Model Law.[1555] Eventually, X terminated the leasing agreement with Z. In the respective arbitration, Z claims the rent and submits that the equipment was objectively not deficient. Y invokes that the court has previously affirmed the deficiency.

596. If issue preclusion is perceived as admissible, the arbitral tribunal might consider to regard the supplier and the lessor as privies and thus expose the latter to a decision rendered against the supplier. In addition, the arbitral tribunal might consider that by providing a financial leasee with the standing to enforce claims against the supplier, the lessor agreed to be bound by any decision rendered against the supplier. For instance, this is the solution under national judgment principles. From a transnational perspective, both solutions appear feasible since a financial leasing has the primary objective to facilitate the financing of purchases. Accordingly, the parties anticipate that an adjudication on the purchase comprises full efficacy.

[G] Indemnification Amongst Connected Debtors

> Following up on scenario (C.), the tribunal affirmed Z's claim against the guarantor B. Upon conforming to its obligations under the award, B seeks indemnification from the main debtor X before a further tribunal. X invokes that B was not obligated towards Z, because the construction had been constructed adequately. B

1555. 'In a financial lease, the duties of the supplier under the supply agreement shall also be owed to the lessee as if the lessee were a party to that agreement and as if the asset were to be supplied directly to the lessee. [...] At the request of the lessee, the lessor shall assign its rights to enforce the supply agreement to the lessee'.

relies on both, the first arbitral award rendered against X and the second arbitral award rendered against Z.

597. If a co-obligor, a surety or a guarantor have been successfully sued by the creditor and then seek indemnification from the main debtor, they might raise the indemnification claim under their own genuine rights or because they were assigned the creditor's claim. In any case, given that the said parties are no privies and non-mutual preclusion unpreferable, the party seeking indemnity can*not* invoke res judicata. Instead it will be a matter of the contract governing the indemnity whether indemnification for a satisfied award can be claimed immediately or indemnity can only be claimed for substantively justified claims, thus permitting the claim's review. In the former case, the award will establish a permissible, factual effect.

[H] Indemnification in Insurance Case Scenarios

Carrier X agrees to transport automobiles by Y across the Pacific. Upon discharging the freight, Y discovers that certain automobiles were damaged. X invoked that this resulted out of an unforeseeable storm and could not have been prevented by adequate safety measures. Yet, an arbitral tribunal seized by Y rejects any application of *force majeure* and holds X liable for damages. Since X was insured for losses arising out of unforeseeable weather conditions, he claims reimbursement from its insurer Z who invokes, however, that the prior tribunal has already rejected any unforeseeability.

598. When indemnification is requested by or against an insurer, national laws often extend res judicata beyond the prior dispute's parties. This might occur either under privy doctrines (at common law and – concerning lis pendens and irreconcilability – under the Brussels Regime) or, because the insurer can be deemed to have impliedly agreed to a preclusion agreement (under German or US law). Therefore, it is submitted that it is feasible to regard insurers as privies. However, the interpretation of the insurance agreement might comprise additional relevance where the first dispute occurred in arbitration and the insurer would not have been subject to the tribunal's jurisdiction under the principle of subrogation. Then, the subsequent tribunal should interpret the specific insurance contract whether it allows extending res judicata even though the insurer would have been unable to join the arbitration. Regularly, the insured's obligation towards the insurer to conduct an arbitration adequately can serve as a positive indicator. Therefore, Z should be regarded as a privy that can invoke the prior award.

[I] The Introduction's Case Example: Indemnification in Chains of Contracts

599. In the *Introduction* to this book, the case example assumed that an arbitral tribunal awarded damages to a principal against a contractor for a deficient construction project.[1556] If the contractor seeks indemnity from the sub-contractor before an arbitral tribunal, the admissibility of issue preclusion will be an instant obstacle. For instance, the tribunal in *ICC Cases 2475/2762* generally considered a Belgian judgment between a purchaser and a re-seller as applicable in indemnity proceedings against the producer because the latter was an intervener; however, this did not necessitate that the issues adjudicated in court were binding. Instead, merely the re-seller's obligation towards the purchaser as such can establish any third-party effect.[1557]

600. Even if issue preclusion were admissible, none of the examined jurisdictions would affirm a third-party effect. In addition, the preferable restriction of the prior arbitral award's effect by virtue of its jurisdictional boundaries further opposes that the sub-contractor would be exposed to issue preclusion. Accordingly, it is submitted that under transnational principles, prior decisions should not comprise third-party effects in indemnity proceedings along sales or construction chains. Instead, the exclusive means for a binding third-party effect is a preclusion agreement between the contractor and the sub-contractor, which requires specific indications, at least for implied consent. In the absence of such preclusion agreement, chains of contracts thus remain saliently exposed to the risks of multi-fora disputes.

601. The very gravity of such multi-fora disputes can be concludingly illustrated by the *Macao Sardines* case.[1558] In this case, a producer of tins for sardines from Macao was unable to meet a large order and filled the tins with mud instead. After the tins were re-sold many times over to wholesalers, supermarkets and finally customers, the tins' content was discovered in the Philippines during a local food shortage. Before the Hong Kong Commercial Court, over 100 claimants sued their sellers stretching from Japanese merchants to a Manila Supermarket. It was only between the Taiwanese wholesaler and the Macao factory that an arbitration clause had been agreed upon. Their arbitration took more than eleven years. Whilst the Hong Kong Commercial Court awarded damages to the buyers in forty-six judgments on the grounds of the tins' objective deficiency, the sole arbitrator's unpublished arbitral award dismissed the indemnity claims of the Taiwanese wholesaler against the Macao producer on the grounds that the tins were factually merchantable. Implicitly, it did not consider the judgments binding in the absence of party identity. Therefore, the court and the arbitrator reached different conclusions as to the very same aspect, i.e., the goods' objective quality. This might well be undesirable. Yet from a legal perspective, transnational principles of res judicata are not the adequate means to prevent it.

1556. *See supra* [2].
1557. *ICC Cases 2475 & 2762*, Award, (1974-1985) I ICC Collection 325.
1558. Reported by Kerr, (1987) 3 Arb. Int'l 79-86.

§8.05 CONCLUDING PRINCIPLES FOR THIRD-PARTY EFFECTS BEFORE ARBITRAL TRIBUNALS

602. When an international arbitral tribunal has to determine whether a prior judgment or a prior arbitral award can be facilitated for precluding an arbitrating party's claim, request or argument (res judicata), an arbitral tribunal can either apply national law determined by means of private international law (conflictualist approach) or apply transnational principles (substantive approach). This decision should generally be made with regard to the general interests of the parties before the very tribunal considering res judicata.[1559] For reasons of foreseeability, flexibility and consistency, it is submitted that the application of transnational principles is a feasible option.[1560] The content of these principles should be developed in scholarship and jurisprudence by virtue of comparative law. By contrast, privy assessments under international investment treaties are *not* transferable.[1561]

603. If an arbitral tribunal seeks to apply transnational principles for res judicata *and* considers res judicata's general operations requirements met, the examination proposes the following principles on the issue whether res judicata should be inapplicable, because the prior decision has not been rendered between the parties to the subsequent arbitration:

(1) In general, an arbitral tribunal should exclusively preclude any party's request or argument under referral to a judgment or arbitral award rendered in prior proceedings (res judicata), if all parties have also been parties therein or succeeded to a party thereto.

(2) A party that was no party to the prior proceedings and did not succeed to a party thereto (prior third party) should only be exposed to or be able to rely on res judicata, if:
   (a) an agreement concluded between the parties stipulates accordingly; or
   (b) considerung the prior tribunal's jurisdiction as well as the prior third party's legal relationship and effective actions, the prior third party could and should have participated in the prior procedure in order to exercise its right to be heard; or
   (c) specific precedence necessitates such measure in order to prevent a set aside.

(3) Any obligation imposed on and any claim conferred to a party by a prior decision can necessitate further consequences under the otherwise applicable law (factual effect). A prior third party should only be exposed to or be able to rely on a factual effect, if:
   (a) an agreement concluded between the parties stipulates accordingly; or
   (b) the prior third party could have participated in the prior proceedings; or

1559. *See supra* [525].
1560. *See supra* [532-540].
1561. *See supra* [545-552].

   (c) it had no reasonable standing to submit on the prior subject matter; or
   (d) the otherwise applicable law allows to invoke the prior decision's inaccuracy; or
   (e) specific precedence necessitates such measure in order to prevent a set aside.

(4) An arbitral tribunal should refer to any prior judgment or arbitral award establishing, modifying or terminating a person's or an object's legal status.

(5) An arbitral tribunal should exclusively reject any joined party's request or argument by referring to earlier stages of the arbitral proceedings, if that party succeeded to another party thereto, or would be exposed to res judicata under Principle (2).

Chapter 9
The Application of Res Judicata Principles to Jurisdictional Decisions

604. So far, the examination has dedicated its emphasis to preclusive, conclusive and factual effects of decisions *on the substance*. By contrast, this final Chapter examines these very effects with regard to decisions *about arbitral jurisdiction*. Such issue arises when a court decides about jurisdictional aspects (validity or scope of arbitration agreement, arbitrability) for pre-emptive requests (e.g., staying litigation, compelling arbitration or issuing an anti-suit injunction) or in 'award judgments' (e.g., setting aside, confirming or recognizing an arbitral award) and the said jurisdictional issue arises again in follow-up disputes before arbitral tribunals or courts. For multilateral transactions, this matter comprises a preeminent relevance. Given the diverging perceptions on implied consent of non-signatories to arbitration agreements as they have been undertaken by the French and English courts in *Dallah*,[1562] conclusive effects of jurisdictional decisions before foreign courts could be a primary tool for preventing multi-fora disputes. To follow up on *Dallah*, the question whether a French set aside rejection could comprise conclusive effects on the English enforcement courts was *not* raised before the United Kingdom (UK) Supreme Court.[1563] Yet, *obiter*, it mentioned an effect vice versa.[1564]

605. If a conclusive effect of jurisdictional decisions exists, this will raise a follow-up issue, its *third-party effect*. The issue arises when the decision on arbitral jurisdiction concerns an allegedly multilateral arbitration agreement in general (e.g., its validity or arbitrability), some alleged signatories to this very arbitration agreement have not

1562. *See supra* [40-41].

1563. English courts do not apply the doctrine of *iura novit curia* and are bound to the parties' submissions on the law.

1564. *Dallah Real Estate and Tourism Holding Company v. The Ministry of Religious Affairs, Government of Pakistan*, [2010] UKSC 46, [29] per Lord Mance ('[...] an English judgment holding that the award is not valid could prove significant in relation to [the French set-aside] proceedings if French courts recognise any principle similar to the English principle of issue estoppel').

participated and, eventually, the arbitration agreement is invoked against or by such non-participating signatory in follow-up disputes. Then, the previous adjudication on arbitral jurisdiction might comprise a conclusive effect towards that, previously non-participating, signatory. Whilst there are currently no authorities on the latter issue, the increasing relevance of arbitration, in general, and multi-arbitration clauses, in particular - especially following the recent inclusion of multiparty provisions in arbitral rules[1565] - might bring this issue to practical attention soon. This Chapter will address both the general and the third-party issue in differentiating between the subsequent fora: conclusive effects before courts (*see* §9.01, *infra*) and before arbitral tribunals (*see* §9.02, *infra*). It will conclude with the limited relevance of jurisdictional decisions *by* arbitral tribunals (*see* §9.03, *infra*).

§9.01 CONCLUSIVE EFFECTS OF FOREIGN ARBITRATION JUDGMENTS BEFORE STATE COURTS

606. In international arbitration, a range of jurisdictions potentially adjudicates on an arbitration clause. These jurisdictions operate not in a vertical but in a *horizontal system of jurisdictional prerogatives.*[1566] The jurisdictional prerogatives might differ, e.g., on the implied-consent threshold for non-signatories to arbitration agreements.[1567] Then, Forum Coordination could only be achieved if jurisdictional judgments will be conclusive before foreign courts. Currently, the main discussion about conclusive effects of foreign court adjudications on the arbitration agreement concerns revisionary decisions, such as set asides, confirmations or exequaturs. These decisions are often summarized as 'award judgments' (*jugements sur sentence*). Effectively, the degree to which courts seized with annulment or recognition requests refer to such prior award judgments exposes a significant divide amongst arbitration jurisdictions, particularly between civil and common law (*see* [A], *infra*). By contrast, the extent to which pre-emptive jurisdictional decisions might trigger conclusive effects is less debated (*see* [B], *infra*). In any case, *even if* foreign judgment principles were generally to apply to said decisions, the examination submits that neither *erga omnes* nor privy doctrines are applicable. Therefore, a conclusive effect will only exist between the parties to the prior litigation (*see* [C], *infra*).

[A] Status Quo: Award Judgments' Susceptibility to Foreign Judgment Principles

607. The conclusive effect of 'award judgments' (set asides, confirmations, *exequatur* or a rejection of any of these requests) in follow-up litigation about the efficacy of an

1565. *See supra* [37].
1566. *See supra* [87-89].
1567. *See supra* [40-41].

arbitral award at the arbitral seat (annulment, confirmation) or third states (recognition and enforcement) might be a standalone topic of contemporary arbitration discussions. It combines extraordinary practical relevance, implementations of legal-theory perceptions and significant potential for policy considerations. In fact, the topic is manifold, both in terms of case scenarios and opinions. Hence, the topic can only be outlined at this stage. Such outline should commence with the very fact that award judgments are *un*codified. Article V(1)(e) NYC[1568] addresses nothing but the permission to deny recognition to an annulled award. Hence, this very case scenario triggers (overriding) considerations of uniform law. With regard to other considerations, national laws only regulate the recognition of judgments in general:[1569]

> [This] raises the fundamental question whether award judgments are equivalent to other foreign judgments, and if not, in what respects they differ.[1570]

608. If award judgments are susceptible to foreign judgment principles, the conclusive effects before foreign courts will depend on the award judgment's res judicata.[1571]

609. By far the most prominent discussion concerns the recognition of set-aside judgments and Article V(1)(e) NYC. It is well known that French jurisprudence facilitated the leeway under the provision's wording ('may'), Article VII(1) NYC[1572] and a transnational characterization of international arbitration[1573] for enforcing foreign arbitral awards regardless of a prior annulment.[1574] Corresponding decisions could once have been observed in the US[1575] and Belgium.[1576] This handling raised

1568. 'Recognition and enforcement of the award may be refused [...] the award [...] has been set aside or suspended by a competent authority of the country in which [...] that award was made'.
1569. Cf. Besson, (2017) 19 ICCA Congress Series 675-681.
1570. Scherer, (2013) 4 J. Int'l Disp Settlemt 588.
1571. Besson, (2017) 19 ICCA Congress Series 681-682; Hascher, (1993) Rev. Arb. 268; Scherer, (2013) 4 J. Int'l Disp Settlement 605; Petrochilos, (1999) 48 ICLQ 862; Solomon, *Die Verbindlichkeit von Schiedssprüchen* 537.
1572. 'The provisions of the present Convention shall not [...] deprive any interested party of any right he may have to avail himself of an arbitral award in the manner and to the extent allowed by the law or the treaties of the country where such award is sought to be relied upon'.
1573. Gaillard, *Legal Theory of International Arbitration*; Fouchard, (1997) Rev. Arb. 329 and (1998) Rev. Arb. 653.
1574. *Hilmarton Ltd v. OTV*, 23 March 1993, [1994] Clunet 701; Cass. (1e civ.), *PT Putrabali Adyamulia v. Rena Holding and Mnogutia Est Epices*, 29 June 2007, [2006] Rev. Arb. 665; Cass. (1e civ.), *Pabalk Ticaret Limited Sirketi v. Norsolor SA*, 9 October 1984, [1985] Rev. Arb. 431; Cass. (1e civ.), *Polish Ocean Live v. Jolasry*, 10 March 1993, (1994) Y.C.A. 662; CA Paris, *Arab Republic of Egypt v. ChromalloyAero Services*, 14 January 1997, (1997) Y.C.A. 691; CA Paris, *Bargues Agro Industries v. Young Pecan Company*, 10 June 2004, (2005) Y.C.A. 499; CA Paris, *Directorate General of Civil Aviation of the Emirate of Dubai v. International bechtel Co. Limited.*, 29 September 2005, (2006) Y.C.A. 629; CA Paris, *La sté SA Lesbats et fils v. Monsieur Volker Le Docteur Grub*, 18 January 2007, (2007) Y.C.A. 297.
1575. *Chromalloy Aeroservices v. Arab Republic of Egypt*, 939 FSupp 907, 913 (DDC 1996). Notably the case was settled before the appeal decision could have been rendered.
1576. Bruxelles Court of First Instance, (1990) Y.C.A. 370 aff'd CA Bruxelles, *Sonatrach v. ord Bacon & Davis Inc*, 9 January 1990, [1990] J. trib 386.

severe critics.[1577] Amongst the two most important counter-streams, one proposes to distinguish between 'Local Standard Annulments' and 'International Standard Annulments',[1578] a solution followed under Article IX(1) European Convention.[1579] The other seeks to apply foreign judgment principles in that the set aside should be recognized unless the set-aside court violated, e.g., its jurisdiction, due process or public policy. This is the majority position in the US,[1580] other jurisdictions[1581] and scholarship.[1582] In conclusion, the conclusive effect of set asides is considered *either* a matter of the NYC exclusively *or* a matter of foreign judgment principles. Under res judicata notions, the latter solution will pose no obstacle to civil law, since the annulment's dispositif is at stake.

610. Although the enforcement of annulled awards has long constituted an isolated discussion, it is now acknowledged that the situation vice versa has to be examined conjointly, namely where a party seeks to resists either the confirmation at the seat or the recognition and enforcement elsewhere although other courts have already *upheld* the arbitral award. Since the NYC does not address the preclusion of repetitive objections to an arbitral award, the focus lies with foreign judgment principles:[1583] As a starting point, US courts comprehensively allow to enforce confirmation judgments

1577. van den Berg, (1985) 6 Pace L. Rev. 41-42; Berger and Kellerhals, *Arbitration in Switzerland* [2083]; Gharavi, *The International Effectiveness of the Annulment* 114; *Poudret and Besson* [930] ('only depart therefrom […] if the setting aside is a manifest disregard of the arbitration law of the seat').
1578. Paulsson, (1996) 7 Am. Rev. Int'l Arb. 99 and (1998) Rev. Arb. 637; *Born* 3639; Radicati di Brozolo, (2011) 16 ICCA Congress Ser 102. *Crit* Mayer, (2017) 19 ICCA Congress Ser 705 and (2001) 10 ICCA Congress Ser 175 ('drafting of a Convention, along the lines of Art. IX of the Geneva Convention').
1579. 'The setting aside in a Contracting State of an arbitral award covered by this Convention shall only constitute a ground for the refusal of recognition or enforcement in another Contracting State where such setting aside took place in a State in which, or under the law of which, the award has been made and for one of the following reasons […].' App by OGH, *Radenska v. Kajo*, 20 October 1993, (1994) 49(14/15) ÖJZ 513; OLG Dresden, [2007] SchiedsVZ 327 reversed on other grounds BGH, [2008] NJW 2718.
1580. Restatement (Third) Int'l Comm Arb. (TD 2), § 4-16 (b); *Baker Marine (Nig) Ltd v. Chevron (Nig)*, 191 F.3d 194, 196-197 (2d Cir. 1999) ('Recognition of the Nigerian judgment in this case does not conflict with United States policy'); *Karaha Bodas Co. v. Perusahaan Pertambangan Minyak Dan Gas Bumi Negara*, 335 F.3d 357, 367 (5th Cir. 2003); *TermoRio SA ESP et al. v. Electrificadora del Atlantico SA ESP et al*, 421 FSupp2d 87 (DDC 2006) upheld *Corporación Mexicana de Mantenimiento Integral v. PEMEX-Exploración y Producción*, 2013 WL 4517225 (S.D.N.Y.) ('violated basic notions of justice in that it applied a law that was not in existence'). For further US judgments *see Born* 3632-36.
1581. Chile: Supreme Court of Chile, 8 September 2011, Case 4390-2010 (award annulled in Argentina). Germany: OLG Rostock, (2000) Y.C.A. 717; Wolff, [2008] LMK No. 265473. Netherlands: Hoge Raad, *sté europ d'études et d'entreprises v. Socialist Federal Republic of Yugoslavia*, 26 October 1973, [1974] NJ No. 361; Gerechtshof Amsterdam, *Yukos Capital SarL v. OAO Rosneft*, 28 April 2009, (2009) Y.C.A. 703. Switzerland: TF, 8 December 2003, 4P.173/2003, [3.1] (*obiter*).
1582. Bermann, (2015) 381 Rec. des cours [629, 729]; Bollée, in *Procédures parallèles et décisions contradictoires* 107; Park, (1999) 93 Am. J. Int'l L. 813; Petrochilos, *Procedural Law in International Arbitration* 336; Schlosser, in *Stein and Jonas* [311]; Silberman, (2009) 28 Ga J. Int'l Comp. L. 32; Solomon, *Die Verbindlichkeit von Schiedssprüchen* 701.
1583. Cf. Scherer, (2013) 4 J. Int'l Disp Settlement 619. *See also* Nazzini, (2018) 66 Am. J. Comp. L. 603.

of the seat ('parallel entitlement').[1584] For instance, in *Navimpex*, the US Court of Appeals for the Second Circuit allowed the claimant to seek enforcement of the Paris Court of Appeal's confirmation,[1585] although it has previously considered the enforcement of the arbitral award time-barred.[1586] Such solution has also been adopted in England,[1587] Australia,[1588] India[1589] and Israel.[1590] A functionally comparable tool would be to *preclude* enforcement objections under Article V NYC when comparable grounds have been unsuccessfully raised in set asides.[1591] US law applies this preclusion technique in the strongly related case scenario where a third-State judgment has already awarded exequatur to the award: the non-recognition grounds unsuccessfully raised in third States preclude comparable non-recognition grounds under the FAA by virtue of issue preclusion.[1592] This is also the case at

1584. Restatement (Third) Int'l Comm Arbitration, § 4-3 (d) ('If a foreign award has been reduced to a judgment by a court in the arbitral seat, a party may seek either: (1) recognition or enforcement of the award in accordance with the provisions of this Chapter; or (2) recognition or enforcement of the judgment in accordance with the foreign judgment recognition and enforcement standards of the forum in which such relief is sought.') Cf. *Island Territory of Curacao v. Solitron Devices Inc*, 489 F.2d 1313 (2d Cir. 1973); *Fotochrome Inc. v. Copal Co*, 517 F.2d 512 (2d Cir. 1975); *Victrix SS Co. v. Salen Dry Cargo AB*, 825 F.2d 709 (2d Cir. 1987); *In re Waterside Ocean Navigation Co*, 737 F.2d 150 (2d Cir. 1984). *See Oriental Commercial & Shipping Co. (UK), Oriental Commercial & Shipping Co. (Saudi Arabia), Abdul Hamid Bokhari v. Rosseel NV*, 769 FSupp 514, 516 (S.D.N.Y. 1991) (obiter). *Contra Commissions Imp Exp SA v. Republic of Congo*, 13-004, 2014 WL 3377337 (DC Cir. 2014) - FAA was held to require the very opposite result when the claimant sought to enforcement the English confirmation whilst the arbitral award's enforcement was time-barred.
1585. Notably, the refusal of an annulment was under Art. 1498(2) CPC considered to have exequatur effect: '*Le rejet de l'appel ou du recours en annulation confère l'exequatur à la sentence arbitrale ou à celles de ses dispositions qui ne sont pas atteintes par la censure de la cour*'.
1586. *Seetransport Viking Trader Schiffahrtsgesellschaft GmbH & Co. v. Navimpex Centrala Navale*, 29 F.3d 79 (2d Cir. 1994) with reference to *Ilsand Territory of Curacao v. Solitron Devices Inc*, 489 F.2d 1313 (2d Cir. 1973).
1587. *Dicey Morris and Collins* Rule 71 ('If a party obtains a foreign judgment by which a foreign arbitral award is made enforceable, he may enforce that judgment in England [...]. [This] provides for the enforcement of a foreign judgment, which orders the judgment debtor to pay a sum of money in the amount of an award. It does not apply to a foreign *exequatur* under which the leave of the foreign court is given to execute the award as if it were a judgment.') and [16-163] with references to *East India Trading Co. Inc. v. Carmel Exporters and Importers Ltd*, [1952] 2 QB 439; *International Alltex Corp. v. Lawler Creations Ltd*, [1965] IR 264; *E.D. & F Man Sugar Ltd v. Lendoudis*, [2007] EWHC 2268 (Comm). *See Yugraneft Corp. v. Rexx Management Corp*, [2010] SCC 19; *E.D. & F Man Sugar Ltd v. Lendoudis*, [2007] EWHC 2268 (Comm); *ABCI v. Banque Franco-Tunisienne*, [1996] 1 Lloyd's Rep. 495 (Comm) aff'd on other aspects by [1997] Lloyd's Rep. 531 (CA) (Brussels Regime inapplicable).
1588. *Biakh v. Hyundai Corp*, (1990) XV Y.C.A. 360 (SCNSW).
1589. *Harendra H Metha v. Mukesh H Metha*, (2000) XXV Y.C.A. 641 (SCI). *See Cosid Inc. v. Steel Authority of India Ltd*, (1985) XI Y.C.A. 502 (HC India).
1590. Israel Supreme Court, *Puckholz v. Sohachesky*, 13 May 1999, No. 10854/07 cited by Einhorn, (2010) 12 YB Priv Int'l L. 45.
1591. Cf. *Minmetals Germany GmbH v. Gerco Steel Ltd*, [1999] 1 All ER 315, 331 (Comm) ('very strong policy consideration before English courts that [what] has been conclusively determined by the court of the agreed supervisory jurisdiction [on] the award should stand').
1592. *Belmont Partners LLC v. Mina Mar Group Inc*, 741 FSupp2d 743 (WDVa 2010); Restatement (Third) Int'l Comm Arbitration, § 4-8 and comment a ('Under some circumstances, it may be appropriate for the court, in acting upon a motion for post-award relief, to give preclusive effect to an earlier judicial decision that considered the same ground for challenging an

common law.[1593] Particularly, the Court of Appeal's *Yukos* judgment only re-examined the Russian annulment's partial nature and rejected to defer to the Dutch enforcement courts' reading, because it deemed the issue of 'partiality' a matter of genuinely national perceptions.[1594] In conclusion, common law broadly applies foreign judgment principles to award judgments: confirmation judgments rendered at the arbitral seat allow 'parallel entitlement'; annulment rejections at the seat as well as third-State recognitions trigger issue preclusion.

611. By contrast, civil-law courts will *not* preclude an annulment or non-recognition ground that has been previously raised unsuccessfully. The reason is the restrictive operation of res judicata. Excluding issue preclusion, res judicata is exclusively attached to the prior award judgment's dispositif[1595] which would then state nothing but 'the request for set aside is rejected' or that 'the arbitral award is recognized'. Hence, the exclusive question for civil law-courts is whether a confirmation or exequatur judgment can *itself* be a ground for recognition and enforcement. In general, this is rejected.[1596] Most expressly, the German Federal Court of Justice's 2009 judgment lays out the counterarguments.[1597] Yet, any of them meets opposition.

---

arbitration agreement or arbitral award. In other situations, de novo consideration of the recurrent issue is appropriate. The preclusive effect, if any, to be afforded the prior judicial determination will depend on the circumstances of each particular case. [...] Whether a prior judicial determination is given preclusive effect in a post-award action may depend on, among other things, the law that governed that determination in the prior action. With respect to certain grounds for granting or denying post-award relief - such as the invalidity of the arbitration agreement - the law applicable to the ground is the same regardless of whether the ground is raised to defeat a motion to compel arbitration, to vacate the resulting award, or to resist confirmation, recognition, or enforcement of the award. Because the applicable law is identical, the prior determination can readily be given preclusive effect.').

1593. Scherer, (2013) 4 J. Int'l Disp Settlement 593; *Mustill and Boyd* 288 (on grounds of comity). Cf. Harder, (2013) 62 ICLQ 456. For obiters *see Chantiers de l'Atlantique SA v. Ganztansport & Technigaz SAS*, [2011] EWHC 3383, [313-318] per Flaux J. (Comm); *Dallah Real Estate and Tourism Holding Company v. The Ministry of Religious Affairs, Government of Pakistan*, [2010] UKSC 46, [29] per Lord Mance ('[...] an English judgment holding that the award is not valid could prove significant in relation to [the French set-aside] proceedings if French courts recognise any principle similar to the English principle of issue estoppel'); *ABCI v. Banque Franco-Tunisienne and Others*, [2002] 1 Lloyd's Rep. 511 per Chambers J. (QB); not addressed in the appeal, [2003] EWCA Civ 205; *Karaha Bodas Co. LLC v. Perusahaan Pertambangan Minyak Dan Gas Bumi Negara*, [2003] HKCFI 390, [48-53].

1594. *Yukos Capital SarL v. OJSC Rosneft Oil Company*, [2012] EWCA Civ 855, [151]. Reversing *Yukos Capital SarL v. OJSC Rosneft Oil Company*, [2011] EWHC 1461, [107] (Comm). Applied in *Diag Human Se v. Czech Republic*, [2014] EWHC 1639 (Comm).

1595. *See supra* [113].

1596. France: CA Paris, *sté Unichips Finanziaria SPA et al. v. Gesnouin Consorts*, 12 February 1993, [1993] Rev. Arb. 256; *Fouchard Gaillard and Goldman* [1595]; Georgia: Georgian Supreme Court, *Polestar*, 26 March 2010, A 1985-S-68-09; Italy: Corte di Cassazione, *Fratelli Damiano v. August Topfer & Co*, (1992) XVII Y.C.A. 559; Switzerland: TF, 28 July 2010, 233/2010, (2012) 30 ASA Bull. 97, [3.]. Yet, *see* the distinction to modifying judgments, TF, 20 July 2007, 4A137/2007, (2007) 25 ASA Bull. 798, [F.5] ('*Hat das staatliche Gericht - wie hier – das Recht, einen Schiedsspruch in einem Berufungsverfahren abzuändern, stellt sein Entscheid keinen Schiedsspruch mehr dar*').

1597. BGH, 1 September 2009, IX ZR 152/06, (2010) XXXV Y.C.A. 374, [15-24]. Overruling BayObLG, 27 June 1999, XXVIII Y.C.A. (2003), 259; RGZ 49, 45, 51; OLG Hamburg, [1964] MDR 853 (domestic constellations). Shortly rendered before: OLG München, 22 June 2009, [2010] SchiedsVZ 169, 172 = (2010) XXXV Y.C.A. 371, [9] ('[The Spanish annulment]

612. (i) Undisputedly, the NYC sought to prevent double exequatur.[1598] However, as explicitly provided by its Article VII, the NYC does not seek to impede more favourable arbitration law.[1599] Particularly, parallel entitlement promotes arbitration in that it can facilitate the recovery of post-award interests and help to enforce non-signatories to the NYC.[1600]

613. (ii) A confirmation or exequatur does not '*decide afresh the merits*'[1601] and is merely directed at the execution forum. Yet, in opposition to the application of *exequatur sur exequatur ne vaut*[1602] on arbitral awards, scholars point out that arbitration exequaturs create a 'specified legal situation', transposing the contractual award into a procedural right.[1603] Moreover, any judgment is prima facie territorial. Yet, judgments are recognized abroad in order to conform to the parties' specified expectations and the quest for decisional harmony across jurisdictional frontiers.[1604]

614. (iii) As to procedural tactics and fairness, the German Federal Court of Justice expressed that parallel entitlement unduly favoured creditors which could select between several enforcement paths. Correspondingly, Maxi Scherer highlights the forum-shopping dangers arising out of a shift in review, e.g., where an exequatur court exercises a lenient control of Article V(1)(a) NYC as in *Dallah*.[1605] Now, however, prominent common-law authorities have responded to this concern and restricted parallel entitlement: public policy prevents parallel entitlement where the confirmation court's standards fall short of Article V NYC.[1606]

615. (iv) This leaves the focus with the quest for decisional harmony. Whilst a deferral to other enforcement judgments might indeed create disorder and incentives for forum shopping, a deferral of enforcement courts to the set-aside courts serves decisional

decision of 17 June 2008 is binding, pursuant to Sect. 328(1) ZPO [...] as to the preliminary question whether there is a valid arbitral award under national Spanish law.').

1598. Cf. District Court Amsterdam, *SPP (Middle East) Ltd v. Arab Republic of Egypt*, 12 July 1984, (1985) Y.C.A. 287; TF, 3 January 2006, 5P.292/2005; *UNCITRAL Guide to NYC* 207; Liebscher in Wolff (ed.), *New York Convention* Art. V [357].

1599. Cf. Bermann, (2015) 382 Rec. des cours [740-741].

1600. *Schlosser* [908]; Borges, *Das Doppelexequatur* 230-231. Certainly, the rule on interests under *London Chatham and Dover Railway Co. v. South Eastern Railway Co*, (1893) AC 429 (HL) has been reversed by s. 49 1996 Arbitration Act.

1601. Formulation by Scherer, (2013) 4 J. Int'l Disp Settlement 606.

1602. Cf. Gaudemet-Tallon, [1994] Rev. crit. DIP 377; Gottwald, in *Münchener Kommentar* § 722 [32-33]; Kegel, in *Festschrift Müller-Freienfels* 377-384. *See* ECJ, 20 January 1994, *Owens Bank*, C-129/92, EU:C:1994:13, [28-34] (Bruxelles Regime does not apply on Member State Judgments recognising Third-State Judgments). The French phrase has been established by Gavalda, [1935] Clunet 106. *See* on the rule's application at common (procedural) law *Dicey Morris and Collins* [14-036].

1603. Bollée, *Sentences arbitrales* [406-9]. Cf. Solomon, *Die Verbindlichkeit von Schiedssprüchen* 600-3.

1604. Mayer, (2017) 19 ICCA Congress Series 710-711. Cf. Bollée, *Sentences arbitrales* [420-421].

1605. Scherer, (2013) 4 J. Int'l Dispute Settlement 610-611.

1606. Bermann, (2015) 381 Rec. des cours [742]; *Dicey Morris and Collins* [16-165] ('It is suggested that, save in an exceptional case, it is likely to be contrary to public policy to enforce a judgment on an award, where there are proven grounds to refuse enforcement of the award itself under the provisions of Art. V New York Convention.').

harmony when the revocation ground is identical.[1607] Given the perhaps universal examination of arbitral jurisdiction in set-aside proceedings under Article V(1)(a) NYC, one might particularly raise that the concentration of jurisdictional prerogatives with the arbitral seat effectively prevents multi-fora disputes on jurisdictional matters.

616. Hence, even though there are convincing reasons to award confirmation judgments with parallel entitlement in civil law, the latter is *de lege lata* restrictive. In conclusion, award judgments trigger a severe discussion on the applicability of foreign judgment principles. Whilst common law generally applies them, other jurisdictions award them to annulments only and French law rejects any application.

[B] Pre-emptive Jurisdictional Decisions and Foreign Judgment Principles

617. The conclusive effects of judicial supervision in arbitral matters do not only trigger *revisionary* adjudications but also *pre-emptive* adjudications such as orders compelling arbitrations, anti-suit injunctions or decisions about challenges to the arbitral tribunal's independence and impartiality. Can the decisive issues for such decisions, e.g., the validity of the arbitration agreement be re-raised again in subsequent set-aside or recognition procedures or does the prior jurisdictional decision preclude this? Whilst scholarship is not as comprehensive as for award judgments, there appears no doctrinal or practical reason why the parameters of the discussion should differ. Hence, courts faced with the conclusive effects of pre-emptive jurisdictional decisions by foreign courts will address whether (i) the decision is generally susceptible to foreign judgment principles and, if it is, (ii) triggers res judicata.

618. The latter criteria will regularly bar conclusive effects of *preliminary* assessments of the arbitration agreement, since res judicata can only operate for *final* decisions.[1608] This excludes discretionary measures such as stays of litigation at common law and *prima-facie* declarations of incompetence (*competence-competence négatif*) by French courts under Article 1448(1) CPC.[1609] In addition, it will equally exclude anti-suit injunctions. Moreover, when a court declares itself incompetent, the decision will not constitute res judicata on the arbitration agreement before other civil-law courts, since the said agreement is regularly not mentioned in the dispositif. Instead, only a declarative judgment on the arbitration agreement's validity will be a ground for res judicata. For instance, as an amendment to the UNCITRAL Model Law, the German § 1032(2) ZPO codifies such declarative judgments.[1610] It does comprise res judicata effects in subsequent set asides before German courts.[1611] However, if *foreign* courts

1607. Mayer, (2017) 19 ICCA Congress Series 714. *See* Nazzini, (2018) 66 Am. J. Comp. L. 603 et seqq.
1608. Cf. *Born* 3219.
1609. Cf. *Poudret and Besson* [515].
1610. 'Prior to the constitution of the arbitral tribunal, an application may be made to the court to determine whether or not arbitration is admissible.'
1611. Huber and Bach in Böckstiegal et al. (eds), *Arbitration in Germany*, s. 1032 ZPO [57-60].

were to render a declarative judgment on the validity of an arbitration agreement, the above-mentioned rationales of civil-law jurisprudence that seek to prevent procedural tactics might equally apply. Hence, there is a significant ground to assume that they would *not* be recognizable.

619. At common law by contrast, the doctrine of issue preclusion generally guarantees that any judgment about arbitral jurisdiction will be preclusive in eventual set-aside or enforcement proceedings.[1612] As to the susceptibility to foreign judgment principles, there appear no policy reasons why pre-emptive jurisdictional decisions should enjoy less susceptibility than award judgments. Again, common law provides a broader basis than civil law for considering pre-emptive jurisdictional decisions as conclusive.

[C] Signatories to the Arbitration Agreement as Privies?

620. *If* a jurisdictional decision is conclusive upon subsequent litigations such as set asides or enforcement proceedings, the follow-up issue arises whether the conclusive effect also exists towards *third parties* that did not participate in the proceedings leading to the court decision on the arbitration clause. Practically, this issue necessitates that the arbitration clause is prima facie multilateral, yet that not all signatories have participated in the prior proceedings and that a non-participant is exposed to, or relies on the allegedly invalid arbitration clause. Effectively, such case scenarios will be particularly relevant at common law where conclusive effects of prior judgments on arbitral jurisdictions are widely acknowledged.[1613] Yet, it might also arise before civil-law courts if the prior decisions focused on a declaration of the arbitration agreement's validity, yet not all of its signatories participated in it. Finally, it will be relevant for award judgments when the arbitral award has been rendered between more than two parties, one creditor sought enforcement against one debtor, and either of them finds himself in further enforcement proceedings against another party. In all those case scenarios, a jurisdiction admitting arbitration judgments' susceptibility to foreign judgment principles has to address the question whether non-participating signatories to the arbitration agreement are exposed to the conclusive effect under the applicable law, regularly the *lex fori*.[1614]

621. At common law, jurisdictional decisions will regularly operate in personam. When a court is seized with a claim and incidentally assesses an arbitration agreement, there is an ordinary decision operating in person. When the court is seized with the recognition of an award, the decision bars or creates a procedural claim of the award creditor towards the award debtor. Therefore, the decisive issue is whether non-participating signatories to the arbitration agreement can be perceived as privies in

1612. Berman, (2015) 381 Rec. des cours [627]; *Born* 3219 citing *In re Pharmacy Benefit Managers Antitrust Litigation*, 582 F.3d 432, 439 (3d Cir. 2009); *Agrico Chem Co. v. Williams Co, Inc*, 2005 WL 2044942 (ND Fla); *N. River Ins. Co. v. Philadelphia Reins Corp*, 63 F.3d 160, 165 (2d Cir. 1995).
1613. *See supra* [602-611].
1614. *See supra* [371-373].

interest. In this regard, it is submitted that the mere standing as a signatory to a multilateral arbitration agreement should *not* suffice to establish any privy position. Instead, a non-participating signatory might have individual interests not adequately represented by the participating co-signatory. Therefore, the threshold for a privy position should require further indicators such as the non-participating signatory's joint substantive liability/claim, its communality of desired results and an effective communication with a participant. Only if such high threshold is met, a signatory to an arbitration agreement can be exposed to issue preclusion of jurisdictional procedures. In Germanic jurisdictions, the test will be even stricter, since discretionary privy assessments do not exist. Instead, they require that another provision of procedural or civil law itself and generally expose third parties to claim preclusion.[1615] Since such provision does not exist for multilateral arbitration agreements, there is limited ground to consider non-participating signatories bound.

Interim Conclusion

622. In conclusion, subjecting decisions about arbitral jurisdiction to foreign judgment principles only partially establishes Forum Coordination in jurisdictional matters. In general, common law acknowledges parallel entitlement and jurisdictional issue preclusion. By contrast, civil-law jurisdictions are averse to any binding effects beyond annulments and declarations on the arbitration agreement. Hence, when the particular effect of an arbitration agreement towards non-signatories is at stake, the potential for conflicting judgments remains. Moreover, if a general issue of the arbitration agreement's validity concerns multiple signatories, non-participating signatories will not be exposed to the jurisdictional decision's conclusive effect.

§9.02 CONCLUSIVE EFFECTS OF ARBITRATION JUDGMENTS BEFORE ARBITRAL TRIBUNALS

623. Before arbitral tribunals, it is yet again already debated whether prior judicial examinations of the arbitration agreement's validity are generally susceptible to conclusive effects. In particular, this might cause tension with the principle of *competence-competence* (*see* [A], *infra*). Even if this preclusion were permissible, the personal nature of the arbitral obligation to adjudicate demands to strictly adhere to party identity when allowing conclusive effects (*see* [B], *infra*).

[A] Status Quo: Jurisdictional Res Judicata and Competence-Competence

624. In *Chapter 1*, it has been submitted that courts' annulment powers establish a vertical hierarchy over arbitral tribunals in jurisdictional matter.[1616] In addition, it has

1615. *See supra* [202-208].
1616. *See supra* [85].

been outlined that jurisdictions rejecting the principle of *competence-competence négative* allow courts to rule on the arbitration agreement even before the award is rendered; e.g., when being seized with a motion to stay or compel arbitration.[1617] Such measures raise the question as to their binding effect on parallel or subsequent arbitrations. Scholarship primarily stresses the necessity to differentiate. Certainly, res judicata can merely be relevant when the court has fully assessed an arbitration clause and not contended itself with a discretionary stay or a prima facie assessment.[1618] Another aspect particularly relevant for civil lawyers might be whether the arbitration agreement is mentioned within a decision's dispositif.[1619] Whilst there is ample municipal authority on the binding obligations of arbitral tribunals to comply with previous judgments on the arbitration clause,[1620] limitations are raised when (i) the court had merely declined its own jurisdiction by virtue of an arbitration agreement[1621] or (ii) the court was not part of the arbitral seat.[1622] Correspondingly, the tribunal in *ICC Case 6535* considered itself bound to a prior judgment from the arbitral seat affirming the arbitration clause's validity.[1623] Such approach appears well feasible under considerations of opportunism, given that courts will in the end have the last word when set asides are requested (*see* [85], *supra*).

625. By contrast, the sole arbitrator in *ICC Case 5423* assessed the validity of an arbitration clause without any recourse to the Paris Court of Appeal's prior decision holding the clause valid.[1624] Moreover, scholarship opposes binding effects on jurisdiction.[1625] Particularly, Gary Born has raised the argument that courts have to apply Article II NYC. Hence, their rejection of arbitral jurisdiction risked to violate treaty law and thus needed to be reviewable by tribunals.[1626] Another counterargument is the fact that the arbitrators remain obligated towards the parties only.[1627] Moreover, other tribunals have refused to refer to jurisdictional assessments of courts outside the seat,

1617. *See supra* [86].
1618. *See Born* 3778; Schaffstein, *Res Judicata* [6.41].
1619. Cf. *Poudret and Besson* [516-517].
1620. In addition to the previous note England: *Repub. Of Kazakhstan v. Istil Group Inc*, [2008] 1 Lloyd's Rep. 382, 395 (QB); *Nat'l Navigation Co. v. Endesa Generacion SA*, [2009] EWCA Civ 1397. Germany: Schwab and Walther, *Schiedsgerichtsbarkeit* Ch. 7 [3] (judgment declining jurisdiction binding). Italy: Corte di Cassazione, *Italo Meneghetti v. Töpfer*, (1990) XII Y.C.A. 493 (judgment declining jurisdiction binding). Switzerland: Poudret, in *ASA Special Series* 159.
1621. ATF 120 II 155, *United Arab Emirates v. Westland Helicopters*, 164 ('If the court declines its jurisdiction, its decision does not bind the arbitration tribunal seized at a later stage'); ATF 124 III 83, *Compania Minera Condesa SA et al. v. BRGM-Pérou SAS*, 86-87; *Westland Helicopters Ltd v. Al-Hejailan*, [2004] EWHC 1625 (Comm).
1622. Bucher, (2001) Semaine Judiciaire No. 5 191.
1623. *ICC Case 6535*, Award of 1992, (1991-1995) III ICC Collection 495, 496 ('*Le tribunal arbitral considère également que le tribunal étatique [...] a décidé, d'une manière qui lie le tribunal arbitral*').
1624. *ICC Case 5423*, Arbitral Award, 1987, (1986-1990) II ICC Collection 339, 341.
1625. *See* Perret, in *ASA Special Series* 66; Schaffstein, *Res Judicata* [6.49-6.50] (merely persuasive effect of jurisdictional decisions).
1626. *Born* 3782.
1627. *See supra* [519].

which seems valuable, since the argument of opportunism can no longer prevail.[1628] In conclusion, the existence of jurisdictional res judicata is controversial.

[B] The Personal Nature of the Arbitral Tribunal's Obligation to Adjudicate

626. If an arbitral tribunal generally considers a prior determination of a court on, e.g., the arbitration agreement's validity binding, the follow-up issue arises whether this also applies towards a signatory to the arbitration agreement that participates in the proceeding before the tribunal, yet has not participated in the prior proceedings. In this regard, it is submitted that the preferable perspective to perceive res judicata before arbitral tribunals as a restriction of the arbitral obligation to adjudicate[1629] opposes any application towards prior third parties. In particular, with regard to jurisdictional matters, the very core of the arbitral obligation to adjudicate is at stake. This even further increases the threshold for third-party effects. Whilst the threshold under national procedural laws is already significant,[1630] the interrelation with the obligation to adjudicate renders any application unpreferable. Therefore, even if an application of jurisdictional res judicata is regarded as admissible, it should only be applied when all the parties exposed thereto participated in the prior proceedings.

§9.03 CONCLUSIVE EFFECTS OF JURISDICTIONAL DECISIONS BY ARBITRAL TRIBUNALS

627. Finally, the examination mentions whether jurisdictional decision *by an arbitral tribunal* can also trigger conclusive effect. In addition to the above-mentioned considerations, the effectively limited binding force of such jurisdictional decisions additionally opposes any conclusive effects. In domestic settings, jurisdictional determinations by arbitral tribunals have no determinative force on courts. Instead, they can be reviewed in set-aside and recognition proceedings.[1631] Given the powers of courts to reject recognition and enforcement under Article V(1)(a) NYC, this also applies in international case scenarios: courts maintain the jurisdictional prerogative over arbitral tribunals. Thus, the binding force of jurisdictional determinations by arbitral tribunals will primarily be an issue before other arbitral tribunals.

1628. *ICC Case 4862*, (1986-1990) II ICC Collection, 508 (decision from Yemen, arbitration in France); *ICC Case 5294*, (1989) XIV Y.C.A. 137 (decision from Egypt, arbitration in Switzerland); *ICC Case 10623*, Arbitral Award, 7 December 2001, (2003) 21 ASA Bull. 82, [128] (decision from Ethiopia, arbitration in Switzerland); Hague Arrondissementsrechtbank, *Repub. of Indonesia v. Himpurna* Cal. *Energy Ltd*, (2000) XXV Y.C.A. 469 (decision from Indonesia, arbitration in the Netherlands).

1629. *See supra* [519].

1630. *See supra* [612-613].

1631. *See supra* [85].

628. Again, the views are divided. The ILA does '*not exclude giving awards [on jurisdiction] preclusive and conclusive effects*,' since the annulment exposure '*creates a question of validity and res judicata is predicated on the assumption that an award is valid*'.[1632]

629. *Poudret and Besson* consider subsequent tribunals bound when the arbitral seat has accepted the prior jurisdictional decision.[1633] Moreover, the tribunal in *ICC Case 3383* applied jurisdictional res judicata. In this case, an Iranian and a Belgian party to an installation contract agreed on ICC arbitration, yet formed an ad hoc clause during the first arbitration hearing. Since the ad hoc tribunal regarded this clause invalid, the disputed returned to the ICC tribunal considering the ruling on the ad hoc clause binding, yet rejecting the ICC clause to have revived.[1634] By contrast, tribunals in other cases refused to refer to prior tribunals' jurisdictional decisions. This applies to an unpublished Milan Arbitration Chamber Award[1635] – notably containing a dissenting opinion – and an unpublished ICC award eventually leading to an unsuccessful annulment judgment of the Paris Court of Appeal.[1636] In conclusion, it is uncertain whether res judicata should be awarded to prior jurisdictional decisions of tribunals. Even if it were permissible, it should not apply towards third parties for the aforementioned reason (*see* [626], *supra*).

§9.04 CONCLUDING THESES

(1) Multilateral transactions operate against the inherent risk of having jurisdictional issues brought before multiple courts, each of them prima facie exercising its own prerogative on, e.g., the validity of the arbitration clause or the effect on non-signatories.[1637]

(2) If the competent court annuls an arbitral award for jurisdictional deficiency, most jurisdictions will reject to enforce the annulled award, an exception being France.[1638]

(3) Moreover, common-law courts will not only defer to foreign *annulments* but also to foreign confirmations, annulment rejections or exequaturs in that they allow parallel entitlement and jurisdictional issue preclusion. By contrast, civil-law courts exclude parallel entitlement and do not acknowledge issue preclusion.[1639]

1632. *ILA Final Report on Res Judicata* [20].
1633. *Poudret and Besson* [477].
1634. *ICC Case 3383*, Award, 1979, (1974-1985) I ICC Collection 394.
1635. *Milan Arbitration Chamber* Case 2308, Award of 2009, unpublished, reported by Radicati di Brozolo, in *ASA Special Series* 16-17.
1636. CA Paris, *Papillon Group Corporation v. République Arabe de Syrie*, 26 March 2009, [2010] Rev. Arb. 525.
1637. *See supra* [599].
1638. *See supra* [604].
1639. *See supra* [605-611].

(4) Even if the application of foreign judgment principles were admissible, third-party effects should be handled restrictively. Particularly, signatories to an arbitration agreement are not privies per se.[1640]

(5) The binding effect of prior jurisdictional decisions before arbitral tribunals concerns the latter's competence-competence and the obligation to adjudicate. In arbitral scholarship and jurisprudence, the applicability of res judicata is divided.[1641]

(6) Even if jurisdictional res judicata were applicable, the personal nature of the obligation to adjudicate bars the application towards third parties to the prior proceeding.[1642]

1640. *See supra* [613].
1641. *See supra* [616-617, 620].
1642. *See supra* [618].

CHAPTER 10
Conclusions

§10.01 OBSERVATIONS ON ARBITRAL AWARDS' THIRD-PARTY EFFECTS UNDER NATIONAL LAWS

630. The general standard pursuant to which an arbitral award comprises preclusive, conclusive or factual effects in follow-up litigation towards third parties (third-party effect) is not explicitly addressed, neither under national statutes nor in appellate jurisprudence. Yet, two cornerstones can be revealed from jurisprudence and scholarship. Primarily, judgment principles apply. Hence, an arbitral award establishes third-party effects if a comparable judgment would. This concerns four scenarios in particular. *First*, an arbitral award can be invoked erga omnes when it adjudicates a legal status. *Second*, arbitral awards can generally establish non-mutual preclusion at common law in that an arbitral party cannot invoke any unsuccessful argument in follow-up litigation, irrespective of the subsequent opponent. *Third*, res judicata can be invoked against privies. Whilst the privy position of successors is rather uncontroversial, national laws might differ with regard to co-obligors, sureties, guarantors, shareholders and insurers. Yet, they concur that a privy position has to be inferred from either a legal position or effective actions and, in any case, will be an impediment on the right to be heard. *Fourth*, an arbitral award might comprise factual effects in that the existence of the obligations imposed on or the claims conferred to an arbitral party trigger further consequences under other legal provisions, e.g., for objective impossibility or damages quantifications. The exclusive doctrine explicitly stipulating such effect is French law's *opposabilité*. Notably though, jurisprudence has exceedingly applied this concept in functional relation to issue preclusion.[1643]

631. The additional observation is: judgment principles will not exclusively govern arbitral awards' third-party effects. Instead, there is continuous authority that an

1643. *Supra* Chapters 3, 4, 7.

arbitral award cannot affect third parties that have not been bound by the underlying arbitration *agreement*. At common law, there is ample authority that such third parties can generally neither be exposed to issue preclusion nor rely on non-mutual preclusion. The French *Cour de Cassation* has not precluded a guarantor from a third-party appeal against an arbitral award, although judgment principles would have allowed precluding him. An *obiter* of the Swiss Federal Tribunal and German scholarship state accordingly. Conceptually, the examination supports such reconciliation of arbitral jurisdiction and arbitral effects. It is the exclusive means for guaranteeing that third-party effects operate as intended in civil procedure: as a shift of the participatory burden.[1644]

§10.02 PROPOSALS FOR INTERNATIONAL ARBITRAL AWARDS' THIRD-PARTY EFFECTS

632. *Third-party effects of foreign arbitral awards before courts* demand an assessment of the New York Convention (NYC). Even though desirable, it establishes no uniform regime of res judicata yet. Instead, nothing but its recognition mechanism can apply to awards' third-party effects. In this regard, it is submitted that Article V(1)(a) NYC can and should generally restrict arbitral awards' third-party effects towards strangers to the underlying arbitration agreement. This boundary equally applies to non-mutual preclusion. Moreover, it generally applies to status and factual effects unless:

- the third party would have had no standing to submit on the prior subject matter;
- the factual effect does not prevent a review of the arbitral award; or
- the factual effect prevents absolute irreconcilability between the arbitral award and the eventual judgment.[1645]

633. If Article V(1)(a) NYC is no obstacle to an arbitral award's third-party effect, the further operation will be assessed under the follow-up litigation's *lex fori*. Yet, if the *lex fori* comprise a discretionary standard for awards' third-party effects such as common law with regard to non-mutual preclusion and privy positions, the court may take into consideration that certain aspects of the multilateral relationship such as the arbitration agreement, intervention possibilities or the law of the substance are governed by foreign law.[1646]

634. *Third-party effects of prior decisions before international arbitral tribunals* can be assessed under transnational principles. In this regard, the examination proposes to adopt the differentiations revealed by virtue of comparative law. Accordingly, res judicata should only apply if all parties to the arbitration:

1644. *Supra* Chapter 4.
1645. *Supra* Chapters 5, 7.
1646. *Supra* Chapter 6.

- have been parties to the prior proceedings;
- are successors to the parties thereto; or
- have agreed on such preclusion.

Moreover, res judicata can apply towards third parties to the prior proceedings, if the latter could (from a jurisdictional perspective) and should (from a due-process perspective) have participated in the prior proceedings.

In addition, prior decisions on issues of status and factual effects can be referred to, although prior awards' factual effects should be treated under the above-mentioned restriction.[1647]

635. Finally, even if *award judgments and pre-emptive decisions about arbitral jurisdiction* were susceptible to preclusion and foreign judgment principles, the status of a signatory to the arbitration agreement as such does not justify its exposure to such decision.[1648]

§10.03 RETURN ON PRACTICE: AN INCENTIVE PRE-EMPTION OF JURISDICTIONAL TACTICS

636. Given the application of Article V(1)(a) NYC before courts and the application of jurisdictional and due-process principles before arbitral tribunals, this examination has generally taken a restrictive position towards arbitral awards' third-party effects. It largely opposes them where invoked in indemnity matters (against suppliers, subcontractors, potential insurers) or in sequential claims against connected debtors (co-obligors, related companies, main debtor and surety/guarantor). This might expose the proposal to the criticism that res judicata were an ineffective tool against the risks of multi-fora disputes and conflicting decisions as they are particularly pertinent for multilateral case scenarios. Indeed, this is the case. However, the very reason is that res judicata is only *one* out of *several* means of Forum Coordination. Therefore, it is submitted that the analysis of arbitral awards' third-party effects should not occur in an isolated manner. The issue is not as simple as 'is an arbitral award preclusive and conclusive towards all commercially related parties?'. Instead, it is necessary to frame this issue against the bigger picture and ask: *is the third-party effect of arbitral awards the most foreseeable and fairest solution in order to establish Forum Coordination for multilateral transactions*? It is in this regard that the examination answers in the negative.

637. In particular, the primary submission of this examination is that any third-party effect of arbitral awards that exceeds prior potentials for joinders, consolidation and lis pendens will disregard res judicata's procedural origin as a shift of the participatory burden. Moreover, it will open the floodgate for procedural tactics. As long as arbitral

1647. *Supra* Chapter 8.
1648. *Supra* Chapter 9.

tribunals' jurisdiction for such measures is *de lege lata* limited by the arbitration *agreement*'s scope, the latter should also restrict an arbitral award's third-party effect.

638. Certainly though, the 'nightmare of inconsistent decisions'[1649] requires prevention. The examination's core contention is that res judicata should not be the stage to do so. Instead, multiparty case scenarios require carefully drafted arbitration or jurisdiction agreements providing for combined dispute resolutions which prevent any lack of power of tribunals over third parties as identified as on arbitration's key deficits in the 2018 Queen Mary International Arbitration Survey. To facilitate multi-party arbitration, all major arbitral rules have recently updated their rules with multiparty provisions.[1650] Alternatively, they require carefully drafted preclusion agreements. The strict third-party standard introduced is perceived as an incentive for such agreements. Thus, it is submitted that the strict proposal's return on practice is both the prevention of procedural tactics and the emphasized incentive for the conclusion of multiparty arbitration clauses, *forum*-selection clauses or preclusion agreements.

§10.04 RETURN ON THEORY: A MANIFESTATION OF ARBITRATION'S HYBRID DESIGN

639. In general, the position in favour of or against arbitration might expose an author's '*notion of the law*'.[1651] By virtue of its strict proposals on arbitral awards' third-party effects, the instant examination takes a position in favour of arbitration, against its judicialization and in favour of its party-autonomy foundation instead. Moreover, its restrictive positions originate from the understanding that despite interests of justice, consistency, certainty and efficiency, adjudicatory effects can only result out of adjudicatory participation (or the sufficient possibility to participate). Such submission should be perceived as a submission safeguarding due process.

640. Taking the examination's core objective, i.e., to protect party autonomy and due process, a final step further, the examination would like to apply this general position to the fundamental conceptual tension that was underlying this study and arbitration scholarship: the tension between arbitration's contractual foundation and its judicial function. This tension is at the heart of the judicial/contractual/hybrid discussion on arbitration in general and the territorialist/pluralistic/transnational/a-national discussion on the legal theory of *international* arbitration in particular.[1652] In the latter regard, the examination has no ambition to conclusively adopt any standpoint and thereby subject its proposals to one notion. Yet, it may comment on the support that its proposals provide. In general, the examination has continuously expressed that the regime for res judicata cannot be both, a justification for and a consequence of

1649. *See supra* [1].
1650. *See supra* [37].
1651. Mayer, (2017) Rev. Arb. 363 ('[...] *une citation d'un auteur espagnol: Selon qu'une personne se déclarera pour ou contre [l'arbitrage], on aura découvert le fond de sa pensée, métaphysique plus que dogmatique, sur ce que le droit doit être véritablement.*').
1652. *See supra* [119-124].

arbitration's juridicity or territoriality. Instead, res judicata's underlying rationales should guide the discussion. In cross-border case scenarios, these rationales imply that, before courts, the former arbitral seat's law does not govern res judicata and that, before arbitral tribunals, transnational principles can apply. Either proposal can apply as an argument *against* territorialist notions of arbitration.

641. More specifically, it is with regard to arbitration's general character that the examination seeks to contribute. In particular, the standard for determining arbitral awards' third-party effects seeks to reconcile both arbitration's consensual foundation (by focusing on the underlying arbitration agreement's scope) and its judicial function (by applying proceduralist due-process principles). Accordingly, the proposed regime on arbitral awards' third-party effects is the very manifestation of arbitration's hybrid design.

Bibliography

Institutional Publications

American Law Institute

Restatment (Second) Conflict of Laws (1971).
Restatement (Second) Judgments (1982).
Restatement (Third) Foreign Relations Law of the United States (1987).
Restatement (Third) U.S. Law of International Commercial Arbitration - Tentative Drafts No. 1 (29 March 2010), No. 2 (16 April 2012), No. 3 (16 April 2013), No. 4 (17 April 2015), No. 5 (30 March 2017).

European Commission

Hess, Burkhard with Pfeiffer, Thomas and Schlosser, Peter: 'Study JLS/C4/2005/03 - Report on the Application of the Regulation Brussels I in the Member States', published as *The Brussels I Regulation 44/2001* (Beck Hart Nomos 2008).
(*Heidelberg Report*)
Jenard, Paul: 'Report on the Convention on Jurisdiction and Enforcement of Judgments in Civil and Commercial Matters', (1979) *Official Journal of the European Commission* C 59/1.
(*Jenard Report*)

Institut De Droit International

'The Principles for Determining when the Use of the Doctrine of forum non conveniens and anti-injunctions is appropriate' (Rapporteurs: L Collins and G Droz), (2004) 70(II) *Annuaire de l'Institute de Droit International* 252.
(Institut de Droit International, *Forum non Conveniens and Anti-Suit Injunctions*).

International Law Association

'Declining and Referring Jurisdiction in International Litigation' (Committee on International Civil and Commercial Litigation - Chairman: P E Nygh, Rapporteur: C McLachlan), London Conference 2000, (2000) 69 *ILA Reports of Conferences* 137.
(*ILA Report on Declining and Referring Jurisdiction in International Litigation*)

'Final Report on Lis Pendens and Arbitration' (Committee on International Commercial Arbitration - Chairman: F De Ly, Rapporteur: A Sheppard), Toronto Conference 2006, (2006) 72 *ILA Reports of Conferences* 146, (2009) 25(1) *Arbitration International*, 3-34.
(*ILA Final Report on* Lis Pendens)

'Final Report on *Res Judicata* and Arbitration' (Committee on International Commercial Arbitration - Chairman: F De Ly, Rapporteur: A Sheppard), Toronto Conference 2006, (2006) 72 *ILA Reports of Conferences* 186, (2009) 25(1) *Arbitration International*, 67-82.
(*ILA Final Report on Res Judicata*)

'Interim Report on *Res Judicata* and Arbitration' (Committee on International Commercial Arbitration - Chairman: F De Ly, Rapporteur: A Sheppard), Berlin Conference 2004, (2004) 71 *ILA Reports of Conferences* 827, (2009) 25(1) *Arbitration International*, 35-66.
(*ILA Interim Report on Res Judicata*)

'Recommendations on Lis Pendens and *Res Judicata* in Arbitration' (Committee on International Commercial Arbitration - Chairman: F De Ly, Rapporteur: A Sheppard), Toronto Conference 2006, (2009) 25(1) *Arbitration International*, 83-85.
(*ILA Recommendations*)

International Law Commission

'Draft on Arbitral Procedure Prepared by the International Law Commission at Its Fourth Session in 1952', UN Doc A/CN.4/59, (1952) II *Yearbook of the International Law Commission* 60.
(*ILC Draft on Arbitral Procedure*)

UNCITRAL

'Recommendation regarding the interpretation of Article II(2) and Article VII(1) of the Convention on the Recognition and Enforcement of Arbitral Awards', 7 July 2006, UN Doc A/61/17.
(*UNCITRAL Recommendation on Article II, VII NYC*)

'Report on the survey relating to the legilsative implementation of the Convention on the Recognition and Enforcement of Foreign Arbitral Awards - New York 1958', 5 June 2008, UN Doc A/CN.9/656.
(*UNCITRAL 2008 Report on NYC*)

UNCITRAL 2012 Digest of Case Law on the Model Law on International Commercial Arbitration, available at www.uncitral.org.

(*UNCITRAL Case Digest*)
UNCITRAL Secretariat Guide on the Convention on the Recognition and Enforcement of Foreign Arbitral Awards, 2016 Edition, available at www.uncitral.org. (*UNCITRAL Guide on NYC*)

Scholarly Publications

Althammer, Christoph: *Streitgegenstand und Interesse* (Mohr Siebeck 2012).
Althammer, Christoph: 'Unvereinbare Entscheidungen, drohende Rechtsverwirrung und Zweifel an der Kernpunkttheorie', in: R Geimer and R A Schütze (eds), *Recht ohne Grenzen – Festschrift für Athanassios Kaissis zum 65. Geburtstag* (De Gruyter 2012).
Althammer, Christoph and Tolani, Madeleine: 'Neue Perspektiven für einen gemeineuropäischen Rechtskraftbegriff in der Rechtsprechung des EuGH zur EuGVVO?', (2015) *Zeitschrift für Zivilprozess International*, 227-249.
Ameli, Farhad: *La saisie-arrêt en droit international privé* (Dissertation, Paris 1990).
Ancel, Jean-Pierre: 'Une remède: la concentration du contentieux devant l'arbitre', in: B Darmois and É Glucksmann (eds), *Procédures parallèles et décisions contradictoirs* (Bruylant 2015), 141-152.
Andrews, Neil: *English Civil Procedure* (OUP 2003).
Antomo, Jennifer: *Schadensersatz für Verletzung einer Gerichtsstandsvereinbarung* (Mohr Siebeck 2017).
Arroyo, Manuel (ed.): *Arbitration in Switzerland* (Kluwer 2013).
Arrue Montenegro, Carlos Alberto: 'Le nouveau droit panaméen de l'arbitrage', (2014) *Revue de l'arbitrage*, 617-640.
Audit, Mathias: 'La loi applicable à l'autorité de la choise jugée', (2007) 8-9 *Procédures*, No. 16.
Audit, Mathias with Bollée, Sylvain and Callé, Pierre: *Droit du commerce international et des investissements étrangers* (LGDJ 2014).
(Audit Bollée and Callée, *Commerce international*)
Austmann, Andreas: 'Commercial Multi-Party Arbitration – A Case-by-Case Approach', (1990) 1(3) *American Revue of International Arbitration*, 349-372.
Bach, Ivo: *Grenzüberschreitende Vollstreckung in Europa* (Mohr Siebeck 2008).
Bach, Ivo: 'Deine Rechtskraft? Meine Rechtskraft!', (2013) *Europäische Zeitschrift für Wirtschaftsrecht*, 56-59.
Barnett, Peter: *Res Judicata, Estoppel and Foreign Judgments* (OUP 2001).
Bartin, Etienne Adolphe: 'Le jugement étranger considéré comme un fait', (1924) *Journal du droit international (Clunet)*, 857-872.
Bartin, Etienne Adolphe: *Principes de droit international privé selon la loi et la jurisprudence*, Vol I-III (LGDJ 1930-1935).
Basedow, Jürgen: *Die Anerkennung von Auslandsscheidungen* (Alfred Metzner 1980).
Basedow, Jürgen: 'Qualifikation, Vorfrage und Anpassung im International Zivilverfahrensrecht' in: P Schlosser (ed.), *Materielles Recht und Prozessrecht* (Gieseking 1992), 131-156.

Basedow, Jürgen: 'Lex Mercatoria and the Private International Law of Contracts' in: J. Baseow and T Kono (eds), *An Economic Analysis of Private International Law* (Mohr Siebeck 2006), 57-72.

Basedow, Jürgen: *The Law of Open Societies – Private Ordering and Public Regulation in the Conflict of Laws* (Brill 2015), revised publication of 'The Law of Open Societies: Private Ordering and Public Regulation of International Relations – General Course', (2012) 360 *Recueil des cours – Collected Courses of the Hague Academy of International Law*, 9-516.

Basedow, Jürgen: 'Hundert Jahre Rechtsvergleichung', (2016) 71 *Juristenzeitung*, 269-280.

Spühler, Karl with Tenchio, Luca and Infanger, Dominik: *Basler Kommentar – Schweizerische Zivilprozessordnung* (2nd ed., Helbing Lichtenhahn 2013).

([author], in *Basler Kommentar*)

Batiffol, Henri: 'Le pluralisme des méthodes en droit international privé', (1973) 139 *Recueil des cours – Collected Courses of the Hague Academy of International Law*, 75-148.

Beignier, Bernard: 'Assurance et arbitrage – la place de l'assureur dans l'instance arbitrale', (2008) *Revue de l'arbitrage*, 227-262.

Bell, Andrew S: *Forum Shopping and Venue in Transnational Litigation* (OUP 2003).

Ben Hamida, Walid: 'Développment des procédures parallèles et facteurs de désordres proceduraux dans l'arbitrage d'investissement', in: B Darmois and É Glucksmann (eds), *Procédures parallèles et décisions contradictoirs* (Bruylant 2015), 17-28.

Berger, Klaus-Peter: 'The International Arbitrators' Application of Precedents', (1992) 9(4) *Journal of International Arbitration*, 5-22.

Berger, Klaus-Peter: *International Economic Arbitration* (Deventer 1993).

Berger, Bernhard: Note (TF, 29 May 2015, 4A_633/2014), (2015) *ASA Bulletin*, 642-657.

Berger, Bernhard and Kellerhals, Franz: *International and Domestic Arbitration in Switzerland* (3rd ed., Stämpfli et al., 2015).

(Berger and Kellerhals, *Arbitration in Switzerland*)

Berman, George A: 'The "Gateway" Problem in International Commercial Arbitration', (2012) 37(1) *Yale Journal of International Law*, 1-50.

Berman, George A: 'International Arbitration and Private International Law – General Course', (2015) 382 *Recueil des cours – Collected Courses of the Hague Academy of International Law*, 41-484.

Gmür, Max (found): *Berner Kommentar – Schweizerische Zivilprozessordnung*, Vol 1-2 (Schulthess, edition of 2012).

([author], in *Berner Kommentar*)

Besson, Sébastien: 'La Portée Internationale des "Jugements sur Sentence"', in: A Menaker (ed.), *ICCA Congress Series Vol. 19* (Kluwer 2017), 675-690.

Betancourt, Julio César: 'State Liability for Broach of Article II.3 of the 1958 New York Convention', (2017) 33 *Arbitration International*, 203-247.

Bitter, Jan Willem: 'Consolidation of Arbitral Proceedings in the Netherlands – The Practice and Perspective of the Netherlands Arbitration Institute', in: PCA (ed.), *Multiple Party Actions in International Arbitration* (OUP 2009), 221-238.

Black, Vaughan and Pitel, Stephan G A: 'Forum-selection Clauses - Beyond the Contracting Parties', (2016) 12(1) *Journal of Private International Law*, 26-59.

Bléry, Corinee: *L'efficacité substantielle des jugements civils* (LGDJ 2000).

Blomeyer, Arwed: 'Rechtskrafterstreckung infolge zivilrechtlicher Abhängigkeit', (1962) 75 *Zeitschrift für Zivilprozess*, 1-27.

Böckstiegel, Karl-Heinz: 'Einführende Überlegungen zur Beteiligung Dritter an Schiedsverfahren' in: K-H Böckstiegel, K-P Berger and J. Bredow (eds), *Die Beteiligung Dritter an Schiedsverfahren* (Carl Heymanns 2005), 1-6.

Böckstiegel, Karl-Heinz with Kröll, Stephan and Nacimiento, Patricio (eds): *Arbitration in Germany: The Model Law in Practice* (2nd ed., Kluwer 2015).

([author] in Böckstiegel et al. (eds), *Arbitration in Germany*)

Boele-Woelki, Katharina: 'Unifying and Harmonizing Substantive Law and the Role of Conflict of Laws', (2010) 340 *Recueil des cours – Collected Courses of the Hague Academy of International Law*, 275-461.

Bogdan, Michael: *Private International Law as Component of the Law of the Forum* (Nijhoff 2012), Pocketbook Edition of (2010) 348 *Recueil des cours - Collected Courses of the Hague Academy of International Law*, 9-252.

Bollée, Sylvain: *Les méthodes du droit international privé à l'épreuve des sentences arbitrales* (Economica 2004).

(Bollée, *Sentences arbitrales*)

Bollée, Sylvain: Note (Cas 1e civ, 14 February 2006), (2006) *Revue critique de droit international privé*, 827-842.

Bollée, Sylvain: Note (Cass 1e civ, 4 July 2007), (2007) *Revue de l'arbitrage*, 808-820.

Bollée, Sylvain: 'La contrariété de décisions dans le contrôle des sentences arbitrales', in: B Darmois and É Glucksmann (eds), *Procédures parallèles et décisions contradictoirs* (Bruylant 2015), 101-108.

Bollée, Sylvain: 'Les effets des sentences arbitrales à l'égard des tiers', (2015) *Revue de l'arbitrage*, 695-738.

Bollée, Sylvain: 'Les recours et les tiers en matière arbitrage', (2018) *Revue de l'arbitrage*, 139-159.

Bond, Stpehan R: 'The Experience of the ICC International Court of Arbitration', in: ICC (ed.), *Multiparty Arbitration* (ICC Pub No. 480/1 1991), 39-53.

Borges, Georg: *Das Doppelexequatur von Schiedssprüchen* (de Gruyter 1997).

Born, Gary B.: *International Commercial Arbitration*, Vol I-III (2nd ed., Kluwer 2014). (*Born*)

Born, Gary B. and Rutledge, Peter: *International Civil Litigation in United States Courts* (5th ed., Kluwer 2011).

Bosch, Wolfgang: *Rechtskraft und Rechtshängigkeit im Schiedsverfahren* (Mohr Siebeck 1991).

Boyer, Louis: 'Les effets des jugements à l'égard des tiers', (1951) 49 *Revue trimestrielle de droit civil*, 163-207.

Brand, Ronald A: 'Enforcement of Foreign Money-Judgments in the United States', (1991-1992) 67(2) *Notre Dame Law Review*, 253-334.

Brekoulakis, Stavros: 'The Effect of an Arbitral Award and Third Parties in International Arbitration – Res Judicata Revisited', (2005) 16 *American Review of International Arbitration*, 177-208.

Brekoulakis, Stavros: *Third Parties in International Commercial Arbitration* (OUP 2009).

(Brekoulakis, *Third Parties in Arbitration*)

Brekoulakis, Stavros: 'Rethinking Consent in International Commercial Arbitration – A General Theory for Non-signatories', (2017) 8 *Journal of International Dispute Settlement*, 610-643.

Brenner, Susan W: 'Crossing-Over – The Issue-Preclusive Effects of a Civilian/Criminal Adjudication upon a Proceeding of the Opposite Character', (1987) 7 *Northern Illinois University Law Review*, 141-236.

Briggs, Adrian: 'The Principle of Comity in Private International Law', (2011) 354 *Recueil des cours – Collected Courses of the Hague Academy of International Law*, 65-182.

Briggs, Adrian: *Private International Law in English Courts* (OUP 2014).

Briggs, Adrian and Rees, Peter: *Civil Jurisdiction and Judgments* (5th ed., Informa 2009).

Brown, Chester: *A Common Law of International Adjudication* (CUP 2007).

Bucher, Andreas: 'La dimension sociale du droit international privé – cours général', (2009) 341 *Recueil des cours – Collected Courses of the Hague Academy of International Law*, 9-526.

Bucher, Andreas: 'La cométence universelle civile', (2015) 372 *Recueil des cours – Collected Courses of the Hague Academy of International Law*.

Burrows, Andrew (ed.): *English Private Law* (3rd ed., OUP 2013).

Calavros, *Urteilswirkungen zu Lasten Dritter* (Gieseking 1978).

Callé, Pierre: 'L'autorité de la chose jugée et les tiers' (2016) *Revue de l'arbitrage*, 77-90.

Caron, David and Caplan Lee M: *The UNCITRAL Arbitration Rules* (OUP 2006).

Casad, Robert C and Clermont, Kevin M: *Res Judicata* (Carolina Academic Press 2001).

Ceshire, Geoffrey Chevalier and North, Peter (found) with Fawcett, James (consult ed) and Torremans, Paul (ed.): *Ceshire North and Fawcett – Private International Law* (15th ed., OUP 2017).

Chambreuil, Bertrand: 'Arbitrage international et garanties bancaires', (1991) *Revue de l'arbitrage*, 33-68.

Chanais, Cécile: 'L'autorité de la chose jugée en procédure civile – perspectives de droit comparé', (2016) *Revue de l'arbitrage*, 3-50.

Cheng, Bin: *General Principles of Law as Applied by International Courts and Tribunals* (CUP 1953).

Chiu, Julie C: 'Consolidation of Arbitral Proceedings and International Arbitration', (1990) 7(2) *Journal of International Arbitration*, 53-76.

Cohn, Ernst J: 'Parties', in: U Drobnig et al. (eds), *International Encyclopedia of Comparative Law*, Vol. XVI, Civil Procedure (Mohr Siebeck 2014), Ch. 5.

Cooter, Robert and Ulen, Thomas: *Law and Economics* (6th ed., Pearson 2016).

Cound, John J, Friedenthal, Jack H. with Miller, Arthur R. and Sexton, John E.: *Civil Procedure*, Cases and Materials (8th ed., West 2001).

Cox, Kristof: 'Zen and the art of determining the effects of an arbitration award vis-à-vis third parties' in: CEPANI (ed.), *L'arbitrage et les tiers* (Bruylant 2008), 175-213.
Cromwell, Thurston K: 'Arbitration and Its Collateral Estoppel Effect on Third Parties - Vandenberg *v.* Superior Court', [2000] *Journal of Dispute Resolution*, 425-438.
Currie, Brainard: 'Mutuality of Collateral Estoppel - Limits of the Bernhard Doctrine', (1957) 9 *Stanford Law Review*, 281-322.
Currie, Brainard: 'On the Displacement of the Law of the Forum', (1958) 58 *Columbia Law Review*, 964-1028.
di Pietro, Domenico: 'General Remarks on Arbitrability under the New York Convention', in: Lukas Mistelis and Stavros Brekoulakis (eds), *Arbitrability - International and Comparative Perspectives* (Kluwer 2009), 85-98.
de Vareilles-Sommières, Pascal: 'La sentence arbitrale étrangère contraire à une loi d'ordre public du for', (2014) 3 *Journal du droit international (Clunet)*, Doctrine No. 12.
Debourg, Claire: *Les contrariétés de décisions dans l'arbitrage international* (LGDJ 2012).
Debourg, Claire: 'Imbroglio d'outils de résolutin des inconciliabilités de décisions', (2013) *Revue de l'arbitrage*, 420-438.
Debourg, Claire: 'La prévention des contrariétés de décisions arbitrales et étatiques', in: B Darmois and É Glucksmann (eds), *Procédures parallèles et décisions contradictoirs* (Bruylant 2015), 73-86.
Debourg, Claire and Scheffer Da Silveira, Gustavo: Note (Superior Tribunal de Justica, *Ferroatlântica SL v. Zeus Meneracaeo Ltda et al*), (2014) *Revue de l'arbitrage*, 746-752.
Derains, Yves and Schwartz, Eric A: *A Guide to the ICC Rules of Arbitration* (2nd ed., Kluwer 2005).
Desdevises, Yvon: 'Action en justice - Généralités' in, *Juris-Clausseur procédure civile*, Fascicule 500-60 (updated 7 August 2016).
Di Pietro, Domenico and Platte, Martin: *Enforcement of International Arbitration Awards* (Cameron May 2001).
Dicey, Albert Venn with Morris, John H C (founds) and Lord Collins of Mapesbury, Lawrence (gen. ed.): *The Conflict of Laws*, (15th ed., Sweet & Maxwell 2012).
(*Dicey Morris and Collins*)
Domat, Jean: *Les loix civiles dans leur ordre naturel, le droit public, et legum delectus*, Vol. I (1745, LEN 2017).
Domke Martin (found) and Edmonson, Larry C: *Domke on Commercial Arbitration* (3rd ed., Thomson/West 2003).
Douchy-Oudot, Mélina: 'Autorité de la chose jugée au civil sur le civil', in *Juris-Clausseur de Procédure Civile*, Fascicule 554 (LexisNexis updated on 3 July 2015).
Douglas, Zachary: 'The Hybrid Foundations of Investment Treaty Arbitration', (2003) 74 *British Yearbook of International Law*, 151-289.
Douglas, Zachary: *The International Law of Investment Claims* (CUP 2010).
Drobnig, Ulrich: in: J. Basedow et al. (eds), *Aufbruch nach Europa - 75 Jahre Max-Planck-Institut für Privatrecht* (Mohr Siebeck 2001), 745-762.

Drobnig, Ulrich: 'Gaurantee, Independent', in: J. Basedow K J Hopt and R Zimmermann (eds), *Max Planck Encyclopedia of European Private Law*, Vol 1. (OUP 2012).

Drobnig, Ulrich: 'Suretyship (Modern Law)', in: J. Basedow K J Hopt and R Zimmermann (eds), *Max Planck Encyclopedia of European Private Law*, Vol. 2 (OUP 2012).

Duclos, José: *L'opposabilité* – essai d'une théorie générale (LGDJ 1998).

Duve, Christian and Wimalasena, Phillip: 'Arbitration of Corporate Law Disputes in Germany', in: K-H Böckstiegel with S Kröll and P Nacimiento (eds), *Arbitration in Germany* (2nd ed., Kluwer 2015), 927-961.

Ehrenzweig, Albert Arnim: 'Local and Moral Data in the Conflict of Laws – Terra Incognita', (1966) 16 *Buffalo Law Review*, 55-98.

Einhorn, Talia: 'The Recognition and Enforcement of Foreign Judgments on International Commercial Arbitral Awards', (2010) 12 *Yearbook of Private International Law*, 43-67.

El Hakim, Jacques: 'Should the Key Terms Award, Commercial and Beinding be Defined in the New York Convention?', (1989) 6(1) *Journal of International Arbitration*, 161-170.

Erk-Kubat, Nadja: *Parallel Proceedings in International Arbitration* (Kluwer 2014).

Fawcett, James Jeffrey (ed.): *Declining Jurisdiction in Private International Law – Report to the XIVth Congress of the International Academy of Comparative Law* (OUP 1995).

Fentiman, Richard: *International Commercial Litigation* (2nd ed., OUP 2015).

Fohrer-Dedeurwaerder, Estelle: *La prise en considération des normes étrangères* (LGDJ 2008).

Fouchard, Philippe: *L'arbitrage commercial international* (Dalloz 1965).

Fouchard, Philippe: 'Conclusion', in: Institute of International Business Law and Practice (ed.), *Multiparty Business Disputes*, ICC Document No. 359 (1980), 59-67.

Fouchard, Philippe: 'La levée par la France de sa réserve de commercialité pour l'application de la Convention de New York', (1990) *Revue de l'arbitrage*, 571-584.

Fouchard, Philippe: Note (Cass 1e civ, 10 June 1997), (1997) *Revue de l'arbitrage*, 377-379.

Fouchard, Philippe: 'La portée internationale de l'annulation de la sentence arbitrale dans son pays d'origine', (1997) *Revue de l'arbitrage*, 329-352.

Fouchard, Philippe: 'Suggestions pour accroître l'efficacité internationale des sentences arbitrales', (1998) *Revue de l'arbitrage*, 653-672.

Fouchard, Philippe: Note (Cass 1e civ, *Zanzi v. de Coninck et al*), (1999) *Revue de l'arbitrage*, 262-271.

Foskett, David: *The Law and Practice of Compromise* (6th ed., Sweet & Maxwell 2005).

Fry, Jason with Greenberg, Simon and Mazza, Francesca: *The Secretariat's Guide to ICC Arbitration*, ICC Product No. 729E (2012).

Gaillard, Emmanuel: 'L'affaire Sofidif ou les difficultés de l'arbitrage multipartite', (1987) *Revue de l'arbitrage*, 275-292.

Gaillard, Emmanuel: 'Anti-suit Injunctions Issued by Arbitrators', in: AJ van den Berg (ed.), *ICCA Congress Series Vol. 13* (Kluwer 2007), 235-261.

Gaillard, Emmanuel: 'Abuse of Process in International Arbitration', (2017) 32(1) *ICSID Review*, 17-37.

Gaillard, Emmanuel and Savage, John: *Fouchard Gaillard and Goldman on International Commercial Arbitration* (Kluwer 1999) – translated and revised version of Fouchard, Philippe with Gaillard, Emmanuel and Goldman, *Traité de l'arbitrage commercial international* (Litec 1999).

(*Fouchard Gaillard and Goldman*)

Garnett, Richard: *Substance and Procedure in Private International Law* (OUP 2012).

Gaul, Hans Friedhelm: 'Die Rechtskraft und Aufhebbarkeit des Schiedsspruchs im Verhältnis zur Verbindlichkeit des staatlichen Richterspruchs', in: K-P Berger et al. (eds), *Festschrift Otto Sandrock zum 70. Geburtstag* (Recht und Wirtschaft 2000), 285-328.

Gebauer, Martin: 'Uniform Law, General Principles and Autonomous Interpretation', (2000) 4 *Uniform Law Review – Revue de droit uniforme*, 683-705.

Geimer, Reinhold: 'Beteiligung weiterer Parteien im Schiedsgerichtsverfahren', in: K-H Böckstiegel with K-P Berger and J. Bredow (eds), *Die Beteiligung Dritter an Schiedsverfahren* (Carl Heymanns 2005), 71-89.

Geimer, Reinhold: *Internationales Zivilprozessrecht* (7th ed., Otto Schmitt 2015).

Germelmann, Claas Friedrich: *Die Rechtskraft von Gerichtsentscheidungen in der Europäischen Union* (Mohr Siebeck 2009).

Gharavi, Hamid G: *The International Effectiveness of the Annulment of an Arbitral Award* (Kluwer 2002).

Ginsburg, Ruth B: 'Judgments in Search of Full Faith and Credit – The Last-In-Time Rule for Conflicting Judgments', (1968-1969) 82 *Harvard Law Review*, 798-832.

Glenn, H Patrick: 'Exequatur sur Exequatur – Doppelexequatur in Europe and North America', in: J. Basedow et al. (eds), *Aufbruch nach Europa – 75 Jahre Max-Planck-Institut für Privatrecht* (Mohr Siebeck 2001), 705-724.

Goldman, Berthold: 'Les conflits de lois dans l'arbitrage international de droit privé', (1963) 109 *Recueil des cours – Collected Courses of the Hague Academy of International Law*, 347-485.

Goode, Roy: 'The Role of the Lex Loci Arbitri in International Commercial Arbitration', (2001) 17(1) *Arbitration International*, 19-40.

Goode, Roy with Kronke, Herbert and McKendrick, Ewan: *Transnational Commercial Law* (2nd ed., OUP 2015).

Gordley, James: 'Comparison, Law, and Culture: A Response to Pierre Legrand', (2017) (Special Issue) *American Journal of Comparative Law*, 133-180.

Goutal, Jean-Louis: Note (Cass com, 4 June 1985), (1987) *Revue de l'arbitrage*, 139-147.

Goutal, Jean-Louis: 'L'arbitrage et les tiers – Le droit des contrats', (1988) *Revue de l'arbitrage*, 439-474.

Granier, Thomas: 'La jonction de procédures arbitrales dans le règlement de la Chambre de Commerce International', in: B Darmois and É Glucksmann (eds), *Procédures parallèles et décisions contradictoirs* (Bruylant 2015), 123-141.

Greenberg, Simon with Feris, José Ricardo and Albanesi, Christian: 'Consolidation, Joinder and Cross Claims', in: B Hanotiau and E A Schwartz (eds), *Multiparty Arbitration*, ICC Document No. 701E (2010), 161-183.

Grigera Naón, Horacia: 'Choice-of-Law Problems in International Commercial Arbitration', (2001) 289 *Recueil des Cours – Collected Courses of the Hague Academy of International Law*, 5-395.

Grigera Naón, Horacia: 'Competing Orders Between Courts of Law and Arbitral Tribunals', in: G Aksen et al., *Global Reflections on International Law, Commerce and Dispute Resolution – Liber Amicorum in Honour of Robert Brinert* (ICC 2005), 335-345.

Gröschl, Manuela: *Konkurrierende Schiedsverfahren in Investitionsstreitigkeiten* (Shaker 2017).

Guinchard, Serge with Chainais, Cécile and Ferrand, Frédérique: *Procédure civile* (33rd ed., Dalloz 2016).

Guldener, Max: *Schweizerisches Zivilprozessrecht* (2nd ed., Schulthess 1958).

Guzmann, Andrew T: 'Choice of Law – New Foundations', (2002) 90 *Georgetown Law Journal*, 883-940.

Häberle, Peter: 'Grundrechtsgeltung und Grundrechtsinterpretation – Zugleich zur Rechtsvergleichung als "fünfter" Auslegungsmethode', (1989) *Juristenzeitung*, 913-925.

Habersack, Mathias: *Vertragsfreiheit und Drittinteressen* (Duncker Humblodt 1992).

Habscheid, Walter: 'Die Präklusionswirkung des rechtskräftigen Urteils', (1952) 152 *Archiv für die civilistische Praxis*, 169-182.

Habscheid, Walter: 'Quelques questions fondamentales concernant l'autorité de la chose jugée en droit comparé', in: *Liber amicorum – Adolf F Schnitzer offert à l'occasion de son 90e anniversaire le 30 Juillet 1979* (Georg 1979), 179-198.

Habscheid, Walter: *Schweizerisches Zivilprozess- und Gerichtsorganisationsrecht* (2nd ed., Helbing Lichtenhain 1990).
(Habscheid, *Zivilprozessrecht*)

Häcker, Birke: *Consequences of Impaired Consent Transfers* (Mohr Siebeck 2009).

Hall, Michael Scott: 'Issue Preclusion Is No Illusion for Arbitration in Arkansas', (2005-2006) 58 *Arkansas Law Review*, 929-948.

Hanotiau, Bernard: *Complex Arbitrations* (Kluwer 2006).

Hanotiau, Bernard: 'Non-signatories, Groups of Companies and Groups of Contract in Selected Asian Countries', (2015) 32(6) *Journal of International Arbitration*, 571-620.

Harder, Sirko: 'The Effects of Recognized Foreign Judgments in Civil and Commercial Matters', (2013) 62(2) *International and Comparative Law Quarterly*, 407-441.

Harney, Sophie: 'Réputation de l'arbitre et décision arbitrale – Quelques éléments d'analyse économique', (2012) *Revue de l'arbitrage*, 757-768.

Harris, Bruce with Planterose, Rowan and Tecks, Jonathan: *The Arbitration Act 1996 – A Commentary* (Blackwell 1996).

Hascher, Dominique: 'Consolidation of Arbitration by American Courts', (1984) 1(2) *Journal of International Arbitration*, 127-144.

Hascher, Dominique: 'Recognition and Enforcement of Arbitration Awards and the Brussels Convention', (1996) 12 *Arbitration International*, 233-264.

Hascher, Dominique: 'Principes et pratique de procédure dans l'arbitrage commercial international', (1999) 279 *Recueil des cours – Collected Courses of the Hague Academy of International Law*, 51-193.

Hascher, Dominique: 'L'autorité de la chose jugée des sentences arbitrales', in: *Travaux du comité francais de droit international privé – Années 2000-2003* (Pedone 2004), 17-36.

(Hascher, in *Travaux comité francais DIP 2000-2003*)

Hascher, Dominique: 'Recognition and Enforcement of Arbitration Awards and the Brussels Convention', (1996) 12(3) *Arbitration International*, 233-268.

Hausmann, Rainer: 'Die Aufhebung von Schiedssprüchen nach neuem deutschen Schiedsverfahrensrecht', in: G Hohloch et al., *Festschrift für Hans Stoll zum 75. Geburtstag* (Mohr Siebeck 2001), 593-615.

Hay, Peter: 'On Merger and Preclusion (Res Judicata) in U.S. Foreign Judgment Recognition – Unresolved Doctrinal Problems', in: R A Schütze (ed.), *Einheit und Vielfalt des Rechts – Festschrift für Reinhold Geimer zum 65. Geburtstag* (Beck 2002), 325-338.

Hay, Peter: with Weintraub, Russell J. and Borchers, Patrick J: *Conflict of Laws*, Cases and Materials (13th ed., Foundation 2009).

Hazard, Geoffrey C Jr with Leubsdorf, John and Basset, Debra Lyn: *Civil Procedure* (6th ed., Foundation 2011).

Héron, Jacques and Le Bars, Thierry: *Droit judiciaire privé*, (5th ed., Domat 2012).

Hill, Jonathan: 'The Significance of Foreign Judgments Relating to an Arbitral Award in the Context of an Application to Enforce the Award in England', (2009) 8(2) *Journal of Private International Law*, 159-183.

Hobér, Kaj: 'Parallel arbitration proceedings', in: BM Román and JDM Lew (eds), *Parallel State and Arbitral Procedures in International Arbitration*, ICC Publication No. 692 (2005), 243-268.

Hobér, Kaj: 'Res Judicata and Lis Pendens in International Arbitration', (2011) 366 *Recueil des cours – Collected Courses of the Hague Academy of International Law*, 99-404.

Holtzmann, Howard M and Neuhaus, Joseph E: *A Guide to the UNCITRAL Model Law on International Commercial Arbitration* (Kluwer 1995).

Huet, André: 'Procédure civile et commerciale dans les rapports internationaux – Domaine de la "*lex fori*": jugement et voies d'execution', in: *Juris-Classeur de droit international*, Fascicule 582-30 (LexisNexis, update 18 April 2012).

Huet, André: 'Effets en France des judgements étrangers subordonnés à leur régularité internationale – Efficacité substantielle et autorité de chose jugée', in: *Juris-Classeur de droit international*, Fascicule 584-35 (LexisNexis, update 14 November 2015).

Hwang, Michael: 'Commercial Courts and Arbitration – Competitors or Partners?', (2015) 31(2) *Arbitration International*, 193-212.

Hwang, Michael and Chan, Andrew: 'Enforcement and Setting Aside of International Arbitral Awards – The Perspective of Common Law Countries', in: A J. van den Berg (ed.), *ICCA Congress Series Vol. 10* (Kluwer 2001), 145-164.

ICCA (ed.): *ICCA's Guide to the Interpretation of the 1958 New York Convention – A Handbook for Judges* (Kluwer 2011).

Jarrosson, Charles: *La notion d'arbitrage* (LGDJ 1987).

Jarrosson, Charles: 'L'arbitrage et la Convention européenne des droits de l'Homme', (1989) *Revue de l'arbitrage*, 573-607.

Jarrosson, Charles: 'L'autorité de chose jugée des sentences arbitrales', (2007) 8-9 *Procédures*, No. 17.

Jarvin, Sigvard: 'Consolidated Arbitrations – a Critique of Dr van den Berg', (1987) 3(3) *Arbitration International*, 254-257.

Jauernig, Ottmar: 'Die subjektiven Grenzen der Rechtskraft', (1988) 101 *Zeitschrift für Zivilprozess*, 361-389.

Jayme, Erik: 'Ausländische Rechtsregeln und Tatbestand inländischer Sachnormen – Betrachtungen zu Ehrenzweigs Datum-Theorie', in: E Jayme et al. (eds), *Gedächtnisschrift für Albert A Ehrenzweig* (Müller 1976), 35-50.

Jayme, Erik: 'Identité culturelle et intégration: le droit international privé postmoderne – cours général', (1995) 251 *Recueil des cours – Collected Courses of the Hague Academy of International Law*, 9-267.

Jayme, Erik: *Rechtsvergleichung und kulturelle Identität* (Mohr Siebeck 2012).

Jayme, Erik: 'Narrative Norms in Private International Law', (2015) 375 *Recueil des cours – Collected Courses of the Hague Academy of International Law*, 9-52.

Jayme, Erik: 'Les langues au droit international privé', (2017) 381 *Recueil des cours – Collected Courses of the Hague Academy of International Law*, 11-39.

Kaufmann-Kohler, Gabrielle: 'Identifying and Applying the Law Governing the Arbitration Procedure – The Role of the Law of the Place of Arbitration', in: A J. van den Berg (ed.), *ICCA Congress Series Vol. 9* (Kluwer 1999), 336-365.

Kaufmann-Kohler, Gabrielle: 'Arbitral Precedent – Dream, Necessity or Excuse?', (2007) 23(3) *Arbitration International*, 357-378.

Kaufmann-Kohler, Gabrielle: 'Soft Law in International Arbitration – Codification and Normativity', (2010) 1 *Journal of International Dispute Settlement*, 283-299.

Kaufmann-Kohler, Gabrielle and Lévy, Laurent: 'Insolvency and International Arbitration', in: H Peter et al. (eds), *The Challenges of Insolvency Law Reform in the 21st Century* (Schulthess 2006), 257-284.

Kaufmann-Kohler, Gabrielle and Rigozzi, Antonio: *International Arbitration – Law and Practice in Switzerland* (OUP 2015) – translated and revised version of *Arbitrage international*, (2nd ed., Schulthess 2010).

(Kaufmann-Kohler and Rigozzi, *International Arbitration in Switzerland*)

Kegel, Gerhard: 'Exequatur sur exequatur ne vaut', in: A Dieckmann et al. (eds), *Festschrift für Wolfram Müller-Freienfels* (Nomos 1986), 377-395.

Kegel, Gerhard and Schurig, Klaus: *Internationales Privatrecht* (9th ed., Beck 2004).

Kerr, LJ Michael: 'Arbitration v. Litigation / The Macao Sardine Case', (1987) 3(1) *Arbitration International*, 79-86.

Kieninger, Eva-Maria: *Wettbewerb der Privatrechtsordnungen* (Mohr Siebeck 2002).

Kinsch, Patrick: *Le fait du prince étranger* (LGDJ 1994).

Kirchner, Christian: 'An Economic Analysis of Choice-of-Law and Choice-of-Forum Clauses', in: J. Basedow and T Kono (eds), *An Economic Analysis of Private International Law* (Mohr Siebeck 2006), 33-58.

Kischel, Uwe: *Rechtsvergleichung* (Beck 2015).

Klein, Frederic-Edouard: *Considérations sur l'arbitrage en droit international privé* (Helbig Lichtenhain 1955).

Klement, Dorothee: *Rechtskraft des Schiedsspruchs* (Nomos 2018).

Knuts, Giesela: '*Iura Novit Curia* and the Right to Be Heard - An Analysis of Recent Case Law', (2012) 28 *Arbitration International*, 669-688.

Koch, Mathias: *Unvereinbare Entscheidungen iSd Art 27 Nr 3 und 5 EuGVÜ und ihre Vermeidung* (Peter Lang 1993).

Koops, Tilman: 'Der Rechtskraftbegriff der EuGVVO', (2018) *Praxis des internationalen Privat- und Verfahrensrechts*, 11-21.

Krause, Rainer: *Urteilswirkungen gegenüber Dritten im US-amerikanischen Zivilprozessrecht* (Mohr Siebeck 1994).

Kreindler, Richard with Wolff, Reinmar and Rieder, Markus S: *Commercial Arbitration in Germany* (OUP 2016).

Kremslehner, Florian: 'Lis Pendens and Res Judicata in International Commercial Arbitration', in: G Zeiler et al. (eds), *Austrian Yearbook on International Arbitration 2007* (Manz), 127-162.

Kröll, Stefan: 'Recourse Against Negative Decision on Jurisdiction', (2004) 20(1) *Arbitration International*, 55-78.

Kröll, Stefan: 'Materiell-rechtliche Einwendungen im Exequaturverfahren bei Schiedssprüchen - Zeit für eine Neujustierung', in: R Geimer with A Kaissis and R C Thümmel (eds), *Festschrift zum 80. Geburtstag von Rolf A. Schütze* (C.H. Beck 2015), 305-319.

Kröll, Stefan: 'Zur kollisionsrechtlichen Behandlung von Schiedsvereinbarungen', (2016) *Praxis des internationalen Privat- und Verfahrensrechts*, 43-48.

Kröll, Stefan with Mistelis, Loukas and Perales Viscasillas, Pilar (eds): *Convention on Contracts for the International Sale of Goods (CISG) – A Commentary* (2nd ed., Nomos and Hart 2018).

Kronke, Herbert: 'Internationales Zivilverfahrensrecht - Anhang IV zu Art 38 EGBGB', in: Soergel (found), *Bürgerliches Gesetzbuch*,Vol. 10 (12th ed., Kohlhammer 1996), 2030-2190.

(Kronke, in *Soergel*).

Kronke, Herbert: 'Principles Based Law and Rule Based Law - The Relevance of Legislative Strategies for International Commercial Arbitration', in: H Kronke and K Thorns (eds), Grenzen überwinden Prinzipien bewahren - *Festschrift für Bernd von Hoffmann zum 70 Geburstag* (Gieseking 2011), 1002-1011.

Kronke, Herbert: 'Acceptable Transnational Anti-suit Injunctions', in: H Kronke and K Thorns (eds), Recht ohne Grenzen - *Festschrift für Athanassios Kaissis zum 65. Geburtstag* (Sellier 2012), 549-557.

Kronke, Herbert: 'Leichtigkeit und Schnelligkeit des Verkehrs und managing litigation risks - Kriterien für Prorogationsnormen im transnationalen Handelsrecht', in: R

A Schütze (ed.), *Fairness Justice Equity – Festschrift für Reinhold Geimer zum 80. Geburtstag* (Beck 2017), 397-407.

Kronke, Herbert with Nacimiento, Patricia Otto, Dirk and Port, Nicola Christine (eds), *Recognition and Enforcement of Foreign Arbitral Awards – A Global Commentary on the New York Convention* (Kluwer 2010).

Kronstein, Heinrich: 'Business Arbitration – Instrument of Private Government', (1944) 54 *Yale Law Journal*, 36-69.

Kropholler, Jan and von Hein, Jan: *Europäisches Zivilprozessrecht* (9th ed., R&W 2011).

Kulzer, Barbara: 'Some Aspects of Enforceability of Foreign Judgments – A Comparative Survey', (1966) 16 *Buffalo Law Review*, 84-121.

Krueger, Thalia: *Civil Jurisdiction Rules of the EU and their Impact on Third States* (OUP 2008).

Lalive, Pierre with Poudret, Jean-Francois et Reymond, Claude: *Le droit de l'arbitrage interne et international en Suisse* (Payot 1989).

Lakkis, Panajotta: *Gestaltungsakte im internationalen Rechtsverkehr* (Mohr Siebeck 2007).

Lalive, Pierre: 'Transnational (or Truly International) Public Policy and International Arbitration', in: P Sanders (ed.), *ICCA Congress Series* Vol. 3 (Kluwer 1987), 257-320.

Lalive, Pierre: 'Nouveaux regards sur le droit international privé – ajourd'hui et deomain', (1994) 1-2 *Revue Suisse de Droit International et de Droit Européen*, 3-29.

Lalive, Pierre with Poudret, Jean-Francois and Reymond, Claude: *Le droit de arbitrage interne et international en Suisse* (Helbing Lichtenhain 1989).

Landbrecht, Johannes: *Teil-Sachentscheidungen und Ökonomie der Streitbeilegung* (Mohr Siebeck 2012).

Lazic, Vesna: 'The Commission's Proposal to Amend the Arbitration Exception in the EC Jurisdiction', (2012) 29 *Journal of International Arbitration* 19-47.

Le Bars, Thierry: 'Autorité positive et autorité négative de chose jugée', (2007) 8-9 *Procédures*, No. 12.

Leboulanger, Philippe: 'Multi-Contract Arbitration', (1996) 13(4) *Journal of International Arbitration*, 43-97.

Legrand, Pierre: 'Jameses at Play: A Tractation on the Comparison of Laws', (2017) (Special Issue) *American Journal of Comparative Law*, 1-132.

Lenenbach, Markus: *Die Behandlung von Unvereinbarkeiten zwischen rechtskräftigen Zivilurteilen nach deutschem und europäischem Zivilprozessrecht* (Duncker 1997).

Leurent, Bruno: 'Reflections on the International Effectiveness of Arbitration Awards', (1996) 12(3) *Arbitration International*, 269-286.

Lévy, Laurent and Schlaepfer, Anne-Véronique: 'La suspension d'instance dans l'arbitrage international', (2001) *Cahiers de l'arbitrage (Paris Journal of Int'l Arbitration)*, 18-26.

Lew, Julian DM: *Applicable Law in International Commercial Arbitration* (Sijthoff 1978).

Lew, Julian DM: 'Achieving the Dream - Autonomous Arbitration', (2006) 22 *Arbitration International*, 179-294.

Lew, Julian DM with Mistelis Loukas A and Kröll, Stefan: *Comparative International Commercial Arbitration* (Kluwer 2003).

(*Lew Mistelis and Kröll*)

Lewald, Hans: 'Règles générales des conflicts des lois - Contribution à la technique du droit international privé', in: (1939) 69 *Recueil des cours – Collected Courses of the Hague Academy of International Law*, 1-147.

Lobin, Yves and Desdevises, Yvonee: 'Action en justice - Classification des actions en justice', in: *Juris-Classeur de procédure civil*, Fascicule 500-90 (LexisNexis, update 7 August 2016).

Loquin, Eric: 'Arbitrage et cautionnement', (1994) *Revue de l'arbitrage*, 235-252.

Loquin, Eric: 'De l'obligation de concentrer les moyens à l'obligatoin de concentrer les demandes dans l'arbitrage', (2010) *Revue de l'arbitrage*, 201-233.

Loquin, Eric: 'Arbitrage - Compromis et claus compromissoire', in: *Juris-Clausseur de procédure civile*, Fascicule 1020 (LexisNexis, update 31 July 2014).

Loquin, Eric: 'Arbitrage - Sentence Arbitrale', in: *Juris-Clausseur de procédure civile*, Fascicule 1042 (LexisNexis, update 2 February 2016).

Lowe, Vaughan: 'Res Judicata and the Rule of Law in International Arbitration', (1996) 8 *African Journal of International and Comparative Law*, 38-56.

Lühmann, Tobias: *Die Rechtskraft des Schiedsspruchs im deutschen und US-amerikanischen Recht* (Mohr Siebeck 2015).

Lüke, Wolfgang: *Die Beteiligung Dritter im Zivilprozess* (Mohr Siebeck1993).

Magnus, Ulrich and Mankowski, Peter (eds): *Brussels Ibis Regulation* (3rd ed., Sellier 2015).

Mann, Frederick Alexander: 'Lex Facit Arbitrum', in: P Sanders (ed.), *Liber Amicorum for Martin Donke* (Kluwer 1967), 157-183 - A German translation has been published as 'Internationale Schiedsgerichte und nationale Rechtsordnung', (1968) 130 *Zeitschrift für das gesamte Handels- und Wirtschaftsrecht*, 97-129.

Mann, Frederick Alexander: 'Fusion of the Legal Profession', (1977) 93 *Law Quarterly Review*, 367-395.

Mansel, Heinz-Peter: *Personalstatut, Staatsangehörigkeit und Effektivität* (Beck 1988).

Mansel, Heinz-Peter: 'Gerichtsstandsvereinbarung und Ausschluss der Streitverkündung durch Prozessvertrag', (1996) *Zeitschrift für Zivilprozess*, 61-77.

Mansel, Heinz-Peter: 'Vertretungs- und Formprobleme bei Abschluss einer Schiedsvereinbarung', in: B Grunewald and H-P Westermann (eds), *Festschrift für Georg Maier-Reimer zum 70. Geburtstag* (Beck 2010), 407-424.

Mantilla-Serrano, Fernando: 'La contrariété de décisions dans l'arbitrage d'investissement: risques et conséquences', in: B Darmois and É Glucksmann (eds), *Procédures parallèles et décisions contradictoirs* (Bruylant 2015), 29-40.

Marchisio, Giacomo: *The Notion of Award in International Commercial Arbitration – A Comparative Analysis of French, English and the UNCITRAL Model Law* (Kluwer 2017).

Marotzke, Wolfgang: 'Urteilswirkungen gegen Dritte und rechtliches Gehör', (1987) 100 *Zeitschrift für Zivilprozess*, 164-211.

Mayer, Pierre: *La distinction entre règle et décisions et le droit international prive* (Dalloz 1973).

Mayer, Pierre: 'L'autonomie de l'arbitre international dans l'appréciation de sa propre compétence', (1989) 217 *Recueil des cours – Collected Courses of the Hague Academy of International Law*, 319-454.

Mayer, Pierre: 'Revisiting Hilmarton and Chromalloy', in: A J. van den Berg (ed.), *ICCA Congress Series* Vol. 10 (Kluwer 2001), 165-176.

Mayer, Pierre: 'Litispendance, connexité et chose jugée dans l'arbitrage international', in: *Liber Amicorum Claude Reymond – Autour de l'arbitrage* (Litec 2004), 185-203 (P Mayer, in *Liber Amicorum Claude Reymond*).

Mayer, Pierre: 'La 'circulation' des conventions d'arbitrage', (2005) *Journal du droit international – Clunet*, 251-265 – reprinted in *Choix d'articles de Pierre Mayer* (LGDJ 2015), 389-400.

Mayer, Pierre: 'Le phénomène de la coordination des ordres juridiques étatiques en droit privé – cours général', (2007) 327 *Recueil des cours – Collected Courses of the Hague Academy of International Law*, 9-378.

Mayer, Pierre: 'Réflexions sur l'autorité négative de chose jugée', in: *Liber amicorum Jacques Héron* (LGDJ 2008), 331-344 – reprinted in *Choix d'articles de Pierre Mayer* (LGDJ 2015), 477-491.

Mayer, Pierre: Note (Cass com, *ITM v. Prodim*), (2009) *Revue de l'arbitrage* 329-336.

Mayer, Pierre: 'Extension of the Arbitration Clause to Non-signatories under French Law', in: PCA (ed.), *Multi-Party Actions in International Arbitration* (OUP 2009), 189-199.

Mayer, Pierre: 'Conflicting Decisions in International Commercial Arbitration', (2013) 4 *Journal of International Dispute Settlement*, 407-419.

Mayer, Pierre: 'La liberté de l'arbitre', (2013) *Revue de l'arbitrage*, 339-365.

Mayer, Pierre: 'L'autorité de chose jugée des sentences entre les parties', (2016) *Revue de l'arbitrage*, 91-105.

Mayer, Pierre: 'The French Approach as a Starting Point for General Reflections on the Recognition of Foreign Award Judgments', in: A Menaker (ed.), *ICCA Congress Series Vol. 19* (Kluwer 2017), 706-717.

Mayer, Pierre and Heuzé, Vincent: *Droit international privé* (11th ed., LGDJ 2014).

McLachlan, Campbell: *Lis Pendens in International Litigation* (Nijhoff 2009), Pocketbook Edition of (2008) 336 *Recueil des Cours – Collected Courses of the Hague Academy of International Law*, 201-553.

McLachlan, Campbell with Shore, Laurance and Weininger, Matthew: *International Investment Arbitration* (2nd ed., OUP 2017).

Meier, Sonja: 'Solidary Obligation', in: J. Basedow K J. Hopt and R Zimmermann (eds), *Max Planck Encyclopedia of European Private Law*, Vol. 2 (OUP 2012).

Meira Moser, Luiz Gustavo: 'Contracting Parties' Minds – The Decision-Making Process in Cross-Border Sales', (2017) 8 *Journal of International Dispute Settlement*, 250-279.

Michaels, Ralf: 'The Functional Method of Comparative Law', in: R Zimmermann and M Reimann (eds), *The Oxford Handbook of Comparative Law* (OUP 2006), Ch. 10.

Michaels, Ralf: 'Economics of Law as Choice of Law', (2008) 71 *Law & Contemp. Problems*, 73-105.
Mignot, Marc: *Les obligations solidaires et les obligations in solidum en droit privé francais* (Dalloz 2002).
Mignot, Marc: Note (CA Paris, 10 March 2005), (2006) *Revue de l'arbitrage*, 456-468.
Millar, Robert Wyness: 'The Historical Relation of Estoppel by Record to Res Judicata', (1940-1941) 35 *Illinois Law Review*, 41-59.
Mills, Alex: *The Confluence of Public and Private International Law* (CUP 2009).
Milsom, SFC: *Historical Foundations of the Common Law* (2nd ed., Lexis 1981).
Minoli, Eugenio: 'L'Italie et la Convention de New York', in: P Sanders (ed.), *Liber Amicorum for Martin Donke* (Kluwer 1967), 199-214.
Mourre, Alexis and Vagenheim, Alexandre: 'Arbitrage Commercial International', in: *Juris-Classeur de procédure civile*, Fascicule 1067 (LexisNexis, update 11 September 2010).
Mustill, Michael J. and Boyd, Stewart C: *Commercial Arbitration* (3rd ed., LexisNexis 2010).
(*Mustill and Boyd*)
Motulsky, Henri: 'Pour une délimination plus précise de l'autorité de la chose jugée en matière civil', (1968) *Recueil Dalloz*, 1-24.
Muir Watt, Horatia: 'Aspects économiques du droit international privé', (2004) 307 *Recueil des cours – Collected Courses of the Hague Academy of International Law*, 25-383.
Muir Watt, Horatia: Note (Cass com, 4 October 2005), (2006) 95 *Revue critique de droit international privé*, 408-412.
Krüger, Wolfgang and Rauscher, Thomas (eds): *Münchener Kommentar zur Zivilprozessordnung*, Vols 1-3 (5th ed., Beck 2017).
([author], in *Münchener Kommentar*)
Musielak, Hans-Joachim and Voit, Wolfgang (eds): *Zivilprozessordnung* (17th ed., Beck 2017).
Nagel, Heinrich and Gottwald, Peter: *Internationales Zivilprozessrecht* (7th ed., Otto Schmidt 2013).
Nazzini, Renato: 'Enforcement of International Arbitral Awards – Res Judicata, Issue Estoppel and Abuse of Process in a Transnational Context', (2018) 66 *American Journal of Comparative Law*, 603-638.
Nelle, Andreas: *Anspruch Titel und Vollstreckung im internationalen Rechtsverkehr* (Mohr Siebeck 2000).
Newmark, Christopher and Hill, Richard: 'Can a Mediated Settlement Become an Enforceable Arbitration Award?', (2000) 16(1) *Arbitration International*, 81-88.
Niboyet, Marie-Laure: *L'action en justice dans les rapports internationaux de droit prive* (Economica 1986).
Niboyet, Marie-Laure: 'Inconciliabilité d'une sentence avec un jugement étranger exequaturé', (2012) *Revue de l'arbitrage*, 573-586.
Nicklisch, Fritz: 'Multi-party Arbitration and Dispute Resolution in Major Industrial Projects', 11(4) *Journal of International Arbitration* (1994), 57-72.

Nouvel, Yves: 'L'autorité de la choise jugée attachée à la transaction', (2007) 8-9 *Procédures*, No. 16.

O'Hara, Erin A and Ribstein, Larry E: 'From Politics to Efficiency in Choice of Law', (2000) 67 *University of Chicago Law Review*, 1151-1232.

Oppetit, Bruno: 'Philosophie de l'arbitrage commercial international', (1993) *Journal du droit international (Clunet)*, 818-848.

Otte, Karsten: *Umfassende Streitentscheidung durch Beachtung von Sachzusammenhängen* (Mohr Siebeck 1998).

Pair, Lara M and Frankenstein, Paul: 'The New ICC Rule on Consolidation – Progress or Change?', (2011) 25 *Emory International Law Review*, 1061-1092.

Palsson, Lennart: 'The Institute of Lis Pendens in International Civil Procedure', (1970) 14 *Scandinavian Studies in Law*, 59-81.

Park, William W: 'Duty and Discretion in International Arbitration', (1999) 93(4) *American Journal of International Law*, 805-823.

Park, William W: 'Arbitration's Protean Nature: The Value of Rules and the Risks of Discretion', (2003) 19 *Arbitration International*, 279-301.

Park, William W: 'The Arbitrator's Jurisdiction to Determine Jurisdiction', in: AJ van den Berg (ed.), *Back to Basics?*, ICCA Congress Series No. 13 (Kluwer 2007), 55-153.

Park, William W: 'Non-signatories and International Contracts: An Arbitrator's Dilemma', in: PCA (ed.), *Multiple Party Actions in International Arbitration* (OUP 2009), 3-27.

Paulsson, Jan: 'Arbitration Without Privity', (1995) 10 *ICSID Review* 232-257.

Paulsson, Jan: 'The Case for Disregarding LSAS (Local Standard Annulments) under the New York Convention', (1996) 7 *American Review of International Arbitration*, 99-128.

Paulsson, Jan: 'L'execution des sentences arbitrales dans le monde de demain', (1998) *Revue de l'arbitrage*, 637-652.

Paulsson, Jan: 'Arbitration in Three Dimensions', (2011) 60 *International and Comparative Law Quarterly*, 291-238.

Paulsson, Jan: *The Idea of Arbitration* (OUP 2013).

Paulsson, Marike R P: *The 1958 New York Convention in Action* (Kluwer 2016).

Peiffer, Max Christoph: *Grenzüberschreitende Titelgeltung in der Europäischen Union (Duncker Humblodt 2012).*

Péroz, Hélène: *La réception des jugements étrangers dans l'ordre juridique français* (LGDJ 2005).

Petersen, Niels: 'Braucht die Rechtswissenschaft eine empirische Wende?', (2010) 49 *Der Staat*, 435-455.

Petrochilos, Georgios: 'Enforcing Awards Annulled in Their State of Origin under the New York Convention', (1999) 48(4) *International and Comparative Law Quarterly*, 826-856.

Petrochilos, Georgios: *Procedural Law in International Arbitration* (OUP 2004).

Pfeiffer, Thomas: *Internationale Zuständigkeit und prozessuale Gerechtigkeit* (Klostermann 1995).

Pfeiffer, Thomas: 'Datumtheorie und *local data* in der Rom II-VO', in: R Michaels and D Solomon (eds), *Liber Amicorum Klaus Schurig* (Sellier 2012), 229-236.

Pfeiffer, Thomas: 'Gewillkürte Prozessstandschaft im Schiedsverfahren', (2017) *Zeitschrift für Schiedsverfahrensrecht - German Journal of Arbitration*, 135-141.

Pielemeier, James R: 'Due Process Limitations on the Application of Collateral Estoppel Against Nonparties to Prior Litigation', (1983) 63 *Boston University Law Review*, 383-442.

Pika, Maximilian: 'Schiedsspruch ultra partes? - Die subjektive Rechtskrafterstreckung anhand von rechtlichem Gehör und Parteiautonomie', (2018) 131 *Zeitschrift für Zivilprozess*, 225-259.

Pika, Maximilian and Trippel, Pierre: Note (*DIRECTV Inc. v. Imburgia et al*, 136 S.Ct. 463), (2016) *Zeitschrift für Schiedsverfahrensrecht - German Journal of Arbitration*, 292-293.

Poncet, Charles and Mockler, Luisa: 'Res Judicata - A Contribution to the Debate on Claim Preclusion in International Arbitration', in: *Liber Amicorum en l'honneur de William Laurence Craig* (LexisNexis 2016), 309-324.

Pothier, Robert Joseph: *Traité des obligations*, Oeuvres de Pothier II (1821, Dalloz 2011).

Poudret, Jean-François: 'L'exension de la clause d'arbitrage: approches francaise et suisse', (1995) 122 *Journal du droit international (Clunet)*, 893-927.

Poudret, Jean-François and Besson, Sébastien: *Comparative Law of International Arbitration* (2nd ed., Sweet & Maxwell 2007) - translated and revised version of *Droit comparé de l'arbitrage international* (Schulthess 2002).
(*Poudret and Besson*)

Poudret, Jean-François and Cottier, Gabriel: 'Remarques sur l'application de l'article II de la Convention de New Yok', (1995) *ASA Bulletin*, 383-393.

Queen Mary University of London - School of International Arbitration (ed.): *Report on International Arbitration - Corporate Attitudes and Practices.*

Queen Mary University of London - School of International Arbitration (ed.): *2010 International Arbitration Survey - Choices in International Arbitration.*

Racine, Jean-Babtiste: Note (Cass 1e civ, 16 November 2004; CA Paris, 2 June 2004; CA Paris, 30 June 2004), (2006) *Revue de l'arbitrage*, 680-692.

Radicati di Brozolo, Luca: 'Res Judicata and International Arbitral Awards', in: P Tercier (ed.), *Post Award Issues*, ASA Special Series No. 38 (Juris 2011), 127-140 - available as an individual document at SSRN, whose page numbers the examination refers to.

Rauscher, Thomas (ed.): *Europäisches Zivilprozess- und Kollisionsrecht*, Vols. I-V (4th ed., Otto Schmidt 2015-2016).

Redfern, Alan: 'International Commercial Arbitration - Winning the Battle', in: The Southwestern Legal Foundation (ed.), *Private Investors Abroad* (1989), 167-193.

Redfern, Alan with Hunter, Martin J. (found), Blackaby, Nigel and Partasides, Constantine: *Redfern and Hunter on International Arbitration* (6th ed., OUP 2015).
(*Redfern and Hunter*)

Reed, Lucy: 'Ab(use) of due process', (2017) 33(3) *Arbitration International*, 361-377.

Reinisch, August: 'The Proliferation of International Dispute Settlement Mechanisms – The Threat of Fragmentation vs. the Promise of a More Effective System?', in: J. Crawford et al. (eds), *International Law Between Universalism and Fragmentation* – Festschrift in Honour of Gerhard Hafner (Martinus Nijhoff Publishers 2008), 107-125.

Reisman, Michael W: *Systems of Control in International Adjudication and Arbitration – Breakdown and Repair* (Duke University Press 1992).

Reisman, Michael W: 'The Diversity of Contemporary International Dispute Resolution – Functions and Policies', (2013) 4 *Journal of International Dispute Resolution*, 47-63.

Reisman, Michael W with Craig, Lawrence, Park William W and Paulsson, Jan: *International Commercial Arbitration* (2nd ed., Foundation 2015).

(*Reisman Craig Park and Paulsson*)

Ricci, Edoardo F: 'La crise de l'arbitrage juridictionnel en Italie', (2002) *Revue de l'arbitrage*, 841-855.

Romano, Roberta: 'Law as a Product: Some Pieces of the Incorporation Puzzle', (1985) 1 Journal of Law Economics and Organizations, 225-289.

Rose, William with Sime, Stuart and French, Derek: *Blackstone's Civil Practice* (OUP 2008).

Roland, Henri: *Chose jugée et tierce opposition* (LGDJ 1958).

Rosenberg, Leo: 'Die Präklusionswirkung von Urteilen', (1950) 5 *Süddeutsche Juristen-Zeitung*, 313-320.

Rosenberg, Leo with Gaul, Friedrich and Schilken, Eberhard: *Zwangsvollstreckungsrecht* (17th ed., Beck 1997).

Rosenberg, Leo, Schwab, Karl-Heinz and Gottwald, Peter: *Zivilprozessrecht* (17th ed., Beck 2010).

Roth, Herbert: 'Europäischer Rechtskraftbegriff im Zuständigkeitsrecht?', (2014) *Praxis des internationalen Privat- und Verfahrensrechts*, 136-139.

Rubino-Samartano, Mauro: *International Arbitration* – Law and Practice (3rd ed., Juris 2014).

Rubins, Noah and Kinsella, Stephan: *International Investment* (Oceana 2005).

Ruehl, Giesela: *Statut und Effizienz – Ökonomische Analyse des Internationalen Privatrechts* (Mohr Siebeck 2011).

Sanders, Gerard J: 'Rethinking Arbitral Preclusion' (1992-1993) 24 *Georgetown Journal of International Law* (formerly *Law & Policy of International Business*), 101-122.

Sandrock, Otto: 'Arbitration Agreements and Groups of Companies', in: *Etudes de droit international en l'honneur de Pierre Lalive* (Lichtenhain 1993), 625-643.

Schack, Haimo: 'Drittwirkung der Rechtskraft?', (1988) *Neue Juristische Wochenschrift*, 865-873.

Schack, Haimo: 'Widersprechende Urteile – Vorbeugen ist besser als Heilen', (1989) *Praxis des Internationalen Privat- und Verfahrensrechts*, 139-142.

Schack, Haimo: 'Die Versagung der deutschen internationalen Zuständigkeit wegen forum non conveniens und lis alibi pendens', (1994) 58 *Rabels Zeitschrift für ausländisches und internationales Privatrecht*, 40-58.

Schack, Haimo: *Internationales Zivilverfahrensrecht* (7th ed., Beck 2017).

Schaffstein, Silja: *The Doctrine of Res Judicata Before International Commercial Arbitral Tribunals* (OUP 2016).
(Schaffstein, *Res Judicata*)

Schaefer, Hans-Bernd and Ott, Claus: *Lehrbuch der oekonomischen Analyse des Zivilrechts* (5th ed., Springer 2013).

Scherer, Maxi: 'Effects of Foreign Judgments Relating to International Arbitral Awards - Is the "Judgment Route" the Wrong Road?', (2013) 4(3) *Journal of International Dispute Settlement*, 587-628.

Schinkels, Boris: *Normsatzstruktur des IPR* (Mohr Siebeck 2007).

Schlechtriem, Peter (found) and Schwener, Ingeborg (ed.): *Schlechtriem and Schwenzer – Commentary on the UN COnvention on the International Sale of Goods* (4th ed., OUP 2016).

Schlosser, Peter: 'Urteilswirkungen und rechtliches Gehör', (1967) *Juristenzeitung*, 431-437.

Schlosser, Peter: *Das Recht der internationalen privaten Schiedsgerichtsbarkeit* (2nd ed.,. Mohr Siebeck 1989).
(*Schlosser*)

Schlosser, Peter: 'Arbitral Tribunals or State Courts - Who Must Defer to Whom?', in: P Karrer (ed.), *Arbitral Tribunals or State Courts – Who Must Defer to Whom*, ASA Special Series No. 15, 15-34.
(Schlosser, *ASA Special Series*)

Schlosser, Peter: 'Jurisdiction and International Judicial and Administrative Cooperation', (2000) 284 *Recueil des cours – Collected Courses of the Hague Academy of International Law*, 13-276.

Schlosser, Peter: Note (Pakistan *v.* Dallah) (2010) 15 Zeitschrift für Zivilprozess International, 405-411.

Schlosser, Peter: Commentary to §§ 1025-1066 ZPO and International Conventions, in F Stein and M Jonas (found) with R Bork and H Roth (eds), *Kommentar zur Zivilprozessordnung*, Vol. 10 (23rd ed., Mohr Siebeck 2015).
(Schlosser, in *Stein and Jonas*)

Schlosser, Peter and Hess, Burkhard: *Europäisches Zivilprozessrecht* (4th ed., Beck 2015).

Schmidt, Felix: *Die Typologie von Schiedssprüchen* (Carl Heymanns 2012).

Schneider, Michael E: 'Multi-Fora Disputes', (1990) 6(2) *Arbitration International*, 101-121.

Schwab, Karl-Heinz: 'Rechtskraft auf Dritte und Drittwirkung der Rechtskraft', (1964) 77 *Zeitschrift für Zivilprozess*, 124-160.

Schwab, Karl-Heinz: 'Mehrparteienschiedsgerichtsbarkeit und Streitgenossenschaft', in: P Schlosser et al. (eds), *Festschrift für Walther J. Habscheid* (Gieseking 1989), 285-294.

Schwab, Karl-Heinz and Walter, Gerhard: *Schiedsgerichtsbarkeit* (7th ed., Beck 2005).

Schwartz, Eric: 'The Practices and Experiences of the ICC Court', in: *Conservatory and Provisional Measures in International Arbitration*, ICC Publ No. 519 (1993), 46-65.

Schweizer, Phillipe and Olivier Guillod: 'L'exception de litispendance et l'arbitrage international', in: *Le juriste suisse face au droit et jugements étrangers* (Fribourg Univ., 1988), 71-89.

Schuetze, Rolf: *Schiedsgericht und Schiedsverfahren* (5th ed., Beck 2012).

Schuetze, Rolf: Commentary to the 10th Book of the German Code of Civil Procedure concerning Arbitration, in B Wieczoreck and R A Schütze, *Zivilprozessordnung und Nebengesetze*, Vol. 11 (4th ed., De Gruyter 2014).

(Schuetze, in *Wieczoreck and Schütze*)

Schurig, Klaus: *Kollisionsnorm und Sachrecht* (Duncker & Humblot 1981).

Seraglini, Christophe: 'Le droit applicable à l'autorité de la chose jugée dans l'arbitrage', (2016) *Revue de l'arbitrage*, 51-76.

Seraglini, Christophe with Ortscheidt, Jérôme: *Droit de l'arbitrage interne et international* (Domat 2013).

Shany, Yuval: *Regulating Jurisdictional Relations Between National and International Courts* (OUP 2007).

Shapiro, Sheldon R: 'Some Thoughts on Intervention Before Courts, Agencies and Arbitrators', (1968) 81 *Harvard Law Review*, 721-772.

Shapiro, Sheldon R: 'Modern View of State Courts as to Whether Consent Judgment Is Entitled to Res Judicata or Collateral Estoppel Effect', (1979) 91 ALR3d, 1170-1235.

Shell, G Richard: 'Res Judicata and Collateral Estoppel Effects of Commercial Arbitration', (1988) 35 *UCLA Law Review*, 623-675.

Sheppard, Audley: 'Res Judicata and Estoppel', in: BM Román and JDM Lew (eds), *Parallel State and Arbitral Procedures in International Arbitration*, ICC Publication No. 692 (2005), 219-242.

(Sheppard, in *Parallel State and Arbitral Procedures*)

Silbermann, Linda J: 'The New York Convention After Fifty Years', (2009) 38 *Georgia Journal of International and Comparative Law*, 25-67.

Silbermann, Linda J with Stein, Allan R and Wolff, Tobias Barrington: *Civil Procedure – Theory and Practice* (4th ed., Kluwer 2013).

Simons, Thomas and Hausmann, Rainer (eds): *Unalex Kommentar Brüssel I-Verordnung* (IPR 2012).

Sinai, Yuval: 'Reconsiderung Res Judicata – A Comparative Perspective', (2010-2011) 21 *Duke Journal of International and Comparative Law*, 353-400.

Shookman, Jamie: 'Too Many Forums for Investment Disputes? ICSID Illustrations of Parallel Proceedings and Analysis', (2009) 27(4) *Journal of International Arbitration*, 361-378.

Smit, Hans: 'International Res Judicata and Collateral Estoppel in the United States', (1962) 9 *UCLA Law Review*, 46-75.

Smith, Gordon: 'Comparative Analysis of Joinder and Consolidation Provisions Under Leading Arbitral Rules', (2018) 35(2) *Journal of International Arbitration*, 173-202.

Söderlund, Christer: 'Lis Pendens, Res Judicata and the Issue of Parallel Judicial Proceedings', (2005) 22(4) *Journal of International Arbitration*, 301-322.

Söderlund, Christer: 'Multiple Judicial Proceedings an the Energy Charter Treaty', in: C Ribeiro (ed.), *Investment Arbitration and the Energy Charter Treaty* (New York 2006), 237-256.

Solomon, Dennis: *Die Verbindlichkeit von Schiedssprüchen in der internationalen privaten Schiedsgerichtsbarkeit* (Sellier 2007).

Spellenberg, Ulrich: 'Prozessführung oder Urteil – Rechtsvergleichendes zu Grundlagen der Rechtskraft', in: W Gerhard et al. (eds), *Festschrift für Wolfram Henckel zum 70. Geburtstag am 21. April 1995* (De Gruyter 1995), 841-862.

Spencer Bower, George (found) and Handley, Kenneth R: *Res Judicata* (4th ed., LexisNexis 2009).

Spohnheimer, Frank: *Gestaltungsfreiheit bei antizipiertem Legalanerkenntnis* (Mohr Siebeck 2010).

Stapf, Beatrice: *Die Entwicklung der Rechtskraftlehre* (Mohr Siebeck 2017).

Steger, Christian: *Die Präklusion von Versagungsgründen bei der Vollstreckung ausländischer Schiedssprüche* (Mohr Siebeck 2015).

Steingruber, Andrea Marco: *Consent in International Arbitration* (OUP 2012).

Stier, Andreas: 'Preclusive Effects of International Arbitral Awards', (2004) 15 *American Review of International Arbitration*, 321-336.

Story, Joseph: *Commentaries on the Conflict of Laws* (1834).

Strong, Stacie I: *Class, Mass and Collective Arbitration in National and International Law* (OUP 2013).

Stucken, Ralf: *Einseitige Rechtskraftwirkung von Urteilen im deutschen Zivilprozess* (Peter Lang 1990).

Stürner, Michael and Wendelstein, Christoph: 'Das Schiedsvereinbarungsstatut bei vertraglichen Streitigkeiten', (2014) *Praxis des internationalen Privat- und Verfahrensrechts*, 473-480.

Stürner, Rolf: 'Rechtskraft in Europa', in: R Geimer et al. (eds), *Festschrift für Rolf A. Schütze zum 65. Geburtstag* (Beck 1999), 913-934.

Stürner, Rolf: 'The Principles of Transnational Civil Procedure', (2005) 69 *Rabels Zeitschrift für ausländisches und internationales Privatrecht*, 201-254.

Sutton, David St John with Gill, Judith and Gearing, Matthew: *Russel on Arbitration* (23rd ed., Sweet & Maxwell 2007).

(*Russel on Arbitration*)

Symeonides, Symeon C: 'Private International Law: Idealism, Pragmatism, Eclecticism – General Course', (2016) 384 *Recueil des cours – Collected Courses of the Hague Academy of International Law*, 9-409.

Tao, Jinghzou: *Arbitration Law and Practice in China* (Kluwer 2012).

Thomale, Chris: 'Materielle Rechtskraft – Eine kurze Ideen- und Kodifikationsgeschichte', (2018) 73 *Juristenzeitung*, 430-434.

Thomas, Heinz and Putzo, Hans (founds): *Zivilprozessordnung* (38th ed., Beck 2017).

Tomasin, Daniel: *Essai sur l'autorité de la chose jugée en matière civile* (LGDJ 1975).

Train, François-Xavier: 'L'extension de la clause compromissoire – Chronique des années 2012-2017', (2017) 2 *Revue de l'arbitrage*, 389-444.

Tweeddale, Andrew and Tweeddale, Karen: *Arbitration of Commercial Disputes* (OUP 2005).

Usunier, Laurence: 'L'exclusion de l'arbitrage dans la refonte du règlement Bruxelles I', in: B Darmois and É Glucksmann (eds), *Procédures parallèles et décisions contradictoirs* (Bruylant 2015), 87-100.

van den Berg, Albert Jan: *The New York Convention of 1958* (Kluwer 1981).

van den Berg, Albert Jan: 'When Is an Arbitral Award Nondomestic under the New York Convention of 1958', (1985) 6 *Pace Law Review*, 25-68.

van den Berg, Albert Jan: 'Consolidated Arbitrations, the New York Convention and the Arbitration Act 1986 – A Replique to Mr Jarvin', (1987) 3(2) *Arbitration International*, 257-262.

van den Berg, Albert Jan: 'Consolidated Arbitrations and the 1958 New York Convention', (1986) 2(3) *Arbitration International*, 367-369.

van den Helden, Jacob: *Finality in Litigation – Law and Practice of Preclusion* (Kluwer 2017).

van Houtte, Hans: 'May Court Judgments that Disregard Arbitration Clauses and Awards be Enforced under the Brussels and Lugano Conventions?', (1997) 13 *Arbitration International* 85.

Veeder, Van Veechten: 'Issue Estoppel, Reasons for Awards and Transnational Arbitration', in: *Complex Arbitrations, ICC International Court of Arbitration Bulletin – Special Supplement* (2003), 73-79.

(Veeder, in *ICC Bulletin*)

Voet, Johannes: *Commentarius ad pandectus* (orig. 1698, transl. Butterworth 1957).

Vogenauer, Stefan (ed.): *Commentary on the UNIDROIT Principles of International Commercial Contracts (PICC)* (2nd ed., OUP 2015).

von Hein, Jan: 'Einleitung Internationales Privatrecht', in: F-J Säcker et al. (eds), *Münchener Kommentar zum Bürgerlichen Gesetzbuch*, Vol. 11.

von Hoffmann, Bernd: 'Grundsätzliches zur Anwendung der "lex mercatoria" durch internationale Schiedsgerichte', in: H-J Musielak and K Schurig (eds), *Festschrift für Gerhard Kegel* (Kohlhammer 1987), 238-253.

von Hoffmann, Bernd and Thorn, Karsten: *Internationales Privatrecht* (9th ed., Beck 2007).

von Mehren, Arthur T.: 'Recognition and Enforcement of Foreign Judgments – General Theory and the Role of Jurisdictional Requirements', (1980) 167 *Recueil des Cours – Collected Courses of the Hague Academy of International Law* 9-112.

von Mehren, Arthur T.: *Limitations on Party Choice of the Governing Law* (Tel Aviv University 1986).

von Mehren, Arthur T.: 'Arbitration Between States and Foreign Enterprises: The Significance of the Institute of International Law's Santiago de Compostela Resolution', (1990) 5 *ICSID Review – Foreign Investment Law Journal*, 54-64.

von Mehren, Arthur T.: 'Theory and Practice of Adjudicatory Authority in Private International Law: a Comparative Study of the Doctrine, Policies and Practices of Common- and Civil-Law Systems', (2002) 295 *Recueil des cours – Collected Courses of the Hague Academy of International Law*, 13-476.

von Mehren, Arthur T. and Trautman, Donald T: 'Recognition of Foreign Adjudications – A Survey and a Suggested Approach', (1967-1968) 81(8) *Harvard Law Review*, 1601-1696.

Wagner, Gerhard: *Prozessverträge* (Mohr Siebeck 1998).

Wagner, Gerhard: 'Bindung des Schiedsgerichts an Entscheidungen anderer Gerichte und Schiedsgerichte', in: K-H Böckstiegel with K-P Berger and J. Bredow (eds), *Die Beteiligung Dritter am Schiedsverfahren* (Carl Heymanns 2005), 7-54.

Wälde, Thomas W: 'How to Avoid Conflicting Awards - The Lauder and CME Cases', (2004) 5(1) *Journal of World Investment and Trade*, 37-45.

Wehland, Hanno: *The Coordination of Multiple Proceedings in Investment Treaty Arbitration* (OUP 2013).

(Wehland, *Multiple Proceedings in Investment Arbitration*)

Weller, Marc-Philippe: *Die Vertragstreue* (Mohr Siebeck 2009).

Weller, Marc-Philippe: *Die Grenze der Vertragstreue von (Krisen-)Staaten* (Mohr Siebeck 2013).

Weller, Marc-Philippe: 'Die Neue Mobilitätsanknüpfung im Internationalen Familienrecht - Abfederung des Personalstatutenwechsels über die Datumtheorie', (2014) *Praxis des Internationalen Privat- und Verfahrensrechts*, 225-233.

Weller, Marc-Philippe: 'Vom Staat zum Menschen - Die Methodentrias des Internationalen Privatrechts unserer Zeit', (2017) 81 *Rabels Zeitschrift für ausländisches und internationales Privatrecht*, 747-780.

Whitesell, Anne Marie: 'Multiparty Arbitration - The ICC International Court of Arbitration Perspective', in: PCA (ed.), *Multiple Party Actions in International Arbitration* (OUP 2009), 203-212.

Whitesell, Anne Marie and Silva-Romero, Eduardo: 'Multiparty and Multicontract Arbitration - Recent ICC Experience', in: ICC (ed.), Complex Arbitrations - *ICC Bulletin Special Supplement* (2003), 7-23.

Whitman, James Q: 'The Hunt for Truth in Comparative Law', (2017) (Special Issue) *American Journal of Comparative Law*, 181-190.

Williams, David A R and Tushingham, Mark: 'The Application of the *Henderson v. Henderson* Rule in International Arbitration', (2014) 26 *Singapore Academy of Law Journal*, 1036-1058.

Windscheid, Bernhard: *Die actio des römischen Civilrechts, vom Standpunkte des heutigen Rechts* (Buddeus 1856).

Winstanley, Adrian: 'Multiple Parties, Multiple Problems - A View from the London Court of International Arbitration', in: PCA (ed.), *Multiple Party Actions in International Arbitration* (OUP 2009), 213-220.

Wolf, Manfred: 'Rechtliches Gehör und die Beteiligung Dritter am Rechtstreit', (1971) *Juristenzeitung*, 405-409.

Wolff, Reinmar: Note (BGH, 21 May 2008, III ZB 14/07), (2008) *LMK*, No. 265473.

Wolff, Reinmar (ed.): *New York Convention - Commentary* (Beck & Hart 2012).

Wong, Jarrod: 'Court or Arbitrator - Who Decides Whether Res Judicata Bars Subsequent Arbitration under the Federal Arbitration Act', (2005-2006) 46 *Santa Clara Law Review*, 49-92.

Woolf, Jeremy: *Zamir and Woolf - The Declaratory Judgment* (4th ed., Sweet & Maxwell 2011).

Woolhouse, Sarita Patil: 'The Effect of an Arbitration Award on Subsequent Arbitration Between Different Parties – An English Law Perspective', (2004) 7 *International Arbitration Law Review*, 150-156.

Wright, Charles Alan and Miller, Arthur R (eds): *Federal Practice and Procedure* (4th ed., Thomson 2013).

Wu, Elizabeth: 'Addressing Multiplicity of Shareholder Claims in ICSID Arbitrations under Bilateral Investment Treaties – A "Tiered Approach" to Prioritising Claims?', (2010) 6(2) *Asian International Arbitration Journal*, 134-163.

Yaffe, Nathan: 'Transnational Arbitral Res Judicata', (2017) 34(5) *Journal of International Arbitration*, 795-834.

Zajdela, Basile: *L'autorité de la chose jugée devant l'arbitrate du commerce international*, Doctoral Dissertation, Université de Paris I – Panthéon Sorbonne 2015.

Zajdela, Basile: Note (CA Paris, *SNC Forézienne v. SAS Guintoli*), (2017) Rev. Arb. 1217-1229.

Zaugg, Niklaus: 'Objective Scope of Res Judicata of Arbitral Awards – Is There Room for Discretion?', (2017) *ASA Bulletin*, 319-333.

Zeuner, Albrecht and Koch, Harald: 'Effects of Judgments (Res Judicata)', in: U Drobnig et al. (eds), *International Encyclopedia of Comparative Law*, Vol. XVI, Civil Procedure (Mohr Siebeck 2014), Ch. 9.

Zimmermann, Reinhard: *The Law of Obligations* (OUP 1996).

Zöller, Richard (found): *Zivilprozessordnung* (32nd ed., Otto Schmidt 2018).

Zuckerman, Adrian: *Zuckermann on Civil Procedure – Principles of Practice* (3rd ed., Sweet & Maxwell 2013).
(*Zuckermann*)

Zweigert, Konrad and Kötz, Hein: *An Introduction to Comparative Law* (3rd ed., OUP 1998) – translated from *Einführung in die Rechtsvergleichung* (Mohr Siebeck 1996).

Table of Cases*

Arbitral Awards

Ad-hoc

CAS

ICC

* Adhering to the respective traditions, the cases are arranged *either* by their name (common law, arbitral and supranational decisions) *or* the court and date (ECJ and civil-law decisions).

ICSID

Internatioanl Tribunal of the Law of the Sea

ITLOS, *Southern Bluefin Tuna* (*Australia v. Japan, New Zealand v. Japan*), Award on Jurisdiction, 4 August 2000, (2006) XXIII UN Rep Int Arb Awards 3, 222

Iran-US Claims Tribunal

Fluor Corp. v. Islamic Republic of Iran, 7 August 1986, ITM 62-333-1, (1986) 11 Iran-US CTR 296, 38

Iran v. USA, 17 May 1982, DEC 8-A1-FT, (1982) 1 Iran-US CTR 144, 70

Mark Dallal v. Islamic Republic of Iran, Bank Mellat, 10 June 1983, 53-149-1, (1983) 3 Iran-USCTR 10, 152

Reading & Bates v. Islamic Republic of Iran, ITM 21-28-1, Interim Award, 9 June 1983, (1983) 2 Iran-US CTR 401, 38

Milan Arbitration Chamber

Milan Arbitration Chamber Case N2308, Award of 2009, unpublished, citedby Radicati di Brozolo, in *ASA Special Series* 16-17, 299

SCC

SCC Case 24/2002, Arbitral Award, 2003, Bond and Linn Bergman (eds), [2004-2009] SCC Arbitral Awards 127, 243

SCC Case 24/2007, Renta 4 SVSA et al v. Russian Federation, Decision on Preliminary Measures, 20 March 2009, 258

SMA

SMA Case 2065, Pacific Star Corporation (Voyage Charterer) v. Metal Transport Corporation of New York (Voyage Subcharterer), (1987) XII Y.C.A. 172, 42

Decisions Rendered by International and Supranational Courts and Tribunals

Permanent Court of International Justice

Certain *German Interests in Polish Upper Silesia* (*Germany v. Poland*), Judgment, (1925) 6 PCIJ Rep Ser A 20, 37

Charzów Factory (*Germany v. Poland*), Judgment (1927) 9 PCIJ Rep Ser A, 5

Free Zones of Upper Savoy and District of Gex (*France v. Switzerland*), Order,(1929) 22 PCIJ Rep Ser A 22, 69

Lotus (*France v. Turkey*), Judgment, (1927) 10 PCIJ Rep Ser A, 16

International Court of Justice

European Court of Human Rights

European Court of Justice

State Court Decisions

Australia

England and Wales

A v. B, [2007] EWHC 54 (Comm), 45
ABB Lummus Global Ltd v. Keppel Fels Ltd, [1999] 2 Lloyd's Rep 24, 23
ABCI v. Banque Franco-Tunisienne, [1996] 1 Lloyd's Rep 495 (QB), 291
Abu Dhabi Gas Liquefaction Co. Ltd v. Eastern Bechtel Corporation, [1982] 2 Lloyd's Rep 425 (CA), 25, 39
Aldi Stores Ltd v. WSP Group plc, [2007] EWCA Civ 1260, 102, 103
Arnold v. National Westminster Bank plc, [1991] 2 AC 93 (HL), 50
Arthur J. S Hall & Co. (a firm) v. Simons, [2002] 1 AC 615 (HL), 53
Arts & Antiques Ltd v. Richards, [2013] EWHC 3361 (Comm), 128
Asher v. Secretary of State for the Environment, [1974] Ch 208, 101
Ashmore v. British Coal Corp, [1990] 2 QB 338 (CA), 101
Associated Electric and Gas Insurace Services Ltd (AEGIS) v. European Reinsurance Co. of Zurich, [2003] UKPC 11, 66, 184, 66
Astra Insurance v. Sphere Drake Insurance and others, [2000] 2 Lloyd's Rep 550 (QB), 20
AT & T Corporation et al v. Saudi Cable Company, [2000] 2 Lloyd's Rep 127 (CA), 62
Bain v. Copper, (1841) 8 M&W 751, 108
Baratok Ltd v. Epiette Ltd, [1998] 1 BCLC 282 (CA), 144
Bank Mellat v. Helliniki Techniki, [1984] 1 QB 291, 63, 190
Bank of Scotland v. A, [2001] 1 WLR 751 (HL), 58
Barclays Bank plc v. Homan, [1992] BCC 757 (CA), 45
Barrow v. Bankside Members Agency Ltd, [1996] 1 WLR 257 (CA), 60
Bawejem v. MC Fabrications, [1999] BCIC 174 (CA), 21
Baytur v. Finagro, [1991] 4 All ER 129 (CA), 20
Bishop of Salisbury v. Phillips, (1704) 90 ER 927, 105
Blohn v. Desser, [1962] 2 QB 116, 143
Bon Groundwork Ltd v. Foster, [2012] EWCA Civ 252, 67
Booth v. Leycester, (1837) 48 ER 430, 45
Bouygues Offshore SA v. Caspian Shipping Co, [1998] 2 Lloyd's Rep 461, 46
Bradford & Bingley Building Society v. Seddon, [1999] 1 WLR 1482, 102
Bremer Öltransport v. Drewry, [1933] 1 KB 753 (CA), 76
Bruns v. Colocotroonis (The Vasso), [1979] 2 Lloyd's Rep 412 (CA), 138
Bulfracht (Cyprus) Ltd v. Boneset Shipping Co. Ltd (the Pamphilos), [2002] 2 Lloyd's Rep 681, 73
Caledonian Railway Co. v. Turcan, [1898] AC 256 (HL), 61
Carl-Zeiss Stiftung v. Rayner & Keeler Ltd (No 2), [1966] 2 All ER 536 (HL), 52
Carlyle Capital Corporation v. Conway, [2013] 2 Lloyd's Rep 179, 46
Castrique v. Imrie, (1879) LR 4 HL 414, 196, 219
Chantiers de l'Atlantique SA v. Ganztansport & Technigaz SAS, [2011] EWHC 3383 (Comm), 292
Christopher Brown Ltd v. Genossenschaft Oesterreichischer Waldbesitzer Holzwirtschaftsbetriebe GmbH, [1954] 1 QB 8 (QB), 67
Chun Wo Building Construction v. China Merchants Tower Co, [2000] 2 HKC 255, 35

France

Georgia

Germany

Hong Kong

India

Ireland

Isreal

Italy

Kenia

Malaysia

Netherlands

New Zealand

Russia

Singapore

Spain

Sweden

Switzerland

United States of America

[illegible] v. [illegible], [illegible] (5th Cir. 1987), 17
[illegible], 24 [illegible]
(D.D.C. 2015) [illegible] LLC v. [illegible], 587 [illegible] (D.C. Cir. 2009), 190
[illegible] (D. Md. 1978), 23
[illegible] (2d Cir. 1997), 39
[illegible] F.3d 111 (5th Cir. 1997), 81
[illegible] Co., 765 F.Supp. 590 ([illegible]. 1991), 3
U.S. v. [illegible], 758 F.3d [illegible] (7th Cir. 2014), 186
[illegible] (1999), 110
[illegible] (Ct. App. 1993), 131
[illegible] (2d Cir. 1987), 201
[illegible] F.2d 156 (8th Cir. 1979), 94
[illegible] 892 P.2d 1048 (Idaho 1994), 129
[illegible], 74 S.Ct. 188 (1953), 68, 73
[illegible] v. [illegible], 124 F.3d 192 (2d Cir. 1997), 128

Table of Transnational Legislation

Treaties

Arbitration Rules

Model and Soft Laws

Travaux Préparatoires

Index

O

P

R

S

T

INTERNATIONAL ARBITRATION LAW LIBRARY

1. Moshe Hirsch, *The Arbitration Mechanism of the International Center for the Settlement of Investment Disputes,* 1993 (ISBN 07-923-1993-1).
2. Aida B. Avanessian, *Iran-United States Claims Tribunal in Action,* 1993 (ISBN 18-533-3902-4).
3. Isaak I. Dore, *The UNCITRAL Framework for Arbitration in Contemporary Perspective,* 1993 (ISBN 18-533-3573-8).
4. Vesna Lazić, *Insolvency Proceedings and Commercial Arbitration,* 1998 (ISBN 90-411-1115-8).
5. Joachim Frick, *Arbitration in Complex International Contracts,* 2001 (ISBN 90-411-1662-1).
6. Katherine Lynch, *The Forces of Economic Globalization: Challenges to the Regime of International Commercial Arbitration,* 2003 (ISBN 90-411-1994-9).
7. Christoph Liebscher, *The Healthy Award: Challenge in International Commercial Arbitration,* 2003 (ISBN 90-411-2011-4).
8. Hamid G. Gharavi, *The International Effectiveness of the Annulment of an Arbitral Award,* 2003 (ISBN 90-411-1717-2).
9. Abdulhay Sayed, *Corruption in International Trade and Commercial Arbitration,* 2004 (ISBN 90-411-2236-2).
10. Gabrielle Kaufmann-Kohler & Thomas Schultz, *Online Dispute Resolution: Challenges for Contemporary Justice,* 2004 (ISBN 90-411-2318-0).
11. Christopher R. Drahozal & Richard W. Naimark (eds), *Towards a Science of International Arbitration: Collected Empirical Research,* 2005 (ISBN 90-411-2322-9).
12. Ali Yeşilirmak, *Provisional Measures in International Commercial Arbitration,* 2005 (ISBN 90-411-2353-9).
13. Christian Bühring-Uhle, *Arbitration and Mediation in International Business,* second revised edition, 2006 (ISBN 978-9-041-12256-8).
14. Bernard Hanotiau, *Complex Arbitrations: Multiparty, Multicontract, Multiissue and Class Actions,* 2006 (ISBN 978-9-041-12442-5).
15. Loukas A. Mistelis & Julian D.M. Lew (eds), *Pervasive Problems in International Arbitration,* 2006 (ISBN 978-9-041-12450-0).
16. Julian D.M. Lew & Loukas A. Mistelis (eds), *Arbitration Insights – Twenty Years of the Annual Lecture of the School of International Arbitration, Sponsored by Freshfields Bruckhaus Deringer,* 2006 (ISBN 978-9-041-12606-1).
17. Mark Kantor, *Valuation for Arbitration: Compensation Standards, Valuation Methods and Expert Evidence,* 2008 (ISBN 978-9-041-12735-8).
18. Christoph Brunner, *Force Majeure and Hardship under General Contract Principles: Exemption for Non-Performance in International Arbitration,* 2009 (ISBN 978-90-411-2792-1).

19. Loukas A. Mistelis & Stavros L. Brekoulakis (eds), *Arbitrability: International & Comparative Perspectives*, 2009 (ISBN 978-90-411-2730-3).
20. Sam Luttrell, *Bias Challenges in International Commercial Arbitration: The Need for a 'Real Danger' Test*, 2009 (ISBN 978-90-411-3191-1).
21. Monique Sasson, *Substantive Law in Investment Treaty Arbitration: The Unsettled Relationship Between International Law and Municipal Law*, Second Edition, 2017 (ISBN 978-90-411-6103-1).
22. Ileana M. Smeureanu, *Confidentiality in International Commercial Arbitration*, 2011 (ISBN 978-90-411-3226-0).
23. Won Kidane, *China-Africa Dispute Settlement: The Law, Economics and Culture of Arbitration*, 2011 (ISBN 978-90-411-3674-9).
24. Karel Daele, *Challenge and Disqualification of Arbitrators in International Arbitration*, 2012 (ISBN 978-90-411-3799-9).
25. Crina Baltag, *The Energy Charter Treaty: The Notion of Investor*, 2012 (ISBN 978-90-411-3428-8).
26. Alexandra Diehl, *The Core Standard of International Investment Protection: Fair and Equitable Treatment*, 2012 (ISBN 978-90-411-3869-9).
27. Manuel Indlekofer, *International Arbitration and the Permanent Court of Arbitration*, 2013 (ISBN 978-90-411-4766-0).
28. Günther J. Horvath & Stephan Wilske (eds), *Guerrilla Tactics in International Arbitration*, 2013 (ISBN 978-90-411-4002-9).
29. Albert Badia, *Piercing the Veil of State Enterprises in International Arbitration*, 2014 (ISBN 978-90-411-5162-9).
30. Nadja Erk, *Parallel Proceedings in International Arbitration: A Comparative European Perspective*, 2014 (ISBN 978-90-411-5264-0).
31. Simon Vorburger, *International Arbitration and Cross-Border Insolvency: Comparative Perspectives*, 2014 (ISBN 978-90-411-5419-4).
32. Ahmad Ali Ghouri, *Interaction and Conflict of Treaties in Investment Arbitration*, 2015 (ISBN 978-90-411-5417-0).
33. Reto Marghitola, *Document Production in International Arbitration*, 2015 (ISBN 978-90-411-5159-9).
34. Alfonso Gómez-Acebo, *Party-Appointed Arbitrators in International Commercial Arbitration*, 2016 (ISBN 978-90-411-6671-5).
35. Jonas von Goeler, *Third-Party Funding in International Arbitration and Its Impact on Procedure*, 2016 (ISBN 978-90-411-5015-8).
36. Dean Lewis, *The Interpretation and Uniformity of the UNCITRAL Model Law on International Commercial Arbitration: Focusing on Australia, Hong Kong and Singapore*, 2016 (ISBN 978-90-411-6700-2).
37. Stavros Brekoulakis, Julian D.M. Lew & Loukas Mistelis (eds), *The Evolution and Future of International Arbitration*, 2016 (ISBN 978-90-411-7004-0).
38. Rémy Gerbay, *The Functions of Arbitral Institutions*, 2016 (ISBN 978-90-411-6217-5).

39. Maximilian Clasmeier, *Arbitral Awards as Investments: Treaty Interpretation and the Dynamics of International Investment Law*, 2017 (ISBN 978-90-411-8357-6).
40. Tony Cole (ed.), *The Roles of Psychology in International Arbitration*, 2017 (ISBN 978-90-411-5921-2).
41. Pietro Ferrario, *The Adaptation of Long-Term Gas Sale Agreements by Arbitrators*, 2017 (ISBN 978-90-411-8232-6).
42. Jacob B. van de Velden, *Finality in Litigation: The Law and Practice of Preclusion – Res Judicata (Merger and Estoppel), Abuse of Process and Recognition of Foreign Judgments*, 2017 (ISBN 978-90-411-8342-2).
43. Dolores Bentolila, *Arbitrators as Lawmakers*, 2017 (ISBN 978-90-411-8354-5).
44. Giacomo Marchisio, *The Notion of Award in International Commercial Arbitration: A Comparative Analysis of French Law, English Law, and the UNCITRAL Model Law*, 2017 (ISBN 978-90-411-8391-0).
45. Csaba Kovács, *Attribution in International Investment Law*, 2018 (ISBN 978-90-411-9675-0).
46. Mary Mitsi, *The Decision-Making Process of Investor-State Arbitration Tribunals*, 2019 (ISBN 978-90-411-9600-2).
47. Ahmet Cemil Yıldırım, *Interpretation of Contracts in Comparative and Uniform Law*, 2019 (ISBN 978-94-035-1130-6).
48. Beata Gessel-Kalinowska vel Kalisz, *The Legal, Real and Converged Interest in Declaratory Relief*, 2019 (ISBN 978-94-035-1244-0).
49. Maximilian Pika, *Third-Party Effects of Arbitral Awards: Res Judicata Against Privies, Non-mutual Preclusion and Factual Effects*, 2019 (ISBN 978-94-035-1273-0).

www.ingramcontent.com/pod-product-compliance
Lightning Source LLC
LaVergne TN
LVHW020645300926
849161LV00004B/818